Fundamentals of
Financial Planning

Huebner School Series

Gary K. Stone, Editor

Readings in Multiline Insurance Law and Operations
Charles E. Hughes (ed.)
Fundamentals of Financial Planning
Robert M. Crowe (ed.)
Readings in Income Taxation
James F. Ivers III (ed.)
Group Benefits: Basic Concepts and Alternatives
Burton T. Beam, Jr.
Retirement Planning for a Business and Business Owner
Kenn Beam Tacchino
Retirement Planning for Individuals
K. B. Tacchino, W. J. Ruckstuhl, E. E. Graves, and R. J. Doyle, Jr.
Readings in Wealth Accumulation Planning
Robert J. Doyle, Jr., and Eric T. Johnson (eds.)
Readings in Estate Planning I
Ted Kurlowicz (ed.)
Readings in Estate Planning II
Jeffrey B. Kelvin
Planning for Business Owners and Professionals
Ted Kurlowicz, James F. Ivers III, and John J. McFadden
Financial Planning Applications
James F. Ivers III and William J. Ruckstuhl
Retirement Planning Handbook
Robert J. Doyle, Jr., and Donald Wright (eds.)
Tax Planning for Business Operations
Eric T. Johnson
Computerizing a Financial Planning Practice
Edmund W. Fitzpatrick

Robert M. Crowe, PhD, CLU, ChFC, is professor of finance and insurance at The American College. Previous positions he has held include the deanship of the College of Business Administration at Memphis State University and the University of Tulsa. He has also served as an economic affairs officer for the United Nations in Switzerland. He earned his doctorate as a fellow of the S. S. Huebner Foundation for Insurance Education at the University of Pennsylvania. He is the author of the book Time and Money: Using Time Value Analysis in Financial Planning.

Huebner School Series

Fundamentals of Financial Planning

Edited by Robert M. Crowe

The American College/*Bryn Mawr, Pennsylvania*

This publication is designed to provide accurate and authoritative information about the subject covered. The American College is not engaged in rendering legal, accounting, or other professional service. If legal or other expert advice is required, the services of an appropriate professional should be sought.

Library of Congress catalog card number 90-81241
ISBN 0-943590-27-2

Printed in the United States of America

Contents

Preface   *vii*

Meeting Client Needs through Financial Planning
Robert M. Crowe   *1*

Risk-Tolerance in Financial Decisions
Michael J. Roszkowski   *25*

Effective Communication in Financial Counseling
Lewis B. Morgan   *71*

Gathering Client Information
Robert M. Crowe   *99*

Income Tax Planning
James F. Ivers III   *165*

Planning the Client's Estate
Ted Kurlowicz   *184*

Insurance Planning: The Risk Management Process
Charles E. Hughes   *210*

Insurance Planning: Survey of Insurance Coverages
Charles E. Hughes   *237*

Investments and Investment Planning
William J. Ruckstuhl   *265*

Retirement Planning
Kenn Tacchino   *301*

Computerizing the Financial Planning Practice
Dale S. Johnson   *333*

Regulation of Financial Planners
Jeffrey B. Kelvin   **369**

The Ethical Environment of Financial Planning
Robbin Derry   **384**

Sample Planning Case
Dale S. Johnson and Jai P. Sawhney   **406**

Appendix A
Standards for a Comprehensive Financial Plan
Registry of Financial Planning Practitioners   **449**

Appendix B
Time-Value-of-Money Analysis in Financial Planning
Robert M. Crowe   **455**

Appendix C
Risk Identification Questionnaire
Charles E. Hughes   **481**

Appendix D
Define Your Practice
Dale S. Johnson   **489**

Appendix E
Computer Configurations
Dale S. Johnson   **490**

Appendix F
Software Vendors, Systems, and Programs
Dale S. Johnson   **491**

Appendix G
Software and Hardware Buying Tips
Dale S. Johnson   **511**

Index   **515**

Preface

In the last few years of the 1970s and the first few of the 1980s, American consumers were confronted by a "triple whammy"—very high inflation rates, very high interest rates, and very high federal income tax rates. Moreover, at about the same time a trend began at the federal level toward loosening many of the regulatory restrictions on the activities of several types of financial institutions. The financial industry responded by inundating the marketplace with a host of new, often confusing, products and services to help consumers cope.

It was in the midst of all of this turmoil that the terms *financial planning* and *financial planner* really became chic. Trade and professional associations of financial planners grew. Glossy magazines on financial planning sprang up. Professional designations in financial planning became widely used by financial services practitioners. College professors began teaching financial planning at several universities. Many financial services practitioners replaced their old labels—stockbroker, insurance agent, accountant, banker, and so forth—with the new label, financial planner.

The almost frenzied rush to financial planning began to slow down during the last several years of the 1980s. Inflation cooled. Interest rates moderated. Taxes were "reformed." Many of the hot new financial products and services lost their appeal. Financial planning as a field of professional activity began to mature. It probably will continue to do so during the decade of the 1990s.

A major difficulty that has faced those who provide professional education for practitioners in the field of financial planning is the scarcity of suitable literature on the subject. This book is an effort to help fill the gap with basic information about how to use the financial planning process properly to help solve client problems. Four broad areas of client financial concerns are discussed: the fundamentals of tax planning, insurance planning, investment planning, and retirement planning. The book also introduces the topic of using computers and time-value-of-money techniques in financial planning. The ethical and regulatory environment within which financial planning is carried out is also discussed. Finally, all of the dimensions of financial planning are pulled together and reflected in a basic sample financial planning case.

Creation of this book in the short time allotted for it would not have been possible without a concerted effort by several people. My thanks go to those who authored chapters, most of whom are my faculty colleagues at The American College. M. Donald Wright, JD, CPA, has been an important part of this project from its inception. As a practicing financial planner he was able to provide many practical ideas about the content of the various chapters. In addition, I am grateful for the good work provided by our Editorial Services Department, especially Nancy J. Tarquinio and Kay Powell. Several members of the College's secretarial staff, especially Nancy A. Cornman and Neysa A. Westman, were invaluable. Lastly, I owe a great deal to Patricia M. Crowe, my favorite financial planner.

Robert M. Crowe

Fundamentals of
Financial Planning

Meeting Client Needs through Financial Planning

Robert M. Crowe*

Although providing financial planning advice and services to clients is a relatively new and still-emerging field of professional endeavor, very affluent individuals have had access to such help for many years. Moreover, some financial services professionals such as accountants and life insurance agents argue that they have been financial planners all their lives. Perhaps they are correct. However, it is generally recognized that financial planning services that cover a *spectrum* of client concerns have become available to most Americans in the middle and upper-middle income brackets only in about the past 20 to 25 years.

Financial services practitioners claiming to be financial planners first appeared in numbers in the late 1960s, a period of rising inflation and rising interest rates. The financial planning movement grew rapidly during the 1970s as the general trend of prices continued upward. By the late 1970s and into the early 1980s, inflation and interest rates were virtually out of control. Confronted with very high income tax rates along with these inflation and interest rates, American consumers clamored for help. The growth of the financial planning movement was explosive. Often, however, what practitioners labeled as financial planning service consisted mostly of selling "get rich quick" products and elaborate income tax dodges, usually accompanied by an abundance of "hype." A few practitioners, sometimes with near-messianic zeal, preached the message of *comprehensive* financial planning as the financial salvation of the American household.

By the mid-1980s, much of the turbulence in economic conditions began to settle down. In addition, when income tax reform eliminated the most extreme types of tax shelters from the marketplace, many so-called financial planners disappeared from the scene. Many advocates of the comprehensive approach to financial planning, at least when provided solely on a fee-for-service basis, came to realize that this type of financial planning is practical for only a small, affluent clientele.

As the 1990s begin, the financial planning profession appears to be gaining some stability and maturity. Consequently it is now possible to describe in perhaps a more balanced fashion than before what financial planning is and what client needs it can fulfill.

This chapter explains what the author believes financial planning is. It includes a discussion of different views on this subject and a summary of what financial planners actually do. This chapter also describes the recommended content of a *comprehensive* financial plan and emphasizes the important role of time-value-of-money analysis in the financial planning process. Further, some of the key events in the historical development of financial planning as a profession during the past 20

---

*Robert M. Crowe, PhD, CLU, ChFC, is professor of finance and insurance at The American College.

years are summarized. Finally, the chapter discusses the basic conditions in the marketplace that provide opportunities for professional financial planners to serve clients and identifies some of the obstacles planners must help clients overcome if financial goals are to be achieved.

WHAT IS FINANCIAL PLANNING?

One of the factors that has hampered the development of financial planning as a discipline and as a profession is the fact that there has been and continues to be very little agreement among practitioners as to what exactly financial planning is. Indeed, it sometimes seems that there are as many definitions of financial planning as there are people who call themselves financial planners.

Single-Purpose View

Some practitioners take the position that the simple selling of a single financial product or service to a client in order to solve a single financial problem constitutes financial planning. According to this *single-purpose* or *specialist view,* all the following individuals would be examples of financial planners:

- a stockbroker who advises a customer to buy shares of common stock of a particular company
- a salesperson who sells to a client shares in a real estate limited partnership
- a preparer of income tax returns who suggests that a client establish a Keogh plan
- a banker who opens a trust account for the benefit of a customer's handicapped child
- a life insurance agent who sells key person life insurance to the owner of a small business
- a personal finance counselor who shows a client how to set up and live within a budget

Narrow-Focus View

Other practitioners might argue that none or only some of the preceding persons are really financial planners. These practitioners would argue that real financial planning must embrace more than just solving a single financial problem of a client and must extend beyond the selling of a single financial product or service. Practitioners adhering to the *narrow-focus view* might emphasize that there are three basic categories of client financial needs and financial products and services: insurance planning, tax planning, and investment planning. From their perspective, true financial planning should deal with at least a large part of one of these categories and perhaps some aspects of a second category. They might even specify that true financial planning must always include at least some investment planning activity. According to the narrow-focus view, the following individuals would probably qualify as financial planners:

- an insurance agent who sells all lines of life, health, property, and liability insurance

- a tax attorney who assists clients with their income, estate, and gift tax planning
- an investment adviser who is registered as such with the Securities and Exchange Commission
- a life insurance agent who also sells a family of mutual funds to meet both the protection and wealth accumulation needs of clients

Comprehensive-Focus View

Still other practitioners would say that financial planning means and is synonymous with comprehensive financial planning. According to this *comprehensive-focus view,* financial planning must consider all aspects of the client's financial position, which includes all the client's financial needs and objectives, and must utilize several integrated and coordinated planning strategies for fulfilling those needs and objectives. The two key characteristics of comprehensive financial planning are, then, that it

- encompasses all the personal and financial situations of clients to the extent that these can be uncovered, clarified, and addressed through information gathering and counseling
- integrates into its methodology all the techniques and expertise utilized in more narrowly focused approaches to client financial problem solving

Because of the wide range of expertise required to engage in comprehensive financial planning, effective performance virtually always requires a team of specialists. The comprehensive planner's tasks are to coordinate the efforts of the team and to contribute expertise in his or her field of specialization.

In its "purest" form, comprehensive financial planning is a service provided by the planner on a fee-only basis. No part of the planner's compensation comes from the sale of financial products, thus helping to ensure complete objectivity in all aspects of the plan. Some members of the team of specialists also are compensated through fees, while others might receive commissions from the sale of products. In its less "pure" but often more practical form, comprehensive financial planning provides the planner with compensation consisting of some combination of fees for service and commissions from the sale of some of the financial products. Again, members of the team of specialists might receive fees or commissions.

Furthermore, in its "purest" form, comprehensive financial planning is performed for a client all at once. A single planning engagement by the planner and his or her team of specialists creates the one plan that addresses all the client concerns and utilizes all the needed financial strategies. This plan is then updated with the client periodically and modified as appropriate. In its less "pure" form, comprehensive financial planning is performed incrementally during the course of several engagements with the client. For example, the planner in one year might prepare a plan to treat some of the client's tax concerns and insurance planning problems. In another year the planner might focus on the client's investment concerns and then dovetail the strategies for dealing with them with the previously developed tax and insurance strategies. In a third engagement the planner might address the remaining issues in the tax, insurance, and investment planning areas and coordinate all the recommended strategies with each other and with the previously developed plans.

Again, each incremental part, as well as the overall plan, is reviewed periodically and revised as appropriate.

Financial Planning as a Process

What, then, is financial planning? Can the financial services professional whose focus is on only a single type of financial problem and financial product for clients legitimately be called a financial planner? What if the professional's focus is broader than this but less than comprehensive? Is the comprehensive approach the only true form of financial planning? The debate goes on among financial services professionals even now. Moreover, this debate is not merely an exercise in semantics; it becomes intensely practical when questions are raised about such issues as who shall regulate financial planners, who shall set standards for the financial planning profession, what sort of education should financial planners have, or which financial services practitioners may hold themselves out to the public as financial planners.

This author believes that financial planning is a *process*, a methodology. This process for helping clients achieve their financial goals can be applied to the full range of client goals on a comprehensive basis. The process can also be applied on a more narrow basis to only a subset of those goals or even to only a single financial goal of a client. It is not the range of client concerns that is addressed that makes a practitioner a financial planner. Rather, it is the process that is used by the practitioner in addressing client concerns that makes a practitioner a financial planner.

There are six steps to the financial planning process.

1. Gather the relevant information about the client.
2. Analyze the client's present position.
3. Develop a plan for achieving the client's objective(s).
4. Obtain the client's approval of the plan.
5. Implement the plan.
6. Review the performance of the plan periodically and revise the plan as needed.

Each of these six steps is discussed briefly in the following pages.

Gather the Information

After a client has expressed an interest in having a financial plan developed, the planner's first responsibility is to gather all the information about the client that is relevant to the problem(s) to be solved and/or to the type of plan to be prepared. The more complex the client's situation is and the more varied the number of his or her goals is, the greater will be the information-gathering task.

Two broad types of information will need to be gathered: objective and subjective. A few examples of objective (factual) information that might be needed from the client in particular cases are a list of securities holdings; an inventory of assets and liabilities; a description of the present arrangements for distribution of the client's (and spouse's) assets at death; a list of annual income and expenditures; and a summary of present insurance coverages. Of at least equal importance is the subjective information about the client. The financial planner often will need to gather

information about the hopes, fears, values, preferences, attitudes, goals, risk tolerances, and priorities of the client (and spouse).

Obviously, information gathering is far more than asking the client a series of
questions or filling out a form. Certainly some of that is required, but usually
information gathering also requires examination and analysis of documents such as
wills, tax returns, and insurance policies supplied by the client or the client's other
financial advisers. It also requires advising, counseling, and listening during
face-to-face meetings with the client and spouse. These skills are especially important
because the planner needs to help the client and spouse identify and articulate clearly
what they really want to accomplish and what risks they are willing to take in order
to do so.

Chapter 4 of this text, in conjunction with chapters 2 and 3, provides a more
complete discussion of the information-gathering step in the financial planning
process.

Analyze the Present Position

Once the relevant information about the client has been gathered, organized,
and checked for accuracy, consistency, and completeness, the financial planner's
next task is to analyze the client's present financial condition. The objective here is
to determine where the client is now *in relationship to the goals that have been
established by the client during the information-gathering stage.*

This analysis may reveal certain strengths of the client's present position relative
to those goals. For example, the client may be living well within his or her means,
and thus resources are available with which to meet some wealth accumulation goals
within a reasonable time period. Maybe the client has a liberal set of health insurance
coverages through his or her employer, thereby adequately covering the risks
associated with serious disability. Perhaps the client's will has been reviewed recently
by his or her attorney and brought up-to-date to reflect the client's desired estate
plan.

More than likely, however, the financial planner's analysis of the client's present
financial position will disclose a number of weaknesses or conditions that are
hindering achievement of the client's goals. For example, the client may be paying
unnecessarily high federal income taxes or using debt unwisely. The client's portfolio
of investments may be inconsistent with his or her risk-taking tolerance. Maybe the
client's business interest is not being used efficiently to achieve his or her personal
insurance protection goals, or important loss-causing possibilities have been overlooked, such as the client's exposure to huge lawsuits arising out of the possible
negligent use of an automobile by someone other than the client.

One conclusion from the planner's analysis may be that the client's present
financial position does not realistically permit accomplishment of the client's goals
as established earlier. If this is the case and if the client cannot be persuaded to
modify his or her financial life-style, the planner will have to work with the client
to scale back some or all of the goals. Perhaps dollar amounts to be achieved will
have to be lowered; perhaps time frames for the achievement of goals will have to
be lengthened; perhaps priorities among the goals will have to be revised; perhaps
some goals will even have to be dropped for the time being.

Develop a Plan

After the information about the client has been analyzed and, if necessary, the objectives to be achieved have been refined, the planner's next job is to devise a realistic plan for bringing the client from his or her present financial position to the attainment of those objectives. Since no two clients are completely alike, a well-drawn financial plan must be tailored to the individual, with all the planner's recommended strategies designed to be consistent with each particular client's needs, abilities, and goals. The plan must be the *client's* plan, not the *planner's* plan.

Many of the planning strategies that might be appropriate for particular clients are described later in this text. See particularly chapters 5 (income tax planning), 6 (estate and gift tax planning), 7 and 8 (insurance planning), 9 (investment planning), and 10 (retirement planning). Many additional planning strategies are described in more advanced texts.

It is unlikely that any individual planner can maintain an up-to-date familiarity with all the strategies that might be appropriate for his or her clients. Based on his or her education and professional specialization, the planner is likely to rely on a limited number of "tried and true" strategies for treating the most frequently encountered planning problems. When additional expertise is needed, the planner should always consult with an adviser who is a specialist in the field in question to help the planner design the client's overall plan.

Also, there is usually more than one way for a client's financial goals to be achieved. When this is the case, the planner should present alternative strategies for the client to consider and choose and should explain the advantages and disadvantages of each strategy. Strategies that will help achieve multiple objectives should be highlighted.

The financial plan that is developed should be specific. It should detail who is to do what, when, and with what resources. A sample of a completed plan is contained in chapter 14. See particularly pages 423 through 425 for an example of this type of specificity.

Obtain the Client's Approval

The planner's next step is to present the proposed plan to the client for approval. Normally, the report describing the plan should be in writing. Since the objective of the financial planning report is to communicate, its format should be such that the client can easily understand and evaluate what is being proposed. Some financial planners take pride in the length of their reports, although lengthy reports are often made up primarily of standardized, "boilerplate" paragraphs and pages. In general, the simpler the report, the easier it will be for the client to understand and adopt. Careful use of graphs, diagrams, and other visual aids in the report can also help in this regard.

When the financial planning report has been presented and reviewed with the client, the moment of truth arrives. At this time the planner must ask the client to approve the plan (or some variation thereof) and its implementation schedule. As part of this request, the planner must ask the client to allocate money for the plan's implementation. Keep in mind the warning of one college professor of financial planning who pointed out that a mistake he used to make with his students was that he never dared to use the "S" word in class—financial planning involves *selling*. Even for the small number of financial planners who are compensated entirely on a fee-for-service basis, the client must be *sold* on the need to work with the planner to develop and implement a plan.

Implement the Plan

The mere giving of financial advice, no matter how solid the foundation on which it is based, does not, in this author's opinion, constitute financial planning. A financial plan is useful to the client *only if it is put into action*. Therefore, part of the planner's responsibility is to see that plan implementation is carried out properly, according to the schedule agreed upon with the client.

Financial plans that are of limited scope and limited complexity may be implemented for the client entirely by the planner. For other plans, however, additional specialized professional expertise will be needed. For example, legal instruments such as wills and trust documents may have to be drawn up, insurance policies may have to be purchased, or investment securities may have to be acquired. Part of the planner's responsibility is to *motivate* and *assist* the client in completing each of the steps necessary for full plan implementation.

Review and Revise the Plan Periodically

The relationship between the financial planner and the client should be an ongoing one. Therefore, the sixth and final step in the financial planning process is to review the client's plan periodically. Normally this is done at least once each year or more frequently if changing circumstances warrant it. The first part of this review process should involve measuring the performance of the implementation vehicles. Secondly, updates should be obtained concerning changes in the client's personal and financial situation. Thirdly, changes that have occurred in the economic, tax, or financial environment should be reviewed with the client.

If this periodic review of the plan indicates satisfactory performance in light of the client's current objectives and circumstances, no action needs to be taken. However, if performance is not acceptable or if there is a significant change in the client's personal or financial circumstances or objectives, the planner and client should revise the plan to fit the new environment. This revision process should follow the same six steps used to develop the original plan, though the time and effort needed will probably be less than in the original process.

Summary

The financial planning process described above is depicted schematically in figure 1-1. The blocks on the left represent the six steps in the process, while the blocks on the right indicate the main substantive activities that should occur in each step.

FIGURE 1-1
The Financial Planning Process

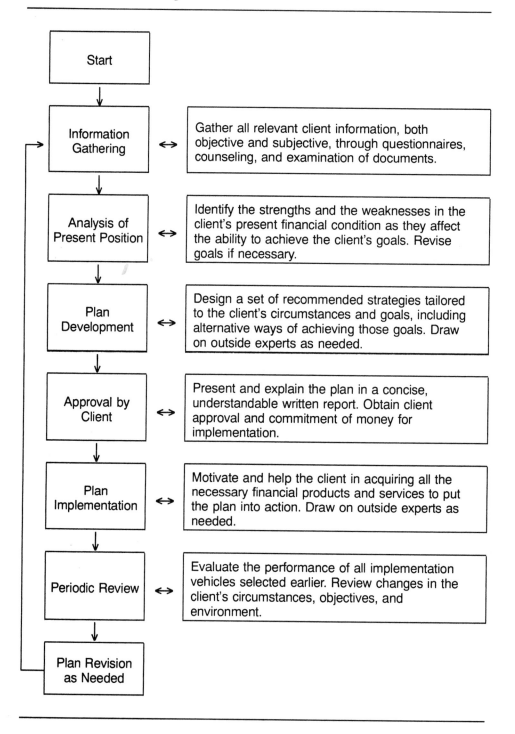

CONTENT OF A COMPREHENSIVE FINANCIAL PLAN

As noted earlier, comprehensive financial planning is only one type of financial planning. In practice, it is the least frequently encountered type for most planners for several reasons. First, not many clients are willing to invest as much of their own time in the undertaking as comprehensive financial planning requires. Second, only quite affluent clients are willing and able to pay for all the time of the planner and his or her staff that is needed in developing a comprehensive financial plan. Third, not many clients can easily deal with the totality of their financial goals, capabilities, and difficulties all at one time. Instead, most prefer to concentrate on only one or a few related issues at a time. (As has been mentioned, however, even clients in the latter group can have a comprehensive plan developed and implemented for them in incremental stages.)

For those cases in which the planner is called upon to prepare a comprehensive financial plan for a client, whether entirely in one engagement or incrementally over a period of years, what should the plan contain? Clearly, comprehensive financial planning is such an ambitious and complex undertaking that it must cover a great deal of ground. The Registry of Financial Planning Practitioners of the International Association for Financial Planning[1] has developed and promulgated a set of standards in this regard. The complete text of the Registry's standards for the content of a comprehensive financial plan appears as Appendix A at the end of this book.

A comprehensive financial plan should address all pertinent areas relating to the client, according to the Registry. If the planner does not personally address each of the areas in the development of the plan (and in this author's experience not many planners have the range and depth of expertise needed to do so alone), the planner should then serve as the coordinator for the development of the other areas of the plan.

According to the Registry, at least 13 pertinent areas should be addressed in a client's comprehensive financial plan. Although the order, depth, and style in which they are discussed in the plan document may vary, these 13 areas are as follows:

- First, a comprehensive plan should include personal data about the client and the client's family, such as names, addresses, dates of birth, social security numbers, phone numbers, and so on.
- Second, the plan should include the client's stated goals and objectives, indicating the priority of each one and the time frame for achieving each one.
- A third topic should be an identification of the various problems in the client's present position, including such things as possible catastrophic medical costs, unplanned high costs of educating children, and unnecessarily high current tax burdens.
- Fourth, any assumptions used by the planner in preparing the recommended strategies, such as assumptions about future inflation rates and investment yields, should be explicitly spelled out in the plan document.
- Fifth, the plan should contain the client's balance sheet, showing his or her assets, liabilities, and net worth.

- The sixth component should be a cash-flow management statement. This statement should identify all the client's sources and uses of cash and indicate his or her net cash flows.
- Seventh, a comprehensive financial plan should include a federal income tax statement and an analysis thereof.
- Eighth, the plan should analyze the client's financial exposure to losses of both a personal and business nature arising from mortality, morbidity, legal liability, and property damage. This section of the plan should also list and analyze the client's insurance coverages for such exposures.
- A ninth item should be a listing of the client's present investment portfolio, including an analysis of its liquidity, diversification, and risk characteristics.
- Tenth, the plan should analyze any future capital needs that the client will have for special purposes, such as retirement planning or children's education costs.
- Eleventh, a comprehensive plan should address the client's estate plan. There should be a review of the assets that will be included in the gross estate and an estimate of the estate tax burden that will be present.
- A twelfth item should be a list of recommendations by the planner for dealing with the issues and problems identified earlier and for achieving the client's goals and objectives.
- Finally, the plan should deal with implementation. It should contain a prioritized list of actions to be taken, including what is to be done, when, and by whom.

WHAT FINANCIAL PLANNERS ACTUALLY DO

In addition to the preceding description of the financial planning process, identifying the kinds of professional activities in which financial planners actually engage is another way to understand what financial planning is. A study conducted in 1987 sheds considerable light on this question.[2] This study surveyed a random sample of individuals who claim to be financial planners, most of them holders of CFP, CLU, and/or ChFC professional designations, who have been active in the field for several years.

The study showed that the job activities of these practicing financial planners fall into six main categories. The principal specific activities within each category are described below.

- *marketing financial planning services* — Although these planners use a variety of techniques for obtaining and serving clients, they rely heavily on published media, such as writing articles and newsletters, as well as advertising. They frequently make personal presentations, such as lectures and seminars, and also obtain referrals from other professionals and from present clients.
- *evaluating client needs* — This category of activity centers on meeting with clients in order to collect information about them. The specific tasks that were considered most important to the survey respondents are interviewing and using questionnaires to explore the background, attitudes, financial resources, and obligations of clients that affect clients' financial goals and needs.
- *explaining financial planning concepts and clarifying client goals* — This set of tasks entails explaining issues and concepts related to such topics as estate plans,

income taxes, insurance, investments, retirement-income plans, asset management, and budgeting. Also included is a discussion with the client of incompatibilities between the client's goals and the resources available for achieving them.

- *analyzing client circumstances and preparing financial plans* — Tasks in this category include an analysis of the client's financial records and documents, such as tax returns, insurance policies, and investment records. Other important tasks are the formulation of recommendations for meeting client goals in such areas as retirement, risk management, taxes, and investments.

- *implementing financial plans* — This task includes the preparation of the written document incorporating the recommended financial strategies and tactics, which are all tailored to meet the needs of the particular client. It also involves explaining the planner's fee structure, the fiduciary responsibilities of the planner to the client, and full and fair disclosure to the client of material facts and opinions about recommended products and services. (Of course, some of this explanation may also take place as part of the marketing activities of the financial planner.) The implementation activities also include selecting and offering alternative financial products to the client and may entail carrying out client requests to purchase or sell them.

- *monitoring financial plans* — A planner's activities in this category reflect the continuing nature of the desired relationship with clients. Planners review and evaluate changes in their clients' personal circumstances (births, deaths, divorces, and so on), changes in laws and economic conditions, and the performance of the plan that has been implemented. Changes in financial plans are recommended to clients as needed.

The reader will undoubtedly recognize the similarity between this set of activities in which financial planners say they actually engage and the six steps in the financial planning process discussed earlier in this chapter.

THE ROLE OF TIME-VALUE ANALYSIS IN FINANCIAL PLANNING

In virtually every financial planning situation, the client is called upon to *give up* money in one or more time periods (money out) in order to *receive* money in one or more other time periods (money in). For example, a financial plan may involve a client depositing a sum of money each month in an individual retirement account (IRA) during the client's working years (money out) in order to provide a monthly income for the client during his or her retirement years (money in); life insurance premiums may have to be paid for several years while a client is alive (money out) in order to provide a life income for the spouse following the client's death (money in); or a gift may be made in trust now to a client's child (money out) in order to reduce the client's federal income tax burden in each of the next several years (money in). These and dozens of other transactions in which financial planning clients engage all involve an exchange — dollars *now* for dollars *later*.

Opportunity Cost and the Interest Rate

However, dollars that are due to be paid or received in different time periods do not have the same value. A rational person would prefer to receive money early, rather than having to wait for it. A given number of dollars received early have a greater value to the person than the same number of dollars received later. Why? This is because money received now can be invested and can earn additional dollars for the recipient. If the person must wait before receiving money, the opportunity to invest it and earn additional dollars in the interim is lost.

Conversely, a rational person would prefer to pay money out later, rather than having to pay it now. A given number of dollars to be paid out later are less costly to the person and have a lower value than the same number of dollars paid out early. Again, the reason for the difference is that the person who can delay paying out money can invest it in the meantime and earn additional money. One who must pay the money out early, on the other hand, loses that opportunity.

The lost opportunity to invest money and earn a profit is called *opportunity cost.* The tool that is used to measure the opportunity cost of paying out one's money early (for example, by putting it into a passbook savings account so that a bank can use it) is the compound annual interest rate that the individual could have earned by investing the money elsewhere with a similar degree of risk.

Importance of Time-Value Analysis in Financial Planning

Whenever a financial planner recommends a transaction to a client that involves an exchange of dollars in different time periods, the opportunity cost must be taken into account. The method for doing so is called time-value-of-money analysis. An understanding of time-value analysis is therefore essential to competent performance by financial planners. The basics of time-value-of-money analysis in financial planning are discussed in Appendix B at the end of this book.[3]

The following are just a few examples of the kinds of questions that a financial planner can answer for a client if the planner is well-versed in time-value analytical techniques:

- Anne wants to know how large a capital sum she must accumulate by age 65 in order to provide her with an income of a specified number of dollars per year that she cannot outlive and to enable her to bequeath the full capital sum to her nephew at her death.
- Brad is putting a specified number of dollars per year into his credit union account in order to pay for his son's college education. Brad asks a financial planner approximately how much will be in the account when his son is ready for college.
- Carol would like to accumulate a specified down payment to buy a home a few years from now. She wants to know how large her monthly savings must be in order to reach the target.
- Dave, who invested a sum of money in mutual fund shares several years ago and has been receiving dividends every year since then, wants to know what

his average annual rate of return will have been if he sells his shares back to the fund at today's higher price.

- Edna's inheritance was put into a bank certificate of deposit a few years ago, and she wants to know how much it will have grown to when the CD matures 2 years from now.
- Frank noticed that his bank advertises that on savings accounts it pays a specified *interest rate* but it also claims that the *yield* on these accounts is more than this rate. Frank asks his financial planner for an explanation of the difference between the rate and the yield.

All these and many more time-value-of-money problems involve using three or four of the following five variables:

- a present amount of money
- a future amount of money
- a series of level or uneven payments
- a period of time
- an interest rate

Developing the skill to work comfortably with the known variables in order to calculate the amount of the unknown variables is a prerequisite to a financial planner's ability to help clients achieve their financial goals.

MAJOR EVENTS IN THE EVOLUTION OF FINANCIAL PLANNING AS A PROFESSION

It was noted at the beginning of this chapter that financial planning is, in general, still a new and emerging profession. Its development as such has been facilitated by a number of organizations during the past 20 to 25 years.

Perhaps the earliest landmark event in the development of financial planning as a profession occurred in 1969 with the formation of the International Association of Financial Planners (IAFP), which was later renamed the International Association for Financial Planning. The IAFP is a trade association that, among other things, promotes financial planning, conducts educational and training programs for members, sponsors market research about financial planning, and promotes ethical conduct among practitioners.

Several colleges and universities have played an important role in the development of the financial planning profession. In 1972 the College for Financial Planning, which is the educational institution that originally awarded the Certified Financial Planner (CFP) professional designation, was formed. (This function was later transferred to a newer organization, the International Board of Standards and Practices for Certified Financial Planners [IBCFP].) In 1973 holders of the CFP designation formed the Institute of Certified Financial Planners (ICFP), a membership organization to help build professionalism in the field.

A number of important developments at what was originally called The American College of Life Underwriters in the mid-1970s and thereafter also contributed to the financial planning movement. The name of the institution was changed to The American College to reflect a broadened educational mission within the financial services field. The College created a graduate-degree program, Master of Science in Financial Services, that included a full six-credit graduate course in Financial Counseling. Discussions by the College's Board of Trustees with various constituencies of the institution led eventually to a broadened array of designation-level courses. This broadening in the curriculum culminated with the creation of a new professional designation in the early 1980s — Chartered Financial Consultant (ChFC). Meanwhile the College's professional sister organization, the American Society of Chartered Life Underwriters, also broadened its mission, membership, and programs, accepting the new categories of graduates of the College into the Society and changing its name to the American Society of CLU & ChFC.

Traditional colleges and universities also contributed to the emerging financial planning profession during the 1970s and 1980s, though on a much smaller scale than the College for Financial Planning and The American College, both of which serve a national student body. A number of schools, such as Golden Gate University, Brigham Young University, Wright State University, and Georgia State University, developed curricula in financial planning at the undergraduate or master's level. These and other schools also began offering courses to help prepare people for the CFP and ChFC examinations.

An important study of the emerging financial planning industry was published in 1979 by the Stanford Research Institute (now called SRI International). The study projected rapid growth of the field and pointed out the need for large numbers of qualified planners to support America's growing need for financial services.

Two other forces that have spurred the growth and professionalization of financial planning have been the American Institute of CPAs (AICPA) and the Life Underwriter Training Council (LUTC). During the mid-1980s the AICPA developed for its members an educational program leading to the designation of Accredited Financial Planning Specialist. At about the same time the LUTC created a Financial Planning Skills course as part of its designation program for life insurance agents. This course teaches life insurance agents how to integrate the sale of noninsurance financial products with their regular portfolio of life insurance products.

A final positive influence to be mentioned in the emergence of the financial planning profession is the Registry of Financial Planning Practitioners. Formed in 1983 under the aegis of the International Association for Financial Planning, the Registry admits and recognizes planners who meet specified requirements relating to knowledge, experience, practice methods, educational credentials, ethical conduct, and client recommendations.

OPPORTUNITIES AND CHALLENGES IN THE FINANCIAL PLANNING MARKETPLACE

A number of broad trends having important implications for financial planning practitioners have been at work in the United States in recent years. They all point to enormous opportunities for financial planners to render valuable service to clients.

One of the most important trends is that the population is growing older. The median age of Americans has risen from 27.5 to 32.5 in the past 20 years, meaning that a larger proportion of the population has moved into the period of highest earnings. Also, as people get older, they tend to devote a smaller share of their income to current consumption and a larger share to saving and investing.

One of the causes of the rising median age of Americans is that the members of the "baby boom" generation are no longer babies. The children born from the late 1940s to the early 1960s are now in the 26-to-44 age bracket and constitute about 30 percent of the U.S. population. Another cause of the rising average age is that Americans are living longer. Approximately 12.6 percent of them are now age 65 or over as compared to 9.2 percent in 1960. This percentage will continue to rise during the decade of the 1990s. Government statistics indicate that the average life expectancy for 65-year-old males is now 14 years and for 65-year-old females is 18 years.

The aging of the American population means that more and more consumers need retirement planning help during both their remaining years of active work and their retirement years. Also, an increasing proportion of the population needs assistance in planning for the cost of their children's college education.

In addition to the aging of the population, a second important trend in the financial planning marketplace is that dual-income families are increasingly common. Mostly this is a result of more and more women reentering the labor force, even during the years when they have young children. Dual-income families typically have higher total incomes, pay higher income and social security taxes, and have less time to manage their finances. The opportunities for the financial planner to assist are obvious.

A third broad trend is the increasing volatility of financial conditions in the American economy. Three indicators of this volatility confronting and confusing American households in the past 25 years are the changes that have occurred in inflation rates, in the level of interest rates, and in common stock prices. For example, during the first half of the 1960s, annual increases in the consumer price index averaged only 1.3 percent, the prime interest rate charged by banks on short-term business loans averaged only about 4.68 percent, and the Standard & Poor's index of 500 common stock prices averaged around 72.0. Consider the dynamic patterns of these indicators since then, as shown in table 1-1.

Inflation and interest rates rose steadily in the late 1960s, and they were undoubtedly a motivating factor behind the growth in the number of financial planning practitioners. Inflation and interest rates then cooled but bounced up again sharply in the mid-1970s. After a 3-year respite, they rose very sharply in the late 1970s and into the 1980s. Throughout this entire period, stock prices rose only modestly.

Inflation rates slowed again during the mid-1980s, as did the prime interest rate. Meanwhile the stock market rose dramatically but erratically. As the 1980s came to a close, inflation and interest rates were creeping up again and average common stock prices were gyrating sharply from day to day.

In addition to the volatility of inflation rates, interest rates, and stock market prices, another destabilizing influence faced by American consumers has been the important annual changes in the U.S. income tax rules. Still another element of instability in the financial environment has been the rapid rise in the failure rate among financial institutions, including some very large ones. In the 1980s failure rates among savings and loan associations, banks, and insurance companies were higher than they have been in many years.

The volatile economic conditions in the United States emphasize the need and opportunity for financial planners to continuously monitor their clients' financial circumstances and to adjust the plans as circumstances dictate. These conditions also make it doubly important that planners thoroughly understand and abide by their clients' risk tolerances.

TABLE 1-1
The Consumer Price Index Changes, the Average Prime Rate, and the Average Standard & Poor's 500 Stock Index: 1965–1989

Year	Percentage Change in CPI	Average Prime Rate (%)	Average S & P 500 Index
1965	1.6%	4.54%	88.2
1970	5.7	7.91	83.2
1971	4.4	5.72	98.3
1972	3.2	5.25	109.2
1973	6.2	8.03	107.4
1974	11.0	10.81	82.8
1975	9.1	7.86	87.1
1976	5.8	6.84	102.0
1977	6.5	6.82	98.2
1978	7.6	9.06	96.0
1979	11.3	12.67	102.8
1980	13.5	15.27	118.7
1981	10.3	18.87	128.0
1982	6.2	14.86	119.7
1983	3.2	10.79	160.4
1984	4.3	12.04	180.5
1985	3.6	9.93	186.8
1986	1.9	8.33	236.3
1987	3.6	8.20	268.8
1988	4.1	9.32	265.9
1989	4.8	10.87	323.1

Source: Statistical Abstract of the United States and *Federal Reserve Bulletin*, various issues.

A fourth major trend in the financial planning market is the technological revolution that has occurred in the financial services industry. This revolution has made possible the creation of many new financial products and has made it easier to tailor these products to individual client needs. Also, the technology has made possible improved analysis of the performance of these products by planners who are technically able to do so.

CONSUMER NEEDS FOR FINANCIAL PLANNING

A basic and inescapable principle of economics is the law of scarcity: in every society human wants are unlimited whereas the resources available to fill those wants are limited, thus requiring that the resources be somehow rationed among the wants. This rationing problem creates the need for financial planning even in affluent societies, such as the United States, and even among all except (perhaps) the super-affluent members of such societies. To put it colloquially, there is just never enough money to go around.

What are the main financial concerns of American consumers? Are they able to handle those concerns on their own or do they need professional help? If they need professional help, with what type of problems do they need help? If they need professional help, do they recognize that they need help? In short, do U.S. consumers have a significant need and effective demand for professional financial planning services in the 1990s?

In each of the past few years, the IAFP has sponsored a survey of American consumers that sheds considerable light on a number of these questions. The most recent of these consumer surveys, entitled "Americans Cope with Their Finances," was conducted in April 1989.[4] Some of the results of this survey are presented below.

Short-Term Financial Concerns of American Consumers

Part of the 1989 survey inquired about the financial concerns of consumers in the short run. The largest single concern among respondents reported in this category was a fear that they would be unable to pay their home mortgages. This fear was ranked among the top two or three financial concerns by 19 percent of all households and by 21 percent of higher-income households. Moreover, the importance of people's concern about their mortgage increased very sharply in 1989 in comparison with the 2 preceding years.

Consumers' fears about their ability to meet their mortgage payments may be due to the increased use of adjustable-rate home mortgages by many members of the baby boom generation in recent years. Many adjustable-rate mortgages provide automatic increases in the interest rate in the early years. In addition, the interest rate may be pegged to changes in some independent economic indicator, such as the prime interest rate charged by banks on short-term business loans. The prime rate moved from 7.75 percent at the end of the first quarter of 1987 to 11.5 percent at the end of the first quarter of 1989. (In the ensuing 12 months, it has fallen back somewhat to 10.0 percent at the end of the first quarter of 1990.)

Other important short-term financial concerns expressed by survey respondents in 1989 were paying the monthly bills, taxes, and the costs of the children's education.

Again the influence of the baby boomers, whose children are or soon will be in college, is reflected in the results. The cost of education was a particularly important worry among higher-income households. Fears about inflation ranked far below most other short-term concerns for both the entire survey group and the higher-income group. Table 1-2 provides details concerning the results of the portion of the survey dealing with short-term financial concerns of the respondents.

TABLE 1-2
Biggest Economic and Financial Concerns Facing Household
(Results of Multiple Responses)

	Total Public			Total Higher-Income		
	1989	1988	1987	1989	1988	1987
Paying back mortgage/payments on house	19%	9%	11%	21%	6%	10%
Paying (our) bills/debts/monthly expenses (general)	11	13	11	7	8	6
Paying taxes/high/rising taxes	11	11	9	11	12	14
Paying for (child's) education/college	11	8	10	17	12	19
Car	10	6	7	9	4	5
Paying medical/doctor bills	9	9	15	4	3	7
Renovating/refurnishing home	7	2	3	7	2	4
Buying food/(rising) grocery bill	5	5	6	1	1	3
Paying for insurance/high/rising insurance rates	4	4	4	4	1	3
Lack of job security—fear of losing job/layoffs	3	4	3	2	3	2
High/rising interest rates	3	4	2	5	8	3
Paying for utilities/(rising) utility bills	3	3	5	2	1	2
Paying the rent	3	3	5	1	–	1
Putting some money away for/need money for retirement	3	1	2	4	2	2
Inflation/high/rising cost of living	2	9	6	5	11	5
Inability to put some money into savings/save some money	1	4	2	2	6	3
(Rising) price of fuel/energy	1	3	3	1	–	2
Paying for clothing	1	1	1	*	–	*
Moving expenses	1	1	1	1	1	1
Car repairs	1	1	1	1	–	*

(continued)

TABLE 1-2 (continued)

	Total Public			Total Higher-Income		
	1989	1988	1987	1989	1988	1987
Paying/saving for a vacation/traveling	1	1	–	2	1	–
Lack of money—having a hard time making ends meet	*	6	3	*	4	1
Concern over my business/company	*	3	2	1	4	3
Low income/inadequate salary	–	4	4	–	4	5
Am unemployed/lacking steady employment	–	3	4	–	–	1
Concern over investments/need for wise investments	–	3	2	–	8	4
Living on a fixed income	–	2	2	–	–	–
Concern over new/change in tax laws	–	1	4	–	3	9
(Possible) loss of second/spousal income	–	1	*	–	1	1
None—no (real) financial concerns	6	15	11	7	23	19
All other mentions	10	4	5	8	8	7
Don't know	18	7	6	15	6	5

*Less than 0.5% mention
–No response

Long-Term Financial Goals of American Consumers

A second major part of the IAFP survey inquired about the top two or three long-term financial goals of Americans. The major objectives for both the entire survey group and the higher-income group were, in order of importance, as follows:

- to save/provide for a comfortable retirement
- to save/provide for the children's education
- to purchase/build a new house

As might be expected, the rankings assigned to these long-term goals did not change much from year to year. Table 1-3 contains details concerning the long-term goals of the respondents. One noteworthy point revealed by this table is that a substantial percentage of the respondents in both groups indicated either that they haven't thought about their long-term goals, don't really have any such goals, or don't know what their long-term goals are.

With respect to the major long-term financial goal, having a financially comfortable retirement, 43 percent of the respondents in the total group and 39 percent of those in the higher-income group said they were very concerned or somewhat concerned that they may outlive their retirement savings. It is also interesting that over half of the respondents in each group were totally unable to estimate what their monthly retirement income will be.

With respect to the second most important goal, providing for the children's college education, the survey revealed several important points. First, only 14 percent of the total group who have dependent children expect their children to qualify for grants or scholarships. In the higher-income group the figure was 9 percent. These expectations contrast sharply with today's pattern in which IAFP states that about 46 percent of college freshmen receive some type of student aid, averaging about $3,800 per student.

Second, although on average the respondents were about 8 years away from paying for college, few of them could estimate what those costs will be. About one-third overestimated the costs, one-third underestimated them, and 20 percent didn't know.

Third, most of those respondents who said they had started a college savings program are probably not keeping up with the annual inflation in college costs. In recent years most estimates place the average annual increase in college tuition rates at 7 to 8 percent and room and board costs at 5 to 6 percent. It is unlikely that the aftertax interest earnings of most who are saving for their children's education are sufficient to keep up with such increases.

TABLE 1-3
Two or Three Long-Term Financial Goals Set for Self
(Results of Multiple Responses)

	Total Public			Total Higher-Income		
	1989	1988	1987	1989	1988	1987
Save/provide for (comfortable) retirement	28%	23%	24%	41%	34%	35%
Save/provide for children's education/college	14	16	14	21	22	20
Purchase/build a (new) house	10	13	16	10	7	11
Increase my savings/build up my savings accounts	5	13	13	5	13	12
Haven't thought about long-term goals/don't (really) have any financial goals	9	12	15	3	5	12
Pay up/off my bills/debts	7	9	9	8	6	6
Want to live comfortably/be able to enjoy life	5	9	5	4	9	7

(continued)

TABLE 1-3 (continued)

	Total Public			Total Higher-Income		
	1989	1988	1987	1989	1988	1987
Gain financial independence/security	6	7	7	8	12	14
Pay off my mortgage/make home payments	3	7	6	4	5	6
(Just) to make ends meet/keep up with bills/cost of living	4	7	5	1	4	2
Increase/better my income/net worth	4	6	6	5	10	6
Achieve (my) professional goals	1	5	4	1	5	2
Start/increase/make lucrative investments	5	5	4	4	8	8
Am retired/old(er), so have no long-term goals	–	4	4	–	3	1
Save/provide for early retirement	2	4	4	4	9	8
Purchase a (new) car	2	4	4	1	2	1
Save/provide for my education/schooling	–	3	3	–	1	2
Already reached my goals/satisfied with my achievements	1	3	2	2	5	1
Start/own a business	2	–	–	3	–	–
Travel	2	–	–	4	–	–
Repair/renovate/improve house	0	1	2	–	1	1
Provide money/financial assistance/inheritance for my children	–	1	2	–	2	3
All other mentions	7	2	6	8	3	7
Don't know	18	3	2	9	2	3

–No response

Plans for Long-Term Medical Care Costs

Another portion of the IAFP survey, which deals with consumers' plans for meeting the costs of long-term medical care, is particularly worthy of note. Over one-third of the total respondent group and almost one-half of the higher-income households said that a family member might need long-term medical care. Within these two groups, almost one-half rated this need as *very likely*. And of these, 25 to

30 percent indicated that they either had no plans or did not know how the costs of long-term medical care for a family member would be covered.

It is likely that many of the respondents who said they have insurance to cover these costs are mistaken or are overestimating the amount of the costs that will be covered. Likewise, some of the respondents probably are under the mistaken impression that the federal medicare program (see chapters 8 and 10) will be of significant help.

Consumer Attitude concerning Professional Help

The last item to be mentioned here that was revealed by the IAFP survey is that many Americans see a benefit to having professional help in managing their finances. About one-half of the general public said that such help would be beneficial. Among higher-income respondents the belief is even stronger; 60 percent said professional help would be beneficial. It should be noted, however, that neither group of respondents was asked whether, how much, or how (fee-for-service or commissions as part of the purchase of financial products) they would be willing to pay for this professional assistance.

Obstacles Confronting Consumers

The results of the annual IAFP survey make it clear that many American households still have not gained control of their financial destinies. Certainly, there are many reasons why they have not developed financial plans that will enable them to do so. Three of the most important obstacles they face are the following:

- *the natural human tendency to procrastinate* — Among the reasons for putting off the task of establishing a financial plan may be a lack of time due to a hectic life-style, the seeming enormity of the task of getting one's finances under control, and the belief that there is still plenty of time to prepare for achieving financial goals.
- *the very common tendency for Americans to live up to or beyond their current income* — The pressure in households to overspend for current consumption is enormous, and many families have no funds left with which to implement plans for the achievement of future goals.
- *the lack of financial knowledge among consumers* — Although in recent years there has undoubtedly been some growth in the financial sophistication of Americans, there is still widespread ignorance about how to formulate financial objectives and how to identify and properly evaluate all the strategies that might be used to achieve them. Compounding this problem has been the continuous introduction during the financially turbulent 1970s and 1980s of "hot" new financial products, many of which disappeared from the scene not long after being introduced.

A major part of the financial planner's challenge is to help clients overcome these obstacles by educating them and motivating them to gain control of their own finances.

A basic conclusion that can clearly be drawn from the results of the 1989 IAFP survey, as well as the ones that preceded it in 1987 and 1988, is that American consumers need help in managing their personal finances to achieve their financial goals. Moreover, many Americans seem to realize that they would benefit from professional help, and others undoubtedly can be educated to reach the same conclusion. (Here, once again, read the "S" word.)

PLAN OF THE BOOK

Proper financial planning for clients is a very demanding field of activity for financial services professionals. It requires an unusual combination of attributes and abilities on the part of the planner. Much of the work calls for the planner to exercise a full range of interpersonal abilities, such as communicating, empathizing, counseling, and motivating. Much of the work also calls for the planner to exercise a number of technical skills, such as minimizing taxes, optimizing investment performance, dealing with pure-risk exposures, and crunching numbers.

A field that is as broad and as deep as personal financial planning cannot be thoroughly covered in a single text. This book attempts to provide only the basics. Chapters 2 and 3 are devoted to some of the interpersonal and psychological aspects of the financial planner's work, particularly improving the planner's ability to communicate with clients and to better understand their risk tolerances. Chapter 4 deals with the first of the six steps in the financial planning process, which is the gathering of all the relevant objective and subjective information about the client.

The next several chapters focus on the basic technical knowledge that a financial planner must have — the elements of tax planning, insurance planning, and investment planning. Aspects of these three broad technical areas, together with some less concrete but equally important areas of knowledge, are combined in chapter 10, where the focus is on retirement plans, which are one of the most important financial concerns of American consumers.

Chapters 11, 12, and 13 address a number of issues important to operating a financial planning practice. These issues are computerizing the practice, meeting regulatory requirements, and planning in an ethically proper manner.

The final chapter brings together much of the material in the preceding 13 chapters into a practical, "live" (though hypothetical) case setting. A series of appendixes rounds out the text with greater detail about comprehensive financial plans, time-value-of-money analysis, pure-risk management, and computerization of a practice.

Is financial planning a demanding, challenging field of professional endeavor? It most certainly is. And, it is also one of the most satisfying when done well because of the significant contribution financial planning can make to the emotional and financial well-being of clients and planners alike. So now, to begin.

Notes
1. Some information about both organizations is provided later in this chapter.
2. Larry Skurnik, "Job Analysis of the Professional Requirements of the Certified Financial Planner" (Denver: College for Financial Planning, 1987).

3. A more complete treatment of the tools and techniques of time-value analysis in financial planning is contained in Robert M. Crowe, *Time and Money,* 2d ed. (Homewood, Ill.: Dow Jones-Irwin, 1990).
4. The telephone survey was conducted by the Gallup Organization. It polled 1,000 households representative of the United States as a whole and an oversample of 300 households with incomes of $50,000 and up. The survey carries an error margin overall of ± 3.1.

2

Risk-Tolerance in Financial Decisions

Michael J. Roszkowski*

INTRODUCTION

The various investment vehicles available today are characterized by different levels of risk and potential return. Both ethical and regulatory principles require that the financial planner recommend only those products and investment strategies that are *suitable* for a given client after considering such factors as the client's investment objectives, financial capacity to absorb a loss, and psychological propensity for risk-taking. The goal is to deliver the most return for the amount of risk the client can tolerate. Proper asset allocation is impossible without factoring the client's risk-tolerance into the equation. Financial services professionals therefore need to be familiar with the concept of risk-tolerance, and likewise, make their clients aware of its significance to their investment decisions.

Helping clients to understand their level of risk-tolerance, while extremely important, is also one of the more difficult tasks facing the financial planner. Done properly, however, it will help foster improved relationships with clients and should mitigate the possibility of litigation by clients who feel that they were placed in investments outside their level of comfort.

This chapter is designed to help the reader better understand the concept of risk-tolerance. Major scientific findings about risk-tolerance are summarized and their practical implications for financial planners are discussed. Although it may at first appear to be a rather simple topic, risk-tolerance has proven to be an extremely complex phenomenon. It is included in many academic disciplines as an area of study—notably economics, psychology, finance, and management science. Each field has a different tradition and tends to approach risk-tolerance from a different perspective, thereby adding something unique to a general understanding of the subject. This chapter attempts to integrate the relevant research from all these disciplines and, in the process, touches on some areas where professional disagreement remains. Unfortunately, in some instances, it is necessary to sacrifice depth of coverage to allow for a greater breadth of coverage. (More detailed knowledge may be obtained by consulting the references listed at the end of this chapter.)

More specifically, this chapter aims to show the financial services professional how people view risk and how they process information about risk factors. Aspects believed to cause people to either minimize or exaggerate the objective level of risk in a situation are explored. Demographic and personality characteristics that have been linked to risk-tolerance are also discussed. Finally, various approaches to assessing a client's risk-taking propensity are considered and their relative merits

---

*Michael J. Roszkowski, PhD, is associate professor of psychology at The American College.

and drawbacks noted. As much as possible, the use of jargon has been avoided in this chapter. However, at times it helps to label some phenomena in order to facilitate a dialogue about the subject and to help make the information more memorable. (Things named are easier to recall.)

The material in this chapter is intended to sharpen the financial adviser's skills in dealing with clients. It should allow him or her to view the problems faced on a daily basis from a theoretical perspective. It is hoped that after completing the study of this subject matter, financial planners will have greater insight into why clients accept or refuse risk. This awareness can be used by financial planners to better serve the needs of their clientele.

RISK-AVERSION, RISK-SEEKING, AND RISK-INDIFFERENCE

It is generally accepted that people react differently to risk. Some are always willing to accept it, others are always ready to reject it. It is best to think of reactions to risk as a *continuum.* Individuals on the one end are known as "risk-seekers" (or "risk-tolerant") while those on the other end are known as "risk-averters" (or "risk-rejecters"). People in the middle are referred to as "risk-indifferent." Frequently the terms *aggressive* and *conservative* are used to describe investors who are, respectively, risk-seeking and risk-averse. According to conventional wisdom, investment decisions involve a trade-off between risk and expected return. Risk-averse investors prefer low risks and are therefore willing to sacrifice some expected return in order to reduce the variation in possible outcomes.

The *majority* of the population is thought to be closer to the risk-averter end of the continuum. For example, a recent study conducted by the Life Insurance Marketing and Research Association (LIMRA) asked survey participants if they would be willing to "take risks for higher yields." The answers were to be given on a 10-point scale where 1 indicated "not willing" and 10 stood for "very willing." Whereas 45 percent of the people rated themselves 1, 2, or 3, only 11 percent rated themselves 8, 9, or 10. The remaining 44 percent used the middle values (4 through 7) to describe themselves.

Security is a fundamental human need, as revealed in various surveys conducted over the years. In 1975, and then again in 1986, a representative national sample of adults were asked to indicate the one most important thing they sought in their lives. In both 1975 and 1986 security was among their top choices (see table 2-1). Similarly, job security is overwhelmingly most workers' top priority, according to a poll conducted by the Roper Organization several years ago. Offered a choice between greater job security with a small pay raise or a higher pay raise but less job security, 83 percent elected the first option, 13 percent chose the second option, and 4 percent were undecided.

The generally negative view people hold about exposing themselves to the risk of loss is, in fact, the basis for all sorts of consumer warranties. Is it any wonder that advertisements allowing for a "risk-free 30-day examination period" are so appealing for all products, including insurance policies?

TABLE 2-1
The Most Important Thing People Want Out of Life

	1975	1986
Self-respect	21.1%	23.0%
Security	20.6	16.5
Warm relationship with others	16.2	19.9
Sense of accomplishment	11.4	15.9
Self-fulfillment	9.6	6.5
Being well-respected	8.8	5.9
Sense of belonging	7.9	5.1
Fun and enjoyment of life	4.5	7.2
	100.0%	100.0%

Note: Adapted from Kahle and Kennedy (1989).

The following characteristics are thought to distinguish between risk-averters and risk-takers in their outlook on life:

Risk-Averter	Risk-Taker
• sees risk as danger	• sees risk as challenge or opportunity
• overestimates risk	• underestimates risk
• prefers low variability	• prefers high variability
• adopts the worst-case scenario (emphasizes the probability of loss)	• adopts the best-case scenario (emphasizes the probability of a win)
• is pessimistic	• is optimistic
• likes structure	• likes ambiguity
• dislikes change	• enjoys change
• prefers certainty to uncertainty	• prefers uncertainty to certainty

Why are some people more willing than others to take risks? Various factors have been hypothesized as playing a role in risk-acceptance. They include biological makeup, upbringing, and other life experiences.

Loss-Aversion

People's unwillingness to accept losses is a fundamental part of their attitude toward risk. As will be evident shortly, although it is typically stated that most people are *risk*-averse, it is really more appropriate to say that they are *loss*-averse.

In finance and related disciplines risk-aversion is defined as the preference for certain outcomes over uncertain outcomes. Conversely, risk-seeking refers to a preference for uncertain outcomes over certain outcomes. Various studies have demonstrated conclusively that people are indeed cautious when faced with a choice between certain and uncertain gains. That is, they most often select the certain gain, even if it is smaller. However, when the two alternatives are a choice between a relatively small but certain loss and a relatively larger but only probable loss, most people are risk-takers. In other words, they are willing to risk a large loss rather than accept a smaller but certain loss. For illustration purposes, consider the following problems posed by psychologists Tversky and Kahneman. First look at problem 1, which consists of the following two choices, A and B.

> A: a sure win of $3,000
> B: an 80 percent chance to win $4,000 (and a corresponding 20 percent chance of winning nothing)

Most people take choice A. That is, offered a choice between a relatively smaller but certain gain, and a relatively larger but nonguaranteed gain, most people elect the smaller but certain prize. Choice A is considered the risk-averse alternative, whereas choice B is the risk-seeking alternative. Now look at problem 2, which consists of choices C and D.

> C: a sure loss of $3,000
> D: an 80 percent chance of losing $4,000 (and a corresponding 20 percent chance of losing nothing)

Note that the only difference between problem 2 and problem 1 is that problem 2 deals with losses. That is, the probabilities and money involved remain the same as in problem 1. Here, alternative C is the certain (risk-averse) choice, while D is the uncertain (risk-seeking) choice. Under the possibility of loss, most people revise their preferences; they now elect choice D. In other words, when both alternatives are unpleasant, most people are inclined to take the 20 percent gamble that they will lose nothing even though the odds are against them. In problem 2, then, they prefer uncertainty to certainty or, in other words, they are risk-seeking.

Both the preference for A and the preference for D are a manifestation of the same psychological mechanism, namely, a reluctance to sustain a loss. It is really the prospect of loss that makes one risk-averse in the first problem and risk-seeking in the second problem. In both cases, people don't want to give up any money. For most people, the extent of risk-seeking that occurs when faced with a choice between losses is much greater than the extent of risk-avoidance that occurs when the choice is between gains.

These laboratory findings have been confirmed by observing real-life activities. At racetracks, a person will gamble larger amounts of money and place more bets on longshots when he or she has been losing that day. Likewise, companies take greater risks when they are in financial trouble, as when their returns are below target.

Cultural Admiration of Risk-Taking

Although for themselves most people desire and value security, they also tend to admire those who take greater risks than they do. In American culture, risk-takers are heroes, seen as possessing the "right stuff." Risk-taking in all spheres of life is supported. For example, U.S. bankruptcy laws encourage risk-taking by forgiving financial mistakes. Most people, given the opportunity to change their nature, would like to be more risk-taking rather than less risk-taking in their everyday behavior.

Furthermore, almost everyone is willing to acknowledge that a certain degree of risk-taking is a critical factor in financial success. Some years ago, readers of *Psychology Today,* for instance, were asked to indicate the importance of various attributes to "making a lot of money." Risk-taking was viewed as *very important* by 44 percent of the respondents. The only other attributes that received more *very important* ratings than risk-taking were ambition (84 percent), hard work (64 percent), and brains/talent (50 percent).

THE FORMAL CONCEPT OF RISK AND PEOPLE'S INTUITIVE UNDERSTANDING OF IT

The term *risk* has many definitions, as is pointed out in chapters 7 and 9. Psychologists and other scientists have compared these definitions to people's intuitive understanding of the concept of risk. There are some striking differences.

In the field of finance, the conventional measure of the risk of an investment is its volatility. For example, assume that Stocks A and B had the following annual rates of return over a 5-year period:

Year	Stock A	Stock B
1986	+10%	+10%
1987	−5	+10
1988	+20	+10
1989	+15	+10
1990	+10	+10
Average	10%	10%

Both stocks produced an average 10 percent annual return for the 5-year period. However, Stock B was steady, producing the same return each year. Stock A, in contrast, yielded markedly different returns in each of the 5 years. Because it exhibited less variation in return, Stock B is considered less risky. In other words, Stock B is safer because its return is more predictable (less uncertain). High variance in past (and projected future) returns is equated with risk.

To the average person unsophisticated about investment matters, however, the most important factor in evaluating the riskiness of an investment is the historical trend line in the return generated by the investment. If the trend is *upward,* the investment is perceived as less risky than if the trend is *downward.* Fluctuations in the return are only a *secondary* consideration. To illustrate, consider the following two securities, C and D, which exhibit the same degree of average return and degree of fluctuation in returns over a 5-year period, but whose trends are mirror images of each other.

Year	Stock C	Stock D
1986	−10%	+10%
1987	−5	+5
1988	0	0
1989	+5	−5
1990	+10	−10
Average	0%	0%

The greater risk is perceived by most people to lie in Stock D, because of the downward pattern.

On an intuitive basis, then, people do accept variability of investment returns as a measure of risk, but the evidence shows that many do not treat uncertainty about *positive* outcomes as an aspect of risk. Rather, most people focus on the probability of negative returns in defining a risk. In other words, in most people's minds, the word risk implies danger or possible loss. A recent survey of public opinion regarding the term risk by the Insurance Information Institute further corroborates this point. Asked to indicate what the word risk connotes, most people said "danger" (84 percent) and "possible loss" (77 percent). Risk is thought to increase as bad outcomes become more likely.

With respect to investments, the danger lies in either getting something less than the expected return, or sustaining a loss of the principal. Surveys have demonstrated that portfolio managers and professionals who must routinely deal with capital budgeting tend to incorporate the probability of not achieving an expected (that is, target) return on an investment into their personal definition of a risky investment. However, in most other people's minds, the loss of principal is closest to their intuitive understanding of the word risk. Therefore any investment product promising no loss of principal will appear safe to most consumers. With respect to this point, it is of interest to note that some individuals tend to draw a distinction between investing and speculating. According to this line of thought, investments assure the safety of principal whereas speculations do not. It is no accident that mutual funds that guarantee the return of the principal appeared after the October 1987 stock market crash.

Another difference between people's intuitive understanding of the word risk and some formal definitions of this term involves the distinction sometimes drawn between risk and uncertainty. About 58 percent of the people questioned in the previously noted Insurance Information Institute survey, dealing with the connotations of the word risk, indicated that they associated risk with the word *uncertainty*. However, in the decision sciences, risk and uncertainty are not considered the same. There, risk refers to situations in which (1) the various consequences of each alternative are known and (2) their exact probabilities can be specified. Uncertainty, in contrast, is said to exist when the possible alternatives and their associated probabilities of occurrence are unknown.

For illustration purposes, consider the possible outcomes that students face when they take an examination. There are two possible outcomes—failing or passing. Assume for a moment that someone is asked to estimate his or her chances of passing the course. If he or she can assign a probability to this event (for example, 60 percent chance of passing/40 percent chance of failing), then the exam represents a risk. If, on the other hand, the person has no way of assigning odds (for example, he or she is not familiar with the instructor's grading policies), then the exam represents an uncertainty. On an intuitive basis, most people are not aware of this distinction and view it as "splitting hairs." The typical argument against this distinction is that *objective* probabilities are difficult to obtain. And, in fact, most of the time people tend to rely on *subjective* probabilities, which are based on beliefs rather than objective information.

Perceived versus Objective Risk

In essence, there are four dimensions to a choice involving risk: (1) the potential amount to be gained, (2) the probability of achieving this gain, (3) the amount that could potentially be lost, and (4) the probability of this loss occurring. Whether a person accepts or rejects a risk depends on his or her analysis of these four elements. In analyzing whether it is worthwhile to undertake the risk, different people tend to focus more on some of these dimensions than on others. Some people look most closely at the probability of winning, while some are fixated on the probability of losing. Still others are mainly concerned with the amounts involved.

It has been demonstrated repeatedly that the objective riskiness of a situation and one's interpretation of it, called "perceived risk," are not necessarily the same. Different people exposed to the same information interpret it differently. The objective odds are either lowered or heightened depending on the person's experiences, inclinations toward risk-taking, and the particular circumstances surrounding a given situation.

Perceived Risk and Buying Behavior

According to results of research on buying behavior, when consumers perceive risk in a purchase, their behavior changes markedly. They are likely to buy well-known brands, stick to the brand of a product that they used previously, and if switching to another brand, they will seek out information about the product under consideration. Products that are most likely to be perceived as risky are ones that are new, expensive, and complex.

Every risky decision produces what is known as "anticipatory regret," which refers to the feeling that the choice may prove to have been the wrong one. Factors contributing to an increase in anticipatory regret:

- The decision is viewed as an important one.
- People important to the decision maker feel that the decision should have been delayed until all possible consequences were evaluated carefully.
- The differences among the choices are not very apparent.
- New information has become available about potential losses.
- Negative consequences could materialize soon after the decision is made.

LIMITATIONS IN RATIONAL THINKING

Debates abound among various academic disciplines regarding the extent of rationality shown in people's economic behavior. While some continue to view people's actions in financial matters as *always* totally rational, more and more evidence of less than totally rational behavior is becoming available. At best, human beings act within what the Nobel prize-winning economist and psychologist Herbert Simon calls "bounded" rationality. That is, there are bounds or limits to how rational people can be. Their choices in financial matters are shaped not only by knowledge and rational thinking but also by their values and emotions. Frequently, instead of trying to *maximize* their economic well-being, people will settle for a course of action that is less than optimal but happens to be good enough to satisfy them. (The term *satisficing* is used to describe such behavior.)

Challenges to rationality are often reported in the behavior of the stock market. Certain research suggests that a large part of the volatility in the stock market is due to fads and mass psychology (that is, people doing something because others are doing it) rather than to changes in the economy or the fundamental soundness of the companies issuing the stocks. It has been observed that attitudes about the economy change faster than the economy itself. Likewise, some have likened the spread of enthusiasm and disenchantment about a given stock to the spread of an epidemic. For instance, in October 1984, a woman in New York City claimed that she found glass slivers in Gerbers baby food. Gerbers Products' stock fell 15 percent in two days. But not long thereafter it bounced back. The market crash of October 1987 can be attributed to numerous factors, but there is no doubt that investors mimicked the behavior of others in the selling frenzy. Two recurrent anomalies that have been observed in the stock market are the "weekend" effect and the "January" effect. The weekend effect refers to the fact that average returns tend to be lower on Mondays than on Fridays (except for Friday the 13th), while the January effect refers to the fact that average returns tend to be higher in January than in other months.

Many studies have been conducted by psychologists on how people perceive and process information about uncertain events. Almost every one of these studies has found that people tend to violate rationality to some degree. These flaws in judgment are due in part to people's limited abilities to process information and in part to the interference of their emotions. With respect to the first limitation, it has been established that at any particular moment, a person — even one considered intelligent — can process only about seven pieces of discrete information; yet, interestingly, most people fail to appreciate this limitation.

Few people have an insight into how they make risky decisions. Many people do not understand the laws of probability, and their ability to combine two or more probabilities is especially flawed. For example, in one study a substantial number of people preferred a lottery in which they were allowed to draw one ticket out of 10 to another lottery in which they would be able to have 20 draws out of 100 tickets. (The 20-draw lottery is, of course, a better deal.) When processing information about probability, most people do it intuitively on the basis of what feels right, rather than on mathematical formulas. Few people have been exposed to courses on how to make optimal decisions using mathematical decision rules.

Some distortions in people's estimation of probability and risk are unique to each particular individual. Such idiosyncratic distortions depend on the individual's particular psychological makeup. Other distortions are quite systematic, influencing most people's perception of risk in a similar manner. Systematic distortions of perceived risk are often due to the operation of mental shortcuts, called *heuristics*. These are rules of thumb that are appropriate in most circumstances, because they act to reduce the cognitive strain that results from too much information (that is, information overload). In certain situations, however, those rules of thumb can be misleading.

Overconfidence in Intuitive Judgments

Most people, laymen and professionals alike, tend to have a degree of confidence in their judgment that is well above that warranted by reality. Studies have been conducted that ask people to make a choice and then estimate their probability of being right. These research findings indicate that if a person believes he or she has an 80 percent chance of being right, in reality this probability is only 70 percent. In other words, people are right in their judgment seven out of 10 times rather than eight out of 10. There is even error when one is totally certain about something. In one study, when people said something "always" happened, it actually occurred only 80 percent of the time. Likewise, when these individuals indicated that something "never" happened, it occurred about 20 percent of the time.

Research has also shown that, typically, people use fewer clues to make a decision than they claim. The importance of minor clues is overestimated in most instances. Presenting people with more facts seems to make people feel more *confident* about their decisions, but generally the accuracy of their decisions is not augmented by the additional information.

Nonrepresentativeness of Short-Run Trends

Most people fail to appreciate what has been called "the Law of Large Numbers." They are willing to make their risk-assessments on the basis of very small samples, not realizing that what is true in the *long run* may not occur in the *short run.* This leads to the well-known "gamblers fallacy," which makes people believe that the probability of heads is more likely after a short run of tails. It has been further observed that, in line with this gamblers fallacy, people are willing to wager a larger amount of money after a sequence of pure losses or pure gains than after a mixed sequence of events (gains on some, losses on others). Some analysts believe that, in line with this fallacy, many investors tend to give disproportionate importance to short-run economic developments. Recent events tend to be given undue emphasis in people's decision-making, such as judgments about the value of a particular stock.

The following experiment illustrates people's failure to appreciate the significance of small versus large samples. In this experiment, people were asked to indicate which of the following is more likely to be an honest coin—coin A or coin B. Remember, in a single flip of an *honest* coin there is a 50-50 chance of the coin falling on its head or tail.

Coin A: 8 heads in 10 flips
Coin B: 70 heads in 100 flips

The honest coin is more likely to be A, but many people say B because the distribution of heads and tails is closer to 50-50 for coin B. These individuals are in error, however, because they fail to appreciate the small number of flips that took place with coin A. In the *short run,* an outcome that defies what one would expect in the long run is quite possible.

Failure to Correctly Evaluate Exposure

Most people have a particularly hard time evaluating the true magnitude of a risk that is not constant. In one study, the participants were asked to estimate the magnitude of risks that varied in both extent of potential harm and exposure time (that is, long-duration high risk; long-duration low risk; short-duration high risk; short-duration low risk). It was discovered that people fail to factor exposure time correctly into their estimates of risk. They tend to *overestimate* the impact of short-duration high-risk events. Being in danger for a very short time is seen as much more dangerous than it really is.

Denial of Risk

Willingness to undertake a high risk could be due to either a failure to accurately evaluate the true level of danger or an accurate evaluation but willingness to nonetheless engage in the activity because the level of danger is acceptable (perhaps even enjoyable). The evidence suggests that people engaging in risky behaviors on a *voluntary* basis often fail to appreciate the true level of danger in the situation. They may know the statistical odds but refuse to believe that these odds apply to them personally.

As an example, consider the results of a study sponsored by the Insurance Information Institute. It was discovered that only 58 percent of people who smoke in bed consider it to be a very risky activity, whereas 92 percent of those who do not smoke in bed find it to be so. Similar patterns were identified for activities such as gambling (35 versus 63 percent), driving a car (27 versus 39 percent), skiing (13 versus 33 percent), and investing in the stock market (26 versus 39 percent).

Frequently, people claim that there is less risk in their own personal case because they possess skills that reduce the risky aspects of the situation. For instance, many sky divers deny that their sport is risky. To them, it is risky only if one "does not know what he or she is doing." Similar attitudes have been documented among people who speculate in the stock market and real estate. A sharp distinction is drawn by such individuals between taking risks and being foolhardy. (This distinction is illustrated well in a Vietnamese proverb: "While it is noble to assist a stricken elephant in rising, it is foolhardy to catch one that is falling down.") As will become apparent shortly, in many cases, people have unwarranted confidence in their skill levels.

Other people deny the risk because they feel especially lucky. They believe that the odds can be beaten. Even if the odds of success are only 10 in 100, such individuals are apt to think, "Somebody has to be in that 10 percent, so why shouldn't it be me?" When the objective probability of an event is unknown, people tend to *overestimate* the probability of a desired outcome and *underestimate* the probability of an undesired outcome. Many an individual who felt that the odds could be beaten has traveled to Las Vegas in a $15,000 car and indeed has come home in a $100,000 vehicle. Unfortunately, in a majority of such cases the $100,000 vehicle was not a new car but a bus.

People's reluctance to buy insurance stems in part from such unrealistic optimism. Some agents present actuarial data to their prospects on the probability of death, disability, and hospitalization, but most prospects feel that such statistics don't really apply to them personally. Most people believe that they are less likely than average to die prematurely, be hospitalized, or become disabled. For instance, in a recent study people were presented with the statistic that during a given year approximately 19 out of every 1,000 persons will sustain a disability lasting over 3 months. (In other words, the odds of disability were 19 in 1,000.) The group was then asked to estimate their personal odds of sustaining a disability. On average, the subjects felt their personal odds to be much lower—only 6 in 1,000.

This same optimism characterizes people's outlook about their own financial future compared to the outlook for the nation as a whole. A Gallup Organization poll conducted in 1989 discovered that only 25 percent of the public believed that the financial state of our country would be better "a year from now." However, as far as their own personal situation was concerned, more than twice as many people (54 percent) felt that their personal financial status a year from the time of the poll would have improved. Similar results were observed over the last 15 years, except for 1982, when the country was in a deep recession.

It has been observed in almost all studies of this topic that people tend to especially discount very small negative probabilities, treating them as if they didn't exist at all. Due to this bias in the processing of risk information, many people are reluctant to insure against low-probability events even if a catastrophic loss potential exists and the insurance is underpriced (in relation to the actuarial risk). For example, flood insurance, despite being federally subsidized, is not easy to sell. Sales do increase after a flood occurs, but only for a few months. Psychologists have examined the style of thinking that supports this undue optimism. In essence, it has been found that people tend to overgeneralize from their previous experiences. The person's thinking goes along the lines of "It hasn't happened to me yet, so it probably never will."

Two techniques have been suggested as a way of encouraging the purchase of insurance coverage for underestimated perils. One, the insurance should be sold as part of a comprehensive package rather than as a separate policy. Two, a partial refund can be offered to the policyholder during years in which no claims occur.

The refunding concept can be used with other coverages as well. For instance, some companies are marketing accidental death protection that offers a refund of the full premium paid if, after a certain number of years of continuous coverage (for example, 15 years), no claim is made. The same concept is being used by others to market a fully refundable homeowners insurance, even if claims have been made.

The plan, of course, requires a single lump-sum, up-front premium payment that is higher than the standard annual premiums would have been.

Complete Elimination versus Reduction in Risk

Research comparing how people react to a *reduction* in a risk relative to its complete *elimination* has been conducted. It has been noted that most people place a disproportionately high value on the latter. Some have suggested that this mindset also has implications for the marketing of insurance products.

The high value people place on the elimination of risk may be the reason why low deductibles on property and casualty coverages are so popular, despite the relatively high premiums. Furthermore, this bias implies that the way a particular coverage's degree of protection is described to a client is very important. For instance, an insurance policy guarding against a particular peril, like fire, may be viewed as either *full* protection against the specific risk or a reduction in the overall probability of property loss. Based on the observed preference for the elimination of a risk compared to its reduction, there is a distinct marketing advantage in focusing on the coverage's *full* protection aspect. Telling a prospective client that buying the policy will lower his or her chances of suffering property damage will have a lower inducement value than will stressing to the client that he or she has *full* protection against fire.

Availability Bias

The most well documented bias altering people's estimates of risk is called "availability bias." It refers to the fact that events that are easy to imagine or recall will be judged as more probable than they actually are. Events that are dramatic and vivid or that receive heavy media attention are easily available to one's mind and are therefore overestimated. In contrast, events that are dull or abstract are underestimated. A few examples should help explain this particular bias.

- When asked to estimate whether the letter "K" occurs more frequently as the first letter or the third letter in an English word, most people say first. In actuality, the letter "K" appears three times more frequently in the third position of a word. The reason why most people believe otherwise is because it is a lot easier for them to think of words that start with "K."
- Which is more frequent, homicide or suicide? Most people believe that homicide is five times more frequent. Yet suicides are 30 percent more common. People tend to believe that the opposite is true because homicides are reported in the news, whereas suicides are generally not (unless the suicide involves a well-known personality).
- People overestimate the probability of dying from accidents in comparison to dying from illness. Again, this is because the media devotes more coverage to deaths resulting from events like airplane crashes than to deaths resulting from heart attacks. Likewise, the amount of coverage afforded different diseases in medical journals leads many physicians to erroneously estimate the risk of death

from a particular disease. The morbidity of diseases that are dealt with frequently in the medical journals is overestimated.

- Seeing the movie *Jaws* made the public much more wary of going in the ocean than the actual probabilities of being attacked by a shark warranted.
- People tend to be more influenced by personal experiences because they are more vivid. Thus research shows that people overestimate the probability of death from diseases that killed people they knew personally. Similarly, people tend to be influenced more by anecdotal evidence provided by their friends than by more representative and trustworthy information contained in statistical reports. Consequently, most people, when they are in the market for a car, will rely more heavily on the experiences a friend has had with a particular model than on a consumer survey report. Similarly, many people who failed to wear a seat belt, despite repeated warnings from various governmental agencies, started to wear one when a friend or neighbor was hurt or killed because a seat belt was not worn. It was only after this personal experience that they began to wear a seat belt. (On a more positive note, because they make information much more vivid, sales presentations incorporating slides or other graphics have proven to be much more successful than purely oral presentations.)

Familiarity Bias

Most people dread the unknown. Risks that are familiar are feared less than risks that are unfamiliar. In other words, people tend to perceive less risk in things they know. The more a person knows about a product, company, or situation, the lower will be his or her perception of risk (all other things being equal). For example, it has been reported that investors who are sophisticated about investment vehicles are more risk-tolerant than investors who are naive about the field. Educating clients about unfamiliar investments may lower their inherent fears about them.

Typically, people overreact to unexpected news. Studies have shown that both securities analysts and the lay public overreact to recent information, giving the new (that is, unfamiliar) information more importance than it really deserves. The impact of familiarity can be discerned clearly in both the financial industry's and investors' reactions to the October 1987 stock market drop of 508 points as compared to the drop of 200 points in October 1989. For example, the publication *Financial Services Week* conducted a random survey after the October 1989 drop. The survey revealed a very unconcerned attitude. Despite reports after the "miniplunge" of 1989 that the market was fragile, most investors and their advisers were unfazed by the drop, and few advisers received any panicky telephone calls from their clients. One financial adviser who was interviewed in the *Financial Services Week* survey summarized the situation in the following terms:

> I was so disappointed. . . . Not only did I not get any calls from clients, but Monday morning I called up a bunch of clients—I was going to calm them down and let them know that the world had not ended—and their consensus was "big deal, so what?"

Another financial services professional taking part in this interview stated:

Three years ago we had a 60-point drop and people thought that was the worst tragedy ever. . . . And now a 60-point drop wouldn't even make the front page.

Hindsight Bias

Most people fall victim to what has also come to be known as the "Monday morning quarterback" bias. This bias makes people believe *after the fact* that many events were more predictable than they were in reality. In retrospect, many people claim that certain events did not surprise them. In fact, they actually claim to have predicted them. For example, many investors and analysts claimed that they "knew all along" that the market was going to crash in 1987 (yet they did not move their money into other investments).

Confirmation Bias

After making a decision, most people are more apt to seek out information that supports rather than refutes their beliefs. If they encounter disconfirming evidence, they are very likely to discount it.

Illusion of Control Bias

People tend to underestimate the risk involved in activities under their control, like driving a car, relative to activities in which the control is given over to someone else, like flying as a passenger in an airplane. A Roper Organization poll taken in 1988 reveals that about 16 percent of the population fears flying on a plane. Ironically, the chance of being involved in a car accident driving to the airport to catch a flight is greater than the chance of the airplane crashing.

Time Horizon

In investments, differences can exist between short-run and long-run strategies to maximize return. Therefore it is critical that a time horizon be specified. It has been reported that for most decisions involving an element of risk, the length of the time elapsing between making the decision and the knowledge of the eventual outcome is very crucial. If the time span between these two events is long, the person is more likely to accept the risk than if the time span is relatively short. In other words, if something is imminent, there is an increased sense of danger.

People tend to psychologically overemphasize short-term risks. Some authorities have suggested that people start smoking because the threat of cancer is so far in the future. The long-term risk, although quite threatening, does not seem real to them. This refusal to consider future risks seriously can be seen in Mark Twain's reaction to being told that, by giving up smoking and drinking, he could add another 5 years to his life. Twain's reaction was that without smoking and drinking another 5 years of living would not be worth it.

Fortunately, there may be some synergy between people's willingness to bear risk under a broad time horizon and the performance of the riskier investment products. Analysis of historical data has shown that, from a long-term perspective, many of these products were not risky. That is, while they show a great deal of volatility in the short run, they are less volatile in the long run. In other words, they are safer when viewed within a broadened investment time horizon.

Unfortunately for their financial well-being, people typically have a short-range rather than long-range planning horizon. The tendency to be myopic about one's investment planning horizon is well illustrated in a study conducted by a psychologist named Herrnstein. Herrnstein presented a group of people with the following situation: Let's suppose that you win a lottery that gives you two alternative ways, A and B, of collecting your winnings.

A: You can collect $100 tomorrow.
B: You can collect $115 a week from tomorrow.

A sizable portion of the group selected option A, despite the fact that by waiting only one more week they would have been able to earn 15 percent. (There are few investments that would pay 15 percent *per week* interest.)

Next, the people who selected choice A were presented with another hypothetical lottery, in which the two payment schedules were C and D.

C: You can collect $100 52 weeks from today.
D: You can collect $115 53 weeks from today.

Interestingly, almost all of those who selected payment schedule A now selected payment schedule D. If they were consistent in their behavior, they would have chosen C. There was the same one-week difference between A and B as between C and D. However, the one-week difference meant much more in the present than it did in the future.

Research-based evidence shows that 10 to 15 years is the longest time horizon that most people consider to be practical for planning purposes of any sort. Surveys of the general public continue to find that people do recognize that upon retirement they may not have enough income to live in the style that they are now accustomed to, but they fail to do anything to remedy the situation. The reason typically offered as justification is something to the effect that they have a more pressing *immediate* crisis or concern (for example, the need to use the money to get the children's braces). Many people who purchase term insurance instead of permanent insurance, intending to invest the difference in premiums, never do so because more immediate concerns always arise. One virtue of permanent life insurance is its built-in saving component. It takes much convincing to have an individual look beyond a rather limited time perspective.

Voluntary versus Involuntary Risk

It has been reported that people are more willing to bear a risk if they assume the risk on their own volition. For instance, if a wife is coerced to go along with the wishes of her husband and invest their funds in a vehicle she is unfamiliar with, she may exaggerate the level of risk in the product. Sometimes, however, when people are placed in a risky situation under less than voluntary conditions, they may deny the existence of the risk in order to avoid feelings of anxiety. For example, it has been observed that workers who must deal with toxic chemicals on a daily basis often refuse to become knowledgeable about the potential hazards they face. An acknowledgment would force them to either quit their jobs or continue working and feel uneasy about it.

A similar reluctance to learn the truth may be found in the case of people who are at risk for Huntington's disease, a progressive and fatal neurological disorder. The symptoms of this disorder do not appear until adulthood. Huntington's disease has genetic roots, and someone whose parent suffers from this disease stands a 50 percent chance of developing it. The gene for this disease can now be identified through genetic testing. However, it has been reported that most people at risk do not want to find out if they will or will not develop the disease. The 50 percent chance of receiving good news is not offset by the 50 percent chance that the news will be bad. It seems that under these circumstances, people prefer to remain in a state of uncertainty.

Mood

Psychologists have been studying the impact of a person's mood on his or her willingness to undertake a risk. The relationship between mood and risk-tolerance is quite complex, given the results of the various studies dealing with this topic. The research shows that a good mood leads to more positive expectations and lower perceived risk. Conversely, a bad mood leads to increased estimates of risk. However, when it comes to actual behavior, a good mood does not necessarily lead to greater risk-taking. While a good mood does increase willingness to take relatively *low risks,* it decreases the person's willingness to accept *high risks.* Perhaps this is because the person does not want to jeopardize his or her good mood.

Some theoreticians attribute the generally lower stock prices on Monday as compared to Friday (the weekend effect discussed earlier in this chapter) to differences in people's moods on Mondays as opposed to Fridays. Monday is said to be an unpleasant day for most people since it is the start of a work week. On Friday, though, most people are in a pleasant mood because they are anticipating the weekend. These differences in mood are believed to be reflected in stock prices. The same explanation can be extended to the January effect. Since January marks the beginning of a new year, people are generally optimistic in outlook, which again shows up in higher stock prices.

Effects of Alcohol on Risk-Taking

A number of studies have shown that alcohol consumption causes people to become reckless and take greater risks than they would ordinarily. An intriguing result of such experiments is that even those people who *believed* that they were drinking alcoholic beverages—when in reality they were not—also increased their risk-taking behaviors.

Parties Bearing the Consequences of a Decision

The answer to the question "Who will be affected by the consequences of my actions?" is a strong determinant of whether a risk will be acceptable or unacceptable.

A decision is most risk-averse in nature if its outcomes will have consequences for both the individual making the decision and those the individual cares about. A decision is somewhat less risk-averse if only the individual decision maker is affected. The *most* risk-prone decisions are made if only others will bear the consequences of the decision. For instance, managers take more risks when they invest their company's money than when they invest their own personal funds. Studies of stock market trading reveal a similar pattern. If the money being invested is his or her own, the investor requires more information before making a transaction and makes significantly fewer trades.

Group Dynamics of Risk-Taking

A phenomenon that has been studied for close to 30 years concerns the differences between individual and group reactions to risk. Originally called the "risky shift," today this phenomenon is also known as the "choice shift." This term refers to the finding that a group decision is usually more extreme than a decision favored by most members of the group when they are polled individually before the discussion. In most cases, the shift is toward more risky action, although in some instances shifts toward a more cautious attitude have also been observed. (Hence, the more neutral term *choice shift* is preferred today.)

Several studies on the choice shift phenomenon bear directly on financial planning. In one study people were asked to identify the investment products that they would be willing to buy. The investments available to them ranged from low-risk (no variability in their historical return patterns) to high-risk (very variable, with low returns in certain years and high returns in other years). First, each person made his or her selection individually. Next, they took part in a group discussion, the group's task being to reach a consensus regarding their choices. While on an individual basis most members of the group wanted the less risky products, the group decision was in favor of the riskier products. Similar results were obtained in another study where the group's task was the selection of an automobile physical damage coverage. When polled individually, the people participating in this study were willing to pay, on average, about another $48 in premiums in order to get physical damage coverage on their cars. As a result of the group discussion, however, the consensus was that they would be willing to pay less — only $31 — for this particular coverage. In other words, the group was willing to bear more of the risk. Group shifts in the risky direction have also been documented in a study concerning decisions about starting a new business venture.

A number of possibilities have been suggested as plausible explanations for the shift in the risky direction, including the following:

- The responsibility for a decision is spread over a large number of people. If the decision turns out to have been a bad one, no one person feels totally responsible for it.
- The risk-tolerant members in the group are influential and are able to sway the others in the group to follow their lead.

666

6

6

6

66666666

6

66

6

66666

6

6

6

6

6

66

6

66666

6

66

66

66

66666

66

- As a result of the discussion, the group members become more familiar with the situation. As noted earlier, familiar situations are not as frightening as unknown ones.

Mental Accounts

Various psychological experiments have been conducted to illustrate how "mental accounts" operate in people's evaluation of monetary gains and losses. One such study shows that the opportunity to save a given amount of money will be viewed quite differently, depending on what mental account a person uses to evaluate the psychological value of this money. A scenario developed by psychologists Daniel Kahneman and Amos Tversky asked people what they would do if they went out to buy a $125 jacket and a $15 calculator, and upon arrival at the main store, were informed by the sales clerk that the calculator was on sale for $10 at a branch store that was 20 minutes away. Under these circumstances, 68 percent of the people studied were willing to drive 20 minutes to save $5.

In a second version of this same story, the $5 in savings is on the jacket rather than the calculator. (That is, the price of the jacket is $120 at the branch store and $125 at the main store. The price of the calculator is $15 at both stores.) The percentage of people willing to drive 20 minutes to save $5 under the second set of circumstances was only 29 percent.

Five dollars would be saved either way, yet the number of people willing to save this amount of money was substantially different. Why? The simple reason is that people maintain different mental accounts for the prices of jackets and calculators. Money to be gained or lost is not evaluated in a vacuum. Rather, there is always some *subjective standard* that is employed as a yardstick to gauge the value.

The concept of mental accounts has many implications for financial services practitioners. The amount of pleasure or displeasure that the appreciation or depreciation in the value of a certain asset will bring to a client is not necessarily determined by the simple dollar amounts lost or gained. Other factors will influence the client's assessment of the event. For example, did the client's neighbor (or brother or sister) do better or worse? How did another security the client was thinking of buying fare?

It is necessary for financial services professionals to recognize that because of mental accounts their clients may have different risk-tolerance levels for different funds, depending on how they acquired the money and what they intend to do with the money eventually. Inherited versus earned money is one factor that may account for different risk-tolerance levels. Some people who inherit hard-earned money from a loved relative refuse to risk losing the principal. With money they earned personally, however, they may have less fear of potential loss. For others, the reverse may be true.

People's mental accounting for posting gains and losses does not treat money earned and money lost as equal units. Money lost carries a much heavier psychological value. For instance, making $5,000 on an investment, provided that this return is equal to what was expected, will make a client happy. Conversely, losing $5,000 on an investment will make a client unhappy. Research shows, however, that the unhappiness experienced at losing the $5,000 is greater than the happiness felt at earning $5,000. Thus clients are apt to be more upset about a given loss than pleased about an equivalent gain. Similarly, most investors feel worse if they sell a security that shortly thereafter increases in value than if they failed to buy the security in the first place.

Mental accounting may also be the underlying cause for the finding that most investors prefer cash dividends over capital gains (even if tax law should point to the opposite as the optimal course to take if one wants to maximize wealth). Dividends and capital gains are placed into separate mental accounts according to some theorists.

IS RISK-TAKING A SITUATION-SPECIFIC OR GENERAL PERSONALITY TRAIT?

Some financial planners tend to describe people as risk-takers or risk-averters, without considering the type of behaviors on which they base such classifications. It is as if they expect people to act in a similar manner in all aspects of life. Yet psychologists are still debating whether most people have a consistent pattern of risk-taking in all realms of their lives or whether the degree of risk they are willing to assume depends on the nature of the situation. Although some evidence suggests that there is a *slight* predisposition to act in either a risk-taking or risk-averse manner in different situations, this predisposition is weak for most persons. Only persons with the personality type psychologists call the "thrill-seeker" (also known as the "sensation" or "arousal" seeker) seem to be relatively consistent.

In general, the more similar any two situations are, the greater is the consistency in risk-taking behavior in these two situations. Research has shown that essentially four major types of life situations involve risk-taking:

- *Monetary* situations involve risks like investments, gambling, or job changes.
- *Physical* situations involve risks that could result in bodily harm, such as mountain climbing or skydiving.
- *Social* situations involve risks that could lead to loss of self-esteem or another person's respect. "Call reluctance" comes from an unwillingness to take a social risk. So does fear of public speaking; a 1988 Roper Organization poll found that 26 percent of the population considers public speaking to be one of the most frightening things in life.
- *Ethical* situations involve risks in which one is faced with the prospect of compromising one's moral or religious standards or society's legal standards. For example, trading on insider information involves an ethical risk.

These four risk contexts have been described, based on their consequences, as the potential loss of capital (monetary risk), the potential loss of life (physical risk), the potential loss of face (social risk), and the potential loss of freedom (ethical risk).

Cases in which the level of risk-taking is quite different across different contexts are not hard to find, as many people change their behavior from situation to situation. The author was told of one, a Navy pilot who had been decorated for heroism during the Vietnam War. After his discharge from the service, this individual was encouraged to begin a career in life insurance sales. His new career proved to be both financially and emotionally unrewarding, however, because he was uncomfortable with prospecting. This came as a surprise to the person's manager since there was clear-cut evidence of fearlessness and risk-taking in the person's war record. The ex-pilot and his manager had a discussion about his fear of prospecting. During the course of the conversation, it became evident to the manager that it was actually a low level of social risk-tolerance that accounted for this person's high physical risk-tolerance during the war. The individual related that what kept him flying was the fear of disapproval by others. As he put it, whenever he got jittery about a mission and thought of turning back, all he had to do was picture the look of disapproval from his commander and fellow pilots that he would get when he landed. In this case, low tolerance for social risk was, in part, responsible for high physical risk-tolerance.

One can also find people who work in physically risky jobs because they have low monetary risk-taking tolerance. The quote below shows how fear of being unemployed influenced an individual to continue working with a hazardous substance:

> If you have a family, two kids, a house, a car, and bills to pay, you forget your personal feelings about certain things. Nobody wants to do things that are wrong, but then again they have the responsibility to provide for their family. We really don't have a choice . . . I can't look for a year and a half for a job. I'd lose everything. [Brown, p. 265]

As the evidence above shows, one should be careful in using risk-taking in nonfinancial matters to infer a level of risk-tolerance for investments. Knowing that someone is a risk-taker in a certain physical activity provides clues about how the individual will react in other situations that involve potential bodily harm. But it gives much less of an idea about whether this person will be willing to invest in a financially risky venture. The latter information is best determined from a knowledge of the person's typical behavior in monetary risk-taking situations. Thus a financial planner who mails a promotion for an "aggressive" mutual fund to a skydiving club should not be surprised if the responses to the ad are not dramatically greater than if the mailing had been made to the public at large. The best predictor of an investor's risk-tolerance in a financial matter is his or her risk-preference in other financial matters, rather than how the person reacts to risk in sports, social situations, and so on.

The client's risk-tolerance in financial matters should be of primary concern to the financial planner, since this is the aspect of the client's situation that is within the planner's purview. However, there may be some value in looking at the client's risk-taking disposition in other aspects of life. First, it may be useful to make the client aware that he or she may not necessarily have the same propensity for risk in money matters as in physical activities or social activities. Often clients assume that there is a general predisposition to assume the same level of risk irrespective of the sphere of life or situation they are dealing with. In other words, it may help clients learn about themselves. Second, consistency across different contexts may alert the financial planner to whether the individual is someone who is a thrill-seeker (discussed later in this chapter).

Although not as critical to investment decisions as financial risk-tolerance, the client's tolerance to risk in physical matters may also be worth considering for another reason. Physical risk-taking could be a relevant issue to take into account when determining the client's insurance needs. It has been shown that risk-taking in the physical realm is a major factor in various types of accidents. Thus people who have high levels of physical risk-tolerance are more apt to die from accidental causes or to suffer disabling injuries from an accident. According to the *Statistical Bulletin* published by the Metropolitan Life Companies, accidents are the *leading* cause of death among children and young adults. When the U.S. population is considered as a whole, accidental death is third in line after death due to cardiovascular diseases or cancer. Some estimates suggest that every hour there are 11 accidental fatalities and about 1,040 accident-caused disabling injuries. Deaths from motor vehicle accidents account for approximately half of the accidental deaths reported in this country. Accidental death riders and disability income insurance may be of interest to the physical risk-taker, especially if the individual has, at the same time, a low level of monetary risk-tolerance.

Physical risk-taking is also a contributing factor in death from nonaccidental causes. Consequently, risk-taking in health-related matters is of increasing concern to insurance companies. It is now standard for insurance carriers to charge lower premiums for nonsmokers, and an emergent trend may be to extend similar premium reductions to people who avoid other health risks as well. Because of the AIDS epidemic, a growing area of research — some sponsored by the insurance industry — is concerned with risk-taking in sexual behaviors (a form of physical risk-taking).

PERSONALITY AND LIFE-STYLE CHARACTERISTICS OF THE RISK-TAKER

A majority of the studies on the personality of the typical risk-taker have been conducted under the assumption that risk-taking is a general personality trait rather than being specific to a particular context. Therefore the measures of risk-taking used in these studies did not differentiate between attitudes toward physical, social, ethical, and monetary risk-taking. As such, one needs to exercise caution in utilizing these findings in financial planning since they may apply more to one of the other categories of risk-taking than to monetary risk-taking in particular.

For example, the following life experiences that some researchers identify as typical of the risk-taker probably apply more to physical risk-takers than monetary risk-takers:

- took dares as a child
- drank and smoked at an early age
- was sexually active at a young age
- enjoys dangerous leisure activities, such as mountain climbing, surfing, hang gliding, scuba diving, racing a car, motorcycling, or skydiving
- is likely to hold a job as a pilot, soldier, fireman, or policeman

Likewise, the following characteristics of risk-takers may be related mostly to social risk-taking:

- has a social presence
- is self-accepting
- is self-confident
- is aggressive
- is independent
- is irresponsible
- is status-seeking
- has strong leadership abilities
- is unaccepting of other people's opinions

Similarly, the finding that risk-takers feel low levels of guilt for wrongdoing probably applies more to the ethical risk-taker than to the physical, monetary, or social risk-taker.

Other characteristics identified in this type of research may, however, also apply to monetary risk-takers. Among these are the following:

- emphasizes merit rather than seniority in job promotions
- enjoys work that allows him or her to make decisions
- requires little time to make a major decision
- when taking tests that have a time limit, completes them very quickly, attempting to compensate for a greater number of mistakes by answering more questions
- takes a chance and guesses on tests that impose a penalty for guessing (such as the Scholastic Aptitude Test)
- is optimistic in outlook, seeing mistakes as setbacks rather than as personal failures (that is, believes that lack of success does *not* doom a person to eternal failure—tomorrow will be better)
- has a low need for an ordered environment
- is able to handle stress
- is persistent

Relatively few studies have focused on the biographical and psychological characteristics of monetary risk-takers per se. Research conducted by Frank Farley, a psychologist at the University of Wisconsin, is an exception. His studies indicated that monetary risk-takers were good money managers who spent considerable time reading about investments and related financial matters and expressed confidence in their money-making abilities. In contrast to the monetary risk-averters, who stated that their long-term goal was happiness, the monetary risk-takers listed success as their primary goal. Farley also found that the people willing to take large monetary risks tended to possess leadership skills and good sales skills. For many monetary risk-takers, money was the center of their lives. Some had a very firm belief in God.

A particularly noteworthy result to emerge from another survey comparing the investment attitudes of risk-tolerant and risk-intolerant investors concerns their satisfaction with the returns they previously received on their investments. Whereas risk-averse investors are generally satisfied, those who are risk-tolerant tend to feel that they were not adequately compensated.

ATTITUDES TOWARD MONEY

Along with knowing a client's risk-tolerance, it is also instructive to understand a client's attitude toward money. Most people try to earn money because of the goods and services it can buy. Some people, however, come to value making money as an end in itself rather than as a means to an end. In the sections that follow, the origins of the latter behavior are considered.

Perception of Being Rich

When faced with some unpleasant task almost every person has at one time or another said to herself or himself: "Someday I'll be rich enough so that I will not have to do this anymore." A fundamental question, then, is how much money is necessary to be rich — that is, to be able to purchase the necessities as well as the luxuries of life. It appears that the answer is quite subjective.

A *Psychology Today* survey conducted in the early 1980s determined that the amount of money needed to feel rich was a function of the person's current level of personal income. In essence, the higher the level of personal income, the greater the amount of wealth (that is, assets) a person required to consider himself or herself rich. More detail about this pattern can be found in table 2-2.

TABLE 2-2
Personal Income and Amount of Wealth Needed to Be Rich

Current Personal Income	Level of Wealth Required to Be Rich
under $10,000	less than $100,000
$10,000–$29,000	$100,000–$500,000
$30,000–$49,000	$500,000–$1,000,000
$50,000–$100,000	over $1,000,000
over $100,000	over $5,000,000

Note: Adapted from *Psychology Today* (May 1981).

Compulsive Drive for Wealth

As the data in table 2-2 implies, most people may never get to the point where they feel rich enough, no matter what their objective level of wealth. Most people, even though they may not feel rich, do not become compulsive in their pursuit of greater wealth. Others, however, become totally preoccupied with this goal. It becomes the center of their lives to the exclusion of all other interests and pursuits. It is said that many such individuals exhibit symptoms of addiction; that is, they are "hooked on money."

Compulsive money-making sometimes results from the need to take risks (that is, thrill-seeking). In such cases, it is *making* money, not *having* money that is important to the individual. In other words, once the money is made, it loses some of its appeal.

Frequently, though, compulsive money-making has other roots. Some people are obsessed with making money because it allows them to "keep score." Accumulation of wealth conveys to both the compulsive money-maker and to others how well the money-maker is doing. Such individuals are willing to take risks that will not enrich them to any appreciably greater level because the more money one has, no matter how small the amount, the higher is one's "score."

People who are concerned with "keeping score" may also be interested in possessing other status symbols as well. A study published by the Roper Organization several years ago identifies the status symbols that people with above average income tend to value (see table 2-3).

TABLE 2-3
Things Valued as Status Symbols

Symbol	Percentage
Owning a business	58
Frequent travel	55
Serving as a trustee of a cultural institution	53
Being a corporate director	50
Shopping in prestige stores	30
Owning expensive jewelry	29
Flying first class	28
Owning an expensive car	28
Belonging to a private club	27
Owning a boat	21

Note: Reported in *The Public Pulse,* the Roper Organization, Inc. (1987).

PROFILES OF SUCCESSFUL AND UNSUCCESSFUL INVESTORS

Risk-tolerance is just one of the human characteristics bearing on investment decisions. Some research exists relating to other aspects of such decisions. The most interesting line of research of this kind deals with psychological differences between people who are successful and people who are unsuccessful in their investment pursuits.

From a group of 538 investors, a research psychologist named Van Tharp selected the 53 most successful and the 53 least successful investors. He developed the following profile of winning and losing investors, based on the psychological attitudes they expressed in a questionnaire.

A very positive image of the winning investor can be found in Tharp's results. In addition to stating that they took carefully planned risks, the successful investors were confident in their ability to make money. They had systematic trading techniques and were able to learn from their mistakes. They attributed both success and failure to their own efforts rather than to other causes. Generally, the successful investors had a positive self-image. Furthermore, the successful investors described themselves as happy and enjoying life to the fullest (for example, taking vacations, looking forward to what each new day will bring, and so on). Such investors also felt that they were able to handle stress well, frequently viewing pressure situations as challenges. They did not, however, trade in the market just for the thrill of it. They diversified their investments, having only a small portion of their capital in any one speculative product. Most important, they claimed to be willing to get out of an investment when things went wrong.

Quite a different composite picture of the unsuccessful investor emerged. The unsuccessful, or losing, investor described himself or herself as trading for the thrill of it, investing for power, to get even, or out of fear. Often, the unsuccessful investor possessed low self-esteem and blamed everybody but himself or herself for investment failures. A generally pessimistic outlook characterized many of the unsuccessful investors, and they did not seem to enjoy life. Unsuccessful investors changed brokers often, hoping to find one that understood their problems, but they did not follow the recommendations given to them by these brokers. The unsuccessful investors rationalized their losses and poor financial status by telling themselves that money was probably the root of evil, or that it was just as well that they were not rich since wealth would bring on additional stresses.

One characteristic has been found that consistently differentiates the successful from the unsuccessful investor—how losing investments are handled. Successful investors are willing to "cut their losses" when an investment is doing poorly, whereas unsuccessful investors tend to hold on to the investment, hoping that it will somehow miraculously turn around. Some writers have labeled this reluctance to realize losses as the disposition to "ride losers too long." A more familiar term is that losing investors have a tendency to "throw good money after bad." Jack Schwanger, author of *Market Wizards,* found that a willingness to cut their losses seemed to be the common link in top traders' attributions of their success. Most noted that with regard to picking winning trades, they were no better than anybody else. What distinguished them from less successful colleagues was their ability to limit their losses by selling the losers quickly. The profits were made on the few stocks that appreciated markedly. One successful commodity trader interviewed by Schwanger indicated that the three elements to successful trading are (1) cutting losses, (2) cutting losses, and (3) cutting losses. Many professional traders automatically sell a security once the loss reaches a certain percentage of the purchase price (for example, 10 percent). (Investors can use stop-loss orders to serve this same function.)

The mental account concept discussed earlier is of relevance here also. Selling a security at a price lower than what was paid for it means that the mental account opened for it would have to be closed with a posted loss. It is hypothesized that people find it extremely difficult to do this. To do so, one can no longer justify it to oneself as a simple paper loss. One's mistakes must now be admitted, and most people would like to forestall this decision for as long as possible.

It has been suggested by some writers in this field that because of people's generally negative feelings about closing a mental account at a loss, financial advisers should try to avoid any references to cutting losses. It is said that the realization of the loss can be made easier psychologically by advising the client to *transfer* his or her assets into another investment. By using the word *transfer,* no loss is implied, and the mental account for the poor investment can remain open.

THE THRILL-SEEKER

The thrill-seeker is the personality type most likely to be *consistently* risk-seeking across all dimensions of life, including financial matters. Sometimes a distinction is made between physical thrill-seekers and mental thrill-seekers, based on the arena of life they may emphasize in their sensation seeking. However, all thrill-seekers abhor routine, be it mental or physical. These individuals are always on the lookout for experiences that offer novelty, ambiguity, complexity, and intensity. If a thrill-seeker can't find excitement, he or she will create it. "In-and-out" trading in the stock market, for instance, provides many such quick thrills. For the thrill-seeker, the uncertainty of an investment decision may hold as much enticement, perhaps even more, than the anticipated payoff. To the thrill-seeker, money made from a safe investment does not hold as much value as the same amount of money made from a risky investment. There is some research showing that thrill-seekers have a biologically based need for greater than normal levels of arousal.

Thrill-seeking can have either very constructive or very destructive outlets. For example, constructive mental outlets are available in the arts or sciences, fields that reward the creative thinking characteristic of the thrill-seeker. Crime, in turn, provides a common destructive outlet for both mental and physical thrill-seeking. Even in prison, thrill-seekers are a problem, because they continually try to escape.

It is important to realize that not everyone who takes many risks is necessarily a thrill-seeker, although by definition, every thrill-seeker must be considered a risk-taker. How can a financial planner spot the thrill-seeker? To a certain extent, the thrill-seeker is a caricature of a risk-taker, showing many of the same basic characteristics, but in a markedly exaggerated form. In addition to the characteristics already mentioned in defining the thrill-seeking personality, the financial planner should be alert to those that follow.

Thrill-seeking is more common among men than women. Thrill-seekers like loud parties. They tend to be outgoing, spontaneous, and fast decision-makers. In looking for a history of sensation seeking, the planner needs to check to see if the person participates in risky sports and likes to gamble, especially at blackjack. Thrill-seekers may associate with unconventional persons and have an intense dislike for people they perceive as boring. The thrill-seeker wants variety in his or her sex life and has had more sexual partners and encounters than most people have. This type of personality also shows greater-than-average interest in all erotic material, including pornography. Many thrill-seekers are reckless drivers—so the planner should look for a history of speeding tickets and traffic violations. If the thrill-seeker uses recreational drugs, a variety of drugs rather than just one drug are taken. While logic would dictate that the thrill-seeker would prefer stimulant drugs over sedative drugs, the evidence for this pattern is not conclusive.

Although thrill-seekers constitute a relatively small proportion of the population, they pose a serious potential threat to the financial planner. They may appear to be perfect candidates for risky investments, given their obviously high tolerance for risk. But this very love for uncertainty, along with a desire for novel, intense, and varied experiences, may lead the thrill-seeker to pursue legal action against the planner for suggesting an overly risky product if the investment does not produce the expected returns. Suing can be a very exciting experience for a thrill-seeker, especially if he or she has not done it before. With this type of client, the planner must take particular care in documenting due diligence.

DEMOGRAPHIC CHARACTERISTICS

Numerous studies have been conducted over the years in which risk-tolerance was related to such things as age, sex, marital status, wealth, and occupation. The results of this research are discussed below.

Wealth

Do wealthy individuals take more risks with their money? Before this question can be answered, a distinction must be drawn between *absolute* and *relative* risk-tolerance. Absolute risk-tolerance is gauged by the *amount* of wealth one allocates to risky assets. Relative risk-tolerance, on the other hand, is measured by the *proportion* of one's wealth allocated to risky assets. It is generally accepted by most investigators of this topic that absolute risk-tolerance increases with wealth. The reason is quite obvious — the wealthy have more money to spend on *everything*. There is some disagreement, though, about whether relative risk-tolerance increases with wealth. Several studies have addressed this question by examining people's investment portfolios. One such study, conducted by Cohn and his colleagues, found that relative risk-tolerance does increase with wealth — the wealthier a person was, the greater the proportion of total wealth that person put in risky assets. For instance, if the individual's assets were above $175,000, on average, 62 percent of his or her investments were risky. If the total value of assets was below $175,000, only 42 percent of the investments were of the risky type. This pattern held even after sex, age, and marital status were taken into account. However, this relationship between wealth and risk-tolerance was strongest among male investors and married investors.

Some researchers have been unable to find relationships of this sort. One reason for the discrepant results in studies is attributable to differences in the type of assets that were considered and how these assets were classified (safe versus risky). The way the primary residence is treated seems to be especially critical. Relative risk-tolerance goes up with increasing wealth if housing is either excluded from the definition of wealth or classified as a riskless asset.

Further support for a positive relationship between relative risk-tolerance and wealth can be seen in studies using questionnaires as the basis for determining the degree of risk-tolerance. In the survey sponsored by the Insurance Information Institute cited at the beginning of this chapter, it was reported that the wealthy were more likely to associate the word *risk* with the word *opportunity* than the other respondents. Similarly, a study of the upper affluent sponsored by CIGNA found that the risk-takers in this group were more likely to have higher incomes and were much more likely to be millionaires. The "chicken and egg" question still remains — did the wealthy become so because of their greater willingness to assume risk, or is it that they are more risk-taking now that they are wealthy? That is, does having money make one more risk-seeking?

How money was acquired may also be a factor in the risk-taking propensity characteristic of the wealthy. Differences in risk-tolerance have been reported between those who inherited their wealth and those who made their fortune themselves. Namely, people who earned their own wealth are more risk-tolerant than those who inherited their wealth.

Some evidence suggests that a majority of the millionaires alive today did not inherit their wealth. In an interview with *Financial Services Week* (March 5, 1990) consultant Steve Moeller reports that 60 percent of millionaires made their fortunes by starting their own businesses. According to Moeller, the profile of the average millionaire is as follows: married, male, 57 years old, some college education, blue-collar family background, annual income of $130,000. Millionaires who acquired their own wealth prefer to make their own decisions, so Moeller recommends that financial planners present such individuals with a variety of investment options. Moeller claims that many of the wealthy prefer to invest in real estate rather than the stock market. Other evidence indicates that those who inherit their money are more receptive to financial planning advice than those who made their money themselves.

Age

A substantial body of research exists on the relationship between age and risk-taking in all sorts of activities, financial as well as nonfinancial. The bulk of this research points to a negative relationship between age and willingness to take risks. That is, as one gets older, one becomes more cautious. Some qualifiers are in order, however.

This relationship between more advanced age and increased caution may not be as strong for monetary risks as it is for physical risks. Moreover, the relationship between monetary risk-tolerance and age may be weaker among the wealthy, according to some studies. It has been suggested that when looking at the impact of age on risk-taking one also needs to consider the client's particular circumstances. For instance, some financial planners report that they have encountered middle-aged couples who were previously very conservative investors but who now take an interest in aggressive investing because their obligations to raise and educate their children are at an end.

Sex

The study of psychological differences between men and women has a long history. Almost all of the research conducted prior to the beginning of the women's movement indicated that men are more risk-tolerant than women in most aspects of life. Both biologically based and psychologically based explanations have been advanced. One psychological explanation is that women have been socialized to be more dependent and risk-averse.

The results of more recent studies are mixed. A number of the newer studies point to the need to consider age and income when looking at sex differences in monetary risk-taking. While older married women are less likely to accept financial risks than their husbands, when younger men and women with the same income levels are compared, the differences in monetary risk-taking tend to be smaller or even disappear.

Recent polls also reveal the changing attitudes toward financial risks among women. For instance, a *Ms. Magazine* poll conducted in 1977 found that only 26 percent of their readers would *invest* a cash windfall rather than keep it in a savings account. When the same poll was repeated in 1988, 40 percent of the respondents indicated that they would be willing to take risks in order to obtain a higher potential return. Also stock ownership in this group was up. About 33 percent of the 1988 respondents owned stocks, compared to 24 percent of the 1977 respondents.

Other sex-related differences between men and women have also been declining. For example, a recent review of the literature found that the difference favoring males in mathematics skills was larger in studies published before 1974 than in studies published after that date.

Birth Order

Although there is only limited research on the topic, it appears that birth order is related to risk-taking. Namely, the firstborn child tends to be less willing to take risks than the later-born children in the same family. The explanation offered most often is that parents exert greater control over the early life of the firstborn child and instill in him or her the need to be dependable and act responsibly. To the child, this means not taking unnecessary chances.

Marital Status

Single individuals have been found, in some studies, to be more risk-tolerant than married individuals. It has been found, for instance, that married individuals are 2.5 times more likely to be repeat purchasers of insurance than single individuals. The key here is the presence of dependents, rather than marital status per se. If the individual feels that his or her actions are going to have negative consequences for dependents, then he or she is likely to be more cautious. For example, in *dual* income families, the level of risk-tolerance of the married individuals may be no less than that of a single person because neither party is the dependent of the other under these circumstances.

Occupation

Most people spend much of their adult life working. It would be surprising if the types of jobs they hold did not in some way relate to risk-tolerance. Several aspects related to occupation and risk-tolerance have been studied and are discussed below.

Public-Sector versus Private-Sector Employment

One important manifestation of financial risk-taking propensity is the need for job security—the greater the probability of becoming unemployed, the greater the financial riskiness in that occupation. Thus one would expect monetarily risk-averse individuals to gravitate toward jobs that offer security, even if the pay is lower. It is generally accepted that the public sector offers greater job security. A number of studies have compared the monetary risk-taking propensities of private-sector and public-sector employees. This research points to greater risk-aversion among public-sector employees.

Professionals versus Nonprofessionals

According to the results of some studies, professionals (physicians, lawyers, managers, and so on) tend to be more risk-taking in investment decisions than nonprofessionals (farmers, unskilled and skilled laborers, clerical workers, and so on). This disparity is perhaps due to differences in the level of sophistication about investment matters. As mentioned earlier, risk-tolerance tends to increase with increased knowledge and familiarity.

Differences within a given profession cannot be explained in these terms, however. Certain reports indicate that professionals in private practice or working for small firms are more risk-tolerant than individuals in the same profession who are employed by large firms. Among physicians, differences have also been observed between surgeons and physicians in other specialties (internists, for example). Specifically, surgeons reportedly are more likely to be risk-tolerant than other physicians.

Length of Job Tenure

Chances of advancement decrease the longer a person remains in one position. Remaining with the same company at the same job especially lowers one's future advancement opportunities. Again, many people remain in positions that offer few possibilities for upward mobility because of financial security needs. Financial risk-takers, in contrast, change jobs quite frequently (that is, they are "job hoppers").

Management Level

Studies comparing the risk-tolerance levels of managers at different levels within an organization usually find that the risk-takers hold more senior level positions, earn higher incomes, and have greater authority. Risk-takers are also more likely to work as managers in small rather than large firms.

Risk Managers

In one compelling experiment it was discovered that individuals who handle the risk-management functions in corporations are similar to the successful traders mentioned earlier in their willingness to cut losses. Namely, when offered a choice between accepting a *certain* but relatively small loss and a *probable* but potentially larger loss, most of the risk managers picked the first alternative. In this respect, the managers in charge of the risk-management function were quite unlike the managers responsible for other corporate functions. Like the public at large, the latter group was unwilling to accept a loss. They went for the "long shot," hoping that they could escape unscathed from the larger loss despite the relatively large odds against that possibility.

Salary versus Commission

Monetary risk-takers are well represented in occupations in which all or a substantial portion of the earnings depend on commissions. Moreover, the more successful performers in such jobs generally take higher risks. It has been found, for example, that the risk-taking individual is more likely to pursue one or two large accounts instead of a large number of small accounts.

Entrepreneurship

According to the Small Business Administration, about 75 percent of new business ventures fail within 5 years. Given the financial risks involved, one would naturally expect people who are successful entrepreneurs to be high risk-takers. Surprisingly, however, various studies fail to support this commonsense assumption. The body of available research points to only a moderate propensity for taking risks among entrepreneurs. In other words, risk-taking is not the characteristic that differentiates entrepreneurs from nonentrepreneurs. What does? It seems to be the need for independence — to be one's own boss — and a need to achieve. This pattern of motivation may explain the preference for moderate levels of risk over low and high levels of risk. People with a strong need to achieve prefer moderate levels of risk because such situations are ones where skill can have a marked influence on the outcome. In low-risk situations, everyone can achieve the desired outcome, whereas in high-risk situations, it becomes more a matter of luck than skill.

COMMUNICATING PROBABILITY STATEMENTS VERBALLY

Poor communication between client and financial adviser is responsible for many of the allegations of investment unsuitability filed against financial services professionals. Typically, the client claims that the risks of the investment were not conveyed adequately. This brings us to the issue of communicating probabilities of success and failure to one's clients.

Research indicates that people are generally more comfortable describing the probability of an event in words rather than in numbers. Perhaps it is because in everyday situations it is not always possible to assign an exact probability to outcomes. But what does it mean to clients if their financial planner tells them that a certain investment will *probably* double their money in 6 years, while another investment offers only a *low chance* of producing this rate of appreciation?

It has been suggested that at least 282 words and phrases can be used to report the likelihood of something happening. A number of researchers have attempted to quantify these expressions by asking people questions like, "If you were told that an outcome was _____ [the blank being filled in by a word or phrase], what percentage would best represent the probability of that outcome occurring?" Table 2-4 shows the percentages that were assigned to the 18 most commonly used expressions. The intent is to provide the financial planner with a basis for determining how these terms would be understood by clients if he or she were to use them in communicating estimates of the probabilities of various investment opportunities. For example, on average, "almost impossible" is understood as having a 2 percent (2 in 100) chance of occurring. The phrases "medium chance" and "even chance," in turn, are understood to represent about a 50 percent chance of occurring.

TABLE 2-4
Correspondence between Numerical Probability and Verbal Probability Statements

Numerical	Verbal
2%	Almost impossible
5	Very improbable
10	Very unlikely; very low chance
15	Improbable; unlikely
20	Low chance
40	Possible
50	Medium chance; even chance
70	Probable; likely
80	Very possible; very probable; high chance
85	Very likely
90	Very high chance; almost certain

Note: Based on Reagan, Mosteller, and Youtz (1989).

ASSESSMENT OF THE CLIENT'S RISK-TOLERANCE

The Purpose of Assessment

So far, some of the factors that exert an influence of one sort or another on a person's willingness to undertake a risky course of action have been examined. Now comes the issue of assessment. How does one go about measuring a client's *typical* level of risk-tolerance? By typical, we mean the level at which the aforementioned distortions do not cause the client to make decisions that are either riskier or safer than would generally be characteristic of that individual.

The best way, of course, would be to observe the client repeatedly over an extended time period in situations that are likely to reveal his or her characteristic risk-tolerance level. Of course, this is not really feasible since it would entail months of observation, something that the financial planner does not have time for and that would constitute an intrusion that no reasonable client would stand for. Consequently, there is a need to find some shortcuts to obtaining a reasonably accurate estimate of the client's risk-tolerance within a relatively short time period. In the sections that follow, some of the available options will be considered. All of these options call for sensitivity to appropriate cues and an ability to integrate them into a total impression of the client. Even though there is some "science" to guide the financial planner, the task is basically still an art.

Whatever method is used, one should never forget the basic purpose of the assessment process; namely, it is meant to help clients *understand* their own level of risk-tolerance. Quite frequently, clients are not aware of how risk-tolerant or risk-averse they are. To them risk-tolerance is a vague concept that requires both explanation and exploration. The purpose of assessment is not, however, to enable to the planner to *impose* his or her perceptions on the client. For example, it is inappropriate to advise the client that the choice is between "eating" (risky investments) and "sleeping" (nonrisky investments). In the end, it is the client who must decide what constitutes an acceptable level of risk. The planner's role is to help the client learn enough about himself or herself to be able to make an informed decision.

Assessment Methods

Many practitioners fail to appreciate the complexity of the task facing them in trying to determine a client's risk-tolerance accurately. Considerable time and effort are required to do it correctly, and even then the results may not be perfect. The primary problem is that, frequently, the various techniques do not give the same picture of a particular person's level of risk-tolerance. All too often the individual may appear to be a risk-taker when assessed with one technique and a risk-averter when looked at with another technique. For example, in one study employing 16 different assessment procedures, the percentage of people who could be classified as risk-takers ranged from 0 percent to 94 percent, depending on the technique used. On a practical level, this means that more than one approach should be employed for an accurate assessment of a client's risk-taking propensity.

Contrasts between Qualitative and Quantitative Assessment

The assessment process can be either *qualitative* or *quantitative* in its orientation. When one relies on a qualitative approach, one typically collects the necessary information primarily through conversations with the client, without assigning numbers to the information gathered. The information is collected in an unstructured format and is evaluated on an intuitive or impressionistic basis, based on the planner's training and experience. A quantitative approach, in contrast, relies on the use of a structured format — questionnaires, for example — that allows one to translate observations into some type of numerical score. These scores are then used to interpret the client's risk-taking propensities.

Most planners do not rely on one approach to the exclusion of the other. For example, few quantitatively oriented planners are willing to surrender their professional judgment to the results of a questionnaire. It is really a matter of degree of how qualitative or quantitative one planner is compared to another. One can use a primarily qualitative approach and still not forfeit some of the advantages of quantifiable information. Questionnaires and other quantitative devices can be valuable tools in the hands of any skilled financial planner.

One major virtue of using a questionnaire, or similar device, to assess a client's risk-tolerance is that it can facilitate the beginning of a dialogue between the planner and the client. The content of the questionnaire serves to bring to the forefront issues that the client may not have thought about. Another merit, perhaps the major one, is that a quantitative approach allows one to standardize the assessment process.

A number of limitations are inherent in a strictly qualitative approach — one in which the financial planner relies solely on the verbal comments made by a client and interprets their significance on an intuitive basis. In a recent study, it was found that financial planners (like all people) are overconfident about their ability to make intuitive judgments. The planners, presented with various statements that clients could make, were asked to evaluate the level of risk-tolerance these statements implied on a 10-point scale, where 1 indicated low risk-tolerance and 10 indicated high risk-tolerance.

It is understandable that an ambiguous statement, such as "Taking calculated risks is different from being rash," would receive ratings as low as 4 and as high as 8. (The average was 6.7.) However, even on more straightforward statements there was also a lack of consensus. The statement — "I like to speculate on my investments" — if made by a client, was interpreted, on average, as an 8.5. However, again there was diversity of opinion about its meaning. Some financial planners saw the statement as meriting only a rating of 5 whereas others assigned it a rating of 10. "Rubber yardsticks" of this type can be minimized in a quantitative-assessment approach.

When using a qualitative orientation to the assessment of risk-tolerance, the planner should be familiar with good interviewing skills, such as those spelled out in chapter 3 of this book. There are standards for quantitative-assessment procedures as well, most of which are beyond the scope of this chapter. Suffice it to say that a quantitative measurement device, such as a test or even a questionnaire, needs to be constructed very carefully. The questions should be written in such a way that they do not lead or bias the individual to answer them in a certain way. Moreover, evidence must be provided to demonstrate that the test or questionnaire does, in fact, assess the attributes it is meant to measure and that it measures them accurately on a consistent basis.

Provided that they are accurate, the best quantitative measurement devices are ones that allow the planner to compare the standing of a particular individual to a representative group. A measurement device of this sort is said to have "norms." Using such norms, one can compare the individual to the public at large, or to some subgroup. For instance, using a normed measure of risk-tolerance, it is possible to see whether the client is more or less risk-tolerant than people in general or, if the client is a 50-year-old male, to compare the client to other people of the same age and sex.

Unfortunately, the majority of the tests, inventories, scales, checklists, and questionnaires employed today by financial planners to measure their clients' risk-tolerance have not been developed under such strict standards. A majority were created for in-house use by individual planners, brokerage houses, or mutual funds. Many of the developers of these assessment devices are probably unaware of such requirements. There is a critical need for well-constructed questionnaires that provide some evidence to support their use as measures of risk-tolerance.

Most of the available assessment devices suffer from the same problems. In some, the wrong questions are asked, or they are presented in a format that is less than optimal. For instance, many of these devices are too short, thereby failing to contain an adequate representation of questions. It has been demonstrated that answers to similar questions about risk-tolerance may not concur. For example, different answers may be given to the question, "What percentage of your total funds would you put in very risky investments?" and the question, "Would you be willing to borrow money to make a good investment?" In a surprisingly large number of cases, the answers are dramatically different. (Of course, this problem exists in qualitative approaches to risk assessment as well.) In order to avoid being misled by the answer to any one question, the financial planner needs to ask a *series* of questions. Some answers may underestimate the client's true level of risk-tolerance, whereas others may overestimate the true level of this attribute. Other things being equal, the more questions that are used to measure a psychological characteristic, the more precise are the results.

Some of these questionnaires do not separate the different contexts of risk-taking, so that a high score on such a questionnaire is probably better at identifying tendencies toward thrill-seeking rather than high risk-tolerance for investment matters. For all these reasons, caution must be exercised in using questionnaires. It is strongly recommended that the financial planner examine the content of the questionnaire rather than relying on it blindly. A "questionnaire" or "checklist" or "inventory" purporting to assess risk-tolerance may, in fact, be measuring some other attribute.

There are a number of techniques that can be used to assess a client's risk-tolerance. Some lend themselves more to a qualitative approach, whereas others call for a more quantitative approach. In the section that follows, a brief overview of the most common approaches is provided. In essence, such techniques consist of looking at the client's

- investment objectives
- preferences for various investment vehicles
- real-life choices involving risk
- attitudes toward risk
- preferences for different probabilities and payoff levels

Examination of Client Investment Objectives

Frequently, clients are asked to identify their financial objectives. For example, the client may be asked to indicate how important the following are to him or her: liquidity, safety of principal, appreciation, protection from inflation, current income, and tax reduction. The client's level of risk-tolerance is inferred from the answers. If the client's primary concerns are safety of principal and/or liquidity, then risk-aversion is assumed. If, on the other hand, the main objectives are protection from inflation or tax relief, then the inference is that the client is risk-tolerant.

Objectives, however, must not be confused with risk-tolerance. There are many individuals who desire tax relief yet are quite risk-averse. One's stated objectives may, in fact, be quite incompatible with one's level of risk-tolerance, and in many cases the client may be unaware of this incongruity. In a sense, the client's level of risk-tolerance should be the basis for evaluating how reasonable the client's objectives are. However, using objectives for the purpose of gauging risk-tolerance, without any further attempts to assess actual risk-tolerance, is a mistake. To do so is to have the tail wag the dog.

Preferences for Various Investment Products

This is the most direct approach to measuring a client's risk-tolerance. With this method, the client is asked to indicate the products that he or she prefers as investments. Several variations of this procedure exist. At the most "bottom-line" level the client is presented with the available alternatives and is then asked how he or she wishes to distribute available assets among these options. The products are usually presented in some rank order, ranging from very safe investments to very risky investments. Either actual (real) or imaginary funds can be used. For the latter variation of this task, the client is asked something like, "What would you do if you got a windfall?" As might be expected, people tend to be more daring with imaginary money than with actual money. A third variation of this approach is to ask the client to rank the products from most preferred to least preferred or to assign to each product some rating that represents the client's level of preference (for example, low, medium, or high).

The accuracy of this procedure (in all its variants) rests on the client's knowledge of the actual risk-return potential of the various investments. Preferably these differences are explained and specified to the client, since many clients may lack even basic knowledge. One should never assume that clients are highly knowledgeable about financial matters. Surveys of the general public, including the wealthy, reveal a startling level of financial ignorance. For example, a survey conducted in 1989 by the Gallup Organization for the International Association for Financial Planning discovered that 75 percent of the respondents had not changed their credit card behavior since the Tax Reform Act of 1986. Another survey—directed at investors—found that 84 percent did not know the "beta," a quantitative measure of the riskiness of their portfolio. While admitting to ignorance about financial matters on surveys, most people are reluctant to be as open with their financial advisers because they are embarrassed by it.

Real-Life Choices Involving Risks

As with investment products, a person's past performance is no guarantee of future performance. But it has been observed that the best predictor of future behavior is typically past behavior. This notion underlies the real-life-choices approach to risk-tolerance assessment. That is, factual information about the client's life is gathered and evaluated. The following life-style characteristics can be used to gauge a client's disposition toward monetary risk.

- *composition of present investment portfolio.* How risky is it? What percentage of total assets are in passbook savings accounts, Treasury notes, mutual funds, stocks, options and commodities, and so on? If stocks are owned, does the person use short selling and margin buying? If an annuity is owned, is it of the fixed or variable type? How satisfied or dissatisfied is the client with this type of portfolio? If changes were made to a previous portfolio, were these changes in a more conservative or more aggressive direction?
- *debt ratio.* The ratio of the client's liabilities to his or her gross assets has been used as a measure of risk-tolerance. It has been suggested by some that a debt ratio over 23 percent reflects risk-taking, under 8 percent is characteristic of risk-aversion, and 8 percent to 23 percent suggests a risk-neutral attitude.
- *ratio of life insurance to annual salary.* The assumption is that the larger the resulting ratio, the higher the client's level of risk-aversion.
- *the size of deductibles on property-liability coverage.* It has been observed that as the amount of wealth allocated to risky securities rises, so does the size of the deductible on the client's insurance coverages. Risk-tolerant individuals elect larger deductibles.
- *percentage of net wealth used for recreational gambling.*
- *job tenure.* The willingness to make a voluntary job change is considered an indicator of a willingness to take financial risks. Therefore clients can be asked how many job changes they have made during the last 15 years. Over three changes is considered by some as a sign of a risk-taking attitude. Quitting a job before one has found a replacement is particularly significant. Job changes at middle age may also be especially noteworthy.
- *variations in income.* Risk-taking individuals may show greater variations in their annual income from year to year, and not always in an upward direction. The financial adviser should also look at the duration of unemployment if the client was ever unemployed. Did the individual take the first job offer he or she received during this period of unemployment or did he or she wait until a job to his or her liking was found? What was the salary of the new job the client took after the period of unemployment? If it was lower than that of the previous job, it could indicate risk-aversion.
- *type of mortgage.* A willingness to undertake a variable rather than a fixed mortgage could be a sign of monetary risk-taking. If the client has chosen a fixed mortgage, did he or she lock in on a guaranteed rate before settlement? Locking in is a sign of risk-aversion.

Attitudes toward Risk

A method frequently used to obtain information about a client's degree of risk-tolerance involves eliciting his or her attitude toward risk. Attitudes toward risk can be elicited by using either a quantitative or a qualitative approach. Questions can take on many different forms. To begin with, clients can be asked *global* questions such as whether they view themselves as risk-averters or risk-takers. (For example,

"On a 10-point scale, where 1 is an ultimate risk-averter and 10 is an ultimate risk-taker, where would you place yourself?")

Second, clients can be asked about their *specific* reactions to risk. (For example, "Do you find that you . . . can't sleep after making a risky investment . . . have persisting second thoughts about the investment . . . view risk as an opportunity rather than danger . . . get more pleasure from making $3,000 on a risky investment than $3,000 on a safe investment . . . are afraid of losing what you have . . . are willing to borrow money to make a good investment . . . believe that it is impossible to get ahead unless you take chances . . . agree with the saying 'Better safe than sorry,'" and so on.)

Earlier it was noted that a sufficiently large number of questions must be asked in order to assess risk-tolerance accurately. This is especially true in the case of the attitude approach to measurement. It has been found that the reason why many attitudes, as measured through questionnaires or other scales of that type, fail to predict actual behavior is because of limitations in the attitude measure. Not enough questions were asked. When the number of questions was increased, there was a much better correspondence between attitude and behavior.

A major problem with the attitude approach to risk-tolerance assessment is that people want to present themselves in the best possible light to others. Any characteristic that is valued is likely to be overstated. As was noted earlier, in America it is considered more desirable to be risk-taking than risk-averse. Clients are therefore likely to exaggerate their willingness to take risks. Consequently, discrepancies between verbally expressed attitudes and behavior are likely to be encountered, even if a sufficiently large number of questions are asked. When using this approach, one needs to ascertain how well the expressed attitudes agree with other evidence, such as factual information about the person's risk-taking proclivities.

Probability and Payoff Preferences

A variety of assessment techniques fall under this classification. Three types will be considered:

- preferences for certain versus probable gambles
- minimal required probability of success
- minimal required return

All of these methods rely on a manipulation of at least one of the four elements found in any gamble: probability of loss, probability of gain, amount to be lost, and amount to be gained. Consequently, the techniques falling under this classification are best used in a quantitative approach to assessment.

Anyone using the probability and payoff-preferences approach to measuring a client's risk-tolerance needs to be aware of how framing a question affects the answer, lest he or she be misled by the results. Framing refers to the finding that the same objective facts can be described either in terms of the probability of gaining or the probability of losing. Although it may not seem that — to use an analogy — describing a bottle as half empty or half full should have any marked consequences on one's choices in a risky situation, the evidence shows otherwise. To illustrate, consider research in which one group of people is informed that there is a 50 percent chance of success in a particular venture. Another group is told that this same venture has a 50 percent chance of failure. Logically, the same proportion of people in each group should be willing to take this risk. Yet this was not the case. When the risk was described (framed) in terms of the probability of success, more people were willing to take it than when this same risk was described in terms of the chances of failure. Other research along this line has shown that describing ground meat in terms of how lean versus how fat the product was made a big difference. Ground meat described as 90 percent lean was seen as a better buy than the same ground meat described as 10 percent fat.

Preferences for certain versus probable gambles. Gambles are believed to represent, in an abstract form, real-life situations. One very common technique is to present the client with two alternatives. One choice is a certain win, whereas the other choice offers only some probability of winning. A series of such pairs of gambles is presented. For example, the person is asked to indicate whether he or she would choose

A: a sure gain of $1,000
B: a 50 percent chance of gaining $2,000

Persons who are risk-averse chose options similar to A, whereas risk-taking individuals chose options similar to B.

On some questionnaires, these choices are woven around a story line. For example, an item of this type may be "Imagine that you are a winning contestant on a game show. Which of the following actions would you take?"

A: Stop playing with a certain prize of $8,000 in cash.
B: Go another round with a 50 percent chance of winning $16,000 and a 50 percent chance of winning nothing.

Minimum probability of success required before undertaking a risky action. A good example of a procedure relying on this approach is the "choice dilemma" questionnaire (Kogan and Wallach, 1964), often used to study the risky shift phenomenon discussed earlier. This questionnaire presents 12 situations. For each situation, two alternatives are described. One choice is risky and the other is safe. In every case, the risky course of action offers a larger potential payoff. Five odds are given for the chance of success for the risky course of action, namely 1 in 10, 3 in 10, 5 in 10, 7 in 10, and 9 in 10. The person answering the questionnaire is asked to select the odds that would make it worthwhile to take the risky alternative instead of the safe one. The situations involve a broad range of dilemmas, such as job change, heart operation, football game, marriage decision, and so on. One such question involves a business investment decision:

Mr. E is president of a light metals corporation in the United States. The corporation is quite prosperous and has strongly considered the possibilities of business expansion by building an additional plant in a new location. The choice is between building another plant in the U.S., where there would be a moderate return on the initial investment, or building a plant in a foreign country. Lower labor costs and easy access to raw materials in that country would mean a much higher return on the initial investment. On the other hand, there is a history of political instability and revolution in the foreign country under consideration. In fact, the leader of a small minority party is committed to nationalizing, that is, taking over all foreign investments.

Imagine that you are advising Mr. E. Listed below are several probabilities or odds of continued political stability in the foreign country under consideration.

Please check the lowest probability that you would consider acceptable for Mr. E's corporation to build a plant in that country.

___ The chances are 1 in 10 that the country will remain politically stable.
___ The chances are 3 in 10 that the country will remain politically stable.
___ The chances are 5 in 10 that the country will remain politically stable.
___ The chances are 7 in 10 that the country will remain politically stable.
___ The chances are 9 in 10 that the country will remain politically stable.
___ Place a check here if you think Mr. E's corporation should not build a plant in the foreign country, no matter what the probabilities.

The higher the odds of success the person requires, the greater the level of risk-aversion. The choice dilemma is an instrument that has been used extensively in research, and much is known about its measurement properties. However, its appropriateness for assessing monetary risk-taking is questionable because this questionnaire looks at risk-taking in all contexts (for example, it looks at risk-taking as if it was a unitary phenomenon — which it is not, as noted in the earlier discussion of the subject). Only a few of the 12 situations are concerned with financial risk-taking. Furthermore, some of the items are quite dated. Nonetheless, some researchers have found it to be useful in picking out investors who are risk-taking from those who are risk-averse.

Minimum return required before undertaking a risky action. What follows is an example of a question that requires an answer in terms of amount to be gained rather than in terms of probability (as was the case in the choice-dilemma task): "You are faced with an investment opportunity in which you stand a 50 percent chance of losing half of your personal net wealth and a 50 percent chance of making a certain amount of money. How much of a return would you require in order to take this risk?" (The answers are evaluated in relation to the person's net wealth.)

Guidelines on Assessment

The following guidelines are based on the preceding discussion of assessment, taking into consideration the information presented about risk and situational influences on risk-taking propensity:

* Assume that the client is risk-*averse,* unless evidence to the contrary can be obtained.
* Remember that people are more likely to *overstate* than *understate* their risk-taking propensity.

- Keep in mind that even risk-averse individuals may be risk-seeking in situations where the choices are between losses. People are reluctant to cut their losses.
- Start your assessment by looking at the client's demographic characteristics and personality makeup. However, remember that you are dealing with an individual rather than a group. Just because a person belongs to a group that is more risk-tolerant or risk-averse than average, it does not mean that the client facing you today will necessarily follow the group pattern. The differences in risk-tolerance between demographic groups are usually small, so there will be many people who do not fit the stereotype. Do not judge the individual merely by the group that he or she belongs to. Group differences simply provide you with some hunches that can be explored through the assessment process; you still need to assess the *individual* client.
- Focus on monetary risk-taking.
- Look for quantitative-assessment devices that are accurate and allow you to compare the client's performance to a norm group.
- Consider the results from a questionnaire or other measurement device as only an approximation of the client's actual risk-tolerance. No assessment procedure is perfect; they are all susceptible to some error.
- Diversify in how you assess. That is, use more than one approach. This will allow you to draw on the strengths of the various techniques.
- Use the information you collect to start a dialogue with the client about risk-tolerance. Be sure to remember that assessing the client's risk-tolerance is a cooperative venture between the two of you.
- Realize that biases may be operating on the client's risk-perceptions (for example, familiarity, availability, and so on), which may be inflating or deflating the client's true level of risk-tolerance.
- Remember that a client's propensity for risk-taking does not necessarily remain constant throughout his or her lifetime. As noted throughout this chapter, changes in personal circumstances such as age, wealth, and number of dependents can produce shifts. Likewise, world events can either increase or decrease a person's level of risk-tolerance. For instance, after the events of October 20, 1987, fewer people owned stocks than prior to that date. Therefore it is prudent to periodically reassess the client's risk-tolerance.

EPILOGUE

One needs to recognize that knowledge about risk-tolerance is still evolving. The amount of information that is available is substantial, even though many unanswered questions remain.

Even the existing body of knowledge is useless if it is not actually applied by financial planners in their dealings with clients. Loren Dunton, one of the early leaders in the development of the financial planning profession, writes that he is frequently asked by the media to describe the difference between the approach used by financial planners and that used by other financial services practitioners. In his reply, Dunton makes the following comment about financial planners: "Most of them, and all of the good ones, will first find out the risk-tolerance of the individual or couple they might be going to counsel." (Dunton, p. 71)

References

Arrow, K. J. "Risk Perception in Psychology and Economics." *Economic Inquiry,* 1982, vol. 20, pp. 1–9.

Baker, M. W., and E. Kramer. *Success in America: The CIGNA Study of the Upper-Affluent.* Louis Harris and Assoc., Inc., 1987.

Barnewall, M. M. "Examining the Psychological Traits of Passive and Active Affluent Investors." *Journal of Financial Planning,* vol. 1, no. 2, pp. 70–74.

Bellante, D., and A. N. Link. "Are Public Sector Workers More Risk Averse Than Private Sector Workers?" *Industrial and Labor Relations Review,* 1981, vol. 34, pp. 408–412.

Bjorkman, M. "Decision Making, Risk Taking and Psychological Time: Review of Empirical Findings and Psychological Theory." *Scandinavian Journal of Psychology,* 1984, vol. 25, pp. 31–49.

Blum, S. H. "Investment Preferences and the Desire for Security: A Comparison of Men and Women." *American Journal of Psychology,* 1976, vol. 94, pp. 87–91.

Bonieki, G. "What Are the Limits to Man's Time and Space Perspectives: Toward a Definition of a Realistic Planning Horizon." *Technological Forecasting and Social Change,* 1980, vol. 17, pp. 161–175.

Brockhaus, R. H., Sr. "Risk-Taking Propensity of Entrepreneurs." *Academy of Management Journal,* 1980, vol. 23, pp. 509–520.

Brown, M.S. "Communicating Information about Workplace Hazards: Effects on Worker Attitudes toward Risks." *Social and Cultural Construction of Risk,* edited by B. B. Johnson and V. T. Covello. Norwell, Mass.: Kluver Academic Publishers, 1987.

Cohn, R. A., W. G. Lewellen, R. C. Lease, and G. G. Schlarbaum. "Individual Investor Risk Aversion and Investment Portfolio Composition." *Journal of Finance,* 1975, vol. 30, pp. 605–620.

Crum, R. L., D. L. Laughhunn, and J. W. Payne. "Risk-Seeking Behavior and Its Implications for Financial Models." *Financial Management,* Winter 1981, pp. 20–27.

DeBondt, W. M. F., and R. Thaler. "Does the Stock Market Overreact?" *The Journal of Finance,* 1985, vol. 40, pp. 793–808.

Deets, M. K., and G. C. Hoyt, "Variance Preferences and Variance Shifts in Group Investment Decisions." *Organizational Behavior and Human Performance,* 1970, vol. 5, pp. 378–386.

Dickson, G. C. A. "A Comparison of Attitudes towards Risk among Business Managers." *Journal of Occupational Psychology,* 1981, vol. 54, pp. 157–164.

Dowling, G. R. "Perceived Risk: The Concept and Its Measurement." *Psychology and Marketing,* 1986, vol. 3, pp. 193–210.

Dunton, L. *About Your Future.* San Diego: The National Center for Financial Education, 1988.

Farrelly, G. "A Behavioral Science Approach to Financial Research." *Financial Management,* 1980, vol. 9, no. 3, pp. 15–22.

Feinberg, R. M. "Risk Aversion, Risk, and the Duration of Unemployment." *Review of Economics & Statistics,* 1977, vol. 59, pp. 264–271.

Fischoff, B., and R. Beyth. "I Knew It Would Happen — Remembered Probabilities of Once-Future Things." *Organizational Behavior and Human Performance,* 1975, vol. 13, pp. 1–16.

Gooding, A. E. "Quantification of Investors' Perceptions of Common Stocks: Risk and Return Dimensions." *The Journal of Finance,* 1975, vol. 30, pp. 1301–1316.

Grey, R. J., and C. E. Gordon. "Risk-Taking Managers: Who Gets the Top Jobs?" *Management Review,* 1978, vol. 67, pp. 8–13.

Grossberg, S., and W. E. Gutowski. "Neural Dynamics of Decision Making under Risk: Affective Balance and Cognitive-Emotional Interactions." *Psychological Review,* 1987, vol. 94, pp. 300–318.

Harris, L. and Associates. *Public Attitudes toward Risk.* Study No. 837008, conducted for the Insurance Information Institute, 1983.

Heflin, T. L., M. L. Power, and W. L. Dellva. "Choice Shift: Implications for Insurance Application." *The Journal of Insurance: Issues and Practices,* 1988, vol. 2, pp. 68–82.

Hensley, W. E. "Probability, Personality, Age and Risk Taking." *Journal of Psychology,* 1977, vol. 95, pp. 139–145.

Herrnstein, R. J. "Rational Choice Theory: Necessary but Not Sufficient." *American Psychologist,* 1990, vol. 45, pp. 356–367.

Hisrich, R. D. "Entrepreneurship/Intrapreneurship." *American Psychologist,* 1990, vol. 45, no. 2, pp. 209–222.

Hogarth, R. *Judgment and Choice: The Psychology of Decisions.* New York: John Wiley & Sons, 1987.

Hunter, J. E., and T. D. Coggin. "Analyst Judgment: The Efficient Market Hypothesis versus a Psychological Theory of Human Judgment." *Organizational Behavior and Human Decision Processes,* 1988, vol. 42, pp. 284–302.

Isen, A. M., and R. Patrick. "The Effect of Positive Feelings on Risk-Taking: When the Chips Are Down." *Organizational Behavior and Human Performance,* 1983, vol. 31, pp. 194–202.

Isen, A. M., T. E. Nygren, and F. G. Ashby. "Influence of Positive Affect on the Subjective Utility of Gains and Losses: It Is Just Not Worth the Risk." *Journal of Personality and Social Psychology,* 1988, vol. 55, pp. 710–717.

Jackson, D. N., L. Hourany, and N. J. Vidmar. "A Four-Dimensional Interpretation of Risk Taking." *Journal of Personality,* 1972, vol. 40, no. 3, pp. 483–501.

Jamison, K. S. "Upscale Consumers in a Changing Marketplace." *Managers Magazine,* August 1988, pp. 20–24.

Johnson, E. J., and A. Tversky. "Affect, Generalization, and the Perception of Risk." *Journal of Personality and Social Psychology,* 1983, vol. 45, pp. 20–31.

Jones, C. P., and J. W. Wilson. "An Analysis of the January Effect in Stocks and Interests Rates under Varying Monetary Regimes." *The Journal of Finance,* 1989, vol. 12, pp. 341–354.

Kahle, L. R., and P. Kennedy. "Using the List of Values (LOV) to Understand Consumers." *The Journal of Consumer Marketing,* 1989, vol. 6, no. 3, pp. 5–12.

Kahneman, D., and A. Tversky. "Choices, Values and Frames." *American Psychologist,* 1984, vol. 39, pp. 341–350.

Kogan, N., and M. Wallach. *Risk Taking: A Study in Cognition and Personality.* New York: Holt, Rinehart and Winston, 1964.

Levin, I. P., R. D. Johnson, C. P. Russo, and P. J. Deldin. "Framing Effects in Judgment Tasks with Varying Amounts of Information." *Organizational Behavior and Human Decision Processes,* 1985, vol. 36, pp. 362–377.

Levin, I. P., M. A. Snyder, and D. P. Chapman. "The Interaction of Experimental and Situational Factors and Gender in a Simulated Risky Decision-Making Task." *The Journal of Psychology,* 1988, vol. 122, pp. 173–181.

Ludwig, L. D. "Elation-Depression and Skill as Determinants of Desire and Excitement." *Journal of Personality,* 1975, vol. 43, pp. 1–22.

Lupfer, M. "The Effects of Risk-Taking Tendencies and Incentive Conditions on the Performance of Investment Groups." *Journal of Social Psychology,* 1970, vol. 82, pp. 135–136.

MacCrimmon, K. R., D. A. Wehrung, and W. T. Stanbury. *Taking Risks: The Management of Uncertainty.* New York: Free Press, 1986.

MacDonald, J. G., and R. E. Stehle. "How Do Institutional Investors Perceive Risk?" *Journal of Portfolio Management,* 1975, vol. 2, no. 1, pp. 11–16.

March, J. G., and Z. Shapira. "Managerial Perspectives on Risk and Risk Taking." *Management Science,* 1987, vol. 33, pp. 1404–1418.

Markese, J. D., and G. W. Perritt. "Investment Attitudes and Portfolio Decisions of Individual Investors." *The Mid-Atlantic Journal of Business,* 1985, vol. 23, no. 2, pp. 21–31.

Masters, R. "Study Examines Investors' Risk-Taking Propensities." *Journal of Financial Planning,* July 1989, pp. 151–155.

Masters, R., and R. Meier. "Sex Differences and Risk-Taking Propensity of Entrepreneurs." *Journal of Small Business Management,* 1988, vol. 26, no. 1, pp. 31–35.

Milburn, T. W., and R. S. Billings. "Decision-Making Perspectives from Psychology." *American Behavioral Scientist,* 1976, vol. 20, no. 1, pp. 111–126.

Mongrain, S., and L. Standing. "Impairment of Cognition, Risk-Taking, and Self-Perception by Alcohol." *Perceptual and Motor Skills,* 1989, vol. 69, pp. 199–210.

Morgan, R. L., "Risk Preference as a Function of the Number of Wins and the Amount Won." *American Journal of Psychology,* 1983, vol. 96, pp. 469–475.

Morin, R. A., and A. F. Suarez. "Risk Aversion Revisited." *The Journal of Finance,* 1983, vol. 38, pp. 1201–1216.

Okun, M. A. "Adult Age and Cautiousness in Decision: A Review of the Literature." *Human Development,* 1976, vol. 19, pp. 220–233.

Plax, T. G. , and L. B. Rosenfeld. "Correlates of Risky Decision Making." *Journal of Personality Assessment,* 1976, vol. 40, pp. 413–418.

Rachlin, H., A. W. Logue, J. Gibbon, and M. Frankel. "Cognition and Behavior in Studies of Choice." *Psychological Review,* 1986, vol. 93, pp. 33–45.

Rapoport, A. "Effects of Wealth on Portfolios under Various Investment Conditions." *Acta Psychologica,* 1984, vol. 55, pp. 31–51.

Reagan, R. T., F. Mosteller, and C. Youtz. "Quantitative Meanings of Verbal Probability Expressions." *Journal of Applied Psychology,* 1989, vol. 74, pp. 433–442.

Rim, Y. "Personality and Risky Shift in a Passive Audience." *Personality and Individual Differences,* 1982, vol. 3, pp. 465–467.

Roszkowski, M. J., and G. E. Snelbecker. "Effects of 'Framing' on Measures of Risk Tolerance: Financial Planners Are Not Immune." *Journal of Behavioral Economics,* 1990, vol. 19, no. 2, in press.

———. "How Much Risk Can a Client Stand?" *Best's Review,* August 1989, pp. 44–46, 118–119.

Schaninger, C. M. "Perceived Risk and Personality." *Journal of Consumer Research,* 1976, vol. 3, pp. 95–100.

Schoemaker, P. J. H. "The Role of Statistical Knowledge in Gambling Decisions: Moment vs. Risk Dimension Approaches." *Organizational Behavior and Human Performance,* 1979, vol. 24, pp. 1–17.

Schwager, J. D. *Market Wizards—Interviews with Top Traders.* New York: Simon & Schuster, 1989.

Sciortino, J. J., J. H. Huston, and R. W. Spencer. "Risk and Income Distribution." *Journal of Economic Psychology,* 1988, vol. 9, pp. 399–408.

Shefrin, H., and M. Statman. "The Disposition to Sell Winners Too Early and Ride Losers Too Long: Theory and Evidence." *The Journal of Finance,* 1985, vol. 40, pp. 777–792.

Sinn, H. "Psychophysical Laws in Risk Theory." *Journal of Economic Psychology,* 1985, vol. 6, pp. 185–206.

Slovic, P. "Information Processing, Situation Specificity and the Generality of Risk-Taking Behavior." *Journal of Personality and Social Psychology,* 1972, vol. 21, no. 1, pp. 128–134.

Slovic, P., B. Fischoff, S. Lichtenstein, B. Corrigan, and B. Combs. "Preference for Insuring against Probable Small Losses: Insurance Implications." *Journal of Risk and Insurance,* 1977, vol. 44, pp. 237–258.

Snelbecker, G. E., M. J. Roszkowski, and N. E. Cutler. "Investors' Risk Tolerance and Return Aspirations, and Financial Advisors' Interpretations: A Conceptual Model and Exploratory Data." *Journal of Behavioral Economics,* 1990, vol. 19, no. 2, in press.

Sutton, N. A. "An Illusion of Control." *Best's Review: Life/Health Insurance Edition,* July 1987, pp. 54–58.

Svenson, O. "Cognitive Strategies in a Complex Judgment Task: Analyses of Concurrent Verbal Reports and Judgments of Cumulated Risk over Different Exposure Times." *Organizational Behavior and Human Decision Processes,* 1985, vol. 36, pp. 1–15.

———. "Time Perception and Long Term Risk." *Canadian Journal of Operations Research and Information Processing,* 1984, vol. 22, pp. 196–214.

Taylor, R. N. "Psychological Determinants of Bounded Rationality: Implications for Decision-Making Strategies." *Decision Sciences,* 1973, vol. 6, pp. 409–429.

Tharp, V. K. "Winners and Losers: Attitude Makes the Difference." *Futures,* 1984, vol. 12, no. 12, pp. 54–56.

Tversky, A., S. Sattath, and P. Slovic. "Contingent Weighting in Judgment and Choice." *Psychological Review,* 1988, vol. 95, pp. 371–384.

Watson, J. S. "Volunteer and Risk-Taking Groups Are More Homogeneous on Measures of Sensation Seeking Than Control Groups." *Perceptual and Motor Skills,* 1985, vol. 62, pp. 471–475.

Weinstein, N. D. "Why It Won't Happen to Me: Perceptions of Risk Factors and Susceptibility." *Health Psychology,* 1984, vol. 3, pp. 431–457.

Wiener, J. L., J. W. Gentry, and R. K. Miller. "The Framing of the Insurance Purchase Decision." *Advances in Consumer Research,* 1986, pp. 251–256.

Winger, B. J., and N. K. Mohan. "Investment Risk and Time Diversification." *Journal of Financial Planning,* 1988, vol. 1, no. 1, pp. 45–48.

Zuckerman, M. "Sensation Seeking: A Comparative Approach to a Human Trait." *Behavioral and Brain Sciences,* 1984, vol. 7, pp. 413–471.

Zuckerman, M., M. S. Buchsbaum, and D. L. Murphy. "Sensation Seeking and Its Biological Correlates." *Psychological Bulletin,* 1980, vol. 88, pp. 187–214.

Effective Communication in Financial Counseling[1]

Lewis B. Morgan*

INTRODUCTION

Many people take communication for granted. After all, it is an activity that most of us have engaged in since our childhood years, so why not take it for granted? The sad truth, however, is that many of us are ineffective communicators simply because we make that very assumption.

Communication is far too important a skill, especially in the field of counseling, to treat lightly. It is the single most critical skill that a counselor brings to a counseling session.

The purpose of this chapter is to examine the communication process as it typically exists in a counselor-client relationship. Our goal is to enable financial planners to become exceptionally effective communicators in their dealings with clients. Perhaps you already consider yourself to be effective in the area of communication; however, there are probably aspects of the communication process in which you can improve. This reading will attempt to bring these aspects into sharper focus and provide you with techniques for becoming the very best communicator/counselor that you have the potential of being.

The reading begins with a delineation of the various types of structured communication: interviewing, counseling, and advising. From there it proceeds to some of the essentials inherent in financial counseling: structuring the counseling relationship; establishing rapport; and dealing with resistance. Next it looks at some of the characteristics of effective counseling: unconditional positive regard, empathy, genuineness, and self-awareness.

The second part of the chapter focuses on basic communication principles and skills such as nonverbal communication, using the skills of attending to a client, listening and then responding to a client, and asking effective questions.

THREE TYPES OF STRUCTURED COMMUNICATION

Laypeople often use the terms interviewing, counseling, and advising inter-changeably; yet each term has characteristics that are uniquely its own and that differentiate it from the other two. Let us look at each of these three terms and see how they are alike and how they are different.

---

*Lewis B. Morgan, PhD, is professor of counseling and human relations, Villanova University.

Interviewing

One of the most common forms of structured communication is interviewing. Interviewing can be defined as a process of communication, most often between two people, with a predetermined and specific purpose, usually involving the asking and answering of questions designed to gather meaningful information. For example, a television sports announcer might interview a coach at halftime to get information about what mistakes his team has made in the first half, what he plans to do differently in the second half, and how he hopes to win. Or an interview might take place in a personnel office where a job applicant is interviewed for a position with the firm. The interviewer will want to know the following: What assets will the applicant bring to the job? What is her employment history? Where does she see herself fitting into the firm? What salary does she expect? In both instances cited, there is a specific purpose to the interview in that relevant information is being sought through a question-and-answer dialogue.

Stewart and Cash, in their book, *Interviewing: Principles and Practices,* refer to two basic types of interviews: the directive and nondirective interview. In the directive interview, the interviewer directs and controls both the pace and the content to be covered. It is a much more formalized and structured style of interaction. Often the interviewer even completes a questionnaire form as the interviewee answers pointed questions—for example, What is your age? Where do you live? Where was your last job? What is the highest level of education completed? The advantages of the directive interview are that it can be brief and that it provides measurable data. Its disadvantages are that it is often inflexible and does not allow the interviewee to choose topics for discussion.

The nondirective interview, on the other hand, allows both the interviewer and the interviewee a wider range of subject areas to be discussed, and the interviewee usually controls the pacing and purpose of the interview. Thus the advantages of the nondirective interview are that there is greater flexibility, more in-depth responses are gathered, and usually a closer relationship between interviewer and interviewee is established. Its disadvantages are that it consumes more time and often generates data that are difficult to measure objectively.

All interviews, whether they are directive or nondirective, share common characteristics. Interviews typically take place in a formal and structured setting. Questions are the primary source of communication used by the interviewer. The subject matter discussed is specific to the overall purpose of the interview, and digressions from the subject are usually not encouraged. Finally, the interview is usually a relatively short-term relationship between interviewer and interviewee.

Counseling

The second term, counseling, is often confused with interviewing, even though they are not synonymous. Counseling implies help giving, often of a psychotherapeutic nature, and the help-giving aspect is more than implied in counseling; it is built-in and an integral part of the process. Simply stated, a counselor's job is to provide assistance to clients as they explore their present situations, begin to understand where they are in relation to where they would like to be, and then act to get from where they are to where they want to be. Even though this may sound like a simple process, it is not. It usually is a long-term process, typified by struggles, setbacks, and, eventually, insights leading to an ultimate change in behavior as clients strive to live more fulfilling lives.

While financial counseling takes place over a period of time, the interview is usually a one-time interaction. As such, an interpersonal relationship develops between counselor and client, something that usually does not occur in an interview. When we discussed interviewing, we stated that the question was the primary stock-in-trade of the interviewer. While questions are also utilized in counseling, they are not the primary response modality. In certain counseling settings such as mental hospitals and mental health clinics, an intake interview constitutes the first step in the therapeutic process. In this intake interview, many personal questions are asked, either in a written or oral format, but once the intake procedure is concluded, the communication assumes a different form. While questions may still be asked periodically, they are not the predominant form of counselor response. A counselor may paraphrase what the client has said, reflect a feeling, share feedback or perceptions, clarify, summarize, interpret, provide information, and confront. In short, counseling is not as stylized as interviewing because the format is less formal and less structured. Much more of the humanness of both the counselor and the client comes into focus, all with the purpose of providing help to the client.

Advising

Still a third type of structured communication is advising, which is often confused with counseling. In fact, many people who are unfamiliar with counseling think that what they will receive is advice. Perhaps one reason for this misconception stems from the journalistic proliferation of advice such as is offered in newspaper columns by "Dear Abby" and her sister, Ann Landers. This is not to say that advice is never offered by counselors, because it is; but most counselors believe that the very best kind of advice is self-advice, rather than expert advice.

Several situations might require such advice. A college student planning a program of studies is typically assigned an academic adviser in his or her major field of study. The adviser's role is, simply, to advise the student about program sequence, course prerequisites, specific course content, graduation requirements, and possible career opportunities in the major area. In short, the adviser is the expert and, as such, provides excellent advice. A tax adviser might provide advice on tax shelters, investments, tax deferral, and so on. In both instances, advisers know much more about their field of expertise than do their clients, and their clients use this knowledge in order to reach decisions.

In financial counseling, there are bound to be occasions when counselors give advice. After all, financial counselors are the experts and thus their advice has proven value. The danger in offering advice too soon in the counseling relationship is that the client's ability to make decisions is discounted in favor of the expert's opinion. Perhaps the best way to give advice, if advice is given at all, is to hear clients out first in order to understand their situation more completely and to assess their goals, and then to explain what alternatives or options are available.

Advice giving remains a controversial issue in the counseling literature. Its critics maintain that advice fosters dependency and robs clients of the right to make decisions for themselves. It is important for each counselor to question his or her haste in offering ready answers to somewhat complex situations. Is there some inner need like dominance or control being satisfied? Is the advice giver willing to assume the responsibility for another person's life? Is the advice giver projecting his or her own needs, problems, or values into the advice?

So while it is true that many people come to a financial counselor ostensibly looking for advice or the right answer, it is also true that many people choose not to take the advice when it is offered, or if they do take the counselor's advice and later discover that it was unsound, they rightfully blame the counselor.

There is a place for tentative suggestions that leave the final decision about courses of action entirely up to the client. In this manner, clients are free to make decisions that are right for them and thus assume the responsibility for their own lives. Advisers who do this are functioning in a wholly professional and ethical manner.

ESSENTIALS IN FINANCIAL COUNSELING

In the preceding section we differentiated the three types of planned, purposeful communication: interviewing, counseling, and advising. Each one of these types of communication can be found in the financial counseling relationship. For instance, interviewing in the form of data collection for a fact finder might well constitute the early stages of the communications process. After the data are collected, the second phase would probably consist largely of counseling—listening closely to the client and trying to understand the client's inner world of needs, desires, fears, attitudes, values, and goals. The third and final stage of communication in financial counseling would undoubtedly include giving expert advice, or at least carefully exploring possible alternatives for achieving the client's objectives. Let us look at the dynamics of communication and how it works in actual practice.

Structure

In any kind of planned and purposeful communication setting, the first element that needs to be attended to is structuring. Structuring serves to determine both the format and the subject matter of the interaction that is to follow. The counselor's task is to make the purpose of the session clear to the client at the outset. This would include the inevitable introductions, an explanation of the process involved, a discussion of forms that will be used and the amount of time that will be required, a discussion of the confidential nature of the relationship, and some prediction of what kinds of outcomes the client might reasonably expect. This structuring need not be lengthy and cumbersome; in fact, it is far better to structure in a clear, straightforward, and succinct fashion. Consider the following example of structuring:

Counselor: "In order for me to be able to provide the best possible service for you, we'll probably need to see each other on three or four separate occasions, although I want you to know that I'm available to you as often as you need me. Today I thought we'd start by getting some information from you about your own financial situation. To do this, I'll use the fact finder pages, which will remain confidential between the two of us. As we go about our business together, I suspect that we'll be able to come up with a financial plan that will be sensible and help you meet your goals. Do you have any questions?"

The counselor's approach in the foregoing example is friendly and promises cooperation. The client is made to feel important; that he or she is the focal point of the counseling situation. The statement offers hope that the results of client counseling will meet the needs and goals of the client.

In the early stages of counseling, the client may be apprehensive or uncertain about how to begin. A good guide to follow is to begin where the client is. If the client is, in fact, anxious at the outset, some time should be spent discussing the mere difficulty of getting started. Talking about this will invariably alleviate most of the client's anxieties. It is important to keep in mind that whenever feelings emerge, it is best to focus upon those feelings rather than ignore them. If, for example, a client, in the middle of a session, appears distressed over some aspect of his or her situation (for example, an impending divorce), some time must be given to discussing these feelings. Until the feelings are addressed and expressed, a further discussion of content is unproductive and meaningless.

Rapport

Rapport is best established through the personhood of the financial counselor. Attributes that go a long way toward a rapprochement between counselor and client would include a friendly and interested concern; an unhurried, leisurely pace; an accepting, nonjudgmental attitude; attentive, active listening; and an egalitarian relationship. In such a climate, clients are free to be themselves, since they don't have to be afraid that what they say will be evaluated in a negative way by the counselor. Furthermore, they begin to realize that the ultimate responsibility for planning, setting goals, and taking action rests with them and not the counselor.

Perhaps the most important attribute of personhood in establishing rapport is the financial counselor's acceptance of the client. This attitude stems from a sincere desire on the part of the counselor to respect the uniqueness of each client and a genuine wish to be of help. And it might be well to add that accepting others is easier said than done, especially with people who are markedly different from us in terms of their values, attitudes, socioeconomic status, and so on. Despite this difficulty, it is absolutely imperative that counselors accept their clients, because unless a client feels accepted by his counselor, the relationship will never really become a partnership of equals.

Resistance

Resistance often occurs in even the best of counseling relationships. It often is expressed in the form of hostility toward the counselor, and the hostility can be either overt or covert. Open hostility is the easiest type to recognize and, in most cases, to handle. We all know what angry people look and sound like: their faces become flushed; their jaws tighten; they clench their fists; their voices rise; their language becomes more expressively angry. The only effective thing to do at this point is to reflect this anger, as in saying "I can sense your anger. You don't like what I've just said, do you?" This allows the client to vent whatever pent-up feelings of anger they have, and the anger slowly begins to dissipate while the behavior becomes more rational.

Covert hostility is more difficult to recognize and can be more difficult to deal with, since clients themselves may not even be aware of their anger. Some examples of covert hostility are missing appointments; being late for appointments; being sarcastic or cynical; being overly genteel or polite; not getting down to business. Whatever the evidence of covert hostility is, the best approach is *not* to interpret the behavior for the client as latent hostility or passive-aggressiveness but simply to focus on the behavior itself and let the client analyze or interpret it. For instance, the counselor might say, "I've noticed that whenever we talk about your spouse's handling of the family budget, you become sarcastic. What do you think might be going on?" Again, this helps the client to focus on the feedback received and allows angry feelings to be vented. Resistance must be addressed as directly as possible if any good is to come of the counseling relationship.

Other types of resistance behaviors that counselors might encounter during counseling relationships would include withdrawal or passivity; dwelling in fantasy or nonreality; ambivalence or vacillation; and the use of inappropriate humor, to name a few. As mentioned, the counselor should not analyze or interpret a client's resistance behavior since analysis tends only to raise the client's defensiveness. Instead the counselor should be aware of what is occurring, note whether it is a recurrent pattern, and at an appropriate point share such observations in a non-judgmental manner with the client.

Common Areas of Resistance

Client resistance is almost a given in a financial counseling relationship, probably because clients, when they enter into a counseling relationship, yield a certain amount of their privacy and personal power over the situation to the counselor. Resistance is a way of defending oneself, or restoring some of the balance of power to oneself. Certain discussion areas, because of their sensitive nature, seem to be particularly vulnerable to client resistance.

One such sensitive subject area is death and dying. Because of its uncertainty, death is extremely anxiety-producing to some people. Dr. Elizabeth Kubler-Ross, an eminent authority on death and dying, postulates that there are five stages that a person facing death passes through: denial, anger, bargaining, depression, and acceptance. The first four of these stages are all different forms of resistance that the person uses for self-protection. Financial counselors, when discussing future plans with older people, need to be particularly sensitive to the feelings of their clients. Counselors must listen and observe very closely what clients communicate when discussing death and dying. Counselors must be empathetic to feelings and communicate accurately what is heard and observed. A genuine concern for the feelings and attitudes of clients must be manifested. Counselors must also be aware of their own feelings about death, so that they do not interfere with what clients are feeling and attempting to communicate.

Counselors can help to restore some control over the future by involving clients fully in decision making and planning for contingencies. This allows clients to feel useful, worthwhile, and somewhat in control of their situation.

Another area where resistance may be encountered involves marital tensions, such as separation/divorce, parent-child disputes, sex, the empty-nest syndrome, and mid-life crises. While financial counselors are not expected to be highly qualified marriage or family counselors, they should be astute enough to recognize when a married couple is resisting because of an underlying, unexpressed marital problem. And once it is recognized, counselors should be willing and able to focus with the couple on the problem area. Otherwise, if the problem is ignored, whatever decisions are reached will be less valid than those that would be reached after a full airing of the problem. Besides providing a welcome catharsis for the couple, focusing on the problem also enables them to muster their forces to arrive at a mutually satisfactory solution. In counseling couples who are in disagreement on a crucial subject, the counselor needs to listen closely to what both partners have to say. It is far too common, unfortunately, to let the more dominant partner do most of the speaking and deciding. Since the outcome of the decision affects both partners, both should be involved in the discussion. To do any less than this almost guarantees an unsatisfactory conclusion.

Another sensitive area involves the executive who has failed to attain the degree of success he had dreamed of in his profession. His dreams shattered and unfulfilled, he may resort to cynicism, biting sarcasm, or empty humor in an attempt to endure it. Rather than laugh along with him, the effective counselor *reflects* the underlying feeling to let the client know that he understands his disappointment. A simple statement like, "I suppose it's a bitter pill to swallow when you've worked so hard to see your personal hopes shattered like that," allows your client to feel understood and appreciated. More often than not, the client will begin to discuss more openly how he feels. And once people are able to express their feelings, they are well on the way to addressing their problems in an effective manner.

Resistance behaviors, in any case, are a certain tip-off that the client is having difficulty subscribing to the counselor's line of reasoning. It does no good for the counselor to proceed with business as usual, ignoring the obvious resistance; nothing can be accomplished as long as the resistance continues. The resistances must be dealt with openly and objectively. Only then is there any chance that they will be diminished and that the participants can get on with the business at hand.

CHARACTERISTICS OF THE EFFECTIVE COUNSELOR

The main thing a counselor brings to the counseling hour is himself or herself. Financial counselors, first and foremost, must be themselves in how they relate to and interact with their clients. Each counselor is a human being, complete with human strengths and frailties. But each counselor is also a professionally trained individual, a person who, ideally, enjoys listening to and trying to understand other human beings and to accept them as they are. The effective counselor is also sincere and genuine in attempting to help others learn how to help themselves. This attitude generates interesting, challenging, and highly gratifying work; and it is—more than anything else—hard work when it is done professionally.

Carl Rogers, in his classic book, *Client-Centered Therapy,* postulated that there are three conditions necessary to bring about constructive client change: (1) unconditional positive regard, (2) accurate empathy, and (3) genuineness. Most counseling theorists agree that if an effective counselor-client relationship is to exist, the counselor must be open and spontaneous (genuine), must value the client as a unique individual (unconditional positive regard), and must be able to perceive and understand what the client is experiencing (accurate empathy).

A constructive counselor-client relationship serves not only to increase the opportunity for clients to attain the goals that are important to them, but also serves as a model of a good interpersonal relationship. Some questions that all counselors ought to ask themselves from time to time are the following:

- Knowing yourself, do you think it will be possible for you to value your clients, especially those who think, feel, and act differently from you?
- How easy or difficult will it be for you to view the world from another's perspective without imposing your own standards, beliefs, and attitudes on that person? Will your own values, ideas, and feelings hinder your understanding of another person?
- How open do you care, or dare, to be with a client? Will you be able to just be yourself, or will you role-play how you think a professional counselor should be?

These are important questions to consider before engaging yourself in the dynamics of a counseling relationship. Far too many financial counselors assume that they have the right kind of personality to counsel others without ever scrutinizing themselves in the same way. Let us look a bit more closely at the core conditions to which Rogers refers.

Unconditional Positive Regard

This quality is often misconstrued as agreement or disagreement with the client. Rather, it is an attitude of valuing the client, or being able to express appreciation of the client as a unique and worthwhile person. Liking and respecting another person have a circular effect. When you value clients, your sense of liking will be communicated to them; this by itself will enhance their feelings for themselves and add to their appreciation of themselves as worthwhile human beings.

Accurate Empathy

Accurate empathy means that your sense of the client's world fits the client's self-image. This gives clients the feeling that you are in touch with them. When clients say something like, "Yes, that's it," or "That's exactly right," it indicates that your response was right on target, and that they feel that you are closely following and understanding them.

Learning to understand is not an easy process. It involves the capacity to lay aside your own set of experiences in favor of those of your clients—as seen through their eyes, not yours. It involves skillful listening so that you can hear not only the obvious, but also the subtleties of which, perhaps, even the client is unaware.

Developing accurate empathy also means identifying and resolving your own needs so that they do not interfere with your understanding of the feelings and concerns of your client. The counselor who identifies too strongly with the client's state, however, impedes rather than facilitates the counseling objective.

Genuineness

Genuineness means, simply, that the counselor is a real person. There is no facade, no role-playing of what a professional counselor should be. Professional counselors are wholly aware of themselves and their feelings, thoughts, values, and attitudes. More importantly, genuine counselors are not afraid to express themselves openly and honestly at all times. Financial counselors do not have to become something different for all clients with whom they have relationships. They are role-free; they are themselves at all times.

A genuine counselor communicates in a spontaneous and expressive manner and does not conceal anything. A genuine counselor is open and willing to listen to whatever the client is willing to discuss. A genuine counselor is consistent. He or she does not think or feel one thing but say another.

One author suggests that effective counselors can

- express directly to others whatever they are experiencing
- communicate without distorting their messages
- listen to others without distorting their messages
- be spontaneous instead of planned or programmed
- respond openly in a specific and concrete manner
- be willing to manifest their own vulnerabilities and frailties
- learn how to be psychologically close to others
- commit themselves to others

A tall order? Perhaps. And yet, for a financial counseling relationship to be effective, it is mandatory that counselors allow themselves to be genuine with their clients. Otherwise, the relationship deteriorates into a charade of two human beings playing prescribed roles with each other, and this defeats the purpose.

Self-Awareness

There is general consensus among counselor-educators that counselors need to be highly aware of themselves and particularly aware of their own attitudes and values. Counselors who are aware of their own value systems have a better chance of avoiding the imposition of their values onto their clients. This quality is of vital importance since we want to help our clients make decisions that stem from their own value systems, rather than from ours. The more we know about ourselves, the better we can understand, interpret, evaluate, and control our behavior and the less likely we are to attribute aspects of ourselves to the client, a rather common defense mechanism known as projection. Before we can be aware of others, it is essential that we be solidly grounded in self-awareness.

Barbara Okun, in her book, *Effective Helping,* suggests that counselors should continually try to determine their own needs, feelings, and values by answering the following questions:

- Am I aware when I find myself feeling uncomfortable with a client or with a particular subject area?
- Am I aware of my avoidance strategies?
- Can I really be honest with the client?
- Do I always feel the need to be in control of situations?
- Do I often feel as if I must be omnipotent in that I must do something to make the client "get better" so that I can be successful?
- Am I so problem-oriented that I'm always looking for the negative, for a problem, and never responding to the positive, to the good?
- Am I able to be as open with clients as I want them to be with me?

The adage "Know thyself" should apply to financial counselors and other helping professionals even more than it does to the population at large. A very large part of our responsibility as counselors is to know ourselves as thoroughly as possible, so that we are then able to provide the very best kind of objective, informed counseling to our clients. A counselor who has "blind spots" about himself or herself will surely be less effective in a helping situation than a counselor who is comfortably self-aware. This is not to say that the counselor is a problem-free, completely self-actualized individual; rather, it means that the counselor is a human being, having a multitude of strengths and even some weaknesses, but that the weaknesses are known by the counselor and do not interfere with the dynamics of counseling another person.

Values Orientations

As human beings, financial counselors have value systems that are the result of years of living on this planet. Many of our values are inculcated in us by our parents, by schooling, by religion, by our peers, and by society. However they come to us, they are as much a part of us as our physical and psychological characteristics. This is not to say that they are a permanent, transfixed part of our being, because our values can, and do, change. A vivid example of this type of change came during the decades of the 1960s and early 1970s when a whole society's value system was rocked to the core by momentous events such as the assassinations of the Kennedys and Martin Luther King, the civil rights movement, the war in Vietnam, the women's rights movement, and the Kent State killings. This truly was a time when an entire nation's value system was being challenged, and as a result, certain of our long-cherished values were thrust into a state of flux and some, ultimately, were changed. And what happened to the nation was repeated many times over with many individuals in our midst. People who at first accepted the Vietnam War as a rightful intervention by a powerful nation into the affairs of a far-off country slowly changed their values about not only that war, but about armed conflict in general. And virtually the same thing happened on other controversial issues as well: abortion, human rights, euthanasia, drugs, and the like.

The point here is that values, while deeply internalized, are not immutable. Counselors need to remind themselves of this fact of life as they work with clients who are confused and afraid in approaching important decisions. While it is true that we are in many ways a reflection of our past history, we are — or can be — much more than that. There is no need to be shackled to our past. We can, if we choose, overcome our past and live new lives, based upon who we are now and what we believe in and hold to be valuable to us now and in the future. This is a liberating concept and, as such, frees individuals to think, feel, and behave in ways that are congruent with their present being, rather than dooming them to repeat the past and live in ways that are no longer meaningful.

The financial counselor's role in this situation is to act as a catalyst rather than as a maintainer of the status quo. The implied danger, of course, is that counselors might try to force change in their clients' values and attitudes where none is desired or sought after, or that counselors might subtly or not-so-subtly try to impose their values on clients. Both of these dangers must be consciously guarded against. What counselors must do is listen carefully to clients as they sift through the various value choices faced, so that when clients must finally make the choice, it can be done freely, without encumbrances from the past. Clients must actually be opened up to the freedom of making choices that are relevant and meaningful to their very existence. Good counselors have a knack of being able to do this.

Values Differences

Each of us has within us a hierarchy of values that makes order of our lives. An older executive facing retirement might, for example, rank security above risk taking in deciding how to invest money. On the other hand, a younger financial counselor might rank risk taking above security in the hierarchy of values. What happens, then, when the risk-taking counselor sits down to counsel the security-minded preretirement executive? If the counselor is sensitive and understanding, he or she will listen to the older person, trying to get a sense of what is important to the client, what the client is willing and unwilling to do. The effective financial counselor does not try to sell the client a product that the counselor believes is right but that the client believes is wrong, unsafe, or risky.

Counseling is caring, and caring means that the counselor cares enough — has enough faith in the client's worth as a unique human being — to permit that client to make value choices that fit his or her value system. The financial counselor can and should provide information that will help the client make the choice, but the choice itself ultimately belongs to the client, not the counselor. Only in this way are we counselors.

Besides the differences in values, which often are reflective of the differences in age between counselor and client, we also ought to consider several other "isms" — sexism and racism — and how they impinge upon the counselor-client relationship. Let us look first at sex differences. Sexist counseling occurs when the counselor uses his or her own sex ideology as a framework for counseling. In the field of financial counseling this might take place when a male counselor discourages a female client from doing something that has traditionally been thought to be in the man's world, such as returning to work while there is an infant at home to be cared for. This kind of subtle advice giving, besides reflecting the obvious sex-role bias of the counselor, is not in keeping with what is happening in many households today. Further, it is intrusive in that the responsibility for making that decision is clearly the client's and not the counselor's. It is critical that counselors learn to recognize their own biases and sex-role stereotypes and not inflict them upon people whom they are trying to help.

Since financial counselors typically counsel both husband and wife, it is important to understand what both partners have to say. It is far too common to defer to the male of the household, the "breadwinner," without taking into consideration what the female spouse has to contribute. When both husband and wife are in complete agreement, no problem exists. But when they disagree — and this is often communicated through nonverbal signals like a sigh, a frown, or an angry glance — it is important to make a point of bringing the subject up for a full discussion. It is far better to spend whatever time it takes to get both partners to come up with a mutually acceptable decision than to proceed with one person's plan of action, knowing that it doesn't satisfy the other person.

Racism, despite notable progress in the civil rights movement over the past two decades, is still with us in many forms. Counselors engage in racism when they limit the choices of their clients based solely on their clients' race, or when they make faulty assumptions about their clients because of racist stereotyping.

The issue of whether white counselors can be effective in a relationship with blacks or Hispanics has been the subject of much research, though no conclusive findings exist. An effective counselor should be able to work with people of all races, since all people seem to have the same basic psychological needs and problems. Counselors should be able to relate to their clients as individuals rather than as blacks, Hispanics, or Asians. Counselors also need to be conscious of their own biases regarding race and to guard against allowing their biases to adversely affect the quality of the counseling relationship. The counseling strategies employed should not differ with regard to what the race of the client is, any more than they should not differ depending on the sex, age, or religion of the client.

BASIC COMMUNICATION PRINCIPLES

In the previous section we discussed the attributes of an effective counselor. In this section we will explore communication as a process and attempt to relate fundamental principles of communication to effective financial counseling. An effective counselor is also an effective communicator.

Communication is often thought of as one person sending a message through both verbal and nonverbal channels to another person or persons with the intention of evoking a response. A speaker asks, "How are you?" and the listener (or receiver of the communication) answers, "Just fine — except for my back." Effective communication takes place when the receiver interprets the sender's message in precisely the same fashion in which the sender intended it. Difficulties in communication arise when the receiver misunderstands and/or misinterprets the sender's message. Since any individual's intentions are private and rarely clearly stated, the receiver of the message has the difficult job of decoding the message without knowing for a fact what the sender's intentions are.

In addition, communication failures can also be attributed to the wide variety of stimuli with which individuals are bombarded during the course of a conversation. People try to communicate while watching television or listening to the radio, or they attempt to conduct two conversations simultaneously. But all noise is not auditory; some is emotional in nature. How effectively, for example, do you think a Ku Klux Klan member communicates with a Black Muslim? Prejudices and biases, then, are emotionally built-in stimuli that interfere with objective listening and effective communication.

Related to this communication failure is the sad but simple truth that individuals listen in order to evaluate and render judgment about the speaker, which, in turn, makes the speaker guarded and defensive about what he or she is attempting to communicate. Perhaps the best example of this type of ineffective communication is a city council meeting, where one side advocates the raising of taxes, while the other side interrupts, casts aspersions, and generally fights for all it is worth against the tax hike. Whenever there are two people, or two groups, each with a strong vested interest in an emotional issue, the likelihood of there being clear communication is virtually nil.

Communication, even in the best of circumstances, should not be taken for granted. Let us look now at some basic principles of communication theory.

- Communication is learned by all of us through experience, but experience itself does not necessarily make one an effective communicator. As children, we learn how to communicate by imitating our models—parents, brothers, sisters, neighbors, playmates, babysitters. Unfortunately, not all of our models are effective communicators; thus, we acquire poor habits of communication early, and those habits, like all habits, are difficult to break. A child reared in a home where everyone talks at the same time and no one listens carries this model upon leaving the home.
- The meaning of words is illusory; words do not mean—people do. Words are merely symbols. Consider, for example, a simple word like rock. The teenager immediately thinks of loud music; the geologist thinks of a hard object created millions of years ago; the burglar thinks of a diamond ring; the old lady thinks of her favorite chair, and so on. The point is that a word can have almost as many meanings as there are people who use it.
- Language is learned; thus, in a sense, we are programmed, and the meaning of words stays within us for future reference. This programming is extremely helpful since, once we learn a word, it usually remains ours for a lifetime. However, this programming can also serve as an impediment to open communication with others, in that we often refer back to our original conceptions of words without thinking how others might interpret them. For example, the word girl, once used to refer to any female, is now clearly inappropriate in referring to an adult woman in this age of ERA and women's rights.
- No two people are programmed alike; therefore no symbol can always be interpreted the same way. Individuals differ in the nature and degree of their understanding. We perceive things differently, from our own frame of reference, so meanings differ.

- It is impossible for any individual to encode or process all parts of a message. Besides the fact that words are often inadequate in describing accurately what we are feeling or thinking, there is also the problem of distortion, that is, an individual's altering the event to suit his or her own purposes. But even if we have the precise word and communicate it without distortion, we still are faced with the problem of the receiver's receiving it in the same way in which it was intended.
- Some experts claim that the single greatest problem with communication is the assumption of it. Too many people assume that their messages are automatically understood. We also sometimes assume that our perceptions are more right than the perceptions of someone else. Where human communication is concerned, no assumptions can or should be made.
- We can never not communicate. Anything we say or do can be interpreted in a meaningful way as a message. Even during periods of silence, communication takes place. Nonverbal behavior (which will be discussed in some detail shortly) such as eye contact, facial expressions, gestures, body posture, voice inflections, hesitations, and the like, all speak volumes. In fact, most sociological research claims that approximately two-thirds of the total message is communicated via nonverbal channels, especially where human emotions are concerned.
- Listening is communication, too. Unfortunately, not everyone is a good listener; yet, that should not be too surprising, since listening as a communication skill is rarely, if ever, taught formally. To speak precisely and to listen carefully present a real challenge to all of us. The way in which we listen and respond to another person is crucial for building a fulfilling relationship. When we listen carefully, with understanding and without evaluation, and when we respond relevantly, we implicitly communicate to the speaker, "I care about what you are saying, and I'd like to understand it."

The most effective communication occurs when the receiver of a message gives understanding responses, sometimes called paraphrases. A client might say, "I don't know . . . . I doubt that we can afford to send both of our kids to college." A financial counselor using an understanding response would respond to the above statement with, "So you're just not sure you have the resources for a college education right now." While it might be tempting to try to convince the clients at this juncture that there is a way to finance their children's college education, the understanding response communicates a desire to understand the clients without evaluating these statements as right or wrong. It also helps the counselor to see the expressed ideas and feelings of clients from their point of view.

Another means available to the counselor to enhance the communication process and the counseling relationship is to personalize messages. The hallmark of personal statements is the use of the personal pronouns, I, me, and my. Using generalized pronouns such as everyone, anyone, or somebody to refer to your own ideas only tends to confuse clients and, hence, results in ambiguity and faulty understanding. Personal statements like, "I can appreciate your concern over not having adequate resources," reveals your own feelings to clients and increases the personal quality of the relationship.

ELEMENTS OF NONVERBAL BEHAVIORS

As mentioned above, clients communicate many feelings and attitudes to counselors through nonverbal behaviors, including (but not limited to) fear, anxiety, sincerity, confusion, anger, aggression, happiness, hostility, interest, boredom, and concern. The two main sources of nonverbal behaviors are the *body* and the *voice*. From these two sources come four types of nonverbal signs of meaning: *body position, body movement, voice tone,* and *voice pitch.* Each of these types of nonlinguistic signs conveys a wealth of information to the observant financial counselor. It should be noted that the counselor's first impressions of the meaning or significance of any body language must be checked out against other clues given by the client.

The Body

When learning to improve one's ability to observe the nonverbal behaviors of clients, it is important to notice the various ways by which the body actually communicates, either in agreement or in variance with what is actually said. In particular, the counselor should notice and learn to interpret the communications that are transmitted by the client's body positions and movements.

Positions

Overall body posture is the first thing the observant counselor notices. Clients who sit erect and comfortably are usually relaxed. If they lean slightly forward, it is usually a sign of interest and involvement in the counseling session. If they slouch, or seem to draw away from the counselor, they may have no interest or trust in the counselor — or they may be bored. Good client posture may indicate self-assurance and positive self-esteem. Poor posture may signal a lack of self-assurance or low self-esteem.

The counselor should also notice the position of the client's arms and legs. When the legs are uncrossed and the arms are positioned comfortably at the sides, the client is usually relaxed and open. Tightly crossed arms and legs, on the other hand, may indicate distrust or unreceptiveness. The facial position of the client should also be noticed. Most people's faces are expressive of a wide range of ever-changing feelings. The client whose face appears frozen in one position may be signaling fear, anxiety, or anger, or some other prepossessing feeling that could become a block or obstacle to open communication with the counselor.

Movements

The client who frequently changes body positions may be indicating physical or emotional discomfort, or a lack of interest. The counselor should take note of such movements and try to relate them to information gleaned later.

There is reason to believe that body language may be more honest or pure than verbal communication. In certain positive, straightforward human experiences we know that it is. The impulsive hug or kiss of greeting for people we care for is the most obvious example. But people also communicate through the body when they don't want to communicate, or when they are hiding or contradicting themselves. For example, a client may say, "No, I'm not nervous about investing in a tax shelter," while biting his nails, pulling at his hair, or fidgeting distractedly. People often say what they think they may be expected to say in a given situation or context, not noticing themselves what they are actually communicating through body language.

Gestures

Hand and arm gestures are usually used to illustrate or accent verbal statements. Hands clasped so tightly that the knuckles are whitened and taut certainly signify something, perhaps fear or anxiety. While jerky hand and arm gestures may indicate anxiety, smooth, flowing gestures usually mean that the client is relaxed and interested in the counseling session. Frequent crossing and uncrossing of the legs, or bouncing a leg that is crossed, may indicate nervousness, boredom, or lack of interest.

Facial Expressions

The financial counselor can learn much from a client's facial expressions. Look for frowns, smiles, or nervous habits, such as biting the lips. Look especially to see if the client's facial expressions change as topics change, and note whether the expression is appropriate or incongruent. For example, if the client talks about anger, does she appear angry? If she facially expresses disgust about her husband's spendthrift ways, do her intentions in her last will and testament reflect that feeling by providing for her children through a trust, rather than leaving everything outright to her husband?

Eye Contact

Eye contact, or the lack of it, in the counseling session can indicate the client's feeling. If the client's eyes are downcast and rarely meet the gaze of the counselor, the client could be shy, anxious, or fearful (though not necessarily toward the counselor). On the other hand, if the client stares or glares constantly at the counselor, anger or hostility could be indicated. If the client's eyes rove all around the room, looking at the walls and ceiling while the counselor is filling out the data-gathering form, there could be a serious lack of interest in the relevance of data gathering. A client who is open and interested in the counseling session will usually meet the gaze of the counselor. This eye contact of the client usually indicates interest in the session and a positive and concerned attitude toward counseling. Needless to say, reciprocity from the counselor is likely to be perceived by the client in the same way.

The Voice

Nonverbal voice clues can be observed in the tone and pitch of the client's voice. Tone and pitch are qualities of the voice that may indicate the speaker's feelings, quite apart from what is actually said. They should be observed closely.

The Tone

Tone is loudness or softness. The client who talks very loudly or shouts may be indicating anger or hostility. The client who talks very softly may be exhibiting fear or shyness.

The Pitch

Pitch is the quality of a voice that indicates how high or low the voice is on a musical scale. A high-pitched voice may indicate anxiety, fear, or anger. A low-pitched voice can indicate either comfort or control of strong emotions.

Obviously, some people's voices are naturally louder than others. The natural pitch of different voices also varies greatly. The point is not to type these differences but to observe and determine which vocal qualities are natural to a particular client so as to recognize variations. If these vocal qualities do vary during counseling sessions in relation to personal and financial details, they can be important clues to the strong emotions that often affect a client's motivations, needs, and objectives. The counseling sessions themselves are often an inducement to clients to open up and give vent to feelings about their financial condition. Thus voice tone and pitch are important factors for counselors to observe and consider in relation to all other clues that characterize the client and reveal the individual's self-image.

Interpreting the Meaning of Nonverbal Behaviors

It is important for financial counselors to note that in all the descriptions above of nonverbal behaviors, of body language, we have stated that a behavior may or usually does indicate one or more feelings. Nonverbal behaviors are clues that must be clearly observed and compared with what the client says in order to determine whether they are appropriate or congruent. For example, if a client blurts out, "I am furious with the broker who sold me that bunch of junk bonds last year!" and strikes the desk, the gesture is congruent with the verbal message — it agrees with what the client says. If the client makes the same statement and sits calmly smiling, however, there is incongruent behavior — the body language does not jibe with the verbal message. When the financial counselor observes incongruent behavior of this sort in a client, it should be mentioned to the client in order to clarify which element of the communication is correct.

Nonverbal behaviors are clues or indicators. While they signify something, their meanings can be clouded by incongruence, distortion, or vagueness. Premature assumptions about what they really mean would be as unprofessional as failing to notice them altogether. For example, a client's palsied hands might be due to one or more of the following causes: nervousness, fear, Parkinson's disease, too much coffee, chemical poisoning, or alcoholism. The client who always talks loudly may be either angry or hard of hearing, or merely an overbearing individual. The client who shows no interest in counseling may be worn out with worrying whether his recent commodities futures trading is going to wipe him out with margin calls, or whether he should buy term or whole life for estate liquidity, or whether he will have an estate. He may be on tranquilizers over worry about a son and heir who himself abuses drugs. For any number of reasons the client may need psychological counseling or therapy before he can undertake financial counseling. In short, not all the problems that clients may bring to financial counseling sessions are financial in origin or nature. When present, these nonfinancial problems will distort client messages and add to the difficulties of clarifying them.

Observant counselors need to be astute enough to discern from among all the verbal and nonverbal clues and be aware that in most client cases there will be a mixture of congruent and noncongruent evidence. Counselors thus understand who clients are, where they are, where they want to go; and can then suggest the optimal ways to help each one get there. *Do not assume that you know what a given behavior means.* Check it out and clarify your perception with each client.

And do not forget that as a counselor *you* communicate in both verbal and nonverbal ways, too, just as the client does, and that your communications behaviors very much affect the client. This is particularly true of nonverbal messages. Therefore any of the communications and psychological considerations in this chapter that you may agree are important with respect to the client are also important for you. As a financial counseling professional you will want to remove from your own behaviors those elements that present obstacles and barriers to successful communication with the client and with other professionals with whom you deal. The client is then more likely to accept your role in the counseling situation and, ultimately, the plan you develop for meeting his or her financial needs and objectives. Similarly, other professionals whose expertise you will often need to call upon in developing and implementing a plan will respect your role as a financial counselor and planner.

THE SKILLS OF ATTENDING AND LISTENING

Paying attention to clients is a first necessary component in good communication. No matter how expert your other communication skills are, if you are inattentive to your clients' verbal and nonverbal behaviors, you are apt to lose them at the very outset. How often have you been in the company of another person who shies away from looking at you, who glances nervously at his wristwatch, who interrupts you, and who, literally and figuratively, turns his back to you? Surely, if you have had this kind of experience, you recall how uncomfortable and ill at ease you were with this inattentive behavior.

If a counselor's goal is to understand clients, the counselor must first pay close attention to or focus on their verbal and nonverbal messages. Poor attending and poor listening lead to poor understanding.

Physical Attending

Gerard Egan, a renowned counselor-educator, categorizes attending behavior into (1) physical attending, or using your body to communicate; and (2) psychological attending, or listening actively. He uses the acronym, SOLER, as a reminder of the five basic attributes associated with physical attending. Let us look at these five attributes.

- S: Face the other person *squarely.*

When there is face-to-face, direct contact, the communication process is enhanced. You communicate nonverbally to the other person, "I'm here with you; I'm tuned-in and ready to face the issues with you head-on." Turning your body away lessens your involvement with the other person.

- O: Adopt an *open* posture.

There is something to be said about receiving a person with open arms. Crossed arms and crossed legs can inadvertently communicate a holding-off of the other person. An open posture—open arms and uncrossed legs and an open smile—communicates receptiveness to the other person and, hence, increases good communication and decreases defensiveness.

- L: *Lean* toward the other.

This is another physical signal of interest, involvement, caring. Two people who care about each other, when involved in conversation, almost always can be seen leaning toward each other. On the other hand, two people who are observed leaning away from one another, or sitting rigidly straight in their chairs, seem to be either bored or disinterested, or extremely cautious and defensive about getting involved with each other.

- E: Maintain good *eye* contact.

Good eye contact consists of looking at another individual when you are in conversation. Poor eye contact consists of rarely looking at the other person, or looking away when he or she looks at you or staring constantly with a blank expression on your face. The eye contact should be natural and spontaneous. Since you are interested in your client, you will want to use your eyes as a vehicle of communication.

- R: Be *relaxed* while attending.

It is possible to be both intense while focusing on the client and relaxed at the same time. A nervous, fidgety, or rigid counselor communicates these feelings to the client. A counselor who sits in a casual fashion, who speaks naturally and spontaneously, and who uses natural gestures has the advantage of being free to focus intently upon the client and his or her communication, as well as helping to facilitate naturalness and spontaneity in the client.

As has been mentioned previously, it is impossible not to communicate, so as a counselor you might as well use your body—gestures, posture, eyes—to communicate whatever message you wish to communicate. Otherwise, the body may communicate something you do not wish to communicate. In other words, try to make your body work for you on behalf of your counseling relationship.

Active Listening

So far, attending has been described as a physical activity; active listening brings in the psychological activity involved in attending. Many of us take listening for granted, but there is a distinct difference between simply hearing and actively listening. Hearing means the receiving of auditory signals. A person says, "I have a bad headache," and we hear that message and respond, "That's too bad," or "Here, have a couple of aspirin." An active listener, on the other hand, might respond, "You look as though it's really getting you down." In short, the active listener responds not only to the verbal message received through the auditory channel, but also to the unspoken, or nonverbal message, communicated by the sender's body, facial expression, or tone of voice.

Active listening, then, means putting the nonverbal behavior, the voice, and words together—all the cues sent out by the other person—to get the essence of the communication being sent. An active listener is an understanding listener, one who attempts to see the world from the other's frame of reference. If you can state in your own words what the other person has said, and that person accepts your statement as an accurate reflection of what he or she has said, then it is safe to say that you have listened actively and understood with accuracy.

But it must be stated that active listening is not merely parroting another's words—a computer can be (and has been) programmed to do that. Active listening means involving yourself in the inner world of another person while, at the same time, maintaining your own identity and being able to respond with meaningfulness to the messages of that other person.

Responding during Active Listening

As indicated above, active listening is hard work and requires intense focusing and concentration. Years of not listening have made most of us poor listeners. We are distracted easily; we tend to evaluate and judge what is being said while it is being said, so that we are framing our own responses to the speaker's statement before the speaker is finished talking and, thus, we miss the message.

There are several simple ways of responding to people so that they feel accepted and understood. Let us look at some of these response modalities.

Perhaps the simplest response modality is what Allen Ivey refers to as "minimal encouragers to talk," or "continuing responses." Nonverbally, if you want someone to continue talking, you might smile or nod your head to communicate agreement and/or understanding. Equally as effective in communicating your understanding is a minimal encourager like "uh-huh," "mmmm," "then?" "and. . . ?" These relatively unobtrusive responses encourage the speaker to continue talking. They communicate to the speaker, "Go on, I'm with you."

Another type of response that enhances communication is the restatement-of-content response. The rationale for restatement is to let speakers hear what they have said on the assumption that this may encourage them to go on speaking, examining, and looking deeper. Restatement communicates to the client, "I am listening to you very carefully, so much so that I can repeat what you have said." The most effective restatements are those that are phrased in your own words, a paraphrase of what the speaker has stated. To do this effectively, we must temporarily suspend our own frame of reference and attempt to view the world from the other person's perspective. Suppose the client says to you, "I'm really in a financial bind, what with taxes, inflation, fuel bills; I don't know how we make it from one month to the next." An accurate restatement might be expressed, "So things are tough for you financially. It seems like you can't make ends meet." The client, hearing this understanding response, is encouraged to delve more deeply into the situation, feeling that the counselor has, indeed, heard the message on the same wavelength upon which it was transmitted. The bond between client and counselor is, thus, strengthened and greater opportunities for creative problem solving are opened up.

Just as we manifest understanding for our clients by responding to the content of the message, so may we also show our understanding of the client's experience by responding to the feelings expressed. Sometimes feelings are expressed directly, and at other times they are only implied or stated indirectly. In order to respond to a person's feelings, we must observe the behavioral cues like tone of voice, body posture, gestures, and facial expression, as well as listen to the speaker's words. Consider this client statement, "Within the next few months, we need to buy a new refrigerator and another car. [Sighs] I just don't know where the money is going to come from." A reflection-of-feeling response might go, "You sound pretty hopeless about your financial state. It sure is hard to break even, let alone get ahead, these days." Again, by responding in an empathic way to the client's statement, you communicate a deep understanding of the person's experience; in addition, you progress one step further by addressing the unverbalized feelings. We illustrate to the client that we understand so well what he or she is stating that we can paraphrase both words and feelings. It is helpful to both the client and the counselor to struggle to capture in words the uniqueness of the client's experience. The most effective types of understanding responses capsulize both the feeling and the content of the client's message. The basic format for this type of response is "You feel _____ [feeling] because _____ [content]."

This response enables clients to get in closer touch with the feelings that are an outgrowth of their situations. And that, in turn, facilitates the working through of the problem, because the counselor involves clients in exploring themselves in the problem. Because you have accurately understood and responded to them, clients will go on to share other personal experiences that bear upon the presented problem.

A word might be added here about the difficulties that some people have in dealing with feelings, either their own or the feelings of others. Problems often arise in interpersonal relationships because one or more of the involved persons choose to repress, distort, or disguise their feelings rather than admit that feelings are present and then discuss them openly. This is particularly true of so-called negative feelings like anger, sadness, anxiety, frustration, discomfort, and confusion. In actuality, no feelings are negative since they all are part of being human. In any case, counselors who wish to communicate effectively need to address their own feelings as well as those of their clients. The mutual expression of feelings is an integral part of building a close, trusting, caring relationship.

Two other types of understanding responses need to be mentioned here. Each is related to the restatement-of-content and the reflection-of-feeling responses; yet, there is a subtle shade of difference. First is the clarifying response that tends to amplify the speaker's statement. The clarifying response does not add anything new to what the speaker has said; it simply expands what has already been stated. The counselor attempts to restate or clarify for the client what the client has had some difficulty in expressing clearly. It is akin to a translation of the client's words into language that is more familiar and understandable to both client and counselor. Suppose a client says, "I'm not sure. Nothing makes sense anymore. Things get more confusing the more I think about them. It's a real puzzle to me." A counselor, by way of clarification, might say, "I can sense your bewilderment. Let me see if I can help out. From what you've said previously, I get the impression that you want to get your mortgage straightened out before you increase your monthly savings. Is that it?" If the financial counselor has, indeed, been following the flow of the client's experience, this statement will help to clarify the client's confusion over the situation. To the extent that the counselor's response is on target, the puzzle becomes suddenly clear and more readily solved.

Another side to the clarifying response concerns the counselor's need to have things clarified. When the counselor is puzzled, then it is certainly legitimate to ask for clarification as, "I'm sorry. I don't follow what you're saying. Can you make that more clear for me?"

Helpful clarifying responses

- facilitate client self-understanding
- attend especially to the client's feelings
- communicate the counselor's understanding
- move the client toward a clearer definition of the problem

The other type of understanding response is the summary. Summaries are especially helpful toward the end of an interview, since they focus and capsulize a series of scattered ideas to present a clear perspective. The summary has the effect of reassuring clients that you have been tuned in to their many messages. For the counselor, it serves as a check on the accuracy with which the various messages have been received.

It is often better to have the client do the summarizing. In this way, the client maintains the responsibility for bringing the messages together into a meaningful conclusion. As in clarifying, themes and emotional overtones should be summarized, and the key ideas should be synthesized into broad statements reflecting basic meanings. An example of an effective summary might go like this: "So today you described your overall financial situation as bleak, although you think that you might be able to increase your savings if you could refinance your mortgage. I know that you're rightly concerned about that." If the financial counselor has accurately summarized the essence of the interview, the client then has a better handle on the intricacies of the situation, and a resolution is closer at hand.

What we have covered thus far are the basics of nonverbal behaviors, the skills of attending and active listening, and the following four basic types of responses associated with active listening:

- restatement of content
- reflection of feeling
- clarification
- summarization

The element common to all four of these response modalities is that the counselor follows, or tracks, the client's lead. A response of this kind communicates a high level of understanding and enables the client not only to experience what it feels like to be understood, but also to progress further toward an ultimate resolution of the situation. Now we will explore other types of counselor responses, responses in which the counselor, to a certain extent, takes the lead and deviates somewhat from the client's preceding responses.

COUNSELOR LEADING RESPONSES

When the financial counselor decides to make a leading response, it is the counselor's frame of reference that comes into focus. Up to this point, the counselor's responses have followed from the client's statements, but here the emphasis shifts. An obvious danger of this shift is that the counselor may move in a direction in which the client is not yet ready or willing to move. Despite this danger, if the counselor has followed the client closely so far, and if a good relationship has been established, then this different kind of response should not threaten the client, as long as it is interposed carefully and tentatively.

The first of the leading responses is known simply as explanation. Explanation is a relatively neutral description of the way things are. It deals in logical, practical, factual information. It is often offered at the client's request, although there are instances when the counselor will offer an explanation without its being requested. A client may be confused by some terminology that the counselor has used and ask, for example, "Exactly what is an annuity?" The counselor's explanation should be simple, concise, and comprehensible. Long-winded explanations tend to become vague and hard to follow. The counselor should also guard against explaining things in a condescending, patronizing, or pedantic tone. The best kinds of explanations are those that are exchanged between equal partners (not superior-subordinates) in a relationship.

Another type of leading response is the interpretive response. Interpretations can be particularly risky when the counselor goes too deep too soon, or when the interpretation is off base. Interpretations often come across as sounding overly clinical, diagnostic, and authoritarian. Despite these drawbacks, interpretations can be extremely effective responses because they often cut to the heart of the matter. When the interpretation makes sense to the client, it definitely accelerates the interview. We should keep in mind that the goal of all interpretive efforts is self-interpretation by the client in order to increase the client's ability to act effectively. An example of a facilitative interpretation would go something like this:

Client: "I'm not sure whether I want to retire early. I like to keep busy, and I don't know what I'd do with all that free time."

Counselor: "So the prospect of an early retirement is a bit frightening. Maybe you're afraid that you'd just waste your time away?"

Notice that the financial counselor's interpretation did not stray too far from what the client had said. The counselor used the words "frightening" and "afraid," but probably did so on the basis of some fear or trepidation detected in the client's voice. Further, the counselor responded tentatively, using qualifiers like "a bit" and "Maybe," and converted the second statement into a question by a raised voice at the end of the sentence. This enables the client to assimilate the counselor's response without feeling as though it has been offered as a fiat from above. The client, thus, is free to accept, modify, or deny the counselor's interpretation, and this is very important. If the counselor's interpretation is inaccurate, it is far better to discover that early than to proceed indefinitely along the wrong path.

A third type of leading response frequently employed by counselors is reassurance, or encouragement. A reassuring response is designed with the intention of making the client feel better, to bolster his or her spirits, and to offer support in a time of need. It communicates clearly to the client that "I am here by your side, ready to aid you in any way that I can." As a means of helping, however, the reassuring response tends to be merely a temporary measure. It is akin to offering a tissue to someone who is crying; the crying may stop temporarily, but the underlying causes have been left untouched. For this reason the counselor must be careful not to use reassurance indiscriminately. The understanding (reflection-of-feeling) response discussed in the previous section on active listening is far more effective when emotions surface. The understanding response communicates accurate empathy; the reassuring response offers only sympathy, and very few people like to feel pitied. Contrast the effect of these two different kinds of responses on our hypothetical client:

Client:	"I get *so* furious whenever my broker ignores me! It's almost as though I don't exist!"
Counselor:	(using reassuring response): "Well, don't feel so bad. It doesn't do much good to get so worked up. Try not to worry about it, and you'll feel better."
Counselor:	(using reflection of feeling): "I can feel the rage as you speak. You feel like a nonperson around your broker, that you are not getting adequate service for the money you are paying, and that infuriates you."

The first counselor response patches a Band-Aid on a deep wound and is therefore ineffectual. The second response reflects the deeply felt anger and, in so doing, helps the client work through the anger. Reassurance, while not a harmful response, promises pie in the sky and delivers nothing.

The final type of leading response is called advice, or suggestion. Many people actively seek the advice of others, possibly hoping that the advice giver will make the difficult decision for them, or solve their problems for them. And, as chance or human nature would have it, there is certainly no dearth of people in this world willing to dole out free advice. In a financial counseling relationship, however, the best kind of advice is self-advice. Counselors who have been responding in an understanding fashion are already well on their way toward helping clients discover, in their own way and in their own time, what advice is best for them. There are times within a counseling relationship when proffering advice is acceptable, but these times are few. When advice is given, it should be offered tentatively, in the form of a suggestion, or several suggestions, about which the client has the final decision. Otherwise, the counselor not only leads, but takes over the ultimate responsibility for the client's financial plan, and each person has the right to formulate his or her own plan. Advice giving robs the client of this right.

In the next section, we will look at still another type of counselor response —
perhaps the most commonly used response — the question. Questions come in all
kinds of hues and colors, some much more effective in communication than others.

THE QUESTION

The question is surely one of the most timeworn response modes used by
financial counselors. Many counselors see their main role as an interviewer or an
interrogator. The question seems appropriate only when it is an honest attempt to
gather information that the counselor requires and to which the client has access.
Unfortunately, the question is not always used in this fashion. Moreover, the
question-answer dialogue sets up a pattern of communication that is difficult for the
participants to break: the client waits for the inevitable question; the question comes,
followed by the answer (and not much more), and then the wait for the next question.
Questioning almost always casts the counselor in the role of authority figure and the
client in the role of somewhat passive subordinate, certainly not the type of
interpersonal relationship conducive to effective counseling.

Despite the disadvantages of the question mentioned above, there are times
when only a well-phrased question will suffice, particularly when we are seeking
data from the client. Even here, though, there is a qualitative difference among the
various types of questions that might be asked. Several categories of questions will
be discussed in the following section.

Open-ended versus Close-ended Questions

Ideally, questions posed by the counselor should be open-ended and should call
for more than just a yes or no response on the part of the client; otherwise, they tend
to stifle interaction. The open-ended question allows the client to select a response
from his or her full repertory. The close-ended question limits the client to a specific,
narrow response, often either a yes or a no. The open-ended question solicits the
client's opinions, thoughts, ideas, values, and feelings. The close-ended question
typically solicits singular facts or one-word replies.

Contrast the differences in the following sets of questions. The first question
in each set is close-ended; the second question in each set is open-ended.

  1. a. Are you ready to start an investment program?
     b. How do you feel about starting an investment program?
  2. a. Have you given any thought to retirement?
     b. What thoughts do you have about retirement?
  3. a. Are you afraid to start saving something now?
     b. Why have you decided to wait to start saving?

As can be readily seen from the above examples, the open-ended questions ask
for more complete, comprehensive information. In a way, they force the client to
formulate thoughts, ideas, and feelings into fully rounded responses. On the other
hand, the close-ended questions solicit only a one-word or short-answer response,
requiring little thought.

Leading Questions

Other types of close-ended questions that are not only ineffective but also manipulative are those termed leading questions. These questions usually begin with, "Don't you think . . . ," or "Do you really feel . . . ." More often than not they lead the client toward a conclusion that the counselor (not the client) has already formulated, so that there is the element of dishonesty in even asking the question. It is far more effective, and honest, for the counselor to rephrase the leading question into a declarative statement in the form of sharing a perception or opinion with the client. Consider the following leading questions:

> "Don't you think you should start an investment program now?"
> "Do you really feel that $100 a month is enough?"
> "Are you sure you've considered all possibilities?"

With just a bit of reflection, we can see that the counselor is actually saying:

> "I think you ought to start an investment program now." ·
> "I don't feel that $100 a month will be enough."
> "I'm sure there are other possibilities you haven't considered."

The latter statements are much more honest and to the point than the questions from which they stem. Generally speaking, declarative statements communicate far more clearly than the manipulative leading questions. A good rule of thumb to follow in everyday intercourse is to make as many statements as possible and save the questions for honest information seeking.

The Either/Or or True/False Question

Another kind of relatively ineffective question is of the either/or or true/false variety. While this question is not quite as close-ended as the leading question, it is only slightly less closed, since it limits the client to only two options. For example:

> "Do you plan to stay in this house or move to an apartment?"
> "Are you more apt to take a risk or play it safe?"

Clients might prefer both options, or neither, or a third or fourth option; but here they are forced to choose from what we have offered them. The world is not simply black or white; there are various shades of gray; yet, when we phrase questions so that clients are forced to choose from one of two options, we are ignoring a basic fact of life. In the preceding examples, we can improve on the question format by asking,

> "What are your plans after retirement regarding housing?"
> "How do you usually make your decisions?"

Again, we see that by opening up the question we allow clients to respond freely from their own frame of reference, and not from ours. And this is what good interviewing is all about.

Why Questions

Even though why questions can be classified as open-ended questions and, thus, theoretically sound, such is not the case. On the surface, questions beginning with why appear to be legitimate enough, signifying the inquiry into causal relationships as in, "Why are you planning to retire at age 62?" Unfortunately, why questions carry with them a connotation of implied disapproval by the questioner, thus forcing the person being asked the question to justify or defend his or her thoughts, ideas, or actions. Even when that is not the meaning the questioner intends, that is generally how the why question is received. The why question tends to question the client's motivation (or lack of motivation) and, thus, creates a certain defensiveness.

Perhaps the chief reason that why questions are received so poorly dates back to the manner in which parents put children on the spot: "Why didn't you pick up your room?" "Why don't you have your shoes on?" "Why can't you be more careful?" And, of course, this line of inquiry is later picked up by teachers with students: "Why don't you have your homework?" "Why didn't you study for this test?" In short, as children we learned that when an adult asked us a question beginning with why, it meant, "Change your behavior; think as I think; behave the way adults do." And we carry that lesson with us throughout life, usually responding to why questions in a defensive, negative manner.

So unless there is a valid reason for asking a why question and when no other type of question will suffice, it is generally better to avoid why questions.

Question Bombardment

Still another kind of faulty questioning technique occurs when we ask double, triple, or even quadruple questions without waiting for a response. This is frequently referred to as question bombardment. As absurd as this may sound, it occurs far too frequently in interviews to escape comment. For example: "What type of investment program appeals to you most — stock, municipal bonds? Or would you rather look into annuities? When do you think you'd be ready to begin?" The first question in the series is open-ended in nature and can stand by itself quite well; yet the interviewer isn't content to let well enough alone, but instead tacks on other, more restricting close-ended questions. The result then is that the client is caught in a hailstorm of questions all at one time and, more often than not, gets the opportunity to respond to only one of the several questions asked. If more than one question needs to be asked, it is better to ask them as separate questions, waiting for a full response to each question before going on to the next one. The other issue to be addressed, though, is whether so many questions need to be asked in the first place.

Concluding Remarks

Questioning is a major component of the repertory of most interviewers. Yet that need not be so. If we wish to become better communicators, one thing that we can do is to convert some of our questions (especially close-ended, leading, either/or, and why questions) into statements. With a statement, we assume responsibility for what we say. With a question, we shift the responsibility to the other person, which may sometimes be necessary. Far too often, however, we simply shirk our own responsibility for, and involvement in, the interaction when we revert to questioning. As stated previously, counseling is not the same as interviewing. If we hope to do counseling, we need to do far more than simply ask one question after another.

Note

1. Portions of this chapter dealing with elements of nonverbal behaviors have been excerpted from a two-part article entitled "Practical Communications Skills and Techniques in Financial Counseling," by Dale S. Johnson, PhD, CFP, published in *The Financial Planner* 11, no. 6 (June 1982): 98–105, and 11, no. 7 (July 1982): 62–71. They are reprinted by arrangement with the editor of that journal.

Gathering Client Information

Robert M. Crowe

IMPORTANCE OF INFORMATION GATHERING

As has been made clear in the preceding chapters, financial planning for clients involves a wide range of financial goals, problems, and solutions. For example, for some clients the process of financial planning may focus on wealth accumulation; for others tax minimization; for others protection of income or assets from loss; for still others liquidation of wealth that has already been accumulated. In the case where a truly comprehensive financial plan is to be prepared, all these areas and more are involved. In more typical cases, the planner is called upon, at least initially, to help with only one or a few such concerns of his or her client.

Because there is such a great variety of client concerns that a financial planner may need to address, there is also a great variety of information that the planner will have to gather from clients. Defining the client's current situation, determining what the client's desired future situation is and when it is to be achieved, and establishing what the client is willing and able to do in order to get there require information. This information must be accurate, complete, up-to-date, relevant to the client's goals, and well organized. Otherwise, financial plans based on the information will be deficient — perhaps erroneous, perhaps inappropriate, perhaps inconsistent with the client's other goals, and perhaps dangerous to the client's financial well-being.

PREREQUISITES TO THE PROCESS

Before the financial planner begins the information-*gathering* process, he or she should *give* certain information to the client. First, the client should be made aware that he or she will have to invest time, perhaps a significant amount of time, in the information-gathering stage of financial planning. Even though part of the financial planner's responsibility is to avoid consuming the client's time unnecessarily, this commitment of time by the client is essential. The magnitude of the needed time commitment will depend on the scope and complexity of the client's needs and circumstances, but the proper development of even a narrowly focused and fairly uncomplicated plan requires information that only the client can furnish.

Second, the client should be made aware that he or she probably will have to provide the planner with some information that is highly confidential, perhaps even sensitive or painful, for the client to reveal. Again, the scope and complexity of the client's needs will influence this matter. The creation of even rather straightforward plans, however, may require clients to disclose such things as their income and spending patterns, their attitudes toward other family members, or their opinions as to the extent of their own financial responsibilities to others.

Another prerequisite for the effective gathering of client information is a systematic approach to the task. Although there are many possible ways to systematize the gathering of information, one way that has been found useful by many financial planners is to utilize The American College's Financial and Estate Planning Fact Finder. A completed copy of this document for a hypothetical client appears at the end of this chapter, following page 120. This fact-finding form provides the structure for the discussion of information gathering presented in the remainder of this chapter.

USING THE FACT FINDER

Before some of the details of this fact finder are discussed, several preliminary comments are in order. First, the reader will note that the fact finder is a lengthy document consisting of, when completed, 39 pages of figures, facts, and opinions. For most client situations, the fact finder elicits considerably more information than will be needed. Only in the rare case where a fully integrated financial plan is to be created for an affluent client will it be necessary to complete all sections of the fact finder. Most of the sections that have to be completed will depend on the particular areas of concern to be addressed in each client's financial plan. A few sections, however, will be applicable for all clients.

Second, as lengthy as this fact finder is, it will be necessary in some cases to gather still *more* information through additional instruments. For example, chapter 2 contains a discussion of instruments that may be used to gather information about a client's risk-tolerance. Likewise, chapter 7 refers to a survey form that is useful in identifying the wide variety of pure-risk exposures that might confront a client.

Third, even when it is necessary to complete all sections of the fact finder, the client cannot be expected to do the entire job, perhaps not even the majority of it. Handing a client a very lengthy form to complete will almost certainly overwhelm him or her and result in the gathering of either no information or only sloppy and incomplete information. Therefore care must be exercised to avoid overwhelming and frustrating the client and wasting his or her time.

On the other hand, the financial planner's time is also a valuable resource. The planner's time should be spent only on the most sensitive and complex parts of the information-gathering task. Also, the planner's support personnel should complete certain sections of the fact finder based on a review of client-supplied documents such as wills, tax returns, or trust instruments.

Fourth, the fact finder discussed here is not computer-based. The financial planner should first consider whether the information gathered from a client should be entered into a computer software system. (See chapter 11 for a discussion of this issue.) Generally, if most of the information is to be used only once, computerization will not be worthwhile. However, if the information is to be used over and over again, for example to generate alternative financial plans or answers to "what-if" questions, computerization may be desirable.

If the financial planner already has a software system for processing client information, he or she should use a form for information gathering that is consistent with the software. The form should be such that a paraprofessional can easily input the needed data from the form directly into the computer system for processing and analysis. On the other hand, if the planner does not already have a satisfactory software system for preparing financial plans, The American College's Financial and Estate Planning Fact Finder can be used as a basis on which to build one. Also, some of the more sophisticated (and expensive) software systems referred to in chapter 11 lend themselves to the inputting of data directly from this particular fact finder.

Fifth, although this form is called a *fact* finder, it contains more than a simple recitation of facts. It is used to record other types of information, including client attitudes, aspirations, and values, as well as observations and opinions of the financial planner himself or herself. Therefore, completion of certain sections of the fact finder will require the planner to exercise the full range of interpersonal communication skills described in chapter 3.

The remainder of this chapter consists of a brief review of various sections of The American College's Financial and Estate Planning Fact Finder. Much of the information that is called for is self-evident and requires no commentary. The reader should merely scan the types of information that are requested in the form. In some cases, however, some explanation is provided as to when or how a particular set of information might best be gathered and why the information is needed or useful.

THE AMERICAN COLLEGE'S FINANCIAL AND ESTATE PLANNING FACT FINDER

Personal Data

Most of the first section of the fact finder, which consists of the three pages calling for certain factual personal information about the client, will be needed for almost all clients. This section can be given to the client to be completed by him or her at the beginning of the financial planning engagement.

With respect to the portion concerning the client's other financial advisers (attorney, accountant, and so forth), the planner should ask the client to notify each of the advisers that the planner may be in contact with one or more of them to obtain documents or other needed information. The brief form on page 23 of the fact finder can be used for this purpose. The planner should also ask the client's permission to send a letter of introduction to the appropriate advisers to ask for their professional collaboration in meeting the client's need for the financial plan to be developed.

Client Objectives and Factors Affecting the Plan

Pages 4 and 5 of the fact finder call for both objective factual information and subjective responses. These portions should be completed for virtually all clients and are best done through a face-to-face interview. In the case of a married client, his or her spouse should normally participate in this interview to not only reveal any inconsistencies in financial objectives of the two people but also enable them to help each other articulate their shared and separate objectives and perceptions.

The financial planner should not be surprised if the client or spouse has difficulty in expressing his or her objectives in precise terms. Nevertheless, good planning requires that the objectives be expressed in specific terms—How much? By what date? In what order of priority? Bringing this type of specificity to the objectives, though often difficult and time-consuming, is essential. Without clearly defined and understood objectives, it will be impossible to (1) settle upon the route toward achieving them, (2) monitor periodically the client's progress toward achieving them, and (3) determine whether mid-course corrections should be made along the way toward achieving them.

In addition, the planner should recognize that the objectives developed with the client in the early interviewing stage are only preliminary. Subsequent discussions or analyses of the client's financial position may make it obvious that, for example, the objectives are too ambitious to be achievable in practice or that the client's financial capabilities require rearrangement of the priorities placed on the various objectives.

Income and Cash-Management Statements

Pages 6 and 7 of the fact finder call for straight factual information that will be needed in most financial planning engagements, especially those in which the focus is on income tax planning or wealth accumulation. Most of the section dealing with the client's sources of income can be completed by the client working alone or by a financial paraprofessional utilizing the client's most recent federal income tax return.

Completion of the cash-management statement, however, may be a bit more difficult for the client. Most people do not keep close track of where all their cash comes from or where it goes. Nevertheless, the best possible estimate of this information is needed to determine what additional resources, if any, the client can commit to the attainment of his or her objectives. No new initiatives can be pursued for very long if the client experiences frequent net cash-flow deficits (or even net cash-flow surpluses that are due solely to liquidating assets or taking on additional debt).

Inventory of Assets

Pages 8 through 11 of the fact finder require an identification and description of each of the client's assets. This information is essential in any client engagement in which the focus is on investment or wealth accumulation (or even wealth liquidation if planning for a retired client). It will also be needed if the focus is on estate and gift tax planning or insurance planning. The client can usually complete this portion of the fact finder without assistance from the financial planner.

The inventory of assets reveals a great deal of information that is useful to the planner. For example, it helps answer the following questions:

- How does the client use financial resources?
- What are the client's preferences and aversions?
- How liquid is the client's financial position?
- How diversified are the assets?
- How consistent are the assets with the client's objectives?
- What is the client's "basis" in assets for income tax purposes?
- What are some of the client's pure-risk exposures?

Business Interest

The inventory-of-assets pages in the fact finder do not contain a specific section where the value of a client's business interest is listed. Yet for some clients an ownership interest in a small business constitutes a large percentage of their total assets. The value of the interest should be shown somewhere on the inventory of assets. The most logical place is on page 10 of the fact finder among the long-term, nonmarketable assets or among the miscellaneous assets.

Because a client's ownership interest in a small business is so crucial to his or her financial well-being, however, the fact finder contains a special section, pages 12 through 14, for recording information about the business interest and the business's employees. Except for the page about employee census data, this section should be completed by the planner during an interview with any client who has a business interest. This information can reveal many opportunities for using the ownership interest to achieve client objectives. For example, minimizing the client's income taxes, enhancing the client's personal insurance program, providing a hedge against losses arising from the death or disability of a key employee, and disposing of the client's business interest for its full value following the client's death can be accomplished in a well-developed financial plan.

Inventory of Liabilities

In any client engagement where the inventory of assets is completed, the inventory of liabilities on page 15 of the fact finder should likewise be completed. Again, this page can usually be completed quickly by the client on his or her own. The financial planner can use this information to see how heavily the client uses debt and for what purposes. Also, the inventory of liabilities may reveal something about the client's life-style or about when present financial commitments will be completed that will allow some of the client's resources to be used for other purposes.

Insurance Benefits

The next several pages of the fact finder, pages 16 through 20, are used to summarize the client's individually owned insurance coverages as well as his or her employee benefit program. The financial planner's paraprofessional can gather the required information from a review of the client's insurance policies and employee benefit manual. This information will be needed for virtually all clients, since almost any financial plan, regardless of its primary emphasis, would be inadequate if it did not include a consideration of the client's present insurance program.

Risk/Return Profile

In chapter 2 the question of measuring a client's risk-tolerance is treated in depth. The financial planner has an ethical and legal responsibility to recommend to a client only investments that are not so risky as to be inconsistent with the client's risk-tolerance. Page 21 of the fact finder provides one way for the planner to obtain a preliminary assessment of a client's comfort level with taking some risks to obtain a higher return from investing. This assessment should be used along with other indicators, such as the client's current mix of assets and liabilities and his or her personal characteristics, as discussed in chapter 2, to measure a client's risk-tolerance.

In the case of a married client, the risk/return profile should be completed independently by both spouses. This exercise often reveals major differences between them in terms of the kinds of saving and investment instruments they prefer or dislike, as indicated in the upper section of the form. Likewise, the husband and wife may discover that they have important differences of opinion about what objectives they value the most or least in their investments, as indicated in the lower section of the form.

Another dimension of the risk/return profile that should be examined is the congruity or lack of congruity between the responses in the upper and lower sections of the page. For example, if liquidity and safety of principal are highly ranked financial concerns of a client, his or her preferred investment vehicles should be such things as savings accounts, money market funds, and U.S. government securities, not real estate or commodities.

Income and Lump-Sum Needs

On page 22 of the fact finder is an identification of the client's estimate of the needs for both income and lump sums of money in the event of the client's death, disability, or retirement. This page should be completed for all clients whose emphasis is on insurance planning and/or retirement planning, and the planner can most easily complete this during an interview with the client. Although the estimates are expressed in current dollars (that is, in amounts that would be needed if death, disability, or retirement occurred today), the amounts will have to be adjusted upward to offset the effect of inflation. Retirement-income needs should be inflated by the planner using the time-value-of-money techniques described in Appendix B at the end of this book. Income and lump-sum needs in the event of death or disability should be reviewed periodically with the client and adjusted upward as necessary.

Other Sections of the Fact Finder

Some of the remaining sections of the fact finder are self-explanatory, but a brief comment is appropriate concerning four of them.

The tax-planning checklist on pages 29 through 33 is not only an information-gathering form, but also a reminder to the planner of a variety of income, estate, and gift tax strategies that might be advisable for a particular client. The planner should complete this form for all clients for whom income tax minimization or estate planning is a major concern.

The financial position statement on pages 35 and 36 shows the client's present and projected balance sheets. It includes the client's assets, which are taken from the inventory of assets described earlier, but they are shown here at current market value rather than at cost. Current market value is the basis deemed proper by the public accounting profession for preparing personal balance sheets. This form is probably best completed by the planner with the assistance of a paraprofessional staff person. Also, the statement shows the client's liabilities, as contained in the inventory of liabilities described earlier, and the client's net worth, which is defined as the difference between the total assets and the total liabilities.

Page 37 lists the client's various types of *resources* that are available to meet the income and lump-sum needs at death, disability, or retirement. This page can be completed by the planner with the help of a paraprofessional. The information should then, of course, be compared with the information on page 22 of the fact finder that describes the client's *needs* in the event of these three events.

The final page of the fact finder contains a checklist for financial planning review. Once a financial plan has been developed and implemented, the planner must review it with the client periodically thereafter. Ever-changing economic conditions, financial markets, and tax laws require the planner to continually monitor and recommend modifications to the plan so that it will continue to meet the client's needs. In addition, the fact-finder checklist of factors in the client's personal situation is a convenient way for the planner to identify personal occurrences that may call for plan modification. Sending this form to the client or simply going through it in a brief telephone call once a year will enable the planner to keep the plan up-to-date.

A SAMPLE DATA-GATHERING EXERCISE

In order to show how the Financial and Estate Planning Fact Finder might be completed, a hypothetical client case, the case of Charles and Barbara Wiggins, is presented below. In 1989 the planner, Mary Jane English, was called in to prepare for them a completely integrated, comprehensive financial plan, thus requiring completion of all sections of the fact finder. The narrative contains all the information gathered during the financial planning engagement and has been recorded by either the planner, the paraprofessional, or the client on the completed forms that follow the narrative. Note that inadequate information has been provided to complete the section of the tax-planning checklist concerned with advisable tax strategies. This portion of the form would be completed only after a full analysis and discussion of their tax situation with the Wigginses.

CASE NARRATIVE

The clients are Charles F. and Barbara B. Wiggins. They live at 421 Briarcliff Drive, Small City, Georgia 30341. Their home telephone number is (404) 433-2742. Charles is an associate professor of architectural design at Homestate Tech, a state university. His office address is Room 426, Engineering Hall, Homestate Tech, Small City, Georgia 30315, and his office telephone number is (404) 895-2550.

Barbara is an editor for the Small City School District. Her office address is Adams High School, Hickman Boulevard and Wavy Lane, Small City, Georgia 30344. Her business telephone is (404) 495-8000, extension 402.

Charles is also a one-third partner in an architectural design and engineering consulting business—Design Engineering Associates. He founded the business in 1975 with two of his colleagues from the university.

The Wigginses use Edward L. Day, of the law firm of Cox, Day, and Elkins, Suite 920, 1000 Parkway, Small City, Georgia 30301, as their personal and business attorney. Edward Day's office number is (404) 895-9450.

Their CPA, Fred Granger, Suite 123, 888 Parkway, Small City, Georgia 30301, does their personal tax returns as well as the accounting work for Design Engineering Associates. His office telephone number is (404) 895-6428. Granger has worked with Mary Jane English, ChFC, before on financial plans and recommended her to Charles and Barbara for their comprehensive financial planning.

Other advisers include the following:

- administrative trust officer, Xavier Young, Universal Bank and Trust, Dallas, Texas, (214) 319-4000, who has responsibility for administering a trust of which Barbara is the beneficiary
- commercial banker, Helen Morgan, First National Bank, First National Bank Tower, Small City, Georgia, (404) 895-9240
- life insurance agent, John King, CLU, Suite 903, 1000 Parkway, Small City, Georgia, (404) 895-5000
- property and liability insurance agent, Larry Mincer, CPCU, 4220 Kingsway, Small City, Georgia, (404) 433-1984
- securities broker, Nancy Osborne, of the firm of Peters, Quigley and Rogers, 100 Broad Street, Small City, Georgia, (404) 895-3622

None of these advisers has ever provided or offered to provide comprehensive financial planning for the Wigginses. Neither Charles nor Barbara is displeased with any of their present advisers, who they feel have served them fairly well. They have asked Mary Jane to cooperate with their existing advisers in developing their financial plan.

The biographical data on the Wigginses are as follows: Charles was born August 14, 1949. His social security number is 063-42-2221. Barbara Wiggins was born June 5, 1957. Her social security number is 114-68-9370. Charles and Barbara were married on January 11, 1979, shortly after Charles's divorce from Cynthia Crowley. They have one child, Charles F. Wiggins, Jr., born May 11, 1981. Charles has two children by his prior marriage: Stephanie R. Wiggins, born August 13, 1974, and Caroline D. Wiggins, born August 25, 1976. All the children attend public schools.

Both Charles's parents are still living. His father, Ted Wiggins, was born July 4, 1924. He is still employed as a machinist. His mother, Mary Wiggins, was born December 25, 1925; she is a housewife. Charles has a brother James, born July 13, 1948, who is a self-employed contractor; he also had a younger brother Edward, who was killed in an automobile accident in 1977.

Barbara's father is William B. Becker, born May 31, 1928. He is an oral surgeon. Her mother, Susan A. Becker, was born March 11, 1928. She owns a gift shop. Barbara has a twin sister, Betty, who is unmarried and is employed as a diplomatic courier for the U.S. State Department.

Both the client and his spouse are citizens of the United States. They file a joint tax return. Barbara has not been married previously; Charles was formerly married to Cynthia Crowley. He no longer pays alimony to Cynthia, who has remarried, but he does pay $250 per month in child support for each of his two daughters. The payments are to continue until the children reach age 18 or marry, whichever comes first. Charles estimates that he provides approximately 70 percent of their support with his child-support payments. In accordance with the terms of the divorce decree,

Charles maintains a life insurance policy to provide this child support in the event of his death. The face amount of the policy is $100,000.

Charles and Barbara have wills that they had drawn in June 1981, but they have no prenuptial or postnuptial agreements. When asked to describe their basic estate plan, Charles tells Mary Jane that his will leaves one-quarter of his estate to each of his two daughters and one-half to Barbara, if she survives him, or otherwise to Charles, Jr. Should Charles die before his daughters reach the age of majority, the will creates trusts for their benefit. Barbara's will leaves all her property to Charles if he survives her. If he does not survive her, all her property is left to a trust for Charles, Jr., until he reaches 21 years of age. In their wills the Wigginses have designated a guardian for Charles, Jr., in the event of their death before his majority. They have chosen Barbara's sister, Betty Becker, who lives in Apartment 3515, Parklane Towers, 100 Parklane Place, Washington, D.C. Neither Charles nor Barbara recalls notifying Betty of this fact when their wills were signed, and no successor guardian was designated. The First National Bank of Small City is named executor of both their wills and trustee for the testamentary trusts.

Neither Charles nor Barbara has ever made a gift under the Uniform Gifts to Minors Act. Charles does not expect to receive any significant inheritance or assistance from his family and does not believe his family will require his assistance in the future. On the other hand, Barbara is the present beneficiary of a trust created for her by her father. The trust corpus is currently valued at approximately $100,000. Barbara also expects to receive a significant inheritance from her parents at their death. She estimates her parents' net worth is probably well in excess of $1,000,000.

Charles has a doctorate in architectural design, and Barbara has a master's degree in education. Neither Charles nor Barbara has ever served in the military.

When asked to rank a standardized list of general financial objectives in direct order of importance to their family (that is, the item numbered 1 has the highest priority and the item numbered 8 the lowest), the Wigginses' response was the following:

1. provide college education for all their children
2. take care of family in the event of the death of a breadwinner
3. take care of self and family during a period of long-term disability
4. reduce their tax burden
5. maintain their standard of living
6. enjoy a comfortable retirement
7. invest and accumulate wealth
8. develop an estate plan

Charles and Barbara tell Mary Jane that they have no formal monthly budget. They save $8,000 annually, of which they invest $5,000 in investments other than savings accounts or CDs. The Wigginses believe they should be able to save and invest 20 percent of their income after taxes. They would use such savings or investments to pay college expenses for the children and to build a cushion for Barbara and the children in case of Charles's death or disability.

Neither Charles nor Barbara has ever given substantial gifts to family members, educational institutions, or charities. However, both are very interested in the Small

City Chamber Music Society and may wish to become more active in supporting it financially in the future. In their wills, they have made no specific bequests, including bequests to charity. They have been basically satisfied or somewhat satisfied with their previous investment results but feel that yields should be higher given current conditions. They are not committed to any one particular form of investment.

Charles states that he feels Barbara is fair at handling money. If he should die, he believes that her judgment and emotional stability would probably serve the best interests of the family. He thinks the emotional and economic maturity of his children is about average for their ages. Further, in the event of his death or a divorce, Charles believes Barbara will remarry, and he feels she should. Barbara hopes that Charles would remarry in the event of her death. Charles says he would probably like to retire from teaching at about age 65 but would not like to retire from his consulting business until at least age 70. Barbara would not like to work past age 65.

Tax considerations aside, Charles would like his estate first to provide for Barbara and any minor children. After Barbara's death he would like any remaining assets distributed equally to his children. Barbara feels that her estate should provide for Charles first and then be left to Charles, Jr. Barbara and Charles are looking at comprehensive financial planning as a cohesive method for understanding and managing their financial affairs on a long-range basis.

Barbara and Charles seem to have a successful marriage, and they believe that all the children are well adjusted. Barbara admires and respects Charles's devotion to his daughters, who spend a lot of time at her and Charles's house. The daughters are fond of her, and she feels that they have a very good relationship. Stephanie and Caroline are especially close to their half brother Charles, Jr., and appear to enjoy playing big-sister roles. Charles and Barbara seem to have a marriage filled with a great deal of affection and mutual respect and very few of the typical stepfamily problems.

Charles is essentially a self-made man who put himself through school with part-time jobs and scholarships and is now an associate professor at Homestate Tech. Charles feels his consulting business has been moderately successful, but he wishes it were more successful and is somewhat frustrated that his business ownership position is not providing more current and long-term financial and tax advantages for himself and his family. The truth of the matter is that, although Charles seems perfectly capable of making the business even more successful, it is already doing quite well despite the relatively limited time he and his two partners devote to its management. Charles believes that the business could be more successful with some effective planning, which is something he and his partners never seem to get around to doing.

Barbara Wiggins is an intelligent, cultured woman whose father and mother provided every advantage for her and her sister. Barbara and Betty are beneficiaries of trusts that their father established for them years ago. Barbara's trust is invested largely in low-yielding longer-term corporate bonds and has a current market value of about $100,000. The corpus of the trust is under management by Universal Bank and Trust in Dallas, Texas, and yields about $5,000 in annual income. The dispositive provisions of the trust provide that one-half the principal is to be paid to Barbara at age 35 and the balance at age 45 if she is living. If she dies prior to distribution, the trust continues for her living children. If she has no children living, the trust is to be distributed to Betty. Barbara believes the terms of Betty's trust are identical.

Barbara also believes that she and Betty are equal remainder beneficiaries of her father's and mother's wills. As already noted, Bill Becker's estate is estimated to be quite large; however, Barbara knows almost nothing else about her father's financial affairs. She says that she lives without any conscious expectations that her father's estate may someday make her quite wealthy. Barbara is accustomed to her present standard of living, which is based primarily on what she and Charles earn. She enjoys her career and takes a good deal of interest in both Charles's teaching career and his partnership. At this time, she would not really feel comfortable questioning her parents specifically about their net worth or their estate plans.

Both Charles and Barbara have felt for some time that they are paying higher than necessary income taxes. They are seeking financial planning advice largely to explore means of reducing their tax obligation and of diverting more of their income toward their financial planning objectives. It is important to note that, although the Wigginses' income is quite large, they are not saving and investing as much as they would like — or as much as they will need if they expect to achieve their objectives without cutting back their standard of living. Because they do not wish to cut back, they are hoping to achieve their savings and investment objectives through reducing their income taxes and increasing the yield on current and future investments.

To assist in defraying the cost of educating Charles, Jr., and Charles's daughters, Charles has free tuition available at Homestate Tech (as a fringe benefit of his employment there) for all his children who wish to attend. Stephanie has indicated that it is likely that she will attend Homestate Tech and take advantage of this benefit. Taking into account the free tuition, Charles and Barbara estimate that 4 years of college for Stephanie will cost no more than $12,000. For Caroline, who may not go to Homestate Tech, they are projecting college costs of approximately $40,000. On the chance that Charles, Jr., may also go elsewhere, they are projecting college costs of approximately $60,000 for him. Charles and Barbara are somewhat concerned that one or more of the children may later wish to attend a private college and that the costs they have projected may not be sufficient in an inflationary economy. In addition, they are projecting graduate or professional school costs of approximately $30,000, $35,000, and $50,000, respectively for each child. Ideally, they would like to be able to assist their children through their entire educational careers, including postgraduate work, even though all three are still too young to make that type of career choice. To fund these costs Charles and Barbara have long-term CDs of $3,000 each for Caroline and Stephanie and $7,000 for Charles, Jr. These CDs will mature by December 1990.

In addition to wanting the necessary capital to fund the children's education, Charles and Barbara hope to build a comfortable, but not luxurious, vacation home on a lake in the nearby mountains. They expect to acquire the lot and begin construction by 1991. They project a cost of $80,000 in current dollars and hope to obtain conventional 30-year, fixed-rate financing for this project. For the down payment they have a long-term CD worth $8,000 that matures in December 1990. They believe that such a home would be a good investment and realize it could be liquidated, if necessary, to provide additional funds for educating the children. If liquidation is not required for this purpose, they would consider the house a possible permanent residence for their retirement years.

The inventory of assets for Charles and Barbara Wiggins consists of the following items supplied by them on an itemized sheet that appears as table 4-1. The stated values represent the fair market value at the time the fact finder was completed.

Charles's business interest consists of a one-third interest in a partnership, Design Engineering Associates, which is a private consulting firm that he founded in 1975 with Steve Thomas and Ursula Von Waldhem, both of whom are one-third partners and Charles's colleagues at the university. The business is located at 1773 Park Place, Small City, Georgia 30318. The business telephone number is (404) 895-2550. Steve Thomas suffered a mild heart attack in 1984 and is rated for that condition in a personally owned term policy he bought in 1986. The principal business activity of the partnership is supervising the design and construction of small commercial buildings, but it is also involved in the inspection and redesign of existing buildings for possible renovation. None of the partners has an employment contract. The partnership is a calendar-year, cash-method taxpayer.

The partners consider three full-time nonowner-employees of the firm to be key employees: Tom Young, John Blake, and Sarah L. McIntyre. Charles believes that the retention of these key employees is very important to the continued success of Design Engineering. None has any insurability problem as far as Charles knows.

Charles Wiggins has expressed the following views about his interest in the firm:

- If he retires, he wants to sell his interest to the other two partners or to a new partner.
- If he becomes disabled, he may want to sell his interest.
- If he dies, he wants his interest sold for his estate.

In case of disability, death, or retirement, Charles assumes that Ursula Von Waldhem will take over his functions in the business. Charles thinks that the business could be now sold as a going concern and that his one-third interest is worth $125,000. He himself would pay $300,000 for the firm if he were an outsider; he would also pay $175,000 for his two partners' interests. No objective valuation of the business has been made. The largest single asset owned by Design Engineering Associates is the building that houses the business. The partnership purchased the building in April 1982 for a total price of $155,000. They financed $125,000 for 25 years at 9 ½ percent interest, and the present mortgage balance is approximately $110,000. The purchase price was allocated in the purchase contract—$120,000 for the building and $35,000 for the land. The building has been depreciated by the straight-line method over a 20-year useful life for tax purposes. It has a salvage value of $20,000. Charles believes the building could be sold for $175,000.

The current indebtedness of the firm is $120,000, including the mortgage on the building it occupies; the highest indebtedness was $135,000 when they bought their building; the lowest indebtedness was $10,000 when the company was founded. None of the partners personally owns any equipment or other property that is used by the business.

TABLE 4-1
The Inventory of Assets for Charles and Barbara Wiggins

Asset	Cost or Basis	Fair Market Value	Yield	Form of Ownership*	Available for Liquidity	Collateralized	Location
Checking accounts	$ 4,000	$ 4,000	—	JT	Yes	No	First Nat.
Savings accounts	8,000	8,000	5.5% ($440)	JT	Yes	No	First Nat.
Money market funds	4,900	4,900	9.0% ($441)	JT	Yes	No	Safety box
Life insurance cash value	12,200	12,200	—	S(H)	Yes	No	Insurance co.
Life insurance cash value	2,800	2,800	—	S(H)	Yes	No	Insurance co.
200 shares of Home Products, Inc. (1980)	8,000	10,000	6.0% ($600)	S(H)	Yes	No	Safety box
400 shares of Octane Oil Co. (1979)	4,000	8,000	10.0% ($800)	JT	Yes	No	Safety box
100 shares of Growth Industries, Inc. (1984)	4,000	5,000	6.0% ($300)	JT	Yes	No	Safety box
1,000 shares of Sunshine Bldg. Corp. (1986)	1,800	1,200	5.0% ($60)	JT	Yes	No	Safety box
135 shares of Mega Growth Fund (1986)	1,200	1,800	8.0% ($144)	JT	Yes	No	Safety box
Long-term CDs (maturing 12/90)	21,000	21,000	10.0% ($2,100)	JT	No	No	Safety box
Pension/ret. benefits (vested) TDA	0	60,000	10.0% ($6,000)	S(H)	No	No	Safety box
Personal residence (1/79)	60,000	95,000	—	JT	No	$48,000	—
Personal assets							
household furnishings	25,000	20,000	—	JT	No	No	At home
auto (2/85)	8,500	4,500	—	JT	No	No	At home
jewelry/furs	15,000	28,000	—	S(W)	No	No	At home

*JT = joint tenants with right of survivorship; S = single ownership; H = husband; W = wife

Each of the three partners expects $35,000 in net taxable income from the partnership in 1989. The partnership's three full-time key employees are each paid $25,000 annually. In addition, there are three clerical/support employees, each of whom earns $12,000 annually.

According to Charles the company has a strong market position and would command a good price if put up for sale. While it is conceivable that some larger firm might be interested in a merger, there is no indication of interest at this time. Also, there is virtually no chance that the company will go public.

Although the partners have agreed that the remaining partners would want to purchase the interest of any one of them who might become disabled, retire, or die, there is no formal agreement to this effect. In the event of death, disability, or retirement of one partner, they have agreed that they would consider selling a one-third interest to a new partner only if the present partners were unable to purchase the interest and only if the "right person" could be found.

When Charles and his partners went into business, it was a fairly informal arrangement. It was formalized in 1977 by a simple partnership agreement under which the partners share income and losses in direct proportion to their capital accounts, which are equal. The business has provided attractive extra income for all three partners. Their partnership arrangement has worked well, and until now the partners have never seriously considered incorporation. However, now that all three are in relatively high income tax brackets, they are looking for ways to use the business to provide themselves with maximum personal financial and tax advantages and have decided that they should look seriously at incorporation.

The liabilities of Charles and Barbara Wiggins as they provided them are noted in table 4-2.

TABLE 4-2
The Inventory of Liabilities for Charles and Barbara Wiggins

Name of Creditor	Original Amount	Max. Credit Available	Present Balance	Mo./Annual Repayment	Interest Rate	Maturity	Secured/ Insured
Various dept. stores and oil companies	—	$ 6,000	$ 1,000	Pay in full each month	18%	—	No
Credit cards, bank	—	10,000	1,500	Pay in full each month	18%	—	No
Federal income tax (1989 projection)	$31,000	—	31,000	—	—	—	—
State income tax (1989 projection)	5,000	—	5,000	—	—	—	—
Property taxes	2,500	—	2,500	—	—	—	—

(continued)

TABLE 4-2
The Inventory of Liabilities for Charles and Barbara Wiggins

1st Nat. Bank (home mortgage)	55,900	—	48,000	$410/$4,920	8%	2009	Secured
Child support	—	—	24,000*	$500/$6,000	—	—	Insured

*At $3,000 per year for both Stephanie and Caroline until each reaches age 18.

In addition, Charles is responsible as a partner for approximately $37,000 of the $110,000 mortgage for the building that houses Design Engineering Associates. (As a legal matter, of course, Charles is ultimately responsible for 100 percent of all partnership debts because of his status as a general partner. At present all partnership debts are being paid by the partnership.) Also, Charles and Barbara plan to build a vacation home in 1991, for which they expect to obligate themselves to a mortgage of not less than $65,000.

Charles and Barbara have provided Mary Jane with income tax returns for the past 3 years. They have also provided the following data on their current year's income:

Charles	$42,000	(salary from Homestate Tech before TIAA/CREF deduction)
	35,000	(net taxable income from Design Engineering Associates)
Barbara	$15,000	(salary from Small City School District)
	5,000	(trust income)

In addition, they expect to receive $1,904 in cash dividends from common stock, $441 in interest from money market funds, and $2,540 in interest from savings accounts and CDs. On a jointly filed return last year, they paid approximately $32,000 in federal income tax and $4,000 in state income tax.

Ten percent of Charles's gross salary from the university is deducted each year and contributed to a TIAA/CREF tax-deferred annuity. The university matches this amount dollar for dollar on a tax-deferred basis. Of this tax-deferred amount, one-half is presently invested in a fixed-rate fund paying 10.25 percent and one-half in a common stock fund. The average combined yield has been about 10 percent annually for the past 3 years. This particular tax-deferred annuity does not permit withdrawals or loans to participants prior to their reaching retirement age. Several settlement options are available, but there is no provision for a participant to elect a lump-sum distribution. Charles has not yet selected a settlement option. Barbara is the named beneficiary of the account.

Charles estimates his quarterly estimated income tax liability at $2,000. He does not expect more than a 6 percent annual increase in his net income from Design Engineering Associates unless he devotes significantly more time to its management.

At present he has no plans to curtail his teaching duties to devote more time to the partnership.

Charles and Barbara expect their combined annual income to be almost $110,000 next year and believe it could approach $120,000 the following year. Charles expects his university salary to increase by 10 percent annually over the next several years, and Barbara expects salary increases of not less than 7 percent annually.

The following figures were supplied by Charles and Barbara and recorded by Mary Jane's paraprofessional on the cash-management statement and income statement:

- income items as recorded in sources of income on page 6 of the fact finder
- expenditures as noted in table 4-3

TABLE 4-3
The Annual Expenditures of Charles and Barbara Wiggins

Expenditure	Amount	Percent Expected Increase over Next 3 Years
Home mortgage	$ 4,920	0
Clothing and cleaning	3,000	8
Life insurance	2,260	0
Vacations	4,000	8
House furnishings	2,000	0
Education fund	2,000	8
Food	7,000	8
Utilities	4,500	8
Income and social security taxes	40,000	0
Property taxes	2,500	8
Transportation	2,000	8
Medical/dental/drugs/health	2,500	8
House maintenance/repairs	2,500	8
Property & liability insurance	850	8
Recreation/entertainment	4,000	8
Contributions	1,600	8
Savings	1,000	8
Investments	5,000	8
Child support	6,000	0
TDA contribution	4,200	0
Total annual expenditures	$101,830	

Although Charles and Barbara have no recent balance sheet, the data for their financial position statement come from their inventory of assets, business interest survey, and inventory of liabilities.

When asked to state his preference for or aversion to the various types of savings and investment vehicles listed below, Charles gave the following ratings from 0 to 5, with 0 representing an aversion and 5 representing a substantial preference:

Savings account	1
Money market fund	3
U.S. government bond	1
Corporate bond	1
Mutual fund (growth)	5
Common stock (growth)	5
Mutual fund (income)	2
Municipal bond	1
Real estate (direct ownership)	4
Variable annuity	2
Limited-partnership units (real estate, oil and gas, cattle, equipment leasing)	1
Commodities, gold, collectibles	0

Barbara said she has so little investment experience and so little knowledge of investment vehicles that it would be pointless for her to rate the investments.

When asked to respond to a standardized list of personal financial concerns (5 indicating a very strong concern and 0 indicating no concern), Charles responded as follows:

Liquidity	4
Safety of principal	3
Capital appreciation	5
Current income	4
Inflation protection	4
Future income	4
Tax reduction/deferral	5

Barbara responded to the same concerns in the following manner:

Liquidity	4
Safety of principal	5
Capital appreciation	3
Current income	3
Inflation protection	3
Future income	5
Tax reduction/deferral	5

Charles and Barbara have provided Mary Jane English with all their individual life as well as personal property and liability insurance policies for review of policy provisions and cost. In addition, they have provided her with sources of information on their group insurance benefits. From these sources, Mary Jane's paraprofessional has extracted the following information:

(1) Disability income

Group policy number:	W376701
Insurance company:	TIAA/CREF
Insured:	Charles Wiggins
Owner:	Homestate Tech
Cost and pmt. period:	fringe benefit, no employee contribution
Definition of disability:	own occupation, 2 yrs.; thereafter any occupation by virtue of training, education, or experience
Monthly benefit:	for illness or accident, 75 percent of salary, offset by social security for employee only
Waiting period:	sickness, 6 months; accident, 6 months
Benefit period:	sickness, to age 65; accident, to age 65

Uninsured salary continuation plan

Covered employee:	Charles Wiggins
Cost and pmt. period:	fringe benefit, no employee contribution
Definition of disability:	own occupation
Monthly benefit:	100 percent of salary, offset by any social insurance benefits
Waiting period:	none
Benefit period:	6 months

Uninsured salary continuation plan

Covered employee:	Barbara Wiggins
Cost and pmt. period:	fringe benefit, no employee contribution
Definition of disability:	own occupation
Monthly benefit:	100 percent of salary for 3 months, 50 percent for next 9 months
Waiting period:	sickness, 7 days; accident, none
Benefit period:	1 year

(2) Medical expense

Group policy number:	W497321
Insurance company:	Blue Cross/Blue Shield
Insured:	Charles Wiggins
Owner:	Homestate Tech
Cost and pmt. period:	noncontributory fringe benefit for Charles; $40 for family coverage. Coverage for children terminates at 19 (23 if in college).
Basic hospital:	90 days coverage in semiprivate accommodations, most hospital extras covered in full

Surgical:	prevailing fee schedule
Major medical:	$200 deductible per person, 80/20 percentage participation, lifetime maximum of $500,000 per person

(3) Life insurance

Policy number:	W216546
Insurance company:	AJAX
Issue age:	25
Insured:	Charles F. Wiggins
Owner:	Charles F. Wiggins
Type of policy:	whole life, nonparticipating
Cost and pmt. period:	$360/annual
Cash value:	$2,800
Extra benefits:	waiver of premium, accidental death
Amount of base policy:	$25,000
Net payable at death:	$25,000 ($50,000 for accidental death)
Beneficiaries and settlement options:	first to Caroline and Stephanie Wiggins—lump sum; second to Barbara Wiggins—lump sum

Group policy number:	W927354
Insurance company:	TIAA
Issue age:	28
Insured:	Charles F. Wiggins
Owner:	Homestate Tech
Type of policy:	term
Cost and pmt. period:	fringe benefit, no employee contribution
Extra benefits:	waiver of premium, accidental death and dismemberment
Amount of base policy:	$42,000 (equivalent to annual salary)
Net payable at death:	$42,000 ($84,000 for accidental death)
Beneficiaries and settlement options:	first to Barbara Wiggins—lump sum; second to Charles F. Wiggins, Jr.—lump sum

Policy number:	W327621
Insurance company:	ALPHA
Issue age:	29
Insured:	Charles F. Wiggins
Owner:	Charles F. Wiggins
Type of policy:	whole life, nonparticipating
Cost and pmt. period:	$1,900/annual
Cash value:	$12,200
Amount of base policy:	$100,000
Extra benefits:	policy waiver of premium
Net payable at death:	$100,000

Beneficiaries and settle-
   ment options: first to Stephanie and Caroline Wiggins (to
                                assure support to age of majority)—lump
                                sum; second to Barbara Wiggins—lump sum

Group policy number: W541834
Insurance company: GAMMA
Issue age: 28
Insured: Barbara Wiggins
Owner: Small City School District
Type of policy: term
Cost and pmt. period: fringe benefit, no employee contribution
Extra benefits: waiver of premium, accidental death and dis-
                                memberment
Amount of base policy: $15,000
Net payable at death: $15,000 ($30,000 for accidental death)
Beneficiaries and settle-
   ment options: first to Charles F. Wiggins—lump sum; second
                                to Charles F. Wiggins, Jr.—lump sum

(4) Property and liability insurance

Homeowner's insurance
Policy number: W726495
Insurance company: DELTA
Address of property: 421 Briarcliff, Small City
HO Form number: 3
Coverage limits: dwelling, $90,000; personal property, $45,000;
                                additional living expense, $18,000
Deductible: $200 (for property coverage)
Cost and pmt. period: $400/annual
Liability included in HO: $25,000

Automobile insurance
Policy number: W526837
Insurance company: EAGLE
Automobile: 1985 Buick
ID number: 464391 BUOY
Named insured: Charles F. and Barbara Wiggins
Bodily injury: $100,000/$300,000
Property damage: $25,000
No-fault benefits: unlimited medical payments; disability benefits
                                up to $1,000 per month
Uninsured motorist: $10,000/$20,000
Collision deductible: $250
Comprehensive deduct.: $50
Cost and pmt. period: $450/annual

Charles has provided some information on the insurance policies of the partnership. Although Charles has been involved in decisions concerning their purchase, this aspect of the partnership's affairs is handled primarily by Steve Thomas. Charles does know that the partnership carries errors and omissions coverage and fire insurance on its building as well as workers' compensation and general liability insurance. In addition, employees of the partnership are provided with a comprehensive plan of group and medical expense insurance and $10,000 of group term life insurance. Both plans are noncontributory except for dependent medical expense coverage. Because contributions for the coverage of partners are not tax deductible and because the partners have employee benefits at their university jobs, they are not covered under these plans.

For their needs (in current dollars) in the event of disability, retirement, or the death of either of them, Barbara and Charles have reached the following conclusion: In the event of Charles's disability, they would need a monthly income of $8,000, and in the event of hers, $1,000 monthly. For retirement, Charles would need $7,000 per month and Barbara, $1,000 per month. In the event of Charles's premature death, his survivors would need about $8,000 per month during an adjustment period of approximately one year, then $7,500 per month for another 13 years (or until Charles, Jr., is 22 years old), and then $7,000 per month. In the event of Barbara's death, Charles would need about $1,500 per month of extra income for the full 14 years until Charles, Jr., is self-supporting.

If Charles should become disabled or retire, his major medical and other health insurance can be continued, and these policies can also be converted by his survivors in the event of his death.

As noted earlier, all resource items shown below are in current pretax dollars. The final amount of several items depends on interest-rate and/or dividend assumptions that may or may not hold at the actual time disability, retirement, or death occurs. (This is one of the main reasons why client financial plans must be continuously reviewed and updated.) For the purposes of this exercise, all calculations for death and disability income resources assume that the specified contingency will happen tomorrow. In computing resources for retirement, all items have been listed in terms of current dollars and purchasing power.

In the event of disability, Charles Wiggins could rely on the following resources:

Approximate monthly income

Social security benefits	$1,300
Group disability income insurance	1,730
Continuing income from investments, including spouse's trust income	824
Earnings of spouse	1,250
Total income	$5,104

If Charles were to retire at age 65, he could rely on the following resources:

Approximate monthly income

Social security benefits	$ 925
Pension plan (TDA)	5,000
Continuing income from investments, including spouse's trust income	824
Earnings of spouse	1,250
Total income	$7,999

If he should die tomorrow, Charles's family could rely on the following resources:

Approximate monthly income

Social security benefits	$ 1,550 [1]
Pension plan (TDA)	600 [2]
Continuing income from investments, including spouse's trust income	824
Earnings of spouse	1,250
Interest earnings of group term life insurance proceeds payable to spouse	350
Total income	$ 4,574

Lump-sum payments

Social security	$ 255
Group life insurance	42,000
Personal life insurance	125,000 [3]
Total	$167,255

Notes

1. The maximum family benefit from social security in the event of Charles's death would be about $1,550. Assuming that both Barbara and Cynthia, Charles's former wife, continue to work, this maximum benefit would be allocated equally to the three surviving children.
2. Interest only — assumes 12 percent rate of return.
3. Payable to Stephanie and Caroline.

FINANCIAL AND ESTATE PLANNING FACT FINDER

The information collected and maintained in this document will be held in the utmost confidentiality. It will not be shared except as may be required by law, or as may be authorized in writing by the client.

(signed) *Mary Jane English, ChFC*

The American College

CONTENTS

Personal Data   1

Financial Objectives   4

Factors Affecting Your Financial Plan   4

Objectives Requiring Additional Income/Capital   5

Sources of Income   6

Cash-Management Statement   7

Inventory of Assets   8

Business Interest   12

Employee Census Data   14

Inventory of Liabilities   15

Life Insurance Benefits   16

Health Insurance Benefits   17

Property and Liability Insurance Coverage   18

Employment-Related Benefits Checklist   19

Employment-Related Retirement Benefits/Deferred Compensation   20

Risk/Return Profile   21

Income and Lump-Sum Needs for Disability, Retirement, and Death   22

Authorization for Information   23

Receipt for Documents   25

Observations from Counseling Sessions   27

Tax-Planning Checklist   29

Financial Position Statement   35

Income and Lump-Sum Resources for Disability, Retirement, and Death   37

Checklist for Financial Planning Review   39

PERSONAL DATA

Name (file no.)	*Charles F. Wiggins*
Spouse's name	*Barbara B. Wiggins*
Legal home address	*421 Briarcliff Drive Small City, GA 30341*
Business address	**Client** *Homestate Tech, Rm 426 Engineering Hall Small City GA 30315* **Spouse** *Small City School District, Adams High School* *Hickman Blvd. + Wavy Lane, Small City, GA 30344*
Phone	**Home** *(404) 433-2742* **Business:** *Client (404) 895-2550* *Spouse (404) 495-8000, Ext. 402*
Dates of counseling sessions	**Initial Interview** *3/7/89*				
Dates Checklist for Financial Planning Review was sent	

Consultants for Financial and Business Planning*

		Name	Address	Phone
Attorney	personal	*Edward L. Day*	*Cox, Day + Elkins, Suite 920* *1000 Parkway, Small City, GA 30301*	*(404) 895-9450*
	business	*same*		
Accountant ✓	personal	*Fred Granger, CPA*	*Suite 123 888 Parkway* *Small City, GA 30301*	*(404) 895-6428*
	business			
Trust officer		*Xavier Young* *Admini. Trust Officer*	*Universal Bank + Trust* *Dallas, TX*	*(214) 319-4000*
Other bank officer		*Helen Morgan* *Commercial Banker*	*1st National Bank, 1st Nat'l Tower* *Small City, GA*	*(404) 895-9240*
Life insurance agent		*John King, CLU*	*Suite 903, 1000 Parkway* *Small City, GA*	*(404) 895-5000*
Property and liability insurance agent		*Larry Mincer, CPCU*	*422D Kingsway* *Small City, GA*	*(404) 433-1984*
Securities broker		*Nancy Osborne*	*Peters, Quigley + Rogers* *100 Broad St. Small City, GA*	*(404) 895-3622*
Primary financial consultant				

*Indicate source of client with a check.

Notes

PERSONAL DATA (continued)

Client and Spouse

	Date of Birth	Social Security Number	Occupation	Amount of Support by Client/ Spouse	Health Problems/ Special Needs
Client* CHARLES F. WIGGINS	8/14/49	063-42-2221	PROF., ARCHI- TECTURAL DESIGN		NONE
Spouse* BARBARA B. WIGGINS	6/5/57	114-68-9370	EDITOR		NONE

*If not U.S. citizen, indicate nationality.

Children†/Grandchildren

CHARLES F., JR.	5/11/81			100%	NONE
STEPHANIE R. *	8/13/74			70%	NONE
CAROLINE D. *	8/25/76			70%	NONE

†Indicate whether by prior marriage, adopted, or stepchild.

Client's Parents, Siblings‡

TED WIGGINS	7/4/24		MACHINIST	0	NONE
MARY WIGGINS	12/25/25		HOUSEWIFE	0	"
JAMES WIGGINS (BROTHER)	7/13/48		CONTRACTOR	0	"
EDWARD WIGGINS "			DECEASED		

Spouse's Parents, Siblings‡

WM. B. BECKER	5/31/28		ORAL SURGEON	0	NONE
SUSAN A. BECKER	3/11/28		GIFT SHOP OWNER	0	"
BETTY BECKER (SISTER)	6/5/57		DIPLOMATIC COURIER	0	"

‡If possible, obtain addresses, phone numbers, and social security numbers of family members, especially those who are, or may become, beneficiaries, executors, guardians, etc.

Notes   * CHILDREN FROM MY PREVIOUS MARRIAGE

Marital status	☑ Married ☐ divorced ☐ widowed (check appropriate status) date: _1/14/79_
	Any former marriages? ☑ yes ☐ no If yes, to whom? client: _CYNTHIA CROWLEY_ spouse:
	Are you paying alimony? ☐ yes ☑ no If yes, amount: Are you paying child support? ☑ yes ☐ no If yes, amount: _$250 PER MO. PER CHILD_
	Are there prenuptial or postnuptial agreements? ☐ yes ☑ no
Estate plan	Do you have a basic estate plan? ☑ yes ☐ no If yes, describe briefly. _¼ OF ESTATE TO EACH CHILD OF PREVIOUS MARRIAGE; ½ TO BARBARA._ _BARBARA'S WILL LEAVES EVERYTHING TO ME IF I SURVIVE HER; OTHERWISE TO CHARLES, JR._
Wills	Do you have a will? ☑ yes ☐ no date of will: _6/81_
	Does your spouse have a will? ☑ yes ☐ no date of will: _6/81_
Executor nominations	Who has been named as executor in your will? in your spouse's will? Name: _FIRST NAT'L BANK_ Name: _SAME_ Address: _SMALL CITY, GA_ Address: Phone: _(404) 895-9240_ Phone:
Guardian nominations	Have guardians been named for your children? ☑ yes ☐ no _(FOR CHARLES, JR.)_ If yes, who? Name: _BETTY BECKER_ _APT. 3515 PARKLANE TOWERS_ Address: _100 PARKLANE PLACE_ _WASHINGTON, DC_ Phone: _(202) 677-5803_
Trust/trustee nominations	Have you created grantor, Clifford, insurance, or <u>testamentary</u> trusts? ☑ yes ☐ no If yes, who is the trustee? _1ST NAT'L BANK SMALL CITY, GA_
	Who are the beneficiaries? _SEE ESTATE PLAN ABOVE_
	Has your spouse created grantor, Clifford, insurance, or <u>testamentary</u> trusts? ☑ yes ☐ no If yes, who is the trustee? _SAME_
	Who are the beneficiaries? _SAME_
Custodianships	Have you or your spouse ever made a gift under the Uniform Gifts to Minors Act? ☐ yes ☑ no If yes, in which state?
	Who is the custodian?
	Who are the donees?
Trust beneficiary	Are you or any members of your immediate family beneficiaries of a trust? ☑ yes ☐ no If yes, who? _BARBARA_
	Amount expected: _$100,000_
Gifts/inheritances	Do you, your spouse, or your children expect to receive gifts/inheritances? ☑ yes ☐ no If yes, who? _BARBARA_
	How much? _AT LEAST $500,000_ from whom? _PARENTS_ when? _AT THEIR DEATH_
Education	What is the level of your education? _Ph D_
	What is the level of your spouse's education? _M. Ed_
Military service benefits	Are you or your spouse eligible for any benefits deriving from military service? ☐ yes ☑ no If yes, explain.

FINANCIAL OBJECTIVES

Rank from 1 to 8 the importance of having adequate funds in order to do the following:

- **5** maintain/expand standard of living
- **6** enjoy a comfortable retirement
- **3** take care of self and family during a period of long-term disability
- **7** invest and accumulate wealth
- **4** reduce tax burden
- **1** provide college education for children
- **2** take care of family in the event of death
- **8** develop an estate distribution plan
- _____ any others important to you (specify)

Do you have a formal monthly budget? ☐ yes ☑ no   If yes, indicate amount:

How much do you save annually? $3,000   in what form? *primarily CDs* why?

How much do you think you should be able to save annually? *10% after tax* what purpose? *College education for children or in case of Charles's disability or death, to use*

How much do you invest annually? $5,000   in what form? *stocks, mutual funds, money-market* why? *same as above*

How much do you think you should be able to invest annually? *10% after tax* for what purpose? *same as above*

FACTORS AFFECTING YOUR FINANCIAL PLAN

Have you or your spouse ever made substantial gifts to family members or to tax-exempt beneficiaries? ☐ yes ☑ no
If yes, give details. *but may wish to contribute to Small City Chamber Music Society in future*

What special bequests are intended, including charity?
none

Are you satisfied with your previous investment results? ☑ yes ☐ no
Explain. *somewhat, but feels that yields should be higher in current conditions*

Are there any investments you feel committed to (for past performance, family, or social reasons)? ☐ yes ☑ no
If yes, explain.

Is your spouse good at handling money? ☑ yes ☐ no   *(fair)*

If you die, would your spouse be able to manage family finances? ☑ yes ☐ no   *(probably)*

In the event of your death, what is your estimate of the emotional and economic maturity of your children?
average

In the event of your death or of divorce, what are your feelings about the possible remarriage of your spouse? *Charles believes Barbara would and should remarry. Barbara hopes Charles would.*

At what age would you like to retire? *Charles: from teaching at 65; from business at 70*
Barbara: 65

Tax considerations aside, in what manner would you want your estate distributed? *first, to provide for Barbara and minor children, then Barbara for her life, then equally to his children*

What do you think financial planning should do for you?
provide a long-range financial management system

OBJECTIVES REQUIRING ADDITIONAL INCOME/CAPITAL

Do your children attend public or private schools? *public*
If private, annual cost: (elementary) _____ (secondary) _____

Do you plan for your children to attend private schools later?   ☐ yes   ☑ no
If yes, when?

Education Fund

Name of Child	Age	No. Years until College	Estimated 4-Year Cost If Private	Estimated 4-Year Cost If Public	Estimated Graduate School Costs	Capital Allocated	Monthly Income Allocated
Stephanie	15	3		$12,000	$30,000	$3,000 (co)	- 0 -
Caroline	13	5	$40,000		$35,000	$3,000 (co)	- 0 -
Charles, Jr.	8	10	$60,000		$50,000	$7,000 (co)	- 0 -

Support for Family Member(s)

Name	Age	Relation	Estimated Cost	Estimated Period of Funding	Capital Allocated	Monthly Income Allocated

Other Objectives

Objective	Target Date	Estimated Cost	Estimated Period of Funding	Capital Allocated	Monthly Income Allocated
vacation home	1991	$80,000	30 years	$8,000 (co)	- 0 -

Notes

SOURCES OF INCOME

Annual Income

	Client	Spouse*	Dependent Children*
Salary, bonus, etc. *(10% SAL. DED. FOR IDA IS NOT TAXABLE INCOME)*	#42,000	#15,000	
Income as business owner (self-employment)	35,000		
Real estate rental			
Dividends			
Investments (public stock, mutual funds, etc.)	1,904		
Close corporation stock			
Interest			
Investments (bonds, money market funds, T-bills, etc.)	441		
Savings accounts, certificates of deposit	2,540		
Loans, notes			
Trust income		5,000	
Life insurance settlement options			
Child support/alimony			
Other sources (specify)			
Other sources			
Other sources			
Other sources			
Total annual income	#81,885	20,000	

*If spouse or children are employed, give details here.

Income Tax Last Year

(JOINT RETURN)

Federal	32,000		
State	4,000		
Local			
Total income tax paid last year	36,000		
Estimated quarterly tax this year	2,000		

Future Annual Income Estimate

	BUSINESS INCOME / SALARIES		
Next year	39,100 / 46,200	16,050	
Three years			
Five years			
How often do you expect a salary increase or bonus? ANNUALLY			
On the average, how much of a salary increase or bonus do you expect annually? CHARLES 10% FROM TEACHING, 5% FROM BUSINESS			
Has your total annual income fluctuated significantly during the past three years? NO BARBARA 7%			

CASH-MANAGEMENT STATEMENT

Annual Income *Joint*

	Current Yr.	Projections for Subsequent Years				
	19 87	Assumptions	19____	19____	19____	19____
Salary, bonus, etc. *CHARLES 42K / BARBARA 15K*	57,000	+ 10%/YR. / + 7%/YR.				
Income as business owner (self-employment)	35,000	+6%/YR.				
Real estate rental						
Dividends						
Investments	1,904	NO CHANGE				
Close corporation stock						
Interest income						
Investments *(MONEY MKT.)*	441	" "				
Savings accts., CDs	2,540	" "				
Loans, notes, etc.						
Trust income *(BARBARA)*	5,000	" "				
Life insurance settlement options						
Child support/alimony						
Other sources (specify)						
Total annual income	101,885					

Annual Expenditures: Fixed

Housing (mortgage/rent)	4,920	" "				
Utilities and telephone	4,500	+ 8%/YR.				
Food	7,000	" "				
Clothing and cleaning	3,000	" "				
Income and social security taxes	40,000	NO CHANGE				
Property taxes	2,500	+ 8%/YR				
Transportation (auto/commuting)	2,000	" "				
Medical/dental/drugs/health insurance	2,500	" "				
Debt repayment	—					
House upkeep/repairs/maintenance	3,500	" "				
Life, property and liability insurance	3,110	(P+L $50) + 8%/YR				
Child support/alimony	5,000	NO CHANGE				
Current education expenses						
Total fixed expenses	78,030					

Annual Expenditures: Discretionary

Recreation/entertainment/travel	8,000					
Contributions/gifts	1,600					
Household furnishings	2,000					
Education fund	2,000					
Savings	1,000					
Investments	5,000					
Other (specify) *TDA CONTRIBUTION*	4,200	10% OF CHARLES'S SAL.				
Total discretionary expenses	23,800					
Total annual expenditures	101,830					
Net income (total annual income minus total annual expenditures)	55					

INVENTORY OF ASSETS *

Cash, Near-Cash Equivalents

| Items | No. Units or Shares | Date Acquired | Amount, Cost, or Other Basis | Market Value and Titled Owners | | | | | |
				Client	Spouse	Joint (survivor rights)	Joint (no survivor rights)	Community Property	Other*
Checking accounts/cash			4,000			4,000			
Savings accounts			8,000			8,000			
Money-market funds			4,900			4,900			
Treasury bills									
Commercial paper									
Short-term CDs									
Cash value, life insurance			15,000	15,000					
Accum. divs., life insurance									
Savings bonds									
Other (specify)									
Subtotal			31,900	15,000		16,900			

*Children, custodial accounts, trusts, etc.

U.S. Govt., Municipal, Corporate Bonds, and Bond Funds: Issuer, Maturity, Call Dates

Subtotal									

Preferred Stock: Issuer, Maturity, Call Dates

Subtotal									

Common Stock: Issuer, Listed (L), Unlisted (U), Nonmarketable (NM)

Home Products (L)	200	'80	8,000	10,000					
Octane Oil (L)	400	'79	4,000			8,000			
Growth Industries (L)	100	'84	4,000			5,000			
Sunshine Bldg. Corp. (U)	1,000	'86	1,800			1,200			
Subtotal			17,800	10,000		14,200			

Warrants and Options: Issuer, Expiration Date

Subtotal									

Mutual Funds and Type: Growth (G), Income (I), Balanced (B), Indexed (IX), Speculative (S)

Mega Growth Fund	135	'86	1,200			1,800			
(G) (Divs. reinvested)									
Subtotal			1,200			1,800			

8

* Value of Business Interest not included here

INVENTORY OF ASSETS

Cash, Near-Cash Equivalents

Annual Yield %	Annual Yield $	Amount Available for Liquidity	Amount of Indebtedness	Location, Description, Client's Reasons for Holding Asset, etc.	Items
		4,000	—	1ST NAT'L	Checking accounts/cash
5½	440	8,000	—	" "	Savings accounts
9	441	4,700	—	SAFE DEPOSIT BOX	Money-market funds
					Treasury bills
					Commercial paper
					Short-term CDs
		15,000	—	INS. CO.	Cash value, life insurance
					Accum. divs., life insurance
					Savings bonds
					Other (specify)
	881	31,900			Subtotal

U.S. Govt., Municipal, Corporate Bonds, and Bond Funds: Issuer, Maturity, Call Dates

					Subtotal

Preferred Stock: Issuer, Maturity, Call Dates

					Subtotal

Common Stock: Issuer, Listed (L), Unlisted (U), Nonmarketable (NM)

6	600	18,000	—	SAFE DEPOSIT BOX	
10	800	8,000	—	" " "	
6	300	5,000	—	" " "	
5	60	1,200	—	" " "	
	1,760	24,200	—		Subtotal

Warrants and Options: Issuer, Expiration Date

					Subtotal

Mutual Funds and Type: Growth (G), Income (I), Balanced (B), Indexed (IX), Speculative (S)

8	144	1,800	—		
	144	1,800	—		Subtotal

Real Estate

Items	No. Units or Shares	Date Acquired	Amount, Cost or Other Basis	Market Value and Titled Owners					
				Client	Spouse	Joint (survivor rights)	Joint (no survivor rights)	Community Property	Other
Personal residence		'79	60,000			95,000			
Seasonal residence									
Investment (residential)									
Investment (commercial)									
Land									
Other (specify)									
Subtotal			60,000			95,000			

Long-term, Nonmarketable Assets

Items	No. Units or Shares	Date Acquired	Amount, Cost or Other Basis	Client	Spouse	Joint (survivor rights)	Joint (no survivor rights)	Community Property	Other
Long-term CDs	VARIOUS		21,000			21,000			
Vested retirement benefits	TAX-DEFERRED SALARY			60,000					
Annuities									
HR-10 plan (Keogh)									
IRAs									
Mortgages owned									
Land contracts									
Limited partnership units									
Other (specify)									
Subtotal			21,000	60,000		21,000			

Personal Assets

Items	No. Units or Shares	Date Acquired	Amount, Cost or Other Basis	Client	Spouse	Joint (survivor rights)	Joint (no survivor rights)	Community Property	Other
Household furnishings			25,000			20,000			
Automobile(s) (PERSONALLY OWNED)		'85	8,500			4,500			
Recreational vehicles									
Boats									
Jewelry/furs			15,000		28,000				
Collections (art, coins, etc.)									
Hobby equipment									
Other (specify)									
Subtotal			48,500		28,000	24,500			

Miscellaneous Assets

Items	No. Units or Shares	Date Acquired	Amount, Cost or Other Basis	Client	Spouse	Joint (survivor rights)	Joint (no survivor rights)	Community Property	Other
Interest(s) in trust(s) *			100,000		100,000				
Receivables									
Patents, copyrights, royalties									
Other (specify)									
Subtotal			100,000		100,000				
Totals of all columns			280,400	85,000	128,000	173,400			

* BARBARA DOESN'T YET POSSESS THE MONEY. IS IT A REAL ASSET?

INVENTORY OF ASSETS (continued)

Real Estate

Annual Yield %	Annual Yield $	Amount Available for Liquidity	Amount of Indebtedness	Location, Description, Client's Reasons for Holding Asset, etc.	Items
		—	48,000	SAFE DEPOSIT BOX	Personal residence
					Seasonal residence
					Investment (residential)
					Investment (commercial)
					Land
					Other (specify)
		—	48,000		Subtotal

Long-term, Nonmarketable Assets

Annual Yield %	Annual Yield $	Amount Available for Liquidity	Amount of Indebtedness	Location, Description, Client's Reasons for Holding Asset, etc.	Items
10	2,100	(YIELD ONLY) 2,100	—	" " "	Long-term CDs
10	6,000	—	—	" " "	Vested retirement benefits
					Annuities
					HR-10 plan (Keogh)
					IRAs
					Mortgages owned
					Land contracts
					Limited partnership units
					Other (specify)
	8,100	2,100	—		Subtotal

Personal Assets

Annual Yield %	Annual Yield $	Amount Available for Liquidity	Amount of Indebtedness	Location, Description, Client's Reasons for Holding Asset, etc.	Items
	—	—	—	RESIDENCE	Household furnishings
	—	—	—	"	Automobile(s)
					Recreational vehicles
					Boats
	—	—	—	"	Jewelry/furs
					Collections (art, coins, etc.)
					Hobby equipment
					Other (specify)
	—	—	—		Subtotal

Miscellaneous Assets

Annual Yield %	Annual Yield $	Amount Available for Liquidity	Amount of Indebtedness	Location, Description, Client's Reasons for Holding Asset, etc.	Items
5	5,000	—	—	UNIVERSAL BANK + TRUST, DALLAS TX	Interest(s) in trust(s)
					Receivables
					Patents, copyrights, royalties
					Other (specify)
	5,000		48,000		Subtotal
	15,885	60,000	48,000		Totals of all columns

BUSINESS INTEREST

General Information

Full legal name Design Engineering Assoc.	Phone (404) 895-2550

Address 1773 Park Place, Small City, GA 30318

Business now operates as ☐ proprietorship ☑ partnership ☐ corporation ☐ S corporation

When does the fiscal year end? 12/31

What accounting method is used? cash

What is the principal business activity? design and construction of small commercial buildings; inspection and redesign of existing buildings for renovation

In what year did this business begin operation? 1975

If it began other than as a corporation, what is the date of incorporation?   state of incorporation?

Classes of stock   No. authorized shares   No. outstanding shares

What is your function in the business? General Partner

Do you have an employment contract? no

Present Owners*

	Insurability Problem?		Form of Business		
			Corporation		Partnership
	Yes	No			
(A) _____Client_____	☐	☐	owns ___ % common ___ % preferred	1/3 %	_____
*(B) Steve Thomas	☑	☐	owns ___ % common ___ % preferred	1/3 %	_____
(C) Ursula Von Waldhem	☐	☑	owns ___ % common ___ % preferred	1/3 %	_____
(D) _____	☐	☐	owns ___ % common ___ % preferred	___ %	_____
(E) _____	☐	☐	owns ___ % common ___ % preferred	___ %	_____

*Indicate relationship to client by blood or marriage.

Key Employees (other than present owners)

	Insurability Problem			Insurability Problem	
	Yes	No		Yes	No
Tom Young	☐	☑	_____	☐	☐
John Blake	☐	☑	_____	☐	☐
Sarah L. McIntyre	☐	☑	_____	☐	☐
	☐	☐	_____	☐	☐

* Steve Thomas was rated following a heart attack in 1984.

BUSINESS INTEREST (continued)

Disposition of Business Interest

Do you want your business interest ~~retained~~ or sold if you   *maybe*
retire? ☑ yes ☐ no   become disabled? ☐ yes ☐ no   die? ☑ yes ☐ no

IF RETAINED
Who will own your interest and how will the person(s) acquire it?

Who will replace you in your job?

IF SOLD
Who will buy your interest? *existing partners/might consider outsider*

How is purchase price to be determined? *no method in place*

What is the funding arrangement? *none*

Do you have a buy-sell agreement? ☐ yes ☑ no

If yes, is it a cross-purchase, entity-purchase, or "wait-and-see" type of agreement?

Where is it located?

Valuation of Business Interest

Estimate the lowest price for which the entire business might be sold as a going concern today. *$300,000*

What is the lowest price you would accept for your interest today? *$125,000*

If you were not an owner, what is your estimate of the highest price you would pay today for the entire business as a going concern? *$300,000*

What is the highest price you would pay to buy the interest of your coowners today? *$175,000*

Has an impartial valuation of the business been made? ☐ yes ☑ no If yes, when?
What valuation method was used?   What value was established?

What is the average business indebtedness? *$120,000 (mortgage on building is major portion)*

Estimate the highest it has ever been. *$135,000*   Estimate the lowest it has ever been. *$10,000*

Are there patents, special processes, or leased equipment/real property used by but not owned by the business? ☐ yes ☑ no
If yes, who owns what, and under what terms is each used or leased?

What are prospects for growth, sale, merger, or going public? *Business has strong market position and should sell if partners so desire. No indication of merger at this time. Will never go public.*

Survivor Control (letters in parentheses refer to owners named above on page 12)

IF (A) DIES	IF (B) DIES	IF (C) DIES	IF (D) DIES	IF (E) DIES
B wants _____ % control	A wants _____ %	A wants _____ %	A wants _____ %	A wants _____ %
C wants _____ % control	C wants _____ %	B wants _____ %	B wants _____ %	B wants _____ %
D wants _____ % control	D wants _____ %	D wants _____ %	C wants _____ %	C wants _____ %
E wants _____ % control	E wants _____ %	E wants _____ %	E wants _____ %	D wants _____ %
_____ wants _____ % control	_____ wants _____ %	_____ wants _____ %	_____ wants _____ %	_____ wants _____ %

EMPLOYEE CENSUS DATA*

	Sex	Marital Status	Name			Date of Birth			Date Em-ployed†			Full-time‡	Hourly	Salaried	Earnings		Member of Collective Bargain Unit?	Occupation or Job Title
			Last	First	M.I.	Month	Day	Year	Month	Day	Year				Annual Salary or Wage	Additional Compen-sation		
1																		
2																		
3																		
4																		
5																		
6																		
7																		
8																		
9																		
10																		
11																		
12																		
13																		
14																		
15																		
16																		
17																		
18																		
19																		
20																		
21																		
22																		
23																		
24																		
25																		

*It is suggested that the client request this data directly from bookkeeper or other appropriate person.
†The date of its incorporation is also the date of employment of former proprietors or partners of a business.
‡A full-time employee is one who works 1,000 or more hours per year.

INVENTORY OF LIABILITIES

Outstanding Obligations of Client or Spouse	Original Amount	Maximum Credit Available	Present Balance	Monthly/ Annual Repayment	Effective Interest Rate	Payments Remaining/ Maturity Date	Secured?	Insured?
Retail charge accounts		5,000	1,000	PAY IN FULL MONTHLY	18%		NO	NO
VARIOUS DEPT. STORES + OIL COS.								
Credit cards		10,000	1,500	" " "	18%		NO	NO
BANK CARDS								
Family/personal loans								
Securities margin loans								
Investment liabilities								
Bank loans								
Life insurance policy loans								
Income tax liability								
Federal (PROJ. '89)	31,000	(FUNDED BY WITHHOLDING +						
State (" ")	5,000	ESTIMATED TAX PAYMENTS)						
Local								
Property taxes			2,500					
Mortgage(s) 1ST NAT'L	55,900		48,000	4/0 4,920	8%	2009	YES	
Family member support								
Child support/alimony			24,000*	500/6,000				YES
Other (specify)								
Total			77,000	910/10,920				

Are there any other liabilities your estate might be called upon to pay? ☑ yes ☐ no
If yes, explain: PARTNERSHIP LIABILITIES, PRIMARILY 1/3 OF MORTGAGE — $37,000

Do you foresee any future liabilities (business expansion, new home, etc.)? ☐ yes ☐ no
If yes, explain: SUMMER HOME 1991 — MORTGAGE OF AT LEAST $65,000

* $3,000/YR. FOR BOTH STEPHANIE + CAROLINE TILL EACH REACHES AGE 18

LIFE INSURANCE BENEFITS*

Item	Policy 1	Policy 2	Policy 3
Policy number	W216546	W927354	W327621
Name of insurance company	Ajax	TIAA	Alpha
Issue age	25	28	29
Insured	Charles Wiggins	Charles Wiggins	Charles Wiggins
Owner of policy	" "	Homestate Tech	
Type of policy	whole life - non par.	group term	whole life - non par.
Annual premium	$360	paid by University	$1,900
Net annual outlay by client	$360	-0-	$1,900
Current cash value	$2,800	-0-	$12,200
Extra benefits (e.g. waiver of premium, accidental death, etc.)	waiver of premium accidental death	waiver of premium accidental death and dismemberment	waiver of premium
Amount of base policy	$25,000	$42,000*	$100,000
Dividends (value & option)	-0-	-0-	-0-
Term rider(s)	none	none	none
Loan outstanding	-0-	-0-	-0-
Net amount payable at death	$25,000	$42,000	$100,000
Primary beneficiary and settlement option elected	Stephanie + Caroline Wiggins - lump sum	Barbara Wiggins - lump sum	Stephanie + Caroline - lump sum
Secondary beneficiary and settlement option elected	Barbara Wiggins - lump sum	Charles Wiggins, Jr. - lump sum	Barbara - lump sum

Item	Policy 4	Policy 5	Policy 6
Policy number	W541834		
Name of insurance company	GAMMA		
Issue age	28		
Insured	Barbara Wiggins		
Owner of policy	Small City School District		
Type of policy	group term		
Annual premium	paid by employer		
Net annual outlay by client	-0-		
Current cash value	-0-		
Extra benefits (e.g., waiver of premium, accidental death, etc.)	waiver of premium, accidental death and dismemberment		
Amount of base policy	$15,000		
Dividends (value & option)	none		
Term rider(s)	none		
Loan outstanding	none		
Net amount payable at death	$15,000		
Primary beneficiary and settlement option elected	Charles Wiggins - lump sum		
Secondary beneficiary and settlement option elected	Charles, Jr. - lump sum		

*Policies and most recent policy anniversary premium notices should be examined for the information recorded on this page.

* equivalent to annual salary — increases as salary increases

HEALTH INSURANCE BENEFITS*

Medical/Dental Benefits

	Policy 1	Policy 2	Policy 3	Policy 4
Type of policy	group			
Policy number	W497321			
Name of insurance company or other provider	Blue Cross/Shield			
Insured	C. Wiggins + deps.			
Annual cost to client	$480 (for deps.)			
Type of continuance or renewal provision				
Deductible	$200 per person			
Percentage participation	80/20			
Stop-loss limit				
Inside limits	90 days hosp. surg. sched.			
Overall maximum	$500,000			

Disability Income Benefits

	Charles	Charles	Barbara	
Policy number		W376701		
Name of insurance company or other provider	uninsured sick pay for 6 mos. - Homestate Tech.	TIAA/CREF	uninsured disability plan 1 year	
Insured		Charles Wiggins		
Annual cost to client	—0—	—0—	—0—	
Type of continuance or renewal provision				
Definition of disability	own occupation	own occupation - 2 yrs any other suitable occupation thereafter	own occupation	
Monthly disability income				
Accident	full salary	75% salary, offset by ss. - employed only	100% salary - 3 mos 50% salary - 9 mos	
Sickness	full salary	same	same	
Partial disability provision				
Waiting period				
Accident	none	6 months	none	
Sickness	none	6 months	7 days	
Benefit period				
Accident	6 months	to age 65	1 year	
Sickness	6 months	to age 65	1 year	

*Policies should be examined for the information recorded on this page.

PROPERTY AND LIABILITY INSURANCE COVERAGE*

Homeowners Insurance

	Principal Residence	Seasonal Residence	Other Property
Policy number	W 726 495		
Name of insurance company	Delta		
Address of property	421 Briarcliff, Small City,		
HO form # (or other type of policy)	3		
Coverage on dwelling	$90,000		
Replacement cost of dwelling	110,000		
Replacement cost of contents	45,000		
Liability limits	25,000		
Endorsements			
Deductibles	$200 (property)		
Annual cost	$400		

Automobile Insurance

	Auto #1	Auto #2	Auto #3 (or other vehicles, trailers)
Policy number	W526837		
Name of insurance company	Eagle		
Automobile make/year	1985 Buick		
Liability limits	100/300/25		
No-fault/medical benefits	unlimited med. benefits; $1,000/mo. disability		
Uninsured motorist	10,000/20,000		
Collision/deductible	$250		
Comprehensive/deductible	$50		
Annual cost	$450		

Other Property/Liability Insurance

	Policy 1	Policy 2	Policy 3
Type of policy			
Policy number			
Name of insurance company			
Property covered			
Limits			
Annual cost			

Umbrella Liability Insurance

Policy number	
Name of insurance company	
Liability limits	
Retention	
Annual cost	

*Policies should be examined for the information recorded on this page.

EMPLOYMENT-RELATED BENEFITS CHECKLIST

Name and address of client's employer _Homestate Tech, Small City, GA 30315_

Name and address of spouse's employer _Small City School District, Small City, GA 30344_

Who can provide detailed information on employee benefits for you and your spouse?

Client Name _University: Alice Blake, Pers. Servs._
Design Engineering: Mary Martin

Title _Personnel Mgr._
Office Mgr.

Department _University: (404) 495-3010_

Phone _Design Engineering: (404) 895-2550_

Spouse Name _____

Title _____

Department _____

Phone _____

	Benefit now provided for client?		Benefit now provided for spouse?		Information/Comments
Life and Health Insurance	Yes	No	Yes	No	
Death benefits	☑	☐	☐	☐	_____
Accidental death/dismemberment	☑	☐	☐	☐	_____
Travel accident	☐	☑	☐	☐	_____
Medical expense benefits	☑	☐	☐	☐	_____
Short-term disability income (sick pay)	☑	☐	☐	☐	_____
Long-term disability income	☑	☐	☐	☐	_____
Retirement Benefits/ Deferred Compensation*					
Qualified pension plan	☐	☑	☐	☐	_All listed benefits are_
Qualified profit-sharing plan	☐	☑	☐	☐	_through Charles's Homestate_
Nonqualified deferred-compensation plan	☐	☑	☐	☐	_employment except company_
Salary reduction plan (401k)	☐	☑	☐	☐	_car furnished by Design_
Simplified employee pension (SEP)	☐	☑	☐	☐	_Engineering_
Stock bonus plan	☐	☑	☐	☐	_____
Employee stock-ownership plan (ESOP)	☐	☑	☐	☐	_____
Employee stock-purchase plan	☐	☑	☐	☐	_____
Incentive stock-option plan [§422A]	☐	☑	☐	☐	_____
Restricted stock plan [§83(b)]	☐	☑	☐	☐	_____
Phantom stock plan [§83(a)]	☐	☑	☐	☐	_____
Tax-deferred annuity plan	☑	☐	☐	☐	_____
Salary continuation after death	☐	☑	☐	☐	_____
Other (specify)	☐	☐	☐	☐	_____
Miscellaneous Benefits					
Excess medical reimbursement plan	☐	☑	☐	☐	_____
Split-dollar life insurance	☐	☑	☐	☐	_____
Auto/homeowners	☐	☑	☐	☐	_____
Legal expense	☐	☑	☐	☐	_____
Company car	☑	☐	☐	☐	_____
Educational reimbursement	☐	☑	☐	☐	_____
Club membership	☐	☑	☐	☐	_____
Other (specify)	☐	☐	☐	☐	_____

*Describe appropriate benefits on page 20.

19

EMPLOYMENT-RELATED
RETIREMENT BENEFITS/DEFERRED COMPENSATION

Type	Employee's Annual Contribution	Benefits to Client			Benefits to Survivors			
		Lump-sum Pmts.	Monthly Income		Beneficiary	Lump-sum Pmts.	Monthly Income	
			Amount	Beginning/Ending			Amount	Beginning/Ending
Qualified pension plan								
Qualified profit-sharing plan								
Nonqualified deferred-compensation plan								
Salary reduction plan (401k)								
Stock bonus plan								
Employee stock-ownership plan (ESOP)								
Employee stock-purchase plan								
Incentive stock-option plan [§422A]								
Restricted stock plan [§83(b)]								
Phantom stock plan [§83(a)]								
Tax-deferred annuity plan	$4,200 (salary reduction)		$5,000 *	2014/?				
Salary continuation after death								
Other (specify)								
Other (specify)								

Explain and describe pertinent details for planning purposes here (e.g., anticipated benefits not yet in place; client's views on relevance, need, and feasibility of these benefits; problems associated with implementing benefits; etc.).

* in current dollars/purchasing power

Social Security Benefits

What are the estimated retirement benefits (in current dollars)?
client only: $925.00 per month   client and spouse:

What are the estimated disability benefits the client is eligible for if disabled today?
client only: client and family: $1,300.00 per month

What are the estimated survivors' benefits payable to the client's family if death should occur today? $1,550.00 per month

RISK/RETURN PROFILE

On a scale from 0 to 5, with 5 representing a strong preference and 0 representing an aversion, indicate your preference for the following instruments of savings and investment by circling the appropriate number.

Savings account	0	①︎	2	3	4	5
Money-market fund	0	1	2	③︎	4	5
U.S. government bond	0	①︎	2	3	4	5
Corporate bond	0	①︎	2	3	4	5
Mutual fund (growth)	0	1	2	3	4	⑤︎
Common stock (growth)	0	1	2	3	4	⑤︎
Mutual fund (income)	0	1	②︎	3	4	5
Municipal bond	0	①︎	2	3	4	5
Real estate (direct ownership)	0	1	2	3	④︎	5
Variable annuity	0	1	②︎	3	4	5
Limited partnership unit (real estate, oil and gas, cattle, equipment leasing)	0	①︎	2	3	4	5
Commodities, gold, collectibles	⓪︎	1	2	3	4	5

On a scale from 0 to 5, circle the number to the right of each of the items below that most accurately reflects your own financial concerns; 5 indicates a very strong concern and 0 indicates no concern.

CHARLES = O   BARBARA = X

Liquidity	0	1	2	3	⊠	5
Safety of principal	0	1	2	③︎	4	✗
Capital appreciation	0	1	2	✗	4	⑤︎
Current income	0	1	2	✗	④︎	5
Inflation protection	0	1	2	✗	④︎	5
Future income	0	1	2	3	④︎	✗
Tax reduction/deferral	0	1	2	3	4	⊠

Planner's comments and observations

INCOME AND LUMP-SUM NEEDS FOR DISABILITY, RETIREMENT, AND DEATH

	Client	Spouse/ Children
Disability Income Needs Monthly income needed in current dollars	$ 8,000	$ 1,000
Retirement Income Needs Monthly income needed in current dollars	$ 7,000	$ 1,000
Survivors' Income Needs* Monthly income needed in current dollars for surviving family members during the following periods after death:		
Adjustment period (adjustment of standard of living in a transitional period, as needed) – 1 year	$ 8,000	$ 1,500
Until youngest child is self-supporting (number of years 13)	$ 7,500	$ 1,500
After youngest child is self-supporting	$ 7,000	$ -0-
Survivors' Lump-sum Needs* Last expenses (final illness and funeral)	$	$
Emergency fund	$	$
Mortgage cancellation fund (if appropriate)	$	$
Notes and loans payable	$	$
Accrued taxes (income, real estate, etc., if not withheld)	$	$
Children's education (if not already funded)	$	$
Estate settlement costs and taxes (if not provided by liquidity)	$	$
Other (specify)	$	$
Total lump-sum needs in current dollars	$	$

*Some survivors' needs may be met by either periodic income or lump-sum payments or by some combination of the two approaches. Double counting in both categories should be avoided.

Notes   Survivors' lump-sum needs are not indicated since the Wigginses wish to have these items coordinated within a total financial plan.

AUTHORIZATION FOR INFORMATION

TO: _____

_____

_____

Please provide any information that is in your possession and that is asked for in connection with a survey of my/our financial affairs to

_____.

Charles F. Wiggins
(client's signature)

Barbara B. Wiggins
(spouse's signature)

_9-7-89_
(date)

TO: _____
        (company)

Please provide any information that is in your possession and that is requested by _____

_____ concerning the following policies of which I am the owner:

_____   _____

_____   _____

_____   _____

Policyowner's
Authorization   _Charles F. Wiggins_
(signature of policyowner)

_9-7-89_
(date)

Notes

RECEIPT FOR DOCUMENTS

Insurance Policies: Life, Health, Property and Liability

Company	Policy Number	☑	Company	Policy Number	☑
Ajax	W216546	✓	Eagle	W526837	✓
TIAA	W927354	✓			
Alpha	W327621	✓			
GAMMA	W541839	✓			
Delta	W726495	✓			

Original policies checked ☑ above have been received for review and analysis: they will be returned upon completion of analysis or client request.

Mary Jane English
(planner)

1888 Parkway, Ste. 203, Small City, Ga
(address)

(404) 897-1234
(phone)

9/7/89
(date)

All original policies and documents checked in this receipt have been returned to me.

_____
(client)

_____
(date)

Personal/Family Documents (copies)	Date	Business Documents (copies)	Date
✓ Tax returns (3–5 years)	1986-88	✓ Tax returns (3–5 years)	1986-88
✓ Wills (client and spouse)	6/89	✓ Financial statements (3–5 years) unaudited	1986-88
☐ Trust instruments		☐ Deferred-compensation plan	
☐ Financial statements		☐ HR-10 plan (Keogh)	
☐ Personal/family budgets		☐ Individual retirement account (IRA)	
☐ Sale/purchase contract		☐ Simplified employee pension (SEP)	
☐ Current insurance offers		☐ Pension/profit-sharing plan	
☐ Current investment offers		✓ Tax-deferred annuity Homestate	1988
☐ Deeds. mortgages. land contracts		☐ Stock-option/purchase agreement	
☐ Guardian nominations		☐ Buy-sell agreements	
☐ Leases (as lessor or lessee)		☐ Employment agreement	
☐ Notices of awards, elections		✓ Employee benefits booklet Homestate	1988
☐ Power of attorney/appointment		☐ Articles of incorporation	
☐ Separation/divorce/nuptial		☐ Merger/acquisition agreement	
☐ Patents/copyrights/royalties		✓ Partnership agreement Design Engr.	1977
✓ Employee benefits statement Homestate	1988	☐ Company patents	
☐ Other (specify)		☐ Equipment leasing agreement(s)	
☐ Other (specify)		☐ Other (specify)	

OBSERVATIONS FROM COUNSELING SESSIONS

As soon after counseling sessions as possible the financial planner should record impressions and observations about the client in terms of the following:

Personal appearance _well groomed, nicely dressed; socially skilled_

Appearance of office or home _N/A_

Personal interests (sports, hobbies, music, etc.) _enjoys music, theater, travel – interested in local chamber music society (Barbara shares these interests)_

Civic-mindedness _average_

Political awareness _above average_

Financial sophistication _fairly unsophisticated; but intelligent, motivated, and willing to learn._

College ties _none noticeable_

Decision-making ability _seems capable in his partnership_

Level of personal goals _high – but willing to work to achieve his goals_

Consistency of verbal and nonverbal behaviors _high – a very self-aware couple_

Condition of health _both say excellent_

Mental/emotional maturity _above average_

Attitude toward spouse _affectionate + respectful_ parents _respectful_

children _responsible, concerned, + loving_ other family members _not observed_

Financial risk-taking propensity _he is fairly aggressive, though inconsistent; she is more conservative_

Attitude toward financial counseling/planning _open – though initially dubious_

Investment decisions client has made and why _primarily CDs + stocks, to accumulate wealth_

Client's financial status (self-made or inherited) _self-made; spouse privileged_

Concern with taking care of self during retirement _not top priority_

Concern with family after own death _top priority_

Concern with self and family during disability _priority_

Concern with self right now _not top priority_

Concern with self and family right now _yes – and for the immediate future (until children are educated) – a top family priority_

Other pertinent observations, particularly concerning spouse: _The Wigginses seem to have a good marriage of equal partners. No one spouse always makes family decisions. Decisions preceded by discussion, review of alternatives. Charles's children by former marriage are not a problem. However, no decision seems to have been made as to whether they will eventually share in assets or monies that Barbara expects to inherit from her family._

TAX-PLANNING CHECKLIST*

Individual Planning

	At Present Yes	No	Advisable Yes	No
1. Does the client itemize rather than utilize the standard deduction?	☑	☐	☐	☐
2. Are all personal and dependency exemptions being taken (children, parents, foster children, etc.)? [§§151, 152]	☑	☐	☐	☐
3. Are maximum deductions for all expenses related to the production of income being taken?	☑	☐	☐	☐
4. a. Is optimum utilization being made of retirement plans for tax advantage?	☐	☑	☐	☐
b. Has the appropriate type(s) of plan been chosen?	☐	☑	☐	☐
5. Are contributions to charitable and other tax-exempt organizations being used as fully as the client is disposed to use them? [§170]	☑	☐	☐	☐
6. Are the client's real property investments being fully used for tax advantages?	☑	☐	☐	☐
7. Is the impact of the alternative minimum tax being considered for transactions involving tax-preference items? [§55] *N/A*	☐	☐	☐	☐
8. Are income and deductions being directed to specific years to avoid drastic fluctuation by				
a. accelerating income	☐	☑	☐	☐
b. postponing deductions	☐	☑	☐	☐
c. postponing income	☐	☑	☐	☐
d. accelerating deductions	☐	☑	☐	☐
e. avoiding constructive receipt	☐	☑	☐	☐
9. To reduce estate taxes				
a. have incidents of life insurance ownership been assigned?	☐	☑	☐	☐
b. is a life insurance trust being used? [§§2035, 2042]	☐	☑	☐	☐
10. Have installment sales of investments, residences, or other property been arranged to minimize tax? [§453] *N/A*	☐	☐	☐	☐
11. Is investment in tax-exempt instruments being used?	☐	☑	☐	☐
12. Is income being shifted to lower-bracket taxpayers through outright gifts or other lifetime transfers such as family partnerships or irrevocable trusts?	☐	☑	☐	☐
13. Is a qualified minors [2503(c)] trust being used effectively for income shifting or other tax advantage?	☐	☑	☐	☐
14. Have gifts been made under the Uniform Gifts to Minors Act (UGMA) or the Uniform Transfers to Minors Act (UTMA)?	☐	☑	☐	☐
15. Are gift/sale leasebacks being used?	☐	☑	☐	☐

*All code section references are to the Internal Revenue Code of 1986 as amended.

TAX-PLANNING CHECKLIST (continued)

Individual Planning (continued)

	At Present Yes	No	Advisable Yes	No
16. Have alternative distribution methods for qualified plans been analyzed for tax consequences?	☐	☑	☐	☐
17. Are capital-loss offsets being used to reduce total income subject to tax?	☐	☑	☐	☐
18. Are qualified plan distributions, rollovers to another qualified plan, or IRAs advisable for the client in the near future? *N/A*	☐	☐	☐	☐
19. Are contributions to a new or existing IRA advisable if a. the client can make deductible contributions? b. the client can make only nondeductible contributions?	☐ ☐	☐ ☐	☑ ☑	☐ ☐
20. Have like-kind exchanges of property been compared with sale and repurchase and utilized when more advantageous? [§1031] *N/A*	☐	☐	☐	☐
21. Is the client paying substantial amounts of nondeductible loan interest that should be consolidated under deductible home equity loans? [§163]	☐	☑	☐	☐
22. Have returns of capital on investment been distinguished from taxable income? (For example, has the client's basis in the investment been ascertained and any special tax treatment to which that investment is entitled determined?) *N/A*	☐	☐	☐	☐
23. Is the client suited for tax-advantaged investments?	☑	☐	☐	☐
24. Indicate any situation unique to this client that does not appear above.				

Business Planning

	At Present Yes	No	Advisable Yes	No
1. Are maximum allowable deductions for all expenses being taken?	☑	☐	☐	☐
2. Are expiring carryovers of credits, net operating losses, and charitable contributions being effectively used through timing of income and deductions? [§§38, 39, 46, 170, 172]	☑	☐	☐	☐
3. a. Is optimum use being made of retirement plans for tax advantage?	☐	☑	☐	☐
b. Has the appropriate type(s) of plan been chosen?	☐	☑	☐	☐
4. Are contributions to charitable and other tax-exempt organizations being used as fully as the client is disposed to use them? [§§170, 501]	☑	☐	☐	☐
5. a. Is the form of client's business or investment being fully utilized to maximize personal deductions and credits (e.g., corporation, partnership, trust, S corp.)?	☐	☑	☐	☐
b. Are the business's investments being fully used to maximize deductions and credits to the shareholder(s)?	☑	☐	☐	☐
6. Are income and deductions being directed to specific years to avoid drastic fluctuation by				
a. accelerating income	☐	☑	☐	☐
b. postponing deductions	☐	☑	☐	☐
c. postponing income	☐	☑	☐	☐
d. accelerating deductions	☐	☑	☐	☐
e. avoiding constructive receipt	☐	☑	☐	☐
7. Is the full range of deductible employment fringe benefits being explored and used within the client's limits?	☐	☑	☐	☐
8. Are gift/sale leasebacks appropriate for this client?	☐	☑	☐	☐
9. Have alternative distribution methods for qualified plans been analyzed for tax consequences?	☐	☑	☐	☐
10. Is sale-or-exchange treatment possible for redemption of equity in a closely held corporation? [§§301, 302, 303, 318] N/A	☐	☐	☐	☐
11. Have nonqualified retirement or deferred-compensation plans been considered? [§83]	☐	☑	☐	☐
12. Are stock options possible and advantageous? [§422A] N/A	☐	☐	☐	☐
13. Have simplified employee pensions (SEPs) been compared with other forms of deferred compensation?	☐	☑	☐	☐
14. Are qualified plans designed for maximum employee advantage during employment as well as at retirement? (For example, do they permit loans and rollovers from other plans, etc.?)	☐	☑	☐	☐

TAX-PLANNING CHECKLIST (continued)

Business Planning (continued)

	At Present Yes	At Present No	Advisable Yes	Advisable No
15. a. Have buy-sell plans to take effect at death been developed and formalized by legal agreements?	☐	☑	☐	☐
b. If yes, have they been appropriately funded?	☐	☑	☐	☐
16. Have lifetime transfer methods been considered to facilitate the orderly continuation of the business, for example, in case of disability?	☐	☑	☐	☐
17. Are employment contracts being used effectively to support the reasonableness of executive compensation?	☐	☑	☐	☐
18. Indicate any situation unique to this client that does not appear above.				

TAX-PLANNING CHECKLIST (continued)

Estate Planning

	At Present Yes	At Present No	Advisable Yes	Advisable No
1. Have the client and spouse considered electing not to fully use the marital deduction if such an election is tax advantageous to their cumulative estates? [§2056]	☐	☑	☐	☐
2. Have life insurance policies been properly positioned to minimize estate taxes?	☐	☑	☐	☐
3. Does the estate appear to have sufficient liquidity to fund postmortem expenses and estate/inheritance tax liabilities?	☐	☑	☐	☐
4. Has optimum use been made of generation-skipping transfer exemptions? [§§2601-2663]	☐	☑	☐	☐
5. Have testamentary charitable dispositions and their advantages been explored? [§2055]	☐	☑	☐	☐
6. Are lifetime gifting programs being used to shift ownership of assets from the client's estate? [§2503(b), 2503(c)]	☐	☑	☐	☐
7. a. Is the client's will current?	☐	☑	☐	☐
b. Does the will dispose of estate assets in accordance with the client's wishes?	☐	☑	☐	☐
8. Has the value of each estate asset been explored in order to obtain an estimate of potential estate tax liability?	☐	☑	☐	☐
9. Has it been determined that the client can qualify for estate tax deferral? [§6166]	☑	☐	☐	☐
10. If the client qualifies for the requisite percentage of ownership in a corporation, can §303 be utilized to assure sale-or-exchange treatment for stock redeemed to pay administration expenses and estate taxes? *N/A*	☐	☐	☐	☐
11. Have the client's personal planning objectives, feelings, and thoughts been given equal weight with tax planning?	☑	☐	☐	☐
12. Has an existing estate plan been evaluated as to the impact of the current unified credit, marital deduction, and gift tax exclusion? [§§2010, 2056, 2503, 2523]	☐	☑	☐	☐
13. Has consideration been given to the potential consequence of certain transfers made within 3 years of death? [§2035]	☐	☑	☐	☐
14. Have rules on valuation of certain property (e.g., family farms and real property used in a closely held business) been considered? [§2032A] *N/A*	☐	☐	☐	☐
15. a. Is there any reversionary interest or power of appointment not on the client's balance sheet?	☐	☑	☐	☐
b. If so, has it been examined for its potential tax impact? [§§2037, 2041]	☐	☑	☐	☐
16. Indicate any situation unique to this client that does not appear above.				

FINANCIAL POSITION STATEMENT

Assets		Projections for Subsequent Years			
Cash, Near-Cash Equivalents	Current Value	Assumptions	19____	19____	19____
Checking accounts/cash	4,000				
Savings accounts	8,000				
Money-market funds	4,900				
Treasury bills					
Commercial paper					
Short-term CDs					
Life insurance, cash value	15,000				
Life insurance, accumulated dividends					
Savings bonds					
Other (specify)					
Subtotal	31,900				
Other Financial Assets					
U.S. government bonds					
Municipal bonds					
Corporate bonds					
Preferred stock					
Common stock	24,200				
Nonmarketable securities					
Warrants and options					
Mutual funds	1,800				
Investment real estate					
Long-term CDs	21,000				
Vested retirement benefits	60,000				
Annuities					
HR-10 plan (Keogh)					
Individual retirement acct. (IRA)					
Mortgages owned					
Land contracts					
Limited partnership units					
Interest(s) in trust(s)	100,000*				
Receivables					
Patents, copyrights, royalties					
Value of business interest	125,000				
Other (specify)					
Subtotal	332,000				

*This trust corpus should be netted out of the client's total assets in order to determine a working net worth or the client's working capital position.

© 1984 The American College

35

FINANCIAL POSITION STATEMENT (continued)

Assets (continued)

Personal Assets	Current Value	Assumptions	19___	19___	19___
		Projections for Subsequent Years			
Personal residence	95,000	10% annual inc.			
Seasonal residence					
Automobile(s)	4,500				
Recreation vehicles					
Household furnishings	20,000	add $1,000 annually			
Boats					
Jewelry/furs					
Collections	28,000				
Hobby equipment					
Other (specify)					
Subtotal	147,500				
Total assets	511,400				

Liabilities

	Current Value	Assumptions	19___	19___	19___
Charge accts./credit cards	2,500				
Family/personal loans					
Margin/bank/life ins. loans					
Income taxes (fed., state, local) ✳	–0–				
Property taxes	2,500	8% annual increase			
Investment liabilities					
Mortgage(s)	48,000				
Child support	24,000				
Alimony					
Other (specify) partnership mortgage	37,000				
Other (specify)					
Other (specify)					
Other (specify)					
Total liabilities	114,000				

Net Worth

	Current Value				
Total assets minus total liabilities	397,400				

✳ Tax liabilities are funded by withholding and by quarterly estimated tax payments

INCOME AND LUMP-SUM RESOURCES FOR
DISABILITY, RETIREMENT, AND DEATH

Sources of Funds	For Disability			For Retirement			For Death		
	Lump-sum Pmts.	Monthly Income		Lump-sum Pmts.	Monthly Income		Lump-sum Pmts.	Monthly Income	
		Amount	Beginning/ Ending		Amount	Beginning/ Ending		Amount	Beginning/ Ending
Continuing income (p. 6)*		824①	1989 /?		824①			824①	1989 /?
Income of spouse		1,250	1989 /?		1,250			1,250	1989/?
Social security benefits		1,300	1989 /?		925	age 65	255	1,550②	1989 /?
Pension plan (TDA)					5,000	age 65		600③	1989 /?
Profit-sharing plan									
HR-10 plan (Keogh)									
Individual retirement account (IRA)									
Nonqualified deferred compensation									
Other retirement benefits/ deferred compensation									
Group life insurance							42,000	350⑤	1989 /?
Personal life insurance							125,000④		
Annuities									
Group short-term disability income									
Group long-term disability income		1,730	1990/?						
Personal disability income insurance									
Asset liquidation									
Proceeds of sale of business interest	liquidation value undetermined								
Other (specify)									
Other (specify)									
Other (specify)									
Totals		5,104			7,999		167,255	4,574	

*Be sure to adjust for income sources from p. 6 of the Fact Finder that will terminate or decrease if client or spouse dies, retires, or is disabled.

① includes Barbara's trust income
② amount will decrease as children reach cut-off ages
③ assumes 710% return on $60,000 balance; available amount may increase if another settlement option is chosen
④ payable to Stephanie and Caroline
⑤ assumes 10% return on proceeds

CHECKLIST FOR FINANCIAL PLANNING REVIEW

Change in	Has Occurred	Is Expected		Has Occurred	Is Expected
1. Marital status			9. Property ownership		
Marriage	☐	☐	Purchase in joint ownership	☐	☐
Separation	☐	☐	Purchase, client owned	☐	☐
Divorce	☐	☐	Purchase, spouse owned	☐	☐
Remarriage	☐	☐	Purchase, dependent owned	☐	☐
			Transfer to joint ownership	☐	☐
2. Number of dependents			Transfer to client	☐	☐
Increase	☐	☐	Transfer to spouse	☐	☐
Decrease	☐	☐	Transfer to dependent	☐	☐
			Transfer to trustee	☐	☐
3. Health status					
Client	☐	☐	10. Liabilities		
Spouse	☐	☐	Leases executed	☐	☐
Dependent	☐	☐	Mortgage increase	☐	☐
			Lawsuit against	☐	☐
4. Residence	☐	☐	Judgment against	☐	☐
			Unsecured borrowing	☐	☐
5. Occupation			Cosigning of notes	☐	☐
Client	☐	☐			
Spouse	☐	☐	11. Business ownership		
Dependent	☐	☐	New business formation	☐	☐
			Interest purchase	☐	☐
6. Family financial status			Sale of interest	☐	☐
Borrowing	☐	☐	Transfer of interest	☐	☐
Lending	☐	☐	Reorganization among owners	☐	☐
Gifts over $1,000 received	☐	☐	Liquidation	☐	☐
Gifts over $1,000 made	☐	☐	Change of carrier	☐	☐
Purchase of property	☐	☐	Termination or lapse	☐	☐
Sale of property	☐	☐	Surrender	☐	☐
Investments	☐	☐			
Inheritance	☐	☐	12. Legal document status		
Deferred income	☐	☐	Change in last will	☐	☐
Pension plan	☐	☐	Change in trust	☐	☐
Tax-deferred annuity	☐	☐	Buy-sell agreement	☐	☐
Dependent's income	☐	☐	Agreement to defer income	☐	☐
7. Sources of income			13. Insurance status		
As employee	☐	☐	Life insurance	☐	☐
From self-employment	☐	☐	Health insurance	☐	☐
From tax-exempt employer	☐	☐	Group insurance	☐	☐
From investments	☐	☐	Other employer plan	☐	☐
Inventions, patents, copyrights	☐	☐	Property insurance	☐	☐
Hobbies, avocations	☐	☐	Liability insurance	☐	☐
			Change of plan	☐	☐
8. Income tax status					
From single to joint return	☐	☐	14. Attitudes toward others		
From joint to single return	☐	☐	In family	☐	☐
Capital gains	☐	☐	In business	☐	☐
Capital losses	☐	☐	In accepting professional		
Substantial contributions	☐	☐	advice	☐	☐
Unreimbursed casualty loss	☐	☐			
Sick pay received	☐	☐	15. Interest in		
Unreimbursed medical			Idea previously discussed	☐	☐
expenses	☐	☐	Plans seen or heard about	☐	☐
Tax-impact investment(s)	☐	☐			

Income Tax Planning

James F. Ivers III*

INTRODUCTION

I am proud to be paying taxes in the United States. The only thing is — I could be just as proud for half the money.

Arthur Godfrey

It is said that the only things that are certain in life are death and taxes. Although death would seem to be more certain than anything, it's likely that even Houdini would have had trouble defying Uncle Sam. At the least, it would take a highly accomplished escape artist to evade both the federal income tax *and* a jail cell.

In any event, such extremes are not advisable, for a variety of legal, ethical, and moral reasons. Yet, it is perfectly acceptable (and perhaps even commendable) to use every legal means to minimize payment of the federal income tax.

This chapter will outline the most important basic concepts of our federal income tax law. It will not deal with advanced tax planning. It will provide, however, a firm grasp of fundamental concepts — always an excellent foundation to build upon. In other more advanced texts, such as those used in several CLU/ChFC courses, the student will become more familiar with techniques that are available to avoid paying taxes. Some of these tax-avoidance techniques (many call them loopholes) must be left to the experienced tax professional to recommend and implement.

However, a working knowledge of the tax law will enable the financial services professional to help clients, as well as to help the professional know what he or she knows or doesn't know. This will help make situations that call for a tax expert more recognizable. Therefore the purpose of this chapter is to explain basic income tax concepts, and to introduce the reader to the ways in which taxpayers can plan for tax avoidance.

THE PRINCIPLE OF GROSS INCOME

To learn about the federal income tax law, the student should begin with an understanding of the term *gross income.* Basically, gross income includes every item of value, whether consisting of money or other property, that is either made available to or comes into the possession of the taxpayer. In other words, anything of value is considered to be gross income for income tax purposes unless — and this *qualification* is very important — the Internal Revenue Code contains a specific provision that *excludes* a particular item from the taxpayer's gross income.

---

*James F. Ivers III, JD, LLM, is associate professor of taxation and director of the Huebner School at The American College.

This is why the provision in the Internal Revenue Code that provides the gross income rule is referred to as a "shotgun" clause. Although the provision lists 15 different items that are includible in a taxpayer's gross income, the provision states that gross income includes, *but is not limited to,* these items. Gross income means "all income from whatever source derived."

However, certain items of money or other property are not includible in a taxpayer's gross income. These items include gifts, income from tax-exempt bonds, worker's compensation benefits, and many other items. Such items are called *exclusions* from gross income. It is important to remember that the reason such items are excluded from a taxpayer's gross income is that there is a specific section in the Internal Revenue Code that says so. In other words, no item of money or other property can be excluded from gross income unless there is a Code provision stating that it is to be excluded. Therefore it is fairly simple in most cases to determine whether an item is includible in the taxpayer's gross income.

It is important to distinguish the concept of an *exclusion* from that of a *deduction* for tax purposes. An exclusion is an item of value that the taxpayer *receives* that is not includible in the taxpayer's gross income. A deduction, on the other hand, is an item of *expense* (not an item of receipt) which reduces the amount of income that is subject to tax.

> *Example:* Cheryl has the following items of income and expense for the current year: $35,000 in salary from her job as a paralegal, a $5,000 gift from her aunt, and an alimony payment of $3,000 to her former husband. The $35,000 of salary is includible in Cheryl's gross income. The $5,000 gift is not includible in her gross income because there is a provision in the Internal Revenue Code that says that gifts are not includible in the recipient's gross income. The $3,000 alimony payment is deductible from Cheryl's gross income in determining how much of Cheryl's income will actually be taxed, because the Internal Revenue Code contains a provision which states that alimony payments are generally deductible.

EXCLUSIONS FROM GROSS INCOME

There are many items which the Internal Revenue Code states are *excludible* from a taxpayer's gross income. Among these items are the following:

- gifts and inheritances
- income from certain bonds issued by states and municipalities
- worker's compensation benefits
- life insurance proceeds
- benefits paid from medical expense insurance policies
- social security benefits (for taxpayers below certain income levels)
- amounts received under certain dependent care assistance programs, group legal services programs, and educational assistance programs
- certain qualified scholarships

The specific rules determining how and to what extent these items are excludible from gross income are covered elsewhere, such as in The American College's course,

Income Taxation. At this point, it is important for the student to understand only the concept of an exclusion, and how exclusions are used in the overall process of computing an individual's tax liability. An item that is excludible generally does not have to be reported in any way on the taxpayer's return.

DEDUCTIONS

As previously stated, a deduction is an item of expense that reduces the amount of the taxpayer's income that is subject to tax. There are many different items that are *deductible* for federal income tax purposes. However, before some of these items are listed and explained, the concepts of *adjusted gross income* and *taxable income* should be understood.

Adjusted Gross Income

Adjusted gross income is an intermediate calculation that is made in the process of determining an individual's income tax liability for a given year. Why is such an intermediate calculation necessary or useful? For purposes of the tax law, adjusted gross income (AGI) is used as a base amount to determine how the taxpayer must treat certain *other* items for tax purposes. For example, adjusted gross income is used to calculate the maximum amount of charitable contributions that may be deducted by an individual in a given year (generally 50 percent of the individual's AGI).

Taxable Income

Taxable income is the amount of income that will actually be subject to tax in a given year. How does taxable income differ from adjusted gross income? Taxable income is the taxpayer's adjusted gross income, reduced by certain deductions that are taken only after the individual's adjusted gross income has been computed. In other words, in the computation of an individual's tax liability, there are two basic types of deductions. The first type consists of those deductions that are subtracted from gross income to determine AGI. The second type consists of those deductions that are subtracted from AGI to determine taxable income. The first type are often referred to as *above-the-line deductions,* while the second type are often referred to as *below-the-line deductions.*

What is the significance of this distinction? There are two basic reasons why the distinction is important. The first is that above-the-line deductions will change how certain *other* items on the individual's return are treated. This is so because, as previously stated, AGI is used as a base for defining or limiting how and to what extent certain other items may be excluded or deducted on the individual's return. The second reason relates to the concept of the standard deduction.

The Standard Deduction

The standard deduction is a fixed amount, indexed for inflation, which the individual may claim in lieu of claiming itemized deductions on Schedule A of Form 1040. *Itemized deductions,* or deductions which are taken on Schedule A, include charitable contributions, deductions for interest payments, taxes, casualty losses, certain business expenses of employees, and other items. The amount of the standard deduction depends upon whether the individual is filing the return as a single taxpayer, an unmarried head of household, a married taxpayer filing jointly, or a married taxpayer filing separately. For 1990, the standard deduction amounts are as follows:

Single taxpayers:	$3,250
Married filing jointly:	$5,450
Married filing separately:	$2,725
Heads of household:	$4,750

If the individual is entitled to claim itemized deductions which, when added together, are more than the amount of his or her standard deduction, then the individual will deduct his or her itemized deductions and not claim the standard deduction.

Example: Valerie has $3,000 of home mortgage interest payments, and $1,000 of real property taxes on her personal residence this year. Both of these items are deductible as itemized deductions on Schedule A of Form 1040. Valerie's standard deduction amount this year is $3,250. Valerie will deduct her interest and tax payments and not claim the standard deduction, because the total of these payments ($4,000) is greater than her standard deduction amount ($3,250).

All itemized deductions are below-the-line deductions (deductions taken in calculating taxable income). However, if these items were above-the-line deductions (deductions taken in determining adjusted gross income rather than taxable income), Valerie would deduct these items *regardless* of whether she claimed the standard deduction. Valerie could take the standard deduction *in addition to* her other deductions. This is the second important difference between above-the-line and below-the-line deductions. The first type are deductible regardless of whether the individual claims the standard deduction. The second type may be claimed only in lieu of the standard deduction.

Categories of Deductions

Before we discuss the various types of deductions that are allowable under federal tax law, it is important to remember that a deduction may be claimed only if there is a specific provision in the Internal Revenue Code that allows it. If there is no provision in the Code regarding a given item, no deduction may be claimed for that item.

Stated broadly, there are three basic categories of deductions allowable to individual taxpayers. The first category includes deductions for expenses that are incurred in the course of carrying on a trade or business. For example, the cost of employees' salaries or advertising would fall into this category. These are referred to as business deductions. The second basic category includes deductions for expenses that are incurred in the course of an activity that is not a trade or business, but is engaged in for the purpose of producing income and making a profit. An example of a deduction falling into this category is an expense incurred in connection with the maintenance of a taxpayer's investments, such as a fee for investment advice. The third basic category includes deductions for expenses that are simply personal, family, or living expenses. Although the Code provides a general rule that these expenses are nondeductible, there are several important exceptions to the general rule. Personal expenses that *are* deductible include charitable contributions, medical expense deductions, and home mortgage interest payments. However, many of these personal deductions are subject to limitations as to what and how much can be deducted.

Whenever the client or adviser is determining whether a given item of expense is deductible, certain questions should always be asked. Obviously, the first and most basic question is whether the Code allows a deduction for the item. A second important question is what basic category the expense falls under; in other words, whether it is a business expense, an expense for the production of income, or a personal expense. A third question is whether the deduction is an above-the-line or below-the-line deduction. It is always important for tax planning purposes to know where an item will appear on the individual's tax return.

A fourth question that should be asked is whether there is a particular restriction or limitation on the deductibility of the item. For example, certain deductions such as the medical expense deduction and the casualty loss deduction are subject to a *floor*. This floor is based upon a percentage of the taxpayer's adjusted gross income. If the taxpayer's expenses in a given category are less than the applicable floor, no deduction will actually be allowed for the expenses.

> *Example:* Trish has medical expenses of $5,000 this year. Medical expenses are deductible, but only to the extent they exceed 7.5 percent of the taxpayer's adjusted gross income. Trish's adjusted gross income this year is $70,000. Although Trish has $5,000 of medical expenses, her deduction for these expenses is zero because the amount of the expenses ($5,000) is less than 7.5 percent of her adjusted gross income ($5,250).

Other types of restrictions may apply to particular deduction items. For example, cash contributions to a public charity are generally deductible, but only up to a maximum of 50 percent of an individual's adjusted gross income for any given year. Contributions in excess of that amount must be carried over to future taxable years. In the case of charitable contributions, the individual's adjusted gross income provides a *ceiling* for the deduction, rather than a floor.

Another type of restriction that may apply to a deduction is a dollar-amount restriction. An example of this restriction is the rule for deducting interest payments on a taxpayer's first mortgage on his or her principal residence. Generally, such payments are deductible, but only with respect to a maximum of $1 million of loan principal. If the first mortgage exceeds $1 million, a corresponding portion of the interest deduction is disallowed. Note that in the case of the deduction for home mortgage interest, the dollar amount limitation is based upon the amount of the loan principal, not the amount of the interest expense itself. Another example of a dollar-amount limitation is the $2,000 limitation on deductible individual retirement account (IRA) contributions which may be claimed by individuals who are not covered by employer-provided retirement plans, and by certain other individuals whose income falls within specified ranges.

Yet another type of restriction on the deductibility of certain expenses is a percentage limitation. For example, business entertainment expenses are generally deductible, but the deduction is limited to 80 percent of the actual expenses.

There are many other ways in which the Internal Revenue Code limits the claiming of deductions. Students who take an interest in the income tax law can learn about these various restrictions, limitations, and qualifications in American College courses such as Income Taxation.

Depreciation: A Special Type of Deduction

Not all tax deductions represent actual out-of-pocket expenses. Some deductions are allowable even though they represent no corresponding cash outlay. These are often referred to as *paper deductions,* because they represent or are related to some entry on the books of a taxpayer's business or investment activity, but they are not a cash flow item.

What is the nature of these items? And why are they allowable as deductions against a taxpayer's income? What these items represent is a measure of a gradual decrease in the value or usefulness of property owned by the taxpayer. But they are only an arbitrary measure of such a decrease in value or usefulness. They are not a real-life measure of such a decrease.

The most important noncash deduction is the deduction for depreciation. The depreciation deduction allows a taxpayer to recover the cost of certain property for tax purposes by allowing the taxpayer to deduct a specified portion of the cost of the property each year against the taxpayer's income. The reason why such a deduction is allowed is that the cost of property that is used in business or for income-producing purposes should be deductible, but the deduction should be spread out over the useful life of the property.

Generally, capital expenditures, such as those made for the purchase of a building or piece of equipment, are not deductible for income tax purposes. This is so because a capital expenditure is not considered to be an operating expense of a business, but a more long-term investment in an asset. As such, the capital expenditure would normally be recovered for tax purposes only when the asset is sold. In other words, the amount of the capital expenditure becomes the taxpayer's *tax basis* in the asset. This basis will be subtracted from the amount realized when the asset is sold to determine how much of the sale proceeds should be taxed.

But the depreciation deduction allows the taxpayer to deduct portions of the capital expenditure *before* the asset is sold, that is, on an annual basis. The theory is that the asset experiences wear and tear while it is being used by the taxpayer, and therefore there should be a deduction allowed for such wear and tear. However, in reality, the asset might actually be *appreciating* in real economic terms in spite of the wear and tear it is experiencing. This can happen with many types of assets, but is particularly common with real estate. In such a situation, the taxpayer is receiving a tax deduction which is supposed to represent a *decrease* in the property's value, while the property is actually *increasing* in value.

Any depreciation deductions claimed with respect to an asset are subtracted from the taxpayer's *income tax basis* in the asset. This means that when the asset is sold later, the amount of depreciation deducted is, in effect, recouped by the government because the portion of the sales proceeds that is taxable will be increased. But, in the meantime, the taxpayer has enjoyed the economic benefit of the tax deductions for depreciation. The concept of basis will be discussed in more detail later in this chapter.

Because depreciation is a deduction that often does not represent economic reality, there is an element of social policy behind its presence in the tax law. That policy is to stimulate investment in business assets and assets held for the production of income.

What types of assets are eligible for this *cost recovery* that results from the depreciation deduction? There are two basic requirements. The first is that the asset must be used either in the taxpayer's business or in some other activity intended to produce income for the taxpayer. Assets held for personal use are not eligible for the deduction. The second requirement is that the asset must have a limited useful life in order to qualify. This requirement explains why land, for example, does not qualify for a depreciation deduction. Land is considered to be an asset that does not wear out.

There are some fairly complicated rules which determine how much of a qualifying asset's cost can be claimed each year as a depreciation deduction. These rules are based upon two factors: the number of years over which the cost of the asset will be deducted, and the percentage of the cost of the asset that will be deducted each year. The details are beyond the scope of this chapter. In summary, however, it is fair to say that the depreciation deduction is especially beneficial to taxpayers because it allows them to save tax dollars without a corresponding cash outlay in the year of the tax saving.

PERSONAL AND DEPENDENCY EXEMPTIONS

Each individual taxpayer is allowed to claim a personal exemption for himself or herself. A married couple filing jointly may claim an exemption for each spouse. The amount of the exemption or exemptions is subtracted from adjusted gross income in the process of computing taxable income. Personal exemptions are *not* itemized deductions claimed on Schedule A of Form 1040, however. Therefore either the standard deduction or itemized deductions may be claimed in addition to the taxpayer's exemptions. Individual taxpayers are also permitted to claim an additional exemption for each *dependent* individual who is supported by the taxpayer. There are strict rules regarding whom a taxpayer may claim as a dependent and under what circumstances. In 1990, the *amount* of the exemption is $2,050. This amount is subject to indexing for inflation in all succeeding years.

TAX RATES

Once the taxpayer's gross income has been determined, all deductions allowable in determining adjusted gross income are subtracted from gross income. Next, all deductions and exemptions allowable in determining taxable income are subtracted from adjusted gross income. The resulting figure is the taxpayer's taxable income. This is the figure to which the income tax rates are applied to determine the amount of income tax payable for the year.

The rate structure in effect under current law is based upon two tax rates: a 15 percent rate and a 28 percent rate. However, a 5 percent *surtax* is applied to certain ranges of taxable income that would otherwise be subject to the 28 percent rate. This results in a 33 percent rate that will be applicable to many taxpayers. This so-called surtax is designed to apply to upper-income taxpayers. For such taxpayers, the effect of the surtax is to eliminate the benefit of the 15 percent rate as compared to the 28 percent rate (a 13 percentage point differential), and also to eliminate the tax benefits resulting from the taxpayer's personal and dependency exemptions. In other words, the 33 percent rate or *bracket* is a method of eliminating personal and dependency exemptions, as well as the 15 percent rate, for upper-income taxpayers. The intent of the law is to tax such individuals (albeit in a roundabout way) at a flat rate of 28 percent.

For individual taxpayers, a 15 percent rate is first applied to a specified amount or bracket of taxable income. Then the 28 percent rate is applied to the next bracket of income. For taxpayers with taxable income above a specified amount, the 33 percent rate is then applied to the next bracket. The rate applicable to each successively higher income bracket is called the *marginal tax rate*. The amount of income taxed at each marginal rate is called the *marginal tax bracket*. If the taxpayer has enough income taxed at the 33 percent rate to allow the 5 percent surtax to recover the benefit of the 15 percent rate *and* the taxpayer's exemptions, the net effect is that *all* taxable income, plus the total amount "sheltered" by the taxpayer's personal and dependency exemptions, has been taxed at an *effective rate* of 28 percent. The effective rate of tax really means the taxpayer's *average* tax rate, as distinguished from his or her marginal tax rate.

What are the brackets of taxable income to which the various rates are applied? The answer depends upon the individual's *filing status*. As previously mentioned, an individual taxpayer is categorized within one of four filing status categories: a single taxpayer, a married taxpayer filing jointly, a married taxpayer filing separately, or an unmarried head of household. The amount of taxable income that will fall into each tax bracket depends upon the individual's filing status.

For 1990, the tax brackets (without regard to the surtax for the taxpayer's personal and dependency exemptions) for each filing status are as follows:

Filing Status	15% Bracket	28% Bracket	33% Bracket	28% Bracket
Single	$0–$19,450	$19,451–$47,050	$47,051–$97,620	over $ 97,620
Married filing jointly	$0–$32,450	$32,451–$78,400	$78,401–$162,770	over $162,770
Married filing separately	$0–$16,225	$16,226–$39,200	$39,201–$123,750	over $123,750
Unmarried head of household	$0–$26,050	$26,051–$67,200	$67,201–$134,930	over $134,930

When examining these brackets, it is important to note that an *additional* amount of taxable income will fall into the 33 percent bracket. The actual *end* of the 33 percent bracket depends upon how many personal and dependency exemptions are claimed by the taxpayer.

TAX CREDITS

Once the tax rates have been applied to an individual's taxable income, the resulting figure is the individual's tentative tax. However, this tentative tax can be reduced if the individual is eligible to claim any income tax credits.

It is important to understand the difference between a tax *deduction* and a tax *credit.* As explained earlier, a deduction is an item of expense that reduces the amount of income that is subject to tax. A credit, on the other hand, is a dollar-for-dollar reduction of the actual tax payable. Therefore a tax credit, if available, is of more value to the taxpayer than a deduction of an equal amount.

> *Example:* JoAnne has $90,000 of adjusted gross income this year. She has a deduction of $5,000 for her home mortgage interest payments. JoAnne is also entitled to claim a tax credit of $5,000 for rehabilitation work she performed on a certified historic structure which she owns. Assume JoAnne's marginal tax rate is 33 percent. Her deduction reduces her income subject to tax by $5,000, thereby resulting in a tax savings of $1,650 ($5,000 × .33). However, her tax credit is applied *directly* to her tentative tax, thereby resulting in a tax savings equal to the amount of the credit, $5,000.

THE ALTERNATIVE MINIMUM TAX (AMT)

The AMT is a *separate* and *parallel* system of income taxation to the regular system. It applies to any taxpayer whose tax liability under the parallel system is greater than the liability for that year under the regular income tax system. In other words, the taxpayer pays the AMT amount if the AMT is greater than the regular tax. Therefore it follows that the computational process for determining the AMT is a different process from that used in determining the regular tax. The deduction rules are different. The credit rules are different. The tax rates are different.

The purpose of the AMT is to make certain that taxpayers who enjoy certain tax benefits will not be permitted to reduce their tax liability below a minimum amount by claiming certain tax deductions. For example, one thing that the AMT rules do is to add back certain deductions for AMT purposes that are allowable to the taxpayer for regular tax purposes. These items that are deductible for the regular tax, but face different rules under the AMT, are referred to as *tax preference items.* These items generally produce no benefit to the taxpayer under the AMT system as they would under the regular system.

The tax rate under the AMT system is a flat rate applied to income subject to the AMT. For individuals, this rate is 21 percent. For corporations, it is 20 percent. Note that although the AMT tax *rates* are lower than in the regular system, the tax *payable* may be greater. If so, the AMT must be paid instead of the regular tax.

For purposes of this chapter, the student should simply be aware that the AMT tax system exists, and that certain taxpayers with certain types of deductions will be subject to it. The details for calculating the AMT and the various rules for determining what goes in and out of the AMT tax base are found in the texts for more advanced tax courses. A basic understanding of these rules is important for the financial services professional.

CONCEPT OF THE TAXABLE YEAR

Individuals file tax returns on an annual basis. For the vast majority of individuals, income tax is calculated based upon a calendar-year period. However, many partnerships and corporations (as well as a small number of individuals) report their tax liability based upon a 12-month period that does not coincide with the calendar year. Such a period is referred to as a fiscal year. In the past, the use of a fiscal year for tax purposes by a business entity provided an opportunity for deferring taxable income. This was accomplished by paying or crediting income to a partner or shareholder in the beginning of a calendar year that was actually earned by the business during its fiscal year, which began several months before the onset of the calendar year. However, such techniques have been virtually eliminated by strict new rules governing the election of a fiscal year for tax purposes.

THREE IMPORTANT ISSUES

The preceding material has been an overview of the process by which an individual's tax liability is computed. To more fully understand the income tax system, it is helpful to think about three basic issues in addition to understanding the computation process. These three issues are (1) what is taxed? (2) to whom is it taxed? and (3) when is it taxed? There are important tax law doctrines that clarify each of these issues.

The What Question: The Economic Benefit Doctrine

The question of *what* is taxed has already been discussed in the section of this chapter that describes the concept of gross income. In general, anything of value received by the taxpayer is taxed. Any event or transaction which confers an economic benefit upon the taxpayer will result in gross income to the taxpayer, so long as the economic benefit is certain and can be measured. For example, suppose the Carroll Corporation sets up a trust for one of its key employees, Toby. The terms of the trust provide that in 2 years Toby will receive $20,000 a year for a 10-year period. Toby's right to the money is nonforfeitable and the trust assets are not otherwise available to the Carroll Corporation in any way. Even though Toby is not receiving any money currently, the Carroll Corporation has conferred an economic benefit upon Toby that is certain and can be measured using time-value-of-money calculations. Therefore Toby will be taxed currently on the present value of the payments to be made in the future. Note that the result would be different if the payments were contingent upon the rendering of future services by Toby, or if the assets of the trust were available to the Carroll Corporation or its creditors for use other than to pay Toby. This is an example of the *economic benefit* doctrine, which holds that a taxpayer must pay tax whenever an economic benefit has been conferred on the taxpayer, regardless of whether the taxpayer has actually received any cash or property. Another example of the application of this doctrine is the case in which an employer pays life insurance premiums on a policy covering the life of an employee who has the right to name the beneficiary under the policy. The employer in such a case has conferred an economic benefit upon the employee (life insurance coverage) which is subject to income tax.

The To Whom Question: The Doctrine of the Fruit and the Tree

There are many types of assets that produce income that is taxed. The asset producing the income may be a corporate bond that pays interest. Or it may be a piece of real estate that generates rental income. Or it may be an individual, whose knowledge or expertise generates income from sales or services. In any event, the tax principle that applies is this: Income is to be taxed to the person who *earns* it, or to the person who *owns* the *asset* that produces it. In other words, for income tax purposes, the "fruit" comes from the "tree" that produced it, and must be taxed accordingly.

> *Example:* Sandra owns a $1,000 bond issued by the Merlin Corporation. Sandra clips the interest coupons from the bond and gives them to her son, Brett. Brett receives the interest income. Sandra retains ownership of the bond itself. In spite of the fact that Brett has received the income, Sandra is still taxed on it because she owns the asset that produced the income.

Similarly, income from personal services is taxed to the person who earns it. The fruits of an individual's labor cannot be assigned to another individual for tax purposes. For example, assume an insurance agent irrevocably assigns in writing her right to future commissions from one of her client's policies to her daughter. Will her daughter be taxed on the income? The answer is no. The individual who earned the income must be taxed on it. This principle is often referred to as the doctrine of *assignment of income.*

The When Question: The Doctrine of Constructive Receipt

The current use of money is valuable. Therefore if taxation can be deferred, the taxpayer gains a monetary benefit through the use of tax money until it is paid to the government later. As a result, taxpayers may try to use techniques which defer the receipt of income until a later tax year in order to defer the payment of tax on the income. An important doctrine which limits the use of such techniques is referred to as the doctrine of *constructive receipt.*

Under the doctrine of constructive receipt, the taxpayer is deemed to have received income for tax purposes when it is either credited to the taxpayer's account, set apart for the taxpayer, or otherwise made available to be taken into the taxpayer's possession.

Example: John, a life insurance agent, filed a policy application with his company in November of last year. In December, the policy was issued, and a commission check was made out to John. John did not pick up the check until January of this year, even though he could have easily picked it up in December. John must report this income on last year's tax return under the doctrine of constructive receipt, even though John did not *actually* receive the income until this year.

It is important to know, however, that if there is any condition or restriction that limits the taxpayer's right to receive the income, the doctrine of constructive receipt will not apply.

Example: Natalie is a real estate agent. In November of last year, her client signed an agreement to purchase a home the client listed with Natalie. The sale is closed on January 2 of this year. Although Natalie was fairly certain in November that she would receive her commission, the client still had to go through with the closing in order for Natalie's rights to her money to become unconditional. Therefore the doctrine of constructive receipt does not apply to Natalie and she will be taxed on the commission in the year she actually receives it.

BASIC INCOME TAX PLANNING CONCEPTS

Although the Tax Reform Act of 1986 was highly touted as a breakthrough in simplifying the federal income tax system, much complexity remains in the understanding and application of the Internal Revenue Code. Because of this complexity, many highly intelligent people devote their professional lives to the process of trying to figure out how the Code can be analyzed (and, in some cases, manipulated) to save some tax money for their clients. This is fine and good, as long as the tax is saved through tax *avoidance* (reasonable interpretation of the tax laws), and not through tax *evasion* (ignoring or flouting the tax laws).

As previously stated, sophisticated tax planning is not the subject of this chapter. However, it should be helpful to outline some of the basic concepts that are used in tax planning to illustrate how tax lawyers and other tax professionals think in their efforts to help clients.

Income and Deduction Shifting

The purpose behind income-shifting techniques is this: Get taxable income into the hands of a taxpayer who is in a lower tax bracket than the taxpayer who would otherwise have to report the income. The result is that less tax is paid on the income. For example, a taxpayer in the 33 percent marginal tax bracket will pay $3,300 in tax on $10,000 of income. However, a taxpayer in the 15 percent bracket will pay only $1,500 of tax on the same $10,000 of income. Expressed as a percentage, the lower bracket taxpayer pays 55 percent less tax on the same income than would the higher-bracket taxpayer. Although the tax rates are much more compressed than they were before the Tax Reform Act of 1986, income shifting can still provide substantial savings.

What, then, are some of the income-shifting techniques that are available? Perhaps the simplest one is an outright gift of property. As previously discussed, income is taxed to the person who owns the asset that produces the income. If the asset is transferred by gift, the donee will be taxed on income generated by the asset. However, the *gift* tax consequences of giving away property to shift the *income* tax burden must always be considered. Gift taxes are introduced in chapter 6 of this text.

For planning purposes, the converse of income shifting is deduction shifting. Deduction shifting is a simple, yet frequently overlooked, planning technique. Here, the idea is to shift deductions to a taxpayer who is in a higher tax bracket than the taxpayer who would otherwise claim the deduction. As a result, the deduction is taken against income that would be taxed in a higher bracket, thereby resulting in a greater tax savings.

> *Example:* Marjorie is ill and must enter the hospital for an extended stay. The cost of her care is only partially covered by insurance. Although Marjorie has some assets, she is not working and does not have much income. Her mother, Ruth, is in the 33 percent tax bracket and also has enough medical expenses of her own this year to claim a medical expense deduction. Marjorie is Ruth's dependent for tax purposes, and therefore, Ruth can deduct medical expense payments she makes for Marjorie's care. If Ruth pays for Marjorie's care, there will be a tax savings of 33 cents for every dollar of expense. If on the other hand Marjorie paid for her own expenses, there would be little or no tax savings.

Avoiding Limitations on Deductions

As was explained earlier in this chapter, although many types of expenses are deductible for income tax purposes, there may be limitations on how much of a given expense may actually be deducted. One common way that the law limits deductions is through the use of a *deduction floor.* You will recall that the taxpayer is allowed to deduct items that are subject to the floor, but only to the extent those items *exceed* a specified percentage of income (specifically, adjusted gross income in most cases).

For example, there is an entire group of deductions that are claimed by individual taxpayers on Schedule A of Form 1040 that are referred to as *miscellaneous itemized deductions.* This group of deductions includes employee business expenses, fees for safe deposit boxes, fees for investment and individual tax advice, and several other items. First, all of the taxpayer's deductions that fall within this group are added together. Then, the taxpayer's adjusted gross income is multiplied by 2 percent. The resulting figure is subtracted from the total of the items in the group to determine how much the taxpayer can actually deduct. The result is that the taxpayer is permitted to deduct miscellaneous itemized deductions only to the extent they exceed this 2 percent floor.

How can taxpayers avoid this floor? With respect to some deductions that fall within this category, it is impossible to avoid the floor itself. However, if adjusted gross income can be *reduced* in a year in which the taxpayer has these items, a greater portion of the items will be deductible, since the floor will be less. How, then, can AGI be reduced? By maximizing above-the-line deductions, as previously discussed. If a taxpayer has miscellaneous itemized deductions, and wishes to minimize the impact of the 2 percent floor, it may be appropriate to *bunch* the taxpayer's above-the-line deductions into a given year to reduce AGI. Conversely, it may also be helpful to bunch a greater amount of the miscellaneous itemized deductions subject to the floor into one year. The result of this technique would be that some deductions which would be lost under the floor if claimed in next year's return can actually be deducted if taken this year, because the floor has already been exceeded.

Other deductions that are subject to a floor include the medical expense deduction (7.5 percent of AGI) and the deduction for personal casualty losses (10 percent of AGI).

> *Example:* Lynn, who is the sole proprietor of a small business, accidentally rinses her diamond ring down the drain this year. Lynn's husband paid $10,000 for the ring as an anniversary present. Lynn and her husband file a joint return and are in the 33 percent tax bracket. The ring is not insured. Lynn and her husband have $60,000 of AGI for the year. Therefore $6,000 of their casualty loss deduction will be lost under the 10 percent floor ($60,000 × .10). However, if Lynn made a deductible contribution of $5,000 to her Keogh account this year, the couple's adjusted gross income would be reduced to $55,000. Then, only $5,500 of the casualty loss deduction would be lost under the floor ($5,500 × .10). As a result, the Keogh contribution produces a tax savings of $165 ($500 × .33) in addition to the tax benefit produced by the Keogh contribution itself.

Deferral and Acceleration Techniques

Deferral of income and acceleration of deductions are basic and common tax planning techniques. These techniques are based upon the time value of money. If income can be deferred to a later year, the tax payable on the income is also deferred and the taxpayer has the use of that money for a longer time. Similarly, if deductible expenses are accelerated into an earlier tax year, the tax saving from those deductions is realized sooner, thereby giving the taxpayer the use of that money sooner. However, it is important to note that most tax deductions are attributable to actual out-of-pocket expenses. Therefore the expense itself involves the loss of use of money, which over the same time period will be greater than the benefit realized by the tax savings. The point is to not let the tax "tail" wag the overall financial "dog."

What, then, is the potential benefit of accelerating deductions? The benefit lies in a differential with respect to the comparative time periods. For example, if a taxpayer makes a deductible expense in December of this year rather than in January of next year, the taxpayer has lost the use of the money spent only for one additional month. However, the tax savings generated by the expense gives the taxpayer the use of the tax savings for an entire additional year, as compared to making the expense in January. In such a situation, the taxpayer does in fact gain a net benefit from accelerating the expense.

Example: Harry makes a $10,000 deductible business expense in December of this year. Harry's marginal tax bracket is 33 percent. By making the expenditure in December of this year rather than January of next year, Harry postpones the payment of $3,300 in taxes ($10,000 × .33) for one year. Assume Harry can invest money for one year at 8 percent annual interest. Harry will have $264 ($3,300 × .08) that he would not have if he had deferred the expense until next year. However, by paying the $10,000 in December instead of January, Harry loses one month's interest on the $10,000. This amount is $67 [($10,000 × .08) ÷ 12]. But note that Harry is still ahead $197 ($264 − $67) by accelerating the deductible expense and, in effect, deferring the payment of taxes on $10,000 of income for one year.

The Passive Loss Rules

There are special limitations on the deductibility of so-called *passive losses.* These tax losses are typically generated by activities in which the taxpayer has an ownership interest, but does not participate in the activity of the business. For example, suppose a taxpayer owns an interest in a limited partnership which invests in rental real estate. Assume that the depreciation deductions and other deductions generated by the partnership properties exceed the income generated by the properties. Therefore for tax purposes, the partnership generates losses.

Under tax laws in effect before the Tax Reform Act of 1986, there were few limitations on the deductibility of such items by taxpayers owning interests in limited partnerships and other activities in which the taxpayer did not participate. Because these investments allowed taxpayers to *write off* the tax losses against salary and other types of income, they were referred to as *tax shelters.* Tax shelters were a very important weapon in the tax avoidance arsenal.

Under current law, however, there are strict limitations on the deductibility of losses generated by tax-shelter investments. These rules are intended to prevent taxpayers from investing in activities merely for tax purposes, as distinguished from the actual economics of the investment. There are complicated rules and definitions as to what constitutes a passive activity that will be subject to the strict deduction rules. The basic rule, however, is that tax losses generated by passive activities can be deducted only against income generated by the taxpayer's passive activities, and not against salary or other income of the taxpayer.

There are qualifications, exceptions, and certain significant loopholes to these rules. This is one of those areas of the tax law that is a specialty in itself. In fact, some specialists in this area have trouble understanding the rules, which are complicated by hundreds of pages of Treasury regulations. For purposes of this chapter, the student should simply be aware that if a taxpayer invests in an activity in which the taxpayer does not participate, and the activity generates tax losses, the deductibility of those losses is limited by some very strict rules. Activities which are deemed to be passive include most rental activities in which the taxpayer owns an interest. However, investments in publicly traded stocks and bonds are not covered by these rules, because these are not the type of investments that usually produce tax losses on an annual basis.

Tax-Exempt Transactions

Perhaps one of the best types of tax planning techniques is that of creating a transaction which produces a monetary benefit without the taxpayer being taxed on that transaction. Within this general category there are two basic types of transactions. The first is where taxation is altogether *eliminated,* and the second is where taxation of the transaction is merely *deferred.* The first type can be described as a tax-exempt transaction. Such transactions are generally based upon some specific exclusion from gross income.

An example of a tax-exempt transaction is the receipt of income from a public purpose municipal bond. The income from such bonds is excludible from the taxpayer's gross income for federal income tax purposes. You will remember that *all* income is includible in gross income unless there is a provision in the Code which specifically excludes it. There is such an exclusion for certain municipal bond income (IRC Sec. 103).

Financial market forces generally dictate that unless the taxpayer is in the highest income tax bracket (currently 28 or 33 percent), the interest rate on such bonds will not be higher than the aftertax rate on taxable obligations. Therefore such investments are generally of interest only to higher-bracket taxpayers.

Another example of a tax-exempt monetary gain is the exclusion of the first $125,000 of gain on the sale of a personal residence by a taxpayer aged 55 or over.

Nonrecognition Transactions

There are many types of transactions in which taxation is merely deferred, rather than eliminated. These transactions may generally be referred to as *nonrecognition transactions.* Typically, such a transaction involves the sale or exchange of property at a gain realized by the taxpayer. However, because of a provision in the Internal Revenue Code, the *realized* gain is not currently *recognized* (reportable on Form 1040).

How do such transactions merely *defer,* rather than *eliminate,* taxable gain? In order to understand the mechanics of the nonrecognition transaction, the basic tax treatment of a sale or exchange of property must be understood.

Computation of Gain or Loss

When property is sold, it is necessary to determine what portion of the sale proceeds will be subject to taxation. In general, the gain realized from a sale of property is equal to the total amount realized from the sale, minus the taxpayer's *basis* in the property.

What does the term *basis* mean? Broadly stated, basis is the amount that the taxpayer has invested in the property. Therefore basis is generally the amount that the taxpayer paid for the property, plus the cost of any improvements to the property.

Stated another way, the basis of property is generally equal to its cost. As a result, the gain realized from a sale of property is the sale price minus the taxpayer's cost.

> *Example:* Nancy bought 1,000 shares of stock in Cleanseco, Inc., a household cleanser manufacturer, in 1988. She paid $5,000 for the stock. In 1990, she sells the Cleanseco stock for $10,000. The amount realized from the sale is $10,000. Nancy's basis is $5,000. Therefore the realized gain from the sale is $5,000 ($10,000 − $5,000).

The fact that the portion of the sales price which represents a recovery of the taxpayer's *basis* is not taxable illustrates a basic principle of tax law, namely, that money received which represents a *return of capital* is not treated as gross income. The Internal Revenue Code contains many provisions which reflect this basic principle. It is really a matter of common sense: Getting back money which the taxpayer has invested in property should not result in taxation because there has been no profit returned to the taxpayer, only the original investment.

How Nonrecognition Transactions Differ from Taxable Transactions

Some sales and exchanges are governed by specific provisions in the Internal Revenue Code which provide that the gain *realized* shall not be *recognized* (that is, reported on Form 1040 and taxed). It has been stated above that the purpose of these transactions is not to *eliminate* taxation, but merely to *defer* it. How is this accomplished?

The answer to this question relates to the taxpayer's basis in property. Generally, a taxpayer's basis in property is equal to the cost of the property. In the case of an exchange of property, the taxpayer's cost for the property received in the exchange is really the fair market value of the property surrendered in the exchange. However, if the exchange is one in which gain is not recognized, the taxpayer's basis in the new property will generally be the *same* as the taxpayer's basis in the old property. This preserves the unrecognized gain and allows that gain to be taxed when the *new* property is later sold in a taxable transaction.

> *Example:* Robert owns a condominium which he holds as a rental property. He paid $100,000 for the property and added $20,000 worth of improvements. The value of the property is now $180,000. Robert exchanges the property for another condominium in a transaction which qualifies for nonrecognition treatment under the Internal Revenue Code. The property received in the exchange is also worth $180,000. Robert's realized gain is $60,000 ($180,000 value of property received minus $120,000 basis in property given up). Robert's recognized gain is zero because the exchange qualifies for nonrecognition treatment. However, Robert's basis in the new property will be the same as his basis in the old property ($120,000). As a result, if the new property is sold later, the gain that would have been recognized if the exchange was taxable earlier will be recognized *later,* when the new property is sold. On the other hand, if the exchange was taxable, Robert would pay tax currently on the $60,000 of gain, but he would have a basis of $180,000 in the new property.

Clearly, the *deferral* of taxation in such a transaction has significant value. Moreover, the deferred gain may never be taxed if the taxpayer does not sell the property received in the exchange later. The intent of the nonrecognition provisions is merely to defer taxation. But there is no assurance that Uncle Sam will ever get his tax money, particularly if the taxpayer keeps the new property until death.

The example above is just one type of transaction that qualifies for nonrecognition. Other examples include exchanges of insurance policies and certain sales of a taxpayer's principal residence. These transactions, and the specific rules which govern their tax treatment, are beyond the scope of this chapter.

Transactions That Result in a Taxable Loss

Some sales of property will result in a loss, rather than a gain, to the selling taxpayer. This will happen when the amount received for the property is less than the taxpayer's basis in the property. In such cases, the amount of the loss will generally be deductible for income tax purposes if the property sold is either business property or property held for the production of income. If the property is held for personal use, the loss resulting from a sale of the property is generally nondeductible.

Example: Alexandra owns stock in the Hi-Five Corporation, a publicly traded corporation that sells sneakers. Alexandra paid $5,000 for the stock 2 years ago. This year, she sells the stock for $3,500. Alexandra has a realized loss of $1,500 ($5,000 basis minus $3,500 amount realized). Alexandra may deduct the $1,500 loss on her tax return this year.

Ordinary versus Capital Gain and Loss

Some different rules apply to sales of a taxpayer's assets, depending upon whether the gain or loss is treated as an *ordinary* gain or loss or a *capital* gain or loss.

Capital Gain versus Ordinary Income

As most financial services professionals know, one of the most important pieces of the federal tax law puzzle is the broad scope of social policy considerations. In other words, what politicians perceive to be a policy that will get them elected often finds its way into the tax laws. One of the policy issues that is a continuous source of controversy and change is the question of whether *capital gain* should be taxed at the same rates as *ordinary income.*

What is the difference between capital gain and ordinary income? Basically, capital gain is income that is realized through the sale or exchange of a capital asset. The definition of a capital asset does appear in the Internal Revenue Code, although the Code defines a capital asset by stating what it is *not,* rather than what it *is.* In any event, a capital asset can generally be described as any property held by the taxpayer other than property held for sale by the taxpayer, or intellectual or artistic property created by the taxpayer. Special tax rules apply to the sale of property used by a taxpayer in a trade or business. These rules will be discussed below.

The social policy issue surrounding the sale of capital assets is this: Should the sale of such assets receive a tax break relative to other kinds of income? Those who answer yes argue that capital gain tax relief encourages savings and investment. They also argue that full taxation of capital gain subjects taxpayers to what is really a tax on inflation, rather than one on real economic gains.

How does a capital gain tax break favor savings and investment? Stocks, bonds, real estate, and other investment-type assets generally are treated as capital assets. When an investor sells such an asset, a greater portion of the amount realized from the sale will remain in the investor's pocket if favorable tax treatment applies to the realized gain. Therefore the investor has a higher rate of return on the investment, which presumably provides an incentive to save rather than spend.

In addition, it is argued that a portion of the increase in value of an investment-type asset is attributable to inflation, rather than to real economic appreciation. Therefore, the argument goes, taxing the full amount of gain when the asset is sold is confiscatory, because the portion of the gain attributable to inflation has conferred no real economic benefit upon the taxpayer who is paying tax on it.

These theories have helped to introduce varying legislative measures over the years which provide relief for the taxation of capital gain. For example, through the use of an exclusion from gross income for a specific percentage of an individual's capital gain, a lower effective tax rate on the overall gain results.

As of the date of this writing, no special tax treatment for capital gain exists. Capital gain is currently taxed in full, and at the same rates as ordinary income. However, it is quite likely that at some point in the future, a capital gain tax break will be brought back into the law.

What are the arguments *against* favorable tax treatment for capital gain? The principal argument is that a preferential treatment for capital gain favors wealthy taxpayers at the expense of the average citizen. The theory goes that most stocks and bonds and other investment assets are owned by the rich, and that by taxing gains from the sale of these investments at a lower effective rate, the government is playing Robin Hood in reverse: stealing from the poor to feed the rich.

Draw your own conclusions.

Tax Treatment of Capital Losses

When a capital asset is sold at a loss, rather than at a gain, special rules do apply under current law. Basically, capital losses can be deducted only against the taxpayer's capital gains. In other words, a taxpayer cannot deduct a large capital loss from the sale of a stock investment against his or her wages for the year. However, in the case of individual taxpayers only, $3,000 of capital losses in excess of capital gains can be deducted against the taxpayer's other income. Any remaining capital losses can be "carried over" to future tax years.

Sec. 1231 Assets: Depreciable Property and Real Property Used in a Trade or Business

This class of assets receives different tax treatment, depending upon whether the asset is sold at a gain or at a loss. If the asset is sold at a gain, the gain is treated as a capital gain. If the asset is sold at a loss, the loss is treated as an ordinary loss, not as a capital loss.

What is the significance of this hybrid form of tax treatment? The most important thing is that the sale of an asset falling into this category is *not* subject to the limitations that apply to the deductibility of capital losses. Therefore if such an asset is sold at a loss, the loss can be deducted against the taxpayer's salary or other income.

If the asset is sold at a gain, the gain will be treated as capital gain. Even though there is currently no partial exclusion or other preferential treatment available for capital gains, capital gains treatment can provide a benefit for taxpayers who have capital *losses* for the year. Why? Because the capital losses can be deducted against capital gains, but not against ordinary income.

> *Example:* Pat sells a piece of machinery this year that is used in his business. The machinery is sold at a gain of $40,000. Pat also has a capital loss of $40,000 this year from a sale of stock from his investment portfolio. Because the gain from the sale of the machinery is treated as capital gain and not ordinary income, Pat can deduct his stock losses in full against the gain from the sale of the machinery.

The assets that receive this hybrid form of tax treatment include all depreciable property plus land that is used in the taxpayer's business (land is not depreciable for tax purposes). These so-called "Sec. 1231" assets provide the best of both worlds for taxpayers, and the rules that govern them are designed to stimulate investment in assets that are used in the conduct of a business.

TAXABLE ENTITIES

Most of the discussion in this chapter has focused on the individual taxpayer who receives income from salary, investment, or a sole proprietorship. However, the individual is not the only taxpayer under the federal income tax system. Trusts, estates, and corporations also are subject to the federal income tax. However, certain corporations can make an election to have their shareholders taxed on the corporation's taxable income. This is called a *subchapter S election.* The effect of such an election is to have the corporation treated for tax purposes very much like a partnership. Like a partnership, a corporation that makes an S election is not subject to income tax at the entity level. Rather, the owners of the business pay the taxes. Partnerships and S corporations are often referred to as *pass-through entities,* because the responsibility for paying their taxes is passed through the entity to the owners of the entity.

However, trusts, estates, and corporations other than S corporations do pay taxes. There are special rules that apply to each of these entities that do not apply to individual taxpayers. In addition, each of these entities has a tax rate structure that is different from the rate structure applicable to individual taxpayers. To learn more about these entities and the tax planning opportunities they present, students should take American College courses such as Income Taxation and Estate Planning I. Both these courses provide valuable information regarding these taxable entities.

CONCLUSION

This chapter has outlined basic income tax concepts and planning techniques that should be familiar to financial services professionals. Much more can be learned about each of these topics by the financial services professional. Although the income tax rate structure was significantly compressed by the Tax Reform Act of 1986, and many loopholes under prior law have been closed, income tax planning is still a crucial element of financial planning.

6

Planning the Client's Estate

Ted Kurlowicz*

THE GOALS OF ESTATE PLANNING

Planning the client's estate is an essential step in the ongoing process of lifetime financial planning. The narrow view of estate planning is that the process merely involves the conservation and distribution of a client's estate. The broader role of the estate planner, however, is to maximize the distributable wealth of a client and transfer the wealth to the client's beneficiaries in an appropriate fashion. The estate plan reflects lifetime financial planning strategies that lead to increases in the client's distributable wealth, in addition to planning for the disposition of such wealth. Thus the estate plan is not independent from lifetime planning with respect to income taxes, investments, insurance, and retirement planning.

Since the lifetime financial planning steps are thoroughly covered in other chapters, this discussion will focus on planning for the conservation and distribution of a client's estate. However, it is essential for the estate planner to bear in mind that the estate plan should be part of a cohesive financial plan for the client.

Selecting the appropriate alternatives and estate plan involves answering "who," "how," and "when" questions. The client must determine who will be the recipients of his or her property. The "who" question is generally the easiest for the client to answer and will often be determined without significant professional advice.

The client must also determine how the transferees will receive the client's property. For example, the property can be distributed outright to the transferees. On the other hand, property could be left to the transferees in trust with various restrictions on the transferee's enjoyment rights. Finally, a transferee could receive a partial interest in property. One example of a partial interest is a life estate.

The client can generally only answer the "how" question with significant professional advice. The estate planner should be able to determine the client's goals and design a transfer mechanism that both meets these goals and complies with state property law.

The transfer taxes imposed on a specific transfer of property often depend on the form of the property transfer. Planning for the resolution of the "how" question will often focus on the minimization of these transfer taxes within the framework of the client's objectives.

Finally, it must be determined "when" a client's estate will be distributed. Typically distributions will not be made from the client's property until his or her death. However, it may be appropriate to transfer specific items of a client's wealth during his or her lifetime. The reasons for lifetime gifts are numerous, but the primary estate planning purpose of lifetime giving is the reduction of the client's estate tax

---

*Ted Kurlowicz, JD, CLU, ChFC, is associate professor of taxation at The American College.

base. Systematic, planned lifetime giving is often recommended to wealthy clients to reduce the amount of death taxes payable upon testamentary dispositions.

STARTING THE PROCESS

The estate planning process begins with gathering data from the client. This is usually accomplished by interviewing the client and completing a fact finder, similar to (or in conjunction with) the fact-finding interviews discussed in chapter 4. Although the estate plan is a subset of the client's lifetime financial plan, estate planning concerns generally gain prominence later in the client's life. Generally the client should be well on the way toward reaching his or her wealth accumulation and retirement planning goals. Since the primary concern of the estate planner is to determine the appropriate responses to the "who," "how," and "when" questions, the process should begin with the fact finder to ensure that both the estate planner and the client have a full understanding of the client's asset inventory. An accurate asset inventory will indicate the composition and magnitude of the wealth available for distribution. This data will help the client and planner determine whether the assets are in the appropriate form for distribution and whether their total value is adequate to provide the desired distributions to the client's heirs. Planning to convert the assets into the appropriate form or to accumulate additional wealth could follow.

Once the client and the estate planner are aware of the assets available for distribution, the dispositive goals of the client must be ascertained. In many cases this is a simple question. For example, a married individual may want to leave all of his or her wealth to a surviving spouse. In other cases the "who" decision is more difficult and will require some soul-searching by the client. The estate planner should be aware that the client may not be able to answer the "who" question immediately. For example, the client may want to disinherit some children or to ensure that children from a prior marriage are provided for.

Finally, the client must determine how the property will be distributed. The client might be aware that some heirs do not have the acumen to handle outright distributions of property. The client may wish to restrict the ultimate right of an heir to dispose of the property received from the client. This is why the estate planner must have an in-depth interview to determine client objectives. It is prudent for the estate planner to make the client aware of the alternative forms of property transfers and the benefits and risks associated with each. This will assist the client in providing the estate planner with the basic objectives and will permit the estate planner to draft a more complete proposal to recommend to the client.

The interview process between the estate planner and the client is often an uncomfortable event. Many clients feel uneasy talking about issues associated with their death and personal family matters. It is not unusual for the client to modify his or her initial intentions during the estate planning process. The alternative distribution choices discussed with the planner will often raise issues that the client had failed to contemplate initially. It may be necessary to interview spouses separately if an estate plan is drawn up for a marital unit. This is particularly true if the goals of the spouses are not congruent. However, a thorough interview with appropriate follow-up will result in the greatest probability that the estate planner will receive an accurate picture of the client's objectives and thus design a plan that will satisfy the client.

OWNERSHIP OF PROPERTY

The asset inventory of the client as indicated in the fact finder may or may not provide the complete picture to the estate planner. The manner in which the client owns the property may also be a factor. It is important for the estate planner to determine the form of property ownership and inquire about any additional property rights held by the client that are not indicated on the asset inventory form. Some forms of property interest provide less than full use and enjoyment rights and may have been ignored by the client in completing the fact finder. Knowledge of the forms of property interest is essential to the estate planner to determine all of the possible property rights held by the client and the possible forms of dispositions the client can ultimately make to his or her heirs.

Forms of Property Interest

Individual Ownership of Property

Fee simple ownership. The most complete interest in property is a *fee simple estate* (outright ownership of property). The individual who holds such an unlimited interest in property owns all the rights associated with the property, including the current possessory rights and the ability to transfer the property at any point during his or her lifetime or at death. In planning the estate of a client a property held outright by the client is an obvious asset to be considered in the dispositive scheme. If the estate of a married couple is being planned, it is possible that either spouse might own substantial property individually.

Life estates. The life estate is a common form of property ownership and provides the life tenant with the right to possess and enjoy the property for a time period measured by the life of an individual (typically the life tenant). The life estate gives the owner the absolute right to possess, enjoy, and receive current income from the property until the life interest terminates.

Term interests. A term interest provides the current tenant with the right to possess, enjoy, and receive income from the property during a specified term. The interest of the current tenant terminates at the end of the specified term.

Future interests. A future interest in property is the current right to future enjoyment of the property. A future interest in property could either be vested or contingent on the occurrence of some future event. The future interest holder has no immediate right to use and enjoy the property. One type of future interest is a remainder interest, which is an interest that takes effect immediately upon the expiration of another interest in the same property. For example, a remainder interest might take effect upon the termination of a life estate or a term of years. A remainder interest is often held by one individual, the remainderperson, on property contained in a trust that currently benefits another individual—for example, a life income beneficiary.

Another type of future interest is a reversionary interest. The reversionary interest occurs when the current property owner transfers current possessory rights to another. The reversionary interest gives the transferor the right to the return of the property at the end of the possessory term of the transferee. For example, a parent could create a trust for a child for a term of years and retain a reversionary interest in the trust corpus following the child's interest.

Joint Concurrent Ownership of Property

Current possessory rights to property may be held by more than one individual. Such a partial current interest in property is often generically referred to as joint ownership of property.

Tenancy in common. Two or more individuals may hold current possessory rights to property without survivorship rights. Such individuals, known as tenants in common, each hold an undivided interest in the property and may transfer their interest during their lifetime or at their death. Both related and unrelated individuals may hold property by tenancy in common.

Joint tenancy with right of survivorship. Two or more individuals may hold property jointly with their survivors ultimately receiving the entire interest in the property. Both related and unrelated individuals may hold property jointly with rights of survivorship. Since this property interest transfers automatically at the death of a joint tenant to his or her surviving tenants, the property is not subject to disposition by a decedent at his or her death. Usually a joint tenant may transfer his or her interest during life without consent of the other joint tenants. Such a transfer will generally sever the joint tenancy and destroy the survivorship rights of the joint tenants.

Tenancy by the entireties. A tenancy by the entirety is a property interest restricted solely to spouses. It is joint ownership of the property by the spouses with rights of survivorship. A tenancy by the entirety creates a unique situation with respect to disposition of the property. Property is transferred automatically to the surviving spouse at the death of a joint tenant. Thus the property is not subject to disposition by will of a deceased spouse. In addition, the property cannot be transferred during the lifetime of the spouses unless both tenants consent. Tenancy by the entirety is severed automatically upon divorce. An estate planner must know the laws within his or her state jurisdiction with respect to joint property since property held jointly by spouses may or may not be presumed to be held with such rights of survivorship.

Community property. Nine states—Arizona, California, Idaho, Louisiana, Nevada, New Mexico, Texas, Washington, and Wisconsin—have some form of community-property laws with respect to spousal property. Property in such states is treated as either separate or community property. Generally speaking, property acquired during marriage is treated as community property and is equally owned by the spouses. Although community property is not technically jointly held, the law limits the ability of each spouse to transfer community property to individuals other than his or her spouse.

Other Property Rights

Other property interests may be held by a client and used as a vehicle for the transfer of a client's wealth. These other rights generally provide varying restrictions on the ability of the holder to enjoy or transfer the property. These forms of property ownership should be used when the restrictions are appropriate for the objectives of the client.

Beneficial interest in property. Certain property interests may provide one individual with a beneficial interest in property, such as the right to current income or principal distributions. An example of a beneficial interest is the interest owned by the beneficiary of a trust. The trust is created by a grantor who transfers title to the trust property (corpus) to a trustee. The trustee's function is to hold legal title to and administer the trust property for the benefit of the beneficiary. The trustee's ability to make distributions to the beneficiary is determined by the terms of the trust. The trustee may be required to make specific distributions or may be given broad discretion as to the size or timing and to the identity of the beneficiaries. Thus the trustee could possibly be left with substantial dispositive decisions. Trust beneficiaries themselves are generally limited in their ability to transfer their interests until trust distributions are actually received.

Powers. Certain powers to make property decisions may be held by (or transferred by) the client. A *power of appointment* provides the holder of a power with the ability to transfer the property subject to the power. The holder may have a broad power to transfer the property to virtually any recipient. This is known as a *general power.* Or the holder may have a *special power,* which typically provides the holder with a limited class of potential recipients of the property. Any powers of appointment held by a client should be considered in his or her dispositive plans. In addition, a client may wish to grant a power of appointment to another to delegate the ability to transfer the client's property.

Another power that can be held or granted by a client is a *power of attorney.* A power of attorney gives the holder of the power (the attorney-in-fact) the ability to stand in the place of or represent the grantor of the power (the principal) in various transactions. Among the possible transactions is the ability of the attorney-in-fact to transfer property for the principal. The advantages of using a power of attorney will be discussed below.

TRANSFERS AT DEATH — AN OVERVIEW

Knowledge of how property is transferred at death under the laws of the jurisdictional state is necessary to plan an estate. A common misconception is that the decedent's will determines the distribution of the estate. Under most circumstances the will actually affects the distribution of only a small portion of the decedent's property. This fact does not minimize the importance of a carefully drafted will, but merely emphasizes the importance of coordinating all of the client's testamentary transfers, including the client's will, in the estate planning process.

Probate Property

Transfers through Will Provisions

Many misconceptions exist with respect to the various terms associated with the estate planning process. Popular opinion of estate planning is that a primary goal is to reduce the size of the probate estate. The probate estate includes all assets passing by will or intestacy. Probate property is owned outright by the decedent and is not transferred by operation of law or contract, as discussed below. For married individuals probate property is generally limited to the individually owned property of a deceased spouse. Thus the probate estate is often minimized by the usual form of property ownership between spouses—tenancy by the entirety.

Probate (which technically means the process of proving the validity of the will) begins when the original will is deposited in the court with jurisdiction over the decedent's estate. The probate court oversees matters involving the settlement of the estate, distribution of probate property, appointment and supervision of fiduciaries, and disputes concerning the decedent's will. If a valid will exists, the probate court will ensure that the probate property is distributed according to the terms of the will after all estate settlement costs are paid. Although the court has jurisdiction solely over probate property, the state and federal taxing authorities may have the statutory authority to collect any unpaid taxes from nonprobate property if probate assets are insufficient.

Transfers by Intestacy

If a decedent dies without a valid will, all probate property passes under the laws of intestate succession of the jurisdiction state. The intestate laws are deemed to replace the intent of a decedent in the distribution of his or her probate property. The default mechanism provided by the intestacy laws may be of little significance since the probate assets are not substantial in the typical estate.

States vary with respect to intestate laws. Distribution under the intestate laws will depend upon the related individuals who survive the decedent. A decedent's spouse receives primary consideration and will receive the decedent's entire probate estate if the decedent is not also survived by children or parents. If the decedent is survived by children, the surviving spouse and children will generally receive 50 percent each of the estate. The parents of a married decedent will generally get a share only if the decedent is not also survived by children. If the decedent is not survived by any of these related individuals, the next closest related survivors will inherit.

State intestacy laws also apply to a transfer under a will or contract that is deemed invalid.

Transfers by Operation of Law

The nature of certain ownership interests in property causes the property to pass automatically at the death of a decedent. Such property is not subject to the laws of probate and does not pass under the will or intestacy rules. The most significant example of property that is transferred by operation of law is property held jointly with rights of survivorship. The survivorship provisions cause such property to automatically pass to the surviving joint tenant at the death of the joint tenant. As discussed earlier, property held as tenants by the entirety is also an example of an operation-of-law transfer. Many married individuals own property acquired during their marriage in this fashion. For example, the family home, automobile, and significant investments are often held jointly by spouses. At the death of one spouse the property passes automatically to the survivor outside the jurisdiction of the probate court.

In addition, it is quite common for elderly parents to reduce their probate estate by creating operation-of-law transfers to their descendants. One such transfer is the establishment of joint bank or securities accounts with their children or grandchildren with survivorship rights. A similar vehicle for transfer by operation of law is the *Totten trust.* A Totten trust occurs when an individual (generally a parent or grandparent) opens up a bank account in trust for a named individual. At the death of the account holder this property passes automatically by operation of law to the named beneficiary. It should be noted that both such transactions are incomplete gifts and, while effective in reducing probate, have no impact on the taxable estate.

Transfers by Operation of Contract

Another form of nonprobate transfer is transfer by contract. The most common form of transfer by contract involves the transfer of life insurance or employment benefit proceeds to a named beneficiary. The policy proceeds of a life insurance policy will be distributed to the beneficiary designated by the owner of the policy. The same result occurs if an employee has named individuals as beneficiaries of various employment benefits, such as death benefits from retirement plans. These benefits will pass by operation of contract and will not become part of probate unless they are made payable to the executor (or the estate) in lieu of a named beneficiary.

OVERVIEW OF TAXES IMPOSED ON TRANSFERS OF WEALTH

The most significant costs of transferring wealth are the various transfer taxes imposed at the federal and state levels. The tax rates applicable to affected transfers can be quite high (the marginal rate can exceed 100 percent under certain circumstances). The relatively large impact of these transfer taxes makes tax reduction a primary focus in the estate plan with respect to the conservation of a client's wealth. By optimizing the solutions to the "who," "how," and "when" questions the client may be able to implement a plan that approximates his or her stated objectives and holds the transfer-tax reduction of his or her estate to a minimum. The primary focus of this discussion will be the federal estate and gift transfer taxes, but the federal generation-skipping transfer tax (GSTT) and state death taxes will also be discussed.

The Federal Transfer Tax System

The federal tax system consists of three components — gift taxes, estate taxes, and generation-skipping taxes. The federal estate and gift taxes are separate tax systems imposed on different types of transfers, but the systems are unified with respect to tax brackets and tax base. The generation-skipping transfer taxes are separate taxes applied under different rules in addition to any applicable estate or gift taxes.

Federal Gift Taxes

Federal gift taxes will apply only if the following two elements are present:

- there is a completed transfer and acceptance of *property*
- the transfer is for less than full and adequate consideration

These two essential elements of a taxable gift reveal some noteworthy facts. First, only property transfers are subject to gift taxation. Thus the transfer of services by an individual is not a taxable gift. In addition, all completed transfers including direct and indirect gifts of property are taxable. Finally, the less than full and adequate consideration requirement does not contain an element of intent. Therefore it is not necessary that the grantor intends to make a gift. It is merely required that the transfer be for less than full consideration. Generally speaking, transfers between unrelated individuals in a business setting are treated as "bad bargains" and are not treated as taxable transfers.

Exempt transfers. Certain transfers are exempt from the gift tax base by statute. First, a transfer of property pursuant to a divorce or property settlement agreement is deemed to be for full and adequate consideration under some circumstances. Second, transfers directly to the provider of education or medical services on behalf of an individual are not taxable gifts to the recipient of the services. Finally, gifts that are disclaimed by the donee in a qualified disclaimer are not treated as taxable gifts.

The annual exclusion. Much of the design and complexity involved in gift tax planning involves the annual exclusion. Qualifying gifts of $10,000 or less may be made annually by a donor to each of any number of donees without gift tax. The exempt amount can be increased to $20,000 if the donor is married and the donor's spouse elects to join in making the gifts on a timely filed gift tax return.

To qualify for an annual exclusion the gift must provide the donee with a present interest. Outright interests or current income interests in a trust will provide the beneficiary with a present interest. Trust provisions giving the beneficiaries current withdrawal powers can be used to qualify gifts to a trust for an annual exclusion even if the trust provides for deferred benefits. Use of the annual exclusion in the estate planning process will be discussed below.

Deductions from the gift tax base. Two types of gifts are fully deductible from the transfer tax base. First, the *marital deduction* provides that unlimited qualifying transfers made by a donor to his or her spouse are fully deductible from the gift tax base. The marital deduction will prove quite useful if it is necessary to rearrange ownership of marital assets in the implementation of the estate plan. This deduction is similar to the marital deduction against federal estate taxes discussed below.

The *charitable deduction* provides that qualifying transfers to a legitimate charity will be deductible against the gift tax base. Thus all qualifying transfers made to charity will avoid transfer tax.

The unified credit. A cumulative credit of $192,800 is currently available against federal gift tax due on taxable transfers. Under the unified nature of the federal estate and gift taxes this credit provides a dollar-for-dollar reduction of transfer tax otherwise payable against taxable transfers either during lifetime or at death or both. The credit of $192,800 can be used against each dollar of transfer tax until it is exhausted. The tax credit of $192,800 is equivalent to an exemption of $600,000 of taxable transfers from the federal estate or gift tax. Thus the credit is often commonly but mistakenly referred to as the $600,000 unified credit. Since no taxes are due on transfers until aggregate transfers by the donor have exceeded $600,000, the first tax rate bracket applicable to a transfer actually subject to tax is 37 percent. The unified credit is discussed further below.

The Federal Estate Tax

Often the most difficult task in calculating the estate tax is determining the assets that are included in the decedent's estate tax base. Some of the included assets are obvious, such as individually owned property. However, the estate tax rules often cause the inclusion of property in surprising circumstances. For example, property previously transferred by a decedent can be brought back to the estate tax base by provisions of the statute.

The gross estate. The starting point in the estate tax calculation is determining the property included in the gross estate for federal tax purposes. The gross estate includes the property included in the probate estate, but it also includes property transferable by the decedent at death by other means. The decedent's gross estate includes

- property individually owned by the decedent at the time of death
- (some portion of) property held jointly by the decedent at the time of death
- insurance on the decedent's life if either (1) incidents of ownership are held by the decedent within 3 years of death or (2) the proceeds are deemed payable to the estate
- pension or IRA payments left to survivors
- property subject to general powers of appointment held by the decedent at the time of death
- property transferred by the decedent during his or her lifetime if the decedent retained (1) a life interest in the property, (2) a reversionary interest valued greater than 5 percent of the property at the time of death, or (3) rights to revoke the transfer at the time of death

As the list above indicates, the gross estate of the decedent is defined much more broadly than the probate estate, and a reduction of the probate estate will often have little effect on the size of the federal estate tax paid.

Items deductible from the gross estate. Analogous to the federal gift tax rules, certain items are deductible from the gross estate for estate tax calculation purposes. First, legitimate debts of the decedent are deductible from the gross estate if these debts are obligations of the gross estate. Second, reasonable funeral and other death costs of the decedent are deductible from the gross estate. Third, the costs of estate settlement, such as the executor's commission and attorney fees, are deductible to the extent such fees are reasonable.

Marital deduction. As with the gift tax, qualifying transfers to a surviving spouse are deductible under the marital-deduction rules. Since the marital deduction is unlimited, the usual dispositive scheme (100 percent to the surviving spouse) will result in no federal death taxes for a married couple until the death of the survivor of the two spouses. As a client's wealth increases, sophisticated planning is needed to make optimal use of the marital deduction. Planning for the marital deduction will be discussed below.

Charitable deduction. The federal estate tax charitable deduction provides that transfers at death to qualifying charities will be fully deductible from the estate tax base. The charitable deduction is an excellent device to reduce the gross estate of a wealthy individual. As we will discuss below, the transfer of a remainder of current term interest to charity can substantially reduce the estate tax burden of a wealthy client without significantly disrupting his or her dispositive goals.

Credits against the estate tax. The unified credit discussed above with respect to gift taxes is similarly applicable to transfers occurring at death. If the unified credit has not been exhausted by sheltering lifetime gifts, it is available against transfers made at the death of a decedent. The optimal use of a unified credit in conjunction with the marital deduction will be discussed below.

The state death tax credit provides a dollar-for-dollar reduction (within certain limits) against the federal estate tax due for any state death taxes paid by the estate. The state death tax credit is limited, and the maximum state death tax credit available to a particular estate is provided for by a progressive rate schedule in the federal tax code. The size of the credit against the federal estate tax is equal to the lesser of the state death tax actually paid or the maximum state death tax allowable under the progressive credit schedule. State death taxes are usually equal to at least the maximum state death tax allowable under the federal estate tax rules.

Generation-Skipping Transfer Tax (GSTT)

The GSTT was created by the Tax Reform Act of 1986 to prevent the federal government from losing transfer tax if a transferor attempts to skip one generation's level of transfer tax by transferring property to a generation more than one generation below the level of the transferor (for example, when a grandparent makes a gift of property to a grandchild). Although the GSTT is designed to prevent a transferor from finding a transfer tax loophole in the federal estate/gift tax system, it is different from the unified estate and gift tax system in many ways. The GSTT is applied at a flat rate equal to the highest current estate or gift tax bracket on every taxable generation-skipping transfer. Thus any taxable transfers will be currently subject to a 55 percent rate if the GSTT applies. This GSTT is applicable in addition to any estate or gift tax that might otherwise be applicable to the transfer. Thus if the GSTT applies, a transfer could easily be subject to a tax rate in excess of 100 percent of the value of the asset transfer. Obviously, planning to avoid the GSTT is of paramount importance for wealthy individuals.

The GSTT applies to three different types of transfers. First, the GSTT applies to a *direct skip,* which is an outright transfer during life or at death to an individual who is more than one generation below the transferor. The direct skip gift tax applies only if the parents of the skip beneficiary are alive at the time of the direct skip.

The GSTT is also applicable to a *taxable distribution*. A taxable distribution is a distribution of either income or principal from a trust to a person more than one generation below the level of the trust grantor. The recipient of the taxable distribution is a skip beneficiary of the trust. Thus a taxable distribution can occur when a trustee makes a distribution to a skip beneficiary even if a nonskip beneficiary still holds a current beneficial interest in the trust.

Finally, a *taxable termination* is also subject to a GSTT. The taxable termination occurs when there is a termination of a property interest held in trust as a result of death, lapse of time, or otherwise and a skip beneficiary receives the remainder interest outright in the trust.

A $1 million exemption is available to each taxpayer to be applied against GSTT for all potential generation-skipping transfers. The exemption can be applied against transfers during life or at death. Thus a married couple can split gifts and make up to $2 million of generation-skipping transfers without incurring the GSTT. The exemption must be affirmatively allocated to specific transfers in the transferor's appropriate tax return. If this GSTT exemption is not allocated on a gift tax return during the life of a transferor or in the transferor's will, the taxing authorities will allocate the exemption by default. A client would be making a substantial mistake by failing to appropriately allocate the GSTT exemption.

State Death Taxes

Most material on estate planning minimizes the discussion of state death taxes. Although state death taxes are generally applied at a lower rate than the federal estate tax, these taxes should not be ignored for many reasons. First, the majority of estates will not be subject to federal death taxes due to the $600,000 unified credit equivalent. The average estate will, however, be subject to state death taxes. In large estates the federal estate death tax is admittedly the largest expense. However, the state death taxes will also be quite significant. Finally, the state death tax base is defined differently from the federal estate tax bases in many states. Planning for state death taxes should not be ignored since the taxable transfers for state purposes can often be avoided by simple planning that might otherwise be ineffective (and thus disregarded) for purposes of federal estate tax planning. For example, many states exempt life insurance benefits paid to a named beneficiary.

State Inheritance Taxes

Some states impose a tax on the right of a beneficiary to receive the property from the estate of the decedent. The tax rate is based on the amount of property received by each beneficiary and is often based on the relationship of the beneficiary to the decedent. An inheritance received by a close relative is generally subject to a lower rate than an inheritance received by a more distant relation. In many cases the inheritance tax on property received by relatives outside the decedent's immediate family (surviving spouse or children) is subject to a tax that exceeds the federal state death tax credit. In many circumstances the state inheritance tax could be more significant than any federal estate tax due. Despite the fact that inheritance taxes are imposed on the right to receive property, payment of these inheritance taxes is usually the responsibility of the estate.

State Estate Tax

A state with an estate tax is similar to the federal system in that both taxes are imposed on the privilege of transferring property by the decedent. These taxes are generally imposed at progressive rates and apply to a tax base similar to the federal system.

Credit Estate Tax

All states currently impose a credit estate tax (also known as a sponge tax) to bring the total state death tax liability up to the maximum federal death tax credit. In many states this sponge tax is the sole form of state death tax. Thus the state death taxes paid will generally be at least as great as any federal death tax credit allowable.

Factors to Consider in Planning for State Death Taxes

A detailed analysis of each state's inheritance or estate tax is beyond the scope of this discussion. However, there are some peculiarities in the state death tax base that an estate planner should be aware of in the state where his or her clients are located. First, it is important to note that some states will not tax property held jointly by a decedent at the time of his or her death. As we have discussed above, jointly held property is included in the federal estate tax base. Quite often a decedent can avoid estate death taxes without affecting federal taxes by transferring property to joint ownership prior to his or her death.

In addition, some states provide for no marital deduction for individually owned property transferred to a surviving spouse. Therefore severing a joint ownership of property with a surviving spouse may create state death taxes even if that property is transferred to the surviving spouse in a transfer deductible from the federal estate tax base.

Finally, life insurance is often not taxable at the state level if payable to a named beneficiary. It is important to note that life insurance can often avoid state death taxes even if owned individually by an insured at the time of his or her death provided the estate is not the named beneficiary.

PRESERVING THE CLIENT'S WEALTH

There are many techniques that can be used to reduce the tax associated with transferring a client's wealth to his or her heirs. The appropriate answer to the "who" question may be used to reduce tax. For example, qualifying transfers to a surviving spouse are fully deductible from the gross estate. The optimal resolution of the "how" question could also reduce estate taxes. For example, transferring assets to a family trust takes advantage of the unified credit against federal estate taxes. Finally, if the "when" question is answered appropriately, the gross estate of a grantor can be substantially reduced through a systematic lifetime gifting program, and substantial wealth can be transferred free of all transfer taxes.

The Advantages of Lifetime Gifts

Nontax Advantages of Lifetime Gifts

Clients give away property during their lifetime for many reasons. The advantages of making lifetime gifts are as follows:

- The donor can provide for the support, education, and welfare of the donee.
- The donor gets the pleasure of seeing the donee enjoy the gift.
- The donor avoids the publicity and administrative costs associated with a probate transfer at death.
- The donated property is protected from the claims of the donor's creditors.

Tax Advantages of Lifetime Gifts

Although the federal gift and estate taxes are unified for tax purposes, there are some distinctions that make lifetime gifts favorable from a tax standpoint. The tax advantages of lifetime gifts include these:

- The annual gift tax exclusion for gifts of $10,000 or less provides a complete loophole from federal and estate taxes. Each year any number of $10,000 gifts ($20,000 if the spouse joins in them) can be made to reduce the ultimate transfer tax base of a donor.
- The gift tax is imposed on the value of the gift at the time a completed transfer is made. Thus any posttransfer appreciation on the property avoids all transfer tax.
- Any gift tax payable on gifts made more than 3 years prior to the donor's death is removed from the donor's estate tax base.
- The income produced by gifted property is shifted to the donee for income tax purposes. Lifetime gifting may be used to move taxable income from a high-bracket donor to a lower-bracket donee. (This advantage is somewhat limited by special tax rules related to unearned income of children under age 14.)
- Unlimited qualifying transfers can be made between spouses without incurring gift taxes. Spouses can advantageously shift assets between themselves to meet the needs of the estate plan of each spouse.

The Opportunities Created by the $10,000 Annual Gift Tax Exclusion

As discussed above the annual exclusion allows the donor to make up to $10,000 worth of gifts tax free to any number of donees each year. If the donor's spouse elects to split gifts with the donor for the tax year, the annual exclusion is increased to $20,000 per donee. If the client has a substantial estate and several individuals to benefit, the systematic use of annual exclusion gifts can cause the transfer of substantial wealth free of transfer tax.

> *Example:* Tom Taxplanner, a 65-year-old widower, has two children and four grandchildren. Tom can make up to $60,000 of qualifying transfers annually to his heirs without ever subjecting the transfers to federal gift or

estate taxes. If Tom lives an additional 16 years (his actual life expectancy), he can give away $960,000 and save up to $528,000 of estate tax (assuming a maximum 55 percent bracket). The actual tax savings are even greater since the appreciation on the property transferred also escapes gift and estate taxes.

The annual exclusion is available only for gifts that provide the donee with a present interest. For example, an outright transfer of property provides a present interest. Since the outright transfer is often unfavorable (for example, the donee is a minor), significant planning is often necessary to design gifts that restrict the donee's current access to the funds while qualifying for the annual exclusion.

Gifts to Minors

Quite often annual exclusion gifts will be made to minor children or grandchildren as part of the estate plan of a wealthy client. This creates problems for the donor and donee. First, there are restrictions on a minor's ability to hold or otherwise deal with property under state law. In addition, the donor will naturally be concerned about the safety of the funds if the minor has significant access rights. Fortunately there are several methods for making annual exclusion gifts to minors with restrictions on the minor's access to the property.

Uniform Gifts to Minors Act (UGMA) or Uniform Transfers to Minors Act (UTMA). The UGMA and UTMA statutes are model laws that have been adopted in various forms in individual states. They permit the transfer of funds to a custodial account for the benefit of a minor. The custodian of the UGMA or UTMA account manages the property under the rules provided by state law. There are restrictions on the type of property permissible as an investment for these purposes. The original model act, UGMA, has been expanded in many states to increase the types of permissible investments. In a majority of states the newer model act, UTMA, has been adopted, and relatively few restrictions exist in these states on the permissible investments. A UGMA or UTMA transfer is particularly favorable for smaller gifts because it provides for the protection of the assets without the expense of the administration of the trust. The provisions for distribution from the UGMA are provided under the various state laws. Generally speaking, the UGMA funds can be accumulated during the minority of the donee, but the custodial assets must be distributed to the beneficiary upon majority.

Sec. 2503(b) trust. A Sec. 2503(b) trust is an irrevocable trust created by a donor during his or her lifetime to receive annual exclusion gifts. The trust requires that income be distributed at least annually to (or for the benefit of) the minor donee. The minor would receive distribution of the trust principal whenever the trust agreement specifies. A distribution of principal does not have to be made at the majority of the donee. The annual gift tax exclusion is limited to the value of the income interest provided by the trust. The Sec. 2503(b) trust should be invested in income-producing property and is less favorable in some respects than the UGMA gift because income cannot be accumulated.

Sec. 2503(c) trust. A Sec. 2503(c) trust is another type of irrevocable trust designed to receive annual exclusion gifts for a minor. This type of trust requires that income and principal be distributed to the minor at age 21. However, the trust is allowed to accumulate current income prior to the termination of the trust.

Irrevocable trust with current withdrawal powers. A client often wishes to make gifts to a trust with the purpose of accumulation. If the trust provides for accumulation and does not currently benefit the donee, the annual gift tax exclusion would normally be forfeited. Provisions of the law, however, permit the annual exclusion if current beneficial rights are given to the donee. An annual exclusion is permitted if the donee is granted at least temporary withdrawal rights to the deposits to the trust. Under these rules a gift to a trust will qualify for the annual exclusion if the donee has the noncumulative, temporary (for example, 30 days) right to demand the least of (1) the annual addition to the trust, (2) $5,000, and (3) 5 percent of the trust corpus.

Irrevocable trusts with withdrawal powers are often used for the purposes of holding life insurance on the life of the grantor. Since the life insurance will be paid with annual premium additions to the trust, it is intended that these premiums will accumulate in the policy and no distributions will be made until the death of the grantor. If each beneficiary is provided with the ability to withdraw a pro rata share of the annual premium addition to the trust, the annual premium will qualify as an annual exclusion gift to the beneficiaries. Thus a life insurance trust can be created without gift tax costs. The estate tax advantage of the life insurance trust will be discussed below.

Federal Estate Tax Planning

Despite the advantages of systematic annual gifting most individuals will desire to retain a significant portion of their wealth until death. To the extent this wealth is included in the gross estate of the decedent, it will be included in the estate tax calculations. Due to the deduction and credits provided by the estate tax laws, a properly designed estate can distribute significant wealth to the decedent's heirs while minimizing or deferring federal estate taxes.

Planning for the Marital Deduction

The marital deduction provides that certain transfers at death from a deceased spouse to a surviving spouse are fully deductible from the gross estate for estate tax purposes. This deduction is unlimited as long as the property is included in the gross estate of a deceased spouse and is transferred to a surviving spouse in a qualifying manner.

Through *maximum* use of the marital deduction a married couple can, at their option, eliminate all federal estate taxes due at the first death of the two spouses. The estate plan of a marital unit making full use of this marital deduction merely defers the estate taxes until the second spouse dies. The marital deduction will be available at the second death only if the surviving spouse remarries and transfers the property to his or her new spouse. Thus a decedent can avoid all federal estate taxes on his or her estate by making a qualifying transfer of all property included in his or her gross estate (both probate and nonprobate property) to the surviving spouse.

Transfers qualifying for the marital deduction. Simply answering the "who" question in favor of the surviving spouse will not necessarily qualify such transfers for the marital deduction. Tax laws provide that only qualifying transfers will be eligible for this deduction. Thus the "how" question must also be answered appropriately.

The simplest and most common method of transferring property to a surviving spouse — the unrestricted transfer — is eligible for an unlimited marital deduction. This includes all property included in the gross estate of the decedent that passes directly to the surviving spouse. Therefore outright transfers of probate assets by will or intestacy qualify for the marital deduction. In addition, transfers by operation of law or contract that pass outright to the surviving spouse at death similarly qualify. Thus life insurance proceeds payable to the surviving spouse or jointly held property received by survivorship by the deceased spouse qualify for the marital deduction.

Property transfers that place restrictions on the surviving spouse's use or enjoyment of the property may or may not qualify for the marital deduction. The marital deduction was envisioned to prevent a substantial first-death tax to a married couple if the usual dispositive scheme (100 percent to the spouse) is followed. However, Congress intended that the estate taxes would be payable at the second death of the two spouses. Thus a general rule of thumb is that the marital deduction is available only for transfers to a surviving spouse that would cause the ultimate inclusion of the property in the surviving spouse's gross estate. Property transferred to a surviving spouse will not qualify for the marital deduction if the interest is terminable at the death of the surviving spouse.

An interest in property left to a surviving spouse will be nondeductible if

- it terminates upon the occurrence of an event or a contingency, such as death, and
- a third party gains possession of the property after the surviving spouse's interest terminates

A common example of a nondeductible terminable interest is the transfer of a life estate to the surviving spouse with the remainder interest being paid to the couple's children under the terms of the deceased spouse's will. Such a transfer would not create a second-death tax since the surviving spouse's interest terminates and therefore would not be included in his or her estate. However, a first-death tax would be payable since the life estate transferred to the surviving spouse would not qualify for the marital deduction.

Congress recognized that many married individuals prefer leaving property in trust for the surviving spouse. The transferor may be concerned that the spouse may be unable to properly manage the trust property. Or the transferor-spouse might want to limit the invasion rights of the surviving spouse. In addition, it is generally the intent of individuals to ultimately leave their property to their children. The transferor-spouse may want to control the ultimate disposition of the property to preserve the rights of his or her children. This is particularly true if the transferor-spouse has children from a prior marriage. Fortunately the marital-deduction rules have created several opportunities that meet many of these objectives.

Estate trust. A transfer to a surviving spouse through an estate trust qualifies for a marital deduction. Under this arrangement a deceased spouse leaves a life estate in trust to the surviving spouse. The surviving spouse's estate is the remainderperson of this trust. Income from the estate trust can either accumulate or be paid to the surviving spouse at the discretion of the trustee. Since the remainder interest is transferred to the surviving spouse's estate, the property will be included in his or her gross estate, and a second-death estate tax may be payable at that time.

Power-of-appointment trust. Another common marital-deduction trust is the power-of-appointment trust. This trust is designed to distribute income to the surviving spouse during his or her life and provides the surviving spouse with a general power of appointment over the trust property. The general power of appointment may be exercisable by the surviving spouse in all events, or may be exercisable only at the death of the surviving spouse. Since the surviving spouse has a general power of appointment over the trust principal, the principal is included in his or her gross estate for federal tax purposes.

QTIP marital-deduction trust. A special provision of the tax law provides for a marital deduction if qualifying terminable interest property (QTIP) is left to a surviving spouse. Under these rules a terminable property interest can be transferred to a surviving spouse and such interest will qualify for the marital deduction. The QTIP deduction is available if the executor of the deceased spouse elects for QTIP treatment on the estate tax return. The QTIP trust can be funded by probate assets or other types of testamentary dispositions. The surviving spouse must have the right to all income annually from the QTIP for life. At the death of the surviving spouse the QTIP election provides that the property will be included in the surviving spouse's gross estate.

The primary advantage of the QTIP is the ability of the transferor-spouse to control the transfer of his or her assets. The ultimate disposition of the QTIP property would be predetermined by the terms of the trust created by the original transferor-spouse. Thus the QTIP trust permits a transferor-spouse to provide for his or her surviving spouse but still preserve the ultimate interests of his or her children.

Planning for the Unified Credit

The unified credit against estate or gift tax is designed to prevent the imposition of these transfer taxes on moderate-sized estates. As noted earlier, the credit is currently $192,800 and is applied dollar-for-dollar against any estate or gift tax due. This credit provides a shelter against approximately $600,000 of taxable transfers during a transferor's lifetime or at death.

For the unified credit to be applicable to a transfer, the transferor must first create estate or gift tax. Thus the unified credit is not applicable to a transfer that is exempt or deductible from the tax base as a result of other provisions of the federal transfer tax rules. For example, if a transfer is exempt from estate or gift tax as a result of the marital deduction or annual exclusion, the transferor's unified credit will not be applicable.

Coordination of the Marital Deduction and Unified Credit

The maximum use of a marital deduction is the typical dispositive scheme for most married individuals. All property is generally left either outright to the surviving spouse or in other manners qualifying for the marital deduction at the first spouse's death. Since no estate tax will be payable under these circumstances, the unified credit available at the death of the first spouse to die will be wasted.

With appropriate planning each spouse can make maximum use of the unified credit, and the marital unit as a whole can shelter up to $1.2 million in marital wealth from federal estate taxes. This shelter can only be accomplished if each spouse makes maximum use of the $600,000 unified credit equivalent. As discussed above the usual marital dispositive scheme does not take advantage of the $600,000 unified credit equivalent available to the first spouse at his or her death. Thus all assets transferred to the surviving spouse under the marital deduction will be sheltered by only one unified credit available at the second spouse's death.

The usual dispositive scheme can be altered to make maximum use of each spouse's unified credit and optimal use of the marital deduction. Again, this requires appropriate answers to the "who" and "how" questions. With some restrictions, all the objectives of the usual dispositive scheme can be accomplished without wasting the unified credit of either spouse. This maximum estate tax shelter is accomplished by designing each spouse's estate plan to transfer property to both a marital and unified credit trust. This arrangement is commonly referred to as an AB trust arrangement. The AB trust arrangement is designed to operate as follows:

- The A trust is some form of marital-deduction trust. This trust receives assets in a manner qualifying for the marital deduction and provides for maximum use of these assets by the surviving spouse. The remainder of the assets transferred by the decedent are placed into the B trust.
- The B trust is designed *not* to qualify for the marital deduction. The B trust, funded with approximately $600,000, will be part of the taxable estate since it was not deductible under the marital deduction. Thus this trust will create tax and use the unified credit of each spouse.

The "how" question must be answered by designing the transfer to the B trust in a nonqualifying manner for the marital deduction. Therefore the surviving spouse's interest in the B trust must be limited to a life estate, perhaps with some limited invasion rights. Since the B trust is designed as a nonqualifying terminable interest, the assets in the B trust will not be included in the surviving spouse's gross estate and the remainder interest can be reserved for the children.

The "who" question must be answered with respect to the B trust, often referred to either as the family trust or the credit-shelter-bypass trust. The B trust can be used to provide substantial rights to the surviving spouse but must fail to qualify for the marital deduction. If the client is extremely wealthy, the B trust could entirely avoid benefiting the surviving spouse, and is an excellent way to provide for other heirs at the first death.

The AB trust arrangement makes maximum use of each spouse's unified credit, and since the A trust qualifies for the marital deduction and the B trust is sheltered by the unified credit, no estate tax will be paid at the first spouse's death. Thus the

AB trust arrangement does not change the usual first-death tax results. However, the second-death taxes are reduced since an additional $600,000 unified credit has been used at the time of the first death.

Planning Charitable Contributions

Qualifying gifts of property to charities may generate deductions against federal income, gift, and estate taxes. Although some limitations exist for the charitable deduction for income tax purposes, qualifying gifts of property are deductible in full against either the federal gift or estate tax base.

Charitable contributions are deductible for federal income, estate, and gift tax purposes only if made to qualified organizations. Generally speaking, an organization is qualified if it is operated exclusively for religious, charitable, scientific, literary, or educational purposes. In addition, the charity must hold such qualified status under the rules of the Internal Revenue Service. A list of qualified charities is published by the IRS and may be inspected by any individuals interested in making a charitable contribution.

Advantages of gifts to charity. The value of property gifted to a qualified charity is fully deductible from the federal gift or estate tax base. In addition, the value of property gifted to charity will be deductible from the federal income tax base of the donor. (Some limitations exist on the size of the income tax deduction, but they are not discussed here.) Thus a donor can reduce current income taxes and the eventual size of his or her estate. Quite simply, any property gifted to charity will remove the property (including any postcontribution appreciation) from the transfer-tax base of the donor. Since the charitable gift tax deduction is unlimited, charitable contributions can be even more effective than gifts to noncharitable donees in reducing the size of the gross estate of a wealthy client. The charitable deduction is similarly unlimited for testamentary bequests to charities. Through the techniques discussed below, charitable contributions can significantly reduce the decedent's estate tax liability without completely divesting other heirs of the donated property.

Gifts of remainder interests to charity. One disadvantage of an outright lifetime contribution of property to charity is that the donor loses the current enjoyment of the property. Fortunately there are methods to take advantage of the tax benefits provided to charitable contributions while retaining the donor's use or enjoyment of the property. Certain types of trust arrangements, known as *charitable remainder trusts,* can be employed to retain the current enjoyment of the property for the life of the donor (or lives of the donor's family members) while providing gift, estate, and income tax advantages. The charitable remainder trust can be established during the donor's lifetime or at his or her death. The charitable remainder trust permits the donor to retain the current income for the donor or his or her family. The income from the trust corpus will be retained for a time period (usually measured by the life of the donor or lives of selected family members) with the charitable institution holding the remainder interest. The current tax deduction is measured by the present value of the remainder interest held by charity. Thus the donor (or possibly members of the donor's family) receives current benefit of the trust property and current tax advantages, while the charity receives the benefit of the property outright when the remainder interest is distributed. To prevent abuses of the transfer tax system, tax rules carefully specify the types of charitable remainder trusts eligible for such tax benefits.

Donating income interests to charity. Under some circumstances a client may donate a current income interest to charity as opposed to a remainder interest. Under this arrangement, known as a *charitable lead trust,* a trust is established to provide a charity with a current term income interest. The remainder interest in the trust is retained by the grantor (or for his or her family). For income tax purposes the charitable lead trust is a grantor trust, and the current income on the trust is taxable to the grantor. However, the grantor gets a current income and gift or estate tax deduction equal to the present value of the income interest gifted to the charity.

The charitable lead trust is generally used for testamentary dispositions. If the current income interest bequested to the charity is substantial, the estate will receive a deduction in an amount equal to a large portion of the value of the property placed in the trust. Thus the taxable estate is significantly reduced while the family retains the ultimate control of the trust property through its remainder interest. The charitable lead trust is an excellent tool for extremely wealthy individuals who have other substantial assets to leave to their heirs currently, since the assets placed in the charitable lead trust may not be available for several years.

The Role of Life Insurance in the Estate Plan

Life insurance can serve either as an estate liquidity or estate enhancement tool. The most appropriate use of life insurance in the estate plan depends upon the age, family circumstances, and financial status of the particular client.

Life Insurance for Estate Enhancement

Life insurance is generally used for estate enhancement for (1) younger clients, (2) clients with dependent family members, and (3) clients with small to moderate-sized estates. Clients in these categories generally have protection as the primary need for their life insurance coverage. These individuals need to protect their families from the loss of future earnings with which to support the family members. These clients are either in or are headed toward their peak earning years, and their families rely on these future earnings for such things as the educational and medical needs of the children, the support needs of the client and his or her spouse, and the eventual retirement needs of the client and his or her spouse.

The death taxes facing a younger client with a small to moderate-sized estate are relatively minor. The unified credit and marital deduction will generally remove the danger of federal estate taxes for these individuals. Thus estate liquidity is not the primary concern. It is highly improbable, however, that these individuals have accumulated enough wealth to replace future income and support of a prematurely deceased breadwinner. Life insurance is the perfect estate enhancement tool to replace some or all of the financial loss created by the premature death. The use of life insurance coverage to provide for such a loss is discussed in chapters 7 and 8.

Life Insurance for Estate Liquidity Purposes

For older clients with larger estates estate liquidity becomes a primary focus in the use of life insurance. Older clients have generally completed or nearly completed the heaviest support and educational expense years for dependent children. These individuals are usually well along in the funding of their retirement plans and have fewer years of employment ahead of them.

Since these clients may have accumulated substantial wealth, the protection offered by the marital deduction and unified credit may be inadequate to shelter their estates. Although the marital deduction will generally shelter all of the estate from tax at the death of the first spouse, the second death creates a substantial tax problem in the foreseeable future (if the spouse is of similar age). As noted earlier, with optimal planning the unified credit and marital deduction can shelter only $1.2 million of total family wealth from taxes.

In addition, an affluent client may have accumulated substantial wealth that is not liquid. For example, an interest in a closely held family business is often assigned a high value for the purposes of the federal estate tax. However, the business interest may be unmarketable to purchasers outside the family group. If the heirs are to remain in the business, they must discover a method to pay any estate taxes due.

Under the circumstances described above, life insurance is quite useful in providing for estate liquidity. Life insurance can be secured by a client to provide death proceeds equal to the size of the wealth lost in the form of the substantial state death taxes and federal estate tax. In addition, the life insurance proceeds provide cash, which, as opposed to illiquid estate assets, is more readily available to provide for the liquidity needs of settling the estate.

The estate tax treatment of the life insurance selected by these individuals is critical. Since affluent clients are hoping to solve liquidity problems rather than add to a tax burden, life insurance should be purchased and owned in a manner that keeps the death proceeds out of the gross estate if at all possible. Thus these individuals often have ownership arrangements for the life insurance that provide the insured with no incidents of ownership. This can be accomplished by having either the spouse or children of the insured apply for and own the life insurance policy. Or, as discussed below, a trust can be designed to own the life insurance policy. However, the estate or the executor should never be the beneficiary of the proceeds since this beneficiary designation would place the proceeds in the gross estate for tax purposes.

Life Insurance Trusts

Revocable trusts. A revocable life insurance trust is designed to own and/or be the designated beneficiary of life insurance coverage on the grantor's life. The revocable life insurance trust serves no estate tax planning purposes. Since the trust is revocable, the insured is treated as the owner of the policy and the death proceeds will be included in the insured's gross estate. The revocable trust is ordinarily used when a specific, perhaps temporary, protection need exists.

The revocable trust is an excellent method for providing life insurance benefits for the protection of young children. If the insured dies, the trust becomes irrevocable and the children can be provided for by the beneficial terms of the trust. The revocable life insurance trust is also an excellent method of providing protection for children following a divorce.

Irrevocable life insurance trusts. An irrevocable life insurance trust is generally used by older clients who have a more stable family and financial situation. The irrevocable trust can be designed to provide life insurance benefits for heirs outside of the gross estate. In addition, contributions to the trust can be designed to avoid gift or generation-skipping taxes. Thus the irrevocable life insurance trust is a perfect tool for the estate liquidity needs of older wealthy clients without adding to the tax burden. Since the trust is irrevocable, the client should be certain of his or her beneficial intent at the time the trust is drafted.

ESTATE PLANNING DOCUMENTS

The estate plan is a roadmap directing how the client's wealth will be assembled and disposed of during the client's life or at his or her death. The plan itself is useless unless the documents of the plan have been drafted appropriately. The documents must be drafted carefully to avoid hidden traps and to provide direction to the appropriate personal representatives, fiduciaries, and beneficiaries of the client. These directions must be drafted according to the principles of state law and should unambiguously state the intent of the client. Since these documents necessarily involve compliance with state law, they should be prepared by an attorney who specializes in estate planning in the local jurisdiction.

The Client's Will

Despite the importance of the will in a client's estate plan, it is estimated that seven out of ten Americans die without a valid will. Unfortunately these individuals have left the disposition of their estates to the provisions of state intestacy law. In addition, the estates of these individuals will be handled by a court-appointed administrator. In many cases the estate will be subject to unnecessary taxes and administration expenses. In any event, a valid will is necessary for the implementation of a cohesive estate plan.

Requirements for a Valid Will

Although the requirements for wills are provided by the laws of the various states, several items are universal. With some minor exceptions for rare circumstances the following are required for a valid will:

- The will must be in writing.
- The testator, or creator of the will, must sign the will at the end of the document, usually in the presence of witnesses.
- A number of witnesses (generally two or three) must sign the will after the testator's signature. The witnesses are attesting that the signature of the testator is in fact his or her signature.

What Can a Valid Will Accomplish?

The client's will is the centerpiece of the estate plan. Although its primary function is to direct the disposition of the client's wealth, it serves other purposes as well. A properly drafted will can accomplish the following objectives:

- Direct the disposition of the client's *probate* assets.
- Nominate the personal representative of the testator, known as the executor, who will handle the administration of the client's estate.
- Nominate the guardians of any minor children of the testator.
- Create testamentary trusts that will take effect at the testator's death to hold the property of the testator for the benefit of named beneficiaries.
- Name the trustee of any trust created under the will.
- Provide directions to the executor and/or trustees named in the will indicating how these fiduciaries will manage assets contained in the estate or testamentary trust. (The directions could be quite specific or provide broad powers to the fiduciaries.)
- Provide directions for payment of the estate's taxes and expenses. (Care should be taken in naming the components of the estate that will be responsible for taxes and expenses. Incorrect designation of the component obligated to pay such expenses could result in increased death taxes or inappropriately diminished shares of specific beneficiaries.)
- Establish the compensation of executors and/or trustees named in the will.

Living Wills

A living will is a document indicating the client's intentions should the client become disabled and lack the legal capacity to make decisions for himself or herself. Generally speaking, the living will deals with the health care measures that the client wants imposed should he or she become legally disabled. If a living will is desired, the document should carefully spell out whether or not the client desires that heroic measures be taken should he or she experience a life-threatening accident or illness. Living wills are not valid in all states, and local counsel should be obtained if the client wishes to state his or her intentions in this regard.

Trusts

A trust is a relationship (generally in the form of a written document) that divides the ownership of property. Legal title to the trust is held by one party, known as a trustee. The beneficial or equitable interest in the trust property is owned by the beneficiaries of the trust. The trustee has the duty to manage the trust property provided by the grantor of the trust for the benefit of the beneficiaries. The trust is used to provide for beneficiaries when, for one reason or another, they are unable to administer the trust assets for themselves. For example, a trust may be created to provide for minor beneficiaries. Minor beneficiaries are incapable under state law of holding property in their own name and perhaps lack the necessary experience and financial acumen to manage the trust property. The trust is an excellent tool for handling and/or consolidating accumulations of wealth.

The trustee manages the trust property under the terms of the trust. The trust terms are the directions and intentions of the grantor with respect to the management of the trust. For example, there may be directions with respect to the investment of trust assets. More importantly, there are directions with respect to providing for the beneficiaries of the trust. The trust terms may be restrictive and provide the trustee with very little discretion. For example, the terms may provide for specified distributions of income and/or principal to designated beneficiaries at various points in time. Or the trustee may be provided with "sprinkle" powers permitting the trustee to determine when distributions of either income or principal are appropriate for the various beneficiaries. The trustee has the legal obligation to manage the trust prudently and, to the extent the trustee has discretionary powers, to act impartially with respect to the beneficiaries.

Since the trust terms describe the intentions of the grantor, a trust should be drafted carefully under the direction of an attorney who specializes in such matters. In addition, the grantor should select the trustee, whether a private individual or a corporate trustee, with great care.

Living (Inter Vivos) Trust

A trust can be created during the lifetime of a grantor. It could be created for several reasons. The trust could hold property and operate prior to the death of the grantor. Or a trust could be created during the lifetime of the grantor simply to receive assets at the grantor's death. Such a trust is known as a "pour-over" trust.

A trust could be either revocable or irrevocable. A revocable trust is created when the grantor transfers trust property to the trust but reserves the power to alter or revoke the agreement. Since the revocable trust is an incomplete transfer, the creation of a revocable trust has no effect on the client's income, estate, or gift tax situation. The revocable trust gives the grantor the ability to observe the management of the trust assets without relinquishing ultimate control of the assets. Thus the grantor can reclaim the trust assets at any time. The revocable trust becomes irrevocable only when the grantor modifies the trust to become irrevocable or dies and therefore is no longer able to modify the trust.

The revocable trust has gained popularity in recent times as an estate plan in itself. It is drafted to provide the dispositive directions normally contained in a client's will. The client will then transfer all appropriate assets to the trustee to be retitled in the trustee's name. At the grantor's death the trust becomes irrevocable and all property contained in the trust is managed or disposed of under the terms of the trust. The revocable trust is popular as an estate plan since property disposed of by the revocable trust avoids the publicity, delay, and some expenses associated with the probate process.

A living trust can also be designated as irrevocable by the grantor. Since the irrevocable trust is a completed gift, it is effective for gift and estate tax purposes. A properly designed irrevocable trust can receive property from the grantor which, as a completed gift, will avoid the gross estate of the grantor at his or her death. In addition, funds placed in the irrevocable trust become the property of the trustee and are exempt from the claims of the grantor's creditors. The irrevocable trust is an effective estate planning tool for older grantors who face substantial estate tax burdens.

Testamentary Trust

A testamentary trust is created under the will of the testator. Since the will can be changed as long as the testator retains legal capacity, the testamentary trust is never irrevocable until the client's death (or permanent legal disability). A testamentary trust does not receive property until the client dies and the proceeds are transferred to the trust by the executor. Since the trust is contained in the client's will, it is subject to probate. In a simple will testamentary trusts are often drafted to provide for the testator's children should the spouses die in a common disaster. In a more complex estate plan testamentary trusts are often the vehicles for the marital and family trusts described earlier in this chapter.

Durable Power of Attorney

A power of attorney is a written document that enables the client, known as the *principal,* to designate a holder of the power, known as the *attorney-in-fact,* to act on the principal's behalf. The attorney has the power to act in behalf of the principal only with respect to powers specifically enumerated in the document. A *durable* power of attorney is an estate planning document that is not terminated by the legal disability of the principal. Since this document provides the attorney-in-fact with the potential to abuse the privileges granted by the document, these documents are construed very narrowly in transactions with third parties. Thus any powers that the principal wishes to grant to the attorney-in-fact should be specifically enumerated. The document should also clearly specify whether or not the legal disability of the principal has any effect on the power of attorney.

A power of attorney should be drafted prudently for the specific circumstances of the client. Care should be taken as to the choice of the attorney-in-fact, the powers granted to him or her, and when the powers take effect. The advantages of a durable power of attorney include these:

- An older client can execute a durable power of attorney and avoid the necessity of having a guardian or a conservator appointed should the client lose legal capacity.
- The attorney-in-fact can be given the power to manage the principal's assets should the principal suffer a permanent or temporary loss of legal capacity. This is particularly important for owners of a closely held business.
- The durable power can replace or complement a revocable trust. The attorney-in-fact can manage the client's assets subsequent to a client's legal disability and, if empowered, continue the client's dispositive scheme. For example, the attorney-in-fact could continue to make annual exclusion gifts or contributions after the legal disability but prior to the death of the principal.
- In some states the attorney-in-fact can make medical care decisions on behalf of the principal.

CONCLUSION

Although the estate planning process suggests a certain finality, the process should be ongoing. The estate planner should never be satisfied that the client has approved a plan and executed the necessary documents. The estate planner and the client should take the necessary steps to coordinate the estate plan with the client's other personal and financial considerations. For example, property transfers may be necessary to convert the client's property into the appropriate form. Since a will disposes only of probate property, it may frustrate the intent of the plan if the client's property is not converted into a form passing through probate.

In addition, all appointed individuals, such as executors, trustees, and attorneys-in-fact, should be informed of their roles and the intentions of the client. In many cases members of the family will be relied upon to make responsible decisions with respect to the estate plan. These family members should be informed, to the extent necessary, of the client's dispositive intentions.

Finally, periodic follow-up is necessary in a successfully planned estate. Many aspects of the estate plan will be revocable. Such flexibility may provide additional opportunities for the estate planner and the client. Changes in the tax law should be monitored and may necessitate new estate planning steps as a result. The failure to follow up will probably result in client dissatisfaction and perhaps malpractice claims against the estate planner.

7

Insurance Planning: The Risk Management Process

Charles E. Hughes*

Personal financial planning represents an integrated approach to the development and implementation of plans for the achievement of individual or family financial objectives. Although financial objectives may differ in terms of individual circumstances, goals, attitudes, and needs, all integrated plans should include an analysis and recommendations that satisfy the individual protection objectives.

While plans for the accumulation of wealth may be more exciting, the protection of that accumulated wealth cannot be overlooked. Most people work to acquire assets (wealth) such as homes, automobiles, savings, and investments, but the pleasure associated with this wealth is sometimes interrupted by the chilling thought that some event over which there is little or no control could cause assets to be damaged or destroyed. To find some method of protecting assets, or preserving the wealth represented by those assets, is the challenge people face, that is, the risk they face.

As will be seen in more detail in chapter 9, the meaning of the term *risk* as applied to investments relates to the uncertainty of growth or decline in income or principal. Another type of risk, identified as *pure risk,* differs in meaning in that the uncertainty associated with it involves *only the chance of loss.* In this definition the possibility of gain is essentially absent, and all that remains is the alternative of loss or no loss (no change).

To illustrate the concept of pure risk, suppose a client owns a home and is concerned about the possibility of damage or destruction due to fire. What are the possible outcomes? Either a fire occurs and causes damage that results in a loss, or no fire occurs and there is no change or loss. The uncertainty as to the outcome is the pure risk that the client faces. While there is risk in that the home could appreciate or depreciate in market value, this is the investment type of risk and not pure risk. Reference made to risk for purposes of discussion in this chapter and the next will be to pure risk, and this risk is defined as uncertainty as to financial loss.

Technically, a function of insurance is to reduce or replace uncertainty. However, insurance, especially property and liability insurance, is more understandable if its function is stated as a reimbursement for the loss sustained. Loss is the undesirable end result of risk and is defined as the decrease or disappearance of value, usually in an unexpected or relatively unpredictable manner. For example, when fire damages or destroys a home, the owner suffers a financial loss at least equivalent to the cost necessary to repair or replace the damaged property. This type of loss is in the pure risk category.

---

*Charles E. Hughes, DBA, CLU, CPCU, is associate professor of insurance at The American College.

How is the financial services professional to approach his or her clients' pure risk situations? The process of risk analysis and control, normally referred to as *risk management,* has been developed for application in business situations. Much of the same process applies to the management of risk at the individual or family level. This chapter will provide an introduction to the use of the risk management process as an integral part of financial planning for individuals and families. Since the use of insurance is a major tool in managing pure risks, this chapter includes some introductory comments about insurance. Chapter 8 will focus primarily on the insurance coverages available to deal with pure risks that may confront clients.

Risk Management Process

The risk management process is a systematic approach to the discovery and treatment of risks facing individuals and families. It is a modification of the risk management functions performed for business organizations by risk managers, consultants, and practitioners in the field. This process includes three steps:

1. risk analysis
2. risk treatment planning
3. risk treatment plan implementation

Risk Analysis

The first step in the risk management process is to analyze the risks the client faces. The *identification* of risks is the first function in this analysis. Identification might also be considered the most important function, since there is really no need for additional action (until or unless the event does occur) if the risk has not first been identified. A systematic approach is helpful in discovering all of the significant risks the client faces.

The second function in risk analysis is the *measurement* of the losses associated with the identified risks. Once the risks have been identified and an appropriate value determined as a measurement of the possible loss, the final function in risk analysis is to *evaluate* the potential financial impact such losses would have upon the client.

Risk Treatment Planning

The second step in the risk management process is risk treatment planning, which is the evaluation of the alternative techniques for handling risks. Although various methods of loss control and loss financing will be described briefly in this chapter, the major emphasis will be placed on the use of insurance as a risk treatment technique.

Risk Treatment Plan Implementation

The final step in the risk management process involves the collection of data from the first two steps and the formulation of recommendations for the risk treatment plan. In addition, this step includes both assistance in the implementation of the plan and the task of continuously monitoring the selected plan to determine its effectiveness and to review the risks upon which the plan is based.

With this brief overview of the risk management process in mind, each of these three steps will now be discussed in greater detail.

RISK ANALYSIS

As mentioned above, the first step in the risk management process is to analyze the risks that the individual faces. This step includes the identification of risks, measurement of loss, and evaluation of the financial impact of the risk.

Risk Identification

To identify potential risks, a checklist of all the losses that could possibly be incurred by an individual or family is useful to the planner. This provides him or her with a systematic approach to discovering the potential losses faced by the particular client.

The initial step in developing this checklist is to establish some basis for classifying the risks to be identified. For example, one method would be to group the risks into categories according to the general nature of the loss. These categories could include: (1) physical damage to assets, (2) loss of possession by fraud or criminal violence, (3) loss of ownership through an adverse judgment at law, (4) loss of income resulting from damage to the property of others, (5) loss of income because of a personal disablement, and so on. Unfortunately, this technique could become unmanageable and even confusing.

Another method of categorizing risks is to establish general headings under which would be listed events that would (1) decrease assets, (2) decrease income, (3) increase expenses, or (4) increase liability. An advantage of this method is its emphasis on outcomes. For example, under the category Decrease Assets, the planner would be concerned with identifying the assets owned, used, or in the possession of the individual or family that would cause this client to experience a loss should a particular event occur. For example, suppose the client owns an automobile. Could that automobile (asset) be damaged or destroyed? If the answer is yes, the client is exposed to the risk of a decrease in the value of that asset. Therefore, the automobile would be listed under the Decrease Assets category of risk. (At a later stage in the risk management process the planner will also need to examine what could cause this automobile to be damaged or destroyed and to give some thought to the dollar amount of the loss that would be suffered by the client should the event occur.)

The planner should also list ownership of the automobile under the Increase Liability category since an adverse judgment could be rendered against the client because of the ownership of that automobile.

This same process could be completed for each of the four risk categories. As another example, the possibility that a client will be injured or become ill would be listed under both the Decrease Income and Increase Expenses categories of risk. The occurrence of the event would result in an increase in expenses for the client's medical care and the possibility of a decrease in income because of the inability to continue to work during a period of disability.

This whole process can be continued until the planner eventually ends with a rather lengthy list of possible losses or risks that the individual or family faces.

Another method of classifying loss exposure is on the basis of the following outline:

1. property losses
   a. direct losses associated with the need to replace or repair damaged or missing property
   b. indirect (consequential) losses, such as additional living expenses that are caused by the direct loss
2. liability losses arising out of damage to or destruction of others' property or personal injuries to others
3. personal losses
   a. loss of earning power because of premature death, disability, periods of unemployment, or superannuation
   b. extra expenses associated with injuries or periods of sickness

Clients are exposed to direct loss through the ownership of real and personal property. Real property typically consists of the client's dwelling, and personal property includes such items as household goods, clothing, and automobiles. Indirect losses are associated with the loss of use of property (normally indirect losses are associated with real property rather than personal property because of the ease in quickly replacing most types of personal property). In addition to the indirect loss referred to as additional living expenses, other types of consequential losses include debris removal costs, rental income losses, and demolition losses. Of these, additional living expenses and debris removal are the more important losses for most individuals and families.

The ownership, maintenance or use of an automobile is the best known source of liability loss. However, individuals should be aware of the fact that potential losses also arise out of the ownership, maintenance, or use of real property and out of personal activities. It should also be noted that workers' compensation statutes can give rise to an exposure in certain states when a client has household employees.

Examples of personal losses include the loss of continuing income to family members upon the breadwinner's retirement or premature death. In addition, increased expenses associated with medical care for hospitalization and physician expenses are types of personal losses.

When this type of classification system is used, the exposures to risk can be listed in an abbreviated fashion. For example, when the risk involves possible damage or destruction to the dwelling, the use of the word *dwelling* can be appropriate. The underlying questions associated with the single word to identify a risk could include such things as the number of dwellings involved, where the dwellings are located, and, if the dwellings are exposed to loss, what could conceivably cause the loss.

For this last question, some individuals conducting risk surveys prefer to actually list the causes of loss. The advantage in listing the various causes of loss is the ability to better analyze the potential loss associated with a particular risk. However, a primary disadvantage of this approach is the tendency of some financial planners to rely heavily on only those causes of loss that are insurable, and to forget to list causes of loss that are not considered insurable.

The decision of whether to list causes of loss in the identification of risks will be at the discretion of the individual making the risk analysis survey. Those who are skilled in identifying all the possible causes of loss to a particular asset will probably prefer to simply list that asset. An insurance salesperson conducting the survey might prefer to identify causes of loss to help select the proper insurance coverage to meet the particular risk. The financial services professional should select the risk identification procedure with which he or she is most comfortable.

How does the planner go about completing the checklist of potential risks? If a comprehensive checklist is available, and if it has been completed and the information required has been obtained from the client, the completion of the checklist should be rather easy. Since the planner is attempting to identify the client's property and activities that give rise to risk, it might be possible for the planner to simply sit back and think about the risk exposures. However, to ensure that risk exposures will not be overlooked, it is necessary to become more involved. This involvement should include a visual inspection of the client's property or a lengthy discussion with the client in order to obtain answers to the questions in the survey form.

Some risk analysis surveyors like to use an insurance survey form. However, it should be reemphasized that this type of form is normally designed to discover needs for insurance coverages and not to identify all the potential loss situations. Some surveyors prefer their own checklist form, such as the one contained in Appendix C, and financial services professionals would probably incorporate a few additional questions necessary to prepare a complete list of all risks in the client's situation. If there are any doubts about the identification of risks, the financial planner should seek additional assistance from someone experienced in this task.

The first phase of risk analysis can now be completed. To illustrate how this might be done, assume that the circumstances of a client are as follows: Burt Beamer, aged 45, has a wife, aged 43, a son, aged 18, and a daughter, aged 16. Burt is a manager for a local firm and currently earns $78,000 annually. The Beamers purchased a home 5 years ago for $225,000. Last year they purchased a small cabin in the mountains for $45,000. They plan to use this cabin as much as possible during the summer months and occasionally on weekends during the balance of the year. They are also thinking about renting the cabin out periodically during the summer season. The Beamers own two automobiles, a 3-year-old station wagon and a one-year-old foreign compact.

Although this is a simplified example, a partial listing of the risks that the Beamer family faces is shown in table 7-1. In actual practice the planner should seek additional information from the Beamer family to complete the list of exposures. The planner would want to include other assets or property that might be owned or used by the Beamers. He or she would also be concerned with expanding the liability exposure to include any possible business pursuits and to investigate any other liability exposures, such as the use of nonowned autos. In this illustration, personal risks are limited to the premature death of Burt. In practice this area would be expanded to include premature death of Burt's spouse, risks associated with the loss of earning power because of periods of disability, the incurring of additional expenses for medical costs associated with accidents or illnesses, and the need for income at retirement. Even the needs under the premature death category might be expanded beyond those shown in this illustration.

The risk identification process may appear to be a relatively simple task. Some financial services professionals and clients may feel that it is a waste of time to formalize the risk identification process. They need only be reminded that forgetting or neglecting the wrong risk could have disastrous financial consequences.

TABLE 7-1
Risk Identification (Type of Risk)

Property risks
    Direct losses
        Dwelling
        Cabin
        Furniture, clothing, etc. (dwelling)
        Furniture, clothing, etc. (cabin)
        Automobiles
    Indirect losses
        Additional living expenses
        Debris removal

Liability risks
    Owned premises (dwelling, cabin)
    Owned automobiles
    Personal activities

Personal risks
    Premature death (of Burt)
        Cash for clean-up fund
        Education fund
        Mortgage redemption fund
        Lifetime income for spouse

Risk Measurement

The second function of risk analysis is the measurement of the losses associated with the identified risks. As will be shown in table 7-2, the measurement of loss exposures should be the maximum possible loss associated with the event.

Theoretically, risk measurement should include information on loss severity and probability of occurrence. Measuring loss probabilities requires the compilation and interpretation of statistics, and in the single risk situation associated with individuals and families, probabilities have little application. Also, in most single risk situations the frequency of losses is so low that it does not permit the accumulation of sufficient data to have any degree of reliability. Therefore the major emphasis should be on the severity of the loss. When dealing with individual risks, it is safest to assume total loss and identify this as the maximum possible loss.

Property Risks

The easiest asset to measure for loss purposes is cash; each one dollar bill is worth one dollar (except, of course, when it is numismatic property or when problems of foreign exchange enter the picture). For property other than cash, however, risk measurement problems begin to emerge. Three key terms of the measurement process that need to be understood are (1) actual cash value, (2) replacement cost, and (3) depreciation.

Actual cash value is an insurance term used in many property insurance contracts. These contracts often limit the insurer's liability for damaged property to its actual cash value at the time of loss. Actual cash value has generally been defined as replacement cost less a reduction resulting from depreciation and obsolescence. This is normally expressed simply as

$$\text{actual cash value} = \text{replacement cost} - \text{depreciation}$$

Actual cash value is sometimes a difficult measurement to understand, primarily because of the confusion that arises from the interpretations of *replacement cost* and *depreciation.* Although useful life is frequently used as a guideline in measuring depreciation, depreciation as a factor in measuring actual cash value differs from depreciation in an accounting sense. Depreciation is a function of the age of the asset, its use, its condition at the time of loss, and any other factor causing deterioration. In addition, anything that causes the property to become obsolete in any fashion is also included in the depreciation determination for purposes of calculating actual cash value.

Replacement cost is that cost necessary to replace or repair the damaged asset. For personal property this is replacement with a comparable asset at the current price. In the calculation of actual cash value, replacement cost would be reduced for the comparable age of the damaged property. For example, assume that an auto that had been purchased new 3 years ago for $11,995 was completely destroyed in an accident. The same auto purchased today would cost $15,000, which would be its replacement cost. The actual cash value is an amount sufficient to replace the destroyed auto with one of like age and condition. Note, however, that depreciation is deducted from the current price, not the original price. It is immaterial that the damaged auto cost $11,995 new 3 years ago. The actual cash value is $15,000 (replacement cost) less an allowance for depreciation.

When replacement cost is used for real property, such as a dwelling, it is normally interpreted to mean the cost to rebuild the same type dwelling on the same site for the same type of occupancy and with materials of like kind and quality. If the replacement cost for the dwelling was determined to be $160,000 and depreciation was $17,200, the measurement of the actual cash value would be

$$\text{actual cash value} = \text{replacement cost} - \text{depreciation}$$
$$= \$160,000 - \$17,200$$
$$= \$142,800$$

There are several ways of estimating replacement cost. One method used for dwellings is to take the original construction cost and adjust it by one of the published construction cost indexes. A second method is the unit-measurement technique, a tabular process of calculating a base cost value by using a square-foot calculation for a given type of construction and type of dwelling (one-story, two-story, and so on), and then applying a geographic location adjustment factor to that value. A variation of this begins with a counting of rooms in the dwelling. Perhaps the most accurate valuation method is to have a complete survey made by a professional appraiser qualified to prepare replacement cost values. This would probably include a detailed physical inspection and study of any plans available in order that a complete list of labor and material costs could be determined.

Replacement cost has become the more practical measure of the maximum possible loss associated with a client's real property in pure risk situations, especially when insurance is determined to be the technique most appropriate to treat the particular risk. Sometimes there is a temptation to use market value as the measurement of loss for real property. While this is the value that is most familiar to consumers and owners of real estate, market value is closely linked to supply and demand conditions, and caution should be exercised in using this value as the measurement of maximum possible loss for pure risk situations. Remember that pure risk is the possibility of loss or no loss; the concern is for the damage or destruction of property, not its transfer of ownership.

Actually, destruction of real property from a pure risk standpoint might even increase the market value of the property and therefore result in a profit to the owner. For example, suppose a dwelling is situated on a lot at a well-traveled intersection. This property would have market value based on its potential sale as a commercial establishment. If a fire totally destroyed this dwelling, the owner might actually realize an increase in market value for the property since the purchaser would not have to bear most of the cost of demolition in order to prepare the site for a new commercial building. However, if the owner is not interested in selling the property and wants to make the dwelling inhabitable again, the loss is the cost to repair the damage — the pure risk. This is measured on a replacement cost basis, which may differ substantially from market value.

For insurance purposes, the measurement of loss for personal property such as furniture and clothing has traditionally been the item's actual cash value. Actually, however, the maximum possible loss is the replacement cost of the particular item. For an extra premium, most insurance companies will provide replacement cost coverage on personal property. For this reason, and for the purpose of showing the value differences, the maximum possible loss for personal property (and for real property as well) is measured on both a replacement cost and actual-cash-value basis. An example of this is shown in table 7-2.

The loss measurement for personal property is further complicated by the fact that most clients do not keep an accurate list of all the personal property they own. For this reason, it is suggested that the data-gathering questionnaire used in the risk identification function include a listing of specific items of property or clusters of types of property as an aid in formulating a closer approximation of the personal property owned by the client. Then the task becomes one of attaching a value, either replacement cost or actual cash value, to the items of personal property.

TABLE 7-2
Risk Identification and Measurement

Type of Risk	Maximum Possible Loss	
	Actual Cash Value	Replacement Cost
Property risks		
Direct losses		
Dwelling	$160,000	$ 200,000
Cabin	30,000	42,000
Furniture, clothing, etc. (dwelling)	60,000	90,000
Furniture, clothing, etc. (cabin)	4,000	7,500
Automobiles	19,000	28,000
Indirect losses		
Additional living expenses		9,600
Debris removal		3,500
Liability risks		
Owned premises (dwelling, cabin)		unlimited
Owned automobiles		unlimited
Personal activities		unlimited
Personal risks		
Premature death (of Burt)		
Cash for clean-up fund		50,000
Education fund		78,000
Mortgage redemption fund		137,000
Lifetime income for spouse		$1,100,000

The measurement of loss to automobiles tends to be less complex than the measurement of value for a dwelling or personal property. Replacement cost, the cost of purchasing a brand new automobile of the same type, would be the maximum possible loss. However, since physical damage insurance for automobiles is written on an actual-cash-value basis, the loss measurement should be listed on this basis as well as on the replacement cost value. This will indicate for the owner the difference between the actual loss and the amount that the owner can reasonably expect to recover from an insurer. Values for automobiles are published in various "books" that provide a close estimate of the current actual cash value. However, it should be understood that the figures published in these books are for vehicles in average condition and may not apply to specific automobiles.

Finally, for measurement purposes some loss exposures listed under the property risk category are not costs of replacing property but are indirect expenses incurred because of damage to property. The best example of this for most individuals is the category of additional living expenses. These are the costs over and above normal living expenses that would be necessary to provide living accommodations, food, and transportation if a dwelling could not be occupied due to damage or destruction. An estimate of these expenses should be made as the measurement of this loss exposure.

Liability Risks

The measurement of liability risk is somewhat similar to that of indirect additional living expenses since they are both estimates of future dollar amounts. No perfect method has been developed for measuring the maximum possible dollar loss that individuals can suffer from the liability exposure. A client can enter into certain contractual arrangements that will limit the extent of liability, but in most cases the liability loss will depend upon the severity of the future accident and the amount the court awards to the injured parties (or the amount of the out-of-court settlement agreement).

It could be argued that the maximum possible liability loss is limited to the current accumulated wealth of the individual. To a certain extent this is correct since the balance of a judgment could be discharged by a declaration of bankruptcy. Unfortunately, the stigma of bankruptcy that would remain could hamper future business and personal activities. In addition, bankruptcy might not be permitted as a way of discharging some liability judgments. Since a liability loss could range anywhere from a few dollars to $1 million or more, it is appropriate to recognize some uncertainty about the measurement of the liability loss and to identify this amount as "unlimited."

Personal Risks

There are several ways of measuring the loss associated with personal risks. For example, the loss associated with premature death might simply be the aggregate dollar amount that would have been provided to the survivors by the deceased (presumably the breadwinner) on an annual basis over the future productive lifetime of that individual. The human-life-value method of measuring loss due to premature death is based on a calculation of the present value of a given dollar amount annually over a given number of years at some assumed interest rate.

Another common method of measuring the loss associated with premature death is to determine, at some assumed interest rate, the principal sum necessary to provide interest earnings comparable to the dollar contributions that would have been made to the survivors by the deceased. When this method is utilized, other sources of income and other income-producing assets can be considered in arriving at the final capital sum required.

Another method of determining the loss associated with premature death (and the method used in this chapter) is to identify and attach a dollar amount to the specific financial needs of the survivors. For the Beamer family, the lump-sum cash needs are identified in table 7-2 as a clean-up fund, education fund, and mortgage redemption fund. The income need was identified as a lifetime income for the surviving spouse.

In table 7-2, the dollar amount shown for the clean-up fund is an estimate of the amount needed for last illness expenses, funeral costs, outstanding debts, probate expenses, federal and state estate and inheritance taxes, and so forth. The dollar amount for the education fund is the present value of the projected future costs of educating the two Beamer children. Planning for future education expenses has become a common part of the financial planning process, and the dollar amount needed for this item would most likely be provided in some other part of the total financial planning process. If not, some time should be spent in developing an estimate of these costs. The amount for the mortgage is typically the current unpaid balance shown in the amortization schedule.

The measurement of the amount needed to fund the lifetime income for the surviving spouse requires calculations beyond the scope of this chapter. In the planner's discussions with the client it was determined that, in the event of his premature death, Burt wanted his widow to have the equivalent purchasing power of $4,000 per month throughout her lifetime. To calculate the present value of a principal sum needed to satisfy this objective, it is necessary to make assumptions regarding future rates of inflation and future rates of interest earnings. For this case, these assumptions were 4.5 percent and 6.5 percent, respectively. It was also assumed that upon reaching age 65 Mrs. Beamer would qualify for an inflation adjusted benefit equal to $1,000 per month from Burt's social security. Based on these assumptions and a projection of Mrs. Beamer's longevity of life, the current principal sum needed is calculated to be $1,100,000. This is the amount entered in table 7-2 as the maximum possible loss for the personal risk exposure.

At this point, the risk identification and measurement functions can be completed. Table 7-2 illustrates the maximum possible loss values that were determined for the partial list of risks facing the Beamer family.

Risk Evaluation

Once all the risks have been identified and an appropriate value has been determined as the measure of the maximum possible loss, the final function in risk analysis is to evaluate these risks from the standpoint of their potential financial impact upon the client. The financial services professional can assist in this process by having the client assess the seriousness of each potential loss on his or her financial status and by ranking the various risks according to their severity. One method of showing this is to categorize losses as *serious, moderate,* or *minimal* depending on each client's circumstances. The risks listed for the Beamer family in table 7-2 are evaluated using this method in the Risk Impact Chart (table 7-3).

One additional comment should be made about the evaluation of risks. It is a mistake to view these risks as isolated individual events; for example, the fire that causes damage to the dwelling should not be considered as a loss isolated from the concurrent loss due to fire damage of the furniture contained in that dwelling. All the losses that may result from a single event should be combined into one unit to obtain a true measure of the maximum possible loss. Therefore the fire damage to the dwelling and furniture should be considered as one loss and the combined total should be utilized to determine the total financial impact on the individual or family.

TABLE 7-3
Risk Impact Chart

<u>Serious</u>
    Liability losses
        Owned premises (dwelling, cabin)
        Owned automobiles
        Personal activities
    Property losses
        Dwelling
        Cabin
        Furniture, clothing, etc. (dwelling)
    Personal losses
        Cash for clean-up fund
        Mortgage redemption fund
        Lifetime income for spouse

<u>Moderate</u>
    Property losses
        Furniture, clothing, etc. (cabin)
        Automobile (foreign compact)
        Additional living expenses
    Personal losses
        Education fund

<u>Minimal</u>
    Property losses
        Debris removal
        Automobile (station wagon)

RISK TREATMENT PLANNING

The second step in the risk management process is determining what to do about the risks enumerated in the risk analysis step, that is, evaluating the alternative techniques for handling risks. The techniques typically available to individuals and families are grouped in two categories: loss control and loss financing.

Loss Control

Loss control (sometimes referred to as risk control) is concerned with the precontact, contact, and postcontact stages of losses that could have an adverse financial impact upon the individual or family. Loss control is concerned with reducing the probability that events resulting in financial loss will occur and minimizing the magnitude of those losses that do occur.

Many items of real or personal property can be repaired or replaced if they are damaged or destroyed, but even when property is covered by an insurance policy financial loss may result since many insurance policies leave a portion of the loss unreimbursed. In some cases, damaged property cannot be repaired or replaced, nor can a proper substitute for that property be found. Losses associated with injury or death can be compensated for by money, but regardless of the sum, money is frequently not the true measure of the loss in these situations. Therefore as these brief examples indicate, loss control activities are an important part of risk management. Three loss control techniques are examined: risk avoidance, loss prevention, and loss reduction.

Risk Avoidance

The objective of risk avoidance is the elimination of the given activity or condition that gave rise to the risk so that the possibility of a loss becomes nonexistent. While this method is potentially the most powerful risk treatment action, in many ways it is a very difficult treatment technique for an individual or family to practice. For example, if an individual is concerned about the liability loss exposure that arises from the ownership or use of an automobile, the application of risk avoidance would call for the complete elimination of the ownership and use of automobiles. In today's society this could be an extremely difficult objective to accomplish. Furthermore, if an individual currently owns an automobile, a strict interpretation of the avoidance technique would require the individual to demolish the automobile rather than to sell it and thereby transfer the risk to someone else, a practice that is difficult to accept in reality.

To take a more practical case, the existence of a swimming pool in one's backyard increases the liability exposure on the premises. An individual concerned about this liability exposure would practice avoidance by never purchasing a home that had a swimming pool in the backyard, never installing a swimming pool in the backyard, or filling in or destroying a swimming pool that currently exists in the backyard.

Similarly, certain types of animals are known to be vicious or to become vicious at times. Risk avoidance would be practiced by never owning such an animal or by destroying such an animal if currently owned. Concern about the possibility of a valuable fur coat being damaged or stolen would cause an individual practicing risk avoidance to resist purchasing a fur coat or to destroy any such coat that is currently owned. The same would be true for many other types of personal property.

Sometimes individuals can practice risk avoidance when the risk concerns the ownership of real property, for example, by living in rented property rather than owning a home. Although the individuals in this example avoid the loss exposures associated with the ownership of real property, they should be made aware that some of the same types of loss exposure may be acquired through the rental of property. In other words, the avoidance of one risk may create another.

Obviously then, risk avoidance can be a difficult risk treatment technique to apply. It is most effective if considered in the planning stages, that is, when a client is contemplating the purchase of a home or an auto, rather than after the fact when demolition of the asset might be the only avoidance alternative. In any case, it is virtually impossible to avoid all risks and it is therefore necessary to consider techniques that will forestall or minimize the losses.

Loss Prevention

Loss prevention, the attempt to control inescapable risks and forestall losses, must precede the occurrence of a loss and is directed at reducing the frequency of loss. Loss-prevention actions tend to be directed at hazards or conditions that increase the likelihood of a loss occurring. For example, since smoking in bed tends to increase the likelihood of fire, and smoking itself tends to increase the likelihood of future medical complications, a loss prevention action for both of these risks would be to stop smoking. Similarly, since consumption of alcohol combined with driving can increase the likelihood of an automobile accident, loss prevention would be practiced by not consuming alcoholic beverages or by not driving after having done so.

While these examples are "don't do" activities, loss prevention actions can also be positive in nature. For example, the construction of a fence around the swimming pool in one's backyard is an action designed to make it more difficult for individuals to gain access to the pool and therefore reduces the likelihood of a liability loss due to someone's use of the swimming pool without the property owner's knowledge. Some other examples of loss prevention activities include the following: proper servicing of one's automobile in order to reduce the possibility of an accident due to mechanical failure, taking a driver education program in order to reduce the frequency of accidental losses, keeping matches out of a child's reach in order to prevent fire, and picking up a child's toys from the floor and the steps to prevent someone from stepping on one of the toys and causing a fall and a potential injury.

It is sometimes difficult to measure the effectiveness of loss prevention activities since most types of losses occur infrequently. It is also difficult to know how many times loss did not occur because prevention measures were introduced. The goal of loss prevention activities is to eliminate the occurrence of the event, but since not all loss exposures can be totally prevented, some effort should also be made to minimize the magnitude of the loss.

Loss Reduction

Loss reduction is a technique directed at reducing loss severity. It can be used before, during, or after a loss has occurred and is designed to minimize the magnitude of the loss and its financial impact on a family or individual.

Two examples of loss reduction actions directed at the possibility of fire are maintaining fire extinguishers in the home to extinguish flames before they spread and cause extensive damage to the property and installing smoke detectors to alert inhabitants that there is a fire so that they may extinguish the fire or call the fire department. Note, however, that these methods have no value as loss reduction unless they are properly serviced and all household members are instructed in their use. Also, although it is discussed here as a risk reduction action, installing smoke detectors also serves as a loss prevention action since individuals should be instructed to vacate the property when the alarm sounds, thereby reducing the likelihood of death or injury due to fire. Most insurance companies now give a small discount in the premium for the proper installation of smoke detectors.

Loss Control Planning

The techniques of risk avoidance, loss prevention, and loss reduction should not be considered separately; the best alternative is often a combination of these actions. In the evaluation of a particular risk, three questions should be asked. Can this risk be avoided? If not, how can the loss be prevented? If the event and a loss do occur, how can the loss be minimized?

There are costs associated with initiating and maintaining loss control activities. These costs should be compared with the benefits of the loss control action. This may be difficult to evaluate, and some judgment may be necessary to make a positive decision to engage in loss control when costs appear high relative to benefits.

Loss Financing

Since some losses will occur, it is necessary to plan how to fund these losses. Although several techniques are used by individuals, the primary methods are retention, insurance, and, in some situations, noninsurance transfer. This last technique is examined first.

Noninsurance Transfer

Although insurance is the form of risk transfer most commonly practiced, there are noninsurance means of transferring risk. Noninsurance transfers are useful but are more often initiated by businesses than by individuals; individuals are more frequently the recipients of the transfer. For example, when someone orders merchandise through a catalog, the supplier may ship the goods F.O.B. point of origin. This means that the supplier has transferred to the purchaser responsibility for damage to the goods while in transit. As a second example, transportation companies may use a bill of lading to limit their liability. The limit is usually expressed in dollars per unit of weight, and if the limitation is low, some of the risk of damage to the goods being transported may have been shifted to the owner of those goods. A third case may occur when property is left in the custody of others for such purposes as storage, cleaning, or repair. Normally, it is possible to have the bailee, the temporary custodian of the property, assume full responsibility for such property.

When one party assumes the liability of another for bodily injury or property damage as an incidental obligation in contracts dealing with services, premises, or products, the transfer is typically referred to as a *hold harmless agreement.* Such agreements are common in business-to-business dealings, and perhaps more common than generally realized in business-to-individual dealings. One example of the latter is the leasing of dwellings or apartments. Under the lease the landlord may be able to transfer to the tenant financial responsibility for damage to the property and for bodily injuries to third parties that, in the absence of the lease, would be borne by the landlord. Although the landlord is still legally liable to these third parties, the tenant can agree by means of the lease to finance any losses that may otherwise have to be paid by the landlord.

Retention

Many individuals purchase insurance for pure risks and fail to consider other loss-financing techniques. Yet it is obvious that everyone retains some risks, either consciously or unconsciously. Voluntary risk retention can be a useful tool of risk management. However, involuntary or unintentional risk retention due to failure to identify exposures can be a serious problem.

Risk retention is the process of financing or paying one's own losses, and as such is frequently referred to as self-assumption of risk or self-insurance (although this is technically incorrect). In cases where retention is consciously practiced, an individual may set aside funds earmarked for a particular risk. When the loss occurs, these funds are available to pay for the amount lost. However, this formal method of employing retention is rarely practiced — most retention is practiced informally by covering losses with funds in a savings account, by borrowing, or by paying for the loss on an out-of-pocket basis.

People may choose risk retention when the maximum possible loss is too small to cause financial hardship — few people would insure against the risk of accidental loss of a 98 cent ballpoint pen. Conversely, risks for which the maximum possible loss is quite large may be retained because the probability of the loss is extremely small. There is some danger in this practice for individuals since the application of probability is not appropriate for the single exposure unit of the individual. For example, a young person might decide not to purchase life insurance because of the small probability of death at a young age. Retention of the risk for this reason could have very serious consequences.

Retention is frequently practiced even when insurance is purchased for a particular risk. For example, a deductible may apply to losses covered by the insurance policy purchased, in which case the insured is retaining the first dollar amount of the loss. Similarly, the exposure to loss by causes excluded under an insurance contract is retained by the policyowner. These loss exposures may have to be retained by the policyowner simply because there is no alternative. Retention is also practiced when insurance policies exclude the loss to certain types of property or property at certain locations. Other provisions or exclusions in insurance policies may also preclude coverage for particular types of loss. Explaining the need for this sort of retention to purchasers of insurance is an important service provided by the financial services professional.

Insurance

The discussion of insurance in this chapter is designed to provide an understanding of insurance as a risk treatment technique. As a risk-financing method, insurance involves a transfer of the financial burden of risk through a contract for a price (premium). In addition, insurance is a loss-sharing device and a system for reducing risk. This and the following section briefly examine some of the fundamental principles underlying the insurance technique. Applications of the insurance technique will be the topic of chapter 8.

Definition of insurance. There are many definitions of insurance. Insurance is sometimes defined as the business of transferring pure risks by means of a two-party contract. Transfer, then, is the primary function according to this definition, and this is accomplished through use of a contract. A characteristic that distinguishes the insurance technique from other transfer devices is that insurance is practiced as a business.

In the two-party contract, the person who transfers the risk is known as the *insured,* and the party who assumes the risk is the *insurer.* The function of the insurer is to accept the pure risks of many individuals. Since the act of transferring risk does not affect the possibility of the loss, insurance does not replace the need for loss control. However, an interesting phenomenon takes place as the insurer accepts a greater number of similar risks: risk is actually reduced.

To understand this last statement, it is necessary to review the insurance process. As insurers accept insureds, they pool those with similar characteristics and the combination of many similar exposure units permits the operation of the law of large numbers. From a statistical standpoint, as the number of exposure units increases, the deviation of actual from expected experience diminishes. As the potential margin of error decreases, so also does uncertainty about losses. This increased knowledge allows the insurer a greater predictability of probable losses and results in a reduction of risk for the insurer.

This increased knowledge of probable loss frequency and severity also means that the insurer can determine a more suitable charge (premium) for accepting the transfer of risk from the insured. The premium becomes a known cost (in most cases), which replaces the unknown cost of a potential loss. The insurer, in effect, collects a small premium from many and redistributes most of it to the few who suffer loss.

The definition of insurance can be summarized in either a process or functional fashion. As a process, insurance is a transfer of pure risk to a professional risk bearer. From a functional standpoint, insurance is the substitution of a small, certain loss for the possibility of a large, uncertain loss.

Subjects for insurance. During the risk identification function, dwellings, personal property, automobiles, and similar items were listed as risks subject to damage or destruction. However, the underlying question is, what would cause these losses to occur? The causes of loss must be considered in order to determine whether the insurance technique is actually available as a method for treating these particular risks. Insurance does not cover every loss that can occur: insurers look for characteristics that allow a given cause of loss to qualify as an insurable one. Although there are insurable causes of loss that fail to meet every requirement, the following are examples of characteristics that insurers find desirable.

The first desirable characteristic for an insurable cause of loss is the existence of a large number of homogeneous exposures (exposures that have approximately the same expectations of loss). This is necessary to permit the operation of the law of large numbers, discussed earlier, and to allow the insurer to achieve a meaningful estimate of probable losses and to maintain equity among insureds.

A second desirable characteristic is that the cause of loss insured against should be accidental and unintentional; that is, the insured should not have control over when the loss occurs. It should be fortuitous or subject to chance. If a deliberately caused loss were to be paid, moral hazard would be substantially increased.

Third, an insurable cause of loss should produce a loss that is definite as to when it occurred and how much was lost. While difficult to satisfy, these requirements are nevertheless important since their absence may introduce an element of moral hazard and make coverage questions difficult to resolve.

A fourth important characteristic of an insurable cause of loss is that the exposed units should be independent. For example, the destruction of one insured dwelling should not affect the probability that another will burn. The group of insureds should not be exposed to an incalculable catastrophic hazard. If catastrophic occurrences are predictable, however, the cause of loss may be insurable.

Loss-Financing Planning

The evaluation of loss-financing techniques is an important step in risk treatment planning. It begins with an evaluation of the client's capacity to safely assume certain risks so that retention can be practiced at its most effective level. Where retention cannot be practiced, the transfer technique can sometimes be applied.

Although noninsurance transfer of risk is not widely used by individuals, it can be an effective means of financing losses. However, noninsurance transfers should be approached cautiously. The parties to whom risk financing is transferred may be unable to fund losses, thereby rendering the transfer ineffective. Finally, the price of transfer should be compared to other techniques for treating the risk.

There is also a price associated with the use of insurance as a loss-financing technique. The premiums for insurance should be reasonable in relation to the potential financial loss, and the cost should be compared with the cost of alternative techniques. Most individuals have only a limited number of premium dollars with which to purchase protection against insurable losses. The use of premium dollars to protect against relatively small potential losses generally results in failure to cover more significant loss causes. This problem can be overcome by employing the *large-loss principle.*

The use of insurance is best suited to the handling of low-frequency, high-severity risks. The large-loss principle suggests that, in the purchase of insurance, first priority should be given to exposures that might cause significant financial loss. As noted earlier, the definition of a large loss differs among individuals. However, risks listed as serious during the risk evaluation process should, by implication, be large losses and should receive first priority in the use of insurance.

Risk treatment planning is an extremely important stage in the risk management process. The evaluation of risk treatment alternatives leads to decisions on implementation of specific programs that may affect the continued solvency and well-being of families and individuals.

SELECTING THE INSURANCE TECHNIQUE

Insurance will play a major role in risk treatment for most families and individuals. Because of this, it is imperative that all financial services professionals have some understanding of how insurance functions and of the principles underlying insurance contracts.

Many questions arise about the use of insurance as a method of treating risk. For example: Under what circumstances would the insurer be responsible for the loss? What events, causes of loss, property, or sources of liability are covered? Whose life or health is covered? What persons, losses, locations, and time period are covered? Are there any special conditions that do not fall into any of these categories that may suspend or terminate the coverage? If the insurer is responsible for the loss, how much will it pay? And finally, what steps must the insured take following a loss? These are just a sampling of questions that may arise in any discussion of insurance. They cannot all be answered here, but the next section of this chapter will review some of the basic components of an insurance contract, the important principle of indemnity, and some material vital to the adjustment of losses under insurance contracts.

Insurance Contract Components

The provisions in an insurance contract are typically classified into four categories: declarations, insuring agreements, exclusions, and conditions. Some contracts clearly label these categories. In others, the divisions are not clearly discernible, but the content of these categories can be found in the contract.

Declarations

The declarations page is extremely important and should be reviewed thoroughly whenever an insurance contract is issued. This page clearly identifies the insured, describes the property, activity, or life being insured, and states the types of coverages purchased, the applicable policy limits, and the term of the coverage. The information that completes the declarations page is typically obtained from the application for the insurance coverage. It is typically the only material that is typed in the printed policy. It is important that this material be verified for its completeness and accuracy.

Insuring Agreement

The insuring agreement states what the insurer promises to do. In a life insurance policy, for example, the insurer simply promises to pay the face amount on due proof of the death of the insured. An automobile insurance policy may have several insuring agreements—for example, for liability coverage the agreement might state that the company will pay damages for which the insured becomes legally responsible because of an auto accident. The homeowners policy states that the insurance company insures against risks of direct loss. Typically, the insuring agreement describes the characteristics of the events covered under the contract. Certain terms used in the contract may also be defined in this section.

Exclusions

The coverage provided by an insurance contract is limited by exclusions. They may exclude certain causes of loss, property, sources of liability, persons, losses, locations, or time periods.

There are many reasons for exclusions in insurance policies. An exclusion may be contained in one policy because it is more appropriate for coverage to be provided in a different policy. For example, damage to automobiles is excluded from homeowners policies because such damage would more appropriately be covered in an automobile insurance policy. Some losses are excluded because the cause of loss does not meet the characteristics for being insurable (as discussed earlier), and some losses, such as ordinary wear and tear of property, should not be expected to be covered by insurance. Another example, the freezing of an automobile radiator, is not covered because an insured could easily prevent this loss with proper servicing of the automobile. Other types of losses are excluded because they are the concern of only a handful of people who can obtain separate coverage on those specific exposures. An example of this would be the exclusion in automobile policies for travel in Mexico.

An understanding of exclusions by financial services professionals and their clients is even more important when a particular policy is an "all risks" contract. Policies that purport to cover all risks typically do not really do so; they usually state that they cover all risks "except," and then go on to list exclusions. The homeowners policy is a good example of this. For years some forms of homeowners policies were referred to as providing all risks coverage. Although the exclusions were clearly indicated, the implications associated with providing all risks coverage created loss adjustment problems and litigation. The broad coverage now provided by these homeowners policies is against the "risks of direct loss." The policy then goes on to list causes of loss that are not covered.

Sometimes the wording of an exclusion is difficult for the purchaser of the insurance to understand. For example, the purchaser of a health insurance policy may not understand that preexisting conditions are not covered. Exclusions provide an excellent opportunity for the financial services professional to educate consumers by going through the exclusions listed in the client's policy.

Conditions

The conditions define terms used in other parts of the contract and may describe the rights and obligations of the insured and the insurer following a loss. They may also prescribe certain events or actions that must be satisfied before the insurer is liable for a loss. Examples of some conditions are discussed later in this chapter.

Other Components

There are many other provisions in the insurance contract that are important to an understanding of the coverage provided (one of these, policy limits, will be discussed later in this chapter). In addition, it is common to have one or more endorsements or riders attached to the insurance policy. Endorsements and riders modify the contract in some fashion such as by adding or deleting coverage, changing the description of the locations or property covered, or placing restrictions on what the insurer may or may not do.

Principle of Indemnity

Many property, liability, and health insurance policies are contracts of indemnity. The principle of indemnity, often said to be the cardinal principle of insurance, states that a person may not collect more than his or her actual loss in the event of the occurrence of an insured peril (cause of loss). Indemnity contracts require the insurance company to reimburse the insured for the "actual cash value" of the loss sustained. As noted earlier, some insurance policies, such as homeowners policies, settle losses on the basis of replacement cost rather than actual cash value. Although this is a violation of the principle of indemnity, it has become an accepted practice. Other policies, such as life insurance contracts, simply pay the dollar amount stipulated on the face of the contract since life insurance contracts are not intended to be interpreted as contracts of indemnity.

The enforcement of the indemnity principle in insurance contracts includes three additional concepts: insurable interest, subrogation, and duplicate insurance. The purpose of these concepts is to minimize the possibility that the insured will profit from the occurrence of the event covered in the insurance contract.

Insurable Interest

A legal requirement under the principle of insurable interest is that the insured be able to demonstrate a loss to himself or herself in order to collect under the contract. Insurable interest is that relationship to the person or thing insured that the law requires so that the contract is not a mere wager. The basis for insurable interest in property and liability contracts includes (1) a property right, (2) a contract right, and (3) legal liability. If insurance is to be purchased, an insurable interest is essential (although in property and liability insurance the insurable interest need exist only at the time of loss and not at the inception of the contract).

Although life insurance is not considered a contract of indemnity, the requirement of an insurable interest does apply. It is generally accepted in law that an individual has an unrestricted insurable interest in his or her own life. Beyond this, the basis for the existence of an insurable interest can be found in a close family relationship or a financial relationship. A major difference between a life insurance contract and a property or liability insurance contract is that for life insurance the insurable interest must exist only at the inception of the contract.

Subrogation

Subrogation is a process in insurance whereby the insurer is substituted for the insured for the purpose of claiming indemnity from a third person for a covered loss. Once the insurance company pays a loss to an insured, the insurer takes over the rights of that insured to recover from a third party for the loss. For example, if a client's automobile is damaged in an accident where the other party is clearly at fault, the client may wish to avoid possible delays in repairing the auto by having his or her own insurance company pay for the damage under the collision coverage. Once this settlement has taken place, the client's insurance company can begin proceedings against the party at fault in an attempt to recover the amount paid to the client. The client is not able to recover twice — once from his or her own insurance company and again from the wrongdoer. Subrogation reinforces the principle of indemnity by preventing double recovery.

Duplicate Insurance

Finally, the inclusion of clauses in insurance contracts regarding the existence of other insurance minimizes the possibility that the insured will profit from the occurrence of an event. Typically such clauses provide that policies covering the same risk must share in the loss on some predetermined basis. The purpose is to discourage the insured from taking out duplicate policies with different insurers in the expectation of recovering more than his or her actual loss.

Loss Adjustments

The natural presumption among those who purchase insurance is that the insurance company will pay or reimburse the insured if a loss is suffered. Earlier in this chapter it was stated that insurers collect small premiums from many clients and redistribute them to the few who suffer loss. This functional interpretation of insurance is widely accepted. However, it should also be understood that the insurer is under no obligation to do anything until it has been notified of a loss. When and how this notification takes place and what the amount of the loss payment will be are questions important for the client's understanding of the way insurance contracts fulfill their promises, and for the purpose of counseling clients in their effective purchase of insurance.

Initiating the Loss Adjustment

Insurance contracts contain conditions setting forth the procedures that the insured must follow in submitting a claim. They may be very simple, as in a life insurance policy where the requirement is the submission of due proof of death. While some major medical policies may include a provision stating that a notice of claim must be submitted in writing within 20 days after the commencement of any loss covered by the policy, most current major medical policies simply include a provision stating that notice of a claim may be submitted as soon as is reasonably possible. Once a notice of claim has been received, the major medical policy states that the company will then furnish to the claimant such forms as are necessary to complete the proof of loss. This written proof of loss must then be completed and furnished to the insurance company within 90 days.

Homeowners and personal auto policies contain conditions setting forth the insured's duties after a loss (or accident) occurs. The first requirement is normally prompt notice to the company (or agent). This requirement is followed by a list of additional duties, such as notification of the police if the cause of loss is theft or cooperation with the insurance company in the investigation, settlement, or defense of any claim or suit where third parties might be involved. Eventually, the insurance company requires some form of written proof of loss. If personal property is included in the loss, the insurer will most likely ask for an inventory of the damaged property. Preparing such an inventory can be a difficult task since people tend not to remember all details about all their personal property, as was indicated earlier in this chapter in the identification of risks function in the risk management process.

The period following an event that causes loss can be very stressful. During this period the financial services professional should provide as much assistance as possible to aid the client in processing a claim with an insurance company. If the financial services professional represents an insurance company, he or she should be thoroughly familiar with the requirements of that company in the total claim process in order to readily give a client proper assistance.

Policy Limitations on Amounts Payable

After the required notice of claim and proof of loss have been filed, the insured and insurer move into the settlement phase of the loss adjustment. Unfortunately, insureds are sometimes not happy with the loss adjustment, often because of a general lack of understanding of the provisions and clauses contained in the insurance contract. One of the most common causes of disagreement over the amount of a loss settlement results from the actual-cash-value basis for settling many property damage claims, since insureds prefer that the item be replaced or simply that replacement cost be the basis of settlement.

There are several other clauses contained in insurance contracts that also act to limit the amount payable under the policy. These include deductibles, time limitations, dollar limitations, and coinsurance clauses. Of these, the deductible is perhaps the most visible limiting clause and the most easily understood by insureds. The deductible is simply the amount of money that must be paid by the insured before the insurance company will become liable on the loss. Time limitations also affect the total amount of dollar coverage and are quite common in health insurance contracts, for example, where benefits are payable only for a stated number of days, weeks, or months. Time limitations may also be used to restrict benefits to the amount of time it would take under normal conditions to repair or replace damaged property. Most insurance contracts provide for maximum dollar limits for recovery of losses.

A coinsurance feature means different things in different insurance policies. For example, in major medical health insurance policies, coinsurance refers to a sharing of the costs—for example, 80 percent to be paid by the insurer and 20 percent by the insured—typically between the deductible and the maximum dollar limit in the policy. With this feature the insured is thus required to participate in the costs of medical care.

The coinsurance provision in property insurance policies is quite different. Here, coinsurance penalizes an insured that does not carry a sufficient amount of insurance in relation to the value of the insured property. Under these conditions, the insured shares in the loss only if the requirements of the coinsurance provision are not satisfied.

Although homeowners policies do not contain a coinsurance clause, the loss settlement provisions are very similar. Homeowners policies require that, at the time of loss, the amount of insurance carried on the damaged dwelling be 80 percent or more of the full replacement cost of the dwelling at the time the loss occurs. If the amount of insurance carried is less than 80 percent of the replacement cost, the insurer agrees to pay the greater of the actual cash value of the loss or a proportion of the cost to repair or replace the dwelling determined by the ratio of the amount of insurance carried to the amount of insurance required. This can be expressed as a formula:

$$\frac{\text{amount of insurance carried}}{\text{amount of insurance required}} \times \text{loss} = \text{recovery}$$

The following example will illustrate the operation of this loss settlement provision. As indicated in table 7-2, Burt Beamer's dwelling has a replacement cost value of $200,000. If Burt carried at least 80 percent of this value ($160,000) on the dwelling, a loss to the dwelling would be settled on the replacement-cost basis, subject, of course, to the policy limit. However, if Burt carried less than $160,000, there would be a calculation of both the replacement cost value of the damage and the actual cash value of the damage sustained. Suppose Burt carried $120,000 on the dwelling and suffered a loss with a replacement cost value of $20,000. The application of the above formula would be as follows:

$$\frac{\$120,000}{\$160,000} \times \$20,000 = \$15,000$$

If the actual cash value of the loss is greater than $15,000, the loss is settled on that actual-cash-value basis. If actual cash value is less than $15,000, the loss recovery is $15,000. Note that in this situation Burt Beamer would be sharing in the loss because an inadequate amount of insurance to value was carried. As illustrated in this example, it is important to understand replacement cost on dwellings and to make sure that clients purchase a sufficient amount of insurance for their homeowners coverage on the dwelling.

RISK TREATMENT PLAN IMPLEMENTATION

The final step in the risk management process is implementing the program of loss control and loss financing that has been formulated to meet the identified risks. Here the discussion will be limited to selecting the proper insurance coverage and the role financial services professionals play in this plan implementation.

Preparing the Plan

The financial services professional is now ready to formulate a plan for the utilization of insurance as a technique for treating the risks faced by the client. In performing this step, he or she should be concerned with matching particular insurance policies to the various risks identified and measured in the risk analysis step.

An important step in proposing insurance coverages to meet specified risks is to rank in order of importance the various insurance policies available. One practical approach to identifying a rank or priority for the various insurance coverages is to list the risks according to the seriousness of their financial impact upon the client. This was done for the Beamer family in table 7-3, where risks were listed according to the categories *serious, moderate,* and *minimal.* The first priority in the use or purchase of insurance should be the risks identified as "serious."

One technique for exhibiting a plan of insurance utilization to the client is to list the insurance contracts according to their desirability as methods of meeting identified risks. This can be done by breaking down into the categories of *essential, desirable* and *available* the insurance contracts that would take priority in the utilization of the client's premium dollars.

A sample of a listing of insurance policies for the Beamer family is shown in table 7-4. This list does not mention insurance coverage for two of the loss exposures that were identified as being in the serious category: liability at premises owned and liability arising out of personal activities. A financial services professional who understands the homeowners policy would realize that these liability loss exposures are covered by section II of the homeowners policy, but the client might assume that important risks have been forgotten. For this reason it would be appropriate that the listing of insurance policies, at least in the essential and desirable categories, include a brief description of the recommended insurance contracts. For example, where a homeowners policy has been recommended, the description should include the identification of property covered, limits on property, liability coverage, and the various extensions of coverage provided in this comprehensive package policy.

Since the description of insurance policies is the subject of chapter 8, the descriptions for the Beamer family have been omitted from table 7-4. However, since the current replacement cost of the dwelling does appear, a dollar amount can be shown that will satisfy the loss settlement provision in the contract (a minimum of 80 percent of the replacement cost), with the replacement cost as the maximum. Dollar values can be inserted for the liability limits in the homeowners policy and the personal auto policy, but these will have to be coordinated with the requirement of the personal umbrella liability policy.

The whole life insurance policy on Burt Beamer's life is for the purpose of satisfying the cash need for the clean-up fund. The face amount for this policy was taken from table 7-2, but a different face amount could appear because of other cash needs for the Beamer family that could be integrated into this policy. The amount of the mortgage redemption policy would depend on the current outstanding indebtedness. The income need for Burt's survivors is based on the objectives and assumptions developed earlier in this chapter.

A plan to use insurance as a technique for treating risks cannot be formulated in isolation from other parts of the financial plan or from insurance the client may already have. For example, it is highly probable that the client already has purchased a homeowners policy, an auto policy and life insurance. The client's employer probably provides employee benefits for health care financing, life insurance, income replacement for periods of disability, and retirement, and social security will provide income during retirement. The financial plan may indicate techniques other than insurance for the attainment of desired retirement income levels.

The end result of insurance planning should be an integrative approach to solving the protection needs of the client. It should indicate what gaps or overlaps exist in present insurance coverage, reinforce the value of insurance protection, and enhance the overall validity of the financial services professional's interest in serving the needs of the client.

TABLE 7-4
Insurance Planning

Essential

1. Personal auto policy—$300,000 liability
2. Homeowners form 3—$180,000 dwelling
$100,000 liability
3. Personal umbrella liability—$2 million
4. Dwelling form on cabin—$40,000
5. Whole life insurance policy on Burt—$50,000
6. Life insurance on Burt—$1,100,000 to provide lifetime income to surviving
spouse

Desirable

1. Dwelling form for personal property (cabin)—$4,000
2. Personal auto policy—ACV for physical damage to compact auto
3. Mortgage redemption policy—$137,000

Available

1. Personal auto policy—ACV for physical damage to station wagon
2. Life insurance on Burt—$78,000 for education fund

Role of the Financial Services Professional

The role of the financial services professional in risk treatment plan implementation can take several different directions. First, he or she may feel that the task is complete at the presentation of the risk treatment plan and request that the client implement the plan in conjunction with a professional insurance specialist. A second alternative is to provide complete assistance to the client in the implementation of the plan. If the financial services professional is a licensed insurance agent, the type of assistance provided should be obvious.

The role of the financial services professional who is not a licensed insurance agent will, of necessity, be much more general than the role of a licensed agent. There are three areas in which such a financial services professional can provide clients with information about insurance companies: financial stability, services provided, and premium costs for the coverage proposed.

Although there are various types of insurance companies, as the companies grow in size, the distinction between stock and mutual, for example, tends to become less distinct. Rather than attempting to differentiate between the types of companies, the financial services professional should identify financially stable firms and be able to state with some confidence that the selection of a given company is satisfactory from a financial stability standpoint. As a minimum reference on a particular company, the financial services professional may consult a publication such as *Best's Insurance Reports* for a description of an insurer's management, general underwriting policy, and present financial data.

Service is a second area to consider in the selection of insurance. Service takes many forms, including the ability to provide the type of insurance coverage desired, fairness in settling claims, and provision of efficient policy owner assistance. If the company cannot provide the specific insurance contract that is desired, there is little need to go beyond this point. However, if the desired policy is available, the professional should know how the policyowner is going to be serviced in the future. An important area of service is claims payment and administration. The financial services professional should seek information about the company's ability to handle all claims and its inclination to provide the proper claim service. The client will also be interested in miscellaneous administrative services, such as changes in the policy, the address, or the named insureds. The company should be able to provide prompt and courteous service. For claims and policyowner services the client will deal with an agent or a company representative.

The third area to consider is cost. In insurance planning for individuals, the only element of cost is typically the premium outlay (perhaps net of dividends) necessary to purchase the desired insurance protection. This may involve some balancing between the insurance transfer and the level of retention (deductibles and policy limits). In reality, decisions of this nature would be considered in the risk treatment planning step of the risk management process. To assist the client, the financial services professional should provide representative insurance premium figures, or at least establish a contact with someone who could provide the appropriate premium quotations.

The financial services professional has identified and measured risks and recommended a risk treatment plan. Proper assistance in the purchase of insurance protection and other risk treatment techniques must follow.

ROLE OF RISK MANAGEMENT IN FINANCIAL PLANNING

Risk management has become integral to maintaining the financial stability of business enterprises. An adaptation of the risk management process is also an appropriate vehicle to combat the undesirable consequences of pure risk situations facing individuals and families. However, the management of property, liability, and personal risks is an area that is sometimes overlooked in financial planning, especially by those professionals who are not specialists in insurance. It is, nevertheless, a vital function in the overall planning process.

Premium expenditures are small in comparison to the disastrous financial effects that accompany the occurrence of insurable risks that are inadequately protected against. It is as important that accumulated wealth be protected as it is for that wealth to grow and provide income. Risk management is the vehicle with which to properly structure that protection.

8

Insurance Planning: Survey of Insurance Coverages

Charles E. Hughes

As pointed out in the preceding chapter, insurance is an appropriate technique for treating many of the pure risks facing most individuals and families. For this reason the financial services professional needs an understanding of what insurance contracts provide and cover and how insurance premium dollars can most effectively be utilized in treating a client's identified risks. The previous chapter contained a brief introduction to insurance. This chapter takes the next step by providing an overview of several types of insurance policies and describing some of the possible problem areas and special situations that may require further examination before recommending an insurance solution. The purpose is to provide the financial services professional with knowledge that will be of assistance in the counseling of clients and in dealing with insurance specialists brought in to assist in this process.

Unraveling the complexity of insurance coverages would require more than a few pages in one chapter. Since this chapter covers several major lines of insurance, the detail in the analysis of specific contracts is minimized so that a greater variety of contracts can be included within a limited space. The chapter begins with homeowners insurance, followed by auto insurance and excess liability coverage, and then treats life insurance, disability, and medical expense insurance coverage.

HOMEOWNERS INSURANCE

A few years ago purchasing property insurance on a dwelling simply meant buying a fire insurance policy. Today, the convenience and cost savings of packaging together various types of insurance coverage has won wide acceptance among the buying public. Most individuals now purchase homeowners policies.

The homeowners policy is a package of insurance coverage on the dwelling and personal property combined with liability coverage. There is more to the purchase of a homeowners policy, however, than simply an individual's wish to buy one. These policies come in a variety of forms, and it is necessary to understand the differences among them to be able to recommend the form that provides the coverage the client desires. All homeowners forms include liability coverage, so much of the decision of which form to recommend is based on differences in the property coverage section of the policy. However, as will be illustrated later, proper liability coverage is vital to the final composition of the policy.

The basis for the discussion of homeowners insurance policies in this chapter is the program introduced and made available by the Insurance Services Office (ISO). The ISO format has been adopted by many insurance companies throughout the country. There are, however, insurance companies that use their own policy forms, and regional or state variations that modify the basic forms.

Homeowners policies are available for owner-occupied dwellings (defined as containing one or two living units) used principally as private residences. Although endorsements are available to provide coverage for three- or four-family dwellings, the owner-occupant of a larger building cannot purchase a homeowners policy on the building. In this situation a tenants form is available. Likewise, unit owners of condominiums or cooperative apartments have a special homeowners form available.

The first decision to make is which homeowners policy to recommend. For the nonowner client this is no problem since the only form available is the broad Form HO–4 (sometimes referred to as the *renters policy*). Condo and cooperative unit owners should use Form HO–6. The broad Form HO–2, special Form HO–3, and modified basic Form HO–8 (basic Form HO–1 has been withdrawn in most states) are available for owner-occupants of dwellings. One basis for determining which form to recommend is to compare the breadth of coverage for losses to the dwelling.

Causes of Loss

The descriptive titles given to homeowners forms — basic, broad, and special — help to identify a basic difference among homeowners policies, at least as far as breadth of coverage on the dwelling is concerned. The major concern here is the determination of the causes of loss provided by the policy. Since, if the policy has not been endorsed, the causes of loss for damage to personal property are virtually the same in all forms, the selection process centers on dwelling coverage.

At one time, property insurance policies were written on the basis of a single cause of loss, such as fire or windstorm. If protection against damage caused by some other peril (defined as *cause of loss*) was desired, it could be added by endorsing the policy. As more and more perils were added they began to be grouped together. For example, several perils, including wind, hail, explosion, riot, and smoke, were grouped together in what was referred to as the *extended coverage endorsement.* The basic form of the homeowners (HO–1) provided coverage for a combination of fire, the extended coverage perils, and a few other perils. The present Form HO–8 is a modification of the basic form.

The *broad form* used in homeowners policies is simply the basic form with an addition of several perils and an expansion of the scope of others. For example, in the basic form loss caused to the dwelling by a vehicle is excluded if the vehicle is owned or operated by a resident of the premises. The broad form removes that exclusion and extends coverage to damage caused by vehicles. Examples of perils added by the broad form include the weight of ice, snow, or sleet and the accidental discharge or overflow of water or steam.

The financial services professional should read policy provisions concerning these and other perils very carefully to determine exactly which losses are covered and under what conditions such coverage is afforded. While this chapter does not go into that detail, the financial services professional should realize that these policies will respond only to losses caused by the specific perils identified in the policy. This is referred to as the *named-peril approach* to providing insurance protection.

The *special form* of the homeowners policies is written on what is called an "all-risks" basis. However, this is a misnomer since not all losses are covered. *All risks* really means that a loss is covered unless it is specifically excluded, which is how the insuring agreement of the special form now reads. Insurance is provided against risks of direct loss to property, and the policy then goes on to indicate that losses caused by listed occurrences or circumstances are not insured. Although the first list that appears is not lengthy, a later part of the homeowners policy lists exclusions applicable to all forms. Therefore, although the special form provides the broadest coverage available on dwellings, it does not cover all risks. While the term *all risks* is still widely used by insurance people, the use of *special form* is more appropriate with the general public.

The comparison of homeowners forms normally results in a choice between the broad Form HO–2 and the special Form HO–3. While the difference in premiums between these two forms is generally moderate, and either would suffice for most clients, recommending the broader coverage provided by HO–3 is usually preferable. The important point is that the client understand that there is a possibility that a given loss to the dwelling might not be covered even by this policy.

Property Coverages

Homeowners policies contain two sections: section I for property coverage and section II for liability coverage. Unless indicated otherwise, the following discussion of property coverages is limited to Forms HO–2 and HO–3. The five major categories of coverage contained in section I of these policies are

- coverage A — dwelling
- coverage B — other structures
- coverage C — personal property
- coverage D — loss of use
- additional coverages

Dwelling — Coverage A

Dwelling coverage requires the selection of a limit or dollar amount of insurance coverage. This is the only part of section I for which the insured *must* choose a limit of coverage. The limits for all other property covered by the homeowners policy are either a fixed-dollar amount or a fixed percentage of the limit on the dwelling. However, some of these limits can be changed by the insured.

A recommendation of the proper limit of coverage that the client should purchase on the dwelling should be made with care. If a loss should occur to the dwelling it will be settled on a full replacement-cost basis if, at the time of loss, the amount of insurance carried is equal to 80 percent or more of the full replacement cost of the dwelling (see chapter 7 for a discussion of this loss-settlement provision). If the current replacement cost of the dwelling is $200,000, a minimum limit of coverage on the dwelling of $160,000 and a maximum limit of $200,000 should be recommended. In most cases it would be appropriate to recommend the selection of a limit closer to the top of the range.

One reason for recommending a limit of coverage on the dwelling close to the dwelling's replacement cost is the fact that the insured must practice retention for any amount not insured. Second, the cost of replacing the damaged property will be measured at the time of loss, and costs could rise between the inception of the policy and the time of loss. This could result in a loss penalty if the amount of insurance carried is not sufficient to satisfy the loss-settlement provision. One way to protect an insured against such a penalty is to place an inflation guard endorsement on the policy. This endorsement periodically and automatically increases the limit of coverage on the dwelling, typically on a specified percentage or construction-cost-index basis. The purpose is to maintain adequate coverage when inflation increases replacement costs. Some insurance companies are now offering coverage that guarantees the full cost of replacing the damaged dwelling even if that cost exceeds the coverage A limit. When this coverage is available, the company typically requires an original coverage A limit equal to 100 percent of the value of the dwelling.

Other Structures—Coverage B

Coverage B provides insurance on other structures located on the premises that are not attached to the dwelling. These include detached garages or toolsheds and such things as fences, driveways, and retaining walls. Unless increased by the insured, the amount of coverage is 10 percent of the limit on the dwelling. Losses to these other structures are settled on a replacement-cost basis.

Other structures on the premises used for business purposes are excluded and must be insured separately. Structures rented to others are also excluded; however, coverage is provided if the structure is rented to a tenant of the dwelling or if the structure is used solely as a private garage.

Personal Property—Coverage C

Personal property includes the items normally contained in a dwelling, such as furniture, appliances, and clothing, and property stored in a garage, other structure, or outdoors. Unless increased, the limit of coverage on personal property is 50 percent of the dwelling limit, and coverage is provided worldwide. However, when an insured has personal property normally situated at a secondary residence, coverage on such property is limited to either 10 percent of the coverage C limit or $1,000, whichever is greater.

Internal limits. Personal property is subject to internal limits of coverage on various items. Some examples of these internal limits include

- $200 on money, bank notes, bullion, gold other than goldware, silver other than silverware, platinum, coins, and medals
- $1,000 on watercraft, including their trailers, furnishings, equipment, and outboard motors
- $1,000 for loss by theft of jewelry, watches, and furs
- $2,500 for loss by theft of silverware, silver-plated ware, goldware, gold-plated ware, and pewterware
- $2,500 on property on the *residence premises,* used at any time or in any manner for any *business* purpose
- $250 on property away from the *residence premises,* used at any time or in any manner for any *business* purpose

For the average homeowner, these internal limits create little concern either because such property is not owned or because, if it is owned, values tend to be within the set limits. When the financial services professional identifies situations where client asset values exceed these limits, it is appropriate to suggest alternative ways of treating the exposure. For some property, such as money, it may be impossible to insure the potential loss above some moderate limit. Other types of property on which these internal limits apply can more appropriately be covered in an insurance policy separate from the homeowners policy. This is true, for example, of a watercraft that exceeds the value of coverage provided in the homeowners policy. (The liability exposure discussed later in this chapter is another reason for the use of a separate policy for watercraft.) Another example includes all the property items where the internal limit applies only to theft. Items of jewelry, furs, and silverware, for example, are common targets of theft. When the values of these items exceed the internal limits, a recommendation of separate and increased coverage would be appropriate.

The limits for some of these types of property can be increased by endorsement to the homeowners policy. Whether the property is covered by an endorsement or by a separate insurance policy, it is important to remember that such property may no longer be covered by the provisions of coverage C. The limit selected for this property should therefore be the full desired limit of that property.

The internal limit on business property is somewhat broader than some homeowners may believe. It applies not only to the conduct of a business on the premises, but also to work brought home from the office, which sometimes includes expensive equipment. While some business property, such as books of account, drawings, and computer tapes or other software media that contain business data, is specifically excluded, the cost of blank recording or storage media and prerecorded computer programs available on the retail market is covered.

Another class of business property specifically excluded is any personal property owned by the insured that is located in an apartment regularly rented or held for rental to others. This exclusion applies whether the apartment is on or off the residence premises. Furthermore, personal property belonging to roomers, boarders, and other tenants is not covered (unless the person is a relative of the insured).

Modifying coverage C. Personal property is covered on an actual-cash-value basis. Sometimes it is desirable to place this coverage on a replacement-cost basis, which can be done by endorsement for an additional premium. To qualify for this broader loss-settlement protection, many companies require either that the limit of coverage on the dwelling equal 100 percent of the dwelling's replacement value or that personal property coverage equal 70 percent of the amount carried on the dwelling (coverage C is normally 50 percent of coverage A). Since the replacement cost of personal property will be greater than its actual cash value, it makes sense to increase coverage C when loss settlement will be based on replacement cost.

Another modification that can be made in coverage C is to extend coverage to a "risks of loss not otherwise excluded" basis. This modification, available only for HO–3, makes coverage on personal property comparable to the coverage on the dwelling.

Loss of Use — Coverage D

The primary loss-of-use coverage is for additional living expenses — those increased costs necessary to maintain normal living standards when the insured's dwelling is uninhabitable because of damage caused by a covered cause of loss. The automatic limit for this coverage is 20 percent of the coverage applicable to the dwelling, subject to a time limit of the period required to repair or replace the damage or to permanently relocate, whichever is shortest.

If a part of the residence premises is rented or held for rental to others, loss-of-use coverage is extended to the fair rental value of the rented portion. In effect, this coverage provides a continuation of the rent payment, less a deduction for expenses that do not continue. Coverage for additional living expenses or fair rental value is also provided if action by a civil authority prohibits the insured from using the residence premises because of direct damage to a neighboring premises that was caused by a covered peril in the insured's policy.

Additional Coverages

There are several additional coverages included in the property section of homeowners policies, some of which provide an additional amount or limit of insurance. Each of these additional coverages should be reviewed carefully to determine what is and is not provided. For example, additional coverage is extended for trees, shrubs, and plants, but only when damage is caused by a list of specified perils. Unfortunately, wind, a common cause of damage to trees, is not among the listed perils.

The cost of removing debris following a loss is another additional coverage. The reasonable expense of removal is paid as part of the loss. However, if the direct loss to the property equals or exceeds the policy limit applicable to that property, an additional amount of coverage is granted for the cost of removing the debris. The additional amount in these situations is limited to 5 percent of the amount of coverage applying to the direct loss.

Another example of the additional coverages contained in homeowners policies is a provision that pays up to $500 for losses resulting from theft or unauthorized use of credit cards or fund-transfer cards, for losses from forgery or alteration of any check or negotiable instrument, and for losses related to the acceptance of counterfeit currency (U.S. or Canadian). While some people may believe there is no need for this coverage because of the apparent limitation of $50 that a card issuer may recover from the cardholder in cases involving lost or stolen cards, this $50 applies per card, and a loss could be substantially greater than anticipated. Moreover, with the extension of this coverage to fund-transfer cards, forgery, and counterfeit paper, this can be a valuable extension of coverage.

Property Coverages — Other Forms

In addition to homeowners Forms HO–2 and HO–3, there are several other homeowners forms and other ways of writing property coverages.

Form HO–4

This form is designed primarily for tenants who occupy residential rental property. It parallels HO–2 except that there is no coverage on the dwelling or other structures. The purchaser of HO–4 selects an amount of coverage on personal property (coverage C), and loss of use (coverage D) is then 20 percent of this amount.

There is typically no need for tenants to purchase insurance on the building. However, tenants sometimes install, at their own expense and for their exclusive use, improvements and alterations to the apartment or dwelling. The tenant's interest in these additions is covered up to 10 percent of the personal property limit. This amount may be increased by endorsement.

Sometimes an owner-occupant of residential property that is not eligible for homeowners coverage, such as a multiple-unit apartment building, will purchase a Form HO–4. Property coverage on the building would be purchased separately on a non-homeowner policy basis.

Form HO–6

HO–6 is for condominium unit owners and cooperative apartment occupants. Although the building itself is not covered (this is the association's responsibility), there is coverage for additions and alterations similar to those mentioned above for HO–4. The limit for this coverage is $1,000. Whether this amount is sufficient depends largely on how the association insurance on the building is written.

If the association insurance covers the entire unit, including all interior fixtures, wiring, decorating, etc., the unit owner may not need more than the $1,000 limit. However, if the association insures only the original construction and not improvements or additions made by the unit owner, the unit owner may need additional coverage. Sometimes the association insurance is what is referred to as "bare walls" coverage. If so, the unit owner must insure the entire interior, including all fixtures, interior partitions, paint or paper on the walls, etc. Since much more than $1,000 of coverage may be necessary to cover the unit owner's interest adequately in this case, the limit can be increased to meet this need.

The purchaser of Form HO–6 must select the amount of the limit on personal property coverage C. Then, 40 percent of that amount is automatically provided for loss-of-use coverage D.

Form HO–8

As discussed earlier, the loss settlement provision applicable to dwellings covered by homeowners policies requires insurance equal to at least 80 percent of the replacement cost of the dwelling. In some cases, especially for older homes, replacement cost might be considerably higher than the market value of the home. Since it would not be logical for many homeowners to purchase insurance on a home in an amount two or three times its market value, Form HO–8 provides a partial solution to the problem.

HO–8 provides insurance on the dwelling and other structures on the basis of the cost of repairing or replacing the property using common construction materials and methods. Since this eliminates the replacement-cost condition, the owner can purchase a lesser amount of coverage on the dwelling without being exposed to the penalty for underinsuring.

The HO–8 form is not as broad as other homeowners forms — for example, only the basic perils apply to this form, coverage on personal property is not worldwide, and theft coverage is more limited — yet HO–8 can serve a useful purpose in the right situation.

Dwelling Program

Many dwellings do not meet the eligibility requirements to qualify for homeowners insurance coverage. As one way of making property coverage available for such dwellings, the Insurance Services Office developed a series of forms in what is called the *dwelling program*. Under this program, property coverage on dwellings, other structures, and personal property, as well as additional living expenses and rental value can be provided. In general, the coverage provided under the dwelling program is narrower than that provided by the homeowners program. A fundamental difference is the fact that the dwelling program does not include the theft, liability, or medical payments coverage that homeowners policies do. Another difference is that in the dwelling program, an insured who desires to include personal property in a policy covering the dwelling must separately select a stated limit, whereas in the homeowners policy the selection of a limit on the dwelling automatically establishes a limit on the personal property.

As an example of how this dwelling program might be used, recall the cabin owned by the Beamer family as a secondary residence (see chapter 7). Although the cabin might qualify for homeowners coverage, the Beamers had already purchased a homeowners policy on their principal residence, so a homeowners policy on the cabin would duplicate some coverage. (Some companies will write a homeowners policy on the secondary residence and give a premium credit for the section II coverage discussed below.) An alternative solution for the Beamers is to purchase a dwelling program policy on the cabin. Also, since the homeowners policy contains only a small amount of coverage on personal property located at a secondary location, the Beamers could add a separate amount of additional personal property coverage for the cabin on the dwelling program policy.

Liability Coverages

Personal liability insurance provides protection for activities and conditions at the premises where the insured maintains a covered residence and for personal activities of the named insured and members of the insured's family anywhere in the world. All homeowners policies contain the same liability coverage. Section II of the homeowners policy contains two principal parts, coverage E — personal liability, and coverage F — medical payments to others. As with the property section, this section also includes some additional coverages.

Coverage E is similar to other liability insurance policies. Protection is provided for legal liability involving bodily injury or property damage, but not for personal injury. The latter includes such injuries as libel, slander, violation of privacy, malicious prosecution, and wrongful entry. These may be added by endorsement or covered under the umbrella liability policies discussed later in this chapter. The standard liability limit is $100,000 per occurrence, but may be increased for a relatively small additional charge.

Coverage F provides medical benefits to persons, other than residents of the insured household, who suffer bodily injury at an insured location or who are injured because of an insured's activities away from the insured location. The basic limit for coverage F is $1,000 per person. This amount is available for all necessary medical expenses incurred within 3 years of the date of the accident. Benefits under this coverage will be paid whether or not the insured is legally liable.

Exclusions

The liability section of the homeowners policy has always been considered as providing very broad coverage. In fact, when this coverage is purchased as a separate insurance policy it is referred to as comprehensive personal liability. Nevertheless, as with all policies that are considered to provide broad coverage, what is not covered is of extreme importance. Some of the exclusions found in homeowners policies should be expected, such as war and nuclear exposure. Others should be anticipated because the exposure can be covered with a different policy, such as the motor vehicle, aircraft, and workers' compensation exposures. It should also be anticipated that losses that are intentionally caused should not be covered, nor should bodily injury to an insured.

Certain exclusions are particularly important for the financial services professional to understand in order to assist a client in reorganizing or modifying coverage or in obtaining the proper coverage in some other fashion. Three of these exclusions relate to business pursuits, watercraft, and property damage.

Business pursuits. Bodily injury or property damage arising out of or in connection with a business engaged in by an insured is excluded under the liability and medical coverages of homeowners policies. Most people are unaware that such part-time activities as baby-sitting, lawn mowing, and snow shoveling, or even ongoing hobbies or child care might result in liability losses that are not covered by the homeowners policy. The business exclusion centers on the definition of *business activity*. Basically, if there is an expectation of profit or gain, and evidence of continuity of the activity, the exclusion can be expected to apply and either a separate liability coverage or an endorsement to the homeowners policy will be needed.

Many home-business liability exposures can be covered by using endorsements to the homeowners policy, such as the permitted incidental occupancies residence premises endorsement or the business pursuits endorsement. However, care should be exercised in the use of endorsements since, for example, the business pursuits endorsement does not provide coverage if the business is owned by the insured. It is applicable to those situations where an insured is conducting business in the home for an outside employer. If the business is owned by the insured, a separate business-liability insurance policy should normally be obtained, but liability coverage for something like child care in the home can be covered by an endorsement to the homeowners policy.

A second part of the business exclusion applies to the rental or holding for rental of any part of any premises by an insured. This exclusion does not apply, however, if the rental is (1) on an occasional basis if used only as a residence, (2) in part for use only as a residence as long as the renting family unit has no more than two roomers or boarders, and (3) in part as an office, school, studio, or private garage. For an example of this last case, if the garage is rented out to a person for the purpose of conducting a radio repair shop, no coverage is provided. If the garage is rented for the purpose of parking an automobile, coverage is extended to the property owner. In some cases an endorsement for structures rented to others will be necessary.

Finally, it should be understood that the homeowners policy does not provide coverage for loss arising from the rendering of or failure to render professional services. Separate professional liability insurance is required for clients who have this exposure.

Watercraft. The homeowners policy provides only limited liability coverage for ownership or use of watercraft. No liability coverage applies to any watercraft owned by an insured if it is an inboard or inboard-outdrive type of any size, a rented inboard or inboard-outdrive boat with more than 50 horsepower, or an owned or rented sailboat 26 feet or more in length. Also, if the boat that is owned by the insured is powered by outboard motors with more than 25 total horsepower, there is coverage only if the boat is acquired during the policy period or, if acquired prior to the policy period, if the boat was declared at the inception of the policy or if the insured notified the insurer in writing within 45 days of acquiring the outboard motors. Use of borrowed, nonowned watercraft is covered, and use of rented watercraft is covered if size specifications are met.

The liability coverage provided by homeowners policies for watercraft is suitable for many owners of small boats. However, as the size increases, so does the need to change the insurance coverage. Although liability coverage can be added by endorsement to the homeowners policy, individuals who also want coverage for damage to the boat in excess of that provided under the property section of the policy should be advised to purchase a separate boat or yacht policy.

Property damage. There are some exclusions contained in section II that are directed specifically at damage to property. One of these states that property damage to property owned by the insured is not covered, which seems logical since such property should be covered in section I. This exclusion does not, however, prevent recovery by one insured for damage to that insured's property by another person who also is an insured under the policy.

Another liability exclusion applies to damage to property rented to, occupied by, used by, or in the care of the insured. This exclusion does not apply if the damage is caused by fire, smoke, or explosion (some insurers include water damage in this list). This exclusion is most significant for tenants who may be liable for damage to the apartment they rent and less significant when personal property is involved because coverage C insures personal property owned or used by an insured.

Additional Coverages

As with section I there are several additional coverages contained in section II. Two of these are examined here.

Damage to property of others. This provision makes it possible to pay small property damage claims without needing to prove the loss was caused by the negligence of the insured. Payment of up to $500 per occurrence is made on a replacement-cost basis.

Since property subject to this provision may already be covered under section I of the homeowners policy, payment under this additional coverage is in addition to any section I coverage. As might be expected, this provision does not apply to property owned by an insured or for any loss arising out of a business engaged in by an insured.

Loss assessment. One exclusion that was not discussed earlier is for the insured's share of any loss assessment that would be charged against any member of an association, corporation, or community of property owners. For example, if a liability claim has been successfully made against a condominium association, the association assesses its members for any sum needed to satisfy the claim. This type of assessment is excluded from coverage by the homeowners policy.

An additional coverage contained in the homeowners policy gives back to the insured the benefit of payment for assessments of the nature just excluded above. This coverage will pay up to $1,000 as the insured's share of a loss assessment resulting from bodily injury or property damage not excluded by the policy. This benefit also covers assessments based on the association's liability arising out of an act of an unpaid elected director, officer, or trustee of the association.

This completes the discussion of homeowners insurance coverage. The homeowners policy has become a major risk financing tool for property and liability risks facing individuals and families. It is important that financial services professionals, even those who have no direct relationship to the sale of insurance, have some knowledge of the breadth and complexity of this major insurance policy.

AUTOMOBILE INSURANCE

There are various forms of automobile insurance available today. However, like the homeowners policies just discussed, the Insurance Services Office (ISO) form will be the basis for description in this chapter. This is called the Personal Auto Policy (PAP). In most cases, the policy forms used by insurance companies that do not use the ISO form are very similar to this form. The PAP contains four coverages:

- part A—liability coverage
- part B—medical payments coverage
- part C—uninsured motorists coverage
- part D—coverage for damage to your auto

In addition to the basic coverages, several states have enacted statutes requiring that so-called no-fault benefits be added to the policies. Also, because of the many variances among state requirements, most PAP policies contain endorsements that modify the standard policy to satisfy local requirements regarding terminology or provisions in the policy. Finally, the PAP differs from the homeowners policy in that the insured, for the most part, may choose the coverages he or she desires and must choose an amount of insurance for each coverage.

Liability Coverage

The insuring agreement for the liability coverage provided by the PAP states that the insurance company will pay damages for bodily injury or property damage any insured becomes legally responsible for because of an auto accident. Part A of the PAP contains a single limit, such as $100,000 or $300,000, as the maximum amount that will be paid for all damages resulting from any one accident.

Who Is an Insured?

The PAP identifies the named insured (the person named on the declarations page) and any other family member as insureds for the liability exposure arising from the ownership, maintenance, or use of *any* auto. This means that autos both owned and not owned by the named insured are covered. A family member in this case is anyone who is related to the named insured by blood, marriage, or adoption and who resides in the named insured's household. Other persons are also covered by the named insured's PAP for liability arising out of the use of the insured's *covered auto.*

A covered auto is any vehicle shown in the declarations of the policy. It also includes any trailer the named insured owns. If the insured purchases an additional vehicle during the policy period, it will be covered automatically so long as the insurance company is notified of this addition within 30 days. If the new vehicle is a replacement auto, the insurance company must be notified within 30 days only if the insured desires to add or continue coverage for damage to the auto.

As can be seen, then, the insuring agreement for the liability coverage portion of the PAP is broadly stated to provide coverage for a wide mix of individuals and autos. As might be expected, there are several exclusions applicable to this broad coverage.

Exclusions

Examples of exclusions contained in the liability section of the PAP include intentionally caused bodily injury or property damage, damage to property owned or transported by an insured, and vehicles with fewer than four wheels. There are other exclusions, but only two of these are discussed here.

The PAP excludes coverage for property damage to property rented to, used by, or in the care of an insured. However, this exclusion does not apply to a residence or private garage. In other words, there is coverage if the insured rams a covered auto into the door of a garage he or she rents. At one time another exception to this exclusion applied to autos that were borrowed or rented; although this has since been removed, a few insurance companies have retained the old exception. Therefore the financial services professional should look closely at this exclusion. The current PAP does not provide liability coverage for damage to borrowed or rented vehicles. (See the discussion under Damage to Your Auto later in this chapter.)

The second exclusion has two parts. The first part excludes liability coverage for the ownership, maintenance, or use of any vehicle owned by the named insured or spouse that does not qualify as a covered auto. The intent here is to avoid situations where an insured might own two vehicles but insure only one of them with the expectation that he or she would be covered regardless of which vehicle was being driven. Both vehicles must be insured for coverage to be applicable.

The second part of this exclusion applies to an auto that is furnished or available for the regular use of the named insured or spouse, such as an auto provided by an employer. The insured's PAP excludes liability coverage in such situations. Although the employer's policy would probably provide adequate coverage, this exposure should be examined very carefully. If needed, there are endorsements to the PAP that will provide additional liability coverage for this type of situation.

Medical Payments Coverage

Under the medical payments coverage of the PAP, the insurer will pay reasonable expenses incurred for necessary medical and funeral services because of bodily injury *sustained by an insured.* Subject to certain exclusions, benefits are payable to the named insured and family members if injured while occupying any motor vehicle designed for public roads or if struck by a motor vehicle. This coverage differs from medical payments coverage under the homeowners policy where the named insured and members of the household are not covered, and coverage applies to other persons injured on the premises or because of an insured's activities. In the PAP, medical expenses of other persons are also covered, but only while they are occupying the covered auto. Where no-fault benefits are required, medical payments coverage is normally replaced by the no-fault coverage.

Uninsured Motorists Coverage

Uninsured motorists coverage is a rather unique addition to the PAP policy. It basically provides that if an insured sustains bodily injury (some states also include property damage) in an auto accident where the other driver was at fault (negligent), but where that driver does not have insurance, the insured may recover from his or her own insurance company those sums he or she is legally entitled to recover. In effect, the insured looks to his or her own insurance company to receive what a negligent, uninsured motorist cannot provide.

An uninsured motorist is the owner or operator of an uninsured motor vehicle, which includes vehicles for which there is no applicable liability insurance, as well as hit-and-run vehicles and vehicles for which the liability coverage is not available because the insurer is insolvent or denies coverage. An uninsured motor vehicle also includes vehicles that are insured but have liability limits less than the bodily injury liability specified in the financial responsibility law of the state in which the insured's covered auto is principally garaged.

Some states require that uninsured motorists coverage be included in all auto insurance policies containing liability insurance. Some states stipulate that this coverage is mandatory unless the insured rejects it in writing, while still other states simply consider this an optional coverage.

The limit of liability for uninsured motorists coverage is typically the required limit of the financial responsibility law in the insured's state. However, an option to increase this limit up to the limit the insured has purchased for part A – Liability is available. When this limit is increased, the policy is normally changed by endorsement to provide a combination benefit called *uninsured/underinsured motorists coverage.* The uninsured benefit remains as above. The underinsured benefit provides payment when the at-fault driver or owner has liability insurance at least equal to the financial responsibility limit but less than the limit carried by the insured.

The underinsured motorist benefit becomes an excess amount over the at-fault party's liability insurance up to the amount of the loss or maximum limit carried by the insured. For example, suppose the required liability limit is $25,000 and the named insured carries $100,000. If the named insured suffers bodily injuries in an auto accident and the at-fault driver has no insurance, the named insured would receive $25,000 from his or her own insurance company under the uninsured motorists coverage and the balance of the loss, up to $75,000 (for a total maximum of $100,000), from the underinsured motorists benefit. If the at-fault driver carries liability insurance of at least $25,000, that person's insurance would respond to that limit and the injured party's underinsured motorists coverage would pay the balance of the loss up to the policy limit.

Damage to Your Auto

The physical damage coverage of the PAP is referred to as part D – Damage to Your Auto. The two primary coverages in this part of the policy are *collision* and *other than collision.* The latter has historically been called "comprehensive" and is still referred to in this way by many in the insurance business. *Collision* is defined as the upset of the covered auto or its impact with an object or another vehicle. *Other than collision* is every other cause of loss except collision. In effect, the combination of the two parts provides coverage on an all-risks basis. This, however, means that exclusions listed in the policy should be carefully examined.

Exclusions and Limitations

Several exclusions in this part of the PAP are directed at special types of equipment that may be included within or as part of the auto. For example, damage to custom furnishings or equipment, such as facilities for cooking or sleeping frequently found in pickups or vans, and loss to electronic equipment that receives or transmits audio, visual, or data signals are not covered. This exclusion applies to the increasingly popular telephone in the auto. Coverage for this type of property can be provided by an endorsement to the PAP or by separate insurance coverage. Other types of exclusions in the physical damage part of the PAP include damage caused by wear and tear, freezing, breakdown, and war.

The limit of liability for physical damage claims is the lesser of the actual cash value of the stolen or damaged property and the amount necessary to repair or replace the property. In addition, the damage amount is subject to a deductible that, within limits, can be selected by the named insured. A single deductible may apply to all losses or different deductibles may apply to collision losses and other than collision losses. An increase in the amount of the deductible can often result in a substantial premium savings.

Nonowned Autos

Although this part of the PAP is called Damage to *Your* Auto, coverage is also extended to nonowned autos. A nonowned auto is defined as any private passenger auto, pickup, van, or trailer not owned by or furnished or available for the regular use of an insured. By definition, nonowned auto also includes a temporary substitute auto, used when a covered auto is out of normal use because of breakdown, repair, servicing, loss, or destruction. In one of the strange anomalies of the PAP, a temporary substitute auto is defined as a covered auto in the liability part of the policy, but becomes a nonowned auto in the physical damage part. This underscores the need to study the PAP in its entirety.

Under the physical damage part of the PAP, coverage for nonowned autos is equal to the broadest of any auto having physical damage coverage. This means that when an insured has only other than collision on one auto and both other than collision and collision on another auto, both the collision and the other than collision coverages would apply to a nonowned auto. The coverage provided by this policy is excess over other applicable physical damage insurance. For example, if an insured borrows a neighbor's auto to run an errand and carelessly collides with a tree, the neighbor's physical damage coverage applies first, and the insured's coverage is excess. However, if the neighbor did not carry physical damage coverage, the insured's policy would pay for the collision damage.

Automobiles that are leased on a long-term basis (6 months or more) should be described on the declarations page just as an owned auto would be. Physical damage to an auto that is rented on an occasional basis is covered by the PAP if the insured carries the physical damage coverage. Sometimes a client will ask if it is necessary to purchase the collision damage waiver (CDW) when renting an auto on a short-term basis. This is a difficult question to answer. It would appear that it should not be necessary to purchase the CDW because of the duplication of coverage with the client's PAP. However, the physical damage coverage of the PAP does not provide for the loss-of-use claims that car rental agencies consider a part of the loss to be reimbursed by the renter. Also, the rental agency typically wants payment on the spot to repair or replace the auto immediately, while the client's insurer might want to assess the damages and circumstances before approving payment. For these reasons, the purchase of the CDW may be justified. The cost of this coverage over the duration of the rental must also be considered.

The wording of the CDW varies among auto rental agencies. In most cases there are conditions under which the waiver does not apply, such as while driving in a reckless manner, driving under the influence of drugs or alcohol, or even using the vehicle off paved roads. In these cases the CDW would not respond, but the client's PAP has no similar restrictions. Therefore, the CDW should be recommended to the client, since overlapping coverage is preferable to a gap in coverage. A "yes" to the client's question contains much protection for both the client and the financial services professional.

No-Fault Benefits

Approximately half the states have adopted some form of no-fault automobile insurance plan. Under a pure no-fault plan, legal liability arising out of automobile accidents would be abolished, and anyone suffering a bodily injury loss in an automobile accident would collect from his or her own insurance company. None of the plans now in existence have gone to this extreme. Rather, the right to sue another party either has not been altered or has been modified to eliminate suits for which losses are below a certain dollar limit (called a *threshold*) or below some verbalized statement regarding the severity of the injury. No-fault benefits typically include some combination of medical expenses, lost wages, replacement of services, survivors' benefits, and funeral expenses.

In those states with no-fault laws, individuals either must be offered the coverage or are required to carry insurance to compensate themselves, their families, and possibly passengers in their autos for their own bodily injuries. This is accomplished by adding the required endorsement to the PAP.

UMBRELLA LIABILITY INSURANCE

The homeowners and automobile insurance policies are the basic coverages for most individuals and families. There are situations or possible loss exposures where these two policies are not adequate, and additional types of policies, such as for aircraft, watercraft, business pursuits, or other exposures are needed. Sometimes it is the need for liability limits greater than these two basic policies provide that creates a demand for additional coverage. One policy that is becoming increasingly popular for this purpose is the personal umbrella liability policy, also called *excess liability* or *personal catastrophe liability insurance.*

While there is no standardized personal umbrella liability insurance policy, a few generalizations can be made.

These policies provide excess liability limits over underlying liability coverage limits and, in most cases, broader coverage than the underlying policies. Umbrella liability policies typically provide a liability limit of $1 million or more, often up to a maximum of $5 or $10 million. The insured is required to carry certain underlying liability policies and limits — for example, a homeowners policy with a liability limit of $100,000 and an automobile liability policy with a single limit of $300,000. Other coverages may also be required if the exposures exist.

With respect to the underlying coverages, the umbrella liability policy provides excess coverage. For example, if an individual has an automobile liability policy with a single limit of $300,000 and an umbrella liability policy with a limit of $1,000,000, the first $300,000 of any claim arising out of an automobile accident would be payable under the automobile policy, and the balance (up to the policy limit) would be payable under the umbrella policy. Therefore, the insured would have total coverage amounting to $1,300,000.

An important point to remember about underlying coverage is the fact that the agreed-upon limit of the underlying coverage *must* be maintained by the insured. If the insured in the above instance had reduced the auto liability limit to $100,000 rather than the required $300,000, the umbrella coverage would still pay toward the claim as if the $300,000 limit had been maintained — in other words, the insured would have to pay $200,000 of the claim.

The umbrella policy also covers situations not covered by underlying insurance policies, such as personal injury in the form of libel, slander, and invasion of privacy; auto liability outside the United States and Canada; or liability for damage to property in the insured's care, custody, or control. When the umbrella policy does provide coverage in these cases, it drops down to provide primary coverage over the insured's retained limit. A retained limit is like a deductible that must be paid by the insured. This can be as low as $250, but is typically in the $500 to $1,000 range.

Umbrella liability policies do contain some exclusions. Some typical ones are intentional acts, amounts payable under workers' compensation laws, business pursuits, and damage to the insured's own property. Professional liability may also be excluded, but insurance companies are now offering this coverage if the insured carries an underlying professional-liability policy.

The umbrella liability policy enables an individual to have virtually all-risk liability insurance at a very reasonable cost. The financial services professional should consider recommending this coverage to all clients.

LIFE INSURANCE

The purchase of life insurance should focus on satisfying the financial needs identified for individuals and families. Some of these needs, such as cash for the clean-up fund or for lifetime income for a surviving spouse, continue to exist for many years and can be considered permanent needs. Others, such as the income need during the dependency period or the financial need associated with fixed periods of indebtedness, tend to disappear eventually and are considered temporary needs. These two types of needs influence the choice of an appropriate type of life insurance to recommend.

The insuring agreement in life insurance policies states that the company will pay the face amount (or some designated amount) upon the death of the insured. This death benefit can be viewed simply as the claim payment that is to be made if the contingency insured against occurs, much like a claim payment on a homeowners policy for damage to a dwelling. Just as property insurance is thought of as providing protection, this same approach can be applied to life insurance where the amount to be paid at death can be viewed as protection. Some forms of life insurance place primary emphasis on this protection element.

There is another side to life insurance, however. A client purchasing life insurance frequently gives consideration to the desire for the accumulation of wealth or the need for a cash fund at some known future date, such as retirement. In this instance life insurance is similar to a savings fund, and some forms of life insurance combine this savings element with the protection element.

The process of selecting the appropriate life insurance policy to meet the identified needs and objectives of the client is complicated by the vast array of life insurance policies available in the marketplace. It is important to understand the differences between the various types of life insurance policies in order to make the proper recommendation.

Types of Life Insurance

This section reviews the basics of traditional term and whole life policies and discusses universal life policies. There are numerous variations between these three types of life insurance, and there are many other policies that do not fit precisely into one of these categories. It is impossible to cover all of them in the short amount of space available in this chapter.

Term Life

Term life insurance provides protection for a limited period of time. If the insured dies during that period, the specified amount (normally the face amount of the policy) will be paid to the designated recipient (beneficiary). If the insured survives for the stated period of time, the policy expires and all obligations of the insurance company terminate. The stated period of time in term life insurance policies is expressed as a number of years (such as 1, 5, or 20), or until a certain age of the insured (such as to age 60 or age 65). Because of these features, term insurance is well suited to situations where there is a temporary need for protection.

The death benefit, or face amount of the policy, normally remains constant throughout the life of the term policy. However, term life is also written on a decreasing death benefit basis or, with some companies, on an increasing basis. Sometimes, term insurance is written as a rider or supplement to another life insurance policy, normally to a policy of the whole life variety.

A decreasing term policy may be appropriate for needs that decline over time — such as the principal sum necessary to provide income over a shorter and shorter dependency period or a debt that is being liquidated, such as a mortgage. However, since the principal sum of a mortgage does not reduce on a straight-line basis, a mortgage life insurance policy should have a similar death benefit structure.

An increasing term life insurance policy might be used (typically in conjunction with a whole life policy) when the insured wants the death benefit to equal the original face amount of the policy plus all premiums that have been paid. Another use is when the insured would like to have the death benefit keep abreast of some index, such as the cost of living.

Because it provides protection only for a limited period of time, initial premium rates per $1,000 of coverage are lower for term life insurance than for other life products issued at the same age. If the term coverage is to be continued for another term, the premium rate will increase to reflect the current age of the insured. Although these increases may be nominal at the younger ages, they increase rapidly at older ages.

If an individual has purchased a short time span for the term policy, such as 1, 5, or 10 years, the inclusion of a renewability provision should be considered. This provision allows the insured to renew the policy without showing evidence of insurability. This could be a valuable provision if the insured's health should begin to deteriorate when there is still a need for the protection.

Another provision that should be considered for inclusion with the issuance of a term policy is the conversion privilege. This feature permits an insured to exchange the term policy for a whole life policy or another cash-value insurance contract without evidence of insurability.

In addition to the uses of term life insurance already mentioned, it should be recognized that term insurance can be the basis for one's future permanent insurance program. This is true, for example, when a client needs a large amount of life insurance but can afford only relatively small premiums at the present time. For this reason financial services professionals should conduct periodic reviews with their clients.

Whole Life

There are two features that distinguish whole life from term life insurance. One is, as the name implies, that it is insurance for the whole of life. The policy provides for the payment of the face amount upon the death of the insured regardless of when death occurs. A second feature is the fixed-premium nature of the policy. The premium remains constant throughout the premium payment period of the contract, rather than increasing periodically as is the case with term insurance. (Some whole life policies, such as modified whole life insurance, change premiums as specified in the contract.)

The existence of a fixed premium over a long period of time results in the establishment of the predominant feature of whole life insurance — a savings element. Since premiums during the early years of a whole life policy exceed what is necessary to pay death claims, this excess is set aside and accumulates for the benefit of the insured. This savings element is normally referred to as the policy *cash value* (policy reserves are not discussed in this chapter).

The existence of the cash value buildup alters the structure of the death benefit under whole life policies and provides special benefits to the policyowner. The death benefit for whole life policies remains constant through time. However, since the cash value, or savings element, of the policy increases through time, the protection element decreases. In effect, whole life insurance is a combination of decreasing protection and increasing savings, with the sum of the two elements equaling the face amount of the policy.

The other important aspect of the existence of cash values is the fact that policyowners may have access to those funds. One way to do this is to utilize the policy loan values, which may be borrowed at the request of the policyowner. Although interest is charged on the amount borrowed, there is no requirement that the principal or interest on a scheduled basis be repaid. Any unpaid policy loan or interest will, however, reduce the future death benefit.

The second way to access the savings or cash values is through exercising the policy nonforfeiture options. One of these options is for the policyowner to surrender the contract and receive its surrender value, which is the cash value. Since surrender of the policy cancels the protection element of the insurance when there may still be a need for the coverage, two additional nonforfeiture options are designed to continue a death benefit for the policy. The first of these permits the policyowner to elect to exchange the cash surrender value for paid-up insurance of the same type as the original policy. Paid-up insurance means that no more premiums will be required. As should be expected, since no further premiums will be paid, the face amount of the paid-up policy will be less than the original policy face amount. However, this nonforfeiture option may be appropriate where a smaller amount of whole life insurance would be satisfactory and the client desires to discontinue premiums, for example, when he or she reaches retirement age.

The second option permits the policyowner to exchange the cash value for term insurance for the full face amount of the original policy. As with all term policies, the length of the term coverage will be determined by the age of the insured and the premium dollars available from the cash value. The important point here is that the full face amount continues for some specified period of time. Therefore this option may be appropriate when the need for maximum protection continues to exist, but the premium-paying capacity does not.

Whole life insurance policies can be distinguished by the length of the premium-paying period. When the premium is to be paid as long as the insured is alive, the whole life policy is referred to as a *straight life policy* (sometimes called *ordinary life* or *continuous premium whole life*).

When an applicant, prior to the issuance of a life insurance policy, decides that he or she would prefer to pay premiums only for a specified number of years, a policy can be issued to satisfy that desire. A policy of this nature is referred to as a *limited-payment policy*. Premiums can be scheduled to be paid for a specified number of years or until the attainment of a specified age, typically age 65. These policies involve a higher premium and a more rapid buildup of cash values than a straight life policy. Also, when the premium-paying period is completed, the policyowner has a paid-up policy for the original face amount. This contrasts with the reduced paid-up policy that results from exercising the nonforfeiture option.

The most extreme form of limited-payment life insurance is single premium whole life. This policy involves one premium payment at the inception of the contract. As might be expected, the emphasis in this type of life insurance policy is the savings element rather than the protection element. In fact, because of interest rate levels that were available during the 1980s, the savings element was viewed more as an *investment* than as long-term savings. Changes in certain aspects of the federal income tax treatment of life insurance in 1988 have taken most of the luster from single premium whole life insurance policies.

The shorter the premium-paying period for whole life insurance, the smaller the face amount that can be purchased for a given amount of premium. Therefore, in planning for the use of whole life insurance it is necessary to clearly identify the client's objectives. Since whole life is most appropriate for permanent needs, the trade-off between a high amount of protection and a rapidly accumulating savings element should be considered carefully.

Universal Life

Although universal life policies can properly be classified as whole life policies, they are singled out in this chapter as an example of the flexible premium variety of life insurance policies. Universal life policies require a stipulated premium payment during the first year of coverage. After the first year, the premium on this type of policy is truly flexible. Policyowners may pay whatever amounts at whatever times they wish, or even skip premium payments, as long as the cash value is large enough to cover required policy charges.

Each year the policyowner of a universal life policy receives a report illustrating the flow of funds during the year. This report shows the amount in the cash value account at the beginning of the period, the reduction in this account due to mortality charges and expenses (if any), and the interest earnings credited to the account. This type of detailed information is not generated for traditional whole life policyowners.

Universal life policies offer two death benefit designs, usually labeled as options A and B. Option A provides a constant or level death benefit, like that of traditional whole life policies. However, at older ages the death benefit begins to increase because of the technical need to satisfy the Internal Revenue Code definition of life insurance. Option B provides a death benefit that at any time is equal to the sum of the original face amount of the policy and the accumulating cash value. The death benefit continues to increase as long as the cash value increases.

In addition to flexibility with regard to premium payments, universal life policyowners may also change the face amount of the policy. Decreases in the policy death benefit can be made by policyowner request at any time. However, evidence of insurability may be required if an increase in the death benefit, other than that indicated above, is requested.

Some argue that the universal life policy is the only policy a person will need over an entire lifetime. They base the argument on the flexibility in the premium payments and death benefits, which allows adjustments to be made to fit the client's needs at any time in the life cycle. Therefore, the universal life policy is one that should be understood by all financial services professionals.

Annuities

Life insurance can be considered a technique used to accumulate or create wealth. The growth of cash values can be considered the accumulation of wealth while the cash payment upon the death of the insured is the creation of wealth. Sometimes the wealth already exists for a client, and there is a desire to systematically liquidate that wealth. That is a function that can be performed by annuities.

An annuity provides for the systematic liquidation of a principal sum over a period of time, usually for the lifetime of the annuitant (the recipient of the payments). Annuities are similar to life insurance in that they can be purchased either by a single premium or on an installment premium basis. When annuities are purchased by a single premium, periodic benefit payments to the annuitant can either begin immediately or be deferred to commence at some future specified time. Annuities can be purchased to provide periodic payments of a guaranteed fixed amount or a variable amount. When the variable annuity is elected, the period payment depends on the performance of an underlying investment portfolio, typically common stocks.

Under a pure or life annuity, payments cease upon the death of the annuitant, with no further obligations placed on the insurance company. Most annuity purchasers dislike this contingency basis and prefer arrangements that will guarantee payments to the annuitant's survivors on some basis. This can be accomplished through the election of guaranteed payments for a certain period of time or through the selection of a cash or installment refund arrangement. Another alternative is the joint-and-survivor annuity based on the lives of two or more annuitants, such as a husband and wife.

A knowledge of annuities is important in understanding some forms of pension plans. Their general use in retirement planning is discussed in chapter 10. However, since cash values in life insurance were discussed in this chapter, the financial services professional should recognize that retirement purposes can be served through the purchase of individual life insurance policies. At some time in the future, the accumulated savings element in whole life policies can be exchanged, typically at net cost, for an annuity to provide income to a client for the purpose of supplementing social security and other sources of retirement income.

DISABILITY INCOME INSURANCE

One of the more frequently overlooked personal risk exposures is the loss of wages or earnings during periods of disability. Most people seem to be aware of the medical care costs associated with accident or illness and of the total discontinuation of earnings because of premature death, but tend to overlook the seriousness of the possible loss of income because of disability. At most ages the likelihood of a serious, long-term disability is considerably greater than the probability of death.

The financial services professional should begin the process of satisfying the need for income replacement due to serious disability by examining the client's employee benefit package. This was not suggested for life insurance because group life benefits tend to be small in relationship to the total need. However, in disability income replacement situations, the combination of social security disability benefits and employer-provided salary continuation or disability income benefits may provide most or all of the replacement income needed. Individual disability income insurance is one tool that can be used as an additional source for the replacement of earnings lost during periods of disability.

Definition of Disability

When it is determined that there is a need for additional income replacement protection, the financial services professional should review the key features of disability income insurance policies before making a recommendation to the client. One of these features is the definition of *disability*.

Total Disability

Definitions of disability in disability income policies are based on the ability of the insured to perform certain occupational tasks. One definition, typically called the *any occupation* definition, states that insureds are considered to be totally disabled when they cannot perform the major duties of any gainful occupation that their education, training, or experience makes them reasonably suited for.

A somewhat less restrictive definition is usually referred to as the *your occupation* definition. According to this definition insureds are deemed to be totally disabled when they cannot perform the major duties of their regular occupation. For purposes of this definition, the regular occupation is the one engaged in when the disability begins. Since this definition would allow an insured to work in some other capacity and still be entitled to benefits, insurers modify the definition slightly by adding that the insured may not work in any other occupation. In virtually all definitions of disability, insurers add a provision stipulating that the disabled person must be under the care and attendance of a physician.

Partial Disability

After the totally disabled person has begun the recovery process, there may be a period of time during which he or she may be able to return to work on a limited basis. Since the person no longer satisfies the definition of total disability, partial disability coverage was designed to provide a reduced benefit during this period of recovery. Partial disability is usually defined in terms of time as well as duties: a typical definition may state that, although the insured has returned to work, he or she is unable to perform all of the major duties of his or her occupation or is unable to work on more than a half-time basis.

Partial disability benefits are typically a percentage of the total disability benefit. They are also paid for a limited time period, typically 6 months.

Residual Disability

The concept of residual disability is used as a replacement for the partial disability provision as a method of paying benefits to a disabled insured who has returned to work with a reduced capacity. Although the definition of residual disability may include terms regarding occupational performance like those in total or partial disability, an added dimension refers to a reduction in income. For example, a definition might state that residual disability means that the insured can engage in his or her regular or another occupation, but because of the accident or sickness, income has been reduced by at least 20 percent of the insured's prior income.

Residual disability benefits are payable in proportion to the reduction in earnings and are usually limited to the benefit period of the basic plan. Residual and partial disability coverages are separate add-ons to the total disability income insurance plan.

Key Coverage Provisions

There are several key coverage provisions that should be considered in evaluating the suitability of an individual disability income insurance plan for a client. These include the elimination period, the benefit period, the amount of monthly indemnity, and the terms of renewability.

Elimination Period

The elimination period is the number of days that must elapse between the start of disability and the start of benefit payments. It is sometimes called the waiting period or simply the deductible stated in time rather than dollars. The intent of this provision is to avoid coverage of the short-term illness or injury that temporarily disables an insured and for which retention is more economical than insurance.

Elimination periods are generally available for periods ranging from 30 days to one year. The length of time recommended to a client should depend on the availability of other funds to support a risk retention program. For example, if a client's employer provides a salary continuation plan that will compensate the employee in full for 6 months, there is little need to add an individual disability income insurance policy that will pay benefits at the end of 30 days. However, if a short-term disability would cause financial hardship, a 30-day elimination period might be very appropriate. As with any deductible, the longer the elimination period selected, the lower the premium.

Benefit Period

The benefit period is the length of time during which income benefits will be paid. This ranges anywhere from 2 years in duration to until the insured reaches age 65, or even for the insured's entire lifetime. Historical data indicate that most disabilities are of short duration, but the likelihood of full productive recovery diminishes as the length of the disability increases. This means that long-term disabilities will be more devastating and that insurance is usually the best tool for dealing with this contingency. Therefore the recommended benefit period should be of long duration. Of course, the longer the benefit period, the higher the premium, but a long elimination period might offset part of this higher cost.

Benefit Amount

Individual disability income policies are written to provide a fixed amount of monthly benefit. When disability income insurance is provided on a group basis, it is common to include reference to the total of all such benefits not exceeding some percentage of the insured's earnings. Some policies purchased on an individual basis may still contain a similar reference to a relationship of earnings to insurance. For most individually purchased policies, however, the benefit amount is not adjusted for changes in the insured's earnings or for other disability income insurance that may be payable, except as discussed earlier for residual disability benefits.

Insurance companies limit the amount of disability income coverage they will write so that the total benefit from all sources does not exceed a given percentage of the insured's earned income — about 65 percent for individuals in higher income brackets. One reason for this limitation is the fact that individually purchased disability income benefits are not taxable income to the recipient. Another reason is the potential disincentive for a disabled person to return to work if benefit payments are too high relative to predisability income.

Another limiting factor in purchasing disability income insurance is the maximum dollar benefit that companies are willing to write. This creates problems for higher income clients since they are unable to purchase an adequate level of benefit amount. The maximum benefit available tends to be in the $10,000 to $12,000 per month range for the more favorable risk classifications. The higher the benefit amount, the higher the premium.

Terms of Renewability

State laws specify that individually purchased disability income policies (and medical expense policies) must indicate the basis upon which the insured can continue the contract, a very important consideration to the insured.

Many disability income policies can be canceled or renewal refused at the option of the insurer. If the client wishes to have some assurance of continuation, either a guaranteed renewable or a noncancelable contract should be purchased.

Under a guaranteed renewable contract the insurer reserves the right to change premium rates for all insureds of the same class but cannot cancel or refuse to renew the policy. Under a noncancelable policy the insurer can neither change premium rates nor cancel the policy. A noncancelable policy costs more than a comparable guaranteed renewable one.

MEDICAL EXPENSE INSURANCE

The second major type of health insurance coverage is medical expense insurance. This is the insurance to pay hospital bills, physicians' costs, and various other expenses related to periods of sickness or injury. For many individuals and families this coverage is provided through an employer-sponsored employee benefit program, though in some cases it will be necessary to supplement the benefits provided by such a plan. Usually the only way for a financial services professional to analyze the benefits provided is through reading the employee handbook. If there are gaps or insufficient coverage, proposals should be made to overcome deficiencies.

One factor that may create problems in analyzing and making coverage recommendations of medical expense insurance is the lack of uniformity among individual medical expense insurance policies. Although certain state-mandated benefits or required provisions must be included, many variations still exist.

A strategy that should be considered in reviewing and recommending medical expense insurance is to give first priority to protecting against catastrophic loss. For this reason, the discussion that follows emphasizes major medical coverage.

Major Medical Coverage

Basic medical expense insurance policies typically cover only one or two kinds of medical expense. An example of this is the separate policy issued to provide benefits for expenses associated with hospital confinement. This policy, referred to as a *basic hospital expense policy,* reimburses the insured for room-and-board charges up to a specified number of dollars per day for a specified number of days. As an additional benefit this policy might pay for general nursing, medicines, and other miscellaneous hospital charges. A separate basic surgical expense policy might also be purchased to cover fees charged by a surgeon, normally on some specific schedule basis. Other single-purpose medical expense policies might also be purchased.

In this kind of setting, the concept of major medical expense insurance was developed. Although separate basic medical expense policies could have been, and often were, combined into one policy, gaps or overlaps often existed. Because of the need to overcome this problem and to provide coverage broader in scope than that provided by these basic expense policies, major medical expense insurance policies were designed and introduced. They provide a broad range of coverage for virtually all kinds of expenses associated with illness or injury. Another, and perhaps more compelling reason for the emergence of major medical policies, was the limited dollar amount provided for benefits under the basic policies. Major medical expense policies offer much higher limits on benefit amounts.

Major medical policies are issued in two formats: as a supplemental policy superimposed over existing basic policies or as a combination of the basic and major medical into one policy. The latter is normally called *comprehensive major medical expense coverage.* Although major medical policies differ among companies they tend to have several characteristics in common.

Maximum Limit

The first characteristic of major medical expense policies is the high aggregate limit available for benefits. These limits range from $10,000 to $1 million or more and some policies provide an unlimited benefit amount. The limit stated in the policy can be applied on a per disability basis, a calendar year basis, a lifetime basis, or on some other basis.

Most major medical policies contain certain internal limits, such as a maximum rate for daily hospital room-and-board charges or for charges for surgical procedures. These internal limits are designed to minimize possible abuses of the broad coverage and benefits in major medical policies and to keep premiums within acceptable limits.

Deductibles

The second characteristic common to major medical policies is the deductible. Several types of deductible provisions are found in individual major medical policies. A deductible may apply to each separate illness or may have to be satisfied once in any given calendar year. The policy may include a family deductible that requires a flat dollar amount per year for a family regardless of the number of claims or that eliminates the deductible after two or three members of the family have paid it. Individual major medical policies may also contain a common accident provision stipulating that only one deductible has to be satisfied if two or more family members are injured in the same accident.

The deductible for comprehensive types of individual major medical policies might range from $500 to $10,000 or more. A very high deductible might be appropriate for a client who has ample financial resources to absorb large medical expenses or for a client who has group medical expense coverage that provides only limited benefits. When a major medical plan is superimposed over a basic plan, the deductible is normally quite small ($100 or $250) and applies after basic benefits are exhausted and before major medical benefits begin. This type of deductible is referred to as a *corridor deductible.*

Coinsurance

The third key characteristic of major medical expense insurance is the coinsurance provision (sometimes called a *percentage participation clause*) that requires the insured to pay part of eligible medical expenses in excess of the deductible. A typical provision requires the insured to pay 20 percent (or 25 percent) of the expenses eligible for payment by the insurer. For example, if a client who has a $250,000 major medical policy with a $1,000 deductible and a 20 percent coinsurance provision incurs $21,000 of eligible medical expenses, the client will pay the $1,000 deductible plus 20 percent of the remaining $20,000 of expenses or a total of $5,000.

Some major medical policies contain a stop-loss limit, which modifies the coinsurance provision when an insured's out-of-pocket eligible expenses reach a designated level. At that point the percentage participation by the insured ceases, and the insurer begins paying 100 percent of the eligible expenses. In the above example, if the client had a stop-loss limit of $2,000 including the deductible, the client's total payment for the claim would have been $2,000 rather than $5,000.

An understanding of these three common characteristics of major medical expense insurance—maximum benefit amounts, deductible, and coinsurance—is fundamental to an appreciation of this important coverage. Any individual medical expense coverage, like disability income insurance, must be closely integrated with employee benefit packages provided through the workplace.

Planning for Older Ages

As individuals approach age 65 they may have a tendency to downplay the need for medical expense planning because of the mistaken belief that medicare takes care of everything. It does not, as can be seen in the discussion in chapter 10. This means that financial services professionals and their clients must understand medicare benefits and plan how medical expenses that are not covered can be dealt with in the most effective way. This also means that the financial services professional must keep abreast of frequent changes in the medicare benefit structure, such as the legislation of 1988 and its repeal in 1989.

Insurers provide medicare supplements or medigap policies to cover expenses not paid by medicare. These policies vary from those that cover just the hospital deductible and copayment requirements of medicare to those that provide broad benefit structures covering expenses that exceed medicare allowances, and in some cases, health care expenses that are not covered at all by medicare.

Another segment of medical care that is now receiving greater emphasis is the expense of long-term stays in nursing homes. Medicare provides limited benefits for these expenses at best, and in some situations no benefits are provided at all. Insurance policies have been developed to provide the funding for long-term care not covered under medicare or other medical expense policies. For the most part these policies are new and evolving, and coverage is gradually becoming broader and less expensive. Any policy that alleges that it meets the need for long-term care costs, however, should be examined carefully to make sure it actually does meet the client's needs.

A CAUTIONARY NOTE

A survey of insurance coverages such as the one presented in this chapter can only begin to touch on the basics of individual insurance coverages available to meet the pure risk situations facing clients. Furthermore, each client situation presents different problems to solve. For the financial services professional, this chapter should be considered only as a brief introduction to insurance that provides a basic foundation for the discussion of insurance with clients and a sense of how insurance can be used to meet client needs. It is not, however, a solution to all the questions that arise about insurance.

9

Investments and Investment Planning

William J. Ruckstuhl*

THE MEANING OF INVESTMENT

Often we hear comments such as, "My investments in municipal bonds have performed spectacularly," or "I think that investments are just too risky for me." Rarely, if ever, do we hear, "I invested money in my savings account today." That is because most people do not view a savings account as an investment. They are inclined to think that investments must be stocks, bonds, or some other exotic item, such as futures, options, or master limited partnerships. What actually is considered an investment depends on the definition employed by the individual investor.

When economists define the term *investment*, they focus on additions to the nation's stock of capital assets. Thus new buildings, equipment, and additions to inventory constitute the major elements of the economic definition. This view, however, is too narrow for an understanding of personal investments.

For the purpose of this chapter, investment is defined as the purchase of an asset by an individual or an institution with the expectation that the asset acquired will increase (or hold) its value and will usually generate a positive return commensurate with its risk. The asset may be tangible or intangible. Examples of tangible investment assets include land, buildings, art objects, antique furnishings, set and unset jewels, precious metals, and collectibles such as stamps and coins. Intangible assets are shares of stock, bonds, money in a savings account, or other financial assets. Money in a non-interest-bearing checking account, however, does not qualify as an investment within this definition because its value can be reduced by the ravages of inflation and the account does not provide any return (income) to the depositor.[1]

Investment versus Speculation

When an investment is made, there is the anticipation that a return commensurate with the investment's risk will be earned. This is also true for speculation. Moreover, both investment and speculation can have a short-term time horizon. What, then, is the basic difference between investing and speculating? Short-term investments entail relatively low risk and therefore earn a relatively low return. Speculation, on the other hand, is an effort to obtain a high return in a short period of time by purposely buying (selling) tangible or intangible assets whose value is very uncertain over the next few days, weeks, or months. An example of speculation is buying stock

---

*William J. Ruckstuhl, MBA, CLU, ChFC, is associate professor of finance at The American College.

in a corporation considered to be the object of a bidding war between two or more potential acquirers.

Since the distinction between investment and speculation rests on the expected return in the short run, a particular asset could be acquired by both an investor and a speculator at the same time for different reasons. The speculator anticipates a short-term movement of the asset's market price and expects to dispose of the asset when the price change occurs. The investor, on the other hand, seeks a long-term return and expects to dispose of the asset only in the long run.

Personal Financial Objectives That Require Investment Instruments

Many clients have personal financial objectives that require the accumulation of funds. These objectives were reviewed in earlier chapters of this book. For various reasons such as age, family size, income level, or amount of accumulated wealth, these objectives have different degrees of importance to clients. Objectives that have a high priority with many clients include the desire to be able to

- meet emergency expenditures (for example, due to serious illness)
- acquire expensive personal assets (for example, a new home or automobile)
- pay the education expenses of children
- provide a sufficient retirement income
- accumulate wealth

Clients also possess different views as to the importance of the various outcomes achievable from owning investment instruments. For some clients, high current income received in cash that is spendable now is a paramount consideration, whereas current cash income ranks very low in importance for other clients who have a different time perspective and prefer long-term growth in value. Some clients may require stability of asset value so that they can withdraw monies from the investment at any time without any loss in value. Others may emphasize the need for stability of the yearly income from the investment. Some clients may opt for investments that provide some tax advantages, while others believe this to be a low priority.

Thus, in addition to having different objectives for acquiring investment instruments, clients expect different outcomes from their investment portfolios. The successful financial planner must know each client's personal financial objectives and investment expectations so that he or she can advise whether investments already owned or being considered by a client are appropriate.

CATEGORIES OF INVESTMENT ASSETS

Before one can fully understand investment risks and the measurement of returns (discussed later in this chapter) some basic knowledge concerning different types of investment instruments and their distinguishing characteristics is essential. This section divides these alternatives into four broad categories — cash equivalents, long-term debt instruments, equity securities, and real estate and other investments — and then describes some critical characteristics in each category.

Cash Equivalents

To satisfy the need to make transactions and to have readily accessible money in case of an emergency, many individuals use investments that are known as cash equivalents. Typically cash equivalents either have no specified original maturity date or have one that is one year or less in the future. Since the major purpose for using cash equivalents is ready access to the investment principal, the user's overriding concern is safety of principal. However, investments in this category provide only a modest current income and typically have little or no potential for capital appreciation.

Bank Deposits

The most widely known and used types of cash-equivalent investments are savings accounts and certificates of deposit (CDs) at banks, savings and loans, and credit unions. Since these investments are usually insured to a limit of $100,000 for each different account by an agency of the federal government, they have minimal risk. In addition, few restrictions are placed on withdrawals of deposits in savings accounts.

CDs, which are deposits for a specified period of time such as 3, 6, or 12 months (although maturities of up to 10 years are available), generally impose a loss of a portion of the interest earnings as a penalty for a withdrawal before maturity, although some banks have reduced this to a minimal or zero amount. Because of the time commitment made by the investor, the interest rate earned on CDs exceeds that earned on savings accounts.

Another characteristic of savings accounts and CDs is their ease of acquisition and disposal. Both can be opened or closed at any office of the issuer with little delay and at no cost. Savings accounts can be increased or decreased in virtually any desired sum. CDs can be acquired in sufficiently varied dollar amounts and with staggered maturities that make conversion to cash relatively easy and virtually penalty-free.

Money Market Instruments

Money market deposit accounts (MMDAs) and money market mutual funds (MMMFs) are other popular cash equivalents. For both types of investments, minimum initial dollar amounts are typically required to open the account. In the case of MMDAs offered by banks, virtually any amount can be added to the account. MMDAs typically are insured like savings accounts and CDs. MMDAs allow withdrawals at the bank window or by check. However, a limit is imposed on the number of checks that are allowed at little or no cost per month, and additional checks can be costly. The earnings rate obtained from these instruments often increases depending on the size of the investor's account.

In contrast, MMMFs frequently require minimum dollar deposits and are always uninsured. MMMFs provide access by check, by wire transfer, and, in some cases, by phone. MMMFs are technically mutual funds, and investments therein are technically used to buy shares in the fund. Since MMMFs often belong to a commonly managed family of funds, these MMMF shares can be readily exchanged for shares in other funds within the family with little or no delay or cost.

Both MMDAs and MMMFs hold portfolios of short-term obligations of the federal government and its agencies, of state and local governments, and of businesses. The securities usually have maturity dates averaging under 30 days.

Another popular cash-equivalent investment is U. S. Treasury bills (T-bills). These are obligations of the U. S. government that have maturity dates, when issued, of 30, 60, 90, or 180 days, or one year hence, and are backed by the full taxing authority of the government. With this backing, T-bills are the safest investment available and thus pay investors the lowest interest rate of alternative money market instruments. When the term *risk-free* investment is used, it refers to T-bills. These instruments, sold on a discount basis, require a minimum purchase of $10,000, making them difficult to acquire for clients of modest means. They can be readily sold and converted to cash at a modest cost to meet client needs.

Many other investments have the characteristics of cash equivalents, such as the short-term obligations of state and local governments and of businesses and the long-term obligations of governments, businesses, and nonprofit institutions that are to mature within one year. Some of the characteristics of these types of securities are described below.

Long-Term Debt Instruments

Owners of long-term debt instruments are creditors of the issuing institution, whether it is a government, business, or nonprofit organization. This status grants the investors the legal right to enforce their claims to interest income and principal repayment as contained in the indenture (agreement) that specifies the terms and conditions of the debt issue. In the case of business debt instruments, debt claims have priority over any claims of the owners of the firm.

Bond issues of state and local governments (called municipals) and of businesses typically are quality rated by Standard and Poor's Corporation (S&P) and/or Moody's Investors Service as to the likelihood that the issuer will default on the timely payment of interest or principal. Based on a financial analysis of the issuer, a letter grade is assigned to each bond issue. Bonds rated at the top of the B grade (BBB for S&P, Baa for Moody's) or higher are considered to be "investment quality." Lower ratings are assigned for bonds assessed as "speculative." These rating organizations evaluate the bond when it is issued and continue to monitor the issuer during the bond's life. The lower the quality rating, the greater is the risk of default and the higher will be the interest rate that the investor will expect to earn.

Government Debt Securities

Governmental debt includes securities of the federal, state and local governments, and their agencies. Some federal bonds are backed by the full faith and credit of the U. S. government. For example, all U. S. Treasury obligations have such backing. Other U. S. government bonds issued by federal agencies or organizations, such as the Tennessee Valley Authority or the U. S. Post Office, are not direct obligations of the U. S. Treasury. These bonds, known collectively as *agency bonds,* provide investors with a return greater than that available on U. S. Treasury bonds. A few of these agency bonds have guarantees that effectively place the full faith and credit of the U. S. Treasury behind the bonds.

Some state and local government securities, known as *general obligations,* are backed by the taxing power of the government. Others, usually issued by agencies of a state or local government, are known as *revenue bonds.* They are backed by the revenues earned from such ventures as turnpikes, airports, and sewer and water systems. Without the taxing authority behind them, these revenue obligations are viewed as riskier and pay investors a somewhat higher interest rate than do general obligation bonds.

Typically interest earned on debt issues of the federal government, although subject to federal income taxation, is exempt from income taxation by state and local governments. Exceptions to the exemption from state and local income taxation include mortgage-backed securities issued by federal agencies such as the Government National Mortgage Association (Ginnie Mae) or the Federal National Mortgage Association (Fannie Mae). Interest earned on most, but not all, municipal bonds is exempt from federal income taxation and income taxation by the state in which the bond originates. States generally tax interest earned on municipal bonds issued by other states or their political subdivisions.

Maturities of governmental debt instruments vary from more than one year to 30 years. Bonds with maturities of 10 years or less are often referred to as having an intermediate-term duration and have somewhat less risk than longer-term bonds. If such a risk difference does exist, intermediate-term obligations would pay a slightly lower rate than would a longer-duration bond.

Corporate Debt Securities

Businesses are major contributors to the supply of debt securities available in the marketplace. These securities, either notes if intermediate term or bonds if long term, have various characteristics, which are detailed in the indenture. Some of the more frequently encountered characteristics include the following:

- *secured*—a promise backed by a mortgage on specific assets as further protection to the bondowner should the corporation default on payment of interest or principal
- *debenture*—an unsecured promise, based only on the issuer's general credit status, to pay interest and principal
- *callable*—an option exercisable at the discretion of the issuer to redeem the bond prior to its maturity date at a specified price
- *convertible*—an option exercisable by the bondholder to exchange the bond for a predetermined number of common or preferred shares

For bonds of the same quality rating, these features affect the interest rate available to the investor. If the feature provides a benefit to the bondowner, such as being secured or convertible, a lower interest rate is paid. If the feature provides a benefit to the issuer, such as the absence of specific assets pledged as collateral (debenture) or the presence of a call feature, the interest rate is higher.

The market often assigns labels to securities. One label frequently heard in the news is *junk bonds.* These bonds have low quality ratings from S&P or Moody's and are risky because the firm either has a very large amount of debt outstanding relative to its equity base or has suffered financial reverses and may be headed for serious trouble or bankruptcy. Because the risk is high, the return on junk bonds also is high.

Equity Securities

Equity investments represent an ownership position in a business. As such, they represent a higher risk for the investor than do the previously described debt investments. Although an equity interest can be as the sole owner of a proprietorship or as one of several partners in a partnership, this discussion will focus on equity as evidenced by shares of stock, either preferred or common, issued by a corporation.

Corporations acquire equity funds by selling ownership shares to either a very few individuals or to the public. In the former case the individuals often agree not to sell the shares to others, hence keeping the firm closely held and the shares not marketable. When equity shares are sold to the public, a market for their resale emerges, and the ownership interest can be readily sold or purchased. Corporations can and often do offer different types of ownership interests of which the two most popular are common and preferred shares.

Common Stock

Investors in common stock have the ultimate ownership rights in the corporation. They elect the board of directors that oversees the management of the firm. Each common share receives an equal portion of the dividends distributed as well as any liquidation proceeds. If the firm is unsuccessful, losses will occur that can lead to a cessation of any dividend payments and, if losses continue, to an eradication of the common equity ownership and eventual bankruptcy.

The current income distributed to the shareholder is at the sole discretion of the board of directors. The board is under no legal obligation to make dividend payments to the common shareholder and may instead retain the profits within the business. Only by threatening to or actually electing a new board can the common shareholders be in the position to force a dividend payment, regardless of the profitability of the business.

The owners of common stock also vote on major issues such as mergers, name change, sale of a major part of the business, or liquidation. Lastly, common stockholders usually have a *preemptive right,* which is the right to maintain their relative voting power by purchasing shares of any new issues of common stock of the corporation.

Preferred Stock

Preferred stockholders usually have two privileges that provide them with a preferential position relative to common stockholders. The first privilege is the right to receive dividends before any dividends are paid to the common shareholders. This preference is usually limited to a specified amount per share each year. As previously stated, dividends are payable only if declared by the board. If the preferred shares are noncumulative and no dividend is paid to the preferred shares in any one year, the dividend is skipped and doesn't ever have to be paid. In the next year the corporation can pay the specified annual preferred dividend and then pay a large dividend to the common shareholders. To prevent this from happening, many preferred stocks have a cumulative provision associated with the issue. This provision requires the corporation to pay all the skipped preferred dividends as well as the current year's preferred dividend before any dividends can be paid to the common shareholders.

The second privilege of preferred stockholders is the right to receive up to a specified amount for each share (plus current or cumulative dividends) at time of liquidation. This liquidation value must be paid to the preferred stockholders in full before anything can be paid to the common stockholder.

In exchange for these two preferences, preferred stockholders surrender the basic rights of common shareholders, which were previously described. Occasionally preferred stocks may have callable or convertible provisions such as those for bonds. The effect of these features on the amount of the preferred dividend is the same as on the bond interest rate. In some cases preferred stockholders elect some or all members of the board of directors if dividends have not been paid to them for a specified number of years.

American Depositary Receipts (ADRs)

Many investors desire to own shares in foreign corporations. These shares can be purchased abroad in the same way that domestic corporation shares are purchased in the United States. However, problems, such as fluctuating foreign exchange rates and trading at inconvenient hours due to time differences, make these transactions somewhat complex. To overcome these problems, some U. S. banks have acquired shares in foreign corporations and hold these shares in trust in one of their foreign branches. Then they sell negotiable instruments, called American Depositary Receipts (ADRs), that represent a specified number of shares in a foreign company. ADRs are the equivalent of ownership of the stock, trade as such in domestic markets, and have such rights and privileges as are accorded common shareholders in the country of issue.

Investment Companies

Investment companies can be distinguished in several ways. For example, there is a distinction between closed-end and open-end investment companies. At formation a *closed-end* investment company issues a given number of shares. Rarely, if ever, are additional shares issued. These shares are traded in the stock markets in exactly the same manner as those of operating corporations, such as General Motors. That is, the forces of demand and supply for the stock determine the share price.

The closed-end investment company uses the proceeds from the initial sale of its stock to acquire a portfolio of securities. The market value of this portfolio influences, but does not directly determine, the market price of the closed-end company's shares. Theoretically the value of a share in a closed-end investment company should equal the net asset value of the portfolio. The net asset value is calculated as follows:

$$\text{Net asset value} = \frac{\text{Total assets } - \text{ total liabilities}}{\text{Number of shares outstanding}}$$

However, the shares of most closed-end investment companies sell at a discount of about 5 to 15 percent below their net asset values. When stock market prices in general are buoyant, the discount, as a percentage of net asset value, typically declines. The reverse occurs during periods when general stock market prices decline.

An *open-end* investment company, popularly called a mutual fund, continually sells and redeems its shares at net asset value. Hence the shares are not sold on the stock market. Similar to closed-end companies, mutual funds acquire a portfolio of securities in which each of the fund's shares owns a proportionate interest. As sales and redemptions of the fund's shares take place, the size of the fund's total portfolio changes, increasing when additional shares are sold and decreasing when shares are redeemed.

The nature of the acquisition fees is another distinguishing characteristic among investment companies. Buyers of closed-end shares, since the shares are traded on securities markets, are subject to normal stock-brokerage commissions for both purchase and sale transactions. Some mutual funds charge a sales fee and are called *load* funds. The loading is regulated, and it can be as high as 8.5 percent of the value of the investment. If no sales fee is levied, the fund is called a *no-load* fund.

Technically this distinction should refer not only to an initial sales fee but also to other fees that carry different names but are used to compensate individuals for selling and marketing efforts. One of these fees is the 12-b(1) fee, which is an annual charge against the net assets of the fund that typically ranges from 0.1 to 1.6 percent. A second type of marketing fee is called an exit fee or deferred-sales charge. This is not a modest charge simply to cover the expenses of processing a redemption transaction. Rather, the exit fee is sometimes as high as 4 or 5 percent of the dollar value of the shares being redeemed and is used to pay the costs of the marketing and selling.

Under the federal laws that regulate security transactions, a prospectus (a document that gives a potential buyer the relevant information about a newly issued security) must be delivered to mutual fund buyers before a purchase takes place. The first page of the prospectus includes required tables showing the amount of all expenses associated with the purchase, holding, and sale of the fund's shares. Therefore the magnitude of these additional fees can be determined by the investor who chooses to do so. In addition, the National Association of Securities Dealers is now seeking comments on a proposal: when open-end load funds are bought through a stockbroker, the confirmation sent to the customer must explicitly state the amount, if any, of any exit fees that will be charged when the shares are redeemed. Unfortunately this is a notification *after* the investor has already bought the shares.

Investment companies can also be differentiated on the basis of their portfolio objectives. Although more than 1,500 investment companies exist, they can be segregated into several broad categories based on their portfolio objective. For most of the portfolio categories, subcategories exist. Except for two categories, money market and index funds, the investment company can be either open-end or closed-end. These major categories are as follows:

- *money market mutual funds* — These own a portfolio of short-term interest-bearing securities. As mentioned earlier, they are used by investors as an alternative to cash. They operate only as open-end funds. Subcategories include funds that focus mainly on nontaxable securities or federal securities only or on diversified portfolios.
- *index funds* — These funds own a portfolio of common stock that replicates a major market index such as the S&P 500. They operate only as open-end funds.
- *bond companies* — These companies own a portfolio of bonds. Subcategories include some that invest only in U.S. government issues, municipal issues, or low-quality (junk) bonds.
- *common stock companies* — These companies hold a portfolio of common stocks and perhaps a small number of preferred stocks. Subcategories include those that invest primarily in conservative (defensive) stocks, growth stocks, aggressive growth stocks, or foreign stocks.
- *mixed portfolio companies* — These companies own a portfolio of bonds, stocks, and other investment instruments. Subcategories include balanced companies and income companies.
- *specialty companies* — These companies have very specialized portfolios designed for investors who seek special investment opportunities. One such company might invest in precious metals, a second might focus on commodities or commodity trading, and a third might engage in option trading.

In some cases, an investment company is a totally separate organization that has no links to any other business venture. More often, to enable the fund sponsors to serve a wide range of possible clients, a fund is a part of a family of funds representing several of the above categories or subcategories of portfolio objectives. This feature permits investors to move their investment from stocks to bonds to money market instruments as conditions change. Small fees are sometimes charged when a switch is made within the family of funds.

Several reasons have been advanced as to why investment companies have become popular. The first is that each share in an investment company benefits from the pooled diversification of the portfolio. In addition, the professional management that selects and continuously monitors the securities and the appropriate securities markets should provide better overall portfolio performance than can the typical individual investor. A third reason is that many investors lack the time to properly select securities and can better delegate this responsibility to others. A fourth reason is that the wide diversity of investment companies allows an investor to select the diversified portfolio that best suits his or her investment objective. The tax and record keeping provided by the fund management is another reason for the popularity of investment companies.

Real Estate and Other Investments

Real Estate

Many forms of real estate ownership are available to investors. One such form is the purchase of property directly, either as an individual or as a managing partner in a partnership. One way that requires less active management by the investor is owning shares in a real estate investment trust (which is similar to an investment company but the trust either owns property it manages or owns a portfolio of real estate mortgages). A second way is by owning a limited-partnership interest in a general partnership. This limited-partnership interest has no active role in the firm's management. Real estate investments usually involve more complexities than the previous investment categories because of

- the uniqueness of each property
- the differing rights associated with ownership of each property
- the absence of organized markets for the ready sale and purchase of the property, and the general market risks associated with debt and equity securities. (These risks will be covered in the next section.)
- the complexity of the federal taxation of the income and appreciation from real estate (other than the investor's primary residence) since the passage of the Tax Reform Act of 1986

Most individuals do not purchase their homes primarily for the purpose of realizing a current return or an appreciation in its value. Rather, the main purpose has been to provide shelter for oneself and family. However, ownership of one's home, with few exceptions, has over the past 40 years been one of the most secure and most rapidly rising investment opportunities. As with all investments, market conditions can change. If expenditures for the primary residence are being made because the major objective is to achieve the benefits from an investment, then the property must be examined from that perspective.

Other Investments

Virtually any asset can be used for investment purposes. Over the years, such activities as cattle feeding (usually a farming or feed lot operation) or oil-and-gas drilling and exploration activities have been used as limited-partnership tax-advantaged investments. The growth of the options and futures securities and of the commodities markets has spawned investment instruments that offer different objectives within those markets. The Cold War whetted investor preferences for ownership of precious metals that might rise sharply in value if relations between countries deteriorate. The federal government's granting permission for U. S. citizens to own gold was instrumental in expanding markets for investment instruments such as gold bullion, gold coins, gold futures, and gold-mining stocks. Although general coins and stamps have long been collectibles, more recent types of collectibles have become popular because of the strong economic performance of stamps and coins. Art, ceramics, and china have captured the fancy of many individuals due to the appreciation in certain segments of these markets.

Similar to real estate, each of these investments is a specialty field unto itself. Any technical treatment of the characteristics of these investments is beyond the scope of this introductory discussion.

Summary

This overview described the investment instruments that most clients use. The markets offer other alternatives that appeal to some investors. However, these alternatives either are very risky, require specialized knowledge, or require a minimum expenditure that is beyond the means of most clients.

INVESTMENT RISK AND RETURN

Susan and Bob keenly desire to purchase a home 3 years hence and expect to need $25,000 for the down payment and closing costs. They visited the local savings and loan association (S&L) and were informed that, ignoring taxes, they would need to begin now by depositing $645 monthly for the next 36 months into the S&L's savings account to meet their objective. They went to a mutual fund representative who recommended a fund that invests solely in obligations of the U.S. Treasury. This strategy would require Susan and Bob to invest about $620 per month which, if current rates were maintained over their 3-year planning horizon, would have a terminal value of $25,000. However, even this amount exceeded their ability to save. Then the representative inquired how much they could save each month. When they replied that $560 would be the absolute maximum, the representative recommended a high-income corporate bond fund that would enable their monthly savings to accumulate to the target amount within the 3-year period.

What returns are being offered to Susan and Bob? The following table shows the interest rate represented by each of the investment alternatives.

Investment	Monthly Investment	Interest Rate
Savings and loan	$645	4.75 percent
U.S. Treasuries	$620	7.25 percent
High-income corporate bond fund	$560	13.60 percent

Why does such a variation in rates of return for different types of investments exist? One reason centers on differences in the risk, either real or perceived, associated with different types of investments. If no such differences exist, earnings on investments will not vary. Once risk becomes a distinguishing feature among alternative investments, the investor must consider the potential effect of that risk. To induce investors to purchase assets possessing some degree of risk, sellers must pay a *risk premium* or a return adequate to compensate for the asset's actual or perceived risk.

Meaning of Investment Risk

In the field of insurance, risk typically is viewed as the potential for loss. However, investment assets are acquired with the expectation of receiving some type of gain, thereby causing the insurance-oriented definition to be inadequate for the purpose of explaining investment risk.

Since gain can result from owning investment assets, a more useful definition of investment risk must include positive, zero, and negative gains (losses). Further, the magnitude of positive and negative gains can vary rather sizably from one period to the next. If both elements (positive-negative gains and variation in magnitude) are considered, investment risk can be defined as the variability in the expected return to be obtained from an investment. The greater the actual or perceived potential variation in the return, the greater is the risk of the investment.

Causes of Investment Risk

Variation in an investment's return is the result of one or more distinct forces affecting the particular asset. These forces have an unequal impact on the variation in the return on different investments. In addition, some of these forces affect investment return on an almost daily basis, whereas others do so only infrequently. The combined effect of all these risks constitutes the total investment for a particular real or intangible asset.

These forces, or causes of investment risks, can be divided into three categories that reflect their relative scope and frequency. The first category is called The Big Three. These forces tend to affect most investments and occur with the greatest frequency. They may have the greatest impact on the variation in investment returns. In the short run, less common forces, called The Modest Three and The Minor Three, contain the potential to create very large changes in an investment's return.

The Big Three

The first of The Big Three causes of investment risk is *purchasing-power risk,* sometimes called inflation risk. Inflation is the increase in the general level of prices. Purchasing-power risk also includes the variation in return that can be caused by deflation, which is the decline in the general level of prices. With rising prices, the value of an investment asset or of the income earned thereon, or both, must increase at a rate equal to or greater than the inflation rate. Otherwise the purchasing power of the dollars invested or earned on the asset will decline.

Investment assets that are most susceptible to this risk include the full range of fixed-dollar investments such as savings accounts, certificates of deposit, bonds and other debt instruments, life insurance cash values, and fixed annuities. During a time of rapid inflation these investments' potential for increase either in the real value of the assets or in the return earned from them varies from slight to none. On the other hand, when deflation occurs (twice in the last 50 years), these same investments have the potential for positive returns in value. This occurs because the annual income does not vary with economic conditions (as is the case with the interest on a bond) and the purchasing power of that income stream rises.

For other investment assets the effect of purchasing-power risk is quite different. Some assets increase in their value or return, or both, during periods of inflation. Such assets include real estate, precious metals, and business ownership interests such as common stock. Not all these assets move up in value with inflation in the short run, but over long periods of time the direction of the prices these assets command in the marketplace tends to parallel that of the general price level. Therefore these assets tend to provide greater protection against the inflation risk, but they are more susceptible to the risk of deflation.

The second of The Big Three is *interest-rate risk.* Due to many forces at work in the economy, such as the actions of the Federal Reserve System to control the money supply, the changes in the demand for borrowed funds for consumption or investment purposes, or the movement of foreign exchange rates, the interest rate for any level and duration of risk will change over time. The result is a change in either the value of securities, the income earned on securities, or both. This effect, known as the interest-rate risk, has two segments: capital and reinvestment.

In the *capital segment,* any change in market interest rates typically leads to an opposite change in the value of investments. When interest rates rise (fall), the value of an investment declines (increases). This inverse relationship is most pronounced for financial instruments, such as bonds, mortgages, and U.S. Treasury bills, that have a contractually specified rate of interest or return and a specified duration. Any change in interest rates for these investments will generate some opposite change in their market value (price). The longer the duration until maturity, the greater will be the resulting change in market price. For other instruments, such as common stock or real estate, the relationship is not as pronounced. For example, a small increase (decrease) in interest rates may have little effect on stock market prices. However, a series of small changes or one sizable change in interest rates can cause many stock market prices to move sharply in the opposite direction.

The following example will illustrate why the value of an investment changes when interest rates change. Suppose that an investor purchased a bond when the market interest rate for the bond's risk was 8 percent and that this $1,000 face-amount bond has a maturity date one year hence and pays interest of $80 annually. Next assume that on the following day the market interest rate for bonds of this degree of risk and duration rises to 9 percent. Of course this investor would now like to sell this bond for $1,000. However, the investor will not be able to do so because a potential buyer can obtain $90 interest (instead of $80) by purchasing a newly issued, one-year maturity bond. However, a price can be determined that would make the total return, interest income, and appreciation in the market price of the 8 percent bond such that a potential buyer would be virtually indifferent to either the existing 8 percent or a newly issued 9 percent bond. This price would have to be less than $1,000 so that the buyer's total return would be about 9 percent. Alternatively, if the market interest rate had fallen to 7 percent, for example, the value of the 8 percent bond would rise above its $1,000 face amount so that the total return to the buyer would be equal to 7 percent.

Rather than the one-year maturity used in the previous example, suppose the security had a 10-year maturity. With a 9 percent market interest rate, a buyer would have $10 less interest each year for 10 years if he or she buys the 8 percent debt instrument. Therefore the resulting market price change for this 8 percent security with a 10-year maturity date must be greater than for the one-year maturity in the previous example. This potential change in the market price of debt securities takes on importance if a sale of the security is anticipated prior to its stated maturity date. The longer the time remaining until maturity, the greater will be the resulting market price change. If no sale is planned, the market price's ups and downs are of little consequence to the investor unless an unexpected event creates the need to sell.

How can a financial planner make use of this relationship between the interest rate and the market price of debt securities? If it is anticipated that the forces affecting interest rates are working to increase interest rates, the planner should advise the investor to sell the debt instruments in his or her portfolio. If interest rates do in fact rise, securities similar to those that were disposed of can be repurchased at lower prices. If interest rates are expected to decrease, the investor should be advised to purchase debt securities that, after interest rates rise, can be sold at a gain.

The *reinvestment segment,* which is the second segment of the interest-rate risk, comes into play when debt securities have matured. At this point the investor must reinvest the principal in new securities. Of course, if current interest rates exceed those earned on the matured security, the investor realizes higher future income. What is the result if current interest rates are below those on the matured instrument? The reinvestment element of the interest-rate risk is present because the investor will now realize less income from the reinvested money. The way to minimize the reinvestment element is to stagger the maturities of the securities held in the portfolio so that only a small percentage will mature in any one year. Thus only a long year-to-year downward trend of interest rates would be detrimental to the investor's income stream.

The last of The Big Three causes of investment risk is called *market risk.* Participants in the market for investments should continuously monitor and assess events occurring in the total environment that affect the particular investment asset. These events could be political, economic, demographic, or social in nature and are important because they can affect the expected returns from an investment. The inferences drawn from this monitoring form the basis for decisions to buy, hold, or sell selected or all investment assets. When a sufficient number of market participants act in a similar fashion, market prices for a particular investment (or investment assets in general) can react rather sharply, as the stock market did in October 1987 and 1989. Estimates are that the one-day market price decline in October 1989, which was less than one-third the 1987 decline, resulted in investment losses in excess of $150 billion to holders of equity securities.

Although stock market events capture the attention of the news media, similar declines can occur in markets for other investment assets. For example, at the time of this writing, the markets are experiencing rather sharp price declines for certain types of hotels and department stores. Some analysts are forecasting a long-term decline in residential real estate prices due to changing demographic patterns in the population. Since not all investment sectors are affected to the same degree at the same time, a strategy that spreads an investor's assets over numerous investment markets can mitigate the effect of market risk in one or two investment sectors.

The Modest Three

The next broad category of causes of investment risk, here labeled as The Modest Three, has less overall than The Big Three on the value of investment assets in general. When present, however, they can affect the value of certain investment assets to a sizable degree. For some types of investments, however, The Modest Three do not apply at all.

The first of The Modest Three is *business (default) risk.* For whatever reason, such as a change in consumer preference away from a particular good or service, ineffective management, law change, or foreign competition, some enterprises will experience financial difficulties and will eventually fail. Frequently debt principal or interest payments will not be made on a timely basis, and the organization will be in default. This result can occur in both profit-seeking businesses and nonprofit institutions such as colleges or municipalities. In addition to loss of current and future interest payments, investors in these bonds often lose some or all of the initial sum invested. Because all debts must be paid in full before any funds can flow to the stockholders, rarely is anything left to the owners of profit-seeking firms that have failed. (There is no equity ownership in nonprofit or governmental organizations.) Of course, this risk is not associated with debt instruments of the U. S. Treasury because they are backed by the full faith, credit, and taxing power of the federal government.

Investment tactics to minimize the business risk or default risk include the purchase of investments only from organizations having a high credit rating. As mentioned earlier, both Moody's and Standard & Poor's provide assessments of the issuing organization for securities such as bonds. Obtaining the information for other forms of investments, such as limited partnerships, requires a more diligent investigation by the financial planner and the investor.

The second of The Modest Three is *liquidity risk.* An investment asset is deemed to be liquid (that is, there is no liquidity risk) if the asset can be converted to cash (sold) quickly at any time and without any loss of principal. Generally funds can be withdrawn from a savings account any time the bank is open, and some funds can be withdrawn through automatic tellers any time of the day or night. Thus this asset is liquid. However, the requirement of a 30-day wait to withdraw from a savings account would make the account less liquid. The ability to sell an asset quickly but only at a market price substantially below investor cost is also a characteristic of a nonliquid investment.

Liquidity, as defined above, is a critical concept when evaluating the appropriateness of investment assets for a client's emergency reserve. These funds may be needed quickly, and the client does not want to suffer a loss. Only highly safe, highly liquid assets such as savings accounts, some CDs, life insurance cash values, Treasury bills, and similar investments are recommended.

The next cause of investment risk is called *marketability risk.* Somewhat similar to liquidity risk, this risk occurs when an investment asset cannot be sold quickly at its current market price. This situation arises if, for example, a large block of a thinly traded security comes to the market and significantly depresses its market price. If a more leisurely sale spread out over a period of time had been feasible, the market price might not have dropped at all. For example, at almost any time 100 shares of a Fortune 500 firm's stock can be sold without affecting the market price; however, selling 20 million shares might depress the price substantially.

Some investments, such as homes and other real estate, are affected by marketability risk to a greater degree than those traded on some form of organized market. Admittedly real estate or other assets can always be sold, but a price other than one associated with a distress sale probably cannot be realized.

Because of the existence of marketability risk for some types of investment assets, it does not follow that investors should be advised to completely avoid assets that are not readily marketable. Rather, only a portion of a client's total portfolio should be so positioned.

The Minor Three

Although the effect of the last three causes of investment risk, called The Minor Three, can be just as severe as those described above, the relative infrequency of their occurring causes them to be assigned to this grouping.

The first of The Minor Three is *tax risk.* Virtually all investments have some tax consequences. Income and appreciation in value will at some time be subject to income taxation. In addition, investment assets may be subject to estate and inheritance taxation and gift taxation when ownership is transferred.

In some instances the tax code provides specific incentives to encourage certain types of investments as desirable public policy. However, "what the government granteth, the government can removeth." In 1986 the favorable federal income tax treatment of capital gains was removed, and restrictions were placed on the exclusion of certain municipal bond interest from federal income taxation. (At the time of this writing, proposals have been introduced to reinstate a form of the capital-gain exclusion removed by the 1986 tax act.) Other provisions within the tax code still favor certain investments, but these provisions could be removed by subsequent legislation. New laws could also penalize certain investments by imposing special tax consequences on income or appreciation derived therefrom.

When the tax laws remove some favorable, or add some unfavorable, tax consequences, the value of the affected investment assets falls. To cope with the effects of this type of investment risk, financial planners and investors must monitor events occurring in the national tax arena and make investment decisions accordingly. Investments should be based primarily on their economic value and contribution to investor's goals and should *not* be based solely on their tax advantages.

The second of The Minor Three is called *event risk,* which refers to a variety of possible occurrences that can significantly affect the riskiness of a specific investment asset. One example of such an event is a takeover move.

During the 1980s some individuals and corporations went on a buying spree and acquired some of the largest corporations in the United States. For example, a corporation would perhaps purchase less than 5 percent of the targeted corporation's common stock and then announce its intention to complete the acquisition, using borrowed funds to finance the purchase of the remaining shares. Investors may view this as a decline in the quality of the targeted corporation's previously issued bonds. Why does this occur? Typically a new, nonoperating corporation is created as the mechanism to arrange the financing of the acquisition. The acquirer will generally buy the total equity interest with about 90 or more percent of debt and the remainder with his or her own funds. This tactic is known as a leveraged buyout (LBO). Shortly after the acquisition takes place, the acquired firm is usually merged into the newly formed corporation. As a result of this merger, the bonds from the acquired corporation have the same status as the bonds recently issued by the acquiring corporation. A business that has a high ratio of debt to equity can encounter financial difficulties if it does not have sufficient earnings to meet the interest obligations of the debt. Because this situation could occur, the previously issued bonds are perceived to have higher risk, thus requiring a higher return. Since the interest rate is fixed for the life of the bond issue, the only way for these bonds to provide a higher return is for their price to fall. Thus, when a corporation becomes the target of a takeover attempt, its bonds tend to fall sharply in value.

The last cause of investment risk is called *additional commitment risk.* Some investments may require the buyer to put additional money into his or her investment when certain conditions occur. This additional funding requirement may arise at an inopportune time for the investor. If funds are not available, the investor might be forced to sell the asset at an unfavorable market price. Investments such as certain limited partnerships that can require additional contributions are viewed as being more risky than those that require no further investment.

Summary

As we have seen, investment risk arises for many reasons. Each of these reasons may not be as totally independent of each other as these descriptions make it seem. For example, investors may view inflation as a major forthcoming issue and begin to sell bonds, thus driving down bond prices. Should the monetary authorities seek to mitigate the potential inflation by raising interest rates, bond prices will tumble even further. In addition, if the firm is an announced target for an LBO, the bonds of the targeted firm could plummet in value.

Investment Return

Although most investments do not guarantee that an investor will obtain a return, the expectation of obtaining a return is a primary reason why individuals make investments. As was suggested in the definition of an investment, total investment return has two major components: current income and capital appreciation. Not all investments produce both forms of return. Some investments, such as savings accounts, can produce only current (interest) income. Others, such as undeveloped land, can produce only capital appreciation (unless the land can be farmed or rented). Still others, such as borrowing to purchase corporate common stock, can produce negative current income if the interest expense is greater than the dividend, but they could provide capital appreciation.

Regardless of the possible combinations of returns, a method for comparing the investment returns from different investment assets is an absolute necessity. Over the years and before computers or calculators, three methods for performing quick calculations of investment return acquired widespread acceptance within the investment community. These three measures are still widely used and are (1) the current yield, (2) the holding-period return (HPR), and (3) the approximate yield.

Current Yield

The current yield is perhaps the most widely used measure of financial return. This measure relates the current annual income from an investment to the price of acquiring the asset at today's market price, shown as follows:

$$\frac{\text{before-tax}}{\text{current yield}} = \frac{\text{current annual income}}{\text{current market price}}$$

For example, assume that an investor plans to purchase a corporate bond currently selling at $1,050. The bond will pay the investor an annual interest income of $98. If the bond is purchased, its current yield to the investor would be

$$\frac{\text{before-tax}}{\text{current yield}} = \frac{\$98}{\$1050}$$

$$= .0933 \text{ or } 9.33 \text{ percent}$$

One advantage of the current yield is that it provides a quick way to compare different investments being considered for purchase, retention, or sale. Its major shortcoming is that it fails to look beyond the present date. The investments being compared may have different potentials for future increases or decreases in their market prices. This element is not considered when calculating the current yield. A second shortcoming is that the calculation is made on a before-tax basis. To calculate the aftertax current yield, the above formula must be modified so that the current annual income is reduced by the investor's marginal income tax rate. The following formula makes this adjustment:

$$\frac{\text{aftertax}}{\text{current yield}} = \frac{\text{current annual income} \times (1 - \text{MRT})}{\text{current market price}}$$

$$\text{where MRT} = \frac{\text{investor's combined federal and state marginal}}{\text{income tax rate}}$$

If a 40 percent marginal income tax rate applies to this investor, the aftertax return would be

$$\frac{\text{aftertax}}{\text{current yield}} = \frac{\$98 \times (1 - .40)}{\$1050}$$

$$= .056 \text{ or } 5.6 \text{ percent}$$

The before-tax current yield as shown on the previous page can be multiplied by one minus the investor's marginal tax rate to adjust for taxes (9.33 percent × (1 – .40) = 5.6).

Holding-Period Return (HPR)

Although its name may imply that the holding-period return is a measure of the return over *any* holding period, it is only appropriate for investment periods of one year or less. This is because no consideration of the timing of the investment returns, and therefore of the time value of money, is made. The holding-period return relates the total amount of current income plus the total amount of capital appreciation to the beginning dollar value of the investment. The following formula will determine the before-tax HPR for a one-year period:

$$\frac{\text{before-tax}}{\text{HPR}} = \frac{\text{total current income} + \text{total capital appreciation}}{\text{total initial investment}}$$

For example, assume that Charles purchased an investment on July 1, 1990, for $800. It is now July 1, 1991, and he wants to know what has been the return on his investment. During his one-year holding period, he has received $50 of current income. In addition, the market price of the investment has increased to $840. Based on this information, the before-tax HPR for this investment is

$$\frac{\text{before-tax}}{\text{HPR}} = \frac{\$50 + (\$840 - \$800)}{\$800}$$

$$= \frac{\$90}{\$800}$$

$$= .1125 \text{ or } 11.25 \text{ percent}$$

If an aftertax basis is desired, then the HPR formula becomes

$$\frac{\text{aftertax}}{\text{HPR}} = \frac{\text{total current income} \times (1 - \text{MRT}) + \text{total capital appreciation} \times (1 - \text{MRT})}{\text{total initial investment}}$$

If Charles is in a combined federal and state income tax bracket of 30 percent, then his aftertax return would be

$$\frac{\text{aftertax}}{\text{HPR}} = \frac{\$50\ (1 - .30) + [(\$840 - \$800)\ (1 - .30)]}{\$800}$$

$$= \frac{\$35 + \$28}{\$800}$$

$$= .07875 \text{ or } 7.85 \text{ percent}$$

At the current time, the federal income tax rules do not apply different tax rates to current investment income, such as dividends or interest, and to capital appreciation. Periodically presidential, congressional, or popular sentiment favors such a policy. The aftertax HPR formula provides for differential taxation should it be reinstated into the tax code.

For holding periods shorter than one year, the HPR as calculated above requires modification. If, for example, Charles held the investment for only one-half of a year and achieved the same results, his HPR should be annualized by multiplying 11.25 by 2. This results in an annualized HPR of 22.50 percent. Or, if Charles had achieved his gains in 3 months or in 2 weeks, his annualized HPR would be found by multiplying by 4 or 26, respectively.

Approximate Yield

The true yield on an investment can be described as that rate of interest or discount rate (called the internal rate of return) that makes the present value of the benefits derived from the investment exactly equal to the present value of the cost to purchase that investment. The approximation of that yield or discount rate can be found by using the following formula:

$$\text{before-tax approximate yield} = \frac{\text{annual income} + \dfrac{\text{future price} - \text{current price}}{\text{number of years}}}{\dfrac{\text{future price} + \text{current price}}{2}}$$

Suppose Elly has been advised that a particular stock that is currently selling for $50 a share is expected to increase in value to $68 by the end of 3 years. The annual dividends are expected to be $3 for each of the next 3 years. Based on this information, Elly's approximate yield for the holding period is

$$\text{before-tax approximate yield} = \frac{\$3 + \dfrac{\$68 + \$50}{3}}{\dfrac{\$68 + \$50}{2}}$$

$$= \frac{\$3 + \$6}{\$59}$$

$$= .1525 \text{ or } 15.25 \text{ percent}$$

With no difference in tax rates, multiplying the approximate yield by one minus the investor's marginal tax rate (1 − MRT) will provide the aftertax approximate yield. If the earned income tax rate and the capital appreciation tax rate differ, then each segment of the numerator must be multiplied by one minus the investor's marginal tax rate.

The approximate-yield concept can provide a meaningful estimate of an investment's yield over both short and long holding periods. Applications of this approach include (1) estimating the yield over a planned investment horizon, as shown in the previous illustration, (2) determining the yield from the date of acquisition to the present on a currently owned investment, or (3) determining what the yield was for an investment that has been sold. Only the purpose of the calculation changes; the formula remains unchanged.

REAL AFTERTAX RATE OF RETURN

Earlier it was noted that inflation has been almost continual over the last 50 years. Therefore any analysis or recommendation to a client concerning particular investments should include inflation as a factor. One useful method adjusts the annual aftertax rate of return for inflation. If the holding-period return is used, for example, the real aftertax rate of return can be calculated using the following formula:

$$\frac{\text{real aftertax}}{\text{rate of return}} = \frac{(1 \ + \ \text{aftertax HPR})}{(1 \ + \ \text{current rate of inflation})} - 1$$

Both the aftertax HPR and the rate of inflation must be expressed as decimals in this formula.

For example, if an investor earned an aftertax HPR of .08 (8 percent) during a year when the inflation rate was .04 (4 percent), the investor's real aftertax rate of return would be

$$\frac{\text{real aftertax}}{\text{rate of return}} = \frac{(1 + .08)}{(1 + .04)} - 1$$

$$= 1.038 \ - \ 1$$

$$= .038 \text{ or } 3.8 \text{ percent}$$

Whenever the rate of inflation exceeds the rate of return obtained over a holding period, the investor will realize a negative real aftertax rate of return. This was the result for many investments during the late 1970s and early 1980s, when inflation rates in the United States neared and even exceeded 10 percent and the before-tax return on some investments was 5 percent. Even today savings accounts often pay about a 5 percent before-tax rate of return. If the investor is in the 28 percent income tax bracket, the real aftertax return sinks to zero if the inflation rate is 3.6 percent.

TAXABLE INCOME COMPARED TO TAX-EXEMPT INCOME

Some municipal bonds provide their owners with interest income that is exempt from federal income taxation. Often clients desire to know what would be the equivalent taxable rate for the purpose of making comparisons between these municipals and corporate or Treasury bonds. The following formula will convert a tax-exempt yield to an equivalent taxable yield as follows:

$$\frac{\text{equivalent fully}}{\text{taxable yield}} = \frac{\text{tax-exempt yield}}{(1 - \text{MRT})}$$

A fully taxable yield can be converted to an equivalent tax-exempt yield as follows:

$$\frac{\text{equivalent tax-}}{\text{exempt yield}} = \text{fully taxable yield} \times (1 - \text{MRT})$$

To use these formulas, the tax-exempt yield or the fully taxable yield must be expressed as a percentage, whereas the marginal tax rate must be expressed as a decimal.

For example, assume that Bruce inherited some municipal bonds that have a current yield of 6.5 percent. Recently it was recommended that he purchase taxable corporate bonds as a means of increasing his income. He wonders if it would be worthwhile to sell these municipals and purchase corporate bonds with the proceeds. His marginal income tax rate is 28 percent. Bruce will not have any capital appreciation in the municipal bonds and does not expect any appreciation in the corporate bonds. Based on this information, the equivalent fully taxable yield would be

$$= \frac{6.5 \text{ percent}}{(1 - .28)}$$

$$= 9.03 \text{ percent}$$

If one ignores transactions costs, Bruce would be no better or worse off if he continues to hold the municipal bonds or if he sells them and purchases corporate bonds paying 9.03 percent. His aftertax income would increase only if he can earn a fully taxable return in excess of 9.03 percent.

To verify this, suppose that the corporate bonds paid 9.04 percent. Use of the equivalent tax-exempt yield formula would produce

$$= 9.04 \text{ percent} \times (1 - .28)$$

$$= 6.509 \text{ percent}$$

This yield is slightly more than the 6.5 percent currently being earned. If transactions costs (usually $10 per bond for the first five bonds and less as more bonds are purchased or sold) are taken into consideration, an increase this small cannot justify the sale and purchase.

HISTORICAL PATTERNS OF BEFORE-TAX RETURNS

At this point, the question might arise as to what returns can be expected from different investments. This depends on the time frame used in the analysis and the particular events occurring during the time frame. One might, for example, examine the returns of different types of assets in the 1970s and 1980s and compare these returns to the consumer price index (CPI). The 1970s were a decade for tangibles, such as collectibles, commodities, and real estate. These assets had compound annual rates of growth ranging from 12 to 35 percent and outperformed both the CPI and financial assets such as stocks, bonds, and Treasury bills. However, the 1980s tell a different story. During that decade stocks, bonds, and Treasury bills outperformed the CPI and the tangibles.

Table 9-1 displays several asset categories and includes those assets most likely to be part of client portfolios. The most sophisticated types of investments, such as master limited partnerships, commodity mutual funds, and equipment-leasing partnerships, appeal only to a very small percentage of clients and are purposely omitted.

TABLE 9-1
Historical Investment Returns for Periods Ending December 31, 1988

Asset	Total Annual Return (in Percent)			
	5-Year	10-Year	15-Year	20-Year
Savings accounts	5.50	5.35	5.23	5.02
Fixed income				
U. S. Treasuries/CDs				
Under 1 year	6.83	8.88	8.05	7.49
1–3 years	7.55	8.44	8.19	8.59
3–10 years	8.49	10.04	9.13	8.44
Over 10 years	9.11	10.33	9.38	8.64
Municipals	8.26	9.09	8.15	7.52
Corporates				
A–AAA	10.09	11.29	10.39	9.65
Under A	11.37	12.84	11.81	10.97
Equities				
Blue-chip stocks	14.87	15.67	11.89	9.35
Other stocks	6.53	15.06	13.61	7.38
Growth funds	11.67	15.51	11.66	7.48
Income funds	13.52	14.70	12.86	9.82
Real estate	1.96	4.93	6.90	6.77

Source: Reprinted with permission of Practitioners Publishing Company, Fort Worth, Texas. From the *CPA Financial Planner,* November 1989.

The total return includes both current income (dividends or interest) and capital appreciation when appropriate. The data for municipal bonds, however, include only the current yield since trading before maturity is relatively unusual for municipal bonds. For the various categories, the data shown represent a before-tax return. As a consequence, the data are not exactly comparable since the municipal-bond yield should be adjusted to an equivalent fully taxable yield, as shown previously.

In general, the longer the time to maturity for debt instruments, the larger will be the total return, as shown for CDs and U. S. Treasury securities. When risk rises, such as that for corporate debt rather than U. S. Treasuries, the before-tax return rises. However, despite their lower risk, corporate bonds outperformed blue-chip common stocks over the 20-year holding period. This was not the case for shorter holding periods.

As the data in table 9-2 suggest, when a longer holding period is examined, riskier investments provide the higher return. However, as shown in table 9-2, the return for these assets is much lower over the 63-year period than has been experienced in the last 5 to 15 years.

INVESTMENT PRINCIPLES, STRATEGIES, AND TACTICS

Now that both the types of investments frequently used and the various investment risks and returns have been examined, this section will describe some of the policy recommendations and techniques that are recommended by successful financial planners and used by many successful investors. Not all are appropriate to all situations, but collectively they provide the planner with some guidelines so that clients will receive prudent advice concerning investment strategies and tactics.

TABLE 9-2
63-Year Compound Annual Return (Before Tax) Ending December 31, 1988

Standard & Poor's 500 Stocks	10.0%
Long-term U. S. bonds	4.4%
Treasury bills	3.5%

Meet Emergency and Protection Needs First

No investment should be undertaken unless the investor has first accomplished two highly important personal objectives: emergency needs and protection needs. The consequences of not having satisfied these objectives are too great, as are the risks associated with investments. Obviously some of the client's emergency funds should be placed in investments that will provide some current return. However, these should be limited to the first category of investments (cash equivalents), as previously described.

Match Investment Instrument with Investment Objective

Any investment must be appropriate for the personal financial objective that is being sought. For example, individual retirement accounts (IRAs) accumulate interest on a tax-free basis until the monies are withdrawn. Therefore using tax-free municipal bonds as the funding instrument in an IRA is not a prudent course of action. Seeking the highest rate of return commensurate with the client's risk preferences would be a better course of action due to the tax-free buildup.

When funds are being accumulated for purposes that are not deferable, it is essential to have virtually the precise amount available at the needed time. For example, investments whose market price fluctuates sharply or investments that are not readily salable would not be appropriate for funding a child's expected education expenses. For this type of objective, the proper approach should include matching the investment's maturity with the date the funds will be needed.

As another example, a young client's funding for retirement should not use short-term investments, since these usually are at the low end of the structure of interest rates and offer little opportunity for appreciation over the planning horizon. Instead, investments that have as their objective long-term capital growth are more effective in offsetting the inflation that is likely to occur over the next 30 or 35 years.

Equity Investments Require Extended Holding Horizon

Investments in common stocks that are owned individually or through investment companies should generally have a planned holding period of at least 3 years. Any period shorter than this subjects the investment to increased risk. The problem of market timing, or when to buy or sell, and the transactions costs of the purchase and sale work to make success quite difficult with shorter-term holding horizons.

In addition, the behavior of the stock market favors at least a 3-year planning horizon. Combined with the dividend income earned on a portfolio of common stocks, the ups and downs of the market typically are such that only a few 3-year holding periods fail to provide a positive return. For a horizon of 5 years, even fewer periods fail to provide a positive return. Many shorter periods, however, for example one year or less, have produced a negative total return.

Other equity investments, such as real estate, require even longer planned holding periods due to their relatively larger transactions costs and their general lack of marketability. Indeed, for some limited partnerships financial advisers often advocate at least a 10-year planned holding period.

Change with the Times

Grandpa said, "Never sell the XYZ stock"; but Grandpa has died and conditions have changed. Wise investors monitor the economic, financial, and security markets and continually utilize the new information to restructure their portfolios as conditions dictate. All too often individuals are wedded to a particular investment for emotional, rather than rational, reasons. Other individuals do not sell a particular asset because of the income tax consequences associated with the transaction. However, the time comes when the best course of action is to sell, take the gain, and pay the tax. Perhaps even more difficult is the decision to sell at a loss. No one likes to see a personal decision turn sour, but future conditions might only increase the loss if the asset is not sold.

Beware of Tax-Saving Rationale

Investment analysis and decision making should focus on the underlying economic facts. Sometimes planners who recommend investments focus on the tax benefits that will accrue to the client rather than on the economic soundness of the venture. The Tax Reform Act of 1986 stands as a monument to the fact that the government can change the tax rules rather drastically. Many investments made solely on the basis of tax considerations have generated problems and losses for their owners. Certainly tax considerations influence investment decisions, and their effect must be analyzed. However, tax considerations are only one of many factors that determine the economic soundness of an investment.

Understand the Investment

A financial planner should never recommend to a client any investment that is not fully understood by both the planner and the client. Both ethical and legal factors make this imperative. The hidden consequences arising out of the investment can be significant. For example, purchasing a real estate or oil-and-gas limited-partnership interest results in the need to file at least six additional tax forms each year. Other examples include understanding the consequences of purchasing taxable zero coupon bonds or the risks of investing in newly formed businesses.

Diversify the Portfolio

Diversification of an investment portfolio is a matter of degree. The old adage, "Don't put all your eggs in one basket," never provided the answer to the question, "In how many baskets should the eggs be put?"

Effective portfolio diversification can be viewed as a hierarchy. The narrowest perspective at the bottom of the hierarchy is based on modern portfolio theory. Under this view a security is selected on the basis of how its return varies as compared to the variation in the return on other securities in the portfolio. Ideally the return for each security should vary with respect to the other securities in the portfolio so that the only risk remaining for the portfolio as a whole is market risk. All other risks, such as business risk or interest-rate risk, are virtually eliminated through diversification. Experts suggest that approximately 20 carefully selected securities will largely achieve this result.

Further up the hierarchy, a somewhat broader view of diversification would expand the scope of this process to include investments other than securities that are owned by the client. This wider spectrum could include the client's home, other real estate investments, collectibles, and precious metals. Investing in gold as a precious metal and in gold-mining stocks as a security would not provide additional diversification and, unless compelling reasons existed, one of these two investments should be sold.

The apex of the hierarchy represents the broadest view of diversification and recognizes the client's occupation, the nature and stability of his or her employer, and the investments used in such employment-related benefits as pension and 401(k) plans. For example, a client who is employed as a commission sales representative by a firm whose sales move up and down with the business cycle and who has selected employer stock as the investment instrument for contributions to the 401(k) plan has little diversification should the economy enter a recession. Sage advice might be to reduce the dependence on the employer by using some different investments for the 401(k) plan. In addition, the client should place other funds into investments whose performance varies in a manner markedly different from that associated with his or her employment-related income sources.

Recognize the Role of Intuition

Hard financial and economic analysis by itself is not always sufficient to determine what the appropriate investment is. Some other element, perhaps neither quantifiable nor ascertainable from sophisticated analysis, can provide the hunch that a particular investment will be successful. A recently related story concerns a financial planner who, after purchasing a particular brand of running shoes, noticed that many acquaintances were wearing the same product. Intuition said to recommend a purchase, and investigation confirmed the producer to be a healthy, profitable corporation. The result was a most successful investment for some clients who benefited from a period of rapid growth in the firm's sales and profits.

Expect Mistakes

Not all investments will perform as expected. The planner and client must recognize that mistakes will occur and then dispose of the asset, take the loss, and move on to more successful investments. However, every mistake should provide some insight or information that will benefit future investment analysis and decision making.

Use a Consistent Pattern of Investing

Trying to outguess the market or predict the start of the next downturn or upturn and thus win by having excellent market timing for each and every investment may not be worth the effort. For example, over the period 1968 to 1988, naive client A invested $5,000 each year at the precise moment when stock prices were at that year's peak. More astute client B spent 15 hours per week evaluating market conditions. Over the same 20-year period, client B invested $5,000 each year at the time when stock prices were at that year's absolute bottom. What was the difference in their performance? Client A, at the end of 1988, had a portfolio worth $620,868 and realized a compound annual return of 16.6 percent. Client B did better. The portfolio grew to $799,614 with a compound annual return of 18.5 percent. Both attained highly acceptable returns. Was the effort worth it for B? That depends on the value of his or her time or on how profitably that time could have been used elsewhere. Moreover, in the real world how likely is it that a client will always, over a 20-year period, invest precisely at the peak or trough of stock prices?

Results such as these show the benefit of an investment program that is less concerned with when the investments will be made and more concerned with making investments on a regular and periodic basis. The technique of dollar-cost averaging, which is based on such a pattern of investing, usually achieves satisfactory results.

Take Advantage of the Power of Compounding

Compound interest, or interest earned on interest, is a powerful force in determining the size, at some future time, of an accumulation of funds. The importance of this concept should not be ignored in a client's investment program. Many investments provide easy reinvestment of current income that results in the benefit of compounding. Some of the more frequently encountered examples are as follows:

- *passbook savings accounts* — The interest is automatically added to the account, and the investor must take specific action by withdrawing the interest to prevent compounding from occurring.
- *certificates of deposit* — Small CDs typically do not distribute interest during the life of the instrument. Rather, the interest is automatically reinvested, most often at the same rate being earned on the principal amount invested in the CD.
- *mutual funds* — Most mutual funds allow for the automatic purchase of additional shares whenever current income or capital gains are credited to a shareholder's account.
- *common stocks* — Many large corporations permit the investor to reinvest dividends in additional shares of that corporation's common stock. Often no brokerage charges are levied, and in rare cases the corporation subsidizes the purchase by providing up to a 5 percent discount from the average market price of its stock over the past 3 months.
- *zero coupon bonds* — Bonds that do not make an annual interest payment to the bondholder, such as all U. S. Government Series EE bonds and selected issues of corporate and municipal bonds, have a built-in automatic compounding of interest over their life.

Work with Professionals

The appropriateness of an investment to the client's objectives and the degree of diligence used to verify that an investment is, in fact, appropriate are forces that are imposing a higher standard today on those providing investment advice than was true in the past. Working with investment professionals, particularly those who specialize in specific investments, helps to ensure that the recommended investments are appropriate for the achievement of client objectives. Therefore the abilities of investment counselors, brokers, and bankers should be drawn upon by financial planners.

Beware of High-Pressure Sales Tactics

Most marketers possess persuasive skills, which sometimes border on pressure selling. Unfortunately marketers of investment products are no exception. Frequently tales of high-pressure, boiler-room, telephone solicitations receive widespread coverage in the news media. These are the blatant examples. Although caution on the part of the financial planner and the client might lead to a missed opportunity, the frequency of that occurring is far less than implied by the solicitations and does not outweigh the benefits of careful investigation.

Expect Markets to Overreact

Investment markets are not perfect, or perhaps the players lack perfection. Since perfect knowledge does not exist, when either good or bad news reaches the marketplace, the market often overreacts. Goods news may produce too much euphoria that initially drives prices up disproportionately. Conversely bad news may bring out high degrees of pessimism that drive prices below what are justifiably based on the information. Within a few days the market tends to assess the news more accurately and prices adjust to reflect the reality of the information. Therefore a financial planner's knee-jerk reaction to market behavior fails to provide clients with the advice needed to make proper decisions. Of course, when either upward or downward *trends* emerge in the market, appropriate action must be taken.

Avoid Discretionary Power

Many clients prefer to have others perform the necessary work of managing their portfolios and grant broad managerial powers to accomplish this end. Although this may be an indication of trust in the judgment of the person receiving this power, conflict is likely to develop. Portfolio performance that does not meet a client's expectations, such as a sharp decline in market prices that generates portfolio losses, can precipitate this conflict. To avoid this problem financial planners may want to suggest that approval from the client must be obtained before any action is taken. Exceptions to receiving this prior approval might include times when the client cannot be readily reached or when surgery or other medical treatment precludes the client from taking an active role.

Apply the Control Process

Up to this point, emphasis has been on the need for selecting investments that match a client's objectives. To select these investments there must be performance standards. These performance standards are the first step of the control process. Monitoring performance, the second step, provides the data for the third step, the comparison of performance with standards. If targeted results (the standards) are being met, there may be no need for a change within the portfolio. However, if economic forecasts make certain investments questionable, then, despite having achieved the targeted results, the investments should be sold.

If the targeted results are not being met, the client has a problem investment. A problem investment is any investment that is not achieving its expected level of performance. When faced with a problem investment, the client has two choices — retain or sell. The actual choice will depend on the estimate of the investment's *future* performance. If a new acceptable standard, revised due to changed economic or financial conditions, is achievable, then the client should be advised to retain the problem investment. Otherwise, disposal of the problem investment should be recommended.

ECONOMIC ENVIRONMENT AND INVESTMENT TACTICS

Business cycles resemble roller coasters. Both have a long, slow ride up to the peak and then a short, fast trip down to the trough before starting the long upward ride again. In economic terms, the long ride up is called the *expansionary phase* of the cycle. Economic events that typically occur during this phase:

- increases in demand for goods and services leading to increases in output and employment
- widespread optimism among consumers and business firms concerning future economic conditions
- increases in incomes, profits, and dividends
- rising prices for stocks and tangible assets
- inflationary pressures due to productive capacity limitations
- increasing interest rates due to demand for borrowing to finance the expansion, followed by Federal Reserve restrictive monetary actions to reduce inflationary pressures

During the downward phase of the cycle, often called a *recession,* the reverse of the activities in the expansionary stage takes place.

When investors believe that either of these two phases represents the current situation, then the critical question is, "Will this condition continue into the future?" If analysis provides a positive answer, the investment decision is easy: Buy those investments that will perform well under those conditions. In the early expansionary stages, the recommendations would include, for example, convertible bonds, common stocks, real estate, and commodities. In the early stages of a recession, bonds and other debt instruments are more appropriate.

Those periods at or near the peak or trough of the business cycle are the most difficult to assess. How long will this expansion (contraction) continue? If analysis provides no clear signal, this is not a time to either dispose of or acquire new investments except cash equivalents, such as money market mutual funds or short-term CDs. When conditions become clearer, the investor should be advised to dispose of those investments that are not suitable and to acquire those that are appropriate for the forthcoming conditions.

INVESTMENT MARKETS AND REGULATION

Many types of markets exist for investments. This section will first describe major types of markets where investments trading occurs on a regular basis. These markets are (1) true-auction markets, (2) negotiated markets, (3) dealer markets, and

(4) organized-securities markets. Following this material, the purpose and thrust of the major federal laws and regulations affecting investments will be covered.

Investment Markets

True-Auction Markets

In true-auction markets, investment assets such as artwork, collectibles, or real estate are offered for sale to the highest bidder. The bidding continues until no one exceeds the last bid price. When this occurs, the sale is consummated. Since the advent of telecommunications, potential buyers need not attend these trading sessions. Normally only a small number of potential buyers participate in true-auction markets for several reasons. First, buyers might not be aware that such an auction is being held. Second, buyers often prefer first-hand evaluation of the asset, and the cost of attending these auctions can be high. Third, for some of these assets (such as a particular painter's artwork) only a relatively few potential purchasers exist either regionally, nationally, or internationally. Lastly, the unit price of some of these investments dictates that only a handful of bidders will have the financial resources.

A variant of this form of auction market is used by the Federal Reserve System in its marketing of U. S. Treasury T-bills. Although competitive bidding from financial institutions takes place on a regular basis (every Monday for delivery on Thursday), small investors can submit noncompetitive bids specifying the amount (subject to a minimum purchase of $10,000) and the desired maturity. These bids are accepted at the average price (interest return) for all competitive bids accepted in that day's auction. In this manner the small investor has the opportunity to acquire T-bills directly from the issuer and earn a rate competitive with that being earned by financial institutions.

Negotiated Markets

Negotiated markets predominate for the trading of real estate and similar investment assets. In these markets, sellers list their offerings with brokers who then seek to attract buyers through various advertising and other marketing methods. After a buyer has been located, negotiations determine the price.

Large institutional investors such as pension funds and mutual funds often employ brokers to locate buyers or sellers of large blocks of bonds or stocks. When these transactions involve listed securities (see subsequent treatment of organized-securities market), this negotiated market is called the third market because the transaction does *not* take place on the floor of an organized exchange. This market has many of the same characteristics as the true-auction market such as the lack of general awareness that the asset is available for purchase and sale. Also, as in auction markets, there is often a need for physical examination of the asset, especially a piece of real estate. Lastly, the high unit cost that restricts the number of participants in auction markets may have the same effect in negotiated markets.

Dealer Markets

For many securities, one or more dealers make an active market by offering to buy (at a bid price) and sell (at an ask price) as much of a particular security as desired by investors. The difference between the bid and ask price is the dealer's spread, or compensation, for making the market and bearing the risk of holding an inventory of the security. The dealer makes the market. When demand for the security rises, the dealer raises its bid and ask prices; when demand falls, the dealer lowers these prices.

The over-the-counter market, which is a network of securities dealers, includes over 30,000 different securities issues. A numerical majority, but not the dollar-value majority, of all stocks are traded on this market. In addition to the stocks of operating corporations, this market also includes shares of closed-end investment companies and most government and corporate bonds.

Organized Securities Markets

Formal trading locations and markets exist for securities listed on one or more of the national or regional exchanges. The most noted, the New York Stock Exchange, lists the securities of approximately 1,500 firms and actively maintains trading in these corporations' common and preferred stocks and their bonds. Each security is assigned a trading post on the floor of the exchange where commission brokers, employed by the various stock-brokerage firms, meet to engage in auction trading for the buy and sell orders transmitted to them. Each listed security is assigned to a specialist who makes a continuous, fair, and orderly market for the issue. The specialist performs this job by buying or selling the particular issue to offset any imbalance that develops in the number of buy and sell orders coming to the security's trading post from the commission brokers. The specialist maintains records of special orders brought to the market and accommodates members of the exchange for transactions that are less than the standard amount, which for stocks is 100 shares.

All exchanges have membership requirements for individuals trading on the floor of the exchange. Also, exchanges maintain listing requirements that must be met by a corporation before any trading of its securities can take place on the exchange. The New York Stock Exchange has the most stringent requirements, including a national rather than local interest in the security, a minimum number of shareholders and publicly traded shares, and a minimum dollar amount of profits, assets, and market value of the corporation's common stock. Other exchanges, such as the American Stock Exchange, the Pacific Stock Exchange, and the Philadelphia Stock Exchange, tend to pattern their membership and listing requirements after those of the New York Stock Exchange except that their requirements are not as stringent as New York's.

Regulation of the Markets

Both state and federal regulations govern trading terms, conditions, and practices in all four markets. Federal laws dominate the organized securities and dealer markets whereas state laws are of greater importance in the true-auction and negotiated markets. The focus of this discussion centers on the most important federal laws and briefly describes the main purpose of each.

Securities Act of 1933

The Securities Act of 1933 requires issuers of new securities to file a registration statement with the Securities and Exchange Commission (SEC). The issuing corporation may *not* sell the security until the SEC verifies that the information contained in the registration statement is complete and is not false or misleading. Once approval is obtained, a prospectus is prepared that contains a summary of information from the registration statement. Then the securities can be sold to the public if a copy of the prospectus is made available to all interested buyers.

No attempt to evaluate the investment merits of the proposal is made by the SEC. Rather, the SEC merely seeks to verify that the statements are true.

Securities Exchange Act of 1934

As the name implies, the emphasis of the Securities Exchange Act of 1934 is to regulate the various securities markets. Its scope includes the organized securities exchanges, the over-the-counter markets, all stockbrokers and dealers, and the securities traded in these markets. In addition to requiring registration with the SEC, this act requires these institutions, individuals, and issuing corporations to file periodic updated data with the SEC.

The Maloney Act of 1938

The Maloney Act of 1938 permits the establishment of trade associations for the purpose of self-regulation of a segment of the securities industry. The only self-regulating organization (SRO) that has formed is the National Association of Securities Dealers (NASD). This SRO regulates the securities firms, their owners, and stockbrokers, and establishes rules of practice to which members must adhere. Securities firms that are not members of NASD are regulated by the SEC.

The Investment Company Act of 1940

The Investment Company Act of 1940 established rules and regulations that apply to all investment companies with respect to their dealings with and on behalf of their shareholders. This act is designed to require investment companies (1) to provide adequate disclosure to shareholders and (2) to refrain from paying excessive advisory, management, or brokerage fees. Significant amendments to this act, which were passed in the 1970s, regulate fees associated with contractual purchase plans entered into by individual investors.

Investment Advisers Act of 1940

The purpose of the Investment Advisers Act of 1940 is to protect clients from potential abuses by investment advisers. Such advisers must register with the SEC if they are in the business of providing investment advice for compensation. (A full discussion of this act is in chapter 12 of this text.) It should be noted that the SEC does not guarantee the competence of any adviser; rather, it attempts to protect the investor from fraudulent or unethical practices, principally by requiring that the adviser provide full disclosure to clients.

SOURCES OF INVESTMENT INFORMATION AND ADVICE

Investment recommendations and decisions typically are made on the basis of either security analysis or technical analysis. Security analysis starts with an analysis of the economy and its direction, the industry under consideration and its direction, and the firm and the characteristics of the security under consideration. This three-tiered approach also applies to other investments such as real estate. Technical analysis, on the other hand, involves the examination of current market prices, trading volume and direction, and other trends occurring in the marketplace as a means of predicting the future direction of security prices. Regardless of which approach a planner or investor uses, information is an essential ingredient. This section of the chapter will describe various sources of published information and advice that are readily available.

Investment Information

General Information

Many books, written either for the general public or for college courses, provide technically accurate information concerning the field of investment. The scope and depth of their coverage far surpass this brief overview. Both public libraries and bookstores have wide selections. Due to the fact that many new investment instruments keep appearing in the marketplace and that Congress seems to tinker with the tax laws affecting investments on an almost yearly basis, books published before 1988 or 1989 might not provide the most up-to-date information. However, the basic information contained in earlier-dated books will certainly be reliable.

Descriptive Information

This information includes data from which analysis can occur. For security analysis, data published by the Federal Reserve System, the Department of Commerce, or the Department of Labor about the overall economic environment often are available without charge. Industry trade associations, general business and specialized magazines, and the daily and financial newspapers have information on specific industries. A corporation's annual report or the financial statements for a real estate or tax-advantaged investment are sources of data. Corporations must submit to the SEC a special form, Form 10-K, that contains additional information about the corporation and is available by request. If a new security is under consideration, the prospectus becomes a major source of information. Even if an investor is considering the purchase of a corporation's existing securities, a recent prospectus for the corporation will provide insight into the firm beyond that obtainable from other sources.

Data describing the patterns of behavior in securities markets are reported in major newspapers and in the specialized financial press. The latter category includes the *Wall Street Journal, Investor's Daily,* and *Barron's* and provides more complete information than do general newspapers. Information concerning the amount and direction of stock price changes, interest rates, volume of trading, and other similar data is available on a daily basis. In addition, news retrieval systems that are linked into a personal computer instantaneously make information about past and up-to-the-minute events available.

Overall there appears to be no scarcity of descriptive information. Financial planners and investors must ascertain which sources and types of descriptive information are best suited to their purposes.

Analytical Information

The process of analysis involves breaking problems and information into smaller pieces so that they can be more readily examined and understood. Then the pieces must be synthesized (that is, put back into the whole) to reach an integrated conclusion. Many of the sources referred to in the previous section also provide analytical information. In addition, many financial subscription services perform analyses and sell the results to subscribers. Summary information is also available from full-service brokerage firm reports.

Investment Advice

Investment Newsletters

Numerous investment newsletters, available on a subscription basis, make evaluations as to the attractiveness or unattractiveness of the markets as a whole or of specific industries or firms. These newsletters advise subscribers as to whether a buy, hold, or sell strategy is most appropriate.

Sales Personnel

Regardless of the type of investment under consideration, individuals involved in its marketing offer recommendations for its purchase or sale. Many of these individuals suggest prudent courses of action; however, others place personal gain ahead of customer needs or objectives.

Bankers and Specialized Money Management Firms

Individuals within this group provide single-purpose planning and advice with respect to a client's investment needs. Some overlap within this group exists, such as bankers recommending the use of the bank's specialized money management unit, the trust department, for managing a customer's portfolio. Portfolio management is now also being offered by some stock-brokerage firms.

Financial Consultants

A relatively new field emerged and began to gain acceptance during the 1970s and 1980s. This field, comprehensive financial planning, focuses on the total set of client needs, objectives, and means of achievement. One important element in the comprehensive financial planning process is the use of investments to accumulate funds for education, retirement (financial independence), and other objectives. The financial consultants have a legal and ethical responsibility to their clients to recommend only those investments whose risk-return characteristics match the client's risk-taking profile and financial objectives.

A FINAL WORD

The intent of this chapter has been to provide basic information on many dimensions of the knowledge needed for effective investing. The reader should recognize that no simple solution is appropriate for all client situations. We shall end with the late financier Bernard Baruch's response to the question of how to become rich through investing: "If you have the tenacity of the barnacle, the strength of the elephant, and the courage of a lion, then you have a chance!" And you thought investment involved only bulls and bears.

Note
1. The reader might ask: "Wouldn't money in such a checking account experience an increase in its value during a period of deflation and therefore qualify as an investment?" Indeed it would, but in only 2 of the last 50 years has the year-end consumer price index (CPI) been lower than the beginning-of-the-year CPI. Even in those 2 years the decrease was very slight.

10

Retirement Planning

Kenn Tacchino*

Not too long ago retirement meant being given a gold watch and then quietly living out one's remaining few years with family. But changing life-styles, increased longevity, and improved expectations have drastically altered the nature of retirement. Today, people anticipate active, vibrant retirements in which they enjoy life and economic self-sufficiency. They see retirement not as the short final phase of life but as the reward phase of life—the icing on the cake. What's more, a significant percentage of the population has become increasingly interested in achieving the financial independence currently associated with retirement. Put another way, the so-called graying of America has resulted in a maturing retirement planning movement.

Retirement planning is no easy process, however. Financial services professionals who engage in retirement planning must be prepared to answer some tough questions. Several of these questions concern their role as a retirement planner, the amount of income their clients will need for retirement, the sources of retirement income available from employers and Uncle Sam and strategies for maximizing retirement income. This chapter will explore these questions with the intent of providing financial services professionals with the knowledge and tools they need to properly serve their clients' retirement needs.

WHAT IS THE ROLE OF THE RETIREMENT PLANNER?

Holistic Retirement Planning

Retirement planning is a multidimensional field. As such it requires that the planner be schooled in the nuances of many financial planning specialties as well as other areas. Unfortunately, many so-called planners approach retirement planning from only one point of view, investments, for example. This perspective, the perspective offered by specializing in just one field, is too limited for dealing with the diversified needs of the would-be retiree. A client is better served by a team of planners who have specialized but complementary backgrounds or by a single planner who is experienced in a variety of important retirement topics.

Whether the retirement team or the multitalented individual is the vehicle, the holistic approach to retirement planning is the only means by which a client's needs can be fully and adequately met. Under the holistic approach to retirement planning the planner is required to communicate with clients concerning such topics as

- employer-provided retirement plans
- social security

---

*Kenn Tacchino, JD, is associate professor of taxation at The American College.

- income tax issues
- insurance coverage
- investments
- long-term care options
- retirement communities
- relocation possibilities
- wellness
- nutrition
- life-style choices

Some examples will help to give the flavor of the variety of topics that may be discussed while retirement planning:

Example 1: Adam (aged 65) is retired and receives $30,000 in pension income and $10,000 in social security income. Adam would like to know how he will be taxed for federal tax purposes. Adam is married and files jointly.

The general rule that applies to all retirees, including Adam, is that pension income is fully taxable. However, a married taxpayer can exclude all social security benefits from his or her income for tax purposes if the taxpayer's modified adjusted gross income (which includes pension income and any interest or dividends earned — even on otherwise tax exempt bonds), plus one-half of the social security benefits does not exceed the base amount of $32,000 ($25,000 for single taxpayers). If the base amount, $32,000, is exceeded, the taxable amount of social security benefits will be the lesser of one-half of the social security benefits or one-half of the combined income (one-half of the social security benefit plus the entire amount of modified adjusted gross income) in excess of $32,000. In this case, Adam's combined income is calculated by adding his $30,000 pension to one-half of his $10,000 social security benefit ($5,000). Since $35,000 ($30,000 + $5,000) exceeds the base amount of $32,000 by $3,000, Adam will be taxed on one-half of this amount or $1,500. Thus, Adam must pay federal taxes on his $30,000 pension and on $1,500 of his social security benefit. Adam can take heart, however, in the fact that married taxpayers 65 or over are each entitled to an increase of $600 in their standard deduction ($750 for single taxpayers).

Example 2: Barbara (aged 58) has questions about investing for retirement. Barbara is currently heavily concentrated in aggressive growth equities. Barbara's planner should advise her that she should become less growth oriented and begin to be more concerned with a portfolio that provides enough income for retirement needs. This change in emphasis from aggressive growth to more conservative income stocks is needed for two important reasons. First, since Barbara has only a few years until retirement, she has less time to recover losses should the higher-risk growth stocks suffer reverses. Second, Barbara should become increasingly concerned about having sufficient income in the retirement years.

Barbara's planner cannot, however, just offer her one-time advice to change portfolio strategies. Her planner must help Barbara to implement his or her suggestions and must continue to offer investment advice. A change to income-oriented stocks combined with the downward risk profile of the portfolio will have the effect of generating more *current annual income* for Barbara but less *total return* each year from the portfolio. As a consequence, until retirement actually takes place, the reinvestment of the portfolio's annual income stream becomes an ever increasing segment of total portfolio management for Barbara.

Example 3: Charlie and his wife, Ann, have heard about long-term care insurance from a friend and wonder if it would be right for them. Charlie, aged 65, has recently retired and his personal disability income policy has just expired. Ann, also retired with no personal disability income policy, is slightly older than Charlie and has a family history of poor health. Charlie and Ann have a retirement income of $35,000 per year and are not in a position to spend down (that is, shed income and qualify for medicaid to pay for nursing home care). Charlie and Ann are covered by medicare but their planner informs Charlie that nursing home stays are not covered by medicare to any significant degree.

Charlie and Ann are good candidates for long-term care insurance. Long-term care insurance pays cash benefits of a stipulated amount for every day that the insured utilizes nursing home facilities. Without a long-term care policy the costs of a nursing home would quickly deplete Charlie's and Ann's assets.

Charlie and Ann are uncertain about what level of benefits to purchase. The average cost for a nursing home stay is $22,000 annually, but the facilities that Charlie and Ann would be comfortable with cost $30,000 to $40,000 per year. Charlie's retirement planner advises him that premiums for, say, a $100 a day policy ($36,500 annually) would be approximately $1,800 per year each ($3,600 total). Charlie and Ann can then decide at the appropriate time whether they would prefer to take the $30,000 nursing home and use the extra income ($6,500 per year) for annual living expenses or choose the more expensive home and supplement the difference from their other sources of income.

Applying Knowledge to Client Objectives: The Art of Retirement Planning

The successful retirement planner must not only have a working knowledge of a large variety of financial planning and retirement related topics but must also know how to apply the knowledge to a client's particular situation. This requires understanding a client's objectives, attitudes, and personal preferences. For example, retirement planners should be prepared to help clients meet the important general objectives of maintaining their preretirement standard of living during retirement, becoming economically self-sufficient, minimizing taxes on retirement distributions, adapting to the retirement life-style, and the client's individual objectives, such as taking care of a dependent parent or dealing with special health needs (see table 10-1, which is based on an American College study). In addition, planners should be prepared to deal with a variety of attitudes on how long the client wants to work, what the client's prospects are for health and longevity, whether the client can be disciplined enough to save for retirement and to what extent the client accepts investment risk. It is this application of a broad range of knowledge to a diverse group of clients that makes retirement planning more art than science.

TABLE 10-1
Ranking of Client Retirement Objectives in Order of Priority by Financial Services Professionals

---

1. Maintaining preretirement standard of living
2. Maintaining economic self-sufficiency
3. Minimizing taxes
4. Retiring early
5. Adapting to noneconomic aspects of retirement
6. Passing on wealth to others
7. Improving life-style in retirement
8. Caring for dependents

For the retirement planner the primary responsibility in the "art of retirement planning" is to make clients aware that they are making choices about their retirement everyday. For example, should the client take an expensive vacation or take a moderately priced vacation and save the difference for retirement? The planner cannot force the client to make life-style choices that will provide an adequate source of retirement funds. The planner can, however, make the client aware of the large amount of funds needed for retirement and point out that a spendthrift life-style (one which uses the full aftertax income to support the current standard of living) hurts a retiree in two ways.

First, a spendthrift life-style minimizes the retiree's ability to accumulate savings that will produce an adequate income stream to complement his or her employer pension and social security. These three elements — private savings, employer pensions, and social security — are considered essential for a secure retirement. If any leg on this "three-legged stool" is missing, the client is in danger of falling short of an economically secure retirement. Second, the retiree becomes accustomed to an unnaturally high standard of living. By living below their means before retirement, clients will establish a life-style that is more easily maintained in the retirement years.

Forcing clients to think about retirement planning and their life-style choices is a primary responsibility of the retirement planner. However, two other important facets to retirement planning exist. The planner must devise different retirement strategies for clients who are prepared for retirement and for those who are not and the planner must overcome roadblocks to retirement saving.

Clients Are Never Too Young or Too Old

Planners must deal with clients of all ages and retirement planning takes on different characteristics for different age groups. Those new to the retirement planning field soon find out that clients are never too old or too young to plan for retirement. Starting early can mean all the difference in the world, however (see table 10-2).

Unfortunately some clients don't save for retirement until the time to retire is upon them. But even though clients who start thinking about retirement when it is imminent have lost the ability to set aside savings on a systematic basis and to let compound interest work for them, planning can still be conducted for these clients. Important decisions must be made about distributions from qualified plans, liquidation of personal assets, and investment of any private savings. Developing a retirement plan for the client who has procrastinated also includes determining what funds are available for retirement and creating strategies, even if the funds are inadequate.

One such strategy calls for the planner to suggest that the client postpone retirement. The combined effect of lengthening the accumulation period and shortening the retirement period is financially desirable. If delaying retirement from his or her current job is not feasible, the client can achieve similar results by working for another employer after forced retirement. A second strategy is to recommend that the client move to an area with a lower cost of living. This move will enable the client to stretch his or her retirement dollars. What's more, by freeing up some of the equity in the home the client can make assets available for investment purposes.

In addition to recommending these strategies, it is an essential part of the planner's job to help the client change his or her expectations about retirement. By forcing the client to look realistically at the life-style he or she will be able to afford, the planner can save the client from overspending during the early retirement years and avoid becoming financially destitute in the later retirement years.

Overcoming Roadblocks to Retirement Saving

Perhaps the biggest roadblock to retirement planning is the tendency of many working people to use their full aftertax income to support their current standard of living. For this reason clients must be taught when they are young to follow a budget that allows them to live within their means and that also provides for retirement savings. Planners should make their clients aware that at least a 90/10 spending ratio is generally desired. Under a 90/10 spending ratio, 90 percent of the client's earnings are directed toward the current standard of living, and 10 percent is directed toward other long-term financial objectives, such as the children's education and the client's own retirement. For example, a family with a gross annual income of $50,000 should allocate no more than $45,000 (including taxes) of its total income to standard-of-living and life-style items, leaving $5,000 or more for the long-term objectives. Furthermore, planners should recommend that as income rises, the percentage spent on the current standard of living should decline.

A second impediment to retirement saving is unexpected expenses (including expenses arising from inadequate insurance or the cost of major repairs to a home) and unexpected decreases in income (for example, due to unemployment). The client should set up an emergency fund to handle these inevitable problems. Usually about 3 to 6 months' income should be set aside for this objective. In addition, agents should conduct a thorough review of their clients' insurance needs to make sure they are adequately covered. Two often overlooked areas are long-term disability insurance and umbrella liability insurance.

A third roadblock to saving for retirement occurs in the case of a divorced client. Divorce often leaves one or both parties with little or no accumulation of

TABLE 10-2
Funding an IRA: The Advantages of Starting Young*

IRA One			IRA Two		
Age start		18	Age start		35
Age end		21	Age end		65
Amount per year		$2,000	Amount per year		$2,000
Rate of return		8%	Rate of return		8%
Value at age 65		$287,668	Value at age 65		$266,427
Total amount contributed		$8,000	Total amount contributed		$62,000
Age	Amount	Value	Age	Amount	Value
18	2,000	2,160	18	0	0
19	2,000	4,493	19	0	0
20	2,000	7,012	20	0	0
21	2,000	9,733	21	0	0
22	0	10,512	22	0	0
23	0	11,353	23	0	0
24	0	12,261	24	0	0
25	0	13,242	25	0	0
26	0	14,301	26	0	0
27	0	15,445	35	2,000	2,160
28	0	16,681	36	2,000	4,493
29	0	18,015	37	2,000	7,012
30	0	19,456	38	2,000	9,733
•	•	•	•	•	•
•	•	•	•	•	•
•	•	•	•	•	•
•	•	•	•	•	•
61	0	211,445	61	2,000	188,678
62	0	228,360	62	2,000	205,932
63	0	246,629	63	2,000	224,566
64	0	266,360	64	2,000	244,692
65	0	287,668	65	2,000	266,427

*This comparison dramatically illustrates the value of saving for retirement while young. Note that at age 65 IRA One will have accumulated more funds than IRA Two even though the capital contribution for IRA Two is $54,000 more than IRA One.

pension benefits or other private sources of retirement income. These clients may have only a short time to accumulate any retirement income and may not be able to earn significant pension or social security benefits. If the marriage lasted 10 years or longer, however, divorced persons are eligible for social security based on their former spouse's earnings record.

Another common retirement planning problem concerns workers who have frequently changed employers. Generally, these people will not accumulate vested pension benefits because they never stayed with an employer long enough to become vested. Even if they did become vested, they may have received a distribution of their accumulated pension fund upon leaving the job and probably spent this money rather than investing it or rolling it over for retirement. Planners should advise clients who change jobs to roll over vested benefits into an IRA or into their new qualified plan to preserve the tax-deferred growth of their retirement funds. They should also advise clients who have recently changed jobs that if they have not met the participation requirements of their new employer's plan, then annual tax-deductible contributions can be made to an IRA until they do, regardless of salary.

A final impediment to acquiring adequate retirement savings is the long-term accumulation objectives that clients must meet before retirement. The down payment on a primary residence and/or vacation home and the education of children can consume any long-term savings that people have managed to accumulate. Since these objectives have a greater urgency for completion than retirement, they supplant retirement as a saving priority. Although these objectives are worthy, it is important to remind clients that savings must be carved out for retirement purposes in addition to other long-term objectives.

HOW MUCH WILL YOUR CLIENTS NEED?

Another important task in retirement planning is determining how much the client will need to save in order to achieve his or her retirement goals. Estimating a client's financial needs during retirement is like trying to predict the future: such estimates are fraught with complicating factors and clouded by unknown variables. For example, the planner and client must establish what standard of living is desired during retirement, when retirement will begin, what inflation assumptions should be made before and after retirement, and what interest can be earned on invested funds. In addition, for clients who are forced by economic necessity to liquidate their retirement nest egg the client and planner must estimate the life expectancy over which liquidation will occur. Many of these variables can dramatically change overnight and without warning. The following are examples of variables that could change:

- The client may be planning to retire at age 65 but health considerations, or perhaps a plant shutdown, force retirement at age 62.
- A younger client may be planning on a relatively moderate retirement life-style but business success requires that a higher retirement income be planned for.
- Forecasters may predict that long-term inflation will result in an annual 4 percent increase in the cost of living when in reality 6 percent increases occur. (Even a one percentage point disparity can make a significant difference.)

- Clients may hope for an aftertax rate of return of 7 percent when in fact investment returns are adversely affected by a bear market, or the real aftertax rate of return is suppressed by rising tax rates.
- Clients may plan on a short life expectancy and have the "misfortune" of living longer.

While it is important to understand that planning is, at best, an educated guess, it still beats the alternative. What's more, changing variables can be overcome if the retirement plan is revised and adjusted annually. Once the planner has explained to his or her client the tentative nature of the plan and the need for hands-on monitoring, then the task of setting out a plan for the client begins.

Creating a Retirement Plan

There are three basic facets to any retirement plan. The planner must first determine where the client stands financially for retirement purposes. Then the planner must assess where the client wants to be financially during retirement and the client's ability to reach this goal. Finally, the planner must map the way for a client to achieve his or her goals.

Stage 1: Where Are We?

In order to calculate a client's retirement needs, the planner must first add up the client's existing resources. These may include the amount of any social security benefits due, the amount of any pension benefits due, any private savings the client has accumulated to date, including IRAs and personally owned life insurance, and any other sources of retirement income, such as the proceeds from the sale of a home.

Stage 2: Where Do We Want to Go?

Once a financial inventory of possible sources of retirement income has been taken, the next step is to determine how much annual income will be needed in the first year of retirement to achieve the client's goals. There are two common ways of determining this, the replacement ratio method and the expense method.

Replacement ratio method. The replacement ratio method of retirement planning assumes that the standard of living enjoyed during the years just prior to retirement will be the determining factor for the standard of living during retirement. For clients at or near retirement it is much easier to define the target. For example, if the 64-year-old near-retiree is earning $50,000, then the retirement income for that retiree should maintain most of the current purchasing power that that person has. If, however, a younger client is involved, growth estimates should be made to approximate what the salary will be at retirement.

Note that the entire final salary is not needed for determining the proper amount of purchasing power. In general, a 70 to 90 percent replacement ratio of a client's final average salary is typically used for individual retirement planning purposes. Support for this range rests upon the elimination of some employment-related taxes and some expected changes in spending patterns that reduce the retiree's need for income (see figure 10-1).

Reduced taxes. Retirees can assume that a lower percentage of their income will go toward paying taxes in the retirement years because, in many cases, there is an elimination or a reduction of certain taxes that they previously had to pay. Tax advantages for the retiree include the elimination of the 7.65 percent social security tax on the first $51,300 of income, an increased standard deduction depending on the retiree's age and filing status, the exclusion of all or part of the amount of the

---

FIGURE 10-1
Justification of a 70 to 90 Percent Replacement Ratio

Joe Jones (aged 64) has a fixed salary of $100,000 and would like to maintain his current purchasing power when he retires next year. If Joe has no increased retirement related expenses, Joe can do this by having a retirement income of 70 percent of his final salary as illustrated below. If Joe has increased retirement related expenses, a somewhat higher figure should be used. (Note that postretirement inflation will be accounted for later.)

Working salary			$100,000
less retirement savings		18,000	
less social security taxes	(7.65% x 51,300)	3,924	
less reduction in federal taxes	(extra $750 deduction for being 65)	248	
	(no tax on portion of social security received)	1,650	
less annual commuting expenses to work		450	
less mortgage expenses	(mortgage expires on retirement date)	5,728	
Reductions subtotal			30,000
Total purchasing power needed at 65			$ 70,000
Percentage of final salary needed			70%

---

social security benefit from gross income, reductions in state and local income taxes, and an increased ability to use deductible medical expenses.

Reduced living expenses. Retirees face a variety of changes in spending patterns after retirement, and some of these changes will reduce a retiree's living expenses. These reductions include elimination of work-related expenses; elimination of home-mortgage expenses; elimination of dependent care, that is, child-rearing expenses; elimination of long-term savings obligations; and reduction in automotive expenditures.

Additional factors. It is not all good news for the retiree, however. Retirees also face several factors that tend to increase the amount of income they will need during the retirement period. These include possible increases in long-term inflation, increased medical expenses, increased travel expenses, and other retirement-related expenses.

Expense method. The expense method of retirement planning focuses on the projected expenses that the retiree will have. As with the replacement ratio method it is much easier to define the potential expenses for those clients who are at or near retirement. For example, if the 64-year-old near-retiree expects to have $3,000 in monthly bills ($36,000 annually), then the retirement income for that retiree should maintain $36,000 worth of purchasing power in today's dollars. If, however, a younger client is involved more speculative estimates of retirement expenses must be made (and periodically revised).

A list of expenses that should be considered includes expenses that may be unique to the particular client as well as other more general expenses.

Some expenses that tend to increase for retirees include the following:

- utilities and telephone
- medical/dental/drugs/health insurance
- house upkeep/repairs/maintenance/property insurance
- recreation/entertainment/travel/dining
- contributions/gifts

On the other hand, some expenses tend to decrease for the retiree:

- mortgage payments
- food
- clothing
- income taxes
- property taxes
- transportation costs (car maintenance/insurance/other)
- debt repayment (charge accounts/personal loans)
- child support/alimony
- household furnishings

Stage 3: The Retirement Road Map

Both the replacement ratio method and the expense method can be used to determine the income level a retiree will need at age 65. They do not, however, calculate the amount of savings that the client must accumulate in order to achieve a consistent level of financial security throughout retirement. The amount that the client needs to save to achieve his or her goals is a function of two opposing factors: the savings that the client currently has (stage 1) and the income that the client will need (stage 2). Both factors are influenced by inflation. In order to better understand the effect of inflation over time, consider the loss of purchasing power that occurs in the following example.

Example: Al Edwards (aged 65) is retiring this year and needs $50,000 of retirement income to maintain his current standard of living. If the inflation rate is 4 percent per year over Al's retirement period, Al will need to have an increasing amount of retirement income each year of retirement.

Table 10-3 illustrates the amount of annual income Al will need at specified intervals to maintain a consistent amount of purchasing power.

TABLE 10-3
Retirement Income for Al Edwards

Al's Age	Income
65	$ 50,000
70	60,833
75	74,012
80	90,047
90	133,292
100	197,304

To calculate the true retirement income needed the planner must provide inflation protection both before and after retirement for all the client's resources. In order to accomplish this, the planner must decide which of the client's resources are subject to a decline in purchasing power due to the effects of inflation.

Any social security that the client might receive will *not* be subject to a decline in purchasing power, because social security is indexed each year to reflect inflation. Therefore the planner will not have to provide inflation protection for a client's social security benefit. The planner cannot, however, generally assume any inflation protection for pension benefits. For this reason the client will need to fund for an amount that can be used to bolster a non-inflation-protected benefit during retirement.

Another item that will be affected by inflation is the retirement income deficit itself. The retirement income deficit is any shortfall that exists between what the client has (stage 1) and what the client needs (stage 2). This is not inflation-proof before or after retirement. The planner will therefore need to calculate an inflation factor that protects the client's purchasing power for this amount.

The final step in mapping a client's retirement needs is to calculate the target amount of savings needed. In order to do this, work sheets, such as those in figures 10-2 and 10-3, are helpful. The first work sheet, based on the replacement ratio method, produces the estimated income gap between the desired retirement income and the available retirement benefits. That gap is then adjusted for inflation. The amount of additional capital needed to fill the gap and to supplement the pension benefit (inflation-unprotected) is then computed. Finally, the funding pattern that will be used to generate the needed new capital is calculated.

The second work sheet, based on the expense method, calls for an estimate of the client's current monthly and annual living expenses. The total of these expenses (line 10) is then adjusted for inflation to reflect the expected total at retirement date. Next, a capital sum is calculated (lines 15–19) that will be sufficient, together with interest earnings, to provide an inflation-adjusted income during the estimated number of years in the retirement period.

WHAT SOURCES OF RETIREMENT INCOME ARE AVAILABLE?

Understanding how much a client will need for retirement is only one part of sound retirement planning. In addition, understanding the potential sources of retirement income is another crucial function with which the retirement planner must

---

FIGURE 10-2
Replacement Ratio Method Work Sheet

---

1. Current annual gross salary $ _____

2. Retirement-income target (multiply line 1 by 0.8) (80 percent target) $ _____

3. Estimated annual benefit from pension plan, not including IRAs, 401(k)s or profit-sharing plans[1] $ _____

4. Estimated annual social security benefits[1] $ _____

5. Total retirement benefits (add lines 3 and 4) $ _____

6. Income gap (subtract line 5 from line 2)[2] $ _____

7. Adjust gap to reflect inflation (multiply line 6 by factor A, below) $ _____

8. Capital needed to generate additional income and close gap (multiply line 7 by 16.3)[3] $ _____

9. Extra capital needed to offset inflation's impact on pension (multiply line 3 by factor B, below) $ _____

10. Total capital needed (add lines 8 and 9) $ _____

11. Total current retirement savings (includes balances in IRAs, 401(k)s, profit-sharing plans, mutual funds, CDs) $ _____

12. Value of savings at retirement (multiply line 11 by factor C, below) $ _____

13. Net capital gap (subtract line 12 from line 10) $ _____

14. Annual amount in current dollars to start saving now to cover the gap (divide line 13 by factor D, below)[4] $ _____

15. Percentage of salary to be saved each year (divide line 14 by line 1)[5]   _____ %

(continued)

FIGURE 10-2 (continued)

Accounting for Inflation, Savings, and Capital

Years to Retirement	Factor A	Factor B	Factor C	Factor D
10	1.5	7.0	2.2	17.5
15	1.8	8.5	3.2	35.3
20	2.2	10.3	4.7	63.3
25	2.7	12.6	6.9	107.0
30	3.2	15.3	10.1	174.0

[1]Lines 3 and 4: Employers can provide annual estimates of your projected retirement pay; estimates of social security benefits are available from the Social Security Administration at (800) 234-5772. Both figures will be stated in current dollars, not in the higher amounts that you will receive if your wages keep up with inflation. The work sheet takes this into consideration.

[2]Line 6: Even if a large pension lets you avoid an income gap, proceed to line 9 to determine the assets you may need to make up for the erosion of a fixed pension payment by inflation.

[3]Line 8: This calculation includes a determination of how much capital you will need to keep up with inflation after retirement and assumes that you will *deplete the capital over a 25-year period.*

[4]Line 14: Amount includes investments earmarked for retirement and payments by employee and employer to defined-contribution retirement plans such as 401(k)s. The formula assumes you will increase annual savings at the same rate as inflation.

[5]Line 15: Assuming earnings rise with inflation, you can save a set percentage of gross pay each year, and the actual amount you stash away will increase annually.

Note: Inflation is assumed to average 4 percent a year; the annual return on investments and savings is assumed to be 8 percent.

Source: Reprinted with permission of *U.S. News & World Report,* August 14, 1989, issue. Copyright 1989.

be familiar. There are many types of investment vehicles that a client may use for investing retirement assets, many of which were described in chapter 9 of this book. In addition, there are several sources of retirement income that bear close examination in this chapter. These include

- qualified plans
- nonqualified plans
- IRAs
- social security benefits

Qualified Plans

Perhaps the most valuable way to save for retirement is through a qualified plan. The advantageous nature of a qualified plan stems from the fact that, even though the employer is able to take a tax deduction when contributions are made,

FIGURE 10-3
Expense Method Work Sheet

Estimated Retirement Living Expenses and Required Capital (in current dollars)

Per Month × 12 = Per Year

1. Food
2. Housing:
   a. Rent/mortgage payment
   b. Insurance (if not included in a.)
   c. Property taxes (if not included in a.)
   d. Utilities
   e. Maintenance (if you own)
   f. Management fee (if a condominium)
3. Clothing and Personal Care:
   a. Wife
   b. Husband
   c. Dependents
4. Medical Expenses:
   a. Doctor
   b. Dentist
   c. Medicines
   d. Medical insurance to supplement medicare
5. Transportation:
   a. Car payments
   b. Gas
   c. Insurance
   d. License
   e. Car maintenance (tires and repairs)
   f. Other transportation
6. Miscellaneous Expenses:
   a. Entertainment
   b. Travel
   c. Hobbies
   d. Club fees and dues
   e. Other
7. Insurance
8. Gifts and Contributions
9. Income Taxes (if any)
10. Total Annual Expenses (current dollars) $ _____
11. Inflation Rate until Retirement (I)
12. Total Years until Retirement (N)
13. Inflation Adjustment Factor $(1 + I)^N$ × _____
14. Total Annual Expenses (future dollars)   = _____
15. Inflation Rate Postretirement (i)

(continued)

FIGURE 10-3 (continued)

---

16. Aftertax Rate of Return (r)   _____
17. Anticipated Duration of Retirement (n)   _____
18. Inflation-Adjusted Discount Factor $a = \dfrac{1 + i}{1 + r}$ _____
19. Capital Required at Retirement to Fund
    Retirement Living Expenses

    Amt line 14 $\times \dfrac{1 - a^n}{1 - a}$ $ _____
20. One-Time Expenses   + $ _____
21. Total Capital Need at Retirement   = $ _____

---

contributions to the plan are made on a before-tax basis. In other words, the employee does not have to pay income tax on those contributions when they are made. Instead, the employee pays income tax when funds are distributed from the plan some years later. In addition, investment earnings on plan assets are also tax-deferred. This combination of tax-deferred contributions and tax-deferred earnings is like receiving an interest-free loan from the government. In other words, Uncle Sam allows the client to invest funds for retirement that otherwise would be lost to taxation.

A final tax advantage applicable to qualified plans is that distributions from these plans — although taxed at retirement — are subject to special tax treatment. For example, clients might be able either to reduce the taxes they pay out on lump-sum distribution by using forward averaging or to delay paying taxes on a distribution by rolling over the funds into an IRA.

Figure 10-4 demonstrates the income tax advantages of a qualified plan.

Qualified plans can be categorized in several ways. One way they can be categorized is by focusing on what the employer provides. For one category of plans the employer promises to pay an annual retirement benefit (defined-benefit plans). For another category, the employer pays a specified amount of deferred compensation into an employee's individual account (defined-contribution plans). A second way to categorize qualified plans is to distinguish plans that are typically geared to employer profits (profit-sharing plans) from those that are not (pension plans). A third way to categorize qualified plans is to focus on the business entity that is adopting the plan. If a corporate entity qualifies a retirement plan, the plan is simply known as a qualified plan; if a partnership or self-employed person sponsors a qualified plan the plan is known as a Keogh plan. Over the years the rules for Keogh and corporate plans have evolved so that only a few minor distinctions exist between the two plans. Therefore only the defined-benefit/defined-contribution and pension/profit-sharing differences are examined in the following paragraphs.

Defined-Benefit versus Defined-Contribution Plans

Under a defined-benefit plan the required employer contributions vary depending on what is needed to pay the promised benefits. The maximum annual benefit that can be provided in a defined-benefit plan is 100 percent of the employee's average compensation for the employee's 3 consecutive years of highest pay up to a maximum of $90,000 per year (as indexed in 1990 to $102,582). A defined-benefit plan usually uses a benefit formula to stipulate a promised retirement benefit. This

FIGURE 10-4
Tax Advantages of a Qualified Plan

Assume that a client is a professional who is aged 50, is married, and wants to retire at 65. Assume the professional's total earnings after business expenses are $200,000, his or her personal deductions and exemptions are $30,000, and his or her needs for living expenses are $110,000.

	Without Plan	With Plan
Gross earnings	$200,000	$200,000
Pension contributions	0	46,275
Current compensation	$200,000	$153,725
Income taxes (federal only)	66,400	43,725
Net "take home pay"	$133,600	$110,000
Living expenses	110,000	110,000
Personal savings	$ 23,600	$ 0

At Age 65

	Without Plan	With Plan
Pension accumulation at 10%	$ 0	$1,470,272
Savings accumulation at net 7%	593,045	0
Taxes on lump-sum distribution	0	625,986
Net cash after taxes	$593,045	$ 844,286

Gain for Qualified Plan: $251,241

promised benefit is typically a percentage of the employee's final salary (for example, 50 percent of final salary).

Defined-contribution plans, on the other hand, specify the contribution the employer makes annually and provide an unknown benefit to the employee. The maximum annual contribution that can be provided in a defined-contribution plan is the lesser of $30,000 or 25 percent of the employee's salary. By their nature defined-contribution plans base an employee's benefit on the employee's entire career earnings and *not* the employee's final salary. Defined-contribution plans are sometimes called *individual account plans* because they provide an individual account similar to a bank account for each employee.

Retirement planning considerations. Clients covered by defined-contribution plans may find themselves short of retirement income if investment results are unfavorable. This is because, unlike a defined-benefit plan, the employer's obligation begins and ends with making the annual contribution. If plan investments are poor in a defined-contribution plan, the employee suffers the loss and may have inadequate retirement resources. For example, a person who planned on retiring in November 1987 might have had his or her plan assets cut by one-third because of stock market troubles; therefore this client may have to delay retirement for several years. In a defined-benefit plan the employer suffers the loss.

A second problem is that contributions in a defined-contribution plan are based on participants' salaries for each year of their career, rather than on their salary at retirement as in most defined-benefit plans. For example, if inflation increases sharply in the years just prior to retirement, the chances of achieving an adequate income-replacement ratio are diminished because most of the annual contributions were based on deflated salaries that occurred before the inflationary spiral. By contrast, if the participant had been covered by a final-average defined-benefit plan, the *employer* would have had to make significant contributions to account for the increased final-average salary due to higher inflation.

Another instance where either a defined-benefit plan or a defined-contribution plan may provide inadequate retirement income occurs if the client joins the plan late in his or her career. Under this circumstance, since years to retirement are growing short, a defined-contribution plan may not provide enough time to accumulate an acceptable amount of assets. A defined-benefit plan, where the benefit is based in part on length of service, would also provide a relatively small benefit since these plans are geared to provide adequate replacement ratios for long-service employees only.

Pension versus Profit-Sharing Plans

Under a pension plan the organization is committed to making annual payments to the retirement plan, since the main purpose of the plan is to provide a pension benefit. Under a profit-sharing plan, however, an organization can retain the flexibility necessary to avoid funding the plan annually. What's more, a profit-sharing plan isn't necessarily intended to provide a retirement benefit as much as to provide tax deferral of present compensation. To this end, under certain profit-sharing plans employees are permitted to withdraw funds after they have been in the profit-sharing account for 2 years.

Retirement planning considerations. Two important factors should be kept in mind if a client has a profit-sharing plan: First, retirement planners should closely monitor the funding of the plan. It would be an easy mistake to assume that the employer is making scheduled payments when in actuality the employer isn't contributing as expected because employer contributions to the profit-sharing plan are discretionary. It would also be an easy mistake to assume that the employee is allowing the funds to accumulate for retirement when in actuality the employee is depleting the account by taking withdrawals.

Another important factor concerning profit-sharing plans is that the ability to withdraw funds prior to retirement under some profit-sharing plans opens up some interesting planning possibilities for the client and his or her planner. For example, the client may want to gradually take money out while employed (starting after age $59\frac{1}{2}$ to avoid a 10 percent tax penalty) in order to reposition assets or take advantage of an excellent investment opportunity. In addition, the client may want to prepay any debt that would carry over into retirement, such as prepaying a mortgage or reducing interest expenses on a major capital purchase.

Types of Qualified Plans

Once the planner understands the basic characteristics of each category of qualified plans, the planner is well on the way to understanding the specific type of plan that a client has. For example, if a client has a plan that falls into the defined-contribution and pension categories, the planner knows that employer-contributions are mandatory but that the employee takes the risks associated with investment performance and preretirement inflation.

The final component that the planner needs to understand is the plan's benefit or contribution formula. These formulas are unique to the specific type of plan involved.

Defined-benefit pension plans. As its name implies, a defined-benefit pension plan falls within both the defined-benefit and pension categories. In a defined-benefit pension plan the employer's contributions under the plan are determined actuarially on the basis of the benefits expected to become payable. These benefits are determined under a benefit formula. There are four types of defined-benefit formulas. The most popular type, the unit-benefit formula, accounts for both service and salary in determining the participant's pension benefit. For example, a unit-benefit formula might read

> Each plan participant will receive a monthly pension commencing at normal retirement date and paid in the form of a life annuity equal to 2 percent of final average annual salary multiplied by the participant's years of service.

Under this formula an employee with 20 years of service and a $50,000 final average salary will receive $20,000 a year in the form of life annuity payments (.02 × $50,000 × 20).

A second type of defined-benefit benefit formula, found primarily in church plans, is the flat-percentage-of-earnings formula. This formula relates solely to a participant's salary and does not reflect an employee's service in the benefit calculation. A flat-percentage-of-earnings formula might read

> Each plan participant will receive a monthly pension benefit commencing at normal retirement date and paid in the form of a life annuity equal to 40 percent of the final average monthly salary the participant was paid.

A third type of defined-benefit benefit formula, found primarily in union plans, is the flat-amount-per-year-of-service formula, which relates the pension benefit solely to the participant's length of service and does not reflect the participant's salary. The benefit is calculated by multiplying all years of service by a stated dollar amount. For example, the flat-amount-per-year-of-service formula might read

> Each plan participant will receive a monthly pension benefit commencing at normal retirement date and paid in the form of a life annuity equal to $10 for every year of service worked.

A final type of defined-benefit benefit formula is a flat-amount formula. A flat-amount formula provides the same monthly benefit for each participant. For example, "Each plan participant will receive a pension benefit of $200 a month."

Some plans are designed to contain just one of the above types of benefit formulas (most typically the unit-benefit formula). Many plans, however, contain a mix of benefit formulas. For example, the flat-amount formula is seldom used by itself, but is often used in conjunction with the unit-benefit formula to provide a base amount of coverage for all employees regardless of how long they have been employed or the amount of their final average salary.

Another aspect of defined-benefit formulas is that they can be designed to take social security into account by subtracting part or all of the social security benefit from the monthly benefit or by giving highly paid employees greater benefits to compensate for the fact that social security benefits are geared toward lower-paid employees. In this way, most defined-benefit plans are integrated with social security. In addition, the second type of social security integration described is possible under all of the qualified plans that are discussed below.

Target-benefit pension plans. Unlike defined-benefit pension plans, target-benefit pension plans are defined-contribution plans. Under a target-benefit pension plan annual contributions are limited to the lesser of $30,000 or 25 percent of salary, and each employee is given an individual account into which funds are deposited. Target-benefit plans are a unique form of defined-contribution plan because they include some of the features associated with defined-benefit plans. One of these features is that a defined-benefit formula is used to determine the annual contribution. Under a target-benefit plan an actuary determines the amount of funds needed as the level annual contribution by using actuarial and interest assumptions in conjunction with the benefit formula. This amount is then contributed to the employee's account, at which point the investment and actuarial risks shift back to the employee.

A target-benefit plan provides a unique opportunity for a business owner to stockpile retirement funds in a plan installed toward the end of the business owner's career. The benefit formula used in a target-benefit pension plan requires larger contributions for older employees because there is less time to fund the target benefit.

Money-purchase pension plans. A money-purchase pension plan is a form of defined-contribution plan. It is also, as the name states, a pension plan. Under a money-purchase pension plan the company's annual contributions are mandatory and are based on a percentage of each participant's compensation. For example, the money-purchase benefit formula may provide that annual contributions will equal 10 percent of compensation for each participant. The definition of compensation will vary from plan to plan. In some cases it will include overtime, bonuses and the like; in other cases it will be restricted to base salary. In order to correctly estimate the amount of retirement savings that clients will have, the planner must accurately forecast the approximate compensation that is involved in each case.

Profit-sharing plans. A profit-sharing plan falls into both the profit-sharing and defined-contribution categories. There are two types of contribution formulas that can be used in a profit-sharing plan, the allocation formula and the straight percentage of compensation formula. When the straight percentage of compensation formula is used the employer typically commits to make contributions whether the company has profits or not. The amount of the annual contribution may be specified in the employee's plan (for example, 10 percent of compensation) or it may be determined annually by the employer. Under an allocation formula the employer allocates profits to the employees according to a fixed formula which recognizes both service and salary when determining the percentage of profits to which an employee is entitled.

> *Example:* Peggy, Arthur, and Kim are the three owners (and the only employees) of a shoestore. The store declares a profit of $2,000. Its allocation formula stipulates that profits shall be allocated to participants by the ratio that the units allocated to a participant bear to the total of units allocated to all participants, with one unit allocated for each $100 of compensation and two units allocated for each year of service. Peggy has 10 years of service and earns $20,000 (220 units), Arthur has 8 years of service and earns $15,000 (166 units), and Kim has 5 years of service and earns $10,000 (110 units). The total units for all participants is 496. To determine Peggy's allocation multiply her units (220) over the total units by the $2,000 profit ([220 ÷ 496] × 2000). The contribution to Peggy's account will be $888. To Arthur's it will be $669, and to Kim's it will be $443.

401(k) plans. One of the most popular types of qualified plans is the 401(k) defined-contribution profit-sharing plan. A 401(k) plan allows employees to elect deferral of taxation on current salaries or bonuses simply by placing the money into the plan. Participants who forgo receiving current salary or a bonus enjoy abundant tax savings.

In order to understand the state of 401(k) plans today, it's important to look at their history. For many years employers who felt they could not adequately fund their employees' (and their own) retirement needs provided thrift plans. (If employer matching contributions were not involved they were called savings plans.) Under thrift plans employees become partners of the employer in providing for their own retirement needs. A thrift plan calls for employees to contribute a fixed percentage of salary to the plan and for the employer to make a contribution in the same amount or in a reduced amount. Thrift plans, however, are not tax efficient because the employee's contribution is made with aftertax dollars. In November 1981, the IRS issued proposed regulations that allowed employees to make before-tax thrift contributions to a qualified plan and plan sponsors began to adopt the new 401(k) plans.

In today's market, many employers, even those with defined-benefit, target-benefit, or money-purchase plans, opt for a complementary 401(k) plan. These plans are still highly regarded, despite a recent cutback to a maximum of $7,627 in employee deferrals.

One retirement planning consideration planners should keep in mind is that, for clients who were originally involved in a thrift plan and later came under a 401(k) plan, it is likely they will have some cost basis for annuity distribution purposes. Thus, they will not be taxed on the full amount of their annuity because already-taxed amounts won't be taxed twice.

A second retirement planning consideration is that these plans typically ask clients to sign a salary reduction agreement so that employee contributions to the plan can be made with before-tax contributions. From a retirement planning perspective it is important to encourage your client to take full advantage of these tax shelters. The before-tax nature of contributions can provide for significant retirement savings. In addition, these plans often have the added feature of employer matching contributions. A client who turns his or her back on employer-matching contributions is forfeiting the easiest and most profitable way to save for retirement.

In addition to encouraging participation in the plan, retirement planners must also be aware of the following factors concerning 401(k) plans.

- 401(k) salary reductions affect other benefit programs and may reduce benefits available under a group life or health insurance plan.
- 401(k) salary reductions are immediately 100 percent vested and cannot be forfeited.
- Withdrawals under 401(k) plans are different from those under profit-sharing plans, and, in general, money placed in a 401(k) plan is used primarily for retirement purposes since substantial restrictions curtail withdrawals before retirement.

403(b) plans. A 403(b) plan (sometimes referred to as a tax-sheltered annuity [TSA] or tax-deferred annuity [TDA]) is similar to a 401(k) plan in many respects. Both plans permit an employee to defer taxes on income by allowing before-tax contributions to the employee's individual account and by allowing deferrals in the form of salary reduction. However, 403(b) plans are distinguishable from 401(k) plans in several ways.

- The 403(b) market is comprised of public schools and certain types of tax-exempt organizations only. These are the so-called 501(c)(3) tax-exempt organizations.
- 403(b) plans are not viewed as qualified plans, but they contain many of the benefits of a qualified plan (for example, before-tax contributions). Note, however, that lump-sum distributions from a 403(b) plan are not entitled to the special tax treatment of forward averaging.
- If a salary reduction is used, the amount of the 403(b) contribution that can be made by an employee is restricted to $9,500.

A summary of the main kinds of qualified plans is given in figure 10-5.

IRAs

One of the most important sources of retirement income that retirement planners can counsel their clients about is an individual retirement account (IRA). Individual retirement accounts are similar to qualified plans in many respects. Both are tax-favored savings plans that encourage the accumulation of savings for retirement by allowing contributions to be made with pretax dollars (if the taxpayer is eligible) and earnings to be tax deferred until retirement. Also, both plans have stringent rules to ensure that the goal of encouraging retirement savings is achieved and that revenue loss is minimized.

FIGURE 10-5
Principal Types of Qualified Plans: A Recap

Pension	Profit-Sharing	Specialty
Defined-benefit	Profit-sharing	403(b)
Target-benefit	401(k)	
Money-purchase	Thrift	
	Savings	

Defined-Contribution	Defined-Benefit
Target-benefit	Defined-benefit
Money-purchase	
Profit-sharing	
401(k)	
Thrift	
Savings	
403(b)	

Keogh	Corporate
Defined-benefit	Defined-benefit
Target-benefit	Target-benefit
Money-purchase	Money-purchase
Profit-sharing	Profit-sharing
401(k)	401(k)
Thrift	Thrift
Savings	Savings
403(b)	403(b)

The Ground Rules

IRA contributions. IRAs are subject to certain limitations, including the following:

- Contributions to an IRA may not exceed $2,000 a year or 100 percent of compensation, whichever is smaller.
- IRA contributions may not be made during or after the year in which the client reaches age $70\frac{1}{2}$.
- IRA funds may not be commingled with the client's other assets; the funds may contain only IRA contributions and rollover contributions.
- IRA funds may *not* be used to buy a life insurance policy.
- Funds contributed to an IRA may not be invested in collectibles.
- No loans may be taken from IRA accounts.

Who is eligible for deductible IRAs? Any person under age $70\frac{1}{2}$ who receives compensation (either salary or self-employment earned income) may make a contribution to an IRA. For some, the contribution will *not* be deductible, but the interest earnings will be tax deferred. For others, the contribution (as well as any interest earnings) will be tax deferred through an income tax deduction. Deductible IRA contributions are permitted if the client (or the client's spouse) is not an active participant in an employer-maintained retirement plan or if the client's adjusted gross income falls below prescribed limits, which are designed to approximate a middle-class income. In other words, if either the client or the client's spouse (whether filing jointly or separately) is an active participant in an employer plan, the IRA deduction is available only if their adjusted gross income is under certain limits discussed below.

Active participant. In order to be categorized as an active participant a taxpayer must be covered by an employer-maintained plan. Employer-maintained plans include every type of qualified plan, as well as all federal, state, and local government plans. Not included, however, are nonqualified retirement arrangements.

Note that simply being *associated* with an employer-maintained plan does not affect the taxpayer's ability to make deductible IRA contributions. Deductibility of contributions is jeopardized only if the taxpayer is an active participant in a plan. The term *active participant* has a special meaning that depends on the type of plan involved. Generally, a person is an active participant in a defined-benefit plan unless excluded under the eligibility provision in the plan. In general, if the person is an active participant in any type of defined-contribution plan and the plan specifies that employer contributions must be allocated to the individual's account, then the person is an active participant. In a profit-sharing plan where employer contributions are discretionary, the participant must actually receive some contribution for active-participant status to be triggered.

Monetary limits. In addition to the question of whether a taxpayer is an active participant, the taxpayer's income must also be looked at to determine whether the taxpayer is eligible to make a deductible IRA contribution. If a taxpayer is an active participant, fully deductible contributions are allowed only if the taxpayer has an adjusted gross income that falls below a specified level (see table 10-4). The level for unreduced contributions depends on the taxpayer's filing status. Married couples

TABLE 10-4
Adjusted Gross Income Limits for Deductible IRA Contributions

Filing Status	Full IRA Deduction	Reduced IRA Deduction	No IRA Deduction
Individual or head of household	$25,000 or less	$25,000.01–$34,999.99	$35,000 or more
Married filing jointly	$40,000 or less	$40,000.01–$49,999.99	$50,000 or more
Married filing separately	Not available	$0.01–$9,999.99	$10,000 or more

filing a joint return will get a full IRA deduction if their adjusted gross income is $40,000 or less. Married persons filing separately cannot get a full IRA deduction. Single taxpayers and taxpayers filing as heads of households will get a full IRA deduction if their adjusted gross income is $25,000 or less.

For taxpayers whose adjusted gross income falls between the no-deduction level and the full-deduction level, their reduced deduction can be computed by using the following formula:

$$\text{Deductible amount} = \$2,000 - \frac{\text{adjusted gross income} - \text{filing status floor}}{5}$$

> *Example:* Bob and Rita Johnson (a married couple filing jointly) are both working and have a combined adjusted gross income of $46,000. Bob and Rita can each make the full IRA contribution of $2,000 (total $4,000). The formula shows that each can deduct $800 (total $1,600).

$$\text{Bob and Rita's deductible amount} = \$2,000 - \frac{\$46,000 - \$40,000}{5}$$

$$\text{Bob and Rita's deductible amount} = \$800 \ \text{each}$$

Therefore of the $4,000 contributed to an IRA, $2,400 will be on an aftertax basis.

Spousal IRAs

Spousal IRAs provide an opportunity to save an additional $250 and to arrange favorable distribution of IRA assets. A spousal IRA may be set up even if the taxpayer's spouse has received no compensation during the tax year. In addition to allowing an extra $250 in savings, a spousal IRA provides a valuable opportunity to split contributions to meet retirement and tax needs.

> *Example:* Greg and Diane LeRose meet all the requirements for a spousal IRA. Greg is 50 years old and Diane is 53. If the LeRoses wish to withdraw their contributions as soon as possible without penalty, the $2,000 should be deposited in Diane's IRA and the spousal $250 in Greg's. The reason is that Diane will reach the age when withdrawals are allowed without penalty — age $59\frac{1}{2}$ — before Greg. Therefore she will be able to withdraw funds from her account 3 years before Greg. However, if the LeRoses desire to postpone paying tax on the money as long as possible by delaying the distribution of the account, the $2,000 contribution should be placed in Greg's account since he will turn $70\frac{1}{2}$ (when distributions must start) 3 years after Diane. Of course, if Greg and Diane want to hedge their bets, they can split the contributions evenly or place a substantial amount in Greg's account to delay taxation, while also placing enough in Diane's account to start adequate withdrawals during the 3-year period when she can make penalty-free withdrawals and he cannot.

Nonqualified Plans

Another tax-advantaged way to save for retirement is to use a nonqualified retirement plan. In the case of nonqualified plans, the tax savings are not attributable to Uncle Sam but instead stem from the fact that, in most cases, the employer defers his or her business deduction so that specifically chosen employees won't be deemed to be in constructive receipt of deferred compensation promised them.

A nonqualified deferred-compensation plan is an employer-provided retirement benefit that is typically given to highly compensated executives and managers. There are three basic types of nonqualified plans. Under a so-called top-hat plan the executive defers part of his or her salary for retirement purposes. For this reason top-hat plans are sometimes referred to as pure deferred compensation arrangements. Under an excess benefit plan the employer provides benefits beyond the dollar restrictions imposed on qualified plans. And under a supplemental executive retirement plan the employer provides a second tier of retirement benefits in addition to any qualified benefits. In this case, however, qualified benefits are not at their maximum legal limits.

Retirement Planning Considerations

Even though all three of these plans can provide for abundant retirement savings, planners must be wary of certain potential problems for clients covered by them. One trap awaiting clients covered by nonqualified deferred-compensation plans is that distributions from these plans will be subject to significantly more taxes than similar distributions from a qualified plan. The reason for this is that qualified plan distributions are eligible for favorable 5- or 10-year averaging—a technique used to effectively lower tax rates when a large taxable retirement withdrawal is made—whereas nonqualified distributions are not. Consequently, to avoid a tax disaster under a nonqualified plan distributions should be spread over two or more tax years or an annuity should be considered.

A second trap awaiting clients covered by nonqualified deferred-compensation plans is that promised benefits from nonqualified plans are typically subject to loss for a variety of reasons. For example, the nonqualified plan may contain a forfeiture provision stipulating that benefits will be forfeited if certain conditions are not met. In many circumstances the client may be either unwilling or unable to meet his or her part of the commitment. A second way nonqualified benefits can be lost is if the employer sponsoring the plan goes bankrupt. Nonqualified plan funds are typically held as corporate assets which are subject to the claims of corporate creditors in bankruptcy. By contrast, funds in a qualified plan are held in a trust or insurance contract separate from business assets and are not subject to forfeiture in case of bankruptcy.

A final insecurity associated with nonqualified plans is the threat of immediate taxation to the employee which would result in a lower overall retirement accumulation. For example, despite employer contentions to the contrary some plans are construed by the IRS as providing an immediate economic benefit to the employee, or the employee may be deemed to be in constructive receipt of the income. In either case the prefunded benefit will be taxable while the client is still employed and the advantages of tax deferral will be lost.

Despite all these problems, nonqualified plans have an important role in retirement planning for upscale clients. For one thing, they enable these clients to exceed the maximum limits imposed on qualified plans. (Recall that a defined-benefit plan could not fund a benefit greater than $90,000 as indexed and a defined-contribution plan contribution was restricted to the lesser of 25 percent of compensation or $30,000.) Secondly, they allow clients to circumvent a 15 percent excise tax that is applicable to annual distributions from qualified plans which are over $117,529 (as indexed) and lump-sum distributions over $612,900 (as indexed). Distributions from a nonqualified plan are not subject to the excess distribution penalties. For these reasons a client with a two-tier retirement program sponsored by his or her employer, including both a qualified and a nonqualified plan, is in the best position to plan for retirement. Conversely, an upscale client without the second nonqualified tier may be subject to an inadequate replacement ratio because of the caps placed on qualified plan benefits.

Social Security

Another important source of retirement income is social security. When people use the term *social security,* they are actually referring to the old-age, survivor's, disability, and health insurance program of the federal government. For retirement planning purposes planners should be familiar with the entire social security system, particularly the old-age and health insurance programs.

Eligibility

A client is eligible for retirement benefits under the old-age provision of social security if he or she is covered by social security and has credit for a stipulated amount of work. Credit for social security purposes is based on quarters of coverage. For 1990, a worker receives credit for one quarter of coverage for each $520 in annual earnings on which social security taxes are paid, but credit for no more than four quarters of coverage may be earned in any one calendar year. Consequently, a worker paying social security taxes on as little as $2,000 during the year, regardless of when it was earned during the year, will receive credit for the maximum four quarters. A person is fully insured for purposes of receiving social security retirement benefits if he or she has 40 quarters of coverage.

Retirement Benefits

Old-age insurance benefits are based on a worker's primary insurance amount (PIA). The PIA, in turn, is a function of the worker's average indexed monthly earnings (AIME) on which social security taxes have been paid. For retirement planning purposes the planner need not know how to calculate the AIME and PIA. Instead, the best method to estimate a client's expected social security benefits is to request the employee's data from the Social Security Administration. To obtain this information the client can mail in either Form SSA-7050-F3 or Form SSA-7004-

PC-OP1. The social security office will provide data relating to the client's earnings history and estimated primary insurance amount. In addition, table 10-5 can be used to estimate social security benefits.

Retirement planning considerations. Planners should make their clients aware that social security is geared toward providing benefits for those with a lower income and cannot be relied on as a proportionally large source of retirement income for well-off clients. For example, a person with a $10,000 salary prior to retirement will receive approximately a 50 percent income replacement ratio from social security whereas a person with a $100,000 salary will only receive a 10 percent income replacement ratio.

Early and deferred retirement. A worker who is fully insured is eligible to receive monthly retirement benefits as early as age 62. Electing to receive benefits prior to age 65, however, results in a permanently reduced retirement benefit. If a worker elects to receive retirement benefits prior to age 65, benefits are permanently reduced by five-ninths of one percent for every month that the early retirement precedes age 65. For example, for a worker who retires at age 62, the monthly benefit will be only 80 percent of what the worker would have received had he or she waited until age 65.

Workers who delay applying for retirement benefits until after age 65 are eligible for an increased benefit equal to $\frac{1}{4}$ of one percent for each month (or 3 percent per year) of delayed retirement beyond age 65 and up to age 70.

Medicare

In addition to understanding the amount of retirement benefits provided by social security and the people who are covered by social security, retirement planners need to understand the medicare system.

Eligibility for medicare. Part A, the hospital portion of medicare, is available at no monthly cost to any person aged 65 or older as long as the person is entitled to monthly retirement benefits under social security or the railroad retirement program.

Most persons who are 65 or over and do not meet the eligibility requirements may voluntarily enroll in medicare. However, they must pay a monthly premium. This monthly premium, $192.50 in 1990, is adjusted annually to reflect the cost of the benefits provided. In addition, these persons must also enroll in part B and pay the applicable premiums there as well.

Any person eligible for part A of medicare is also eligible for part B. However, a monthly premium must be paid for part B. This monthly premium, $28.60 in 1990, is adjusted annually and represents only about 25 percent of the cost of the benefits provided. The remaining cost of the program is financed from the federal government's general revenues.

Persons receiving social security or railroad retirement benefits are automatically enrolled in medicare if they are eligible. If they do not want part B, they must elect out in writing. Other persons eligible for medicare must apply for part B benefits. Anyone who elects out of part B or who does not enroll when initially eligible may later apply for benefits during the general enrollment period between January 1 and March 31 of each year. However, the monthly premium will be increased by 10 percent for each 12-month period during which the person was eligible but failed to enroll.

TABLE 10-5
Sample Social Security Benefits—As of 1990

		Monthly Benefits at Age 65 (Spouse Same Age)				
		Your Present Annual Earnings				
Your Age in 1990	Who Receives Benefits	$12,000	$20,000	$30,000	$40,000	$51,300 and Up
65	You	$491	$683	$886	$938	$975
	Spouse* or child	245	341	443	469	487
64	You	486	676	877	931	970
	Spouse* or child	243	338	438	465	485
63	You	496	690	896	952	995
	Spouse* or child	248	345	448	476	497
62	You	497	690	898	955	1,000
	Spouse* or child	248	345	449	477	500
61	You	497	692	899	958	1,006
	Spouse* or child	248	346	449	479	503
55	You	503	701	913	993	1,065
	Spouse or child	251	350	456	496	532
50	You	$491^\dagger$	$685^\dagger$	$892^\dagger$	$988^\dagger$	$1,077^\dagger$
	Spouse or child‡	254	354	461	511	557
45	You	$478^\dagger$	$669^\dagger$	$868^\dagger$	$974^\dagger$	$1,079^\dagger$
	Spouse or child‡	256	358	465	522	578
40	You	$483^\dagger$	$676^\dagger$	$873^\dagger$	$986^\dagger$	1,109†
	Spouse or child‡	258	362	467	528	594
35	You	$481^\dagger$	$675^\dagger$	$867^\dagger$	981†	$1,109^\dagger$
	Spouse or child‡	261	366	470	532	601
30	You	$456^\dagger$	$640^\dagger$	$819^\dagger$	$928^\dagger$	$1,050^\dagger$
	Spouse or child‡	263	369	473	535	606

*Benefit at age 65 or at any age with eligible child in care.
†These amounts are reduced for retirement at age 65 because the normal retirement age (NRA) is higher for these persons; the reduction factors are different for the worker and the spouse.
‡The amount shown is for the spouse at NRA or with eligible child in care, or for the child; the benefit for a spouse younger than NRA without a child in care would be reduced for early retirement.

Medicare: Part A benefits. Part A of medicare provides benefits for expenses incurred in hospitals (for stays up to 90 days in each benefit period), skilled nursing facilities (if a physician certifies that skilled nursing or therapeutic care is needed for a condition that was treated in a hospital within the last 30 days), and hospices (for terminally ill persons who have a life expectancy of 6 months or less). In addition, home health care benefits are covered if a patient needs further care at home for a condition treated in a hospital or skilled nursing facility. In fact, part A of medicare will pay the full cost for an unlimited number of home visits by a home health agency. In order for benefits to be paid, the facility or agency providing benefits must participate in the medicare program. Virtually all hospitals are participants, as are most other facilities or agencies that meet the requirements of medicare.

Medicare: Part B benefits. Part B, the supplementary medical insurance portion of medicare, provides benefits for the following medical expenses not covered under part A:

- physicians' and surgeons' fees that result from house calls, office visits, or services provided in a hospital or other institution (under certain circumstances benefits are also provided for the services of chiropractors, podiatrists, and optometrists)
- diagnostic tests in a hospital or in a physician's office
- physical therapy in a physician's office, or as an outpatient of a hospital, skilled nursing facility, or an approved clinic, agency, or public-health agency
- drugs and biologicals that cannot be self-administered
- radiation therapy
- medical supplies, such as surgical dressings, splints, and casts
- rental of medical equipment, such as oxygen tents, hospital beds, and wheelchairs
- prosthetic devices, such as artificial heart valves or contact lenses after a cataract operation
- ambulance service if a patient's condition does not permit the use of other methods of transportation
- pneumococcal vaccine and its administration
- home health services as described for part A when prior hospitalization has not occurred

With some exceptions, part B pays 80 percent of the approved charges for covered medical expenses after the satisfaction of a $75 annual deductible.

Retirement planning considerations. Although the preceding list for part B of medicare may appear to be comprehensive, planners need to make their clients aware that numerous medical products and services are not covered by part B. Some of these products and services that represent significant expenses for the elderly include the following:

- drugs and biologicals that can be self-administered
- routine physical, eye, and hearing examinations
- routine foot care
- immunizations, except pneumococcal vaccinations or immunization required because of an injury or immediate risk of infection
- cosmetic surgery unless it is needed because of an accidental injury or to improve the function of a malformed part of the body
- dental care unless it involves jaw or facial bone surgery or the setting of fractures
- custodial care
- eyeglasses, hearing aids, and orthopedic shoes

In addition, benefits are not provided to persons who are eligible for workers' compensation or treated in government hospitals. Benefits are provided only for services received in the United States, except for physicians' services and ambulance services rendered for a covered hospitalization in Mexico or Canada under part A.

HOW TO HELP CLIENTS OVERCOME INADEQUATE RETIREMENT RESOURCES

In addition to determining how much income a client will need to retire and understanding the various sources of retirement income, the planner must also help clients produce as much retirement income as possible from their existing resources. The final part of this chapter will address four strategies that the planner can recommend to accomplish this goal.

- trading down to a less expensive home
- reverse annuity mortgages
- postretirement employment
- maximizing pension benefits

Trading Down: Relocation to a Less Expensive Home

If your client can be persuaded to sell his or her home and relocate to a smaller, less expensive residence, the money made available from the transaction can be a valuable source of retirement income. For example, if your client can sell his or her house for $200,000 and buy a new residence for $100,000, the $100,000 gain can be used to produce an extra $10,000 a year in income (assuming a 10 percent interest rate). This can be very desirable from a financial perspective because retirees can capitalize on what for many is their single most important financial asset—their home. In addition, this can be very desirable from a tax standpoint because the IRS allows a one-time exclusion of up to $125,000 on the taxation of gain from the sale of a home. The $125,000 exclusion is subject to the following restrictions:

- The individual taking the exclusion must be aged 55 or older.
- If the individual is married and files a separate return the exclusion is cut to $62,500.
- The exclusion only applies if the property has been owned and used by the client as a principal residence for 3 years of the 5-year period ending on the date of the sale or exchange (the years need not be consecutive).
- The client must make an election to exclude the gain from gross income.
- The exclusion can only be made once during the client's lifetime.

Cashing in While Staying at Home—The Reverse Annuity Mortgage

If your client would like to take some equity out of his or her house but is reluctant to leave the home, an alternative that is available is a reverse annuity mortgage (RAM). Under one type of reverse annuity mortgage the client sells a remainder interest in the home but retains the right to occupy the house until death.

The purchaser of the remainder interest acquires the right to take possession of the property after the homeowner's death (or the death of the homeowner and the spouse). The consideration for acquiring the remainder interest in the house is that the purchaser agrees to make periodic payments to the seller during the seller's life. These payments can significantly enhance a client's retirement income.

Under another type of reverse annuity mortgage the annuity payments plus interest are held as a series of loans against the value of the home. In this case, the amount paid out in an income stream plus interest will be recovered by the lender from eventual sale proceeds after the death of the retiree.

Postretirement Employment

A third alternative that can be used to provide the retiree with extra cash is a part-time job during the retirement years. Many retirees find that working on a scaled-back basis meets not only their financial needs but helps them adapt psychologically to the changes that retirement brings. This is especially true for clients whose self-esteem and sense of self-worth were tied to their careers.

Working after retirement poses a potential problem for retirees, however. They can lose social security income benefits if their earnings exceed specified limits, called annual exempt amounts. In general, social security benefits will be reduced by $1.00 for each $3.00 earned in excess of the limit for retirees aged 65 through 69 (or by $1.00 for each $2.00 earned in excess of the limit for retirement benefit recipients under age 65). The earnings limit is indexed, but in 1990 it is $6,840 for clients under age 65 and $9,360 for those aged 65 through 69.

Thus, if a 63-year-old retired client earns $12,000 in 1990, his or her social security benefits for the following year will be reduced by $2,580 (that is, one-half of the difference between $12,000 and $6,840). Or, if a 66-year-old retired client earns $12,000 in 1990, his or her social security benefits for the following year will be reduced by $880 (that is, one-third of the difference between $12,000 and $9,360).

There is good news for clients aged 70 or above, however. There is no reduction in social security income benefits regardless of the amount of their earnings.

Pension Maximization

The final strategy that we will discuss is pension maximization. Qualified plans typically stipulate the type of distribution that your client will receive. The normal form of benefit for a married individual is a joint and survivor benefit of not less than 50 percent or greater than 100 percent. One strategy available for your married clients is to have your client elect a different payment option by electing out of the normal benefit form with the spouse's written consent. If a married individual who would otherwise be locked into a joint and survivor annuity, elects to have his or her benefit paid in the form of a life annuity he or she can increase his or her retirement income significantly. If at the same time life insurance is purchased (or kept in force) on the life annuitant the spouse's future also remains secure.

Example: Joe Jones (aged 65) and his wife Sally (aged 62) are eligible to receive a $1,500 joint and survivor benefit from the $200,000 they have in Joe's retirement plan (qualified joint and survivor 100 percent). If they elect to receive a life annuity based on Joe's life, they will receive $325 more each month ($1,825). The extra $3,900 a year represents a 22 percent increase in annual income for them. If they can purchase (or keep in force) life insurance on Joe that would provide for Sally for anything less than the $3,900 a year, they will stretch their retirement savings and take a big step toward their financial security goals.

11

Computerizing the Financial Planning Practice

Dale S. Johnson*

Part 1 of this chapter provides general guidelines for computerizing the financial planning practice, including types of software that are not limited to financial planning applications (such as word processing). Parts 2, 3, and 4 of the chapter are limited to discussions of software designed specifically for professional financial planning applications. Part 5 summarizes the most important reasons to computerize the practice.

Appendix D provides supplementary information for Part 1. Table 2 in Appendix E contains summary recommendations for three levels of general hardware and software components for installing or upgrading the basic computer system. Appendix F provides lists of software vendors and programs for several types of financial planning applications. Appendix G contains several software and hardware buying tips and suggestions for dealing directly with the marketplace.

PART 1: PLANNING FOR COMPUTERIZED PLANNING

Financial planning is a complex process. It involves a multitude of facts, details, and interrelationships. It requires ongoing management of information on both clients and the marketplace to implement financial plans and keep them current. Most practices also provide other specialized financial services, such as insurance and investment product sales, accounting, income tax return preparation, asset management, estate planning, and employee benefits and retirement planning. These activities add to the complexity of the practice as well as the management responsibilities. They should be included in plans to computerize and integrated as closely as possible with overall hardware and software needs.

Computerizing does not manage anything by itself. On the contrary, everything that is computerized must be managed—preferably, *before* the practice buys any equipment at all. Computerizing is not just a matter of buying a computer and some software, placing it in an out-of-the-way corner of the office, plugging it in, and expecting it to start performing according to expectations and hopes. That does not work. To achieve satisfactory results, the principals must plan how the office is to be run and who is to be responsible for each part of its operations both before and after computerizing.

When the practice computerizes, the computer(s) should be kept in the forefront of the visible office. This enhances the professional image of the office, positions the firm's capabilities as equivalent to those of larger financial organizations, and

---

*Formerly a faculty member at The American College, Dale S. Johnson, PhD, CFP, is a financial planning consultant and writer based in Villanova, Pennsylvania.

promotes the perception that the operation employs high-tech support tools for its activities and services. Make sure that clients know the firm is computerized; make sure from the beginning that the staff knows how this equipment is to be used in managing clients and practice operations.

NOTE: Computers and software applications create efficiencies in a practice that is already well organized. Disorganization worsens when these tools are applied to it.

The following subsections provide guidelines to help principals and staff determine what tools are really needed from the hardware and software marketplace. Planners who are already computerized will find that this discussion is a useful review of the current status of practice computerization. It will also help to determine whether currently used equipment needs to be upgraded for more effective communications and marketing.

Ultimately, the most important reason for computerizing the planning practice is to provide more efficient information processing and management for marketing purposes. Therefore, to implement a more effective practice marketing strategy, the firm's members should determine the extent and type of communications they have with clients, other service and product providers (for example, specialists, broker-dealers, and insurance carriers), and among groups of employees (such as professional planners, associates, and support staff).

Only members of the firm itself can determine how much information collection, processing, and dissemination go on in the practice and how these elements relate to practice marketing strategy. Only these responsible parties can decide how much and what parts of these activities should be computerized for more effective management.

A fully developed practice business plan is beyond the scope of this discussion. In addition, a business plan may not be particularly useful for determining practice computerization needs. Nevertheless, to choose appropriate software and hardware equipment for financial planning applications, principals and staff will find the guidelines in the following subsections useful for determining what parts of the practice's activities need to be evaluated for computerizing. These guidelines relate directly to later discussion of specific types of software.

Define the Practice's Business

Whether the practice computerizes all at once or gradually, it makes sense to plan all moves carefully, establish a budget for computerizing, and submit all purchase and lease decisions to cost-benefit analysis. An outline of the firm's specific planning activities helps enormously in determining the kind of practice conducted now and the procedures required to deliver services and products during its developmental phases. Using this outline, the guidelines below for practice jobs that can be computerized, the discussions of planning software provided in later sections of the reading, and the lists of software vendors and programs in Appendix F will also help in estimating the costs of computerizing compared to current and projected revenues and the firm's budget for equipment.

It is important to define the practice as the principals want it to be perceived by clients and other financial services professionals. It is even more important to make this definition consistent with what the firm actually does. Otherwise, software and hardware may be purchased to computerize activities that are not even conducted. Therefore, start by defining the nature of the practice's business.

If business activities center primarily on financial planning, make that clear and follow through with implementation. If the business is primarily insurance and investment product marketing and sales, make that clear. If the practice specializes in accounting or legal services, qualified plans administration, asset management, estate planning, or some other focus area of financial services, the activities associated with these specializations should determine the search for appropriate software applications.

No single outline can exactly fit every practice's activities. The best use of the one provided below is for getting started in defining what the firm basically does, or what the principals expect it will be doing as it evolves toward the objectives defined for it. To help organize the survey, typical comprehensive practice activities are included in the outline.

Generally, consider the following items and how they relate to the practice.

- The firm's detailed, specific business and planning objectives
- The scope of the firm's financial planning services
  - Comprehensive and/or focus planning
  - Target market(s) for planning services
  - Related specialized services and product distribution activities
- The firm's planning and support staff requirements
  - Evaluation of all professional planners and current paraprofessional and support staff in relation to their education, experience, aptitude, maturity, and leadership
  - The additional staff and professional associate(s) the firm may need to recruit
- The firm's current technological resources
  - Currently installed computer(s) and software
  - Local and remote computer networks, current or planned
  - Other equipment such as typewriters, printers, copy machines, fax machines
- The education and training levels required for the firm members' activities, including exposure to using computers and software
  - Initial and continuing professional staff competencies (degrees, certifications, registrations, licenses)
  - Initial and continuing support staff competencies, including training programs in computers and software
  - Professional society and trade association affiliations
  - Subscriptions to publications, print reference services, newsletters, and online electronic information retrieval systems
- The firm's implementation services, relationships, and associations

- – Working relationships and communications with investment syndicators, broker-dealers, mutual funds distributors, registered representatives, general partners, insurance agents, brokers, carriers, and consultants
  - – Setting, allocating, and providing accounting for fees and commissions payable to associates
  - – Compliance oversight with securities, investment advisory, and insurance laws and regulations, and with professional standards (for example, those of the International Board of Standards and Practices for Certified Financial Planners, the IAFP Registry of Financial Planning Practitioners, and the American Institute of Certified Public Accountants)
  - – Professional liability risks (errors and omissions)
  - – Maintaining and developing product and service knowledge
- The firm's public relations activities
  - – Office image
  - – Public relations brochure
  - – Client newsletter(s)
  - – Press releases
  - – Networking with other financial services firms and professionals
- The firm's marketing activities
  - – Through seminars
  - – To individuals
  - – To professionals
  - – To corporations
  - – To associations
  - – To financial institutions
  - – To NASD member firms
  - – Through articles, speeches, radio and TV appearances
  - – Through client referrals
- The firm's use of or need for audiovisual aids
  - – Seminar slides
  - – Video presentations
  - – Flowcharts
  - – Cassette programs
  - – Interactive software tutorials

Numerous general practice, individual, and professional activities are associated with the items listed above. Most of these activities involve jobs and tasks related to information management, time management, communications, and marketing. Most can be supported to one degree or another by available software programs.

Define the Firm's Information Processing Requirements

The type of planning a firm offers — comprehensive, focused, or specialist — is a key consideration in defining the firm's information processing needs. Another important factor is whether the planners process information at the computer or employ assistants or paraplanners to run computerized equipment. Finally, does the firm provide fee-only planning with no product distribution, product distribution with commission-only income, or some combination of fees and commission-based planning? This is one of the most important considerations. How the planner is compensated is related to the types of activities the firm is engaged in, thus the types of computerization that may be needed to support those activities.

Whether the firm is independent, or provides planning through a broker-dealer, insurance company, bank, or other financial services organization, may predetermine some of its software and hardware choices. These financial services organizations often provide computer and software support to agents and representatives but require adherence to predetermined standards and brands of equipment. Whether the planner is a practicing accountant or attorney who also provides financial planning will certainly influence how the business is defined, its planning practice activities, and its computerization needs.

When only one person in the office uses and depends on computerization, it is rarely used efficiently and effectively. On the other hand, as soon as more than one person uses and depends on the computer equipment, there may be multiuser needs. This could require either that individual computer terminals be linked in a full network or more simply cable-connected for sharing data files and peripheral hardware. If several planners and staff members are to share the same data files and application programs, the firm may need to link individual computers in a local area network (LAN). In some practices, networks can save money by avoiding costly duplication of application programs. A network may also reduce the need for large hard disk storage capacity on each computer and provide for more efficient use of available printers and other hardware components. A multiuser configuration could also require installation of software and hardware that can be accessed by more than one person at a time and that can run several application programs simultaneously.

A practitioner with relatively few clients who is the only user of the computer won't necessarily need a computer or software applications designed for an individual power user, and of course won't require a network system. However, the practitioner may still prefer a system with enough memory and processing power to execute more than one software application simultaneously (often referred to as multitasking).

Whatever jobs are computerized, remember that planning information and practice communications processing and dissemination are broad-based, complex, and often repetitive. The planner or designated associates and support staff must become proficient in managing them.

The following summary guidelines will help each practice determine its information and communications requirements.

- Review the current client base and target additional markets for practice development.
- Determine the kinds of information clients may expect from the practice and the types of information the practice will need from clients and from external sources (for example, print or electronic databases, securities prices, general economic analyses).
- Determine who among the staff will be primarily responsible for collecting, processing, and managing the flow of information and communications in the practice.
- Determine the flow, volume, and growth rate of operational tasks and jobs.

- Establish cost centers for all tasks; measure and allocate tasks against the efficiencies of computerization.
- Develop a preinstallation plan for tasks, task sequencing, staff responsibility, time frame for completion, and the amount of time required for each task by each staff member.
- Develop a pretraining program for tasks followed by a training program for all software applications that perform them. To this end, develop both a manual and a computerized model of task flow.
- Review progress to date and project expanded use of software, new software needs, and expanded hardware capabilities.

To sum up, modify and add to the guidelines presented above for defining the practice's needs and its specific financial planning activities. Substitute the details of its activities as only the principals can know them. Determine the practice's objectives, products and services to be delivered, and financial and human resources required. Decide current and future goals for the practice, the procedures and systems required during this period, and how quickly and by what means to move to that point. Then, the firm's principals will be better prepared to evaluate computerization issues.

A definition of the practice should be such that it can be included in the promotional brochure describing the firm's services (see table 1 of Appendix D). Fully computerizing the tasks and jobs associated with the activities of this firm could require the power-user configuration of hardware and software recommended in table 2 of Appendix E, including a local area network (LAN) of multiple computer terminals.

NOTE: Surveying the activities of the practice should lead the planner(s) to realize that collecting, processing, and maintaining interactive data on clients and prospects, and tracking financial transactions with clients, are the most important of all communications and management tasks, whatever level of financial planning the firm provides. These tasks can be delegated more efficiently and cost-effectively to global practice computerization than they can to partial computerization or to no computerization at all.

Define Jobs to Be Computerized

The computer and software marketplace offers an enormous variety of products and applications for each of the numerous jobs that a financial planning practice creates. However, because each practice is different and has its own marketing strategies and scope of activities, no single product will necessarily satisfy the requirements of every similar job. Thoroughly knowing the practice's activities and computerization needs is the best way to reduce the confusion and intimidation that everyone encounters when faced with the range of choices available in the software and hardware marketplace.

> *NOTE:* A detailed outline of practice jobs and tasks is the most useful way to develop a shopping list of needed equipment. This outline provides a survey of what is actually done in the practice that can be computerized.

The following guidelines will help in determining the practice's computerization needs in relation to specific kinds of jobs and tasks that computers and software can either fully or partially automate. In general, productivity and profitability in the planning practice can be improved through the following carefully computerized procedures:

- gathering, organizing, processing, storing, and disseminating information for each client and prospective client
- analyzing available client data and proposed planning recommendations, developing solutions to clients' current financial problems, and helping clients set appropriate longer-term courses of action
- articulating sophisticated recommendations in clearly supportive, standardized planning reports that clients can understand
- tracking clients' progress toward their financial objectives with periodic performance evaluations, reports on the status of their financial plans, and the results of their financial decisions
- updating and modifying financial plans on a regular basis, either manually or through sharing information between client and asset management software programs and financial planning software
- accessing and transferring to the firm's computer(s) (that is, downloading) information derived from electronic databases (such as Dow Jones News/Retrieval); creating and disseminating economic, financial, planning, and practice marketing information in various practice communications media, including newsletters
- providing financial accounting for planning practice activities, both for the firm as a whole and for its revenue- and cost-producing members
- documenting, rationalizing, and referencing the planning process as it develops, in compliance with the ethics codes and practice standards of several professional organizations and with the Securities and Exchange Commission and the rules and regulations of the Investment Advisers Act of 1940

Software automates tasks and procedures that are otherwise manually conducted (or not conducted at all). For example, software is referred to as applications. Applications direct the computer to perform specific jobs and provide the programming and computations to do them.

Outline — Software Procedures and Production Jobs

In a financial planning practice, software may be assigned the following procedures and production jobs, depending on the scope of services and products offered through each practice.

Client and Practice Management

- Appointment calendar
  - Advance appointment logs
  - Tickler file for upcoming events
  - Automatic telephone dialer
- Client information management
- Asset allocation (apportionment of a client's investable funds among various types of investments [such as bonds, common stock, cash, and so on] in a manner consistent with the client's risk profile and the risk/return characteristics of each type of investment)
- Asset management and status reporting
- Portfolio price updating
- Performance measurement/reporting on investments
- Billing/accounting
- Fee and commission tracking

Financial and Tax Analysis

- Comprehensive financial and tax planning
  - Financial statements
  - Financial analyses
  - Numeric projections and forecasts
  - Tax calculations and projections
  - What-if modeling of strategies and recommendations
  - Investment portfolio modeling and allocation (using results of asset allocation decisions)
  - Periodic updating and plan revision
- Mini and quick planning
- Needs analysis and product distribution planning
- Planning for specialized focus areas (for example, insurance analysis, retirement planning, qualified plans distribution, education funding)
- Service bureau processing (time sharing)
- Income tax return preparation services

Information Processing and Dissemination

- Word processing and electronic publishing
  - Financial planning reports
  - Stored text on planning techniques
  - Marketing brochures
  - Newsletters and other client communications
  - Client presentations
  - Correspondence
  - Memos and draft letters
  - Mailmerge
  - Text and numeric merge
  - Text and graphics merge
  - Spelling, grammar, syntax check; thesaurus

- Automatic indexing, footnoting, table of contents, text formatting
- Page layout, composition, and font control
- Document creation from online information retrieval systems
- Graphics and visual presentations
  - Merged numeric data with graphs, bar charts, pie charts in two and three dimensions
  - Financial analysis program linking for what-if modeling of merged data
  - Integration of graphics with desktop publishing applications
  - Video and slide presentations
- Optically scanned text and graphics
- Electronic printing
  - Draft quality (dot matrix)
  - Letter quality (advanced dot matrix, thermal transfer, inkjet, liquid crystal)
  - Laser printing

Networks, Online Databases, Communications

- Linked computers, networks, and workstations
- Electronic databases and information retrieval
- Communicating with modems and faxes

Productivity Enhancement

- Multitasking DOS interfaces
- Time organization and management
- File and hard disk management and security

Before choosing any software application tool, the crucial question is always, "What does the job I want it to do consist of?" First, the job to be computerized must be defined, to determine whether a specific software program will do the job. If the firm buys a program without defining the task(s) it is expected to perform, the tool may wag the planner.

By using the outline of items above as a preliminary guide and stimulus to the principals' own reflection, they will come to know better than they did before what kind of financial planning practice they have or plan to develop. If it is less comprehensive than the scope implied in this discussion (for example, less comprehensive than the scope illustrated in table 1 of Appendix D), scale back the practice activities, jobs, and tasks until what the planning practice actually does is accurately described. The remaining sections of this chapter are limited to a survey of the essential types of software that are directly related to financial planning applications.

Whether the planner is a new entrant or already has some experience in the computer and software marketplace, he or she will be struck by the confusion of conflicting claims and the lack of readily available, intelligible information that relates directly to the planner's interests and needs. In many ways, it is an industry in which the putative standards provide few practical guidelines for making purchase decisions. It has not yet settled on a common language and terminology for describing its products. As a matter of fact, every vendor, dealer, and salesperson seems to have a slightly different slant on things. It is an extremely competitive industry, and much of the language used by product vendors, dealers, and reviewers of products is characterized by exaggeration and inflated claims.

This industry hype can easily lead the uninformed customer to buy products that will not do the job(s) for which they were purchased — or to overlook available products that will do the job. *Do not expect the people who are selling the products to know what your practice's jobs are.*

On the other hand, the computer and software industry has created a vast array of products that are now essential support tools for financial planning and many other professional activities. The most important preparation for everybody in this new and confusing marketplace is to know the jobs they want to automate and have a working understanding and definition of the tools they are seeking. Ultimately, the buyer is the one who must sort through the confusion, plan to provide adequate support for practice activities, and then manage and control these activities once they are computerized.

NOTE: Despite the technical details of hardware and software, the fundamental issue for the financial planning practice is how to select the right tools to process information and create communications documents. Details are important to help the practice choose the media through which it manages and markets its services and products.

PART 2: MANAGING CLIENTS AND THEIR ASSETS

Even if the planner doesn't yet have a fully developed financial planning practice, he or she almost certainly has numerous prospects and clients for other financial services and products for whom the practice needs to manage extensive information, including appointments and contacts and time scheduling for planning professionals. The firm either already has or will have other practice procedures to manage. As the firm develops a planning clientele, it will need to manage client cases on an ongoing basis. Depending on the degree of asset management services provided, the firm may need software for one or more of the following services: (1) asset allocation and portfolio optimizing, (2) asset tracking and management, and (3) portfolio performance measurement. At the least, the firm will probably want to install software that enables it to provide clients with periodic status and performance reports on their investment assets.

As an alternative to stand-alone databases (or databases integrated with financial planning systems) and customized spreadsheets, several types of software programs are available to meet the needs listed above. Unfortunately, no one program cost-effectively meets all three application requirements. Only by analyzing the firm's needs and matching them against the specific capabilities of a program can a reasonable purchase selection be made. In some cases, more than one program may be required for a range of needed applications. In this case, determine whether the vendors of the programs under consideration have provided interfaces to share entered data with other types of programs.

NOTE: Unless the firm does not plan to use financial planning software, choose an asset and portfolio management program that interfaces with the financial planning system or program selected. Software for tracking and reporting on investment assets and related cash flows on an ongoing basis should have the capability of exporting data files to the financial planning software that is used. This capability minimizes multiple data entries, reduces data entry errors, and increases information management and communications efficiencies.

Databases

Until recently, available client management programs were either customized stand-alone databases or databases included in integrated financial planning systems. These programs can track the status of multiple portfolios for current clients and also help in prospecting for new clients, using entered information on clients' and prospective clients' interests, occupations, investment preferences, and other characteristics. Data can be entered and maintained on the specific investment and other financial products that a planner may market. This feature can facilitate cross marketing — that is, matching clients' and prospects' needs with the means to implement them.

Once the data are entered, database programs allow the user to screen and query categories of information that meet specific criteria, such as those specified for clients interested in selected bond issues or passive-income investments. After screening the data, these packages can generate a list of names and other specified information. Database programs will also produce mailing labels along with personalized letters based on a client's investments and interest criteria.

Most of the client management programs within integrated planning systems are based on the design and structure of relational databases. Relational structure (as opposed to flat-file) permits easier and more variable querying and sorting of stored data. Ashton-Tate's *dBase III Plus* and Informix Software's *Informix* have been so used. In addition, Microrim's *R:Base System 5* and Borland International's *Paradox* are notably adaptable to client management functions. Purchased separately, database management programs range between $300 and $750.

The more popular database management programs can support several add-on products that make them easier to use and extend their utility. For example, templates (predefined and customizable applications already written and ready for use) are available for accounting packages, client management programs, filing programs, and mailmerge programs. They are also available as utilities programs to help load the database system more quickly and efficiently and provide macros (collections of predefined functions and formulas that make keyboarding easier and more efficient), system-specific training tutorials, and graphics programs that can portray information from reports.

Database programs integrated into financial planning software are usually customized to keep extensive notes on telephone conversations with clients and prospects. Many have Rolodex and calendar features for making notes and leaving reminders to follow up on a prospect or client contact. The reminders can be printed on a daily or weekly basis. Programs used as stand-alone applications can be customized to do the same things.

RECOMMENDATION — Databases: Databases have proved cumbersome and difficult to use, even when integrated with financial planning systems. Unless the firm already uses one that meets its needs, consider installing one or more of the alternatives described in the following subsections.

Spreadsheets

Identifying the right package for specific job requirements is a major problem in selecting all client and practice management software. If a database within an integrated planning system, a stand-alone database, or the alternative stand-alone programs discussed below do not suit the practice's needs, consider using a spreadsheet package. It can provide the advantages of ready availability, relative ease of use, and flexibility to set up work sheets that suit a wide range of practice management needs and user styles.

Unlike the predefined and often unchangeable formats that come with some databases and client management programs, a spreadsheet allows the user to construct templates to present information in virtually any format. Add-on templates for customizing to suit the practice's particular applications are also available.

Major spreadsheet packages for the IBM standard include *Lotus 1-2-3* and Borland International's *Quattro.* Microsoft *Excel* is the standard for the Macintosh and is now available in a version for the IBM standard, but requires the 80286 or 80386 microprocessor and must be run under Microsoft *Windows.* It contains many features not included in *1-2-3* and is easier to learn and use. List prices for spreadsheets start at $195.

RECOMMENDATION — Spreadsheets: Unless the firm already has one or more proficient users of a customized spreadsheet program that meets its needs, the programs described in the following subsection may be better suited for managing client communications, general office procedures, and clients' investment assets.

Client and Asset Management Programs

In addition to spreadsheets and stand-alone and integrated databases, several asset allocation programs and online services, client and asset management programs, and portfolio analysis and performance programs have been designed and marketed for the specific needs of financial planning and asset management professionals. Essentially, they employ specialized database applications. They have been widely accepted, and vendors of several have concluded arrangements to provide interfaces for sharing data with financial planning systems and programs as an alternative to built-in full-fledged databases. Interfaces are also available (or soon will be) between some of these specialized programs. This development creates the possibility for more practice-specific information collection, maintenance, dissemination, and marketing.

For maximum cost and time efficiencies, the firm will need to link financial planning application software to a central information system whose primary uses are for client and general practice management, with an emphasis on asset and portfolio management. Even if the firm doesn't provide financial planning, or only basic levels of it, it must manage clients and other practice activities. The general features and selection criteria apply to any client and asset management software, including generic brands of databases and spreadsheets used independently or within comprehensive, integrated financial planning systems.

Basically, client and asset management software should

- support a wider range of services and fee billings to current clients
- target and communicate effectively with potential clients
- track all practice communications, marketing, and follow up
- provide cash and investment allocation, management, tracking, and performance reporting
- provide interface and data exchange with financial planning software (currently or as a planned enhancement)
- account for the entire staff's time and billable hours

NOTE: The importance of client and asset management software is that it can be the critical link for a computerized global communications and marketing strategy in the planning practice.

Because these activities are conducted daily within the planning practice, installed client and asset management software will be used more often and more intensively than financial planning software.

Financial planning software can be essential in developing the initial plan and its periodic renewals, but it provides few tools for efficient client management *after* those dates. In addition, most planning systems are crude and ineffective in helping the planner determine asset allocations based on each client's risk tolerances and expectations of return on investment assets. At best, they allow the user to impose arbitrary rules of thumb for investment allocations, and cannot access or process necessary historical performance data to develop, optimize, and periodically measure the performance of a market-efficient portfolio.

Unless the planning software can automatically update market prices on the client's financial assets, there is a gap in client communications and ongoing marketing of services and products based on continuously updated client and marketplace information. In addition, data gathering for periodic plan renewal is often as tedious and time-consuming as in initial planning.

Several client and asset management software programs and online services are designed to support these practice needs. They can also support additional billable services related to information management and dissemination to support clients' ongoing financial decisions and the practice's marketing strategy.

Before the firm seriously considers client and asset management programs, determine the practice's information processing and dissemination needs; then, evaluate the programs in relation to these needs. The guidelines for features and functions and the selection criteria in the following two subsections can be used to develop a shopping list of features the firm requires. Vendors and programs mentioned in the text, plus numerous additional programs, are listed in Appendix F under "Client and Asset Management."

Evaluating Capabilities and Features

Under several headings that indicate the functional capabilities of these programs, the following summary outlines features to look for and evaluate in a software program.

Automatic "To Do" Calendar

These are time management tools that can include the following capabilities:

- The "to do" calendar lists procedures and activities to be accomplished, prints them by priority, assigns them to a responsible staff member or employee, and automatically prints them out each day.
- This feature batches input capacity for automatically entering a "to do" for each client (for example, for a new client, printing a welcome letter, preparing a file folder, and adding the client to the billing system).
- The calendar lists suspense items by client, the staff person responsible, and the time period for completion.
- The calendar displays time schedules for all office staff, conference rooms, travel plans, and meetings.
- When used in a local area network, this feature provides all staff members with access to the schedules of other network members, at any time.

Client Billing/Staff Time Management

Basically, these are specialized accounting tools for tracking fees, commissions, and client accounts, and may include the following features:

- automatic billings (for example, $50 per month, $300 per quarter, percentage of assets under management)
- billing and accounting by job (for example, financial plan, investment advice, pension administration, risk management consulting)
- billing caps or limits (for example, the lesser of billable hours or stated fee)
- list of billable, nonbillable, and contingent charges
- report of aged accounts
- tracking and billing of staff time by client

- accounting of staff and employee time
- employee compensation based on billable hours

Client Information Management

These are client management and communications tools, directly related to word processing and printing, including:

- all prospect names, client names, and biographical data in one database
- names, addresses, and telephone numbers to manage all communications; new business prospecting and tracking; ability to automate changes of address, broker-dealers, and carriers; and ability to handle postcards
- a calendar and an auto-dialer to access stored telephone numbers; a telephone manager and an area code manager
- automatic, customizable form letters, using either internal or external word processor
- automatic internal and external mailmerge and label functions, including Rolodex, 3 x 5 cards, exportable names and addresses for use by an external word processor
- client profiles generated from any data stored anywhere in the program on the client, his or her spouse, and their children (available in both preformats and user-defined formats), using multiple SORT criteria
- individual or consolidated family reports
- an unlimited number of client cases and/or portfolios
- security passwords in network versions

Asset and Risk Management

These are functions of asset and portfolio management. These functions include asset allocation and portfolio optimizing, asset management, and portfolio performance measurement features. Note that any one software program does not include all three types of applications. Note also that some do not track insurance and annuity products. (See Appendix F under "Client and Asset Management" for lists of specialized software for asset allocation, management, and performance measurement.) Generally, these capabilities include:

- an automatic telephone modem interface with Dow Jones (or other) securities price update services
- revaluation of all client portfolio holdings simultaneously, with global manual or downloadable price updates
- global dividend, interest (coupon, received, and accrued), stock splits, income and capital gain distributions, realized gains and losses, reinvestment of interest and dividends, return of principal, deposits and withdrawals, tax lots/transaction accounting, cash and money fund accounting, margin accounting, audit trail accounting, total income accounting and reporting—entered once, either manually or downloaded, for all clients holding specific securities
- decision-support, reporting on sector analysis/asset allocation, comparative performance of securities held, price stops with warnings, master list/cross

reference of holdings, cash positions in all portfolios, maturity/expiration dates, margin debt-to-equity ratio (some features limited to asset allocation and portfolio performance measurement programs)
- fund-to-fund transfers to eliminate multiple entries of transactions
- a list of trade orders to broker-dealers
- a list of clients by securities issues owned
- a list of percentage of securities by client/by security
- a list of all securities traded by client (SEC/RIA)
- a list of all clients who traded a specific security (SEC/RIA)
- a full range of securities that can be entered (stocks, bonds, mortgage-backed securities, options, mutual funds, CDs, T-bills, commercial paper, and user-defined)
- calculation of time-weighted rates of return on entered assets; periodic and annualized total return; unrealized gains and losses; analysis of current, yield to maturity, taxable equivalent, and aftertax yield (some features limited to portfolio performance measurement programs)
- records of risk management contracts, lists of all policies by type, face amounts, premiums, and policy loans
- storage of sales illustrations and presentations produced by agents or carriers
- statistical information and SORTs on production by carrier/agent/time period (or by broker-dealer and representative)
- an alert function (watchdog) for specified events (for example, maturity dates, price stops, stock splits, distributions, and corporate takeovers)
- an unlimited number of transactions

Reporting

These items include the types of reports client and asset management software typically provides, such as

- periodic financial statements as required by each practice including gain/loss performance, cash flow statement, balance sheet, and year-end reports for income tax (see analysis capabilities under "Asset and Risk Management" above)
- IRS Schedules B and D (Interest and Dividends, Capital Gains and Losses)
- current asset and risk management contracts — list with totals by form of ownership, and totals by category of asset for allocation management
- a liquidity analysis of estate and investment assets
- sort and list any combination of entered and stored data
- user-defined report formats and content
- printing to disk file for merging reports with other financial planning documents
- printer drivers (or printer specification codes in utilities programs) for a range of standard printers, and for draft, letter quality, and laser fonts
- built-in automatic letterhead for letters, billing invoices, and certain reports, allowing the use of plain paper to reduce costs

Interfaces with Financial Planning Software

To avoid multiple entries of data, reduce entry errors, and maintain a central client information base, it is most important that the program be capable of exporting data to financial planning application software, especially these types:

- The first type is the electronic export of data to spreadsheets (such as *Lotus 1-2-3* or Microsoft *Excel*) and word processors, allowing single data entry, and update of financial data.
- The second type is the electronic export of data to financial planning software systems, allowing single data entry, update of financial planning information and analysis (a current trend between these programs and financial planning systems).

Export and Import of Data Files

In addition to data export capability to financial planning software, the program should provide for data export to and import from general applications, as follows:

- Data should be stored in industry standard formats (for example, *ASCII, dBASE III, 1-2-3*) to avoid dependence on the program vendor and provide flexibility in sourcing and managing data.
- All client, asset, and risk management files should be exportable to floppy disk from the main office system for work on another computer, then importable with changes back to the main system.

Selection Criteria

Once the firm has examined and evaluated the features of several programs, its final selection should be integrated with the following hardware, other software, and general practice considerations. The suggestions are intended to illustrate how to put these considerations together rather than to recommend specific products.

The programs in these categories of software are to be used to determine asset allocations, manage client cases and portfolios, and measure the performance of securities rather than for financial planning applications. Expect these programs to support the firm's needs for primary client communications, information management, and investment analysis relative to its marketing strategy rather than crunch numbers (except as needed for asset allocation optimizing and performance analysis).

- For asset allocation software, three cost-effective programs merit serious consideration: Advanced Investment Software's *RAMCAP — The Intelligent Asset Allocator, Capital Asset Management System* by Wilson Associates, and *LaPorte Asset Allocation System* by Burlington Hall Asset Management, Inc. Generally, the firm's choice should be dictated by a cost-benefit analysis relative to the number and quality of investment advisory clients it has and the breadth and depth of historical data on asset classes and issues the firm requires for fully optimizing client investment portfolios. *RAMCAP* is a cost-effective and well designed program for basic applications; the other two programs are better suited to high-level investment management applications; the system developed by

Wilson Associates provides the fullest range of historical data. Note that this program interfaces with *dbCAMS+ Client and Asset Management System*. (See Appendix F for a list of additional programs.)

- Unless only one person will ever use a client and asset management program (an unrealistic assumption), it should be a network version to provide staff access through multiple keyboards and avoid having to install multiple printers and other components for individual users. This capability is especially important in a transactions-oriented practice. Users won't be able to respond immediately to client queries about the status of an account if there is only one keyboard to the software, nor will the staff be able to perform tasks with more than one application simultaneously.

- Even if the firm uses another brand of network software, make sure the client and asset management program is compatible with Novell's *Advanced Netware 286* because it is a benchmark of the network operating system's compatibility with the computer and other hardware.

- Plan to use a client and asset management program as a major application in a multitasking operating environment with windows, so that more than one application program can be run simultaneously and can thus be accessed immediately. Plan to run either *DESQview* by Quarterdeck Office Systems or Microsoft's *Windows 286/386* as a multitasking interface with *DOS,* and make sure that other major software programs are compatible with the multitasking program.

- Asset allocation and portfolio performance measurement programs are not likely to be used on a daily basis. Therefore, they need not be network versions and they need not be run in a multitasking mode. Although their reports can, and in many cases should, be presented to clients, their best use is as analytical tools used by the planner to (1) make investment recommendations within a diversified portfolio modeled on the client's risk and return parameters and (2) measure the performance, over time, of portfolios and individual issues within portfolios.

- Data that can be entered in client and asset management programs should include essential information for updating financial plans with the current status of investment assets. Therefore make sure an asset management program interfaces (or soon will) with the comprehensive financial planning system that is now being used or being considered.

- Ask for demo versions of the software ($20–$30) for a 30-day trial period, get user lists from vendors, and ask users what kind of business they do, how they put it all together, what it costs, what it does and doesn't do, and the mistakes they made. Compare the firm's client management and communications, general practice operations, financial planning procedures, and investment management needs only with similar operations.

- Count on spending several days learning the program in depth. Pay particular attention to the breadth of data entry, the reports available, and the relative ease of use. Then, evaluate other required software and hardware in the complete system the firm is putting together.

- Be aware that not all available client and asset management programs combine the same levels of capabilities and that not all provide the same degree of performance tracking and reporting. For example, one program, *Market Manager PLUS Professional* from Dow Jones, provides very good portfolio management and performance tracking but offers only limited client communications capability and handles only 1,500 portfolios. *Broker's Notebook* from American Financial Systems is far more sophisticated in both features and accepts an unlimited number of portfolios.

  Other programs offer some degree of asset management capability and may enhance their performance analysis capability in subsequent versions. Therefore if the firm needs both client management and high-level asset allocation and portfolio management and performance reporting, choose a program that offers both or consider interfacing two specialized programs.
- If the firm is primarily a life insurance agency that markets portfolio investments to clients and needs basic portfolio management capabilities that include life insurance products, a program originally designed for prospecting and managing clients and product sales like the *Client Data System,* or *dbCAMS+ Client and Asset Management System,* may fully meet its needs for client and asset management. For programs designed specifically for insurance agents (without asset management capabilities), see the lists under "Insurance Planning and Marketing" in Appendix F.
- If the firm's primary activities center on portfolio investments for active trading accounts, seriously consider *Broker's Notebook,* which also provides excellent client management and communications capabilities. Evaluate whether the firm will also need sophisticated portfolio performance analysis and reporting. If it does, include in the survey *CENTERPIECE* from Performance Technologies, *The Professional Portfolio* (Level I) from Advent Software, and *MicroShaw* from Shaw Data Services. (See Appendix F for additional portfolio performance measurement programs.)
- If the firm is primarily or exclusively engaged in fee-based planning and markets no implementation products, but is heavily involved in investment management, it probably needs asset allocation software and high-level portfolio performance measurement software to supplement the reports produced by financial and tax planning software. It may also need a general client and office management program. Therefore consider the *dbCAMS+ Client and Asset Management System* for its global office management capabilities; Wilson Associates' *Capital Asset Management System* and Burlington Hall's *LaPorte Asset Allocation System* for asset allocation support; and *CENTERPIECE, The Professional Portfolio* (Level I), and *MicroShaw* for portfolio performance analysis. (See the list in Appendix F for additional, more expensive asset allocation and portfolio performance measurement programs.)
- If the firm chooses the financial and tax planning software of Integrated Financial Solutions, Inc. (formerly Interactive Financial Services), consider their add-on programs for client and asset management needs. (See the IFS product list under "Comprehensive Integrated Systems" in Appendix F.)

- If the firm already owns and wants to continue using a specific integrated financial planning system, inquire whether an interface has been or will be developed for it by one or more of the client and asset management program vendors.
- In all cases, determine whether the firm wants both extensive client communications and asset management capabilities in the same program. If it needs both asset and extensive client management capabilities, look at *dbCAMS+ Client and Asset Management System* and the *Client Data System* with the Investments Module. If it needs client management capabilities plus portfolio performance measurement and reporting, inquire about the interface being developed by Performance Technologies for *CENTERPIECE* and a current (but as yet undisclosed) client management program. If the firm already uses or will choose the financial planning software of Integrated Financial Solutions, Inc., or Softbridge Microsystems and needs portfolio performance measurement and reporting capabilities, consider the interfaces being developed for these systems and *CENTERPIECE*.

PART 3: FINANCIAL AND TAX PLANNING SOFTWARE

Financial and tax planning software is available in comprehensive integrated systems, as mini systems, and as "quick" planning programs. Mini systems and quick planning programs are often down-scaled and less expensive versions of comprehensive systems. In addition, several programs provide substantial needs analyses that support both product marketing and fee-based client decision making. There are also numerous stand-alone programs available for essentially all specialized focus areas of planning, including tax planning. Finally, there are miscellaneous programs that provide specialized financial calculations for specific purposes (such as education funding, real estate analysis, divorce planning, and loan amortization analysis).

The number of financial planning systems and programs and the functional differences between them make it effectively impossible for any one person or organization to evaluate them separately and make specific recommendations without knowing each potential user's needs. The diversity of stand-alone applications for focus planning and specialized applications also makes the selection process time-consuming and recommendations even more difficult to make.

Comprehensive and fully integrated systems are fewer in number. They are easier to evaluate when approached for their comprehensive and generic features. Because they also include most of the applications required in a practice, this discussion emphasizes them. The other types of planning software are described briefly under separate headings. Readers should consult the categorized lists of software in Appendix F and contact vendors about programs in the areas of their needs.

RECOMMENDATION — Financial Planning Software: No specific product recommendations are made for this type of software. Only the planner can determine what kind of financial planning the practice provides and which activities related to this service can be computerized efficiently and cost-effectively. However, if the practice is providing or plans to provide fee-based comprehensive planning, software support tools that are less capable than those provided by the best of the "premier" comprehensive systems, or by the best of the stand-alone programs for focus planning, will ultimately prove inadequate. Experience shows that even the best "premier" systems do not provide all of the support capabilities that a practice may need.

In addition, if the principals of the firm are committed to guidelines for the form and content of comprehensive financial plans presented to clients (such as those of the IAFP Registry of Financial Planning Practitioners and the Personal Financial Planning Division of the American Institute of Certified Public Accountants), these criteria should be incorporated in the evaluation of systems and programs.

The complex, repetitive, ongoing activities and procedures of providing financial planning services cannot be effectively and profitably conducted unless the practice is prepared to manage them with automated efficiencies. Practice computerization should begin or be upgraded with a flexible, comprehensive information management system that provides for sharing entered information on clients and their assets with financial planning software. Therefore it is strongly recommended that the firm organize and computerize general practice, client, and asset management procedures before purchasing financial planning software or upgrading current equipment.

RECOMMENDATION — Financial and Tax Planning Software: The firm could also recommend to clients who own computers that they use a personal finance and check-writing software program. Clients who use these programs can provide an enormous advantage to planners because a great deal of preliminary financial planning information will already have been assembled. (See the list under "Personal Finance, Cash Flow Analysis, and Check-Writing Programs" in Appendix F for several popular programs.)

Further, computerized clients can also consider using a software program for preparing their federal income tax returns. Several of these programs link with and share processed data from one or more of the personal finance and check-writing packages. (See the list under "Income Tax Return Preparation Programs" in Appendix F.)

Comprehensive Integrated Systems

The term *integrated* as used in financial and tax planning software evolved when software vendors began to integrate individual applications in a packaged system. This system requires the entry of one set of data to be shared throughout the system's computations, calculations, projections, and reporting. Because comprehensive integrated systems are very powerful, they appeal to planners with large client bases who produce and periodically update a large number of financial plans. In this sense, integrated systems have helped standardize comprehensive planning. However, they do have their limitations.

Integrated data entry and processing is variously defined by product vendors. Some imply that the entry of information on a financial asset or transaction automatically generates the tax consequences and consolidates these consequences with those of all similar transactions and applications. Unfortunately, this is not always the case. Frequently, additional information must be entered to produce accurate consolidated financial and tax results.

Integration is meaningful and reliable only when initially entered data include (or can include) all related items required for processing the data, tracking individually entered items, and producing accurate reports. In a truly integrated system, reports should keep continuous accounts of cash flows, investment assets, and their associated tax consequences through all transactions in all planning scenarios. Beware of claims of "complete integration" of entered data items when a close examination of actual data gathering sheets and screen input reveals that they are too simplistic to support the claims. Report output from elementary data entries will inevitably provide incomplete and misleading projections and tax computations for investment assets and cash flows, retirement assets, estate transfers, and other tax-related computations.

NOTE: Integrated data entry in financial planning software should be evaluated in relation to the quality and meaningfulness of system processing, tracking, and reporting of entered items. This means that the two most important criteria in evaluating them are (1) the breadth, depth, and interrelatedness of entry items for assets, cash flows, and taxes, and (2) the breadth, depth, interrelatedness, and accuracy of reporting on these entered items. Data entries for all information for which the practice requires processing and reports for financial planning purposes should be accepted by the system. Generally, the best way to evaluate a system's processing and reporting capabilities is through careful, detailed examination of the data entry sheets provided for collecting client information, the data entry screens in the system itself, and the reports the system produces. The user should be able to track each data item from its initial entry to its appearance or processed result in all relevant printed reports. If these details in the system seem inadequate, extensive hands-on testing will not be worthwhile.

Comprehensive and fully integrated financial planning systems permit the user to choose a configuration of related and linked software applications that will perform most of the tasks normally associated with analyzing, developing, and reporting comprehensively on clients' current and projected financial and tax liability positions.

Their comprehensiveness is measured by the quality and depth of their coverage of all focus areas of planning.

Typically, a comprehensive integrated system includes essential programs that

- collect and organize client information
- prepare financial and tax profiles
- project these profiles into a finite future (at least 5 years)
- create alternative profiles (what-if modeling) for analyzing potential consequences of various planning assumptions (such as death, disability, retirement, estate planning, inflation, and asset growth rates)
- produce a series of textual and numeric reports that recompute and reprocess all information already entered in the system
- merge financial profile computations with formatted text from a word processor

These systems generally include or can be interfaced with

- sophisticated word processing with dictionary, thesaurus, and desktop printing features
- a high-level financial and tax analysis program
- a graphics program to produce graphs, charts, and visual presentation materials
- a client and asset tracking and management program or facility (usually an integrated database)—or, alternatively, an interface capability with stand-alone client and asset management programs (as described in Part 2)

In addition to numerical report content with textual headnotes, most of the systems also provide more extensive analytical text or "client education" boilerplate that can be customized, replaced, or added to by the user.

The most widely integrated systems (such as those marketed by ABACUS Data Systems, International Financial Data Systems, Interactive Financial Solutions, Confidential Planning Services, Leonard Financial Planning Systems, Sawhney Software, Softbridge Microsystems Corporation, and Sterling Wentworth Corporation) are packaged with most of the essential elements of a comprehensive system. Several can be interfaced with industry standard databases and spreadsheets and with alternative word processing and graphics programs. Recently, interfaces with several of these systems have been developed by the vendors of client and asset management programs discussed in Part 2.

Any one of these comprehensive systems could possibly fulfill the basic processing and reporting needs of a financial planning practice. Nevertheless, each should be examined for as close a correlation as possible between the practice's requirements and the capabilities of the system.

Beyond basics, the systems can be quite different from one another. They vary in their planning approach, comprehensiveness, implementation of reliable federal and state tax computations, flexibility, ease of use, and user support. They also vary widely in the breadth, depth (as distinguished from mere volume), and presentational clarity of report output. Some include "expert system" programming. This programming consists of a set of decision rules activated by certain entered information to provide automated analyses and planning recommendations. These recommendations are based on what an expert might recommend as a general rule of thumb. (Expert systems include *PLANMAN PLUS,* from Sterling Wentworth Corporation and *Softbridge Financial Planner,* from Softbridge Microsystems.)

All of the integrated systems mentioned can be run on IBM PC/XT/AT and other fully compatible computers with a hard disk and 640K of memory. They can also be run on IBM PS/2 models. Most can be used in a local area network (LAN); some are available in customized network versions. Integrated systems require considerable disk storage capacity (ranging from 3 to 10 megabytes). Several of them can also be linked through a telephone modem to online securities price update services (such as Dow Jones News/Retrieval). Only one comprehensive integrated system is currently available for running on the Macintosh computer (*Financial Master* from Strategic Planning Systems — it is also available for IBM computers and compatibles, but must be run under Microsoft *Windows*).

The complete versions of comprehensive integrated systems range in price from $995 to more than $6,000. In early 1987, Confidential Planning Services dramatically lowered the price of *ProPlan.* Later, IFDS lowered prices on its graduated Professional Series. Recently, both Sawhney Software and ABACUS Data Systems lowered the price of their premier systems from the $6,000 range to $995. (See vendor information under "Comprehensive Integrated Systems" in Appendix F for exact pricing.)

As of this writing, vendors of other major integrated systems seem committed to maintaining current prices. Nevertheless, the clear trend is toward significantly lower prices than were common just 2 years ago. One effect of this development is that there are now more systems than before in the price range of $1,000–$3,000. This makes selection simultaneously more complicated and more reasonable in relation to user needs and budgets. (See the complete list of planning systems and programs in Appendix F for current prices.)

Mini, "Quick," and Needs Analysis Systems and Programs

Down-sized versions of most integrated systems have been developed by "unbundling" (modularizing) the systems. "Quick planning" versions of integrated systems have also been produced to appeal to users with less than integrated, comprehensive planning needs, or to users engaged in extensive product marketing. These versions require fewer data entries and produce less extensive computations and projections. Thus, the planner can choose a graduated approach to the whole system by starting with the basic computation, projection, and reporting capabilities and adding component modularized applications as they are needed (such as word processing, graphics, long-range planning, estate planning, and client and asset management). In other systems, the planner can graduate from the basic or "quick" version to the whole, or to an intermediate version, in one or two steps.

Mini or "quick" planning systems are available from International Financial Data Systems, Lumen Systems, Leonard Financial Planning Systems, Softbridge Microsystems Corporation, Sterling Wentworth Corporation, Summit Innovative Systems, Inc., Perception Software Systems, Financial Planning Systems, Inc., Micro Planning Systems, First Financial Software, and other vendors. (See the list under "Mini and Quick Planning Systems" in Appendix F.) These are either down-scaled versions of comprehensive integrated systems or less sophisticated, less integrated, less comprehensive, and less expensive systems designed to support planning in the middle markets with volume product marketing. Several are excellent for these purposes. The products from IFDS, Leonard Financial Planning Systems, Financial Planning Systems, Perception Software, and Softbridge Microsystems are particularly worth examining. However, it cannot be overemphasized that the firm should thoroughly test the capabilities of this type of software in relation to carefully determined practice needs.

Putting together an integrated system incrementally usually costs more than buying the complete system initially. However, if the down-scaled version really meets the firm's needs, it may be more cost-effective to begin this way because it reduces initial costs and training time. It also avoids the common tendency to overbuy and underuse the full power of a comprehensive integrated system. Base prices for mini or "quick" planning versions of larger systems usually begin at $1,500–$2,500.

In addition, the category of "Financial Planning Programs and Needs Analyses" in Appendix F includes numerous programs that are not comprehensive or integrated and are not, strictly speaking, mini or "quick" planning systems. Rather, they are essentially needs analysis applications for selected focus areas of planning. These programs fall into two major types. The first type (including most of the programs listed in Appendix F) is designed specifically to support volume product marketing. The second type (including *Future$sight* from Personal $trategic Planners, *Integrate!* from Malgoire Drucker, and *Personal Financial Planning* from Mayer Hoffman McCann) is designed specifically to support interactive client decision making in relation to clearly determined financial goals. (For this reason they are well suited for use in a fee-based practice.) Several programs of both types are well conceived and affordably priced for these purposes.

New practitioners and practitioners primarily involved in product marketing may find that mini and "quick" planning systems provide the optimum level and quality of computerized support for the financial plans they produce. Others who are primarily or exclusively involved in product marketing, or who require only basic calculations and projections directly related to the client's clearly determined financial goals (and who may not require a comprehensive system's voluminous report output capabilities) may find the needs analysis programs more suited to their practice needs.

Stand-Alone Programs for Focus Planning

Stand-alone application programs designed for focus areas of financial planning are too numerous to analyze or even describe separately. If all of them (1) required standardized data entry, (2) were programmed in the same language, (3) produced standardized, cohesive reports using the same terminology and planning concepts, (4) interfaced seamlessly with each other, and (5) were compatible with a specific computer standard and operating system, an ideal planning system could be assembled for each practice's specific needs.

The component parts of a computerized system should be as linkable as those of an audio system. Unfortunately, the industry has yet to produce such commodity choices and shows little interest in doing so. Lack of standardization in software programming is an obstacle, and so is the lack of a standard definition of financial planning and delivery procedures.

Because of these limitations, stand-alone application software cannot be used for more than a limited range of financial planning applications within the comprehensive practice scope. Stand-alone programs represent a compromise — albeit, in some cases, a desirable compromise — by providing software that is specialized in focus areas of planning (for example, investment management, retirement and employee benefit planning, estate planning, tax planning and income tax return preparation, insurance planning) or that require only specific calculational, "number-crunching" support tools.

Many stand-alone programs for focus planning are very sophisticated and well designed; some provide more in-depth analysis than do comparable applications in integrated systems. Their primary disadvantage is that using more than one of them for the same client requires multiple entries of the same data. However, several of these programs provide file formats (or file transfer capability) that are compatible with standard spreadsheets and databases. The sections on programs for focus areas of planning in Appendix F provide vendor and product information for a wide range of stand-alone applications; the last section, "Miscellaneous Applications," lists numerous programs designed for more limited calculational and analytical tasks.

Service Bureaus

An earlier phase of financial planning software is represented by time-sharing systems in which applications are run from powerful mainframe computers maintained by service bureaus. These systems are costly, difficult to use, not easy to customize (if at all), and usually severely limited in what-if modeling capability. They have been largely replaced by the personal computer and its wider range of interactive planning software, by in-house service bureaus (as in certain large insurance companies and broker-dealers), or by service bureaus established by product vendors whose clients use their software (for example, Interactive Financial Solutions).

Another type of service bureau sells a low-cost plan-production capability derived from a data collection questionnaire that permits the financial services representative to make specific implementation recommendations. These service bureaus provide the financial plan itself at either no cost or at a markup (for example, the Consumer Finance Institute, recently acquired by Price, Waterhouse & Co., and The PlanFirst Company). The plans are designed as marketing tools for product sales.

PART 4: EVALUATING FINANCIAL AND TAX PLANNING SOFTWARE

Although specific financial and tax planning software needs vary from one practice to another, the general requirements for a comprehensive integrated system are similar. Many of their features are also applicable to an evaluation of down-scaled "quick" and mini planning systems. Within the focus areas of planning they include, their features can also be used to evaluate requirements in stand-alone programs for specialized focus areas.

Generally, it is time-consuming to evaluate this software and identify the most suitable types for the needs of a particular practice. The evaluation checklists below are not intended to cover every single feature of a system, but rather to provide criteria for specific representative features that can help the firm evaluate overall system capabilities in relation to practice needs. They should save planners time by providing a guideline to hands-on evaluation of any software systems and programs for focus areas of planning. If the checklist features are more advanced than the firm's requirements, scale back the performance criteria expected so that they match actual practice needs.

NOTE: Evaluating any financial planning software that is not fully integrated and comprehensive increases the importance of the user's actual practice needs. Comprehensive systems typically include so many powerful features that they are rarely if ever fully used: a practice can usually grow with them. Mini and "quick" planning programs and systems are often equally well suited for the applications they are designed to support. Nevertheless, most have distinct limitations in what they can do.

General Capabilities

The first item to examine is the system's overall planning support capabilities. Comprehensive integrated systems should support the following focus areas in which the practice currently offers or will offer planning services: cash flow and personal liability management, individual income tax planning, risk management, investment planning and management, business and professional practice ownership interests, deferred compensation and employee benefits, economic independence and retirement, and estate conservation and distribution, with integrated tax computations and projections. The system should provide complete, basic financial statements (such as a cash flow statement, balance sheet, income statement, and supporting tax statement) under alternative planning scenarios.

Evaluate specific systems capabilities as follows:

- Can the system produce personalized financial profiles for a variety of clients with different needs and objectives and project these profiles into future years? If so, for how many years?
- Once data for a client's current status are entered, can the system produce alternative profiles analyzing financial independence in what-if situations for any desired year, such as
  - the client and spouse's retirement
  - the client and spouse's disability
  - the client and spouse's death
- Can the system's alternative profile components show, use, or compute for
  - year-by-year items of income and asset balances after withdrawals begin
  - capital conservation or depletion options in determining cash needs

   – specified client mortality age
   – default standard mortality tables (which ones?)
   – inflation factor in determining the client's cash needs
   – present value of long-range cash needs
   – optional present-value discount factor
   – client's assets segregated into personal and investment use
 • Does the system provide estate distribution reports, marital deduction analysis, simulated estate settlement computations, and estate taxes under different types of wills in two estates?
 • Is there an automatic cash management capability that
   – simulates net aftertax effects of investing surplus cash in a number of different types of investments
   – predefines investments by their characteristics, dollar limits, or percentages of cash allocation in any given year
   – automatically liquidates debt
 • Does the system analyze investments in portfolios by
   – providing year-by-year performance
   – summarizing performance over the planning time frame
   – calculating the present values of cash inflows and outflows
   – calculating and reporting aftertax, internal, and adjusted rates of return for each investment
 • Can the system analyze educational funding alternatives for
   – more than one child with varying expenses and varying numbers of years in college
   – each child on a year-by-year and month-by-month basis
   – total expenses for all children
   – lump-sum payments for expenses now or at any time before the expenses begin
   – aftertax funding versus funding with a gift
   – average costs of schools by type and geographic region from an updated database
 • Can you enter quantitative information in as much or as little detail as you choose, with options to
   – specify the values and growth or decline rates or amounts for each item of information entered
   – enter information on financial products in alternative ways
   – link information to a central information base
 • Short of comprehensive financial planning, does the system provide general utilities programs to
   – analyze mortgages
   – accumulate money at a specified growth and/or contribution rate for a specified time
   – amortize a loan
   – fund various components of future financial events

Comprehensiveness

The system's comprehensive capabilities are equally important. Superficial implementation of necessary capabilities can convey a false sense of security while you are developing a plan.

Evaluate a system for the following representative details:

- Can the individual characteristics of each asset and investment be classified as to
  - form of ownership (client, spouse, joint, community, trust)
  - whether the item passes to the surviving spouse at the owner's death
  - the owner's objective for holding the item
  - the item's market risk level
  - the item's liquidity status for purposes of cash needs
- Can the system accept entries for various cash-equivalent assets and specify their idiosyncrasies, such as
  - withdrawal of interest as cash
  - reinvestment of interest within the asset
  - specified tax consequences of the asset
  - deposits and withdrawals after the first year
  - system computation of capital gain on sales and withdrawals
- Can the system provide detailed data on traded securities and
  - automatically update their current prices from imported information
  - keep track of the cost basis of securities, including each item of each lot
  - account for purchases and sales in projection years
  - automatically compute capital gain or loss
  - apply the FIFO method of accounting for sales
  - substitute the LIFO method or override the FIFO method when needed
  - calculate appreciation and account for buying and selling taking place at the same time
  - specify dividends based on the number of securities or their fair market value
  - automatically reinvest dividends
- How thoroughly are tax-favored investments and limited partnerships handled? Does the system account for
  - depreciation of assets as tax law requires
  - difference between active and passive investment activity
  - investment interest limits and carryovers
  - sales
  - passive loss deductibility
  - balloon payments to liquidate notes
  - the financial relationship of one investment with another for tax purposes
  - current yield, internal rate of return, and adjusted rate of return
- What type of retirement plan formats are built into the system? Is there a generic format used to define unusual situations? Can the system
  - accommodate IRA contributions for deductibility and for maximum permitted contributions regardless of deductibility
    - handle the contributions, deductions, and accumulations of Keogh plans

- account for voluntary aftertax employee contributions to company retirement plans to which an employer company is also contributing
- distinguish between the different retirements of the client and the spouse for purposes of contributions, deductions, and separate accumulation
- account for income from part-time work after retirement
- account for variable postretirement living expenses — that is, expenses that inflate, expenses that don't inflate, expenses that terminate, and so on
- Can the system handle computations triggered by the offering, exercise, execution, or termination of company-provided benefit plans such as incentive stock options, stock appreciation rights, nonqualified stock options, employee stock-purchase plans, deferred compensation, and profit-sharing plans?
- How thoroughly does the system support insurance planning?
  - Does it contain formats for medical, life, disability, homeowners, auto, and general liability insurance?
  - Can it analyze life insurance coverages for the cash needs of a surviving spouse and children?
  - Can it measure and analyze the disability insurance need for both client and spouse?
  - Does it factor liquid assets and retirement plans when determining the need for life or disability income insurance?
  - Does it factor taxes and estate liquidity when determining life insurance needs?
  - Does it permit life insurance proceeds to meet expenses and liability settlements at death?
  - Does it provide for variable asset growth rates within life insurance policies?
  - Does it account for tax-deferred compounding of asset growth and income?
  - Does it provide for using life insurance for purposes of interim goal funding (such as education expenses of children, survivors' limited-term needs)?
- Does the system account for amortized notes receivable, as when cash inflow is interest only or all or part of principal payments is to be treated as capital gain instead of ordinary income?
- Can you enter the details of a client's business partnership and have the system automatically use this information to determine
  - business income subject to self-employment tax
  - a running account of business cash flow and income, or assets purchased or sold
  - value of the business
  - value of a key employee
- Can you indicate the various components of a client's small-business C corporation or S corporation both for the company and the client's individual ownership share? For example, can the system show
  - the corporation's net income
  - a running account of corporate cash flow, including income, expenses, purchases, sales, borrowings, retained earnings, and cash distributions
  - the client's ordinary income

- the pro rata share of capital gain, tax preferences, and tax credits passed through to the client
- Does the system contain integrated amortization computations for
  - automatic tax deductions for home mortgage interest
  - payments made for amortized loans as items of cash outflow
  - variable-rate mortgages
  - the terms of a past or future loan and its effects in the planning period
  - interest-only loans
  - balloon payments on loans
- Can the system show detailed consequences of social security benefits, including the maximum ceiling for wage bases in future years and retirement benefits? Can past wage levels be optionally selected and projections of benefits at less than 100 percent chosen?

Tax Law Implementation

The accuracy and depth of the system's implementation of income tax law and estate tax law is as important as the financial computations on which you base analyses and recommendations. Make sure the system provides the necessary computations and reports that the firm's clientele will want now and as the practice develops.

NOTE: For all systems considered, decide first what level of integrated federal and state income, estate, and social security tax computations the firm requires throughout the system's reporting capabilities. This is one of the most significant variables in the reliability of all available systems and programs.

Evaluate a system for the following features:

- Does the system automatically perform tax computations and print supporting information for
  - regular tax based on filing status
  - social security and self-employment taxes
  - 5- and 10-year averaging tax on lump-sum distributions
  - tax preferences when accelerated depreciation is elected
  - alternative minimum tax
  - passive-loss limitations and carryovers
  - investment interest deduction limitations and carryovers
  - capital loss limitations and carryovers
  - net operating losses with carrybacks and carryforwards
- Are deductibility limits imposed on
  - phased-in personal interest expenses
  - medical expenses
  - charitable contributions with applicable carryovers

- casualty losses
- other Schedule A deductions
- Does the system include detailed state and local tax computations, integrated, as necessary, with federal taxes?
- Can you select the time of payment of federal and state income taxes, and can payments be
  - indicated as predetermined amounts
  - calculated as a percentage of the current or the previous year's tax liability
  - prepaid for state income tax
  - paid as a percentage of taxes owed in a given year and carried by the system for a tax due or a refund amount
- Does the system automatically compute projected estate taxes and the marital deduction based on the information entered and the options selected? Can it
  - indicate estate administration expenses as a predetermined amount or as a percentage of the adjusted gross estate
  - show state estate taxes based on either gross estate, adjusted gross estate, or taxable estate
  - automatically compute the federal credit for state taxes

Flexibility and Ease of Use

Few clients have identical financial profiles. Few planning practices have identical clients. You need a flexible planning system to accommodate different clients and their varying situations. You also need one that is relatively easy to use and whose full features can be implemented as you need them.

Evaluate a system for the following features:

- Can you make multiple entries—without limit, in any order, with intermediate totals computed and shown as entered—for entry items such as assets, income, and expenses, including their growth or decline factors?
- Can you print reports for an opened case at any time before having entered all information? Can you
  - customize or personalize the title of each entry
  - perform a query and search on command for a specific entered item
  - review the type and volume of data entry items contained in an entered case
- Is the entire system menu driven? Does it provide
  - a context-sensitive help key
  - help at each transaction point
  - error checks as data are entered
  - a clear and intelligible user guide with a topical index
- Does the system come with an information questionnaire or fact finder that
  - facilitates clients' furnishing their own information
  - provides a complete set of data entry sheets
  - prints additional data entry sheets
  - provides a page-to-screen format relationship for data entry sheets
  - provides data entry sheets captioned in clear English rather than codes

Reports

The system's planning reports should reflect the firm's professional image and practice style. Both planners and clients should feel comfortable with their format, content, and depth. Content should be designed to motivate clients to decisive action rather than furnish them with superfluous boilerplate and redundant information.

Evaluate a system for the following reporting features:

- Does the system produce a full set of financial statements, including (at least) an income statement, a supporting tax statement, a cash flow statement, a balance sheet, an investment and portfolio analysis, a long-range economic independence analysis, an estate distribution analysis, and a capital needs analysis (including insurance)?
- Do the system's reports cover in sufficient depth the range of reporting criteria supported by professional standards (such as those promulgated by the Registry of Financial Planning Practitioners)?
- Can both planners and clients easily read and understand the format of the financial statements the system produces?
  - Is this format generally acceptable to accountants?
  - Can you change the format?
  - For how many sequential years can the system print reports?
  - Can you select years for reports to be printed?
  - Can you specify reports in varying degrees of detail?
  - Does the system use the high-quality print features of your printer to emphasize headers and titles?
  - Does the system do the same for laser printers?
- Is the system integrated with a word processing program?
  - Does it automatically merge case information in a standardized report text?
  - Does the sample text provided with the system contain what-if logic for automatic selection of appropriate text and numbers for each planning case?
  - Is this text acceptable and usable without modifications?
  - Can text be edited, changed, added to, reformatted?
  - Does the system provide a list of text data variables with descriptions to help you write your own report text?
  - Can you write your own paragraphs and selectively substitute them for rejected report text?
- Does the system interface (link for data transfer) with more than one word processing program?
- Is the system integrated with a graphics presentation program?
  - Does the system automatically produce basic graphs, bar charts, and pie charts?
  - Can these formats be changed?
  - Can you write your own formats for new graphs?
- Does the system interface (link for data transfer) with more than one graphics presentation program?
- Is report printing menu driven?

- Once data are entered, can you produce reports in a batch process without having to go through each report menu?
- Can you preview reports on screen before printing hard copy?
- Can you cancel the printing cycle before reports are completed?
- Do the reports automatically exclude data entry formats that may have been opened but do not contain any entered information?

The Whole System

After you have evaluated specific performance features, carefully examine them as a system of integrated applications covering the focus areas of planning.

Evaluate for the following overall system features:

- Is the system available only as a single package or can it be bought in integrated modules or in an abbreviated version?
  - How much does the basic system or abbreviated version cost (that is, the engine and drive train without comprehensive applications)?
  - What is the average cost per module or increment toward the full system?
  - What are the annual maintenance costs for these scaled-down versions?
  - How much does the full system cost?
  - What is the annual maintenance cost for the full system? What services are included? What contingencies and costs are the responsibility of the user?
  - Is the entire modularized system seamlessly integrated, including word processing and graphics?
  - Is a trial version of the system available?
  - Is there a full refund policy on the purchase price of the system? How long is a refund available?
- How long does it take to enter an average planning case of about 100 pieces of information? How long does the system take to perform computations for a 10-year profile on an IBM AT, or compatible, running at 8 MHz cycle speed?
- What are the system's floppy and hard disk requirements?
  - How many megabytes of hard disk storage are required for the entire system?
  - How much conventional memory is required to run the system?
  - How many bytes does an average planning case require when stored on a hard disk?
  - Can planning cases be stored on diskettes?
  - Is the system available on both $5\frac{1}{4}$ and $3\frac{1}{2}$ inch diskettes?
- Can the system be networked?
  - Is it a multiuser system? What are the additional costs of the network version (or of multiple copies for one site)?
  - Can planners with terminals at various locations run the system?
  - Is a security password access included for multiple users?
- Will the system run compatibly with the leading multitasking interfaces and operating environments (*DESQview* and *Windows*)?
- Does the system interface (link for data transfer) with one or more client and asset management programs? With spreadsheets and databases?
  - Is the interface two-way or one-way?

     – Do other program vendors plan interfaces with the system?
- How long does it take to learn the system before using it the first time?
  - How much formal training will you need?
  - Where is the training available? Who pays for it?
  - Does the system come with tutorial materials?

The Vendor

The system can be only as good as the people who stand behind it. Purchasing an integrated system is an important and expensive decision, and you may have to live with it for a long time.

Evaluate the software vendor on the following criteria:

- How long has the vendor been in business?
  - When did the vendor first publish an integrated financial planning system, and how many enhanced versions has the vendor released?
  - How many federal tax law changes has the vendor implemented since the first version?
  - How long did it take on average to release the update after a tax law change?
  - What was the longest time lag for providing updates?
- What are the financial planning credentials and competencies of the vendor or of the vendor's staff?
- How easy is it to access technical support by telephone (hours available in your time zone), and how quickly can you get an emergency repair or replacement?
- Are local references available from current users? Is there a users' group in your area?

PART 5: COMPUTERIZATION AND PRACTICE MARKETING

The financial planning process is a sophisticated, integrated strategy for effectively marketing a broad range of financial services and products. In whatever way the planning firm uses computerized support to develop a communications and marketing strategy, its ultimate focus will be on a communications document or documents to be disseminated to clients and prospective clients. The information base assembled on each client or prospective client provides the beginning point for developing a focused practice marketing strategy aimed at meeting clients' and prospective clients' needs for financial services and products. The effective link between these two strategies is communications. Implementing this communications link without computerizing the most repetitive aspects of it is unimaginable.

The utilities and efficiencies provided by computerization enable planners to generate specific applications of marketing strategies and techniques. These strategies and techniques must be practice-specific; they must derive from procedures and delivery methods that are consistent with the kind of practice the firm conducts or wants to develop.

Whatever the practice's marketing strategy, its essence is communications. Adherence to the practices and procedures of the planning process with appropriate computerized support can extend the firm's marketing opportunities and enhance its clients' perceptions of the personalized services it offers. In the final analysis, successfully managing the financial planning practice and effectively marketing its services and products cannot be separated from managing the *computerized* practice.[1] Only when the firm has installed the tools needed to implement a marketing strategy can it fully realize the creative potential of those tools.

Note

1. For a systematic treatment of the planning process, including sample planning cases produced with software, see Dale S. Johnson and Jai P. Sawhney, *Financial Planning: Practice and Procedure* (Prentice-Hall, Inc., 1988).

12

Regulation of Financial Planners

Jeffrey B. Kelvin*

It is well settled that financial planning continues to evolve. It is an emergent profession. In the late 1970s and early 1980s when the proliferation of financial planners, plans, and products became evident, several committees in Congress grew concerned that, due to this growth in the industry, additional regulation would be necessary. There was talk in Washington at that time of new statutes and regulations to specifically cover the activities of financial planners so that consumers could be adequately protected. Much of this talk, of course, was precipitated by relatively isolated horror stories involving fraud and abuse.

The United States Securities and Exchange Commission became alarmed at the prospect of new legislation in this area since the agency felt that regulation of financial planners was its turf. When taking this position with Congress, the SEC was urged to develop a clear and concise position on the subject of what specific activities undertaken by financial services professionals would trigger the application of the existing federal securities laws. This was felt by the Congress to be an approach which could remove the need for new legislation.

CONDITIONS UNDER WHICH THE FINANCIAL SERVICES PROFESSIONAL'S ACTIVITIES ARE SUBJECT TO FEDERAL REGULATION

The Securities and Exchange Commission took the position that the Investment Advisers Act of 1940 was the statutory body of law which should control the area of regulation of financial planners. It is true that this legislation had been enacted 40 years earlier in a postdepression era during which a legislative framework to police and control the activities of discretionary money managers was the primary objective. However, the SEC in the early 1980s took the position that this same statute should be applied to the activities of financial planners. In August 1981, the Securities and Exchange Commission released its now famous Release No. IA-770. This pronouncement set forth three separate tests which were to be applied to the activities of financial planners. In the event that all three tests were answered in the affirmative, the SEC took the position that the Investment Advisers Act of 1940 would apply to the planner's activities. If, on the other hand, any one of the three tests could not be answered in the affirmative, the Investment Advisers Act of 1940 would not apply to these professional activities. Let us review these three tests separately.

---

*Jeffrey B. Kelvin, JD, LLM, CLU, ChFC, is associate professor of taxation at The American College.

Advice or Analyses about Securities

The first test under IA-770 set forth the question of whether the financial services professional provides "advice or analyses" about a security. Since the term *security* is very broadly defined for federal securities law purposes, it can include a great many financial instruments in addition to the best-known securities, like common stocks or bonds. For example, the definition includes a certificate of deposit, commercial paper, a limited partnership, or even variable life insurance or variable annuity products. The official definition of the term *security* as set forth by Sec. 80b-2(a)(18) of the Investment Advisers Act of 1940 is as follows:

> Any note, stock, Treasury stock, bond, debenture, evidence of indebtedness, certificate of interest or participation in any profit-sharing agreement, collateral trust certificate, preorganization certificate or subscription, transferable share, investment contract, voting-trust certificate, certificate of deposit for a security, fractional undivided interest in oil, gas, or other mineral rights, or in general, any instrument or interest commonly known as a *security,* or any certificate of interest or participation in, temporary or interim certificate for, receipt for, or guarantee of, or warrant or right to subscribe to or purchase any of the foregoing.

It is clear based on the breadth and scope of the definitions under this first test, that financial services professionals will invariably become involved with providing advice about securities.

The Business Standard

The second test as set forth by SEC Release IA-770 concerns whether the financial services professional is presented to the public as being "in the business" of providing advice about securities. This issue is answered by examining how the practitioner's services are communicated to the public. What is printed on the practitioner's business card or on the front door of the office? What does the telephone book advertisement say? How is the telephone answered? What is stated on the business card and letterhead? In short, does the practitioner raise any implication that he or she provides any advice about securities? All of these factors are pertinent in deciding whether the financial services professional is "in the business" of providing advice about securities.

The Compensation Test

The last test contained in the SEC release is perhaps the simplest one to apply, and yet the least understood. The issue concerns compensation received by the practitioner, and the test is met regardless of the source of payment. Therefore although a practitioner who charges a fee to a client for the provision of investment advice will easily meet the third test of IA-770, one who charges no fee but does receive a commission on the sale of a securities product will also meet this test. In point of fact, in the current environment it is practically impossible for a financial services professional to fail to meet this third test.

If all three of these tests are applicable to the specific activities of a financial services professional, the terms and provisions of the Investment Advisers Act of 1940 will apply.

SUBSEQUENT REAFFIRMATION OF SEC RELEASE NO. IA-770

SEC Release No. IA-770 was a landmark ruling from the SEC. As the financial planning profession continued to emerge in the mid to late 1980s, many individuals and groups called upon the Securities and Exchange Commission to comment once again on the three tests which had been set forth by IA-770 a few years earlier. It was felt by some that the original three-test approach might no longer be held applicable by the SEC. In October 1987, in response to multiple requests from various segments of the financial services community, the Securities and Exchange Commission announced the release of IA-1092. This pronouncement is significant since it totally reaffirms the three-pronged approach which had earlier been set forth by IA-770.

Therefore the original application by the Securities and Exchange Commission of the three-test approach still applies. As a practical matter, any financial services professional who by reason of his or her activities must answer all three tests in the affirmative will have those activities subjected to the Investment Advisers Act of 1940 at the federal level.

In addition to total reaffirmation of the three-step test of IA-770, however, IA-1092 devoted renewed attention to the antifraud provisions of the Investment Advisers Act of 1940. These provisions are designed to protect consumers who use the services of investment advisers.

The 1987 release cites *SEC v. Capital Gains Research Bureau,* a Supreme Court case discussing the antifraud provisions. That case held that "an investment adviser is a fiduciary who owes his [sic] client an affirmative duty of utmost good faith, and full and fair disclosure of all material facts." As a general matter, the release states that an adviser must disclose to clients all material facts regarding potential conflicts of interest. In this way, the client can make an informed decision about entering into or continuing an advisory relationship with the adviser.

The release includes selected interpretive and no-action letters illustrating the scope of the duty to disclose material information in certain situations involving conflicts of interest. Additional disclosure might be required, depending upon the circumstances, if the investment adviser recommends that clients execute securities transactions through the broker/dealer with which the investment adviser is associated. In addition, the investment adviser is required to inform clients that they may execute recommended transactions through other brokers or dealers.

Release IA-1092 goes on to set forth specific examples of situations that require full disclosure on the investment adviser's filing statement with the SEC. Points raised by IA-1092 in the antifraud/full disclosure area include the following:

• An adviser who intends to implement, in whole or in part, the financial plan prepared for clients through the broker/dealer or insurance company with which the adviser is associated, must inform the clients that in implementing the plan the adviser will also act as agent for that firm.

- An investment adviser who is also a registered representative of a broker/dealer and who provides investment advisory services outside the scope of employment with the broker/dealer, must disclose to advisory clients that the advisory activities are independent of employment with the broker/dealer. Additional disclosure might be required, depending upon the circumstances, if an adviser recommends that a client execute securities transactions through the broker/dealer with which the adviser is associated. For example, an adviser is required to fully disclose the nature and extent of any personal interest in such a recommendation, including any compensation that would be received from the broker/dealer in connection with the transaction. In addition, an adviser is required to inform clients that they may execute recommended transactions with other broker/dealers.
- A financial planner who recommends and uses only the financial products offered by the broker/dealer by which the financial planner is employed should disclose this practice and inform clients that the plan may be limited by such products.
- An investment adviser must not effect transactions in which he or she has a personal interest if this could result in the adviser's preferring his or her own interest to that of the advisory clients.
- An adviser who structures personal securities transactions and then trades on the market result caused by his or her recommendation to clients must disclose this practice.
- An investment adviser must disclose compensation received from the issuer of a security that the adviser recommends.

EXEMPTIONS FROM THE INVESTMENT ADVISERS ACT OF 1940

It should be noted that despite the foregoing, there are six exempted areas of activities specifically set forth in the Investment Advisers Act of 1940. These exemptions could have the effect of eliminating the need for the financial services professional to be subjected to the mandates of the statute. The six exempted areas:

- any bank or bank holding company as defined in the Bank Holding Company Act of 1956 that is not an investment company
- any lawyer, accountant, engineer, or teacher, if the performance of advisory services by any of these is solely incidental to the practice of his or her profession
- any broker, dealer, or registered representative thereof whose performance of advisory services is solely incidental to the conduct of his or her business as a broker or dealer and who receives no "special compensation" for his or her services
- the publisher of any newspaper, news magazine, or business or financial publication of general or regular circulation
- any person whose advice, analyses, or reports relate only to securities that are direct obligations of or obligations guaranteed as to principal or interest by the United States of America

- such other persons not within the intent of the law as the Securities and Exchange Commission may designate by rules and regulations or order

There are three other groups of individuals who, although they fall within the definition of investment adviser, are nevertheless exempt from registration. One exemption is for any investment adviser whose clients are all residents of the state within which the investment adviser maintains the principal office and place of business and who does not furnish advice or issue analyses or reports with respect to listed securities or securities admitted to unlisted trading privileges on any national securities exchange. The second exemption from registration applies to investment advisers whose only clients are insurance companies. Third, an exemption is provided for investment advisers who, during the course of the preceding 12 months, have had fewer than 15 clients and who neither present themselves to the general public as investment advisers nor act as investment advisers to any investment company registered under the Investment Company Act of 1940.

In summary, the three groups of individuals discussed in the preceding paragraph are exempt from registration with the Securities and Exchange Commission even though they are considered investment advisers under the act. They must still comply with the act's antifraud provisions. On the other hand, an individual who falls into one of the six exception categories mentioned above will not be covered by the antifraud provisions and the Investment Advisers Act of 1940 does not apply to any of their activities.

RESPONSIBILITIES OF FINANCIAL PLANNERS WHO ARE COVERED BY THE INVESTMENT ADVISERS ACT OF 1940

Assume that the activities of financial planners meet all three of the above discussed tests of SEC Release No. IA-770. What are the specific responsibilities facing the financial services professional in this context? There are seven separate categories of responsibilities that need to be met: registration, record keeping, charging of fees, assignment of contracts, use of labels, delivery of brochures, and avoidance of fraudulent practices. These responsibilities are discussed in the following sections of this chapter.

Registration as a Registered Investment Adviser

For a financial services professional who meets the IA-770 and IA-1092 tests and must therefore comply with the mandates of the Investment Advisers Act of 1940, the chief requirement is that the practitioner become a registered investment adviser (RIA). This is a burdensome administrative undertaking and is accomplished by completing what is known as *Form ADV*. A one-time filing fee of $150 must accompany the application. The form itself is complicated and will be rejected by the Securities and Exchange Commission's Office of Applications and Reports Services unless completed correctly in each and every regard. Form ADV itself is divided into two broad parts.

The first part of the form asks generalized questions, such as the name, location, and fiscal year of the applicant's business, the form of the business (that is, corporation, partnership, or sole proprietorship), the background of the applicant and any others associated with the applicant, and whether the applicant and the people associated with him or her have ever been convicted of crimes or are subject to certain injunctions. Part I also contains questions relative to the types of clients for which the applicant will provide discretionary or any other account management services.

The second part of the form requires more detailed and extensive information. This information includes the specific types of services offered by the applicant, a detailed explanation of the fee structure, the basic method of operation of the applicant's business, and even questions dealing with the kind of direct involvement the applicant has in securities transactions for clients. Part II also asks for the names of business associates of the applicant within the securities industry, additional information on the applicant, and, if certain additional conditions are met, a balance sheet.

If the Securities and Exchange Commission finds that the applicant has satisfactorily met the general standards upon which the registration is normally accepted, it must grant the RIA registration within 45 days of the filing date or, in the alternative, must begin proceedings to determine whether registration should be denied. As a practical matter, registration will be denied if these general standards have not been met or if the Securities and Exchange Commission determines that registration, if granted, would immediately be subject to suspension or revocation. This could be the result if, for example, the SEC discovers that the applicant has failed to disclose a prior securities law conviction.

Record Keeping Responsibilities

Once the application of the registered investment adviser has been approved, the postregistration phase of compliance begins. One of the more significant elements of this postregistration phase is the record keeping responsibility. It must be noted that there is a 16-step record keeping requirement with which financial services professionals who are registered investment advisers must comply. Included as part of this is compliance with the new Insider Trading and Securities Fraud Enforcement Act of 1988.

Specifically, Sec. 204 of the Investment Advisers Act of 1940 provides the following:

> Every investment adviser who makes use of the mails or any means or any instrumentality of interstate commerce in connection with his, her, or its business as an investment adviser shall make and keep for prescribed periods such records, furnish such copies thereof, and make and disseminate such reports as the Securities and Exchange Commission, by rule, may prescribe as necessary or appropriate in the public interest or for the protection of investors. All records of such investors and advisers are subject at any time, or from time to time, to such reasonable periodic, special, or other examinations by representatives of the Securities and Exchange Commission as the Commission deems necessary or appropriate in the public interest or for the protection of investors.

The Securities and Exchange Commission has promulgated a detailed series of record keeping requirements with which each and every registered investment adviser must comply. As mentioned above there are 16 separate things that must be done in order for the registered investment adviser to be totally in compliance in the postregistration phase. These 16 requirements are as follows:

- *Journal requirement:* Keep a journal in accordance with generally accepted accounting principles.
- *Ledger requirement:* Maintain a ledger in accordance with generally accepted accounting principles.
- *Securities purchased record:* Keep a complete record of all securities you have purchased or recommended.
- *Retention of canceled checks:* Save all your canceled checks and bank statements for a 5-year period.
- *Retention of paid and unpaid bills:* Assemble and save all documentation of paid and unpaid bills.
- *Retention of trial balances and financial statements:* Retain all trial balances and financial statements for a 5-year period.
- *Retention of written communication:* Keep records of all written communications you send to advisory clients and sent to you by advisory clients.
- *Records of discretionary accounts:* Maintain a list of all accounts in which you have discretionary power.
- *Evidence of discretionary authority:* Retain all documents that grant you discretionary authority.
- *Retention of written agreements:* Save all written agreements executed between you and the advisory client.
- *Retention of communications recommending specific securities:* Keep a record of all advertisements, notices, or circulars sent to 10 or more persons that recommend specific securities to clients.
- *Record of securities transactions where RIA has direct or indirect ownership:* Maintain a separate record of all of your recommendations that have been made to an advisory client concerning specific securities in which you have direct or indirect beneficial ownership.
- *Record of securities transactions where RIA has direct or indirect ownership but is primarily engaged in business other than advisory services (for example, life insurance, tax planning, etc.):* Comply with the requirements of the previous item even if you are not primarily involved in investment advisory activities.
- *Brochure retention:* Keep copies of brochures given to clients. Keep signed receipts for the brochures from all advisory clients.
- *Retention of disclosure documents:* Retain copies of all disclosures signed by paid solicitors who refer business to you.
- *Insider trading compliance:* Comply in every respect with the mandates of the Insider Trading and Securities Fraud Enforcement Act of 1988, as will be discussed below.

Because each and every practitioner who operates as a registered investment adviser will be subjected to an SEC examination, it is imperative that professional advisers totally comply with these record keeping mandates. There are both civil and criminal penalties available to the regulators as a method of enforcing these rules.

As mentioned above, the Insider Trading and Securities Fraud Enforcement Act of 1988 contains a series of new record keeping mandates with which a registered investment adviser must comply. It is well known that the Congress has become active of late in the policing of insider trading activities. It has in fact been under a fair degree of pressure to enact legislation to deal with a problem that is viewed by some as being a direct threat to the continued integrity of the securities markets. This latest legislative package is, in large measure, Congress's response to such pressure.

The issue of how to deal with the insider trading problem has been a complex and troublesome one for decades. What to do to control the problem has not been clear-cut and solutions have been exceedingly difficult to find. Legislative history shows that when the Securities Exchange Act of 1934 was being debated, this was one of the major issues even back then. However, it was not until 1968 that there finally was a court decision which held that the use of inside information was a violation of federal securities laws (*SEC v. Texas Gulf Sulfur Company*). Since that case was handed down, Sec. 10(b) of the Securities Exchange Act of 1934 and SEC Rule 10(b)-5 have provided a legal underpinning for the majority of the insider trading cases brought by the Securities and Exchange Commission. In 1984, Congress enacted the Insider Trading Sanction Act. Among other things, this statute gave the SEC the authority to seek the imposition of civil penalties against insider trading violations for as much as three times the profit gained (or loss avoided) as a result of the unlawful purchase or sale of securities. The government felt that such a provision would act as a deterrent. Of course, insider trading problems have become much worse and, as a result, Congress enacted the new insider trading statute in 1988. Since registered investment advisers are viewed as being in a particularly vulnerable position within the insider trading context, special provisions of the new statute were enacted to deal specifically with the activities of registered investment advisers. The new legislation does have provisions which will affect an RIA's operation but which have received little or no attention in the RIA context previously because the SEC had neither promulgated regulations under the act nor commented on its possible application to RIAs. However, the new insider trading statute did add Sec. 204A to the Investment Advisers Act of 1940, which provided the following:

> Every investment adviser subject to the Investment Advisers Act shall establish, maintain, and enforce written policies and procedures reasonably designed to prevent the misuse in violation of this act or the Securities Exchange Act of 1934, of material, nonpublic information by such investment adviser or any person associated with the investment adviser. The Securities and Exchange Commission as it deems shall adopt rules or regulations to require specific policies or procedures reasonably designed to prevent misuse in violation of this act or the Securities Exchange Act of 1934 of material, nonpublic information.

The congressional reports accompanying the latest insider trading legislation provide a lot of insight into the new insider trading statute. They reveal, for example, that the new legislation creates an explicit requirement for broker/dealers and registered investment advisers to establish, maintain, and enforce written policies and procedures reasonably designed to prevent the misuse of material nonpublic information and must also vigilantly review, update, and enforce them. The Congress believes that directly imposing such obligations under the federal securities laws will underscore the significance of such policies and procedures and will enhance the ability of the SEC to monitor and promote the effectiveness of supervisory efforts. There are now direct statutory requirements for registered investment advisers to have written policies and procedures and these written policies and procedures are subject to examination by the government. It should further be noted that there are regulatory, civil, and even criminal penalties under the new Sec. 204A for failure to comply with this new statute section of the 1940 law.

There is even a special bounty provision in Sec. 204A which grants authority to the SEC to award payments to persons who provide information concerning insider trading violations. At the sole discretion of the SEC, the individual can receive up to 10 percent of the penalty imposed or settlement reached.

It is clear therefore that the first thing that needs to be done by the registered investment adviser within the insider trading compliance context is to develop specific procedures. Industry commentators recommend the following items for consideration:

- Separate procedures may be required for different departments within a firm, although a single statement of policy regarding the firm's position may be appropriate.
- Separate supervisory procedures will be needed.
- Management should review and update the procedures on a regular basis.
- Policies and procedures should be reviewed with each employee when hired and on a regular basis as continuing education. Employees should indicate that they have reviewed and understand the firm's policies and procedures.
- Policies and procedures should be provided to all employees, officers, and directors of the firm.

As a practical matter, the new insider trading statute imposes liabilities not only on broker/dealers and registered investment advisers but also on their employees for misuse by such employees of confidential information if the employer has failed to have effectively policed employee activities within the framework of insider trading. The new statute requires all employers to develop a compliance plan. Every registered investment adviser must have a plan in place.

It is possible to engage in insider trading in many different ways. Examples would include conversations with officers of a company with whom the adviser regularly deals or just a normal conversation with clients (for example, "I'm taking my company private in a few months").

It is also possible to have employees who are getting inside information and are acting on it without the knowledge of the registered investment adviser. Therefore the RIA must have a plan. Also, when the RIA firm adopts policies, they must actually be adopted with a view that they will genuinely be enforced. If these policies are adopted pursuant to the statute but are never actually enforced, that can be worse than never having adopted a plan in the first place. It is also clear that an actual policy statement needs to be drafted and enforced and it is equally clear that the management of the RIA must provide all employees with copies of the policy statement. This in effect is evidence of compliance.

To summarize, there are four basic types of requirements within the context of insider trading compliance:

- development of written policies and procedures setting forth the legal prohibitions against insider trading, explaining key concepts underlying these prohibitions, and including any additional restrictions of the firm on insider trading and related activities
- communication of those policies and procedures to employees and supervisors throughout the firm who may learn material nonpublic information as a result of their positions at the firm
- implementation of those policies and procedures through assignment of specific responsibilities to supervisory personnel
- establishment of monitoring mechanisms to increase the likelihood that the firm will prevent, or at least detect, trading and tipping that is not in compliance with the policies and procedures

Fee Restrictions

The 1940 Advisers Act prohibited an investment adviser from basing fees on any share of the capital appreciation of all or any portion of the client's funds unless the advisory contract related to the investment of assets in excess of $1 million. In 1985, the SEC adopted Rule 205-3, which allows registered investment advisers to charge "performance fees" (also referred to as "incentive fees"), but only if the RIA is "managing $500,000 of a client's assets" or "reasonably believes" that the client has a net worth of at least $1 million.

Rule 205-3 requires that clients be advised by brochure that the performance based fee arrangement "may create an incentive for the RIA to make investments that are riskier or more speculative than would be the case in nonperformance based situations." The RIA must also give specific details about how the fee is to be calculated. In addition, the contract between the RIA and client must be based on an arm's-length relationship and the incentive fee must be based on at least one year's performance.

Assignability of Investment Advisory Agreements

Sec. 205 of the Investment Advisers Act prohibits an investment adviser from assigning or transferring an investment advisory contract unless the client expressly consents to such transfer. Congress, in enacting such a provision, wanted to make sure that an adviser would not be able to shift his or her existing responsibilities to some other practitioner or adviser without first obtaining the original client's full consent to the new relationship. Therefore if an existing registered investment adviser wants, for example, to retire, shut down operations, or move to some other location, such practitioner cannot assign the existing professional relationship to another without first obtaining the existing client's full consent to the assignment.

Prohibition of Labels

Sec. 208(c) of the Investment Advisers Act of 1940 provides that it shall be unlawful for any person registered as an investment adviser to represent that he or she is an "investment counsel" or to use the name "investment counsel" unless (1) his or her principal business consists of acting as an investment adviser and (2) a substantial part of that business consists of rendering investment supervisory services.

Although in the form of a no-action letter and not as an actual provision of the Investment Advisers Act of 1940, the SEC has also taken the position that a practitioner must not use the initials "RIA" after his or her name. The SEC was aware of a growing trend within the financial planning community of practitioners using the "RIA" initials after their names as some form of designation — such as CLU or ChFC. Specifically, the SEC stated that, since successful acquisition of professional designations such as CLU or ChFC requires the passing of rigorous course examinations, it would be misleading to use the initials "RIA" after a practitioner's name, in light of the fact that no courses or examinations are required (at least at the federal level) in order to obtain this status. However, in a somewhat surprising conclusion, the SEC announced that it would permit use of the complete phrase "registered investment adviser" after a financial planner's name.

Brochure Rule

In SEC Release No. IA-664, the Securities and Exchange Commission set forth Rule 204-3, which has become known as the brochure rule. Essentially any practitioner who is a registered investment adviser must deliver a written brochure to each and every client.

Since January 30, 1979, when the U.S. Securities and Exchange Commission promulgated SEC Release No. IA-664, all registered investment advisers have been required to deliver a written disclosure statement to each and every client. This concept, known as the brochure rule, requires every investment adviser to deliver a special disclosure statement not only to existing clients to whom investment advice has been given, but also to prospective clients. This disclosure must be delivered to clients or prospective clients either (1) within 48 hours of entering into an investment advisory agreement or (2) when the contract is entered into if the client can terminate such contract within 5 days.

Compliance with the brochure rule can be accomplished either by providing the client with a copy of part II of the Form ADV or in the alternative by preparing a separate narrative statement containing each and every piece of data that appears as part of part II of the Form ADV. The SEC seems to prefer the former approach.

There are 13 basic categories of data that the brochure must communicate to the financial planning client:

- types of clients
- source of information, method of analysis, and investment strategy
- business background and education
- other securities industry activities
- conditions for managing accounts

- review procedures
- advisory fee structure
- types of securities about which advice may be provided
- minimum educational standards imposed on associates/employees
- other business activities with which the planner may be involved
- interest in securities transactions
- brokerage discretion
- balance sheet in the event that the registered investment adviser maintains custody or possession of the client's funds or securities or requires prepayment of advisory fees 6 months or more in advance and such fees are in excess of $500 per client

In summary, therefore, the brochure rule requires the registered investment adviser to deliver either part II of the Form ADV or the substitute brochure to the client or prospective client. It must also be noted, however, that if a continuing relationship exists between the registered investment adviser and the client, the RIA must offer to deliver an updated version of the brochure to the client at the end of each fiscal year. This portion of the brochure rule differs from the initial requirement in that, rather than the registered investment adviser being required to actually deliver the brochure disclosure statement to the client, it is satisfactory to merely offer to deliver such brochure in subsequent years.

The Antifraud Provisions

Sec. 206 of the Investment Advisers Act of 1940 has come to be known as the antifraud portion of the act. Specifically, it provides the following:

> It shall be unlawful for any investment adviser, by use of the mails or any means or instrumentality of interstate commerce, directly or indirectly:
> a. to employ any advice, scheme, or artifice to defraud any client or prospective client;
> b. to engage in any transaction, practice, or course of business which operates as a fraud or deceit upon any client or prospective client;
> c. acting as principal for his [sic] own account, knowingly to sell any security to or purchase any security from a client, or acting as broker for a person other than such client, knowingly to effect any sale or purchase of any security for the account of such client, without disclosing to such client in writing before the completion of such transaction the capacity in which he or she is acting and obtaining the consent of the client to such transaction. The prohibitions of this paragraph shall not apply to any transaction with a customer of a broker or dealer if such broker or dealer is not acting as an investment adviser in relation to such transaction.
> d. To engage in any act, practice, or course of business which is fraudulent, deceptive, or manipulative. The Securities and Exchange Commission shall, for the purposes of this paragraph (d) by rules and regulations define and prescribe means reasonably designed to

> prevent such acts, practices, and courses of business as are fraudulent, deceptive, or manipulative.

These antifraud provisions of the Investment Advisers Act of 1940 have been interpreted to mean that the investment adviser becomes a *fiduciary* who owes the client "an affirmative duty of utmost good faith and full and fair disclosure of all the material facts." The antifraud provisions of the act also deal quite extensively with conflict of interest issues and, in general, hold the investment adviser to an exceedingly high standard of fiduciary responsibility.

The antifraud provisions of the act may even become operative in situations in which a securities transaction per se has not taken place. In essence, the SEC has decided that since Sec. 206 of the act does not refer to "dealings in securities" as most other general antifraud provisions in the federal securities law do, Sec. 206 is much broader and can be applied to transactions in which fraudulent conduct arose out of the investment advisory relationship between an investment adviser and his, her, or its clients, even if the conduct did not involve a securities transaction.

PROPOSED CHANGES IN THE FRAMEWORK OF FEDERAL REGULATION OF FINANCIAL PLANNERS

There are a few significant developments afoot at the federal level regarding the issue of regulation of financial planners. Specifically, the United States Securities and Exchange Commission has grown increasingly concerned of late about the fact that the number of registered investment advisers who applied to the agency's office of Applications and Reports Services has dramatically increased over the last decade. At the beginning of the 1980s, there were approximately 4,000 registered investment advisers who were on file with the Securities and Exchange Commission in Washington. Today, there are well over 15,000 such registrants. The Securities and Exchange Commission is not unhappy about the increased level of compliance — they couldn't be since they are the ones who have been encouraging and compelling this result in the first place. What the SEC is concerned about, however, is the fact that funding from Congress has created a situation where the agency cannot be adequately staffed. This situation makes it impossible for the agency to keep up with the increased demand for application review and field examinations.

In response to this problem, on September 16, 1988, the SEC through the release of IA-1140 proposed for public comment two new and dramatic rules that would have expanded the intrastate and small adviser exemptions. As part of these proposed changes there were to be significant amendments made to five separate rules under the Investment Advisers Act to make advisers exempt from the registration requirement, the record keeping rule, the advertising rule, the solicitor's rule, the disciplinary rule, and restrictions on principal and agency cross transactions.

Unlike the current intrastate exemption, the new intrastate exemption would have permitted the recommendation of exchange traded securities by registered investment advisers who operated solely in one state, had no more than 50 clients during the course of the preceding 12 months, and managed securities portfolios with an aggregate fair market value of not more than $10 million at the end of the registered investment adviser's last fiscal year.

The proposed small adviser exemption, rather than prohibiting an RIA from holding himself or herself out to the public as an investment adviser (as the current small adviser exemption does), would have been available to an RIA who had no more than 25 clients during the course of the preceding 12-month period and who managed securities portfolios with an aggregate fair market value of not more than $1 million at the end of the adviser's last fiscal year. This exemption would have applied to those RIAs who had advisory clients in more than one state and therefore could not have relied on the intrastate exemption.

Both new rules would have required the application of a 12-month period in order to determine whether the limit of 25 or 50 clients had been exceeded. The adviser would have been required to count clients on a rolling basis so that any clients the adviser had over the course of the preceding 12 months would have been included in the decision as to whether the qualification for the exemption had been met.

Both of these proposed changes were doomed to failure almost from the start. Every trade group and professional association that was called upon to comment on these proposed changes came back with an exceedingly negative response. The underlying feeling of industry observers was that the proposed approach would unquestionably lead to increased fraud and abuse within the securities field and would do a substantial disservice to the consuming public. In perhaps the most significant comment letter, a United States congressman who chaired one of the House subcommittees which oversees the activities of the Securities and Exchange Commission vowed to fight in every way possible to see that these proposals never became reality. It is now a foregone conclusion that these proposals are defeated although the SEC has never actually acknowledged this to be the fact.

In light of the failure to obtain approval of these new exemptions, the Securities and Exchange Commission went to plan B. Specifically, in June 1989, the SEC's Division of Investment Management went directly to Congress and requested that there be a substantive amendment made to the Investment Advisers Act of 1940. The SEC planned to ask Congress to create a mechanism by which a separate self-regulatory organization (SRO) could be created for the express purpose of policing the activities of registered investment advisers. The idea was that an SRO such as the NASD (National Association of Securities Dealers) would begin to assume total responsibility for the regulation of registered investment advisers and financial planners. Although the SEC would still have ultimate authority over the area, the nuts and bolts of the regulatory process such as registration procedures, audits and examinations, educational standards and the like would pass to the SRO rather than remaining with the Securities and Exchange Commission as is the case under the current system.

In the late summer of 1989, Senate bill S.1410 was introduced into the United States Senate by Senators Dodd and Heinz. Known as the Investment Adviser Self-Regulation Act of 1989, the new statutory approach would allow the creation of multiple SROs to assume all hands-on responsibility within the area of regulation of financial planners.

The new approach has unleashed a fire storm of opposition. Although the influential International Association for Financial Planning (IAFP) has endorsed it, most other trade groups and professional associations intensely dislike the proposed new approach. In that the NASD (a securities product oriented organization) would most likely become the chief SRO, many professional associations representing fee-only and nonproduct related financial planning firms are vehemently opposing this new approach. Other groups dislike the proposed new arrangement because they feel that if the Securities and Exchange Commission were to assume a reduced role within the area of regulation of financial planners, the propensity for fraud and abuse would significantly increase. As of the time of this writing it is too soon to tell if this new approach will meet with any appreciable measure of success.

STATE REGULATION OF FINANCIAL PLANNERS

Thus far this chapter has been focused on the regulation of financial planners within the framework of the federal securities laws. It must be noted, however, that there are a whole separate series of regulatory responsibilities stemming from the various state securities laws and state securities commissions. At this time, 40 states require the registration of investment advisers. Some of the states single out the activities of financial planners as part of this requirement while other jurisdictions merely lump the concept of financial planner and investment adviser together as one. It should be noted, however, that state RIA registration generally involves a series of procedures that are even more difficult than those that exist at the federal level.

For example, many states require a minimum capitalization amount as a prerequisite to granting investment adviser registration approval. Some states require a bond and an audited financial statement to accompany the application as well. Almost every state requires that the participants in the registered investment advisory operation have certain NASD licensing such as the series 63 (uniform state securities test), series 22 (limited partnership/direct participation test), or the new series 65 (investment adviser) examination. In addition, the state securities commissions, unlike the SEC, will want to see all contracts, disclosure statements and documents, and literature used by the RIA/financial planner with the client. It is inadequate for the financial services professional to focus only on the federal regulatory implications of providing financial planning advice since the state component of the overall scheme is just as relevant.

CONCLUSIONS

Any argument that the financial planning industry is unregulated must be dismissed as unfounded. This chapter has focused on the various systems used to regulate financial planning professionals. There is obviously a highly comprehensive system of dual regulation involving a variety of legal and regulatory mandates at both the federal and state level. The financial services professional must become familiar with these responsibilities and must grow accustomed to complying with these mandates on a continuing basis.

13

The Ethical Environment of Financial Planning

Robbin Derry*

What does ethics have to do with a basic textbook on financial planning? Is all this talk about ethics in business just window dressing to give industry a better public image? How is morality related to personal and professional financial decisions?

Ethical or moral judgments are normative: they tell us what behaviors and actions are acceptable in specific situations. Ethical conflicts arise in the practice of financial planning as well as in every other aspect of our personal and professional lives. Resolving ethical dilemmas requires careful analysis of the facts and the potential long-term effects of any actions. There are systematic and reliable methods for making ethical decisions. The application of these methods to specific conflicts inherent in financial planning provides an approach to problem solving that is broadly applicable in the professional realm.

In this chapter we will examine

- the role of ethics in the financial services industry
- the codes of ethics of The American College and the American Society of CLU & ChFC
- what the word *professional* means and requires
- how to make sound ethical decisions
- some financial services industry practices that warrant ethical analysis

THE ROLE OF ETHICS

Ethics is the glue that holds our entire economic and free enterprise system together. Without it business deals would collapse, working conditions would be intolerable, trust would be nonexistent. In innumerable business activities people act on the trust that those they deal with will behave ethically. When an employee is assigned a job, the supervisor trusts that the employee will not misuse the information, the time, or the resources that accompany the task. A life insurance agent and a client make a verbal agreement to meet again after the agent has a chance to analyze the client's needs. The agent trusts that the client will come to the meeting and listen to the needs analysis, while the client trusts that the agent will keep personal information confidential. When a manager offers a bonus for high performance, subordinates trust that the reward will indeed be forthcoming upon achievement of such performance. All day people act in ways that demonstrate a trust in the fundamental

---

*Robbin Derry, PhD, is the Charles Lamont Post Chair professor of ethics and the professions at The American College.

assumptions of fair treatment, honest communications, accurate representations of intentions, and the avoidance of deception.[1]

Certainly there are people we have learned not to trust. There are many situations in which it is wise to be wary. People are not always ethical. But in situations where there is little trust it is more difficult to make agreements or to conduct business. Business diminishes and disintegrates without trust. The behavior of untrustworthy individuals and organizations is too unpredictable to risk involvement. When a person lies (or deceives, cheats, or steals) it is difficult to rebuild trust in that individual. If a business develops a reputation for fraud and deception, it is extremely challenging for that business to overcome that reputation. With the erosion of confidence, customers, suppliers, stockholders, and even potential employees will take their resources elsewhere.

Ethics is not merely public relations. It is not about creating a good image. Nor is it a luxury a company may indulge in after it meets the critical bottom line. Ethics is about how people conduct business, every hour of every day. It is about prompt response to client complaints and honest feedback to subordinates, peers, and superiors. Ethical behavior is being honest with ourselves and others. It involves the quality of the work to which people put their name. It is giving clients all the information they need to make decisions that are in their best interest.

Ethics represents a set of fundamental assumptions that underlie nearly all relationships and transactions within society. These are assumptions about the ways we treat other people, what our rights and the rights of others are, where our individual rights end and the rights of others begin, how individual and community property ought to be treated, and what constitutes fair and equitable treatment of all people. Some of these assumptions are embodied in law, but ethics goes beyond law.

LAW AND ETHICS

The relationship between law and ethics can be represented clearly by a Venn diagram.

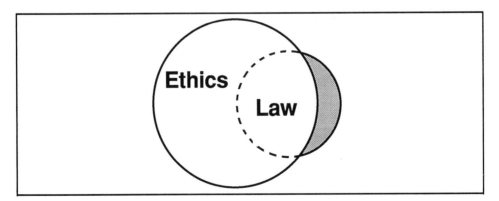

As shown in this diagram, law and ethics overlap but they each have their own domain as well. The dotted line at the intersection of law and ethics represents their mutable boundary. Laws are largely ethical standards that society has codified in order to insist on and enforce these behaviors. Ethical issues that are deemed sufficiently important may become laws, and conversely, laws considered to be excessive or intrusive may be either ignored or struck down in court proceedings.

Business Law and Business Ethics

The specific areas of business law and business ethics overlap in similar ways.

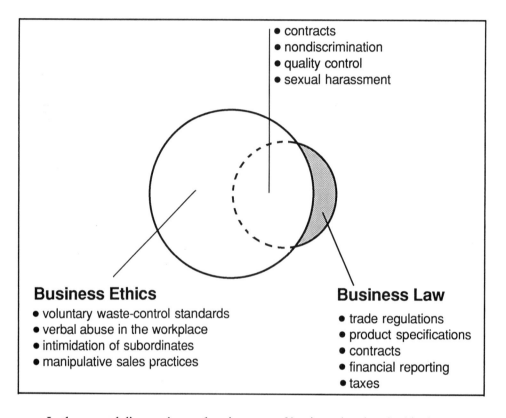

- contracts
- nondiscrimination
- quality control
- sexual harassment

Business Ethics
- voluntary waste-control standards
- verbal abuse in the workplace
- intimidation of subordinates
- manipulative sales practices

Business Law
- trade regulations
- product specifications
- contracts
- financial reporting
- taxes

In the second diagram's overlapping area of business legal and ethical concerns are such issues as fulfilling contractual agreements, nondiscriminatory treatment of different racial groups in hiring and promotion decisions, and meeting minimal quality-control standards in manufacturing processes.

Within the realm of business ethics, outside the realm of business law, would be such concerns as the acceptable level of toxic waste emitted or dumped into the environment if it is known that the legal standards are inadequate or nonexistent, low-level but constant verbal abuse in the workplace, manipulative sales practices, and intimidation of subordinates.

In the purely legal realm are trade regulations, product specifications, and contractual relationships with suppliers, customers, the community, shareholders, and investors. Many "purely legal" rules quickly become ethical issues if they are violated, intentionally misinterpreted, or ignored. In fact, laws represent codified ethical standards. They are the minimum moral requirements that we have agreed to demand for society as a whole.

Can Morality Be Legislated?

"You can't legislate morality" is a popular saying. But morality, or the definition of right and wrong behavior, is precisely the focus of the American legal system. Laws regarding stealing, killing, invading others' privacy, defrauding, and misrepresenting intentions all reflect ethical rules. If these are violated, a penalty is imposed on the violator. So society does, in fact, legislate the most important aspects of morality.

It is true, however, that society cannot legislate *all* of morality. Laws cannot be made to cover every situation that arises. Laws cannot mandate decent treatment and concern for other human beings, although that is certainly an ethical issue. If an attempt were made to define and mandate all moral behavior, it would be impossible to enforce. Furthermore, citizens in democratic countries generally prefer fewer laws and greater personal freedom, rather than more laws and less personal freedom. With a significant increase in laws governing individual behavior, courts and prisons would be even more jammed than they already are. People want a certain amount of personal independence to resolve their ethical dilemmas, but they also need to adhere to some common moral standards, since their decisions about such dilemmas inevitably affect other people. Similarly, of course, their ethical decisions affect us, and we expect them to adhere to a shared morality as well.

The Contrast between Legal Rules and Ethical Rules

The law is relatively clear-cut. Lawyers, the police, and the courts are all employed to provide guidance on how to follow the law. Although lawyers don't always agree and the body of law is always somewhat in flux, there is a concrete and accessible legal system.

Ethical rules, on the other hand, are not as clear-cut. An ethical problem is not even as easily defined as a legal problem. A situation that raises ethical conflicts for Susan may not raise any such conflicts for John. This is because they each have a different sense of responsibility associated with particular moral values. For example, honesty to Susan may mean that she should give her true opinion when colleagues ask her what she thinks. Honesty to John may mean that he is always at work on time and never takes sick days unless he is completely incapable of coming into the office. If Susan doesn't share John's interpretation of honesty, she will feel no ethical dilemma at all about taking a sick day to go for a hike in the woods. And John may feel that it is perfectly acceptable, even moral, to politely lie about a colleague's poor performance. They both would agree that honesty is an important ethical standard, but they would disagree on the situations that raise conflicts over that value.

As this example shows, ethical behavior is not as readily defined as legal behavior. There is no concrete body of ethical standards that serves as recourse in ethical dilemmas. However, there are commonly accepted standards regarding the basic norms governing the moral life. These include such rules as

Don't kill.	Don't deceive.
Don't cause pain.	Fulfill obligations.
Don't disable.	Don't cheat.

Some of these are laws while others are not. They are all commonly held expectations about life in our society, reflecting our values of individual rights and obligations to others. These values and the resulting moral rules extend into the realm of business, since business operates within the larger realm of society as a whole.

Conflicting Moral Rules

Many of the ethical dilemmas that arise are the result of conflicting moral rules. Should Bob tell the truth when it will cause pain to someone? Is Anne's primary duty to complete a major project on time at work or to nurse a sick child at home? Is it right to steal in order to feed one's family?

Clearly the problem is not a shortage of moral rules. Rather it is a problem of deciding which rule is most important in a given situation. As a result, one rule may be compromised in order to meet another. Moral rules are prioritized according to individual needs, experiences, and interests. Often people disagree about the proper priority of moral rules. If these disagreements can be addressed directly, such discussions may facilitate a clarification of ethical standards and serve to communicate expectations for ethical behavior. This is as true in business as it is in personal life.

ETHICS AND THE WORK ENVIRONMENT

Discussing ethical conflicts is one important way that people can express their moral values to those they live and work with. If trust in ethical behavior facilitates and underlies all economic transactions, then people must be sure to build ethical behavior into their business decisions and operations. Only if they integrate an awareness of ethics into their daily work lives will they create a working environment that is founded on strong ethical principles.

What about competitive business practices? Isn't business fundamentally about trying to gain the advantage over competitors? Does ethical behavior put a manager at a competitive disadvantage?

A manager, an insurance agent, a financial planner, or an investment adviser can be ethical, competitive, and tough about goals all at the same time. Business isn't just about competition. It is also about cooperation. It is about meeting the needs of customers. It is about making deals that work for the good of as many people as possible. If a business focused entirely on competing with rivals and neglected its customers, the business would quickly fail.

Honest competition is healthy, contributing to a strong economy, higher quality, and a better selection of consumer products. But competition is not the fundamental purpose of business. The essential business of business is cooperation.

Why is it important to be ethical in business practices? The first reason is that ethical expectations and trust serve to hold business, the economy, and society together. To the extent that people act unethically, these systems fail. The outcome may be that our own business systems falter, now or eventually, as a result of distrust, deception, or a lack of consumer confidence. Adherence to ethical business practices adds a cornerstone to the foundation of any business organization.

The second reason to be ethical in business practices is that individual actions create the work environment in which people spend most of their waking hours. They create their own environments with everything they do and say. What is imposed on people from the outside is not nearly as powerful as the reality they create by their own actions and decisions. People are constantly creating their own living and working context by how they treat others, by statements they make, by attitudes they hold, and by the practices they condone.

Stated most simply, if people lie, cheat, and steal, they are then living in a lying, cheating, and stealing environment. An ethical environment is the only possible one in which society can survive economically, physically, morally, and spiritually. This is the ethical responsibility: to actively create a context in which everyone can survive. The fulfillment of this responsibility requires people to take a careful look at the ethical implications of all actions, the long-term costs, and the alternatives and to listen to the voices of others who are affected.

A person's behavior shapes his or her environment. A person's response to ethical challenges determines the character of all his or her relationships. A person's potential for establishing a strong, thriving business increases with a commitment to ethical action.

CODES OF ETHICS

The American College and the American Society of CLU & ChFC have each developed strong codes of ethics that are binding on students and designees and members, respectively. It is imperative that all American College designation candidates and recipients and American Society members understand and uphold these ethical requirements.

The CLU and ChFC designations have not only educational and experience requirements but also ethical requirements that continue beyond graduation. These requirements mandate the maintenance of ongoing standards of professional conduct. The display of a designation is a continuing representation that the holder will act competently and ethically in all professional relationships.

The American College's Code of Ethics was adopted in June 1984. Although only actions that occur after October 1, 1984, are subject to the code, the standards established by the code apply to students in the CLU and ChFC programs who matriculated on July 1, 1982, or later. All earlier CLU and ChFC matriculants were invited to subscribe to the code and to accept its mandates voluntarily. The jurisdiction of the college does not extend to pre-1982 matriculants who have not consented to be bound by the code.

The American College's Professional Pledge and Canons

Currently every new CLU and ChFC designee is required to take the professional pledge and adhere to the eight canons.

The pledge to which all CLU and ChFC designees subscribe is as follows:

In all my professional relationships, I pledge myself to the following rule of ethical conduct: I shall, in light of all conditions surrounding those I serve, which I shall make every conscientious effort to ascertain and understand, render that service which, in the same circumstances, I would apply to myself.

These are the eight canons:

I. Conduct yourself at all times with honor and dignity.

II. Avoid practices that would bring dishonor upon your profession or The American College.

III. Publicize your achievement in ways that enhance the integrity of your profession.

IV. Continue your studies throughout your working life so as to maintain a high level of professional competence.

V. Do your utmost to attain a distinguished record of professional service.

VI. Support the established institutions and organizations concerned with the integrity of your profession.

VII. Participate in building your profession by encouraging and providing appropriate assistance to qualified persons pursuing professional studies.

VIII. Comply with all laws and regulations, particularly as they relate to professional and business activities.

The certification officer of The American College is empowered by the board of trustees to implement the code by investigating complaints and reports of violations, which may originate with state commissioners of insurance, other public and judicial bodies, individuals, and established institutions or organizations. In certain instances the College itself may initiate action based on an apparent violation.

Violations that may cause the certification officer to begin an investigation include conviction of a misdemeanor or felony, suspension or revocation of a license, or suspension or revocation of membership in an established institution or organization.

Practical Application

What do the professional pledge and the canons mean in terms of daily professional practice? The pledge says, "I shall . . . render that service which . . . I would apply to myself."

To offer a client the same thorough attention to detail that a financial planner would apply to an investment for himself or herself is no small requirement. Think about the kind of service a planner would give to himself or herself and to those closest to him or her. The planner would make absolutely certain to understand all the apparent and hidden costs. The planner would want to know how much it will cost now and whether the cost over the life of the product is fixed or variable. The planner would want to clearly understand the potential risks of the investment or policy. If it is an interest-sensitive product, is the planner (or the client) able to regularly monitor the financial stability of the product? What are the costs of withdrawal? Does the planner understand the potential benefits of the product in the short term as well as in the long term? Does he or she know exactly how to maximize those benefits or what actions to take to reduce the potential harms? The planner would not go into an investment or policy purchase without making use of all possible knowledge about the product.

A financial planner may believe that he or she has a particularly strong interest in knowing all the details because it is his or her profession, while clients simply aren't interested in those details. Or that one of the benefits of being in the financial services business is that the planner has access to information and knowledge that the general public doesn't have. That is one of the perks of the job, the planner may think: the expert knowledge to make better-informed investment decisions.

But the CLU and ChFC pledge says that the financial services professional will render that service to clients that he or she would give to himself or herself. It intentionally uses the professional individual as the standard of comparison precisely because the professional knows how much information is necessary to make a completely informed decision. It is the professional's responsibility to present the information in a way that clients can understand and use in their decision making.

Of course a financial planner cannot *force* someone to understand something, and a client may not even want to know all the details. Nonetheless it is the planner's obligation to provide the client with the needed information, in a manner that the client can understand, and help the client understand why the client needs the information about the product and what its financial effect will be in the short and long term.

Focus on the Client

The pledge also stipulates that the financial services professional will take into account the conditions surrounding the client and that the professional "shall make every conscientious effort to ascertain and understand" such conditions. This refers to the importance of what is known as "consultative" or "client-focused" planning or selling.

Such an approach requires the financial planner to gather as much information as possible from the client about needs, goals, interests, and assets in order to put together an investment or insurance package that will best meet the client's needs. The sale of products is essentially client-driven. As explained in chapter 3, in order for the planner to respond to the client's needs, the planner must approach the client with a willingness to listen carefully. The client can best provide the information regarding his or her own needs and goals. The client may also think that he or she knows which product best fits those goals, but the planner should keep the client focused on articulating needs and goals so that the planner can then find the best product to match those goals.

Consultative planning or selling is a sound approach to building good relationships with clients and selling life insurance and other financial products. It is also an ethical requirement because of the nature of the client-planner relationship. The planner usually has the dual role of agent for a financial services company and agent for the client. As the agent of the company, he or she is expected to accurately represent the products or services sold by the company, their costs and benefits, to the client. Not many life insurance companies still have exclusive relationships with agents, so while agent loyalty is a concern (and will be discussed later), the financial planner who is a life insurance agent is not required to sell only the policies of one or two companies. Most financial services professionals who deal primarily with the products of one company feel that their obligation to the company is to look to those products first to meet their client's needs and go outside their home company for products only if an appropriate policy or investment is not available with that company.

This traditional approach serves several purposes. First the planner is able to gain in-depth knowledge of the products of one or two companies, which would be nearly impossible if a person tried to cover all the products on the market. This knowledge enables the planner to serve the client better. Second, it saves the financial planner extensive research time to be able to work from a body of familiar products. Of course, in some instances this could be detrimental to a client who needs more extensive research to find just the right product. It is important that the planner honestly inform the client of the planner's primary relationship with a particular company. The client should understand that these products are the ones that the planner will research and present in most cases. It is deceptive and clearly unethical to fail to disclose that primary relationship.

The financial planner is also an agent for the client. The client trusts the agent with confidential information. Courts have increasingly found that the common law understanding of the word *agent* is "agent of the client." Courts have held that when a financial services professional induces reliance on his or her expertise, that person incurs liability for decisions made on the basis of the expertise. When a financial planner says in effect to a client, "I am your agent," the planner does indeed take on the responsibilities and liabilities of an agent of the client.

Many educators, speakers, and managers stress the importance of selling a financial service or product solely on the basis of client need. Selling on any other basis, such as the needs and interests of the salesperson, the sales manager, or the company, makes no sense in the long term. The salesperson may be persuasive enough to make fast sales in order to meet a bonus deadline, or the company may be promoting a particular product with higher commission rates. But unless the product really meets the needs of the client over the long term, that client will not keep up the payments, which ends up being costly for the company. Clients who feel that they were sold products that did not meet their needs are not likely to be repeat customers. A client will not refer friends and relatives to a salesperson if the client doesn't believe in the salesperson's ability to listen carefully and respond. So while the short-term sales may look good temporarily, the long-term financial position of the salesperson, the selling agency, and the selling company are hurt by any sales that do not meet clients' needs. The same arguments, of course, support continuing attention to the changing needs of clients over time.

In summary, it is both ethically required and financially wise for the financial planner to thoroughly understand the client's needs. This approach is further corroborated by the Code of Ethics of the American Society of CLU & ChFC. The imperatives and the guides are presented here with the interpretive comments.

The Code of Ethics of the American Society of CLU & ChFC

First Imperative: To competently advise and serve the client.

Guide 1.1: A member shall provide advice and service which are in the client's best interest.

Interpretive Comment

A. A member possessing a specific body of knowledge which is not possessed by the general public has an obligation to use that knowledge for the benefit of the client and to avoid taking advantage of that knowledge to the detriment of the client.
B. In a conflict of interest situation the interest of the client must be paramount.
C. The member must make a conscientious effort to ascertain and to understand all relevant circumstances surrounding the client.
D. A member is to accord due courtesy and consideration to those engaged in related professions who are also serving the client.
E. A member is to give due regard to any agent-principal relationship which may exist between the member and such companies as he may represent.

Guide 1.2: A member shall respect the confidential relationship existing between client and member.

Interpretive Comment

A. Competent advice and service may necessitate the client sharing personal and confidential information with the member. Such information is to be held in confidence by the member unless released from the obligation by the client.

Guide 1.3: A member shall continue his education throughout his professional life.

Interpretive Comment

A. To advise and serve competently, a member must continue to maintain and to improve his professional abilities.
B. Continuing Education includes both the member adding to his knowledge of the practice of his profession; and, the member keeping abreast of changing economic and legislative conditions which may affect the financial plans of the insuring public.
C. A member may continue his education through formal or informal programs of study or through other professional experiences.

Guide 1.4: A member shall render continuing advice and service.

Interpretive Comment

A. Advice and service, to be competent, must be on-going as the client's circumstances change and as these changes are made known to the member.
B. A client with whom a member has an active professional relationship is to be informed of economic and legislative changes which relate to the client-member relationship.

Second Imperative: To enhance the public regard for professional designations and allied professional degrees held by members.

Guide 2.1: A member shall obey all laws governing his business or professional activities.

Interpretive Comment

A. Business activities are non-personal activities carried on outside the life insurance community; professional activities are non-personal activities carried on within the life insurance community.
B. A member has a legal obligation to obey all laws applicable to his business and professional activities. The placement of this Guide within the Code raises this obligation to the level of an ethical obligation.

Guide 2.2: A member shall avoid activities which detract from the integrity and professionalism of the Chartered Life Underwriter designation, the Chartered Financial Consultant designation, or any other allied professional degree or designation held by members.

Interpretive Comment

A. Personal, business, and professional activities are encompassed within the scope of this Guide.
B. Activities which could present a violation of this Guide might include:
   (1) A member's failure to obey a law unrelated to the member's business or professional activities.
   (2) A member impairing the reputation of another practitioner.
   (3) A member unfairly competing with another practitioner.
   (4) Actions which result in the member discrediting his own reputation.
   (5) A member discrediting life underwriting as a profession, the institution of life insurance or the American Society of CLU & ChFC.
   (6) A member advertising the Chartered Life Underwriter or Chartered Financial Consultant designation or membership in the American Society in an undignified manner, or in a manner prohibited by the Bylaws of the American Society.

Guide 2.3: A member shall encourage others to attain the Chartered Life Underwriter and/or the Chartered Financial Consultant designations.

Interpretive Comment

A. Enhancement of the public regard for the CLU and ChFC designations depends upon a continuing increase in the number of holders of the designations who are available to advise and serve the public.
B. Encouraging others who might be qualified to enter into a practice is one hallmark of a professional.

Guide 2.4: A member shall avoid using the Chartered Life Underwriter or Chartered Financial Consultant designation in a false or misleading manner.

Interpretive Comment

A. The CLU and ChFC designations are granted by The American College to specified individuals. Acts which directly or indirectly extend the member's personal designation to others would present a violation of this Guide.
B. Chartered Life Underwriter (CLU) or Chartered Financial Consultant (ChFC) may not be used in a name of a business in a manner which would reasonably lead others to conclude that someone other than the named member held the designation. Example:
(1) John Jones, CLU & Associates is permissible.
(2) John Jones & Associates, Chartered Financial Consultants is not permissible.

Men and women who have chosen to enter into membership in the American Society voluntarily bind themselves to this Code of Ethics of their professional organization.

The purpose of the Code is to give further force to the Pledge taken by all holders of the CLU and ChFC designations and to provide a series of standards by which those involved in providing insurance and financial planning and economic security may conduct themselves in a professional manner. The Code is founded upon the two ethical imperatives of competent advice and service to the client and enhancement of the public regard for the CLU and ChFC designations.

Competent advice and service to the client is at the very essence of any professional calling. Enhancement of the public regard for professional designations gives voice to the concept that in accepting Society membership, an obligation is also accepted to all other holders of similar and allied professional designations and degrees.

In its design, the Code presents the two ethical imperatives, supported by Guides which give specificity to the Imperatives, and interpretive comment which is intended to aid in a uniform understanding of the Guides.

A violation of the Code would expose a member to sanctions which range from reprimand to revocation of membership in the American Society. A member is in violation of the Code when a final judgment is made that the member has breached an ethical imperative through failure to adhere to one or more of the Guides.

The Code of Ethics of the American Society provides clear guidance on professional obligations. These include obligations to clients and obligations to take actions that enhance public respect for professional designations such as Chartered Life Underwriter and Chartered Financial Consultant, as well as for allied professional degrees.

The obligation to competently advise and serve the client underscores once again the importance of the client-focused approach that was discussed in relation to The American College's Code of Ethics. The interpretive comment to guide 1.1 explicitly directs the professional to follow the interests of the client in any conflict of interest.

In some instances, the guides and interpretive comments may contradict common practices or expectations within a financial services practice. Although it may be difficult, the CLU or ChFC should discuss these differences with his or her manager. One potential benefit would be a greater awareness of the ethical standards of the American Society. If there is strong sentiment against these ethical standards on the part of management, it is well for the designee to recognize the prevailing ethical practices and evaluate the consequences of following such practices.

The members of the American Society are expected to be professional standard-bearers. It is in this context that the second imperative is particularly relevant: to enhance public regard for professional designations. This imperative is more than a concern for the image of the American Society and the field as a whole. It also reinforces the importance of acting in ways that will be seen to be entirely ethical even when exposed to the bright light of public scrutiny. Often unethical actions are taken when it is thought that no one will know. Under this imperative actions or decisions that a financial services professional would not want to defend in public are completely unacceptable. In addition the guides elaborate behaviors that the American Society feels are consistent with its goals and standards.

To take actions that would enhance public regard for the profession (which is even more demanding than enhancing public regard for oneself) is to act in ways that are commonly regarded as highly professional. As shown in the next section, professionalism requires competence and reliability. These characteristics are integral to upholding the ethical expectations of The American College and the American Society of CLU and ChFC.

PROFESSIONALISM

Professional is a term of respect and status in society. Traditionally the occupations of law, medicine, and the ministry have commanded this respect. More recently the term has come to represent how people conduct their business in a wide range of fields. One of the important elements of professionalism is the maintenance of ethical standards. For that reason the requirements of professionalism are explored in depth here.

What do people mean when they say, "She is a real professional" or "His behavior was completely unprofessional"? What is commonly understood as professional conduct?

In the first example the positive connotation includes such characteristics as knowing one's job well, reliability, care, thoroughness, dependability, the ability and willingness to perform at the highest level on every transaction, a commitment to providing good service, and an awareness that one represents other people in the same field whose reputations are affected by the quality of performance.

In contrast, the term *unprofessional* commonly carries such meaning as shoddy or careless performance; a lack of concern for customers or clients; unawareness or unconcern for the reputation of a larger group of people; and a narrow, selfish concern for one's own well-being.

To sum up, a professional is commonly expected to have two outstanding characteristics: a high level of competence and reliability and adherence to high standards of ethical conduct.

Burke A. Christensen, JD, CLU, general counsel and vice president of the American Society of CLU & ChFC, suggests that "a professional is a person engaged in a field that requires (1) specialized knowledge not generally understood by the public, (2) a threshold entrance requirement, (3) a sense of altruism, and (4) a code of ethics."[2]

Of these requirements, numbers one and four are immediately evident in the financial services field. Certainly financial consultants and insurance agents have a specialized knowledge not generally understood. Those who are graduates of the CLU and ChFC programs and/or members of the American Society also adhere to professional codes of ethics.

The CLU or ChFC designation represents a kind of threshold entrance requirement, even though there are many successful people working in the field who do not have the CLU or ChFC or an allied professional designation. In addition to a professional designation or degree, however, thorough and continuing education in the fundamentals of the financial services profession is an important aspect of meeting clients' needs. This field is increasingly competitive and complex. Federal and state regulations are in constant flux. Understanding these changes is essential to providing sound advice to clients. The truly professional financial adviser must in some way meet both an entrance requirement of foundational education and a requirement of continuous professional education.

Requirement number three, a sense of altruism, is the characteristic that facilitates adherence to the codes of ethics. Altruism is defined as an unselfish regard for the welfare of others.

The requirement of altruistic behavior may contradict many assumptions about business and competition. But altruism is only one characteristic of a professional, not the only characteristic. A professional is not required to entirely give away services or resources without regard for himself or herself. The professional is required to adhere to ethical standards unselfishly, to take others' needs and views into account. The welfare of others is as important as the professional's own. Altruism does not supplant the professional's own welfare, but it does balance it.

Altruism does not allow one to focus exclusively on one's own success and well-being. Altruism does facilitate the achievement of the characteristics commonly expected of a professional: competence, reliability, and high ethical standards. While altruism is an unselfish concern for others, it is clearly not without its benefits to the altruist. Demonstration of concern for others often wins great trust and reliance. However, it is the worst kind of hypocrisy to feign altruism in order to create the image of trustworthiness and reliability. The image of altruism is quite different from deeply felt altruism, and the false image will inevitably be uncovered to reveal the underlying motivations. Such deception is not worth the personal and professional cost.

The important questions facing professionals are twofold. What environment do we want to create, what environment do we want to work in? This is quite different from the question, How do we want to be perceived? The former question is about daily choices and our expectations of those around us. The latter question is about image.

Insurance and financial services professionals are understandably concerned about their image because it is a poor one among much of American society. But working merely to improve the image is the wrong approach. The critical issue is what these professionals are doing, not what people think they are doing. Professional respect and credibility for this field will follow professional behavior. Adherence to the highest ethical standards as elaborated here will contribute significantly toward the achievement of professional behavior and subsequently to professional respect.

THE PRACTICE OF ETHICAL DECISION MAKING

> Making ethical decisions is easy when the facts are clear and the choices are black and white. But it is a different story when the situation is clouded by ambiguity, incomplete information, multiple points of view, and conflicting responsibilities. In such situations—which managers experience all the time—ethical decisions depend on both the decision-making process itself and on the experience, intelligence, and integrity of the decision maker.[3]

The development of sound moral judgment requires education and practice. Moral education begins in childhood and extends throughout life. The quality of that education varies with many environmental factors. The examples from which people learn to pattern their lives range from tenderness to brutality, from consideration to greed, from fairness to bigotry. How people are affected and how those around them respond teach enduring lessons.

Accordingly the practice of ethical decision making is influenced by environmental pressures and expectations. In work organizations these are aspects of the prevailing "organizational culture." Loyalty, for example, may be more highly valued than candor. Short-term sales performance may be more readily rewarded than superior quality service over the long term. Such rewards teach individuals what is acceptable behavior within that system. These messages may influence the moral reasoning process that is used in ethical dilemmas.

This section addresses how to make ethical decisions, and how organizations can better integrate ethical decision making into their daily operations. The improvement of ethical practice in the workplace must take place on both the individual and the organizational levels. Individuals are ultimately the decision makers, but they are influenced by organizational goals and pressures. Individuals often make decisions within the context of particular organizational roles that they would not make in their personal lives. Therefore it is critical to examine the organizational factors in ethical dilemmas. It is also important that individuals have a reliable method of making ethical decisions. Both the organizational and individual contributions to ethical practice will be addressed here.

Individual Decision Making

For many centuries moral philosophers have debated how to make ethical decisions and how to know what right actions are. Over the years the philosophical theories have been categorized primarily into two schools of thought. The *consequentialists,* including Jeremy Bentham and the utilitarians, have argued that morally right action can be determined by examining the effects or consequences of each action. In order to determine the moral solution to a dilemma one must consider the potential outcomes, weigh the harms and benefits of each alternative, and calculate the right answer on the basis of the greatest resultant benefits. The familiar calculus of the utilitarians was based on "the greatest good for the greatest number."

One drawback of this method is the difficulty of determining how to measure and weigh the good and bad effects against each other. This method has also been faulted for justifying unacceptable evils perpetrated on a minority on the basis of benefits to a large number of people. Surely, the critics of consequentialism argue, there are fundamental human rights for all people that should not be overridden or outweighed by less significant benefits to a great number of people on the grounds that morality is a cost-benefit analysis.

An example of consequentialist reasoning can be found in Ford Motor Company's cost-benefit analysis of the dangers inherent in the exploding gas tank of the Pinto. Management's analysis of their liability costs led them to the conclusion that it was less costly to compensate the victims' families, even to anticipate a continuing cost of death benefits to the families of future victims, than to incur the expense of redesigning the car to relocate the gas tank.

In contrast, the *nonconsequentialists* (or the deontologists, as they are sometimes called) argue that moral action is not determined by consequences but by rules that should be universally applicable to the realm of people affected by the action. Critics of Ford's response to the Pinto design disaster believed that a cost-benefit approach was completely inappropriate and immoral. Allowing an automobile to be built and sold when it was known to be extremely hazardous to the occupants was unconscionable to those who reasoned from a nonconsequentialist perspective.

There are elements of both consequentialist and nonconsequentialist reasoning that are consistently useful for ethical decision making. It is clearly important to weigh the effects of an action and also to consider ethical rules and standards beyond the consequences of the immediate situation. Each approach *alone,* however, can be demonstrated to have significant weaknesses in application.

Presented below is a method of making ethical decisions that has recently been developed to incorporate important elements of both the consequentialist and nonconsequentialist traditions. It is called "the method of impartial legislation," since it is designed to guide the decision maker to an action that would be acceptable as a moral law to all persons affected by the decision. The steps to be taken in assessing the morality of an action are given here.

Morality as Impartial Legislation[4]

1. Accurately state the conduct to be evaluated.
2. Identify all those who are directly and indirectly affected by this conduct.
3. Reason impartially:
   a. Put yourself into the shoes of each of these persons.
   b. *Using as your guide their interests and their beliefs as well as all facts you can obtain,* determine how each person would be benefited or harmed by this conduct, both now and in the foreseeable future.
4. State what you are proposing to do as a general "moral law" (a form of conduct open to all persons).
5. Identify all those who would be directly and indirectly affected if this "moral law" prevailed in society.
6. Reason impartially:
   a. Put yourself into the position of each person affected by this "law."
   b. *Using as your guide their interests and their beliefs as well as all facts you can obtain,* determine how each person would be benefited or harmed by this "moral law," both now and in the foreseeable future.
7. Weigh both the immediate effects of this conduct *and* its impact as a "moral law," considering such matters as the quantity, duration, and likelihood of the harms and benefits involved.
8. Reasoning impartially, as all the persons possibly affected, ask yourself whether on balance you would be prepared to see this "moral law" come into being.
   a. If you would not, you should regard this conduct as *morally wrong.*
   b. If you would, you may regard it as *morally right.*
9. If you have judged this conduct wrong but there are still good reasons for wanting to permit it, consider imaginatively whether there are various alternatives other than simply doing or not doing the action, and carry out a similar analysis for each of the alternatives.

These steps represent a way of approaching ethical problems that considers both the consequences of a given action and its acceptability as a rule or a moral law. The underlying concept is that our system of morality should be a system upon which all rational persons could agree if they could legislate the moral laws together. By trying to take into account each person's perspectives and interests we attempt to reach a solution that is equally partial to every affected person. This method requires a consideration of the effects of the action in the immediate situation and the broader effects if this action were a standard of conduct available to all persons. In this way we weigh the precedent-setting effects over the long term as well as the present consequences.

In order to understand the relevance of the method of impartial legislation in ethical decision making, it will be used to highlight the ethical aspects of several professional issues familiar to many people in the life insurance and financial services industry. However, before we embark on that analysis, some organizational actions that may improve ethical decision making are presented here.

Organizational Requirements for Improving Ethical Decision Making

Organizations, it is sometimes argued, are only paper entities; they do not make policies or shape lives and careers. It is always individuals, not organizations, who make decisions and take actions.

However, when individuals take on jobs and roles in an organization, their decisions and actions are influenced by the goals of the organization. That is as it should be to a large extent. When a person is paid to do a particular job in order to meet the company's stated goals, it is reasonable to expect him or her to perform in accordance with the objectives of the position.

Because of the influence of the organization's expectations on individual action, it is worthwhile to carefully consider the role of the organization in the ethical decision making that occurs in its daily operations. There are three critical steps to follow in analyzing and improving the level of ethical decisions within a work organization:

1. Communicate clear ethical goals and standards.
2. Create positive reinforcement and rewards for ethical behavior.
3. Recognize and remove barriers to good ethical decisions.

Communicate Clear Ethical Goals and Standards

The first step is to communicate ethical standards. They must be practical, specific, and clear. Many corporate mission statements include a commitment to "the highest standards of business ethics." But what does that really mean in practice? In order to fulfill goals set forth in a mission statement, detailed operating strategies need to be established throughout all levels of the company. Broad ethical principles must be defined in more specific terms for each work environment.

There are many issues in our daily work lives that need the spotlight of ethical analysis. Here are some examples of ethical actions that might be taken in specific work situations:

- Solicit and hear constructive criticism from subordinates.
- Respond to customer complaints within 24 hours.
- Be alert to and eliminate destructive stereotypes.
- Give credit for ideas where credit is due.
- Create opportunities for growth for subordinates.
- Develop products and systems which are need-driven.

These might seem to be remarkably small issues, but it is the small daily events that affect the work environment and therefore determine how much work actually gets done every day. When a company is committed to ethical actions and standards on a daily basis, there is no question about how the company is to respond in a time of crisis. Everyone knows what the standards are because the expectations for ethical behavior have been clearly communicated by words and repeated actions.

Reinforcements and Rewards

Once specific ethical standards have been articulated, how can they be implemented? The second step is to create reinforcement and rewards for the desired behavior. A frequent concern about rewards for ethical behavior is the difficulty in measuring such behavior. However, if clear standards and expectations have been set in advance, it is not difficult to assess whether these have been achieved consistently.

A discussion of ethical issues and potential ethical conflicts in an organization's meetings will encourage individuals to raise their concerns and to share their reasoning. This step alone accomplishes small miracles in the workplace. Moral stress results in high turnover rates, while the freedom to discuss ethical issues is a major contribution to alleviating moral stress. This forum also provides the leader of the meeting with the opportunity to articulate ethical standards.

Good ethical decisions and consistent actions can be rewarded with greater access to resources and opportunities. Recognition and appreciation in either a public or private setting increase employees' awareness of the value of ethical behavior to the company.

There are numerous ways to communicate that ethical thinking is critical to the success of the organization. But if clear ethical policies are not established and adherence to them is not rewarded, no one inside or outside the company will recognize the importance of the ethical standards in daily operations.

Recognizing and Removing Barriers

The third step is to observe and revise all organizational practices and systems that are inhibiting good ethical decision making. Consider such things as a widespread inability to talk about ethics in the workplace, a culture that values toughness over the ability to recognize and reason through moral problems, reprimands within departments for raising problems that need to be addressed, closed doors instead of open doors.

In many organizations the reward system, including the compensation system, contributes to unethical behavior because it creates pressures to shortcut ethical considerations if a person is to be successful. When this is the case, it is important to evaluate the barriers to changing those aspects of the reward system that contribute to unethical actions. Why has the system been perpetuated? Who has vested interests in the system as it exists? Have there been any attempts to change it in the past? If there are obvious ethical "costs," what are the offsetting "benefits" to continuing the system as it is?

Barriers to ethical actions may take the form of peer pressure, as is often the case in, for example, the perpetuation of discrimination. Or the barriers may exist because there are financial or other benefits accruing to managers in powerful decision-making positions, who therefore protect their interests in the current system.

Another useful aspect to consider when assessing the barriers is to ask who gets rewarded. What are the characteristics of those who are promoted in this organization? What have they done to earn promotions? What are their selling techniques?

Are they straightforward and honest or manipulative and deceptive? What are the reputations of the successful people?

When one looks around and asks why individuals are not acting up to their highest moral ideals in an organization, there are often many apparent explanations. If these "justifications" for unethical actions are not addressed, the strong ethical standards articulated in the corporate mission statement or code of conduct will never be implemented in practice.

SOME ETHICAL ISSUES IN THE FINANCIAL SERVICES MARKETPLACE

There are many practices in the financial services industry that warrant scrutiny from an ethical perspective. A few of the prominent concerns will be addressed here. These include the use of nonguaranteed and noncurrent rates as illustrations in selling interest-sensitive products, replacement selling, the churning or twisting of clients' accounts, failure to disclose to clients varying levels of commissions on similar products, and unfair discrimination.

The objective of this discussion is to alert the reader to some of the areas in which it would be well to think carefully about the ethical implications of current practices. There is no attempt to analyze each issue thoroughly or to provide solutions. Each of these practices raises complex ethical questions for professionals in this field. As more people are willing to address the ethical costs of these practices, better guidelines will emerge.

High ethical standards are also set by outstanding members of the profession. Leading individuals and organizations must be alert to the opportunities to raise the level of professionalism and ethical actions in order to enhance the respectability and credibility of the profession in society.

In highlighting some of the ethical issues in the financial services industry, we will briefly reiterate the standards of the CLU pledge, The American College's and the American Society's Codes of Ethics, the requirements of professionalism, and the steps in the method of impartial legislation. The purpose is to raise questions for the consideration of the reader.

Illustrations

The use of nonguaranteed and noncurrent rates as illustrations in selling interest-sensitive life insurance and other products can raise conflicts with the CLU pledge and the American Society's Code of Ethics as well as with the standards of professionalism. It is often impossible to argue that the client is being given all necessary information. Sometimes the illustrations are unrealistic. Is the non-guarantee disclosure statement adequate? Often it is not, because of the usual problems with small print. Is the client really clear about the security of the investment and its historic earning record? Only the most honest and realistic illustrations meet the requirements of the codes of ethics and the standards of professional competence and reliability.

If further evidence is needed to demonstrate the unethical foundation of improper illustrations, consider the long-term effects on the companies who mislead clients as to the potential return on their investments. The number and cost of problems facing companies that have consistently oversold clients is staggering.

Replacement Selling or Twisting

Is the new product or policy clearly in the client's interest? If the replacement is not absolutely in the client's best interest, the proposed action is not ethical. The method of impartial legislation requires the creation of an imaginary moral law making the proposed action available to all persons. Would you be prepared to see this action become widely available and practiced by all persons? Reason impartially from the perspective of all persons possibly affected. What could an organization do to create reinforcements for new sales and eliminate rewards for replacement selling?

Churning

Again, the most important and initial question is, Is it in the client's interest? Does this activity fulfill the requirements of professionalism: demonstrating reliability and competence and responding to a client's needs? It often fits none of these. If competent, the financial adviser or sales representative would not be changing advice every few weeks or months.

The temporary success of financial advisers who churn their clients' accounts is based on deception. The adviser induces trust in his or her ability to achieve the client's objectives. Only when this trust is given is the adviser able to persuade the client that constant sales and acquisitions are in the client's interest. In reality these actions only benefit the adviser or broker. The entire practice may be unethical for several reasons: wrongfully inducing trust, breeching that fiduciary trust, and often harming the client financially. Harming the client has long-term detrimental effects on the company and the industry as well.

If we think of churning as a moral law, an action available to all persons, the immorality of this action becomes even clearer. As with all cases of deception, the practice is successful only if people are deceived. If everyone knew and understood that churning was occurring, the adviser would not be able to take advantage of the client.

Disclosure of Commissions

What information does the client need in order to make a good decision about a product or service being recommended? If the financial planner, agent, or adviser has a greater financial interest in one product than another but does not disclose that to a client, is the client misled into believing that an unbiased presentation of the value of each product is being given? What is in the client's interest? What is truly in the professional's interest? Trust is more important than fast sales. Trust is more important to the client, the financial services practitioner, and the company. Reliability and honesty contribute to trust. Does the client always want to know or need to know? Probably not, but the client should know by the professional's behavior that the client can ask for and receive any information that he or she feels is relevant to a decision.

Discrimination and Stereotyping

In all workplaces it is important to be alert to one's own biases and stereotypes. Are we open to hiring, training, and supporting people of different ethnic and religious backgrounds? Do we assume that some people will be more successful than others? Do we provide men and women with similar opportunities and resources? Are we aware of the effects of sexist language? Are we alert to our own assumptions about different groups of people?

The demographics of the work force will change dramatically over the decade of the 1990s. It is projected that by the year 2000 the large majority of the entering work force will consist of groups that are now minorities: women, blacks, Hispanics, and Asians. These groups will bring different backgrounds and cultural training to many relatively homogeneous environments. These groups are still virtually invisible at the higher levels of the corporate world, giving evidence of continuing discrimination.

As has been seen from the codes of ethics, the demands of professionalism, and the method of impartial legislation, ethical judgments require the financial services professional to take into account the perspectives of others, whether they are the needs and interests of the client or those of all affected persons. The professional who learns to do this, should increasingly outgrow discriminatory assumptions and practices. Discrimination and stereotyping are based on ignorance, fear, and inappropriately narrow views of groups different from ourselves. These practices are extremely destructive to society.

Our most significant ethical responsibility is to create an environment in which we can all survive. To achieve this we must take actions that increase trust, meet the needs of those who have put their trust in us, and build organizational systems that encourage reliable, trustworthy, and competent behavior.

Notes
1. The terms *ethics* and *morals* will be used interchangeably. The word *ethic* comes from a Greek root, *ethike,* while *moral* comes from a Latin root, *moralis.* Both words are defined as relating to the principles of right and wrong behavior and to the study of moral obligation. Although they sometimes have different connotations in common usage, they will be treated as synonyms here.
2. Burke A. Christensen, *Journal of the American Society of CLU & ChFC,* January 1990, 21.
3. Kenneth Andrews, "Ethics in Practice," *Harvard Business Review,* September–October 1989, 100.
4. Ronald M. Green and Robbin Derry, *The Ethical Manager* (New York: Macmillan, forthcoming).

14

Sample Planning Case

Dale S. Johnson and Jai P. Sawhney*

INTRODUCTION

In this sample planning case we make recommendations only for generic types of investment vehicles, insurance products, and other planning techniques. We give hypothetical names to recommended instruments and techniques for purposes of identification in planning reports. Although we secured specialist advice in developing our recommendations for the case, in an actual planning practice we would involve these advisers directly with the client in developing more specific recommendations.

Our emphasis in this chapter is on the process of planning rather than specific planning strategies and techniques. Professional financial planners who read this case may think of numerous alternatives for accomplishing the client's financial objectives. Some may work even better than our recommendations. Whatever the alternatives, adherence to the planning process, the integrity of the planning information provided, and the client's objectives is essential.

Limitations of space preclude printing complete before-and-after financial profiles. In practice, you should prepare a Current Financial Profile (base case) for each client that reflects financial information as of the end of the year preceding the current planning year. Then, project these numbers through the agreed-on planning time frame to show the client the future consequences of maintaining this position. Finally, prepare a second Financial Profile that incorporates your planning recommendations, including projections. The two profiles demonstrate the consequences of your recommendations and permit both you and the client to evaluate them.

Limitations of space also diminish our demonstrations of alternative planning scenarios. For example, we could illustrate a client's Financial Profile under the following hypothetical conditions: the client becomes disabled in any year of the planning time frame; the client dies in any year of the planning time frame; the client dies 2 years after transferring ownership of life insurance policies to a trust, and the proceeds are included in the estate; the client retires in any year other than the one projected; the client inherits $1 million in any year of the planning time frame, etc. We could also vary any assumption, the balance in any account or asset item, the inflation factor, anticipated income levels, and all other variables associated with data-entry items to illustrate reconsolidated amounts represented in planning report schedules. There is really no limit to the number of what-if scenarios that could be illustrated.

*Reprinted with permission from *Financial Planning Practice and Procedure,* by Dale S. Johnson and Jai P. Sawhney (Paramus, N.J.: Prentice Hall Information Services, 1988). Copyright © 1988 by Prentice Hall Information Services.

This planning case is for a hypothetical client. Family member names, business entities, and other names are hypothetical. The planning firm — Financial Planning Associates — is fictitious.

CASE NARRATIVE AND PERSONAL PROFILE

Personal Planning Information

Gloria Darsteller is a 36-year-old, single marketing account executive with Brentwood Broadcasting Corporation, a privately held radio broadcasting network located in New York City. Until 2 years ago, Gloria had worked for 4 years in administrative positions at the same company. At that time she moved into marketing and writing public relations and lobbying materials for major corporations and nonprofit organizations for this broadcast network.

Her income has increased dramatically over the past 2 years, with prospects of continuing increases over the next few years. In 1986, Gloria earned $71,000 in salary and bonus. She expects her income to exceed $100,000 by 1988, with a 15 percent annual increase over the next 10 years. She enjoys her work and the increased income her success in this new activity has brought her; however, she now confronts tax and personal financial management problems that she had not previously anticipated.

Gloria has conflicting feelings about her new affluence: on the one hand, she wants to enjoy it in moderation; on the other hand, she wants to create a capital base that, within 10 years, will enable her to radically change her mode of employment and living if she chooses. In current dollars, she would like to have an annual aftertax income of at least $40,000 after 10 more years of working.

Gloria believes that she pays a high price for affluence with the stresses of her job and living in the city. She has little time to pursue her personal interests. (She is a frustrated dramatist who has had one of her plays produced in a small off-Broadway setting.) She has a strong attachment to a house she purchased last year near Woodstock, New York. In 10 years, she might want to relocate to Woodstock and become a part-time real estate broker and a full-time writer. Meanwhile, she wants to explore further real estate investment opportunities in the Catskills.

Gloria seeks ongoing financial counseling to further her basic objectives and define them more precisely. She realizes that her investment experience has been tentative and limited. She must now manage an increasing income, complicated tax considerations, and the temptation to expand her consumer life-style — a temptation all the more enticing because until 2 years ago she had lived modestly on an administrative salary.

Financial Objectives and Assumptions

Gloria's major financial objectives are as follows:

- Establish and maintain an adequate level of liquid reserves through a disciplined cash-management program.

- Increase investment net worth on a systematic basis through a diversified investment program.
- Accumulate enough capital to maintain her life-style and be economically independent before the age of 50.
- Provide for adequate income in case of her disability.
- Minimize taxes while investing for long-range objectives and tax-sheltered income.
- Distribute estate assets (with minimal shrinkage) to her parents (if they survive her) and to her sister and sister's children if her parents do not survive her.

Gloria's Risk Profile indicates that she has a fairly high tolerance for risk. She has a strong preference for growth mutual funds, growth-oriented common stock, and directly owned real estate to build her investment capital base. On the other hand, she expresses a strong concern to preserve her capital, provide for future income, reduce her federal tax burden, and provide inflation protection. In counseling, we determined that, once she was fully aware of the risks associated with her expected return levels (initially 15+ percent), her risk tolerance level falls between 2 and 3 on a 0 to 4 scale. She now understands the need to maintain an appropriate level of liquidity, flexibility, and balance between growth investments and fixed income returns, especially in tax-exempt bonds.

In consultations, we agreed to use an inflation factor of 5 percent throughout the initial 10-year planning time frame. Other planning assumptions are as follows:

- We will seek current returns on municipal bond fund investments of about 8.5 percent and monitor these yields closely for reinvestment purposes.
- We will aim for a growth rate of 12–15 percent annually in common stock-based investments.
- In rental real estate, we will aim for a 15 percent annual growth rate by focusing on investments in the Catskill resort area near Woodstock or in New York City.
- Reinvestment will be in similar vehicles at similar rates of return.
- We will plan for a 4-year horizon initially and use projected checkpoints in 1990 and 1996 for longer-term adjustments to the continuing planning process.
- We will phase in several elements of Gloria's cash management and investment program over the first 4 years of the initial 10-year planning time frame.

Inventory of Assets

Until October 1985, Gloria had done little to bring her personal finances under control or reduce her increasing taxes except contribute to IRA accounts. At the advice of her accountant, in April 1986 she purchased the two-bedroom residential rental property in Woodstock. In October 1986, Gloria invested an additional $12,000 in the property to add a bathroom and laundry room, so that she can rent it year-round.

Gloria actively manages this property. She sets rents, advertises, interviews prospective lessees, collects monthly rental payments, and lets construction and repair contracts. Under a one-year lease, she rents the house for $9,600. She expects to increase annual rent by 10 percent over the foreseeable future.

The purchase price of the house was $95,000. After a $10,000 down payment, she financed the balance with a 30-year fixed-rate mortgage at 10.5 percent. Its depreciable basis, on the 18-year ACRS schedule, is $107,000. She has a homeowner's policy with coverage on the dwelling of $98,000 with no inflation rider and on the replacement cost of contents of $10,000. The annual insurance premium is $261.

In March 1986, Gloria purchased a Honda Accord for $12,500. She allocates it 100 percent to business use, both at Brentwood and for overseeing her rental property. She depreciates the car on the ACRS schedule. She paid $2,500 down and financed $10,000 on a 4-year loan at 11 percent, with monthly payments of $261 beginning April 1, 1986. She pays $1,500 per year for garage space in the city plus $60 per month for gasoline and maintenance. In addition, at a premium of $680 per year (the car is registered in the county where her rental property is located) she carries $100,000/$300,000 liability limits, $150,000 no-fault medical benefits, and $200 deductible comprehensive and collision insurance.

In June 1989, Gloria expects to replace the Honda with a new Sterling that she believes will cost $25,000. She plans to pay $10,000 down and finance $15,000 on a 4-year loan at 11 percent. She will continue to allocate the car to 100 percent business use. She also expects total annual operating expenses of this car to be $3,500 beginning in 1989.

Until 2 years ago, Gloria saved about 20 percent of her gross income, using a savings account and certificates of deposit. In this way, she accumulated about $30,000 before she made her first stock investment. Last year, she established a cash management account with full check-writing privileges at her securities broker-dealer. This account is invested in a tax-exempt municipal bond fund now valued at $19,132. It currently yields 7.5 percent, which is automatically reinvested.

Gloria deposits her monthly salary check and year-end commission-based bonus in the cash management account and writes checks on it to cover her major monthly expenses. She maintains a small checking account at Citibank for odds and ends, with an average balance of $500. In addition, she leaves on deposit with her broker the certificates of common stock in RCI and Flintstone corporations. Neither of these stocks has been a satisfactory investment; RCI (a telecommunications company) has been a disaster. She also owns 200 shares in Brentwood Broadcasting, which she purchased early in August 1986 for $49 per share. She holds these certificates herself.

Over the past 3 years, Gloria has occasionally traded stocks for small short-term gains (or losses) on the recommendation of her account representative. Initially, she thought that as her income rose she would systematically invest in the stock market. She now believes that this type of investing may expose her to unwonted risks and continuing oversight.

She came to this conclusion early last year after considering several investment offerings in both private and public limited partnership real estate syndications. She decided that, if she was going to be serious about real estate, she wanted to choose her own investments and take an active role in managing them. She also decided that she would limit her subsequent direct investments in common stock to no more than 20 percent of her investable funds in any given year. With that decision, she bought the rental house in Woodstock.

Gloria's personal assets are minimal. She has a modest collection of personal jewelry items (to which she adds about $500 worth annually), likes lithographs (she spends about $500 annually to add to her collection), and expects to spend about $1,000 annually to add to and replace household furnishings. Her hobby is photography. She spends about $250 annually on photographic supplies and expects to purchase an enlarger in 1988 for about $1,000.

Gloria's assets include the following:

Cash		$ 500
RCI (300 shares, @ 15.00)		2,175
Flintstone (200 shares, @ 29.00)		5,800
Brentwood (200 shares, @ 49.00)		10,800
TF Cash Mgmt. Acct.		19,132
IRA 1 (9%)		2,818
IRA 2 (10%)		2,928
IRA 3 (11%)		4,684
IRA 4 (8.5%)		2,085
Rental real estate (15%)		121,250
Business automobile		10,000
Personal assets		
Household furn.	15,000	
Jewelry	5,000	
Lithographs	4,000	
Photo equip.	4,000	28,000
Total assets		$210,172

Gloria pays all credit card balances within 2 or 3 months of billing and incurs occasional interest charges on department store charge cards. Her liabilities consist of only the following two longer-term items:

Rental real estate mortgage	$84,717
Business auto loan	8,429
Total liabilities	$93,146

Cash Inflows and Outflows

In 1986, Gloria earned $71,000 in salary and bonus. In 1987, she expects a gross income of more than $90,000, which will include at least $85,000 in salary and bonus. After that, her earnings will be limited only by the time she puts into her work and by account assignments at the company. These assignments are basically designed to encourage account executives to aim for incomes of $100,000–$130,000 annually. Gloria expects her compensation to exceed $100,000 in 1988 and grow at about a 15 percent average annual rate over the next 10 years.

Gloria's financial position in the current year includes the following specific and estimated items:

Salary	$60,000
Bonus	25,000
Rental real estate	9,600
Dividends (Brentwood)	312

| State tax refund | 700 |
| Est. gross income | $95,612 |

Sources of Income

Most of Gloria's income derives from her employment at Brentwood Broadcasting. Each year her salary is scaled to 85 percent of the previous year's gross compensation; bonus compensation above salary is determined at the end of October and paid before the end of each year.

Tax-Deductible Uses of Cash

A financial planning fee of $2,000 for 1987 will decrease to a $750 retainer for 1988. It is aggregated with other employee business expenses (including a $175 income tax return preparation fee) as miscellaneous deductions (subject to the 2 percent floor). Tax-deductible uses of cash (except N.Y. state tax and interest expense) are expected to increase by our assumed inflation factor of 5 percent.

Therapy and counseling	$ 1,500
Medicine and drugs	700
IRA contribution (?)	2,000
New York State tax (est.)	6,000
Interest expense (credit cards)	175
Charitable contributions (50%)	1,000
Miscellaneous deductions	8,500
Gross deductions	$19,875

In addition to these personal deductible expenses, there will be other expenses in 1987 and subsequent years directly attributable to the rental real estate investment. They are estimated as follows:

Advertising	$ 200
Insurance	813
Car and travel	500
Cleaning and maintenance	400
Repairs	500
Supplies	580
Taxes	967
Total expenses (except interest and depreciation)	$3,960

In addition, Gloria estimates that expenses for the Honda in 1987 will total $2,781 (garage in the city, gas, oil maintenance, and insurance); for the Sterling, beginning in 1989, she estimates annual expenses will total $3,500.

We will use our software to compute mortgage interest and depreciation after information is entered for the rental real estate property and the business cars.

Nondeductible Uses of Cash

General living expenses are assumed to increase at 5 percent annually (except furnishings, jewelry, and lithographs, which will remain level). They are estimated as follows:

Food	$ 5,000
Clothing and cleaning	1,500
Entertainment	2,000
Vacations	3,000
Gifts, etc.	1,000
Transportation	900
Repair/maintenance furniture	200
Interior furnishings (annual)	1,000
Photo supplies	250
Rent (NYC apt.)	6,600
Jewelry (annual)	500
Lithographs (annual)	500
Utilities and phone	2,000
Total	$24,450

Risk Coverages, Employee Benefits, and Retirement Assets

At Brentwood, a group-term life insurance contract provides coverage to one and one-half times the nearest $1,000 of her annual compensation; her parents are primary beneficiaries. She is also covered with a group disability income contract for up to $2,500 per month, coordinated with social security benefits for total and permanent disability. This policy pays a maximum of $400 per week for short-term disability of 6 months (with a 7-day waiting period). It will also pay the same for long-term disability if it is certified by a licensed physician that she cannot work. She is also covered by a group health insurance policy to which she makes no premium contributions. This contract provides a stop/loss limit of $250,000 and an overall maximum benefit of $500,000, with a $40 deductible for medical and $50 deductible for dental expenses.

Gloria has no company-sponsored retirement program at Brentwood. Management has discussed a profit-sharing plan, but none has been put into effect. At this point, her only formal retirement plan consists of four individual retirement accounts she opened in 1982, 1983, 1985, and 1986. In 1984, she made a second contribution of $2,000 to the account opened in 1983. She wonders whether it makes sense for her to continue annual contributions to this type of program now that her annual income will soon exceed $100,000.

Estate Conservation and Distribution

Gloria has no dependents. Her retired parents live in Florida and are financially secure. An older sister, Eileen Brennan, is in a second marriage with two children, plus an older child from a previous marriage. At this point, Gloria wants her estate to pass to her parents if they are still living at her death; if not, to her sister and sister's children. She has no will and wonders how it should be drawn, particularly to leave something to her two nieces and her nephew if she should die prematurely. At the death of the second of her parents, she expects an inheritance of approximately $50,000.

PLANNERS' NOTES

General Design of the Financial Plan

In designing Gloria's financial planning for the next 10 years, we conclude that her strong interest in directly owned real estate, with capital growth and tax-reducing advantages coupled with her active participation in managing them, argues for a systematic investment program ultimately involving approximately 40 percent of her surplus cash. We begin this type of investment only in 1990 and will continue it through the initial planning horizon of 10 years and perhaps beyond. We defer further real estate investment in order to (1) maintain a relatively high level of liquidity in the first 4 years of her plan, (2) increase her holding of stock in Brentwood Broadcasting, and (3) buy a condominium in New York City for her personal residence. If interest rates and growth prospects still look good in the Catskills in 1990, she can look seriously for further investment rental property. By that point, her annual cash flow should permit this additional investment. She should also be more diversified in her total investment capital structure by that date.

Until 1990, the 40 percent allocation of surplus cash will be made to tax-exempt municipal bond funds (instead of real estate), one of which will be used as a cash management account. This will provide tax-free accumulation through reinvestment and the liquidity to move to other investments before 1990 should that seem appropriate. It will also provide her with tax-equivalent yields comparable to those of aggressive growth stock and mutual funds. We also suggest that she allocate up to 40 percent of her surplus cash to Orion Shares, beginning in 1990. This is an aggressive growth mutual fund that has averaged 28 percent appreciation over the past 5 years. We recommend that she invest the remaining 20 percent of surplus cash in selected issues of growth common stock, also beginning in 1990. Through installing an automatic cash management feature in her financial plan, each year's surplus cash is allocated to these investments in this order.

Our assessment of this strategy is based partly on the fact that Gloria is not interested in directly overseeing broad-based stock market investments, but wants to put money occasionally into an aggressive or speculative stock. On the other hand, she is interested in managing her own real estate investments. Because she is bright and a quick learner (having already obtained her real estate license), we recommend that she build on her own interests.

Before fully installing the rental real estate segment of her investment program, we believe that Gloria should purchase a condominium in the city for her personal residence. She agrees that this purchase should take precedence over further rental real estate investment until her cash flow improves and she has acquired other substantial equity investments. She has already looked over possibilities and determined price ranges. We recommend that she close by the end of June 1987 and pay $17,000 down on a one-bedroom condominium priced at about $195,000. She should be able to finance the balance on a 30-year mortgage at about 10.5 percent.

By giving up her apartment (it is rent-stabilized and, like most New Yorkers, she considers that an asset) and applying its annual rental to loan amortization, she will secure strong investment potential and several tax advantages of home ownership. In addition, we recommend that Gloria purchase 50 additional shares in Brentwood Broadcasting this year and in each of the next 3 years. This additional stock ownership will permit her to participate more fully in the expected growth of that company.

Planning Objectives

By 1996, if Gloria follows our recommendations, our forecasts indicate that her investment and personal net worth will be sufficient to provide considerably more annual income than the $40,000 minimum she would like. Her assets will support an even higher annual income at that time if she sells the condo or converts it to a rental income unit when she moves to the Catskills. At that point, she should be sufficiently independent to sell and invest further in real estate at her own pace — or to write the plays that may bring her back to New York City for as much time as she would want to spend there in any case.

The Format of the Planning Case

In 3 hours of consultation and information clarification with Gloria, we determined that she expects a comprehensive 10-year planning report confined to essential information, basic financial reports and analyses, and specific recommendations based on this information. We are providing reports for the following years: 1987, 1988, 1989, 1990, and 1996. These reports include current federal tax law and New York State and New York City tax law as of June 1987. This means that our active planning is for only 4 years. The year 1990 and the final year provide sextant readings for the direction of her planning decisions and permit us to foresee (however speculatively) any problem areas that may develop. We could produce a report for each of these 10 years. Doing so, however, would double the number of pages in the report schedules to allow for 10 columns instead of 5.

For help in understanding these reports, Gloria specifically requested that the verbal text our firm provides be included. We agreed that her age, single status, and plans for a major change in her mode of living after the 10-year initial planning horizon nullify most of the value of estate and retirement planning reports. On this basis, we prepared planning reports for Gloria Darsteller as illustrated in her *Personal Financial Plan,* which follows.

PERSONAL FINANCIAL PLAN FOR GLORIA J. DARSTELLER

Table of Contents

Preface

Your Goals and Objectives

Our Summary and Recommendations

An Overview of Your Current Financial Profile

A Graphic Overview of Your Current Financial Profile

Financial Summary

Analyses of Your Financial and Tax Position

   Your Cash Flows and Taxes

   Income Statement

   Supporting Schedule

   Your Cash Flow Management

   Cash Flow Statement

   Your Personal and Investment Net Worth

   Balance Sheet

An Analysis of Your Real Estate Investment

   Investment Analysis

An Analysis of Your Capital Needs

   Capital Needs Analysis

Conserving and Distributing Your Estate

PREFACE

At Financial Planning Associates, we are pleased to participate with you in your financial and tax planning. The reports that follow are your *Personal Financial Plan* as of this date and are based on information you provided. The reports include our forecasts of changes in your financial and tax positions through the years ahead and assume that you will implement the recommendations we make.

We will continue to work with you, your other advisers, and service representatives to help you take the necessary steps to implement your financial decisions. In our professional relationship, the most significant advantages for you will come from continuing access to our financial management experience and counsel. We therefore urge you to use this aspect of our service.

Financial planning is not a specific, one-time event. Rather, it is the continuing application of the same dynamic and interactive process of decision making that brought you to this point in our professional association. Changing conditions and circumstances in your personal life, the financial services marketplace, and tax law are a compelling reality. Charting your financial future through these changes requires that you be flexible and adaptable to ongoing decision making. We have designed our planning recommendations with this need in mind.

The analyses and reports that follow look necessarily to the future and use a number of forecasting techniques. A variety of assumptions and judgmental elements are inherent in any attempt to forecast future results. You should therefore understand that these forecasts are no more than tentative projections from your current position. Differences in tax law, investment climates, interest rates, personal circumstances, and the like will have profound effects on both the accuracy of our forecasts and the continuing suitability of our recommendations for your evolving circumstances.

For these reasons, all of us will need to be sensitive and alert to these changes. Their impact on your ongoing financial profile will require us to reexamine and alter as necessary the strategic course charted from this point. Only thus can you realistically expect to attain the financial objectives toward which we have helped you aim in the process of planning.

As you review our recommendations and supporting reports, remember that the planning process is complete only if financial strategies and tactics are implemented as they are developed. We structured our recommendations around our understanding of your needs, objectives, and resources. You may want to modify some of these recommendations or assign them different priorities. Any changes you make will alter the forecasts and projections and create a different financial plan. That is your prerogative. It is *your* plan.

After you have determined exactly what you want to do, you must then implement your decisions and close your decision-making loop. Then you will begin to move from where you are now to where you want to be. Only through decisive action can you experience the peace of mind that comes from knowing that your financial affairs are under control through your own management. Timely implementation of the decisions you make now and in the future will be the basis for achieving your financial goals and objectives.

While reading and evaluating these reports, you may find it helpful to review the essential elements of personal financial planning that all of us have used to help you chart your financial directions.

[*Note:* Throughout the verbal text of these reports, we purposely print basic terminology and concepts with initial capital letters to draw them to the client's attention and disclose their relationships. These items are referred to repeatedly in numerical schedules and analytical reports as either headings or "bottom-line" categories. In fact, the design and strategy of the client's financial plan is structured within these concepts. For that reason, these concepts and their terminology are most important for fully understanding these reports.]

Comprehensive Personal Financial Planning

When you fully implement comprehensive personal financial planning decisions, you create your own management system. This system focuses on controlling all financial decisions that affect Tax Liabilities, Cash Flows, and Net Worth. Its aim is to integrate Tax Planning, Risk Management, and Investment Planning in a comprehensive planning process. By adhering to this process, we can measure the results of each financial decision through its effects and consequences. In addition, comprehensive planning integrates all personal planning concerns and considerations with determined financial objectives, so that these will be realistic and consistent with who you are and what you want to do with your financial resources.

The comprehensive planning method enables you to make systematic financial decisions by allocating your Cash Flows and Investment Capital Assets toward the achievement of your overall lifetime objectives. To make this method succeed, you must supply the complete information that any good decision-making process requires. From Financial Planning Associates and other advisers, you need support for your decisions through our knowledge of current tax law and suitable alternatives in the financial services marketplace. You also need analyses of your financial information such as we provide. In this sense, you make the decisions and we facilitate your decision making.

In this role, we act solely in your best interests and help you determine and acquire the financial services and products you need on an ongoing basis for a fully developed personal financial management system. In our consultations and in the reports and recommendations included here for your financial plan, we provide you with this support.

To help clarify the main sections of these reports and analyses, the essential elements of financial planning provide useful guidance. Two simple explanatory approaches are particularly helpful. The first is the Allocational Principle of Cash Flows for spending controls. The second is the Production Principle of Investment Capital for structuring spending for investment to produce Cash Flows for specific purposes on an ongoing basis.

The Allocational Principle of Cash Flows

The Allocational Principle of Cash Flows assumes that all personal Cash Inflows are spent in three categories: (1) Personal Spending, (2) Taxes, and (3) Saving and

Investment. Personal spending includes everything purchased for use and consumption—housing, food, clothing, transportation, vacations, hobbies, entertainment, gifts, and premiums for risk management contracts (such as life insurance policies). Spending for taxes includes federal, state, and local income taxes and social security tax. Spending for saving and investment includes every dollar from current Cash Inflows that is allocated to fund specific shorter-term and lifetime objectives, income maintenance during retirement, and distributions to heirs and beneficiaries through estate transfers. Spending for saving and investment is deferred spending because it will actually be expensed at some future date(s).

All Cash Inflows are finally spent. This means that they must be matched and balanced by the sum of all Cash Outflows and outlays. The total Cash Inflow allocated to acquiring assets creates the basis of total Net Worth, which is the difference in dollar value between Total Assets and Total Liabilities. In other words, assets are created through saving (not spending now for consumption and taxes) and investing any annual Cash Surplus after basic living expenses and tax obligations have been paid.

Among the assets that one acquires, successful Investment Assets (explained below) create an increasing capital base that produces additional Cash Flows, either in the form of current income or as future growth in value, or both. Reinvesting Cash Inflows created by investments compounds the growth rate of the Investment Capital base. Over time, an expanding capital base increases Investment Net Worth. Holding constant or reducing liabilities accelerates this increase of Investment Net Worth.

Financial planning attempts to create additional Cash Surplus for investment by employing legal and suitable tax-reduction techniques that convert some of the dollars otherwise spent for taxes into additional dollars to be spent for investment. This effect is also accelerated if spending for life-style maintenance is held constant or reduced as personal income, income from investments, and other Cash Inflows increase.

Effective personal financial planning begins with an analysis of how Cash Flows (both inflows and outflows) are being generated and allocated. Once this analysis is available, we can focus on managing and controlling all Cash Outflows related to living expenses, taxes, and investment—the three parts of the allocational principle in which all Cash Inflows are ultimately spent.

Comprehensive financial planning permits you to use this principle in every area of your financial life. By using it in all of your financial decisions, you can direct appropriate allocations of Cash Surplus and Investment Capital to each of your funding objectives in each area of your primary planning concerns during lifetime employment and retirement. In addition, you can also control the distribution of these Cash Flows and Investment Assets in your estate. Your financial planning reports are structured around cash flow management.

Let's look now at how the Allocational Principle of Cash Flows relates to the second principle we mentioned above: the Production Principle of Investment Capital.

The Production Principle of Investment Capital

Your Investment Capital Asset structure can be compared to that of any business entity. We can usefully think of this business entity as a money factory that consists of all the financial resources that work together to produce a desired amount of money each year. Any organized business consists of several departments that require investment in time or capital to fund their expected production of Cash Flows. For most persons, these "departments" include Job, Investments, Social Security, Pension, and Insurance.

In a sense, it does not matter which department of the business produces the Cash Flows as long as they are adequate to take care of annual requirements: Personal Spending, Spending for Taxes, and Spending for Saving and Investment. However, without planning and proper funding, one or more of these departments may not produce the desired level of Cash Flows as needs arise.

Like any capital enterprise, if this entity is to succeed in producing income over the long term, it must accomplish two main objectives: (1) generate enough output of cash each year to cover your personal spending and taxes payable and (2) produce enough to reinvest in itself for capital growth. Reinvestment in yourself assures that there will be enough Cash Inflow, at every projectable point, to fund your specific financial objectives at a level consistent with your determined needs. If one department of your business shuts down, the other departments must increase their production to maintain the levels of Cash Inflow you need.

When you retire, for example, your Job department closes and your Pension, Social Security, and Investment departments must fill the cash-inflow shortfall that retirement usually creates. Similarly, if you die or become disabled, your Insurance department joins the other still-functioning departments to replace the Cash Inflows of capital production that you lost (or your survivors lost) when your Job department closed down. Your ability to earn money through employment is a capital-producing asset.

Personal Assets — such as your personal residence and automobiles — factor into your Total Asset structure and therefore into your Net Worth. However, they are not included in your Investment Capital Asset structure if you acquire them for use and consumption rather than for the production of Cash Flows. If your Personal Assets have market value — if they have a ready buyer at a price you accept — you can liquidate them for cash. One of the aims of personal financial planning is to ensure that you will not have to resort to this extreme measure to produce the dollars you will need to spend now or later for living, taxes, and investment. On the other hand, at some point in your life, such as in retirement or at your death, you may want to liquidate some of your Personal Assets or convert them to Investment Capital Assets.

Allocating Cash Flows and Investment Capital

To sum up, the relationship between the Allocational and Production Principles of Cash Flows and Investment Capital is central to the basic thrust of personal financial planning. To see yourself — your life circumstances and all of your financial resources — as a business entity assumes that your business is an ongoing Capital Investment Structure designed to produce Cash Flows.

As an individual economic entity, you are initially funded toward the future by the Cash Surplus from your Cash Inflows that you allocate to saving and investment. All of your further investments, plus the reinvestment of the Cash Inflows and realized Capital Appreciation that your current investments produce, are allocated to new departments of your business or to increased funding of currently active departments. In turn, these departments are assigned specific cash-flow-production objectives to meet your lifetime financial needs as well as the financial needs of your survivors.

Comprehensive personal financial planning is actually a method for creating and spending cash flows. We can sum it up as follows: Personal financial planning is the comprehensive, systematic method for establishing, maintaining, nourishing, and eventually liquidating or otherwise disposing of your capital assets to produce desired levels of cash flow for attaining specific financial objectives during your lifetime and within your wishes and intentions for distributing your estate.

This comprehensive personal spending method is employed systematically in the following areas of special planning focus:

- *Tax Planning:* planning for the reduction of tax liabilities to increase cash flows for personal spending and for investment allocation
- *Cash Flow and Liability Management:* maintaining and enhancing personal cash flows through employment, professional practice, or business ownership; controlling allocations of expenditure for life-style maintenance, taxes, and investment; efficiently controlling personal debt levels
- *Risk Management and Insurance Planning:* planning for the protection of cash flows through sound financial management and through cost-effective insuring against risks to income and assets
- *Investment Planning and Management:* planning for and managing the building of a capital base for generating future cash flows by spending current annual surpluses of cash for investment assets; managing investment programs and maintaining appropriate levels of liability associated with investment net worth
- *Business Interests and Employee Benefits:* planning and managing the integration of personal financial planning objectives, the assets and cash flows of business ownership interests, and the various employee benefits typically associated with corporate executives and other salaried employees
- *Retirement and Economic Independence:* planning the allocation of specific investment dollars (in conjunction with social security benefits and pension and other retirement plans) to provide adequate capital to generate the cash flows deemed necessary for economic independence
- *Estate Conservation and Distribution:* planning for the lifetime accumulation and appropriate titling of assets and their distribution according to the individual's intentions at death

To these areas of special emphasis, your own personal concerns, your particular objectives, and your particular circumstances are integrated to create your personal financial management system.

Most of your personal financial transactions generate taxes payable now, next year, or at some deferred taxable event that your capital-production structure creates.

For this reason, comprehensive financial planning integrates tax planning strategies and tactics to foresee and control these Tax Liabilities. As we noted above, comprehensive planning also tries to convert some of what you would otherwise pay as taxes into additional Surplus Cash for investment. Our analyses of both your current and your future financial position carefully track the tax consequences of your financial transactions.

The function of Risk Management in comprehensive financial planning is essentially to provide a hedge against the events (such as death, disability, liability judgments, and major illness) that could threaten the success of your management of Cash Flows and Investment Capital Assets. In this light, we recommend life insurance to replace the Investment Capital that you would not be able to accumulate within your financial planning strategies were you to die prematurely. In some instances, because of the tax-favored accumulation of Investment Capital within life insurance contracts, we may recommend them for investment purposes. Generally, if your Investment Capital program succeeds, the time may come when your only need for pure life insurance protection would be to provide liquidity for settling your estate.

Similarly, all other insurance contracts are used to protect the continuity and conservation of your Cash Inflows and accumulated Investment and Personal Assets. Unless you are a formally organized ongoing business (in which case premiums for insurance contracts would be a tax-deductible business expense), the premiums you pay for contracts of insurance are a nondeductible personal capital expense item. In other words, your spending for insurance premiums is to protect the income-producing potential of your life, and of your accumulated Investment Capital, for the benefit of yourself and your survivors.

Concluding Remarks

If you arrange and manage your financial life in a comprehensive strategy as outlined above, you will have a systematic method for establishing, maintaining, nourishing, and eventually liquidating or otherwise disposing of your Investment Capital Assets and their associated Cash Flows. You will have a personal financial plan.

Your current financial profile reflects your present financial and tax position. The reports that follow are designed to provide you with the systematic method and information support you need for moving your profile toward your personal financial objectives in the years ahead. We urge you to carefully read and evaluate these reports. Our specific recommendations are included in the section entitled "Our Summary and Recommendations."

You are assured of our availability for further consultation, information support, and help with implementing these recommendations to convert them to your personal financial decisions. As you complete that still unfinished task, your current financial profile will become your *Personal Financial Plan.*

YOUR GOALS AND OBJECTIVES

This section recapitulates your financial objectives as we understand them. We make a distinction between your objectives for creating and increasing Investment Capital Assets and your objectives for conserving and distributing these assets from your estate. Your investment growth objectives are taken fully into account throughout the reports covering the next 10 years. Your estate conservation and distribution objectives are taken into account in the Estate Conservation and Distribution section to help you realize your distribution intentions towards heirs and beneficiaries with the least amount of estate shrinkage through taxation and settlement costs.

Lifetime Planning

In our consultations, we refined your short-term and long-range financial objectives. The total horizon in which we are planning consists of only 10 years, or until you reach a level of Investment Net Worth that will support your economic independence.

Following is a summary of your financial objectives as of this date.

1. Establish and maintain an adequate level of liquid reserves through a disciplined cash-management program.
2. Increase your Investment Net Worth on a systematic basis through a diversified investment program focused on real estate.
3. Accumulate enough capital to maintain your life-style and be economically independent.
4. Maintain your current standard of living in the event of your long-term disability.
5. Minimize taxes while meeting Investment Capital accumulation objectives in the most efficient manner; reduce income tax liabilities, if possible, with creative sheltering of investment income.

Estate Planning

Your desires and objectives for conserving and distributing your estate are summarized below.

6. Avoid unnecessary taxes and estate shrinkage at your death.
7. Leave the assets in your estate at death to either or both of your parents if they survive you; if not, to your sister, Eileen Brennan, if she survives you; if not, to the children of Eileen in a manner that preserves the capital for their education or for distribution to them equitably after they reach the age of 23.

OUR SUMMARY AND RECOMMENDATIONS

In our discussions and in the analyses of your current financial profile, there are several clearly indicated steps you now need to take to start moving more directly toward your overall financial objectives. In our planning time frame for 1987 and beyond, we have included our specific recommendations in the computations and forecasts to illustrate their consequences on your financial and tax position if you implement them. We have summarized our specific recommendations for conserving and distributing your estate in the Estate Conservation and Distribution section.

We summarize below our specific recommendations for your overall financial planning. After this summary, we include an Action Checklist to indicate by priority ranking the steps you now need to take to fully implement your personal financial management decisions and provide ongoing oversight.

Specific Recommendations

- Use the Tax-Free Cash Management Account as your investment control account. From its cash surpluses each year, allocate investment funds as indicated in our investment recommendations below.
- Establish an investment program designed to provide an investment portfolio by 1996 that is balanced between real estate investment properties, selected issues of growth common stock, growth mutual funds, and municipal bonds. To achieve this aim, allocate your surplus cash as follows:
  - 25 percent annually to the Tax-Free Cash Management Account, beginning in the current year, at current yields of 8.5 percent or better
  - 15 percent annually to a Tax-Free Municipal Bond Fund beginning in 1990, at yields of 8.5 percent or better
  - 40 percent to an aggressive growth mutual fund, such as Orion Shares, beginning in 1990, at an annual yield of at least 12 percent
  - 20 percent to nondividend Selected Aggressive Stock with anticipated returns of about 15 percent annually, beginning in 1990
  - an additional 50 shares during each of the next 4 years in Brentwood Corporation common stock, for both dividend income and projected appreciation of about 15 percent annually.

    This means that during the next 4 years, we will increase your holdings of Brentwood to 400 shares and build the Tax-Free Cash Management Account to a substantial balance. Beginning in late 1990 or early 1991, we can use this balance as a down payment on further rental real estate investment opportunities — or do so earlier if your evolving circumstances support that plan.

    In any case, by 1991 we will need to rearrange the percentage allocations above to position you to start a concerted real estate investment program, so that by 1996 your investment in this category will be significantly larger than your reports now project. This modification will also diminish your projected holdings in growth common stock, mutual fund shares, and tax-free municipal bond funds in 1996.
- Buy the condominium in the city for your personal residence; use $17,000 from your current balance in the Tax-Free Cash Management Account as a down payment and secure 30-year mortgage financing at 10.5 percent for $178,000 of the $195,000 purchase price of the unit you have looked at.
- Cease your contributions to IRAs. You can do better by contributing to the Tax-Free Cash Management Account as your rising income phases out the former advantages of these contributions. If Brentwood installs a profit-sharing

plan, you will have all the coverage you need in addition to your own investments to provide a comfortable retirement after age 65.

- Continue to actively manage your rental property in Woodstock. After 1990, as positive and fully taxable cash flows begin to be generated by this property, we can evaluate several options for liquidating or exchanging it for similar property to continue the tax-reducing advantages of this form of investment in the light of tax law at that time.

- Liquidate your holdings in RCI and Flintstone common stock. The net capital loss from these two transactions will provide a deduction this year. Neither stock is likely to recover significantly enough to permit a gain over the opportunity cost of having your capital tied up there. The proceeds will add to cash available this year to apply $17,000 to the purchase price of the condo and maintain an appropriate balance in the Tax-Free Cash Management Account.

- Purchase a disability income insurance contract that will provide you $18,000 per year of income in addition to the Brentwood coverage, for a total of $48,000 of replacement income coverage in the event of your disability. Buy only a guaranteed renewable contract with the most liberal definition of disability. The annual premium should be approximately $680.

- Increase your homeowner's insurance coverage on the Woodstock rental property to 100 percent of its replacement value, and have the coverage adjusted each year for approximate appreciation in value. Purchase homeowner's coverage on the condo in the city for at least 80 percent of its replacement value and have the coverage adjusted annually for appreciated value. The premium for $220,000 of initial coverage on the condo should be approximately $980.

- In 1988, drop comprehensive and collision coverage on the Honda and self-insure; this will save you approximately $275 annually in cash outflow.

- In the early years of your plan, we recommend that you slightly reduce or defer some of your planned expenditures for jewelry, lithographs, photography equipment, and household furnishings to direct more cash to investment.

- Have your attorney draft a simple will expressing your estate distribution wishes — specifically, that your entire estate should pass to either or both of your parents jointly if they survive you; if they do not survive you, that your entire estate should pass to your married sister, Eileen Brennan, after bequests to each of your sister's living children (three as of this date) of $25,000; if neither your parents nor your sister survives you, that your entire estate should pass in equal shares to the surviving children of your sister, Eileen Brennan, and that a trust be established for these children from which income and principal can be distributed to them in equitable amounts until they reach the age of 23, after which the remaining trust principal will be distributed to each surviving child equally.

Implementation Schedule

We share with you the responsibility of following through with your decisions and implementing our suggestions and recommendations. We will arrange appointments and be present, as needed, to coordinate activities and provide relevant information for other professionals.

To implement our recommendations, you should take the steps indicated in the checklist below. When you have completed steps scheduled for the current year, your *Personal Financial Plan* will begin.

TABLE 14-1
Action Checklist for Implementation

Recommen-dation	Action Required	Time Frame	Party Responsible	Date Completed
(1)	Change cash management/ investment practices	Now	Client	
(2)	Arrange purchase of 50 shs. Brentwood stock over each of next 4 yrs.	Now	Client/Co.	
(3)	Close on condo	Now	Client/agent	
(4)	Cease contributions	Now	Client	
(5)	Ongoing mgmt.		Client	
(6)	Sell RCI and Flintstone	Now	Client/broker	
(7)	Purchase disab. income policy	Now	Client/agent	
(8)	Acquire/increase homeowners ins.	Now	Client/agent	
(9)	Reduce/defer personal purchases	1987	Client	
(10)	Have attorney draft will	Now	Client/attorney	
(11)	Drop comp/collision coverage	1988	Client	

AN OVERVIEW OF YOUR CURRENT FINANCIAL PROFILE

This section consists of summaries of your current financial profile between the beginning and ending dates of our planning horizon. The purpose of these summaries is to provide you a comparative analysis and evaluation of your present financial position. The summaries include the overall effects of your current financial transactions and assume that you will implement the specific recommendations we have developed for your endorsement.

The information included in this overview is derived from the more detailed tax and financial analyses included in subsequent sections of this document (or in your case file, from which we can provide copies at your request). These summaries outline your interrelated financial and tax transactions over a period of 10 years, starting with 1987.

Your Net Worth

A conservative valuation of your present assets and liabilities reveals that your Net Worth is $190,060. The value of your assets places you in a select group. You are among the wealthiest 2.6 percent of adults in the United States. When your profile is compared with others whose Total Assets exceed $300,000, about 17 percent have a Net Worth similar to yours.

Your Adjusted Gross Income

Your current Adjusted Gross Income indicates that you would be classified as an above-average-income household. According to a review of all individual tax returns filed for the 1983 tax year, your current Adjusted Gross Income is in the top 5 percent reported. You are among fewer than four million individuals and households who show an Adjusted Gross Income of between $50,000 and $75,000 a year. About 90 million individuals show less Adjusted Gross Income than your group reports.

The figures above are based on the latest available information on personal wealth and income published by the Internal Revenue Service.

Your Taxes, Cash Flows, and Purchasing Power

Based on the information you provided and the assumptions we made in projecting your profile for the next 10 years, your Net Worth increases at a rate higher than the anticipated inflation rate. The increase in your Net Worth places you in an even higher group of wealthy individuals and families. However, this increase cannot be accurately categorized as above until more recent statistics are available.

In the first year of your profile, your income is taxed at a Marginal Bracket Rate of 35 percent. Your tax profile is typical for your income level.

This analysis indicates that the overall growth in your Cash Inflows will be sufficient to offset the effects of inflation. Inflation has the effect of progressively reducing the real value or purchasing power of the dollar. In 1996, each current dollar will be worth 59 cents, assuming an average inflation rate of 5 percent. In 1987, you will receive a Gross Real Income of $106,537. From this amount, you will pay an Income Tax of $23,111. Your Net Real Income will therefore be $83,426. This Net Real Income excludes the cash you will receive from liquidating assets as well as the tax losses that will be generated by your tax-favored or direct participation investments.

Real Income represents your current spendable income or purchasing power. Your purchasing power is estimated to increase steadily throughout the 10-year span covered in your financial profile. To maintain your current level of purchasing power in the last year of our planning time frame, you must produce a Net Real Income of $129,422 in 1996 to neutralize the combined impact of taxes and inflation (taxflation) on your Cash Inflows. Your projected Net Real Income of $271,520 in 1996 is derived from $378,637 of Gross Real Income less $107,117 of projected Income Tax. Therefore, your purchasing power will not be adversely affected over the next 10 years.

In the first year of the plan, you are in a sound Cash Flow position. During 1987, you will spend about 20 percent of your total pretax Cash Inflows for living expenses. Your future spendable income will grow faster than your future living expenses. Therefore, the amount of Surplus Cash available for saving and investment will be increasing each year.

A GRAPHIC OVERVIEW OF YOUR CURRENT FINANCIAL PROFILE

The analytical results and observations described in this section are derived from your current financial profile and the projected outlook for your financial position over the next 10 years. Apart from the details and numbers of various financial analyses in subsequent sections, we would like you to *see* your overall financial picture.

The following graphic profile provides you a quick visual grasp of your Cash Flow, Net Worth, and Tax Liabilities. This section contains the following graphs and charts to describe your current and projected financial profile from several important analytical perspectives:

Cash Inflow
Income and Inflation
Cash Outflow
Net Worth
Income Taxes
Income and Taxes

ANALYSES OF YOUR FINANCIAL AND TAX POSITION

The following reports provide more detailed written analyses of your financial and tax position over the next 10 years. The reports assume you will have implemented our recommendations. These analyses are accompanied and supported by your basic financial statements and use terminology and concepts drawn from them to focus your attention on the most important items for you to consider.

Your financial statements include:

Income Statement
Supporting Schedule
Cash Flow Statement
Balance Sheet

YOUR CASH FLOWS AND TAXES

Your Income

You earn a total of $85,000 in Personal Service Income (salaries, wages, bonuses) in 1987. In addition, you earn $2,337 in interest and dividends. The total of your Cash Inflows for this year is $76,041 after considering the loss of $21,596 from your direct participation or other tax-favored investments and before considering any other adjustments or deductions for tax purposes.

In 1996, you are projected to earn a total of $299,021 in Personal Service Income. Your interest and dividend earnings are projected to be $29,340. The adjusted investment earnings for tax purposes is computed to be $353,851. This computation takes into consideration the gain of $2,852 from your direct participation or other tax-favored investments.

FIGURE 14-1
Cash Inflow for Gloria J. Darsteller (1987)

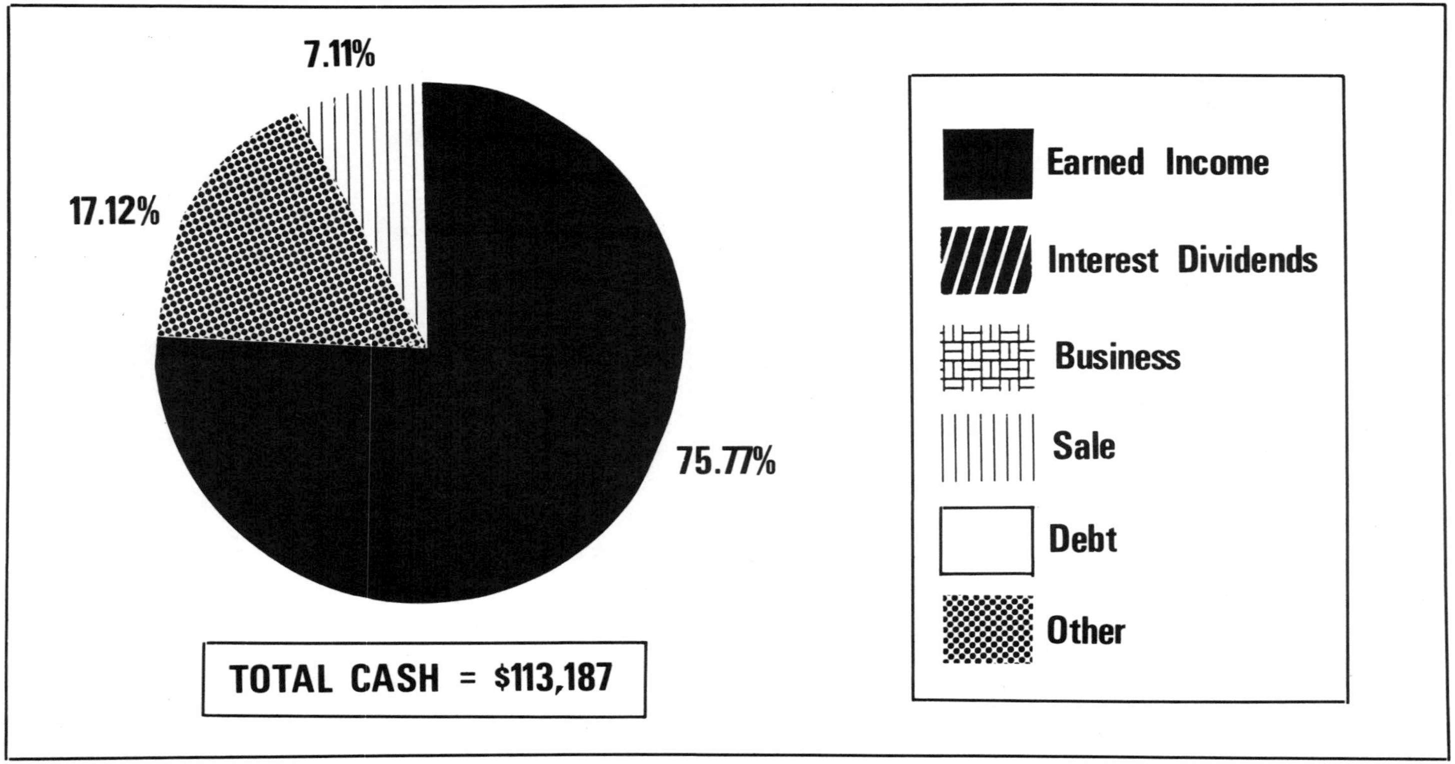

FIGURE 14-2
Income and Inflation for Gloria J. Darsteller

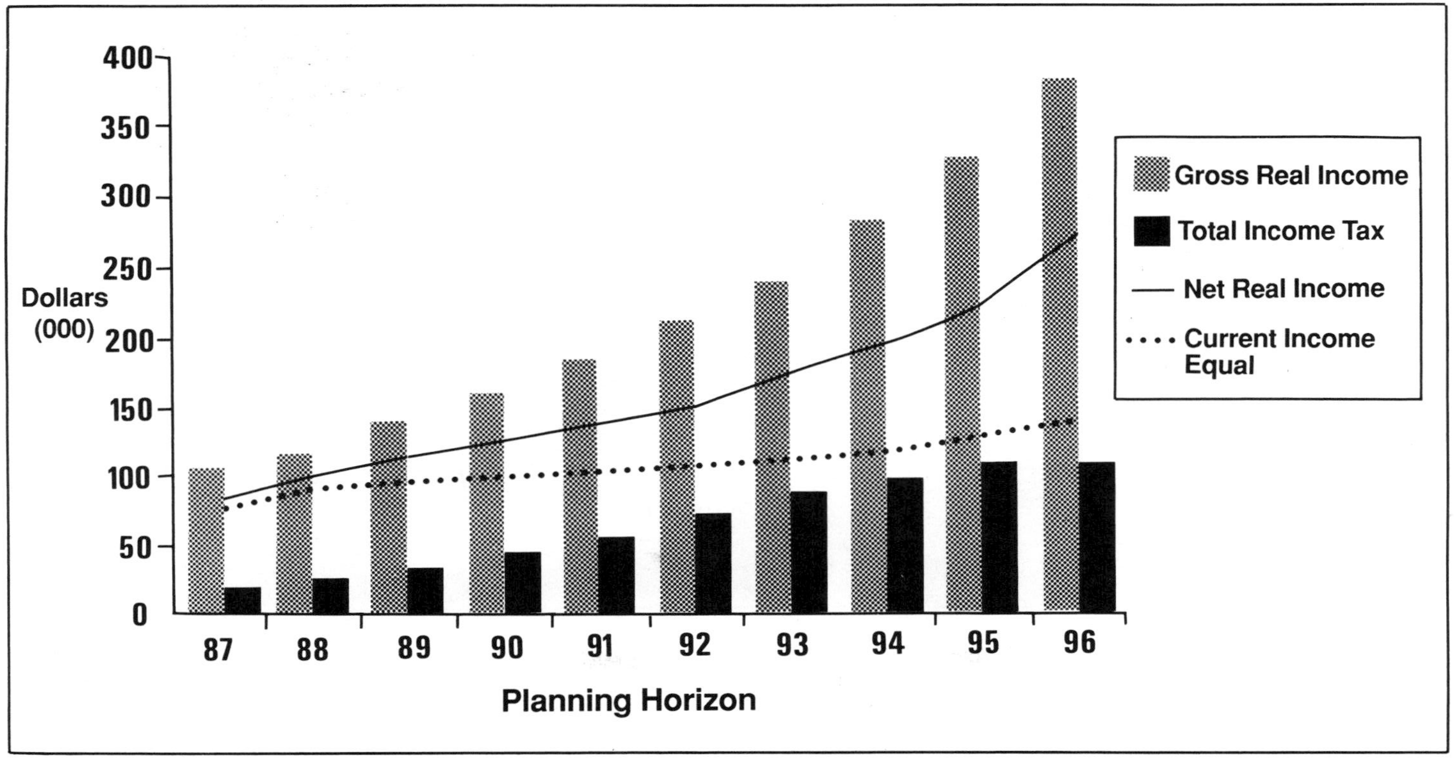

FIGURE 14-3
Cash Outflow for Gloria J. Darsteller

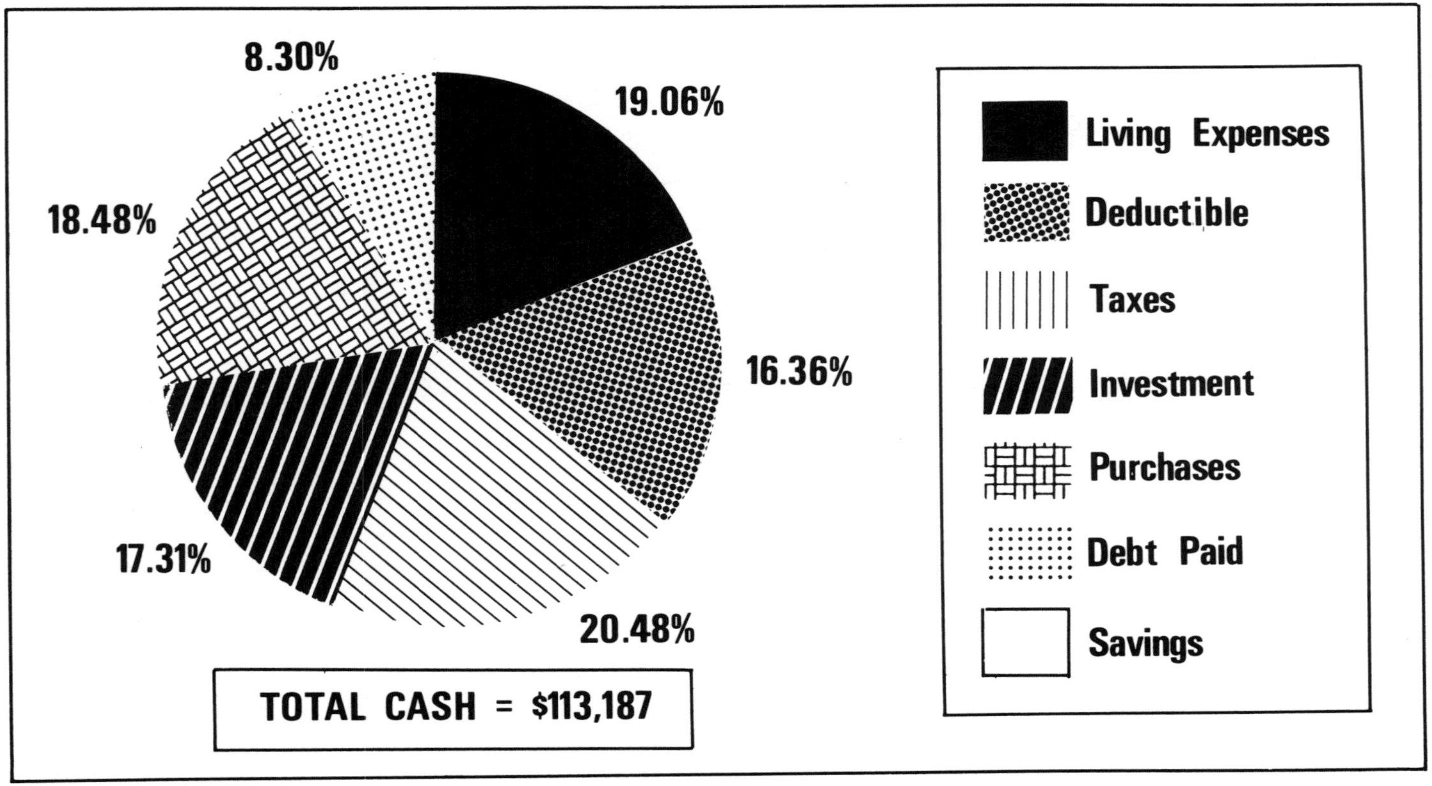

Living Expenses
Deductible
Taxes
Investment
Purchases
Debt Paid
Savings

19.06%
16.36%
8.30%
20.48%
18.48%
17.31%

TOTAL CASH = $113,187

FIGURE 14-4
Net Worth for Gloria J. Darsteller

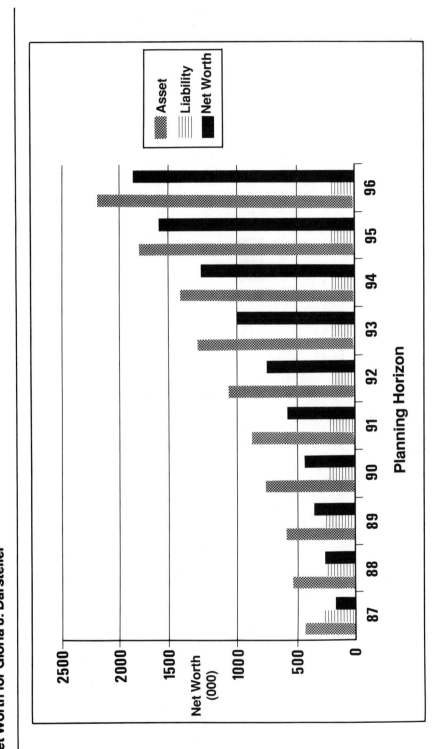

FIGURE 14-5
Income Taxes for Gloria J. Darsteller (1987)

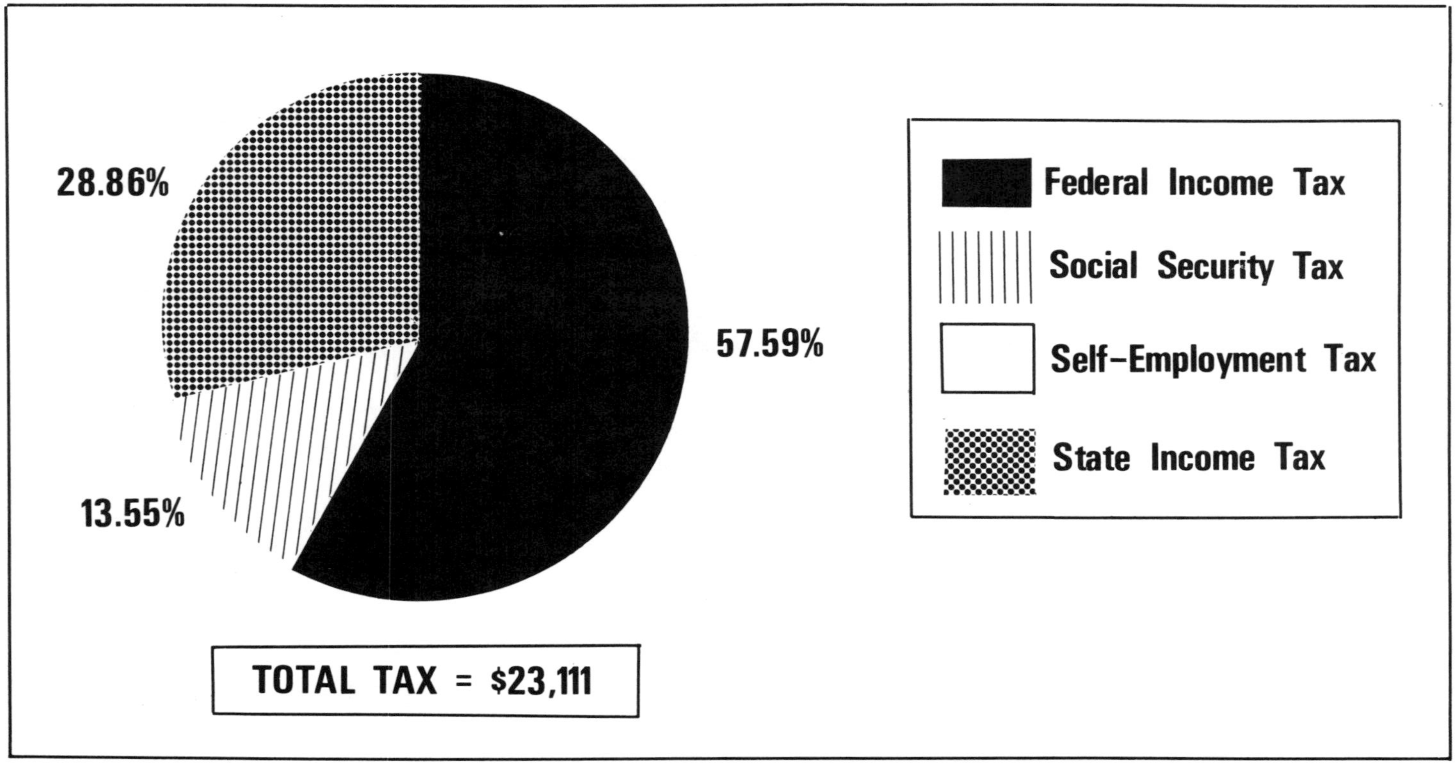

Legend:
- Federal Income Tax
- Social Security Tax
- Self-Employment Tax
- State Income Tax

57.59%

28.86%

13.55%

TOTAL TAX = $23,111

FIGURE 14-6
Income and Taxes for Gloria J. Darsteller

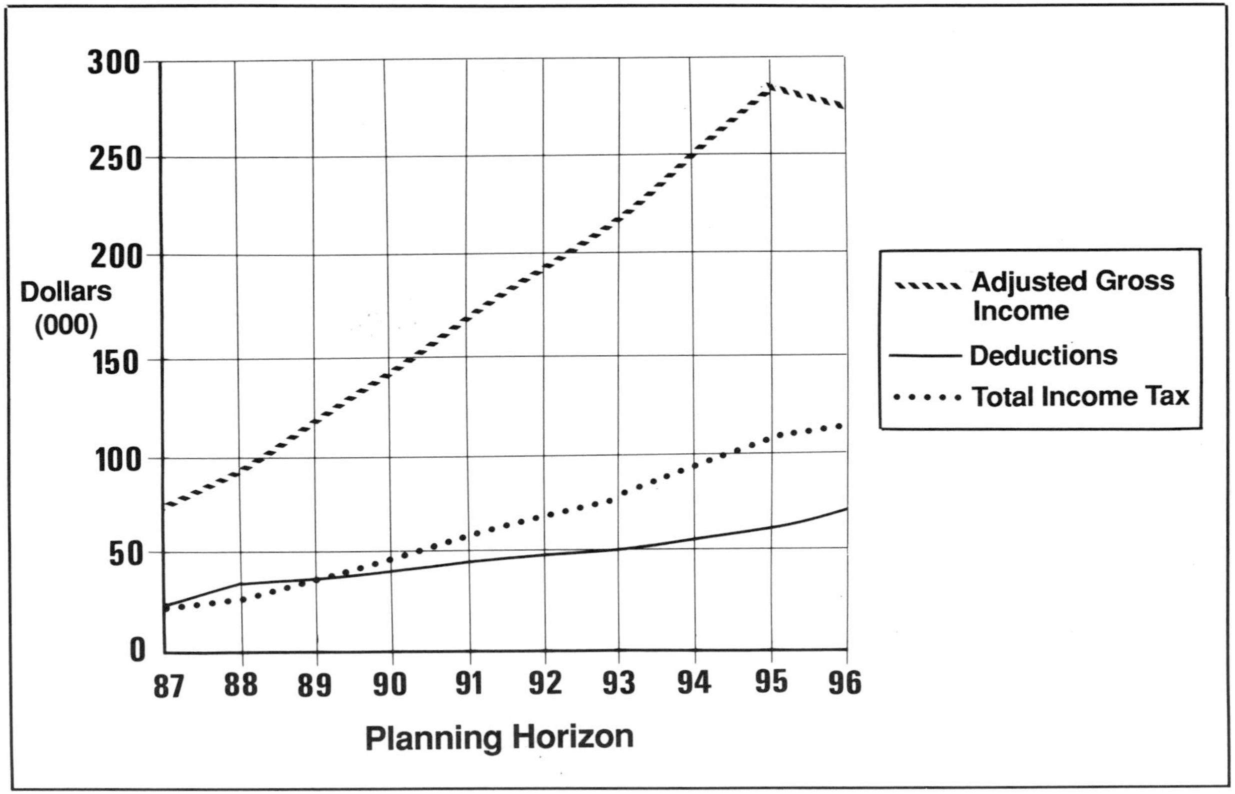

TABLE 14-2
Financial Summary for Gloria J. Darsteller (June 1987)

	1987	1988	1989	1990	1996
Gross Real Income					
Personal earnings	$ 85,000	$ 97,750	$112,413	$129,275	$299,021
Interest income	2,025	3,265	4,672	5,858	28,540
Dividends rcvd	312	375	560	640	800
Rental income	9,600	10,560	11,616	12,778	22,638
Business auto 2	0	0	0	0	5,000
Business auto 1	0	0	5,200	0	0
Rental real est	9,600	10,560	11,616	12,778	22,638
	$106,537	$122,510	$146,077	$161,329	$378,637
Income & Inflation					
Gross real income	$106,537	$122,510	$146,077	$161,329	$378,637
Total income tax	−23,111	−24,359	−35,588	−43,426	−107,117
Net real income	$ 83,426	$ 98,151	$110,489	$117,903	$271,520
Cur real income	$ 83,426	$ 87,598	$ 91,977	$ 96,576	$129,422
Inflation rate	5%	5%	5%	5%	5%
Cash Flow					
Citibank checking	$ 500	$ 500	$ 547	$ 487	$ 538
Normal cash inflow	113,187	119,245	141,405	155,471	350,097
Normal cash outflow	103,819	99,399	128,165	128,509	196,503
Cash invested	9,368	19,800	13,300	27,000	153,600
Cash balance	$ 500	$ 547	$ 487	$ 449	$ 532
Net Worth					
Personal assets	$266,662	$302,984	$343,365	$389,755	$ 854,225
Investment assets	191,473	236,489	304,882	359,510	1,326,271
Personal liabilities	−177,640	−176,710	−175,676	−174,529	−164,448
Investment liabilities	−90,435	−87,422	−97,276	−92,577	−77,577
Personal net worth	89,022	126,274	167,689	215,226	689,777
Investment net worth	101,038	149,067	207,606	266,933	1,248,694
Net worth	$190,060	$275,341	$375,295	$482,159	$1,938,472

Your Tax-Favored/Direct Participation Investments

The total value of your tax-favored or direct participation investments changes from $147,438 in 1987 to $495,526 in 1996. These investments produce a gross positive pretax Cash Flow of $9,600 in the first year of your financial profile, while pretax Cash Flow from your investments will be $27,638 in 1996. Your investments also produce a taxable loss of $21,596 in the first year of your profile. In 1996, your taxable gain from investment will be $2,852.

Your Tax Preferences amount to $3,210 and the total amount of Investment Interest you pay to produce the loss is $7,825, subject to deductible limits, in 1987. However, $272 of your Investment Interest exceeds the deductible limits and has therefore been disallowed. Your Investment Interest will be $8,601 in 1996. All of your Investment Interest expense will be fully deductible that year.

For financial details on your rental real estate investment, please review the Investment Analysis report.

Your Individual Retirement Plans

As of the end of 1987, you have accumulated $13,662 in your Individual Retirement Plans. You are not making any tax-deductible contributions to these plans in 1987.

You will have accumulated $32,088 in your Individual Retirement Plans as of the end of 1996. You are not making any tax-deductible contributions to these plans in 1996.

Your Income Taxes

We compute your 1987 Income Tax to be $23,111. This tax consists of $13,310 in Federal Regular Tax and $3,132 in Social Security tax. In addition, your Total Tax Liability includes $6,669 in state and local income taxes.

The federal income taxes computed above are based on your 1987 Single Status while claiming one Exemption for yourself. In addition to the Exemption, a total of $21,401 is applied against your Adjusted Gross Income as Itemized Deductions. After adjusting your Itemized Deductions for the current standard deduction or Zero Bracket Amount, your Taxable Income is $49,862.

Your Marginal Federal Tax Bracket is 35 percent in 1987. This tax rate is applied to $22,862 of your current Taxable Income of $49,862. An increase of Taxable Income of $41,138 or more will move you into the 38 percent bracket. In this case, the higher rate is applicable only to the amount of income that falls in the higher bracket. If you decrease your federal Taxable Income by $22,862 or more, you will fall into the 28 percent bracket.

Your income tax liability is projected to be $107,117 in 1996, based on a Taxable Income of $205,210. This tax consists of $58,243 in Federal Regular Tax and $4,774 in Social Security tax. Your Total Tax Liability also includes $44,100 in state and local income taxes.

Your federal income taxes in 1996 were calculated using the Single Status and one Exemption for yourself. Your Itemized Deductions are projected to be $67,782. In 1996, your Marginal Federal Tax Bracket will be 28 percent. This is the highest tax bracket. Your federal income taxes in that year were computed using a cumulative indexing factor of 47.74 percent, applied to the base tax rates of 1984 as required by current income tax law.

TABLE 14-3
Income Statement for Gloria J. Darsteller (June 1987)

	1987	1988	1989	1990	1996
Earned Income					
Compensation—c1	$ 85,000	$ 97,750	$112,413	$129,275	$299,021
	$ 85,000	$ 97,750	$112,413	$129,275	$299,021
Interest/Dividends					
Brentwood Corp	$ 312	$ 375	$ 560	$ 640	$ 800
Orion shares	0	0	0	162	7,191
	$ 312	$ 375	$ 560	$ 802	$ 7,991
Investments					
Rental income	$ 9,600	$ 10,560	$ 11,616	$ 12,778	$ 22,638
Rental real est	−13,289	−11,408	−9,437	−8,433	2,543
Business auto 1	−8,307	−8,068	3,424	−13	0
Business auto 2	0	0	−8,914	−14,285	309
Carryover sch E	0	−272	−586	0	0
Inv int disalwd E	272	586	0	0	0
Passive loss c/o	0	0	0	−8,914	−71,654
Disallowed	0	0	8,914	27,568	14,944
	$−11,724	$ −8,602	$ 5,017	$ 8,701	$−31,220
Other					
State tax refund	$ 700	$ 0	$ 0	$ 0	$ 0
	700	0	0	0	0
Net capital gain	−1,125	0	0	0	0
Adj gross income	$ 73,163	$ 89,523	$117,990	$138,778	$275,792
Deductions					
Charitable 50%	$ 1,000	$ 1,100	$ 1,210	$ 1,331	$ 2,357
State tax paid	4,666	5,168	7,047	8,082	30,610
Local tax paid	2,003	2,263	3,165	3,676	13,490
Condo mtge interest	7,781	18,609	18,505	18,392	17,391
Personal interest	114	70	35	18	0
Misc expense ded	5,837	5,875	5,689	5,675	3,934
Gross deductions	$ 21,401	$ 33,085	$ 35,651	$ 37,174	$ 67,782
ZBA/Standard ded	2,540	3,000	3,150	3,300	4,400
Allowed deductions	$ 21,401	$ 33,085	$ 35,651	$ 37,174	$ 67,782
Pers exemptions	1,900	1,950	2,000	2,100	2,800
Taxable income	$ 49,862	$ 54,488	$ 80,339	$ 99,504	$205,210
Fed income tax	$ 13,310	$ 13,503	$ 21,816	$ 27,904	$ 58,243
Fed tax bracket	35%	33%	33%	33%	28%

TABLE 14-4
Supporting Schedule for Gloria J. Darsteller (June 1987)

	SINGLE 1987	SINGLE 1988	SINGLE 1989	SINGLE 1990	SINGLE 1996
Income					
Earned income	$ 85,000	$ 97,750	$112,413	$129,275	$299,021
Adj gross income	73,163	89,523	117,900	138,778	275,792
Allowed deductions	21,401	33,085	35,651	37,174	67,782
Pers exemptions	1,900	1,950	2,000	2,100	2,800
Taxable income	$ 49,862	$ 54,488	$ 80,339	$ 99,504	$205,210
Capital Gains					
RCI Corp	$ −1,800	$ 0	$ 0	$ 0	$ 0
Flintstone Tire	675	0	0	0	0
Net capital gain	−1,125	0	0	0	0
Capital gains—AMT	$ −1,125	$ 0	$ 0	$ 0	$ 0
Investments					
Ordinary income	$ 9,600	$ 10,560	$ 11,616	$ 12,778	$ 22,638
Depreciatn/dpltn	14,380	13,185	8,540	16,990	350
Invstmt interest	10,075	9,773	10,354	10,435	8,601
Other expenses	6,741	7,078	7,649	8,084	10,835
Alt min tax adjs	3,210	2,140	1,070	1,070	0
Inv int disalwd E	272	586	0	0	0
Investment income	$−21,324	$−19,162	$−15,513	$−22,731	$ 2,852
Passive Losses					
Passive loss c/o	$ 0	$ 0	$ 0	$ −8,914	$−71,654
Psv ls ald—Rental	13,289	11,408	9,437	3,579	0
Psv ls ald—phs-in	0	0	0	485	0
Disallowed	0	0	8,914	27,568	14,944
Psv loss c/o—AMT	0	0	0	−8,914	−71,069
Psv ls ald—AMT	10,079	9,268	8,367	3,579	0
Disallowed	$ 0	$ 0	$ 8,914	$ 26,983	$ 14,359
Investment Interest					
Inv int sch E	$ 10,075	$ 9,773	$ 10,354	$ 10,435	$ 8,601
Carryover sch E	0	272	586	0	0
Inv int disalwd E	272	586	0	0	0
Inv int disalwd	$ 272	$ 586	$ 0	$ 0	$ 0
Tax Preferences					
Rental real est	$ 3,210	$ 2,140	$ 1,070	$ 1,070	$ 0
Total tax prefs	$ 3,210	$ 2,140	$ 1,070	$ 1,070	$ 0
Federal Tax Liab					
Regular tax	$ 13,310	$ 13,503	$ 21,816	$ 27,904	$ 58,243
Gross fed inc tax	13,310	13,503	21,816	27,904	58,243
Fed income tax	$ 13,310	$ 13,503	$ 21,816	$ 27,904	$ 58,243

(continued)

TABLE 14-4 (continued)

	SINGLE 1987	SINGLE 1988	SINGLE 1989	SINGLE 1990	SINGLE 1996
Fed Tax Analysis					
Indexing factor	$ 0	$ 0	$ 5	$ 10	$ 48
Fed tax bracket	35%	33%	33%	33%	28%
$ to next bracket	$ 4,138	$ 45,992	$ 24,781	$ 10,896	$ 0
Next bracket	39%	28%	28%	28%	28%
Previous bracket	28%	28%	28%	28%	33%
$ to prev bracket	$ 22,862	$ 11,338	$ 35,039	$ 51,954	$ 57,270
Alt Minimum Tax					
Adj gross income	$ 73,163	$ 89,523	$117,990	$138,778	$275,792
Inv int exp sch E	776	523	243	13	0
Carryover sch E	0	272	586	0	0
Inv int disalwd E	−272	−586	0	0	0
Contributions	−1,000	−1,100	−1,210	−1,331	−2,357
Condo mtge interest	−7,781	−18,609	−18,505	−18,392	−17,391
Other qual int	−776	−795	−803	−39	0
Adjusted AMTI	64,110	68,956	97,715	119,029	256,044
Passive loss c/o	0	0	0	8,914	71,654
Disallowed	0	0	−8,914	−27,568	−14,944
Psv loss c/o—AMT	0	0	0	−8,914	−71,069
Disallowed	0	0	8,914	26,983	14,359
Net capital gain	1,125	0	0	0	0
Capital gains—AMT	−1,125	0	0	0	0
Rental real est	3,210	2,140	1,070	1,070	0
Pers exemptions	−1,900	−1,950	−2,000	−2,100	−2,800
AMT exemptions	−30,000	−30,000	−30,000	−28,772	0
AMT taxable inc	$ 35,420	$ 39,146	$ 66,785	$ 88,643	$253,244
Gross alt min tax	7,438	8,221	14,025	18,615	53,181
Fed tax less FTC	$−13,310	$−13,503	$−21,816	$−27,904	$−58,243
Other Tax Liabs					
FICA/soc sec tax	$ 3,132	$ 3,425	$ 3,560	$ 3,764	$ 4,774
NYS PSI (clnt/jt)	81,100	93,655	108,113	124,760	292,971
Other income (c/j)	−9,587	−5,162	1,135	−3,655	54,630
Ded & exmpt (c/j)	−15,632	−26,554	−26,339	−26,316	−24,582
NYS txble inc (c/j)	55,881	61,939	82,909	94,789	323,019
NYC income (client)	55,881	61,939	82,909	94,789	323,019
NY tax prefs (c/j)	3,410	2,340	1,270	1,270	200
NYS income tax (c/j)	4,666	5,168	7,047	8,082	30,610
NYC income tax (c)	2,003	2,263	3,165	3,676	13,490
NY tax (clnt/jt)	6,669	7,431	10,212	11,758	44,100
New York city tax	2,003	2,263	3,165	3,676	13,490
New York state tax	4,666	5,168	7,047	8,082	30,610
Total st/local tax	$ 6,669	$ 7,431	$ 10,212	$ 11,758	$ 44,100
Total inc tax	$ 23,111	$ 24,359	$ 35,588	$ 43,426	$107,117

YOUR CASH FLOW MANAGEMENT

An Analysis of Your Cash Flows

Your Cash Inflow of $113,187 in the first year of your profile changes to $350,097 in 1996. During this period of 10 years, you will receive a total of $2,057,219 in cash. Cash Inflow includes all cash received in a year before your spending for investment resulting from our installation of Automatic Cash Management, as explained below. You receive your highest annual Cash Inflow of $350,097 in 1996, whereas your lowest annual Cash Inflow of $113,187 occurs in 1987. If all the varying amounts of cash you receive over the years are discounted by a factor of 5 percent, the Net Present Value of this stream is $1,509,227. In other words, $1,509,227 today will produce all of the cash you will receive in the next 10 years if it yields a net return of 5 percent.

Similarly, your annual Cash Outflow of $103,819 in the first year of your profile changes to $196,503 in 1996. The total of all your cash expenditure items in the 10-year period adds up to $1,464,019. The highest level of your annual spending of $196,503 occurs in 1996. Your smallest annual Cash Outflow amounting to $99,399 occurs in 1988. Your annual Cash Outflow includes all of your noninvestment spending, such as for household expenses, education, cash purchases, donations, paydown of debt, and taxes. Discounted by the factor of 5 percent, the Net Present Value of your total cash expenditures over our planning horizon is $1,096,742. This means that $1,096,742 today, yielding 5 percent, will take care of all your projected noninvestment cash spending for the next 10 years.

The total of your Nondeductible Living Expenses changes from $21,510 in the first year of your profile to $30,938 in 1996. Over the 10-year span, your Nondeductible Living Expenses total $251,358, with a Net Present Value of $190,498 if we use 5 percent as the discounting factor. In relation to your Gross Real Income, the total of your Nondeductible Living Expenses decreases from 20 percent in 1987 to 8 percent in 1996.

The total of your Income Tax changes from $23,111 in the first year of your profile to $107,117 in 1996. Over the 10-year span, your Income Tax totals $622,378, with a Net Present Value of $448,918 if we use 5 percent as the discounting factor. Incidentally, you pay the highest amount of Income Tax in 1996, $107,117. You pay the lowest amount of Income Tax in 1987, $23,111.

Your Net Cash Flow in 1987, after spending for taxes, living expenses, paydown of debts, and purchases, is $9,368. Your Net Cash Flow after spending for taxes, purchases, and living expenses will be $307,194 in 1996.

Managing Your Cash Flows for Investment

To reflect your financial position as realistically as possible in the years ahead, we created simulation models of your expected Cash Flows, Income Taxes, Investment Net Worth, and the effects of each on the other in view of your specific objectives and cash allocations for investment. We performed this simulation with proper consideration for all of your interrelated and dynamic financial activities that may not actually occur simultaneously, but should be assumed to do so to disclose the consequences of their relationships when they do happen.

In your Automatic Cash Management simulations, we employ an automatic control to limit the amount of your noninvested cash to an average of $500. This noninvested cash can be considered as cash on hand or in a non-income-producing checking account. Your Citibank checking account serves this purpose.

We employ an additional allocational tactic in the Automatic Cash Management simulation. Surplus Cash available for investment is directed to municipal bonds (TF Cash Management Account and Tax-Free Municipal Bond Fund) and to a growth mutual fund (Orion Shares) in each applicable year of your profile. This investment is projected to yield 8.5 percent in tax-exempt interest and about 13 percent growth, respectively.

Based on the saving and investment criteria defined in your Automatic Cash Management simulations, a total of $593,168 will be invested over the 10 years of your planning horizon. Your annual Cash Surplus for investment peaks at $153,600 in 1996. The lowest Cash Surplus for investment takes place in 1987 and is $9,368. The Net Present Value of all the Surplus Cash you will spend for investment during these years is $412,465, discounted at 5 percent.

TABLE 14-5
Cash Flow Statement for Gloria J. Darsteller (June 1987)

	1987	1988	1989	1990	1996
BEGINNING OF YEAR					
Citibank checking	$ 500	$ 500	$ 547	$ 487	$ 538
SOURCES OF CASH					
Cash Income					
Compensation—c1	$ 85,000	$ 97,750	$112,413	$129,275	$299,021
Interest + dividends	312	375	560	640	800
	$ 85,312	$ 98,125	$112,973	$129,915	$299,821
Investments					
Business auto 2	$ 0	$ 0	$ 0	$ 0	$ 5,000
Business auto 1	0	0	5,200	0	0
Rental real est	9,600	10,560	11,616	12,778	22,638
	$ 9,600	$ 10,560	$ 16,816	$ 12,778	$ 27,638
Sale/Withdrawals					
RCI Corp	$ 2,175	$ 0	$ 0	$ 0	$ 0
Flintstone Tire	5,800	0	0	0	0
	$ 7,975	$ 0	$ 0	$ 0	$ 0
Tax Refund					
State tax refund	$ 700	$ 0	$ 0	$ 0	$ 0
	$ 700	$ 0	$ 0	$ 0	$ 0
Other Income					
Rental income	$ 9,600	$ 10,560	$ 11,616	$ 12,778	$ 22,638
	$ 9,600	$ 10,560	$ 11,616	$ 12,778	$ 22,638
Total cash inflow	$113,187	$119,245	$141,405	$155,471	$350,097
Total cash available	$113,687	$119,745	$141,952	$155,958	$350,635
USES OF CASH					
Not Tax Deductible					
Food	5,000	5,250	5,513	5,789	7,757
Clothing	1,500	1,575	1,654	1,737	2,329
Entertainment	2,000	2,100	2,205	2,315	3,104
Vacations	3,000	3,150	3,308	3,473	4,654
Gifts/celebrations	1,000	1,050	1,103	1,158	1,552
Transportation	900	945	992	1,042	1,395
Condo ins prem	980	1,078	1,186	1,305	2,313
Pers disab inc ins	680	680	680	680	680
Rent	3,300	0	0	0	0
Condo rep/maintnce	900	1,800	1,890	1,985	2,660
Utility/phone	2,000	2,100	2,205	2,315	3,104
Interior furnish	0	0	1,000	1,000	1,000
Photo supplies	250	263	276	290	390
	$ 21,510	$ 19,991	$ 22,012	$ 23,089	$ 30,938

(continued)

TABLE 14-5 (continued)

	1987	1988	1989	1990	1996
Tax Deductible					
Emp bus expense—c	$ 3,900	$ 4,095	$ 4,300	$ 4,515	$ 6,050
Medicine & drugs	700	735	772	811	1,088
Therapy/counseling	1,500	1,650	1,815	1,997	3,540
Condo mtge interest	7,781	18,609	18,505	18,392	17,391
Credit card int	175	175	175	175	175
Charity contrb—50%	1,000	1,100	1,210	1,331	2,357
Misc ded—2% limit	3,400	3,570	3,749	3,936	3,400
	$ 18,456	$ 29,934	$ 30,526	$ 31,157	$ 34,001
Income Taxes Paid					
Fed tax paid	$ 13,310	$ 13,503	$ 21,816	$ 27,904	$ 58,243
State tax paid	4,666	5,168	7,047	8,082	30,610
Local tax paid	2,003	2,263	3,165	3,676	13,490
FICA/soc sec tax	3,132	3,425	3,560	3,764	4,774
	$ 23,111	$ 24,359	$ 35,588	$ 43,426	$107,117
Purchase/Deposits					
Brentwood Corp.	$ 3,105	$ 3,571	$ 4,106	$ 4,722	$ 0
Furniture/fixture	0	0	0	1,000	1,000
Jewelry	250	250	250	250	250
Lithographs	500	500	500	500	500
Photography equip	0	0	1,000	0	0
Condominium	17,000	0	0	0	0
	$ 20,855	$ 4,321	$ 5,856	$ 6,472	$ 1,750
Investments					
Rental real est	$ 13,674	$ 13,872	$ 14,080	$ 14,298	$ 15,858
Business auto 1	5,853	5,992	4,605	768	0
Business auto 2	0	0	14,464	8,152	4,691
	$ 19,527	$ 19,864	$ 33,149	$ 23,218	$ 20,549
Liability Liqudtn					
Condominium	$ 360	$ 930	$ 1,034	$ 1,147	$ 2,148
	$ 360	$ 930	$ 1,034	$ 1,147	$ 2,148
Surplus Cash					
Cash invested	$ 9,368	$ 19,800	$ 13,300	$ 27,000	$153,600
	$ 9,368	$ 19,800	$ 13,300	$ 27,000	$153,600
Tot cash outflow	$113,187	$119,199	$141,465	$155,509	$350,103
End of Year					
Cash balance	$ 500	$ 547	$ 487	$ 449	$ 532

YOUR PERSONAL AND INVESTMENT NET WORTH

Your Assets

We compute your Net Worth at the end of 1987 to be $190,060. This total consists of $458,135 in assets and $268,075 in liabilities. Your Total Assets at that time will include $44,535 of Liquid Assets and $413,600 of Nonliquid Assets.

At the end of 1996, your Net Worth is projected to be $1,938,472. This total consists of $2,180,497 in assets and $242,025 in liabilities. Your Total Assets at that time will include $831,277 of Liquid and $1,349,220 of Nonliquid Assets.

For purposes of analysis and planning, we have separated your Total Assets into two categories according to their potential for producing current or future Cash Flows. These categories are conventionally defined as follows:

Personal Assets

These assets are normally not allocated for conversion to investment capital for the production of income in the event of premature death or retirement; they are acquired and held for use and consumption.

Investment Assets

These assets are normally acquired to produce income or future capital growth, or both; they are available to you in retirement or if you become disabled, and are available to your survivors in the event of your premature death.

The value of your Personal Assets in 1987 totals $266,662. With the exception of $500 in cash, all of this amount is considered nonliquid. When netted against your Personal Liabilities of $177,640, these Personal Assets yield a Net Worth of $89,022.

The value of all your Investment Assets in 1987 is $191,473. Your Investment Liabilities amount to $90,435. Therefore, your Investment Net Worth is $101,038.

The growth of your total Investment Net Worth is the most reliable gauge for measuring and evaluating the effectiveness of your Investment Capital Production structure and thus your progress toward achieving your strategic financial objectives. At some point in the future, it may become necessary or desirable to move assets from the Personal category to the Investment category to meet your objectives and needs.

Your Liabilities

The total amount of your outstanding debt at the end of 1987 is $268,075. The amount of $177,640 is considered personal debt and $90,435 is considered investment-related liabilities. You have $177,640 in outstanding mortgage loans on your residence. For these and other personal loans, you are making payments in 1987 totaling $8,316. Of this amount, $360 reduces the outstanding principal balance of your personal debt. The remaining amount of $7,956 is the interest you pay on this debt. As shown on the Income Statement, the interest paid on home mortgages is deducted in computing your income taxes.

The total amount of your outstanding debt at the end of 1996 will be $242,025. The amount of $164,448 is personal debt and $77,577 is investment-related liabilities. You will have $164,448 in outstanding personal amortized loans at the end of this period. In 1996, you will be making payments on these loans totaling $10,279. Of this amount, $2,148 reduces the outstanding principal balance. The remaining amount of $8,131 is deductible interest to the extent that it is allocable to residential mortgages.

TABLE 14-6
Balance Sheet for Gloria J. Darsteller (June 1987)

	1987	1988	1989	1990	1996
LIQUID ASSETS					
Cash balance	$ 500	$ 547	$ 487	$ 449	$ 532
Stocks & Bonds					
TF Cash Mgmt Acct	$ 28,510	$ 48,310	$ 61,610	$ 68,360	$199,285
TF Muni Fund	0	0	0	4,050	82,605
Brentwood Corp	15,525	21,425	28,745	37,779	87,860
Orion shares	0	0	0	11,448	299,185
Sel Aggressive Stk	0	0	0	5,805	161,810
	$ 44,035	$ 69,735	$ 90,355	$127,442	$830,745
Liquid assets	$ 44,535	$ 70,281	$ 90,842	$127,891	$831,277
NONLIQUID ASSETS					
Retirement Plans					
IRA 1	$ 3,072	$ 3,348	$ 3,649	$ 3,978	$ 6,671
IRA 2	3,221	3,543	3,897	4,287	7,594
IRA 3	5,199	5,771	6,406	7,111	13,300
IRA 4	2,170	2,354	2,555	2,772	4,522
	$ 13,662	$ 15,017	$ 16,507	$ 18,147	$ 32,088
Investments					
Rental real est	$139,438	$160,354	$184,407	$212,068	$490,526
Business auto 1	8,000	6,400	5,120	0	0
Business auto 2	0	0	25,000	20,000	5,000
	$147,438	$166,754	$214,527	$232,068	$495,526
Personal Property					
Condominium	$224,250	$257,888	$296,571	$341,057	$788,886
Furniture/fixture	15,000	15,000	15,000	15,000	15,000
Jewelry	5,250	5,513	5,789	6,078	8,145
Lithographs	4,200	4,410	4,631	4,863	6,516
Photography equip	3,800	4,610	4,380	4,161	3,059
	$252,500	$287,421	$326,371	$371,159	$ 821,606
Nonliquid assets	$413,600	$469,192	$557,405	$621,374	$1,349,220
Total assets	$458,135	$539,473	$648,247	$749,265	$2,180,497

(continued)

TABLE 14-6 (continued)

	1987	1988	1989	1990	1996
LIABILITIES					
Mortgage Loans					
Condominiums	$177,640	$176,710	$175,676	$174,529	$164,448
	$177,640	$176,710	$175,676	$174,529	$164,448
Investments					
Rental real est	$ 84,302	$ 83,838	$ 83,321	$ 82,744	$ 77,577
Business auto 1	6,133	3,584	755	0	0
Business auto 2	0	0	13,200	9,833	0
	$ 90,435	$ 87,422	$ 97,276	$ 92,577	$ 77,577
Total liabilities	$268,075	$264,132	$272,952	$267,106	$ 242,025
Net worth	$190,060	$275,341	$375,295	$482,159	$1,938,472

AN ANALYSIS OF YOUR REAL ESTATE INVESTMENT

Your rental real estate property in Woodstock represents a significant beginning in your desire to focus your investment program in this type of asset. As we plan for further investments in the years ahead, it is important for you to become accustomed to analyzing them for their net effects as investments.

The following analysis provides you a breakdown of how this investment produces various economic and tax consequences.

TABLE 14-7
Investment Analysis for Gloria J. Darsteller (June 1987)

	1987	1988	1989	1990	1996
Rental Real Est					
Asset value	$139,438	$160,354	$184,407	$212,068	$490,526
Liability	84,302	83,838	83,321	82,744	77,577
Cash contributed	13,674	13,872	14,080	14,298	15,858
Cash received	9,600	10,560	11,616	12,778	22,638
Ordinary income	9,600	10,560	11,616	12,778	22,638
Depreciatn/dpltn	9,630	8,560	7,490	7,490	5,350
Inv int sch E	9,299	9,250	9,197	9,137	8,601
Cash expenses	3,960	4,158	4,366	4,584	6,144
Net inv inc—ncsh	−13,289	−11,408	−9,437	−8,433	2,543
Passive loss c/o	0	0	0	0	−17,487
Disallowed	0	0	0	4,369	14,944
Inv exp tax prefs	3,210	2,140	1,070	1,070	0
Psv loss c/o—AMT	0	0	0	0	−16,902
Disallowed	0	0	0	3,784	14,359
Business credit	0	0	0	0	0

(continued)

TABLE 14-7 (continued)

Comprehensive Analysis (1987–1996)

	Cur Value	% of Tot	PV @ 5%
Total cash contributed	$146,949	80.09%	$118,360
Initial net asset value	36,533	19.91%	36,533
Total contribution	$183,482	100.00%	$154,893
Projected appreciation	$376,416	68.85%	$231,087
Total cash received	153,007	27.99%	119,420
Accumulated tax savings	17,274	3.16%	15,925
Total benefit	$546,697	100.00%	$366,431

Current aftertax yield:	20.71%
Internal rate of return:	17.58%
Adjusted rate of return:	15.12%

AN ANALYSIS OF YOUR CAPITAL NEEDS

In this section, we describe your needs for capital in the event of your premature death or disability. At death, current life insurance proceeds are included in the computation of Cash Flow to provide for current expenses and set up investments for future cash needs of survivors and beneficiaries. In the case of disability, the amount of annual payments provided by your disability income insurance will be included in the computation of Cash Flow and the analysis of possible need for additional capital.

If your cash needs are in excess of available income and liquid assets, the shortfall may be offset by increasing your life or disability income insurance coverages. The amount of risk you feel comfortable assuming yourself can reduce the additional insurance coverage you might otherwise need. Keep in mind that the analyses shown on the following page include all of your current assets and the growth expectations we discussed during consultation.

The Cash Flow report shows your detailed cash needs for the next 10 years. The Capital Needs report is less detailed; it shows the overall capital you need compared with the income and investments available. Both reports provide important information for evaluating the consequences of losing your income and capital production through disability or death.

TABLE 14-8
Capital Needs Analysis for Gloria J. Darsteller (June 1987)*

	Total Amount	Present Val @ 3%	Present Val @ 5%	Present Val @ 7%
Cash Needed in Next 10 Years				
Mortgage payments	$183,992	$157,940	$143,520	$131,012
Household costs	60,363	51,840	47,145	43,088
Medical expenses	32,734	27,779	25,064	22,727
Food, clothing, transportation	118,247	101,171	91,773	83,656
Other living expenses	72,748	62,164	56,343	51,318
Nonliquid assets purchased	255,525	223,838	206,189	190,802
Income taxes paid	622,378	517,258	460,141	411,323
Other	102,528	88,019	80,017	73,094
Total cash needed	$1,448,515	$1,230,008	$1,110,192	$1,007,020
Cash Available in Next 10 Years				
Personal service income	$1,725,823	$1,445,310	$1,292,611	$1,161,886
Interest & dividends	119,521	97,652	85,883	75,901
Other investment income	153,007	129,461	116,577	105,501
Nonliquid assets sold	10,200	8,606	7,751	7,024
Other income	153,007	129,461	116,577	105,501
Total income available	$2,162,258	$1,811,179	$1,620,081	$1,456,490
Needs in excess of income	$ –713,743	$ –581,172	$ –509,889	$ –449,470
Net ret plan investments	$ 0	$ 0	$ 0	$ 0
Net other investments	713,743	581,172	509,889	449,470
Additional capital needed	$ 0	$ 0	$ 0	$ 0

You have sufficient capital to meet your short-term cash needs.

*This report does not consider the purchase of liquid assets or investments in retirement plans as cash needs. Similarly, cash generated by borrowing or selling assets is not considered a source of cash for the purposes of this report. Therefore, the results shown here should be viewed from a different perspective than in the Cash Flow Statement.

CONSERVING AND DISTRIBUTING YOUR ESTATE

The financial and tax consequences of your untimely death are described in this section. In fact, of course, none of us knows when this event will happen. The importance of seeing its consequences is to notice the difference between them when they flow from decisions made within a lifetime financial plan that anticipates this event and when they are not planned for at all.

The differences can be measured in very substantial dollars. They can also be measured in the profound negative emotions and frustrations that survivors and beneficiaries often experience when the decedent has made no intentional plans to distribute estate assets.

The shrinkage of your estate values will result primarily from the need to pay any personal debt, administration expenses, and federal, state, and local death and estate taxes. Before death occurs, there are many alternatives for arranging these matters to the greatest advantage of all interested parties, especially your estate tax liabilities (if any).

Estate Analysis

The reports, analyses, and computations of your estate settlement costs and taxes would be drawn from the integrated information and forecasts of your overall financial position for a year selected as the hypothetical date of your death. As we agreed, however, a complete analysis of your estate conservation and distribution objectives would be of little value to you at this time.

Right now, our primary concern is to build a living estate. The objectives associated with that aim are reflected elsewhere in these reports and in our recommendations. To assure that your accumulated assets pass with a minimum of shrinkage to beneficiaries you wish to designate, you should consult with your attorney for drafting a simple will and explore means to reduce the New York State inheritance taxes that might be imposed.

As of 1987 and thereafter, current federal estate tax law passes $600,000 free of tax. Through the early years of your living plan, your total Net Worth should be well within this figure. However, as your forecasts show, your Net Worth is expected to increase substantially over the next 10 years.

To fully realize your desires for distributing your estate assets, you should carefully monitor your taxable estate as your Net Worth rises. As your estate values increase and become subject to taxation, you may want to consider certain bequests or testamentary trusts in your will, such as for your sister, Eileen, or for her children.

Your Current Will

As of this date, you have no formal will. This is a serious deficiency of your current financial profile. Without a valid will, your estate would be distributed under the intestacy laws of the state of New York. This would not satisfy your estate distribution intentions. You should execute a simple will as a priority item. (See "Our Summary and Recommendations" section above.)

Standards for a Comprehensive Financial Plan

Registry of Financial Planning Practitioners*

INTRODUCTION

The Registry of Financial Planning Practitioners announces its Standards for a Comprehensive Financial Plan, which provides a basis for evaluation of a comprehensive service to clients. It also offers a focal point for dialogue and written commentary to the Registry regarding the evolution of these standards in the months and years ahead. The Registry's goal is to have the public accept financial planning as a profession; these standards are another step toward this objective.

Many clients do not need or want a comprehensive review in all areas covered by these standards. In fact, modular financial plans are more common today and will continue to grow in popularity due to the cost savings of an abbreviated plan or the client's lack of desire for a complete or comprehensive financial plan. It is therefore very likely that areas covered in the plan would be comprehensive in nature but the plan would not be considered a comprehensive financial plan as defined by the Registry. It must be understood that each financial plan and the standards, actions, and elements appropriate to each plan will vary depending upon the individual characteristics or circumstances of the client, the objectives to be reached, and the needs, desires, and requests of the client as presented to the planner.

For example, a financial planner may strictly limit his or her practice to corporate CEOs who do not have a cash-flow problem and who would not want or be willing to pay for a cash-flow analysis. The plan drafted for this type of client would therefore not fall within the Registry definition of a comprehensive financial plan. This does *not* mean that the plan produced was not excellent and appropriate in the areas covered or that this client was not served professionally, ethically, or competently.

A comprehensive financial plan should contain analysis of all pertinent factors relating to the client. While order and style of presentation may vary, the plan should include, but not be limited to, the following elements:

1. personal data
2. client goals and objectives
3. identification of issues and problems
4. assumptions
5. balance sheet/net worth
6. cash-flow management
7. income tax
8. risk management/insurance

---

*Copyright © 1987, Registry of Financial Planning Practitioners. Used with permission.

9. investments
10. financial independence, retirement planning, education, and other special needs
11. estate planning
12. recommendations
13. implementation

In the development of a comprehensive financial plan, the planner is responsible for the above elements of the plan from data gathering through analysis and presentation to the client. Those elements of the plan that the planner *does not personally perform* remain the responsibility of the planner to coordinate.

When technical elements such as legal and insurance areas are not personally performed by the planner, the financial plan or supplement should include supporting documentation that these areas have been or will be coordinated by the planner.

Analysis of each element of the plan should consist of a review of pertinent facts, a consideration of the advantage(s) and/or disadvantage(s) of the current situation and a determination of what, if any, further action is required. The plan should include a summary statement providing the planner's comments on the analysis and his or her recommendations where appropriate for each element of the plan.

STANDARDS FOR A COMPREHENSIVE FINANCIAL PLAN

Personal Data

Should include relevant personal and family data for parties covered under the plan.

Comment

- This should include, but not be limited to, name, address, social security number, birthdate, and other relevant data.

Client's Goals and Objectives

A reiteration of the *client's stated* goals and objectives, indicating their priority and including a time frame where applicable.

Comments

- The statement of goals and objectives will form the basic framework for the development of the financial plan.
- The client's goals and objectives should be expressed in language as specific and precise as possible. For example, a statement of a goal should read "retire at age 62 in present home and maintain current standard of living" rather than "a comfortable retirement."

Identification of Issues and Problems

A plan must address relevant issues and problems identified by the client, the planner, and/or other advisers.

Comments

- List personal and financial issues and problems that affect the client, such as major illnesses, education costs, and taxes. While the client may be aware of many, if not all, of the issues, the planner may discover other areas that are, or could develop into, a problem.
- These issues and problems, when combined with the client's goals and objectives, will complete the framework and direction for the financial plan. Since style and order are not the primary consideration, the analysis or recommendation section(s) of the plan may be more appropriate for identifying issues and problems.

Assumptions

Identify and state material assumptions used in the plan's preparation.

Comment

- Assumptions should include, but not be limited to, inflation, investment growth rate, and mortality.

Balance Sheet/Net Worth

A presentation and analysis to include, but not be limited to, a schedule listing assets and liabilities with a calculation of net worth and itemized schedules of liabilities and assets to be included as appropriate.

Comment

- In addition to the schedules, footnotes should be included as appropriate.

Cash-Flow Management

Statements and analysis to include, but not be limited to, a statement of the client's sources and uses of funds for the current year and for all relevant years, indicating net cash flow, as well as a separate income statement, where appropriate.

Comments

- sources — earned income, investment income, sale proceeds, gifts, etc.
- uses — living expenses, debt service, acquisition of assets, taxes paid, etc.
- net cash flow — both positive and negative

Income Tax

An income tax statement and analysis to include, but not be limited to, the income taxes for the current year and for all relevant years covered in the plan.

Comments

- Projections should show the nature of the income and deductions in sufficient detail to permit calculation of the tax liability. The analysis should identify marginal tax rate for each year and any special situations such as alternative minimum tax, passive-loss limitations, etc., that affect the client's tax liability.
- The financial plan should include footnotes to let the client know which taxes (for example, state or city) have not been addressed.

Risk Management/Insurance

Analysis of a client's financial exposure relative to mortality, morbidity, liability, and property, including business as appropriate.

Comments

- mortality—survivor income and capital needs analysis
- morbidity—impact of loss of health
- liability—legal exposure
- property—loss of value
- business—loss due to business involvement

Listing and analysis of current policies and problems to include, but not be limited to, life, disability, medical, business, property/casualty, and liability.

Comments

- Analysis of existing coverage and/or risk exposure in relationship to the client's needs, goals, and objectives.
- If any area of insurance is not within the competency range of the financial planner, the planner has the responsibility to coordinate with other professionals and document such coordination in the financial plan. Documentation of the above areas can include the insurance professional's summary, if completed, or the professional's name and the time frame when such review will be completed.

Investments

A listing of the current investment portfolio and an analysis or discussion of the liquidity, diversification, and investment risk exposure of the portfolio. In addition, the suitability of the investments in relationship to the client's needs, goals, and objectives should be addressed. To include, but not be limited to, risk tolerance, risk management of investments, suitability, liquidity, diversification, and personal management efforts.

Comments

- risk tolerance — addresses the client's willingness to accept investment risk
- risk management — analysis of the client's exposure relative to loss of invested capital
- suitability — appropriateness of the investment for the client
- liquidity — the availability of assets that can be converted into cash at acceptable costs
- diversification — appropriate mix of assets to meet the client's needs, goals, and objectives
- personal management efforts — the degree to which the client wants to manage and is capable of managing his or her assets

Financial Independence, Retirement Planning, Education, and Other Special Needs

An analysis of the capital needed at some future time to provide for financial independence, retirement, education, or other special needs. The analysis should include a projection of resources expected to be available to meet these needs at that time.

Comments

- In achieving the above, inflation, growth of assets, and company benefits should be considered where applicable.
- Special sections of the above topics may require a separate heading in the financial plan. For example, company benefits may require an analysis of types available, pretax and posttax contributions needed, tax treatment of plans and investment of benefit plan assets.

Estate Planning

Identification of assets includible in the client's estate and an analysis of the control, disposition, and taxation of those assets.

Comments

- control — authority to manage or direct the use of assets by means of title, trusteeship, power of attorney, etc.
- disposition — transfer of ownership by will, trust, beneficiary designation, or operation of the law
- taxation — taxation of the client's estate and the income tax and estate tax consequences to the beneficiaries

Recommendations

Written recommendations that relate to goals and objectives as well as to financial issues and problems.

Comment

- Written recommendations should specifically address the client's goals and objectives and all issues and problems identified in the plan as well as determine the actions necessary to compensate for any shortfalls. Recommendations should be clearly identified and stated; they should not be conveyed by implication or inference.

Implementation

A prioritized list of actions required to implement the recommendations, indicating responsible parties, action required, and timing.

Comment

- Implementation should include a schedule reflecting actions to be taken as well as priority, dates, and responsible parties.

Time-Value-of-Money Analysis in Financial Planning

Robert M. Crowe

Virtually all of the work that financial planners perform for their clients involves an exchange of present dollars for future dollars. For example, a plan may be established in which the client sets aside funds *now* in order to pay college tuition bills for the children *later*. Or a client's funds may be paid out *now and in several future time periods* in the form of life insurance premiums in order to provide periodic income to the insured's spouse beginning at the death of the insured and continuing throughout *several future time periods*. Money may be borrowed by a client *now* in order to make a purchase, with the loan to be repaid in *one or more future time periods*. These and dozens of other transactions involving financial services professionals and their clients entail an exchange: *dollars now for dollars later.*

However, as will be explained, dollars now do not have the same value as dollars later. Money now is worth more than money later. Therefore the parties on each side of these financial transactions need a technique for making the value of dollars now equal to the value of dollars later. Otherwise one party will be cheated, giving up more value than he or she receives back. That technique, called time-value-of-money analysis, is thus central to the work of all financial services professionals, whether they are bankers, insurance agents, investment specialists, estate planners, accountants, tax specialists, financial planners, or any of a host of others. The objective of this appendix is to provide the reader with an understanding of the basics of time-value-of-money analysis.

DOLLARS NOW VERSUS DOLLARS LATER: OPPORTUNITY COST

The reason why dollars in the present are more valuable than dollars in the future is that one who has dollars now can invest them and realize a rate of return on them. One who waits before receiving dollars, on the other hand, is denied that opportunity and he or she incurs a cost, called an *opportunity cost*. The opportunity cost of an activity (in this case, waiting to receive a specified number of dollars) is defined as the value of the lost opportunity to engage in and receive a value from the best similar alternative available activity (in this case, investing the money and earning a return on it) with the same resource (in this case, the specified number of dollars).

For example, assume that a financial planning client, Vera Vincent, inherited $50,000. The money has been sitting idly in her checking account earning no interest for the past 6 months while Vera has been shopping around for the best long-term place to invest it. If, during that period, Vera had temporarily invested the $50,000 in, for example, a money market deposit account, she could have received investment earnings of about $2,500. Having failed to invest the funds as soon as they were available and, instead, having waited 6 months before putting them to work, Vera incurred an opportunity cost in the amount of $2,500.

The way in which the opportunity cost of waiting for money is measured in financial transactions is by means of an annual interest rate. In the Vera Vincent case, for example, the annual interest rate that reflects her opportunity cost is 10 percent (that is, $2,500 on $50,000 for one-half of a year).

To take another example, a financial planning client who deposits $10,000 in a savings account and leaves it there for 3 years undoubtedly expects to have more than $10,000 in the account at the end of that time. He or she has allowed someone else, the bank, to use this money for 3 years. As compensation for incurring an opportunity cost, he or she expects interest to be credited to the account by the bank. Conversely, someone who borrows money from, for example, a credit union expects to repay not just the amount borrowed but interest as well. The credit union must be compensated for its opportunity cost, for giving up the opportunity to invest this money elsewhere and earn a return on it.

Simple Interest versus Compound Interest

There are two ways of computing interest, simple interest and compound interest. Simple interest is calculated by applying the interest rate to only the original principal amount. Compound interest, on the other hand, is calculated by applying the interest rate to the sum of the original principal amount and all of the interest that has been earned on it in previous time periods.

To illustrate, assume that a client, Adam Alvarez, places $5,000 in a 5-year certificate of deposit at a bank. The CD is credited with 8 percent interest per year, and all interest earnings are left in the account. How much will Adam's CD be worth at the end of the 5 years? The answer depends on whether the 8 percent rate is a simple or a compound interest rate. Table 1 shows the difference between the two.

TABLE 1
Accumulation of $5,000 in 5 years at 8% Simple and Compound Interest per Year

	Simple Interest			Compound Interest		
Year	Principal Amount	Interest	Ending Balance	Principal Amount	Interest	Ending Balance
1	$5,000	$400	$5,400	$5,000	$400	$5,400
2	5,000	400	5,800	5,400	432	5,832
3	5,000	400	6,200	5,832	467	6,299
4	5,000	400	6,600	6,299	504	6,803
5	5,000	400	7,000	6,803	544	7,347

As this table indicates, at 8 percent simple interest Adam's account balance will grow by a constant amount each year, $400, and will total $7,000 at the end of 5 years. At 8 percent compound interest, however, the account balance will grow by an increasing dollar amount each year, beginning at $400 and rising to $544, and will total $7,347 at the end of 5 years. The difference in the ending account balances, $347, represents interest earned on prior interest earnings that were added to, or converted to, principal.

Most practical situations that require recognition or calculation of the time value of money involve compound interest, not simple interest. Therefore the balance of this appendix will deal only with compound interest.

To summarize, then, a compound rate of interest measures the opportunity cost of waiting for money and letting someone else use it in the meantime. It is thus the link between the worth of dollars now, called the *present value* (PV), and the worth of dollars later, called the *future value* (FV). Figure 1 shows the difference between the two values, with compound interest as the link between them. Notice that the line linking the two values is a curve, not a straight line, because compound interest, not simple interest, is being used. This means that, whatever the rate being used, as time goes on the amount of the difference between present and future values increases each year, as was shown in the example in table 1.

FIGURE 1
Compound Interest as the Link between Present Value and Future Value

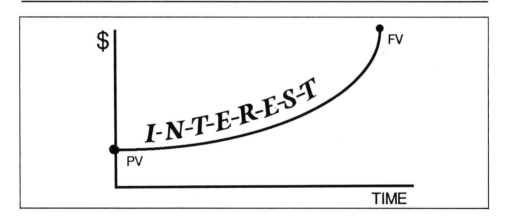

Compounding versus Discounting

The process by which a present value grows over time to a larger future value is called *compounding*. This was the process used in Adam's certificate of deposit example in the right-hand portion of table 1. It is depicted by a movement *up the curve* in figure 1.

The reverse of compounding is called *discounting*. It is the process of reducing a sum of money not due until some time in the future (a future value) to today's lesser value (a present value). Discounting is depicted by a movement *down the curve* in figure 1.

The following is an example of a problem calling for discounting. Assume that a financial planning client, Beverly Blair, is considering the purchase of an attractive piece of raw land. She believes that in 10 years it will be worth $100,000. What should she be willing to pay for the land today? Although the answer to this question cannot be determined without some additional information, this information can be used to demonstrate the need for discounting. In any case, it is obvious that she should be willing to pay less than $100,000. If Beverly is going to tie up her money in land today for 10 years, at which time she expects that it will be worth $100,000, she will be incurring an opportunity cost for which she will insist on compensation. That compensation will be in the form of a discount from the expected future value of the land. Determination of the price she should be willing to pay, therefore, will involve discounting the future value back to a present value at some compound rate of interest. The way to do this will be explained later.

There are two major factors that determine the shape of the curve in figure 1 and that affect the size of the difference between the present value and the future value. One is the length of time over which compounding or discounting occurs. The longer someone must wait for the use of money, all other things being equal, the greater the total opportunity cost is and, therefore, the greater the gap between the present and future values. Since time is reflected on the horizontal axis in figure 1, the longer the time, the longer the curve is, and the greater the difference between the two values is. To refer back to Adam Alvarez's CD in table 1, if the principal sum were left to accumulate for 12 years rather than 5, the ending account balance, the future value, would be more than it was at the end of 5 years. Or, if Beverly Blair's real estate is not expected to be worth $100,000 until after 15 years instead of 10, the price she should be willing to pay for it, the present value, would be lower than under the 10-year scenario.

The second key factor is the particular compound interest rate used in the compounding or discounting process. The higher the interest rate, all other things being equal, the steeper the slope of the curve will be. The steepness of the curve reflects the dollar amount of the difference per time period between the present and future value, as depicted on the vertical axis in figure 1. Thus, for example, if Adam's 5-year CD had been credited with a 9 percent rate rather than 8 percent, it would have grown to a larger future value. At 6 percent it would have grown to a smaller future value.

Choosing the Appropriate Interest Rate

The specific compound annual interest rate that should be used to measure the opportunity cost in the compounding or discounting process is made up of two components: a risk-free rate and a risk premium. *At a minimum,* the opportunity cost one incurs in letting someone else use his or her money is the rate of return that could have been earned by investing the funds in a perfectly safe vehicle, such as 30-day U.S. Treasury bills. They are always available and, for all practical purposes, are risk-free.

But when one allows someone else to use his or her money there is usually some risk involved. A few of the types of risks that may be present are the following:

- the risk of default in the repayment of principal or interest
- the risk of loss of purchasing power due to inflation
- the risk that as the funds are returned they will be able to be reinvested only at lower rates of return
- the risk that tax laws may change in such a way as to reduce the aftertax rate of return being earned

These and other types of risks associated with investing (that is, letting someone else use one's money) are described more fully in chapter 9.

If waiting to receive money involves risk, the compound annual interest rate used in the compounding or discounting process should be increased by adding a risk premium to the risk-free rate. Adam Alvarez, for example, earned 8 percent on his CD, slightly above the 7.5 percent 30-day T-bill rate at the time. The .5 percent risk premium reflects the fact that the CD is a bit more risky than T-bills. And when Beverly Blair selects a rate at which to discount the $100,000 expected future value of the real estate, she might choose 10 percent, 15 percent, or 20 percent, depending on how she assesses the risks. The greater the risk, the greater should be the add-on to the T-bill rate.

THE VARIABLES IN TIME-VALUE-OF-MONEY PROBLEMS

In most time-value-of-money problems there are four variables, of which three are known and the task is to calculate the fourth. The four variables are a present value (PV), an interest rate (i), a number of periods over which compounding or discounting occurs (n), and a future value (FV). The following are examples of various combinations of the known and unknown of these four variables.

- Chuck Conway invests $50,000 (a known PV) in Gro-Mor common stock. He holds the stock for 3 years (a known n) and then sells it for $72,000 (a known FV). In the meantime the stock paid no dividends. What has Chuck's compound annual rate of return been (an unknown i)?
- Denise DiLullo is scheduled to receive $100,000 (a known FV) as a distribution from a trust when she reaches age 30, 6 years from now (a known n). She would like to sell her rights to this money for cash today and is willing to discount the funds at a 7 percent compound annual interest rate per year (a known i). How much would Denise be willing to accept (an unknown PV)?
- Eric Evans is willing to loan a friend $15,000 today (a known PV) for 5 years (a known n). The loan is to be repaid in a lump sum, including compound interest of 14 percent per year (a known i). How much will the borrower have to repay (an unknown FV)?
- Fran Fitzgerald's weekly grocery bill is now $125 (a known PV). If inflation in her grocery costs is averaging 5 percent per year (a known i), how many years will it be (an unknown n) before her weekly grocery bill will be $200 (a known FV)?

Later an explanation will be presented as to how each of these types of problems can be solved.

Some time-value-of-money problems are a bit more complex than these and involve another variable, a stream of payments (PMT) in or out. The task may be to compute

- an unknown PV of a series of payments, given the number of payments (n) and a discount rate (i)
- an unknown FV to which a series of payments will grow, given the number of payments (n) and an interest rate (i)
- the amount (PMT) or number (n) of payments needed to reach a target future sum (FV), or the interest rate (i) that will have to be earned on these payments to reach the target
- the amount (PMT) or number (n) of payments needed to repay or liquidate a capital sum (PV), or the interest rate (i) that will be needed in order to do so

The solution of these types of problems will also be explained in this appendix.

USING TIME LINES TO DEPICT PROBLEMS

In all time-value-of-money problems it is essential that n, the number of time periods, be measured accurately. Often this is a simple task, especially where single sums of money, rather than periodic payments, are involved. For example, if a problem calls for determining the present value of a sum of money due to be received in 8 years, n is obviously 8, measured as the length of time from today, the beginning of year one, till the end of year 8. However, when more complex problems are encountered, measuring n accurately is not so easy and the possibility for calculating an incorrect answer increases. The use of time lines such as those shown in figure 2 can be of considerable help in solving such problems accurately.

Time lines are horizontal lines on which the number of periods in a problem is represented. In figure 2, all the time lines are 5 years long. The present value, future value, and payments are depicted on the time line at the applicable point in time for each. It is customary to depict certain values in a problem below the time line and other values above it. The purpose of this is to reflect the basic tradeoff in time value problems: *Money in* at certain times and *money out* at other times. Whenever time lines are used in this appendix, present values will be shown below the line and future values above it. Payments will be shown below the line if they are *being made* by the individual and above the line if they are *being received* by the individual.

In figure 2, then, the time line in the top left corner represents a problem in which the task is to compute the present value of three equal cash inflows of a given amount to be received at the end of years 1, 2, and 3. The time line in the top right corner represents a problem in which the task is to compute the present value of two equal cash inflows of a given amount to be received at the end of years 3 and 4. In the lower left corner of figure 2 a problem is shown in which cash outflows of a given amount (for example, deposits into a savings account) are made today, one year from now, and two years from now. The task is to compute their future value 5 years from now. Finally, in the lower right corner of figure 2 the time line depicts three cash outflows of a given amount that are made today, 2 years from now, and 4 years from now. The task is to compute the future value of these payments, including the third one, as of the end of year 4 (which is the same, of course, as the beginning of year 5).

FIGURE 2
Use of Time Lines to Depict Time-Value-of-Money Problems Accurately

---

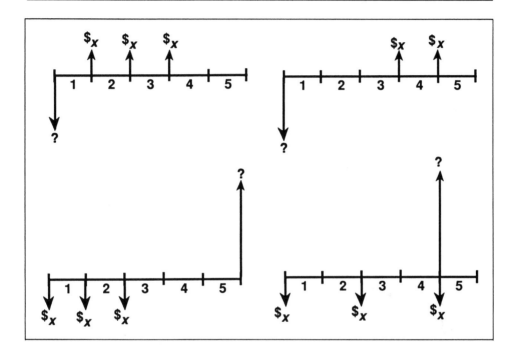

FREQUENCY OF COMPOUNDING, DISCOUNTING, AND PAYMENTS

As will be explained later, there is one more factor, in addition to the stated rate of interest, that affects present and future values. That factor is the number of times per year that the stated interest rate is applied in the compounding or discounting process. Until specified otherwise, however, all of the explanations in this appendix will be based on the assumption that the stated interest rate is applied only once per year.

In addition, some time-value-of-money problems involve a series of payments that are made or received more than once per year, such as monthly or semiannually. These problems also will be addressed later. For the present, however, it will be assumed that all periodic payments referred to in any problems are made once per year, either at the beginning or end of the year.

FUTURE VALUE OF A SINGLE SUM PROBLEMS

Finding the Future Value of a Single Sum (FVSS)

One of the most frequently encountered and most easily understood categories of time-value-of-money problems involves the future value of a single sum (FVSS). For example, if Gerry Gaines places $7,500 in a 6-year, 9 percent certificate of deposit and all interest earnings are left in the account, to what amount will her CD grow by the time it matures?

The basic formula for calculating the future value of a single sum, from which all other time-value-of-money formulas are derived, is as follows:

$$FVSS = PVSS (1 + i)^n$$

where FVSS = the future value of a single sum

PVSS = the present value of a single sum

i = the compound annual interest rate, expressed as a decimal

n = the number of years during which compounding occurs

That is, add the interest rate (expressed as a decimal) to one, and raise this sum to a power equal to the number of years during which the compounding occurs. Then multiply this by the present value of the single sum, or deposit, in question to compute the future value of that single sum.

Depicted on a time line, the FVSS problem being used as the illustration here is as shown in figure 3.

The basic compound interest formula can be used to solve the problem as follows:

$$FVSS = \$7,500 (1.09)^6$$

$$= \$7,500 \times 1.6771$$

$$= \$12,578.25$$

To reiterate a point made earlier, what would happen if i were more than 9 percent or if n were more than 6 years? In either case, the value of $(1 + i)^n$ would be larger than 1.6771, so the FVSS would be more than $12,578.25. That is, FVSS rises as either i or n is increased, and it falls as either of them is decreased.

FIGURE 3
Time Line Representation of an FVSS Problem

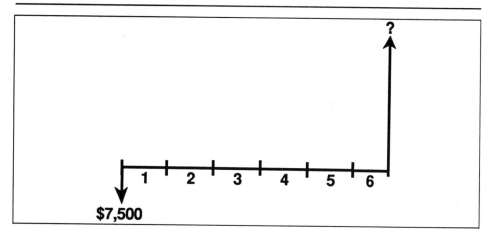

The use of the formula to solve FVSS problems can be time consuming and may lead to errors. To simplify the task, most finance textbooks contain tables showing the value of $(1 + i)^n$ for various rates of interest and numbers of periods. An excerpt from one of these tables is shown in table 2. All that needs to be done is to select the correct factor from the table and multiply it by the PVSS in question to compute its future value. Time-value-of-money tables of several types will be used as the principal tool for solving problems throughout the balance of this appendix. An alternative that some may wish to use is an electronic calculator with finance functions.

TABLE 2
Future Value of a Single Sum (FVSS) Factors

n/i	7%	8%	9%	10%	11%
1	1.0700	1.0800	1.0900	1.1000	1.1100
2	1.1449	1.1664	1.1881	1.2100	1.2321
3	1.2250	1.2597	1.2950	1.3310	1.3676
4	1.3108	1.3605	1.4116	1.4641	1.5181
5	1.4026	1.4693	1.5386	1.6105	1.6851
6	1.5007	1.5869	1.6771	1.7716	1.8704
7	1.6058	1.7138	1.8280	1.9487	2.0762
8	1.7182	1.8509	1.9926	2.1436	2.3045
9	1.8385	1.9990	2.1719	2.3579	2.5580
10	1.9672	2.1589	2.3674	2.5937	2.8394

In the present example, the factor for 6 years and 9 percent is 1.6771. Multiplying this by the $7,500 present value produces the future value of Gerry's CD, $12,578.25.

Notice also in table 2 the effect of changing i or n. Moving across the table to higher interest rates produces higher FVSS factors. Likewise, moving down the table to higher numbers of periods produces higher FVSS factors. Again, FVSS rises as either i or n rises, and vice versa.

Finding n

In some types of future value of a single sum problems FVSS, PVSS, and i are known and the unknown variable is n, the number of periods. For example, assume that Hank Hopkins plans to deposit $5,000 in a savings account and to let it accumulate at an 8 percent compound annual rate of interest. He plans to withdraw the funds when the account balance reaches $8,000, the down payment he wishes to make on a vacation home. How long will Hank have to wait before he has his down payment?

The procedure for solving this type of problem using table 2 is first to divide the FVSS, $8,000, by the PVSS, $5,000, to produce a growth factor of 1.6000. Then look down the 8 percent column to find the factor nearest to 1.6000. The closest factor is a bit lower than this, 1.5869. This means that the actual n is more than 6 years but less than 7 years, and it is closer to 6 years.

One could use a process of interpolation to find the more precise value of n. Specifically, the factor 1.6000 is about 11 percent of the way between the factors 1.5869 and 1.7138. Therefore the more precise n is 11 percent of the way between 6 years and 7 years, or 6.11 years.

Finding i

In other types of future value of a single sum problems it is i, the interest rate, that is the unknown of the four elements. For example, assume that Irene Ingalls bought a home 9 years ago for $110,000. Today she had the home appraised and it was judged to be worth $225,000. What has been the compound annual rate of growth in the value of Irene's home?

The procedure for finding i in this type of problem is similar to that for finding n. Divide the ending value, the FVSS, $225,000, by the beginning value, the PVSS, $110,000, to produce a growth factor of 2.0455. Then look across the 9-year row to find the factor nearest to 2.0455. The closest factor is 1.990, in the 8 percent column. This means that the i was more than 8 percent per year but less than 9 percent, and it is nearer to 8 percent. If a more precise value of i is desired, a process of interpolation between the 8 percent and 9 percent factors in the 9-year row could be used to show that i is about 8.27 percent.

PRESENT VALUE OF A SINGLE SUM PROBLEMS

Finding the Present Value of a Single Sum (PVSS)

A second category of common time-value-of-money problems involves the present value of a single sum (PVSS). For example, assume that Jarrett Jenkins wishes to set aside today in a savings account an amount which, together with compound interest earnings of 10 percent per year, will be sufficient to purchase in 3 years what he thinks will then be a $50,000 automobile. What amount should he place in the account?

The factor for finding the present value of a single sum is mathematically the reciprocal of that for finding the future value of a single sum. Specifically, the formula for finding PVSS is

$$PVSS = FVSS\left[\frac{1}{(1 + i)^n}\right] = \frac{FVSS}{(1 + i)^n}$$

That is, FVSS multiplied by the reciprocal of $(1 + i)^n$, which is the same as dividing FVSS by $(1 + i)^n$, produces the PVSS. Discounting a future sum to the present is, thus, the reverse of compounding a present sum. In order to compound, the known amount is multiplied by $(1 + i)^n$. In order to discount, the known amount is divided by $(1 + i)^n$.

Depicted on a time line, the PVSS problem involving Jarrett Jenkins is as shown in figure 4.

FIGURE 4
Time Line Representation of a PVSS Problem

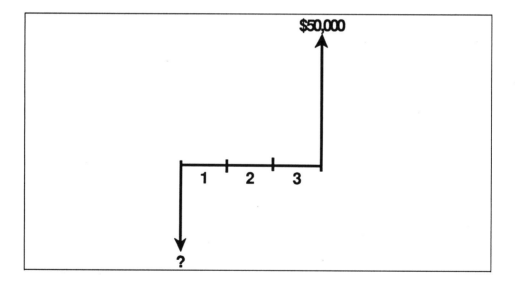

The PVSS formula can be used to solve the problem as follows:

$$\text{PVSS} = \frac{\$50,000}{(1.10)^3}$$

$$= \frac{\$50,000}{1.3310}$$

$$= \$37,565.74$$

That is, if Jarrett deposits this amount today and makes no withdrawals, and if 10 percent compound interest is credited each year, he will have the targeted $50,000 in his account 3 years from now.

What would be the impact on PVSS if the interest rate were more than 10 percent or if the number of periods were more than 3 years? In either case, the value of $(1 + i)^n$ would be larger than 1.3310 so that, when divided into $50,000, it would produce a smaller PVSS. Notice, then, that increasing i or n has the opposite effect on PVSS from the effect it has on FVSS. Increasing these two variables *reduces* PVSS, whereas it *increases* FVSS.

As with FVSS problems, use of a formula to solve PVSS problems is time consuming and may lead to arithmetic errors. Use of a table of PVSS factors is usually more practical. Table 3 shows the value of the quantity

$$\frac{1}{(1 + i)^n}$$

for several interest rates and numbers of periods. (More extensive tables of this type are available in most finance texts.) All that is needed is to select the correct factor from the table and multiply it by the FVSS in question to produce the PVSS.

TABLE 3
Present Value of a Single Sum (PVSS) Factors

n/i	7%	8%	9%	10%	11%
1	0.9346	0.9259	0.9174	0.9091	0.9009
2	0.8734	0.8573	0.8417	0.8264	0.8116
3	0.8163	0.7938	0.7722	0.7513	0.7312
4	0.7629	0.7350	0.7084	0.6830	0.6587
5	0.7130	0.6806	0.6499	0.6209	0.5935
6	0.6663	0.6302	0.5963	0.5645	0.5346
7	0.6227	0.5835	0.5470	0.5132	0.4817
8	0.5820	0.5403	0.5019	0.4665	0.4339
9	0.5439	0.5002	0.4604	0.4241	0.3909
10	0.5083	0.4632	0.4224	0.3855	0.3522

In the present example, the factor for 10 percent and 3 years is .7513. Multiplying this by $50,000 produces the PVSS, $37,565.00. (The .74 difference between the answer found through the formula versus the table is due to rounding.)

Notice also in table 3 that as one moves across the column to higher and higher interest rates the PVSS factors become smaller so that, when multiplied by FVSS, they produce smaller and smaller values for PVSS. The same result occurs as one moves down each column to higher numbers of periods. Again, increasing n or i reduces PVSS, and vice versa.

Finding n

As is true of future value problems, sometimes it is useful to be able to calculate n, given the values for FVSS and PVSS. For example, assume that Kate Kiernan's goal is to have an emergency fund of $5,000. All that is in the fund at the moment is $4,000. If the fund earns 7 percent compound interest per year, when will it reach $5,000?

The procedure to be used is very similar to that for finding n in FVSS problems. (See the Hank Hopkins illustration.) However, in this case, table 3 will be used to produce the answer. Begin by dividing the PVSS by the FVSS to produce a discount factor. Then look in the appropriate interest rate column of table 3 to find the n whose PVSS factor comes closest to this discount factor.

In the present illustration, $4,000 divided by $5,000 produces a factor of .8000. In the 7 percent column of table 3, the closest factor is .8163, which is in the row for 3 periods. This means that n is between 3 and 4 years, and it is closer to 3 years. By interpolation a more precise n, 3.30 years, could be found.

Finding i

In other types of PVSS problems the task is to compute i, given the PVSS, FVSS, and n. For example, assume that Larry Langhorne's net worth has risen from $115,000 to $170,000 during the past 4 years due to his shrewd investing. What has been the compound annual rate of growth in Larry's net worth during this period?

The procedure for solving this type of problem using table 3 is similar to that for finding n. It involves dividing the present value by the future value to produce a factor, and then finding the closest factor to it in the 4-year row of table 3. When $115,000 is divided by $170,000, a factor of .6765 is produced. The closest factor in the 4-year row is .6830, which is in the 10 percent column. This means that Larry's net worth has grown by between 10 and 11 percent per year, closer to 10 percent. Interpolation would show a more precise growth rate of about 10.27 percent per year.

FUTURE VALUE OF AN ANNUITY/ANNUITY DUE PROBLEMS

The next category of time-value-of-money problems to be dealt with involves the future value of a series of periodic payments. An *annuity* is defined as a series of payments of equal amounts that are made at the *end* of each of a specified number of periods. An *annuity due* is defined as a series of payments of equal amounts that are made at the *beginning* of each of a specified number of periods. To repeat a point noted earlier, it will be assumed for the time being that the periods involved are years, that is, that the payments occur annually. It will also be assumed that all of the payments are compounded at the same annual rate of interest, although obviously each payment will earn interest for a different length of time.

It is particularly important in problems involving annuities or annuities due to accurately measure the number of periods during which each deposit earns interest. Time lines such as those in figure 5 will be of great help in doing so.

FIGURE 5
Time Line Representation of Problems Involving the Future Value of an Annuity or Annuity Due

---

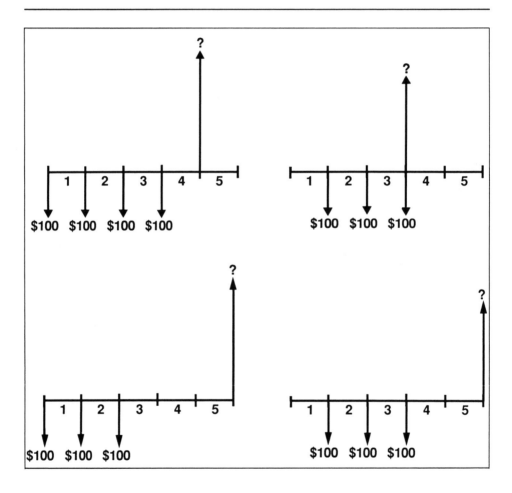

The time line in the upper left portion of figure 5 depicts a 4-year (because four payments are involved) $100 annuity due (because the payments are made at the beginning of each of the 4 years). The problem is to calculate the future value of these payments as of the end of the annuity period. Note that the end of the period for an annuity due is the end of the year in which the final payment occurs, here the end of year 4.

In the upper right quadrant of figure 5 is a time line depicting a 3-year (because three payments are involved) $100 annuity (because the payments are made at the end of each of the 3 years). The problem calls for calculation of the future value of these payments as of the end of the annuity period. Note again that the end of the period for an annuity is the end of the year in which the final payment occurs, here the end of year 3. Thus the end of the period for an annuity always coincides with the date of the final payment.

In the lower left portion of figure 5 a 3-year annuity due is shown. However, the problem calls for finding the future value of the three payments not at the end of year 3 but 2 years later, at the end of year 5. And in the lower right corner a 3-year annuity is shown, with the task being to compute the future value of the annuity at the end of year 5, 2 years after the end of the annuity period.

Finding the Future Value of an Annuity (FVA) and Annuity Due (FVAD)

Calculation of the future value of an annuity (FVA) or annuity due (FVAD) can be treated as a collection of FVSS problems. For example, in the top left portion of figure 5 the FVAD as of the end of year 4 is simply the sum of four calculations: $100 compounded at a given rate of interest for 4 years, plus $100 compounded for 3 years, plus $100 compounded for 2 years, plus $100 compounded for one year. Or, in the top right corner, the FVA can be found by totaling the results of three compoundings: $100 for 2 years plus $100 for one year plus $100 for zero years (which is $100).

The annuity due in the lower left could be treated as follows: find the FVAD by summing the results of $100 compounded for 3 years, 2 years, and one year; then compound this total for 2 more years. Similarly, the annuity depicted in the lower right quadrant could be treated as follows: find the total of $100 compounded for 2 years, one year, and zero years; then compound this total for 2 more years.

As an alternative to these multistep processes, use of an annuity formula can simplify the calculations. The formula for finding the future value of an annuity is as follows:

$$FVA = \left[\frac{(1 + i)^n - 1}{i} \right] \times \text{amount of one payment}$$

The formula for finding the future value of an annuity due is similar:

$$FVAD = \left[\frac{(1 + i)^n - 1}{i} \right] \times \text{amount of one payment} \times (1 + i)$$

The only difference between the two formulas is that the FVAD is larger than the FVA by the amount of one year's additional interest. This result occurs because in an annuity due each deposit earns interest for one extra year (because it is made one year earlier than in an annuity).

To illustrate the calculation of the future value of an annuity, assume that Mary Martinez plans to open an individual retirement account (IRA) at her bank one year from now. She expects to deposit $1,500 per year for 7 years and retire when the last deposit is made. If the IRA is credited with 9 percent compound annual interest, how much will be in Mary's account when she retires? Substituting the known values in the formula, we have

$$FVA = \left[\frac{(1.09)^7 - 1}{.09} \right] \times \$1,500$$

$$= \left[\frac{.8280}{.09} \right] \times \$1,500$$

$$= 9.2000 \times \$1,500$$

$$= \$13,800.00$$

If instead of waiting a year to open the IRA account Mary opens it today, and if she makes the same total of seven $1,500 deposits, how much will be in her account when she retires? Her account balance will be 9 percent higher, as shown in the FVAD formula.

$$FVAD = \left[\frac{(1.09)^7 - 1}{.09} \right] \times \$1,500 \times 1.09$$

$$= \left[\frac{.8280}{.09} \right] \times \$1,500 \times 1.09$$

$$= 9.2000 \times \$1,500 \times 1.09$$

$$= \$15,042.00$$

For those who prefer a simpler approach to calculating the future value of an annuity or annuity due than applying these formulas, there is an easier way. A table of FVA factors appears in most finance books showing the value of the quantity

$$\left[\frac{(1 + i)^n - 1}{i} \right]$$

for various rates of interest and numbers of periods. An abbreviated version of such a table is presented in table 4.

TABLE 4
Future Value of an Annuity (FVA) Factors

n/i	7%	8%	9%	10%	11%
1	1.0000	1.0000	1.0000	1.0000	1.0000
2	2.0700	2.0800	2.0900	2.1000	2.1100
3	3.2149	3.2464	3.2781	3.3100	3.3421
4	4.4399	4.5061	4.5731	4.6410	4.7097
5	5.7507	5.8666	5.9847	6.1051	6.2278
6	7.1533	7.3359	7.5233	7.7156	7.9129
7	8.6540	8.9228	9.2004	9.4872	9.7833
8	10.2598	10.6366	11.0285	11.4359	11.8594
9	11.9780	12.4876	13.0210	13.5795	14.1640
10	13.8164	14.4866	15.1929	15.9374	16.7220

All that is needed is to select the proper FVA factor from the table and multiply it by the amount of one payment to produce the future value of the annuity. If the problem involves an annuity due, the solution is found by first calculating the FVA and then multiplying the result by $(1 + i)$.

In the Mary Martinez illustration, then, the correct FVA factor is 9.2004, a slightly more precise factor than that generated through rounding in the formula. This factor, when multiplied by $1,500, produces an FVA of $13,800.60. If Mary's IRA is opened immediately, her account balance at retirement, the FVAD, will be $13,800.60 × 1.09 = $15,042.65.

If, when Mary reaches the planned retirement date, she changes her mind and decides to wait 3 more years without making any further deposits in the IRA account, how much will she have at retirement? The time line depiction of this case would be analogous to those in the lower half of figure 5. The future value of her annuity or annuity due would be compounded as a single sum for 3 more years as explained earlier in connection with FVSS problems. Based on the factor from table 2, Mary would have either $13,800.60 × 1.2950 = $17,871.78 as the FVA or $15,042.65 × 1.2950 = $19,480.23 as the FVAD.

Finding the Amount of the Payment

Another frequently encountered type of problem involving annuities arises where the future value is known, as are n and i, and the task is to determine the size of the annuity payment. This problem most often involves a preestablished target amount to be achieved at some point in the future. It is solved by dividing the target future amount by the appropriate FVA factor (if the first payment toward the target is to be made at the end of the first period) or by the product of the FVA factor and $(1 + i)$ if it is to be made at the beginning of the first period.

For example, assume that Nate Norris wishes to accumulate $75,000 in order to buy a yacht in 6 years. He plans to make six annual deposits, starting in one year, into an account that will earn 10 percent compound annual interest. How large must each deposit be in order for Nate to reach his goal? Divide the $75,000 target amount by the FVA factor in table 4 for 6 years and 10 percent, 7.7156. The answer is $9,720.57 per year. Or if Nate wishes to make the first of his six annual deposits now, divide the $75,000 target by the quantity (7.7156 × 1.10), or 8.4872. Starting a year earlier will lower the required size of each deposit to $8,836.84.

Finding n

Occasionally time-value-of-money problems are found in which the known variables are the target future value, the interest rate, and the amount of the annuity payment, with the task being to determine n, the number of payments needed to reach the target. The solution is found by dividing the target future amount by the size of one of the payments to produce an FVA factor (for end-of-year deposits). Then, in the applicable interest rate column of table 4, find the factor closest to this and read across the row to find n.

To illustrate, if in the preceding example Nate decides that he wishes to make annual deposits, starting in one year, of $10,000 each, how many years or deposits will be needed to reach Nate's $75,000 goal if the account earns 10 percent per year? Divide $75,000 by $10,000 to produce a factor of 7.5000. In the 10 percent column of table 4 this factor falls between 6.1051 for 5 periods and 7.7156 for 6 periods. It is closer to the factor for 6 periods, meaning that in a bit less than 6 years Nate will reach his goal. (More precisely, by interpolation the answer would be found as 5.87 years.)

Use of table 4 for this type of problem is a bit more complex if the annuity payments are to be made at the beginning of each year. Again, divide the target future amount by the payment to produce a factor, 7.5000 in the current example. Then find the factor in table 4 which, when multiplied by (1 + i), comes closest to this factor. In Nate Norris's case 7.500 is between 1.10 × 6.1051, or 6.7156, and 1.10 × 7.7156, or 8.4872. Thus, n in the beginning-of-year scenario is still between 5 and 6 years, but it is now a bit closer to 5 years than to 6 years. (Actually, n now becomes 5.45 years.)

Finding i

The last type of future value of an annuity/annuity due problem to be discussed here is that in which the known variables are n, FV, and the size of the payment, and i is the unknown variable. The solution is found by dividing the target future amount by the payment to produce an FVA factor (for end-of-year payments). Then, in table 4 look across the row for the applicable n to find the factor closest to this one. For beginning-of-year payments, find the factor which, when multiplied by (1 plus the interest rate in that column) comes closest to this factor.

For example, assume that Olivia Ormsby's goal is to save up $20,000 for an around-the-world vacation trip. She can afford to set aside only $3,300 per year, beginning a year from now, and wants to embark on her trip when she retires in 5 years. What compound annual rate of interest must she earn on her deposits in order to reach her goal? Dividing $20,000 by $3,300 produces a factor of 6.0606. In the 5-period row of table 4 this factor falls between those for 9 percent and 10 percent, and it is a little closer to 10 percent. Olivia must earn almost 10 percent per year (actually, 9.63 percent) to reach her $20,000 goal.

If instead of waiting a year Olivia can begin now to make 5 annual deposits of $3,300, her needed interest rate will be lower. The 6.0606 factor in the 5-period row falls below even the lowest factor shown, 5.7507 × 1.07, or 6.1532. That is, she could earn even less than 7 percent per year (actually about 6.48 percent) and still reach her goal if she starts immediately.

PRESENT VALUE OF AN ANNUITY (PVA) AND ANNUITY DUE (PVAD) PROBLEMS

The fourth broad category of time-value-of-money problems discussed in this appendix involves the present value of an annuity or annuity due. The explanation of how to solve these types of problems is similar to much of what has been discussed in the preceding sections.

FIGURE 6
Time Line Representation of Problems Involving the Present Value of an Annuity or Annuity Due

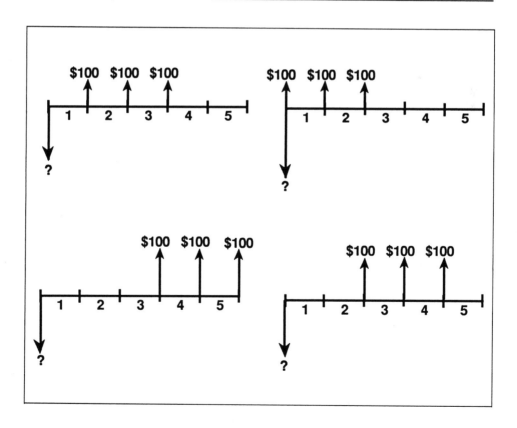

Finding PVA and PVAD

Problems that call for calculation of the present value of an annuity (PVA) or annuity due (PVAD) can be depicted on time lines such as those in figure 6.

The time line in the top left quadrant depicts a problem calling for calculation of the present value of a 3-year, $100 annuity, while that in the top right calls for the present value of a 3-year, $100 annuity due. The time line in the lower left section of figure 6 calls for calculation of the present value of a so-called deferred annuity, which requires a two-step solution process. First calculate the present value of a 3-year, $100 annuity. This gives a value as of the beginning of year 3 (or the end of year 2). That amount is then discounted as a single sum for 2 more years using the PVSS procedures described earlier to calculate the annuity's value as of the beginning of year 1.

The time line in the lower right corner of figure 6 also is a deferred annuity. It is shown here, however, to demonstrate one additional point. This stream of payments can be viewed as either a 3-year annuity deferred for one year or as a 3-year annuity due deferred for 2 years. Both interpretations are correct, and the methods of solving the problem under both interpretations will yield identical results, as will be shown below.

As was true for the solution of FVA and FVAD problems, calculation of the present value of an annuity or annuity due can be treated as a collection of single sum problems. For example, the problem in the upper left portion of figure 6 can be solved by adding up the present values of $100 discounted for 1, 2, and 3 years. The other annuities in figure 6 could be treated in a similar manner.

As an alternative to this multistep approach, formulas can be used to simplify the process. The formula for computing the present value of an annuity is as follows:

$$\text{PVA} = \left[\frac{1 - \left[\frac{1}{(1 + i)^n} \right]}{i} \right] \times \text{amount of one payment}$$

The formula for the present value of an annuity due is similar:

$$\text{PVAD} = \left[\frac{1 - \left[\frac{1}{(1 + i)^n} \right]}{i} \right] \times \text{amount of one payment} \times (1 + i)$$

As can be seen from a comparison of the two formulas, PVAD is larger than PVA by the amount of one year's interest. This is due to the fact that in an annuity due each payment is discounted, or reduced, one year less than in an annuity because it is made one year earlier.

To illustrate the calculation of the present value of an annuity, assume that Peter Piper has won a contest and is scheduled to receive $10,000 per year, beginning in one year and continuing for a total of 7 years. Contest officials have given Peter permission to sell his winnings for a lump sum to an interested investor. If Peter and the investor agree on an 8 percent discount rate, what will be the selling price? Substituting the known values in the PVA formula, we have

$$\text{PVA} = \left[\frac{1 - \left[\dfrac{1}{(1.08)^7} \right]}{.08} \right] \times \$10,000$$

$$= \left[\frac{1 - \left[\dfrac{1}{1.7138} \right]}{.08} \right] \times \$10,000$$

$$= \left[\frac{1 - .5835}{.08} \right] \times \$10,000$$

$$= 5.2063 \times \$10,000$$

$$= \$52,063.00$$

If Peter and the investor decide to delay the transaction for a year, until just before the first $10,000 payment is due, what will be the selling price? The value of this annuity due is 8 percent higher.

$$\text{PVAD} = \left[\frac{1 - \left[\dfrac{1}{(1.08)^7} \right]}{.08} \right] \times \$10,000 \times 1.08$$

$$= \$52,063.00 \times 1.08$$

$$= \$56,228.04$$

For those who prefer a simpler way of solving PVA and PVAD problems, tables of factors can be found in most finance textbooks. A segment of one such PVA table is presented in table 5.

TABLE 5
Present Value of an Annuity (PVA) Factors

n/i	7%	8%	9%	10%	11%
1	0.9346	0.9259	0.9174	0.9091	0.9009
2	1.8080	1.7833	1.7591	1.7355	1.7125
3	2.6243	2.5771	2.5313	2.4869	2.4437
4	3.3872	3.3121	3.2397	3.1699	3.1024
5	4.1002	3.9927	3.8897	3.7908	3.6959
6	4.7665	4.6229	4.4859	4.3553	4.2305
7	5.3893	5.2064	5.0330	4.8684	4.7122
8	5.9713	5.7466	5.5348	5.3349	5.1461
9	6.5152	6.2469	5.9952	5.7590	5.5370
10	7.0236	6.7101	6.4177	6.1446	5.8892

As with the FVA factor table, all that is needed is to select the correct PVA factor and multiply it by the amount of one payment. If it is an annuity due problem it should also be multiplied by the quantity $(1 + i)$. In Peter Piper's case, his annuity would sell for

$$5.2064 \times \$10,000 = \$52,064.00$$

or his annuity due would sell for

$$5.2064 \times \$10,000 \times 1.08 = \$56,229.12$$

To illustrate the solution of a deferred annuity problem, assume that Quincy Quesnay is scheduled to receive as an inheritance $50,000 per year for 10 years, beginning 5 years from today. What is the present value of this income stream discounted at 9 percent per year?

The income stream constitutes a $50,000, 10-year annuity due deferred for 5 years or, what amounts to the same thing, a $50,000, 10-year annuity deferred for 4 years. Here it will be treated as the latter. From table 5 the correct PVA factor is 6.4177. From table 3 the correct PVSS factor is .7084. Therefore the present value of Quincy's deferred annuity is

$$6.4177 \times \$50,000 \times .7084 = \$227,314.93$$

Finding the Amount of the Payment

Another common problem involving the present value of annuities arises where the present value, n, and i are known, and the task is to determine the size of the annuity payment. These problems most often arise out of loan transactions and out of the desire to liquidate a capital sum over a period of years. They are solved by dividing the loan amount or capital sum by the appropriate PVA factor if the first payment is to be made at the end of the first period or by the product of the PVA factor and $(1 + i)$ if it is to be made immediately.

For example, assume that Rita Richardson wishes to borrow $45,000 in order to add a wing onto her home. She plans to repay the loan in five equal annual installments, beginning one year from now. The bank is willing to make the loan at an 11 percent rate of interest. What will be the size of each of Rita's five loan payments? Divide the $45,000 loan amount by the PVA factor for five periods and 11 percent, or 3.6959. The answer is $12,175.65 per year.

Or assume that Stan Shapiro has just retired and has a savings account balance of $250,000. The account will earn 7 percent compound annual interest, and Stan wants to liquidate it gradually over the next 10 years. How large an annual income can he withdraw from the fund per year, starting now? Divide the capital sum, $250,000, by the product of 7.0236 and 1.07, or 7.5153. The answer is $33,265.47.

Finding n

Sometimes it is n, not the size of the payment, that is to be calculated in present value of annuity/annuity due problems. For example, in the Stan Shapiro case, assume that $33,265.47 per year is not enough income for him, and that he wants to withdraw $40,000 per year. How long will the capital sum last under this set of circumstances? Or assume that Rita Richardson cannot afford to repay $12,175.65 per year on her loan. The most she can pay is $10,000. How long will it take to repay the loan under these circumstances?

The solution is found by dividing the loan amount or capital sum by the size of one of the payments to produce a PVA factor (for end-of-year payments). Then, in the applicable interest rate column of table 5 find the factor closest to this and read across the row to find the n. For beginning-of-year payments find the factor that, when multiplied by $(1 + i)$, comes closest to the PVA factor that has been calculated.

In the case of Rita's loan, $45,000 divided by $10,000 produces a PVA factor of 4.5000. In the 11 percent column of table 5, this factor lies about halfway between those for 6 and 7 years, so the loan's new duration will be a bit more than 6.5 years (actually, 6.55 years).

In the Stan Shapiro case, $250,000 divided by $40,000 produces a PVA factor of 6.2500. In the 7 percent column of table 5 the closest factor is that for 8 years $(5.9713 \times 1.07 = 6.3893)$. This means that Stan's capital sum will last a bit less than 8 years (actually, 7.77 years) under the new situation.

Finding i

Finally, in some present value of an annuity/annuity due problems it is i that is the missing ingredient. For example, if starting next year Terry Thompson pays $5,000 per year out of her annual bonus for 8 years in order to fully retire a $27,500 loan, what annual rate of interest will she be paying on the loan? The solution is found by dividing the loan amount, $27,500, by the size of the payment, $5,000, to produce a PVA factor of 5.5000. Then find the factor in the 8-period row of table 5 that comes closest to 5.5000. The closest factor is 5.5348, which is in the 9 percent column. Terry thus will be paying a little over 9 percent (actually, 9.17 percent) for this loan.

If the problem involves beginning-of-year payments, the procedure is similar. For example, if Stan Shapiro wishes to withdraw $40,000 at the start of each year from his $250,000 savings fund and wants the money to last for 9 years, what compound annual rate of interest will have to be earned? Divide $250,000 by $40,000 to produce a PVA factor of 6.2500. Then read across the 9-period row of table 5 to find the factor which, when multiplied by $(1 + i)$, will come closest to 6.2500. In this case, it is in the 10 percent column, since $5.7590 \times 1.10 = 6.3349$. Thus, Stan will have to earn over 10 percent (actually, 10.44 percent) per year in these circumstances.

OTHER-THAN-ANNUAL COMPOUNDING, DISCOUNTING, OR PAYMENT FREQUENCY

Up to this point it has been assumed that compounding or discounting occurs only once per year. Also, in all of the discussion of annuity problems it has been assumed that the annuity payments occur only once per year. It is time now to drop both of these assumptions.

Frequency of Compounding or Discounting

If a stated annual interest rate is applied to a sum of money in compounding or discounting more than once per year, the true or effective interest rate is increased. For example, if a bank advertises that the interest rate on its certificates of deposit is 7 percent compounded weekly, the actual interest rate that will be earned in the course of a year is almost 7.25 percent.

The effective interest rate for any compounding or discounting frequency per year can be computed by means of the following formula:

$$i_{eff} = \left[1 + \frac{i_{nom}}{f} \right]^f - 1$$

where

i_{eff} = the actual or effective annual interest rate

i_{nom} = the stated or nominal annual interest rate

f = the number of times compounding or discounting occurs per year

For example, if a 6 percent nominal rate is compounded quarterly (that is, four times per year), the effective rate is

$$i_{eff} = \left[1 + \frac{.06}{4} \right]^4 - 1$$

$$= 1.0150^4 - 1$$

$$= 6.14 \text{ percent}$$

Therefore any time-value-of-money problem in which compounding or discounting occurs more than once per year can be solved by using the effective rate, rather than the nominal rate, as the value of i.

The greater the frequency of compounding or discounting is per year, the greater the effective interest rate is; therefore the greater the future value being computed or the lower the present value. The following are examples of this principle:

- If a 7 percent nominal annual rate is compounded semiannually, the effective rate is approximately 7.12 percent, and the future value of a $100 single sum after 5 years will be $141.06.
- If the 7 percent nominal rate is compounded daily (360 times per year), the effective rate is roughly 7.25 percent, and the FVSS will be $141.90.
- If a 9 percent nominal annual discount rate is applied semiannually, the effective rate is about 9.20 percent, and the present value of a $100 single sum due 5 years hence is $64.39.
- If the 9 percent nominal rate is applied weekly, the effective rate is approximately 9.41 percent, and the PVSS is $63.79.

Table 6 contains a listing of several common nominal annual interest rates and the effective rates they produce when applied with typical compounding or discounting frequencies per year.

TABLE 6
Effective Interest Rates for Selected Nominal Rates and Compounding Frequencies per Year

Nominal Annual Interest Rate	Compounding Frequency per Year				
	Semi-annually	Quarterly	Monthly	Weekly	Daily (360 days)
7%	7.12%	7.19%	7.23%	7.25%	7.25%
8	8.16	8.24	8.30	8.32	8.33
9	9.20	9.31	9.38	9.41	9.42
10	10.25	10.38	10.47	10.51	10.52
11	11.30	11.46	11.57	11.62	11.63

Frequency of Payments

Many types of annuity payments are made more frequently than annually. For example, home mortgage payments are usually made monthly. Bond interest payments are usually made semiannually. Many individuals make savings deposits from their weekly or biweekly paychecks.

The solution to annuity and annuity due problems when the payments are more frequent than annual requires two adjustments in the procedures. First, the figure that is used or computed as n is the total number of *payments* in the problem, not the number of years. Second, the figure that is used or computed as i in the problem is the *periodic* interest rate, not the annual rate (for example, one-fourth of the annual rate for quarterly payments, one-twelfth of the annual rate for monthly payments, and so on).

To illustrate, assume that Ursula Uhlig plans to save $300 per month, starting next month, for 3 years in an account at her credit union. If the account is credited with an annual (nominal and effective) interest rate of 8 percent, how much will be in Ursula's account at the end of the 3-year period?

Since tables of time-value factors often do not contain a very wide range of interest rates and a very long range of numbers of periods, the FVA formula, with the two adjustments described above, will be used to solve this problem. Substituting the known values in that formula, we have

$$FVA = \left[\frac{\left[1 + \frac{.08}{12} \right]^{3 \times 12} - 1}{\left[\frac{.08}{12} \right]} \right] \times \$300$$

$$= \left[\frac{(1.0067)^{36} - 1}{.0067} \right] \times \$300$$

$$= \left[\frac{1.2718 - 1}{.0067} \right] \times \$300$$

$$= 40.5672 \times \$300$$

$$= \$12,170.16$$

Notice that the value used for n was 36 payments, not 3 years. Also notice the value used for i was .0067, not .08, because the monthly interest rate in the problem is one-twelfth of 8 percent.

CONCLUDING COMMENT

There are many more types of applications of time-value-of-money techniques in the field of financial planning. For example, TVM analysis can be used to determine the actual rate of return on an investment that provides a varying amount of dividend payments or appreciation in capital each year. Or it can be used to prepare a complete amortization schedule for a home mortgage, showing the amount of each monthly payment that is paid in interest and that is applied against principal. These and other advanced applications are beyond the scope of this introductory discussion. A mastery of time-value-of-money analytical techniques, however, will provide an important set of tools for financial services professionals in helping clients meet their financial goals.

APPENDIX C

RISK IDENTIFICATION QUESTIONNAIRE
(Individual Form)
Developed by Charles E. Hughes

_____
(Name)

_____
(Mailing Address)

_____

_____
(Phone Number)

REAL PROPERTY

Address of principal residence _____

_____

This is a single family dwelling_____ duplex_____ apartment unit_____ condominium_____

other (describe)_____

Address of all additional locations:

Seasonal residence_____

Farm_____

Income property_____

Vacant land_____

Other property interests_____

Property Owned	Principal Residence	Other (identify)	
Residence—square ft.			
Number of stories			
Type of construction			
Year built			
Original building cost			
Date purchased			
Purchase price			
Actual cash value			
Replacement cost (excl. land value)			
Current mortgage			

Describe detached garage or other buildings on the same premises.

_____

If any of these properties were rented rather than owned, what amount of rent would probably be charged?

_____

If any occupied property would become untenantable because of damage or destruction, what monthly expenses over and above current living expenses would be incurred?_____

_____

Provide a copy of the latest appraised value excluding land on each property._____

Property Rented

Single family dwelling_____ duplex_____ apartment_____

Monthly rent_____

Lease termination date_____

If premise becomes untenantable because of damage or destruction, does lease require continuation of rent?

_____

Income Property

	Location 1	Other
Number of units		
Type of commercial use		
Rental income—annual		
Monthly rates		

If all leases could be cancelled and rewritten today, what change would there be in annual rental income and

rate per unit?_____

Land

	Farm	Vacant Land
Number of acres		

General

Occupation and other business pursuits (describe duties)_____

_____

Amount of largest personal check likely to be drawn_____

Number of credit cards_____ Number of fund transfer cards_____

Number of full-time servants_____ part-time_____

Number of caretakers or other household employees_____

PERSONAL PROPERTY

Estimated Value of	Principal Residence		Secondary Residence	
	Actual Cash Value	Replacement Cost	Actual Cash Value	Replacement Cost
a. Silverware, pewter				
b. Linens (including dining and bedroom)				
c. Clothing (men's, women's, children's)				
d. Rugs (including floor coverings and draperies)				
e. Books				
f. Musical instruments (including pianos)				
g. Television sets, radios, record players, and records				
h. Paintings, etchings, pictures, and other objects of art				
i. China, glassware (including bric-a-brac)				
j. Cameras, photographic equipment				
k. Golf, hunting, fishing, and other sports equipment				
l. Refrigerators, washing machines, stoves, electrical appliances, and other kitchen equipment				
m. Bedding (including blankets, comforters, covers, pillows, mattresses, and springs)				
n. Furniture (including tables, chairs, sofas, desks, beds, chests, lamps, mirrors, and clocks)				
o. Business property				
p. All other personal property (including wines, liquors, foodstuffs; garden and lawn tools and equipment; trunks, traveling bags; children's playthings; and miscellaneous articles in basement and attic)				
Total Estimated Value				

Special Items

Jewelry and watches:

    a. Describe each item_____

    b. Original cost of each_____

    c. Appraised value (obtain appraisal)_____

    d. Where kept (safe-deposit box)_____

Furs:

    a. Describe each article of fur_____

    b. Original cost of each_____

    c. Appraised value (obtain appraisal)_____

    d. Where stored (limit of liability per receipt)_____

Describe and value other items of unusual value:

    a. Stamp collections_____

    b. Fine arts_____

    c. Paintings_____

    d. Antiques_____

    e. Securities_____

Boats or marine equipment:

    a. Length and type of boat_____

    b. Size of motor_____

Miscellaneous Items

    Dogs, saddle horses, and other pets (pedigreed)_____

_____

    Contents of barns, sheds, and other outbuildings_____

_____

    Value of children's property away at school_____

_____

    Airplanes, motorcycles, and motorized scooters_____

_____

    Location, nature, and value of property in storage warehouses: furs in storage, sports equipment at clubs,

    silver in safe-deposit vaults, etc._____

_____

Cash on hand_____

Automobiles

	#1	#2	#3
Year and make			
Body style/model			
Identification number			
Name of registered owner			
Purchase date (new/used)			
Purchase price			
Actual cash value (current)			
Use of automobile			
Distance to work			
Where garaged (if other than principal residence)			
Trailers—Type			
Weight			
Axles			

Describe all recreational vehicles _____

_____

_____

Do you ever rent an automobile? _____ Length of typical rental period _____

Describe your use of company-owned vehicles _____

_____

PREMATURE DEATH

	You	Spouse

Lump-Sum Cash Needs

Cleanup fund. Includes unpaid last illness expenses, burial costs, federal and state taxes, probate costs, and other unpaid bills or debts $ _____ $ _____

Mortgage. The remaining balance. (Assumes that preference is to pay off mortgage. If not, mortgage payments should be included in income needs.) $ _____ $ _____

Education fund. Estimated present value of future costs to educate children $ _____ $ _____

Emergency fund. Used for unexpected expenses not readily payable from current income $ _____ $ _____

Other $ _____ $ _____

Totals $ _____ $ _____

Income Needs

Level of income desired for each category (based on current purchasing power)

Survivors
Lifetime monthly income to surviving spouse $ _____

Additional monthly income to family during child-raising years (dependency period) $ _____

Monthly income during first 2 years after death (readjustment period) $ _____

DISABILITY

Estimated monthly income needed if disability occurs today $ _____

MEDICAL EXPENSE

Estimated cost of major illness requiring extended hospitalization and physician care $ _____

RETIREMENT

Desired monthly income at retirement $ _____

Define Your Practice

Dale S. Johnson

TABLE 1
Financial Planning Associates—Client Services

Consulting and Advisory	Comprehensive Financial Planning	Investment and Insurance Products	Asset Management
–Financial consulting –Investment advising –Income tax planning –Accounting –Estate administrator –Income tax return preparation	–Written plan –Personal data –Objectives –Assets and debts –Cash flows –Income tax management –Risk management and insurance –Retirement planning –Estate distribution planning –Education funding –Recommendations –Implementation –Progress monitoring –Annual review –Investment reviews –Ongoing planning	–Mutual funds –Stocks –U.S. bonds –Muni bonds –Partnerships –Real estate –Tangibles –Life and disability insurance –Annuities –Retirement plans	–Asset allocation –Tracking returns –Ongoing planning –Portfolio performance measurement –Personal meetings –Quarterly reports

Computer Configurations

Dale S. Johnson

Component Item	Basic	Intermediate	Power-User
–Machine standard (IBM/ISA/EISA)	100% compatible	100% compatible	100% compatible
–Microprocessor Clock speed	80286 10-12 MHz	80386SX/80386 12-16 MHz	80386/80486 16-33 MHz
–Bus architecture Clock speed	16-bit 6-8 MHz	16-bit 6-12 MHz	32-bit 6-12 MHz
–Hard disk	30-40Mbyte (40 ms.)	40-60Mbyte (40-28 ms.)	60-80Mbyte (28-15 ms.)
–Floppy drives	1.2/1.44Mbyte	1.2/1.44Mbyte	1.2/1.44Mbyte
–Memory LIM 4.0 EMS	640K	640K-2Mbyte	2.5+ Mbyte
–Static/Cache RAM	Software	Machine/ Software	Machine/ Software
–Operating system	*DOS* 3.3	*DOS* 3.3	*DOS* 3.3
–Ports	2 serial + 1 parallel	2 serial + 1 parallel	2 serial + 1 parallel
–Expansion slots	8-bit/16-bit	8-bit/16-bit	8-bit/16-bit
–Power supply	150 watts	200 watts	225-250 watts
–Keyboard	101-key	101-key	101-key
–Multitasking (with LIM EMS)	N/A	*DESQview 2.2/ Windows 286*	*DESQview 386/ Windows 386*
–Network	N/A	Artisoft's *Lantastic*	Novell/Ethernet ARCnet
–Display monitor	Mono/Hercules; Color/CGA/EGA	Mono/Multiscan; Color/EGA	Color/VGA; Multiscan
–Warranty	1 yr. parts and labor	1 yr. parts and labor	1 yr. parts and labor

Appendix F

Software Vendors, Systems, and Programs

Dale S. Johnson

Below is a selected list of financial planning software applications. The category headings are meant to be helpful rather than definitive of value or usefulness. Certain programs and systems could be categorized under other headings. For example, the terms *comprehensive* and *integrated* may mean different things to both vendors and users and could include some of the programs listed under "Mini and Quick Planning Systems"; some client and asset management programs also include certain features and reports of portfolio performance software. Brief parenthetical annotations are provided for program titles that are not self-explanatory.

The list includes only systems and programs available for running on or online link with IBM standard personal computers and compatibles — the de facto standard for financial services application software. In some programs, updating is through online link with the vendor's mainframe computer.

Supplemental programs and add-on modules are listed with the system or program to which they directly relate. Check other category headings for additional specialized programs from the same vendor and for system-related programs that can be used as stand-alone specialized applications.

The lists do not include general application software (such as word processing programs, databases, spreadsheets, and multitasking interfaces) that may also be included in a computerized practice. General application software programs are available through local software dealers and national discount software outlets.

List prices can change quickly. Some are related to levels of service and single or multiuser versions. Others are for updatable user diskettes or online use at licensing fees, or for various combinations of available packages. Inquire with vendors for full details and for annual maintenance and update fees for other than the systems and programs for which annual maintenance is figured in the quoted list price. A low-cost program presentation diskette or functional demonstration version is available for most major programs and systems.

Comprehensive Integrated Systems

This category includes systems designed to support comprehensive financial planning. In general, these are the "premier" systems. Examine these systems in relation to the checklists in Part 3, "Evaluating Financial and Tax Planning Software."

- ABACUS Data Systems, Inc., 2775 Via de la Valle, Suite 101, Del Mar, CA 92014, (619) 755-0505: *FastPlan III,* $995 (first-year maintenance included; annual maintenance thereafter, $400); or lease at $210 per quarter plus annual maintenance charge; same charge for each additional user version (as in a network).

- Confidential Planning Services, Financial Planning Building, Middletown, OH 45042-0430, (513) 424-1656: *ProPlan,* $495 + $95 per month maintenance and initial training; *Business System Software,* $49; *Financial Text Library System,* $395; *Education Funding Analysis,* $99; *Defined Contribution Analysis,* $99. Inquire about interface with *dbCAMS+ Client and Asset Management System.*
- Financial Planning Technologies, Inc., 4710 Ruffner St., Suite B, San Diego, CA 92111, (800) 643-6431, (800) 824-4302 (CA): *FPTech* (PFP system plus broker-dealer plus back-office support), $20,000+ with hardware.
- Integrated Financial Solutions, Inc., 1130 Northchase Pkwy., Suite 200, Marietta, GA 30067, (800) 831-7636, (404) 952-4721: *Financial Planner,* $5,995; *Financial Planner Plus* (includes *Chart Master, Report Writer, Office Manager*), $6,995; *Financial Manager,* $2,995; *Report Writer,* $495; *Financial Advisor,* $595; *Asset Manager,* $1,495; *Office Manager,* $995; *Chart Master* (Ashton-Tate), $395. Service bureau is available. (Formerly available through a subsidiary of Interactive Financial Services, Atlanta.)
- International Financial Data Systems, Inc. (IFDS), P.O. Box 888870, Atlanta, GA 30356-0870, (800) 554-8004, (404) 256-6447: *Professional Series/3,* $1,499; *Supporting Schedules,* $499; *Text Library System,* $349. Inquire about interface with *dbCAMS+ Client and Asset Management System.*
- Leonard Financial Planning Systems, 68 Alexander Dr., Research Triangle, NC 27709, (800) 632-3044, (919) 549-9853: *Leonard 5000,* $5,000; *Leonard 6000,* $6,000 (network version). Inquire about interface with *dbCAMS+ Client and Asset Management System.*
- Sawhney Software, Inc., 888 Seventh Ave., New York, NY 10106, (800) 752-6344, (212) 541-8020: *ExecPlan II,* $995 + $500 annual maintenance (first 90 days free). Inquire about interface with *dbCAMS+ Client and Asset Management System* and other database programs.
- Softbridge Microsystems Corp., 125 Cambridge Park Dr., Cambridge, MA 02140, (800) 325-6060, (800) 325-5959 (MA): *Softbridge Financial Planner,* $6,000; *FP-Assistant,* $1,495; *Softbridge Business Planner* (ask vendor for exact date of availability).
- Sterling Wentworth Corp., 2319 Foothill Dr., Suite 209, Salt Lake City, UT 84109, (800) 752-6637, (801) 467-7510 (UT): *PLANMAN PLUS,* $4,500 ($6,000 with *DATABASE* and *GRAPHICS*); *GRAPHICS,* $500; *DATABASE,* $2,000; *BUSINESS-PLAN,* $2,995.
- Strategic Planning Systems, 15233 Ventura Blvd., Suite 708, Sherman Oaks, CA 91403-2293, (818) 784-6863: *Financial Master,* $4,000 (versions for both Macintosh and for IBM compatible computers running under *Windows*).

Mini and "Quick" Planning Systems

This category represents planning systems that may be comprehensive and, in some cases, integrated, or partially so. Some are down-scaled versions of systems listed above. In general, they are designed to support planning and product implementation in the middle to upper middle markets (as defined by income and/or net worth). They do not include the range of features and capabilities of comprehensive integrated systems. See the checklists in Part 3, "Evaluating Financial and Tax Planning Software."

- CLR/FASTTAX, 2395 Midway Rd., Carrolton, TX 75006, (800) 642-7689, (214) 404-8444: *Financial Sense,* $1,995; *Marketing Kit,* $995; *Total Practice System,* $2,495. Service bureau plans are available at variable pricing.
- Financial Planning Systems, Inc., 537 E. 300 South, Salt Lake City, UT 84102, (800) 245-1991, (801) 322-0527: *Life Planner System,* $530 + $50 monthly maintenance, update, technical support.
- First Financial Software, 137320 Veterans Memorial Highway, Hauppage, NY 11788, (516) 724-8282: *FPLAN,* $1,295.
- International Financial Data Systems, Inc. (IFDS), P.O. Box 888870, Atlanta, GA 30356-0870, (800) 554-8004, (404) 256-6447: *Professional Series/2,* $999; *Supporting Schedules,* $499; *Text Library System,* $349. Inquire about interface with *dbCAMS+ Client and Asset Management System.*
- Leonard Financial Planning Systems, 68 Alexander Dr., Research Triangle, NC 27709, (800) 632-3044, (919) 549-9853: *Leonard 2000,* $2,000. Inquire about interface with *dbCAMS+ Client and Asset Management System.*
- Lumen Systems, Inc., 4300 Stevens Creek Blvd., Suite 270, San Jose, CA 95129, (800) 233-3461, (800) 321-2959 (CA), (408) 984-8134: *Financial Planning Professional,* $1,495; *Client Tracker,* $500; *Graphics,* $500; *Planner's Alert* (rules, library), $500. Inquire about interface with *dbCAMS+ Client and Asset Management System.*
- Micro Planning Systems, 1499 Bayshore Highway, Suite 214, Burlingame, CA 94010, (415) 692-0407: *Professional Financial Planning System,* $895 ($995 (CA)); *Super Planner,* $395.
- Money Tree Software, 1753 Wooded Knolls Dr., Suite 200, Philomath, OR 97370, (903) 929-2140: *MoneyCalc PLUS* (integrated *1-2-3* templates), $1,595; *MoneyCalc Premier,* $975; *Easy Money,* $675. Inquire about bundled prices and interface options with client and asset management programs.
- Perception Software Systems, 1010 Hurley Way, Suite 300, Sacramento, CA 95825, (916) 965-8094: *Master Plan: The Analyst,* $1,495.
- Sawhney Software, Inc., 888 Seventh Ave., New York, NY 10106, (800) 752-6344, (212) 541-8020: *ExecPlan II* (Financial Profile Module of complete system), $495 + $250 annual maintenance. Inquire about interface options with client and asset management programs.
- Softbridge Microsystems Corp., 125 Cambridge Park Dr., Cambridge, MA 02140, (800) 325-6060, (800) 325-5959 (MA): *Softbridge QuickPlan,* $2,295 ($2,495 with *Lotus 1-2-3*).
- Sterling Wentworth Corp., 2319 Foothill Dr., Suite 209, Salt Lake City, UT 84109, (800) 752-6637, (801) 467-7510 (UT): *STEP 1,* $2,495; *NEXT $,* $1,995.
- Summit Innovative Systems, Inc., One Grand Centre, Suite 211, Sherman, TX 75090, (800) 527-4132, (800) 442-3407 (TX): *Summit Financial Writer,* $495.

- Dennis E. Wilt, 911 West 8th Ave., #8, Suite 201, Anchorage, AK 99501, (907) 276-4610: *Pyramid* (integrated financial diagnostics), $2,495.

Financial Planning Programs and Needs Analyses

The following programs are more difficult to classify. They are neither comprehensive nor integrated. Some provide extensive financial planning analyses and reports, others provide needs analyses in focus areas of planning. Most are designed to support product marketing. See the checklists in Part 3, "Evaluating Financial and Tax Planning Software."

- Blankenship & Co., P.O. Box 69016, Houston, TX 77269, (713) 370-0006: *The Professional Plan,* $149.95.
- Brentmark Software, P.O. Box 9886, Suite 2, Newark, DE 19714, (302) 366-8160: *Financial Planning Toolkit* (49 financial calculations in seven categories), $225.
- Consumer Finance Institute (a division of Price Waterhouse), 2 University Park, 51 Sawyer Rd., Waltham, MA 02154, (617) 899-6500: *Personal Financial Strategies* (service bureau reports with recommendations, client reference materials), $225–$300 per client.
- Dataplan, Inc., 7616 LBJ Freeway, Suite 400, Dallas, TX 75251, (214) 960-2516: *Modular Planning System* (investment oriented), $250.
- FAX International, 4724 S.W. Macadam Ave., Portland, OR 97201, (800) 654-8938: *FINA◆EASE* (family income needs analysis/estate analysis), $195.
- Financial Data Corp., P.O. Box 1332, Bryn Mawr, PA 19010, (800) 392-6900, (215) 525-6957: *Financial and Estate Planners' NumberCruncher-1,* $199; *Financial Planning Toolkit* (death, disability, retirement, education), $199. Estate planning module, $300. (Both programs use *Lotus 1-2-3* templates.)
- Financial Planning Information, Inc., Riverbend Office Park, 9 Galen Street, Watertown, MA 02172, (800) 448-8112, (617) 924-6939: *The Personal Financial Planning Program* (20-page report with recommendations for client, 4-page needs summary for planner), $475.
- First Financial Software, 137320 Veterans Memorial Highway, Hauppage, NY 11788, (516) 724-8282: *FPLAN* (Basic Plan module), $695.
- International Financial Data Systems, Inc. (IFDS), P.O. Box 888870, Atlanta, GA 30356-0870, (800) 554-8004, (404) 256-6447: *Penny Pincher II Software* (reports for product marketing support), $499.
- Lumen Systems, Inc., 4300 Stevens Creek Blvd., Suite 270, San Jose, CA 95129, (800) 233-3461, (800) 321-2959 (CA), (408) 984-8134: *Quiklook* (capital needs, sales-oriented, base for additional planning), $750; *Toolbox,* Vols. 1 & 2, $125 each. Inquire about bundled pricing.
- Malgoire Drucker Inc., 7315 Wisconsin Ave., Bethesda, MD 20814, (301) 469-3999: *Integrate!,* $495. Requires *Lotus 1-2-3*.
- Mayer Hoffman McCann, 420 Nichols Rd., Kansas City, MO 64112, (800) 433-2292, (816) 753-3870: *Personal Financial Planning* (targeted to CPAs), $295.

- Personal $trategic Planners, Inc., 109 Park Washington Ct., Falls Church, VA 22046, (800) 266-6571, (703) 241-0122: *Future$sight,* $1,500 ($600 annual maintenance). System requires Microsoft *Windows,* Microsoft *Excel* spreadsheet, and 1 megabyte of expanded memory; also available for Macintosh SE computer.
- The PlanFirst Co., 6 North Park Dr., Suite 103, Cockeysville, MD 21030, (301) 683-0600: *PlanFirst* (financial needs analysis for middle markets, service bureau preparation), $198.
- Provisor Corporation, 2105 112th Ave., N.E., Suite 100, Bellevue, WA 98004, (206) 462-7890: *Provisor* (lists of recommended investment and insurance products, service bureau preparation), $395.
- Ryan Software, Inc., 901 North Broadway, North White Plains, NY 10603, (800) 447-8338: *Ryan Projections* (10-year projections of financial statements, income tax, cash flow; passive activity loss limitations, carryovers, and dispositions; effects of education expenditures), $235; *Ryan Investment Plan,* $95. On *Lotus 1-2-3* templates.
- Successful Money Management Software, Inc., 10180 S.W. Nimbus, Suite J-6, Portland, OR 97223, (503) 620-8284: *Life Goals,* $695.
- Tax Calc, 4210 W. Vickery Blvd., Fort Worth, TX 76107, (800) 527-2669, (817) 738-3122: *Tax Calc Personal Financial Planner,* $750; *Financial Decisions Planner,* $100. Both run off *Lotus 1-2-3.*

Asset and Portfolio Allocation

These programs are designed to help the planner create market-efficient asset and portfolio allocations in relation to investment return objectives, risk levels, market indexes, and investment classes. Except as noted, they are based on diversification models of modern portfolio theory. See the evaluation criteria in Part 2 of the chapter.

- Advanced Investment Software, 8101 E. Prentice Ave., Suite 310, Englewood, CO 80111, (303) 773-8500; *RAMCAP–The Intelligent Asset Allocator,* $595 ($49 per quarter update); *Cash Flow Analyzer,* $49.
- Black River Systems Corporation, 4680 Brownsboro Road, Building C, Winston-Salem, NC 27106, (919) 721-0928: *MACRO* WORLD INVESTOR,* $699.95 ($399.95 annual update). Includes over 100 economic indicators, prices of stocks with highest return on equity.
- Burlington Hall Asset Management, Inc., 126 Petersburg Rd., Hackettstown, NJ 07840, (201) 852-1694: *LaPorte Asset Allocation System,* $1,975 annual license fee, $695 annual fee for over 2,000 mutual funds performance data sent quarterly ($1,695 sent monthly), $195 for commodities data sent quarterly ($475 sent monthly).
- Callan Associates, Inc., 71 Stevenson St., Suite 1300, San Francisco, CA 94105, (415) 974-5060: *ASSETMAX,* $3,000 annual.
- CDA Investment Technologies, Inc., 1355 Piccard Dr., Rockville, MD 20854, (301) 975-9600: *CDA Asset Mix Optimizer,* $2,800 annually (31 investment classes, monthly update), $700 annually (quarterly update); *CDA Mutual Fund*

Hypotheticals, $575 annually (quarterly update); *CDA Mutual Fund Optimizer,* $500 annually (quarterly update); *CDA Micro Universe* (all mutual funds, 60 indexes, etc.), $6,000 annually (monthly update), $4,000 annually (quarterly update); *CDA Micro Performance,* $250 + monthly (service/lease, quarterly update). All updates with diskettes (except online subscriptions at different pricing).

- Gentry and Associates, 7473 E. Butler Drive, Building B, Scottsdale, AZ 85258, (602) 998-8046: *Asset Mix Optimization,* $495.

- Computer Handholders, Inc., P.O. Box 59, Arcola, PA 19420, (215) 565-7467: *Portfolio Management Software Package,* $375. Designed initially to teach various techniques of modern portfolio theory in university curricula, the current version is better adapted for professional use.

- C.R. Hunter & Associates, 1176 Inner Circle, Cincinnati, OH 45240, (513) 825-8669: *The Permanent Portfolio Analyzer* (based on Harry Brown's *Inflation-Proofing Your Investments*), $99; *The Dual Portfolio Manager* (long-term, short-term tracking, based on Harry Brown's *Why the Best-Laid Investment Plans Usually Go Wrong*), $99. Based on client-provided parameters rather than modern portfolio theory diversification model.

- Ibbotson Associates, 8 South Michigan Ave., Chicago, IL 60603, (312) 263-3434: *Asset Allocation Tools* (requires *Lotus 1-2-3,* version 2.01), $5,000 ($4,000 annual update). Differs from the Scientific Press version listed below in its much more extensive historical database.

- Investment Company Data, Inc., 406 Merle Hay Tower, Des Moines, IA 50310, (800) 255-2255 (ext. 5222), (515) 270-8600: *ICD Online* (rate of return and selected fundamentals on 2,000 mutual funds), $50 for password and setup, $1 per minute; *ICD Spreadsheet* (*1-2-3* templates for rate of return, fundamentals, addresses of 2,000 mutual funds), $475–$2,400 for selectable categories of monthly updated diskettes on equities, fixed-income assets, and mutual funds; *ICD Hypothetical Investment Program* (investment and reinvestment optimizing strategies based on 25-year investment data). Inquire with vendor for pricing.

- Morley and Associates, Inc., Suite 400-Kruse Woods One, 5285 S.W. Meadows Rd., Lake Oswego, OR 97035, (800) 548-4806, (503) 635-5414: *COMPASS Portfolio Planning System,* $2,800, $280 annual maintenance (includes quarterly updates, support).

- PAAR Systems, P.O. Box 356, Cotati, CA 94931-0356, (707) 576-7227: *Personal Asset Allocation Report,* $275; *Pension Asset Allocation Report,* $275; *Planned Asset Acquisition Report,* $125; all three programs, $495. Sales oriented, based on client-provided parameters rather than modern portfolio theory diversification model.

- Russell Analytical Services, P.O. Box 1616, Tacoma, WA 98401 (206) 591-3556: *Russell Asset Allocation Model,* $7,000 ($3,500 annual update).

- Sponsor Software Systems, Inc., 860 Fifth Ave., New York, NY 10021, (212) 724-7535: *Asset Allocation Expert,* $5,000 ($2,500 annual update).

- The Scientific Press, 507 Seaport Ct., Redwood City, CA 94063, (415) 366-2577: *Asset Allocation Tools* (requires *Lotus 1-2-3,* version 2.01), $2,500.

- Irwin Tepper Associates, 77 Oak St., Suite 2, Newton, MA 02164, (617) 244-6747: *Investment Policy Analyst,* $2,500. Includes no historical data but accepts imported data.
- Vestek Systems, Inc., 353 Sacramento St., Suite 2100, San Francisco, CA 94111, (415) 398-6340: *Asset Allocation Model,* $5,000 annual.
- Wilson Associates, 4653 Vanalden, Tarzana, CA 91356, (818) 999-0015: *Capital Asset Management System* (asset allocation, periodic historical data updates), $1,500 annual license fee and $200 monthly maintenance (76 asset classes, 300 mutual funds, asset optimizer, performance analysis); $500 annual license fee and $110 month maintenance (same as above, no mutual funds). Inquire about interface with *dbCAMS+ Client and Asset Management System* (see listing in the next section).

Client and Asset Management

These programs are designed primarily for managing information and communications with clients and prospects; managing and status reporting on investment assets and insurance coverages, and supporting general planning practice communications and reporting procedures. When compared, the programs are rarely equal over the whole range of these capabilities. Each was initially designed as a "niche" market product; each is characterized by some outstanding features, others that are more or less standard. Some do not track insurance and annuity products. Inquire with vendors about interfaces with financial planning software systems and programs and with asset allocation and portfolio performance measurement programs. See the evaluation criteria in Part 3 of the chapter.

- American Financial Systems, Inc., 17 Haverford Station Rd., Haverford, PA 19041, (215) 896-8780: *Broker's Notebook* (client communications, portfolio management system for active trading accounts), $1,295 (network version price depends on number of users); $1,495 with module to download back-office account data.
- Contact Software International, Inc., 1625 W. Crosby Rd., Carrollton, TX 75006, (800) 228-9228, (214) 929-4749: *ACT!* (sophisticated database, sales and marketing, activity history, communications), $395.
- Dow Jones & Company, Inc., P.O. Box 300, Princeton, NJ 08543-0300, (609) 520-4641, (609) 520-4642: *Market Manager PLUS Professional* (portfolio management), $499 (plus subscription to Dow Jones News/Retrieval for down-loaded price updating).
- E-Z Data, Inc., 533 S. Atlantic Blvd., Monterey Park, CA 91754, (800) 777-9188, (818) 281-2296, (818) 913-2683: *Client Data System* (client and asset management), $699; network version, $1,199; New Business Tracking Module, $249; Investment Tracking Module, $199; Commission Accounting Module, $199. Inquire about interfaces with financial planning systems.
- Financial Computer Support, Inc., Route 4, Box 527, Deer Park, MD 21550, (301) 387-4445: *dbCMS+ Client Management System, Plus* (client and asset

management), $575 or $50 plus $395 initiation fee, $40 per month membership in FCSI; *dbCAMS+ Client and Asset Management System* (client, asset, and portfolio management plus transaction log), $875 or $100 plus initiation fee and monthly membership fee; *Billing and Time Management Module,* $320; Dow-Jones Interface, $125. Inquire about interfaces with financial planning systems and other programs.

- Halperin & Lax, 335 Centerville Rd., Warwick, RI 02886, (401) 738-2350: *The Total Client Management System* (client and asset management, including mutual funds and insurance), $600.
- KN Systems, 6114 LaSalle Ave., Suite 255, Oakland, CA 94611, (800) 356-2259, (415) 339-3606: *The Financial Planner's Desktop Companion* (client and asset management, basically a customized desktop organizer), $149.
- Alan Mayer Enterprises, 6413 Congress Ave., Suite 200, Boca Raton, FL 33487, (800) 533-3640: *Broker Portfolio System* (client and portfolio management), $1,500.
- M & M Software Co., Inc., 2720 Stemmons Freeway, Suite 902, Dallas, TX 75207, (314) 346-6248: *Client's Financial Profile: Investment Monitoring Program* (basic, unsophisticated client contact and asset tracking), $475.
- North American Software, Inc., 4140 Crossgate Sq., Cincinnati, OH 45236, (513) 793-2240: *Broker's Helper* (client and portfolio management), $995.
- Plaid Bros. Software, 17952 Sky Park Circle, Suite K, Irvine, CA 92714, (714) 261-7255: *Prospect* (sales prospect tracker), $295; *Portfolio Manager* (portfolio tracking and reporting), $995.
- Sales and Marketing Systems, Inc., 1950 Old Gallows Rd., Vienna, VA 22180, (800) 832-0030, (703) 790-3422: *SalesCONTROL 2* (sophisticated database, sales and marketing, activity history), $695 single user, $2,795 five or more users. Inquire about interface with *Shaw Microserv* portfolio analysis and performance software.
- SaleMaker Software, 402 South Center Street, Grand Prairie, TX 75051, (800) 766-7355, (214) 264-2626: *SaleMaker Plus* (client management and telemarketing), $695 single user, $2,495 5-user network.
- Scherrer Resources, Inc., 8100 Cherokee St., Philadelphia, PA 19118, (215) 242-8740: *Broker's Ally* (client management and prospecting), $395; MATE (add-on module for appointments, time logging, and expense reporting), $99.
- Charles Schwab and Co., 101 Montgomery St., San Francisco, CA 94104, (800) 334-4455, (415) 627-7000: *Equalizer Personal Investment System* (securities and mutual funds portfolios, trading, tracking, orders, reports), $269.
- Successful Money Management Software, Inc., 10180 S.W. Nimbus, Suite J-6, Portland, OR 97223, (503) 620-8284: *SMART Practice* (client and asset management), $995.
- TECHSERVE, INC., P.O. Box 70056, Bellevue, WA 98007, (800) 826-8082: *PFPRO Professional Portfolio Software,* $695.
- Time Trend Software, 337 Boston Rd., Billerica, MA 01821, (508) 663-3330: *Fund Master TC* (mutual funds technical analysis, selection, reporting, portfolio management), $289; *The Enhanced Fund Master Optimizer,* $150; *Fund Pro* (for professional user with multiple portfolios), $425; *Warner Data Retriever*

(module for down-loadable prices, distributions via Warner Computer Systems), $45. Inquire about interface with *dbCAMS+ Client and Asset Management System.*

Portfolio Analysis and Performance Measurement

These programs are designed for sophisticated portfolio management, performance measurement, and reporting, based on modern portfolio theory and calculations of time-weighted returns as recommended by the Bank Administration Institute for pension funds. They also provide varying client communications capabilities. The programs are targeted primarily to specialist investment advisory and asset management firms, including institutions, but may also be suitable for financial planning firms that provide asset management services. Inquire with vendors about interfaces with other programs and investor services. See the evaluation criteria in Part 3 of the chapter.

- Advent Software, 512 Second St., San Francisco, CA 94107, (415) 543-7696, (212) 398-1188 (NY Office): *The Professional Portfolio,* $2,700 (Level I), $6,700 (Level II, institutional).
- Gentry and Associates, 7473 E. Butler Drive, Building B, Scottsdale, AZ 85258, (602) 998-8046: *The Intelligent Investor,* $950.
- Performance Technologies, Inc., 4024 Barrett Dr., Suite 202, Raleigh, NC 27609, (800) 528-9595, (919) 787-2911: *CENTERPIECE Portfolio Performance Software,* $895. Inquire about interfaces with financial planning systems.
- Shaw Data Services, Inc., 122 East 42nd St., New York, NY 10168, (212) 682-8877, (201) 882-1034 (NJ office), (617) 367-3200 (Boston office): *MicroShaw,* $2,000 (basic portfolio management, without performance measurement and client billing); $3,000 (without client billing); $4,000 full system. Inquire about online services from a mainframe computer, interfaces with other programs.
- West Coast Software, 1211 Southwest 5th Ave., Suite 1250, Portland, OR 97204, (800) 622-1046, (503) 796-1046: *AIM* (Asset Investment Management, including asset allocation, portfolio management, portfolio performance measurement), $7,500 annual subscription (includes enhancements, monthly index updates, and consulting). This is the only program known to the author that includes high-level capabilities in all three specialized areas of asset management.

Personal Finance, Cash Flow Analysis, and Check Writing

The following financial accounting and cash flow programs are suitable for personal and/or small business use. They are not financial planning programs but provide support for its beginning phases. For some financial planning clients, these programs could be very useful and would supply the planner with a great deal of initial and updated financial data. Several of the programs also provide check-writing features. As indicated, some programs interface directly with selected income tax return preparation software designed for personal use.

- Armstrong's Financial Organizers, Inc., 5950 Berkshire Ln., LB #59, Dallas, TX 75225, (214) 987-1414, (800) 451-2856: *Armstrong's Home Financial Organizer,* $69.95.
- ChipSoft, Inc., 5045 Shoreham Pl., San Diego, CA 92122, (800) 782-1120, (619) 453-8722: *Personal Finance Manager* (links with ChipSoft's *TurboTax* income tax return preparation program), $99.00.
- Column One, Inc., P.O. Box 2607, Gaithersburg, MD 20879, (301) 948-9599: *CashTrac* (financial tracking in check register format), $45.
- Dac Software, Inc., 4801 Spring Valley Rd., Dallas, TX 75244, (214) 458-0038: *Dac-Easy Light* (personal, small business financial accounting, check writing), $69.95.
- Jay Gold Software, 2311 40th St., Box 2024, Des Moines, IA 50310, (515) 279-9821: *Home Finance System-III* (includes check writing), $99.
- Intuit, Inc., 540 University Ave., Palo Alto, CA 94301, (415) 322-0573: *Quicken* (personal, small business financial accounting, check writing), $49.95. Links directly with *J. K. Lasser's Your Income Tax* return preparation program.
- Lumen Systems, Inc., 4300 Stevens Creek Blvd., Suite 270, San Jose, CA 95129, (800) 233-3461, (800) 321-2959 (CA), (408) 984-8134: *Personal Financial Manager,* $200.
- MECA Ventures, 285 Riverside Ave., Westport, CT 06880, (800) 835-2246 (ext. 12), (203) 226-2400: *Managing Your Money* (personal, small business financial accounting), $219.95 (includes *Checkwrite Plus*); *Checkwrite Plus* (personal, business bookkeeping, and check writing), $69.95. Both link with MECA's *Tax Cut* income tax return preparation program.
- MoneyCare, Inc., 253 Martens Ave., Mountain View, CA 94040, (800) 824-9827, (415) 962-0333: *Financial Navigator: Professional Version* (personal, small business cash flow and financial asset accounting, tax tracking, includes *Tax & Year-End Tool Kit*), $399; *Financial Navigator: Personal Version* (cash flow accounting), $99; *Navigator Access* (securities price updates via Warner Computer Systems), $99; *Tax & Year-End Tool Kit* (closes out *Financial Navigator* totals, opens new year, links with ChipSoft's *TurboTax*), $49 ($99 with *TurboTax*).
- Monogram, 8295 South La Cienega Blvd., Inglewood, CA 90301, (213) 533-5120: *Dollars and Sense* (personal, small business financial accounting, check writing), $179.95.
- Parsons Technology, 375 Collins Rd., NE, Cedar Rapids, IA 52402, (319) 395-7300: *Moneycounts Plus* (personal financial accounting, check writing), $58. Links with Parsons's *1989 Personal Tax Preparer.*
- Sapana Micro Software, 1305 S. Rouse, Pittsburg, KS 66762, (316) 231-5023: *Expense-Track II,* $69.95.
- Softquest, Inc., P.O. Box 3456, McLean, VA 22102, (703) 281-1621: *The Smart Checkbook* (personal, small business financial accounting, check writing), $100.
- Tax Calc, 4210 W. Vickery Blvd., Fort Worth, TX 76107, (800) 527-2669, (817) 738-3122: *Individual Cash Flow Planner,* $75; *Business Cash Flow Planner* (FASB 95), $95; *Business Planning Model* (forecasts and projections), $195. Programs run off *Lotus 1-2-3.*

- Technology Media Services Group, 1721 E. Frankford Rd., Suite 2421, Carrollton, TX 75007, (214) 492-5779: *Home Finance Organizer,* $69.95.
- Timeworks, Inc., 444 Lake Cook Rd., Deerfield, IL 60015, (312) 948-9200: *Sylvia Porter's Your Financial Planner* (personal, small business financial accounting), $99.95.

Personal and Small Business Income Tax Planning

These programs are designed for personal tax planning and forecasting rather than income tax return preparation, and for small businesses such as might be owned by financial planning clients. See Part 4 of the chapter, including the evaluation checklists for integrated financial and tax planning systems.

- Aardvark/McGraw-Hill, 1020 N. Broadway, Milwaukee, WI 53202, (800) 292-2962, (414) 225-7500: *Professional Tax Planner,* $395.
- Apt Software Corporation, Hicksville, NY 11801, (516) 931-2516: *The Tax Estimator* (income tax estimates based on 3 years' returns), $245.
- Best Programs, Inc., 2700 S. Quincy St., Suite 270, Arlington, VA 22206, (800) 368-2406, (703) 820-9300: *Tax Partner Planner* (5-year projections), $395.
- BNA Software, 2300 M St., NW, Suite 660, Washington, DC 20037, (800) 424-2938: *BNA Income Tax Spreadsheet,* $495; with 50-state planner, $890.
- CPAid, Inc., 1061 Fraternity Circle, Kent, OH 44240, (800) 227-2437, (216) 678-9015: *CPAid Tax Planner,* $300.
- EZWare Corp., 29 Bala Ave., Suite 206, Bala Cynwyd, PA 19004, (800) 7543-1040, (215) 667-4064: *EZTax-Plan Business Edition,* $295; *EZTax-Plan Personal Edition,* $95.
- Integrated Financial Solutions, 1130 Northchase Pkwy., Suite 200, Marietta, GA 30067, (800) 831-7636, (404) 952-4721: *Tax4Caster* (15-year projections of tax, cash flow, net worth), $475.
- IRIS Systems, 2966 Diamond St., Suite 200, San Francisco, CA 94131-3287, (800) 852-4747 (CA), (415) 432-4747: *IRIS Professional Tax Forecaster* (federal and CA or NY), $595; federal and other states, $695.
- Money Tree Software, 1753 Wooded Knolls Dr., Suite 200, Philomath, OR 97370, (903) 929-2140: *Money Tree Tax Planning* (*1-2-3* templates for income and estate tax), $250.
- Park Technologies, Inc., P.O. Box 1317, Clifton Park, NY 12065, (800) 423-3189, (518) 877-5881: *Tax Planner,* $79.95; *Corporate,* $149; *S-Corporations,* $149. Programs require *Lotus 1-2-3* or compatible spreadsheets.
- Research Press, 4500 W. 72nd Terr., Prairie Village, KS 66208, (913) 362-9667: *SHORTAX+PLUS* (*Lotus 1-2-3* work sheets for 6-year analyses of IRS 1040 data, schedules), $295.
- Ryan Software, Inc., 901 North Broadway, North White Plains, NY 10603, (800) 447-8338: *Ryan Income Tax* (3-year projections on *Lotus 1-2-3* templates), $95; *Ryan S Corp.,* $95.
- Sawhney Software, Inc., 888 Seventh Ave., New York, NY 10106, (800) 752-6344, (212) 541-8020: *Planmode* (advanced individual income tax

planning, investment oriented), $395; *Taxmode* (individual income tax planning and calculation), $295.

- SoftView, Inc., 4820 Adohr Ln., Suite F, Camarillo, CA 93010, (805) 388-2626: *TaxView Planner,* $119.
- Tax Calc, 4210 W. Vickery Blvd., Fort Worth, TX 76107, (800) 527-2669, (817) 738-3122: *Professional Tax Planner,* $395; *Combined Federal and State Tax Planner* (module for NY and CA), $100. Programs run off *Lotus 1-2-3.*
- Tax Help, 6 Hopkins Rd., Peabody, MA 01960, (508) 535-0688: *TAXPLAN91* (3-year what-if comparisons, graphics), $70.
- 1040 Solutions, Inc., 3460 Torrance Blvd., Torrance, CA 90503, (213) 543-4002: *Tax Projection Worksheet,* $195.

Income Tax Return Preparation

The programs listed include packages suitable for personal use; in some instances, the vendor indicates the program is also suitable for professional use. Ask vendors about laser printer support, electronic filing capability, the number of federal forms and schedules supported, the actual state modules available, and annual update costs. Programs that provide links for data transfer with personal finance and check-writing programs may be particularly well suited for use by financial planning clients.

- AM Software, P.O. Box 25010, Kansas City, MO 64119, (816) 241-0014: *AM-TAX,* $45; state modules, $30 each.
- Austin Scientific, Inc., P.O. Box 1146, Menlo Park, CA 94026-1146, (800) 433-1608, (415) 323-6338: *TaxTime 1040,* $95–$195; state modules, $50–$95.
- CDE Software, 4017 39th Ave., SW, Seattle, WA 98116-3848, (206) 937-8927: *Checks and Balances,* $74.95.
- ChipSoft, Inc., 5045 Shoreham Pl., San Diego, CA 92122, (800) 782-1120, (619) 453-8722: *TurboTax* (links with ChipSoft's *Personal Finance Manager* and MoneyCare's *Financial Navigator*), $75; state modules (41 available), $40 each. With Interface module, can import data from *Quicken, Dollars and Sense,* and *Managing Your Money* personal finance programs, or from a spreadsheet that produces ASCII files.
- Double Eagle Software, 2340 Plaza del Amo, Suite 215, Torrance, CA 90501, (213) 212-6611: *The Tax Advantage,* $59.95; CA module, $45.
- EZWare Corp., 29 Bala Ave., Suite 206, Bala Cynwyd, PA 19004, (800) 543-1040, (215) 667-4064: *EZTax-Prep 1040,* $129.95; modules for CA, NY, PA, $69 each. Runs off *Lotus 1-2-3.*
- Legal Knowledge Systems, P.O. Box 695, Drexel Hill, PA 19026, (215) 789-3679: *Ask Dan about Your Taxes,* $89.95; modules for CA, MA, and NY, $12.95 each.
- MECA Ventures, 285 Riverside Ave., Westport, CT 06880, (800) 835-2246 (ext. 12), (203) 226-2400: *Tax Cut,* $79.50. Links with MECA's *Managing Your Money* personal finance program.
- Myrick Computer Services, Inc., 1250 Tower Ln., Erie, PA 16505, (800) 854-3709, (814) 455-6610: *E-Z Tax Filer,* $69.

- Park Technologies, Inc., P.O. Box 1317, Clifton Park, NY 12065, (800) 423-3189, (518) 877-5881: *TaxEase System,* $79.95. Requires *Lotus 1-2-3* or compatible spreadsheets.
- Parsons Technology, 375 Collins Rd., NE, Cedar Rapids, IA 52402, (800) 223-6925: *1989 Personal Tax Preparer,* $29. Links with Parsons's *MoneyCounts* personal finance program.
- Rockware Data Corporation, 2817 Regal, Suite 105, Plano, TX, (214) 596-0588: *Supertax,* $59.
- Simon & Schuster Software, 1 Gulf & Western Plaza, New York, NY 10023, (212) 378-8142: *J. K. Lasser's Your Income Tax,* $75; modules for CA and NY, $39.95 each. Links with Intuit's *Quicken* personal finance program; available from Intuit for $65.
- SoftView, Inc., 4820 Adohr Ln., Suite F, Camarillo, CA 93010, (805) 388-2626: *TaxView,* $119; modules for CA and NY, $65 each.
- Tax Help, 6 Hopkins Rd., Peabody, MA 01960, (508) 535-0688: *1040 Preparation,* $25–$150 (federal plus selected states); *Corporation or S Corporation Tax,* $99.
- Tax Shop, 7668 Municipal Dr., Orlando, FL 32819, (407) 351-0966: *Tax Shop 1040,* $59.
- Timeworks, 444 Lake Cook Rd., Deerfield, IL 60015-4919, (312) 948-9200: *Swiftax,* $69.95.
- Valley Management Consultants, 3939 Bradford Rd., Huntington Valley, PA 19006, (215) 947-4610, (215) 947-2507: *EASYTAX,* $89; $49 for NY and CA, $35 for PA and NJ modules. Requires *Lotus 1-2-3.*

Insurance Planning and Marketing

These programs are designed primarily for and marketed to insurance professionals involved in various focus areas of financial planning in which insurance applications are relevant.

- Advanced Financial Systems, 173 E. College St., Covina, CA 91723, (818) 339-7456: *Pension Maximization* (using life insurance), $295.
- Benefit Analysis, Inc., 996 Old Eagle School Rd., Suite 1105, Wayne, PA 19087, (215) 293-0808, (800) 223-3601: *Family Financial Review* (for estate planning), $1,000; *Family Income Continuation Plan* (life and disability income needs), $395.
- James R. Carl, CPA, Miller Energy, Inc., 229 E. Michigan Ave., Suite 220, Kalamazoo, MI 49007, (616) 343-0582: *Life Insurance Return Analysis,* $125.
- Client Marketing Systems, 895 Oak Park Blvd., Pismo Beach, CA 93449, (800) 643-4488, (805) 473-0550: *The CIC System* (prospecting and client management database), $395.
- COMPULIFE Software, Inc., 4248 Ridge Lea Rd., Amherst, NY 14226 (800) 265-2763, (716) 831-9943: *Compulife Quotation System* (quotations, proposals on whole life and term insurance, cost comparisons with alternative policies and companies), $295 plus $49 monthly update fee; *Compulife Analysis Series* (analyses of interest-adjusted cost, income from capital, retirement investment),

$190; *Prospect/Client File Manager,* $395. Inquire about multiple-copy discounts.

- Coss Corporation, 9040 North 51st St., Milwaukee, WI 53223, (414) 354-6663: *LIFESCAPE* (insurance proposals and graphics, including comparisons with investment products), $495 (stand-alone, user data entry), $745 (linked directly to print file data from another program).
- Diversified Insurance Software Corporation, 2437 U.S. 19 North, Suite 410, Clearwater, FL 33575, (813) 799-4113: *Group Rater* (downloaded rate book), $250 plus $125 monthly for monthly updated rate data, $950 one-time charge for version for user-updated data; *Health Rater* (individual health policies), $350 annual including monthly updated rate data; *Term Rater* (individual term policies, various companies), $400 annual including monthly updated rate data; *Brokerage Production Database* (for GA/brokerage network), inquire with vendor for pricing.
- Financial Data Corp., P.O. Box 1332, Bryn Mawr, PA 19010, (800) 654-2227, (215) 526-1361: *Financial Fire Drill* (insurance marketing report-generating program), $1,000.
- Financial Data Planning Corporation, 2140 South Dixie Highway, Miami, FL 33134, (305) 858-8200: *FinPac B* (financial needs analysis, income tax, AMT, averaging tax, business valuation, etc.), $795; *Agency Database* (client/prospect, insurance/investments, and commission tracking), $795 single user, $2,495 network version; *FDP/125* (cafeteria plan feasibility, enrollment, administration), $1,000–$2,995 (modular); *Easy Laser* (pension plan integration analysis), $595–$795.
- Financial Profiles, Inc., 5964 La Place Ct., Suite 100, Carlsbad, CA 92008, (800) 237-6335, (800) 822-8302 (CA): *Financial Profiles* (extensive needs analyses and reports), $1,495; *Business Profiles System* (client business planning), $1,495; *Profiles Productivity System* (client and practice data management), $295; *Risk Profiles System* (insurance needs analyses—life, homeowner, property and casualty, liability, medical), $295.
- Foster Software, Inc., 6361 Presidential Ct., Ft. Myers, FL 33919, (800) 922-8722: *Comm-Trac* (sophisticated agent/broker commission tracking), $879.
- InsMark, Inc., 2274 Camino Ramon, San Ramon, CA 94583, (415) 866-1050: *InsMark* (stand-alone marketing, illustration, proposals program), $95–$795; *InsMark Proposal System (IPS); Executive Benefits System (EBS),* $95–$795; *InScribe* (graphics interfaces with IPS/EBS system), $195–$795; *Documents on a Disk* (170+ documents and legal agreements), $95–$495. Variable pricing depends on whether bought through home office (which includes link with mainframe data) or by individual agent for stand-alone program with manual data input.
- ISIS Incorporated, 260-A Coney Island Dr., Reno-Sparks, NV 89431, (702) 358-7400: *ISIS Plus* (family, estate tax, business insurance sales illustrations), $800; system unbundles into three separately priced modules at $295, $395, and $495, respectively.
- LIMRA's Trac-It, Inc., P.O. Box 7829, The Woodlands, TX 77387, (800) 822-8003, (713) 358-7400: *Client Marketing Management System* (agent's

prospect/client tracking), $695; *Agency Planner* (agency manager's agent production tracking), $1,095; *Brokerage System* (brokerage operations), $1,495.

- Longman Financial Services Publishing, P.O. Box 2200, Vernon, CT 06066, (203) 643-7799: *Asset Management Plan*, $695; *Financial Need Analysis II*, $495.
- Money Tree Software, 1753 Wooded Knolls Dr., Suite 200, Philomath, OR 97370, (903) 929-2140: *Money Tree Planning* (*1-2-3* templates for insurance analysis), $500. Philibert Software Group, Inc., 980 Canton St., Suite 100, Atlanta, GA 30075, (404) 642-2056: *PSG-Planner* (life insurance needs analyses), $295; *Prism* (life insurance needs analyses and sales illustrations), $295; *Universal Life System* (deferred compensation, split dollar, executive bonus), $1,500.
- Scherrer Resources, Inc., 8100 Cherokee St., Philadelphia, PA 19118, (215) 242-8740: *Agent's Ally* (client management and prospecting), $395; MATE (add-on module for appointments, time logging, and expense reporting), $99.
- SDG Innovations, Inc., 10615-G Tierrasanta Blvd., #122, San Diego, CA 92124, (619) 565-1200: *SDG Prospector* (client/prospect administration system), $695.
- SEE Computer Services, Inc., Suite 204, 930 Clifton Ave., Clifton, NJ 07013, (201) 471-8044: *SEETERM* (up to 8 competitive term illustrations), $395; (16 illustrations), $695.
- Specialists in Financial Planning, 2309 Renard Pl., SE, Albuquerque, NM 87106, (800) 523-7987, (505) 242-1998: *MACH 7* (database and prospecting system, optional prospect lists), $20 monthly subscription or $200 per year.
- Worksheets, Ltd., 12133 Tall Trees, Dunlap, IL 61525, (309) 243-9057: *MPlan* (needs analyses), $150; *Database*, $150.

Estate Planning, Taxation, and Administration

These programs are designed as stand-alone estate planning programs. See the sections on "Comprehensive Integrated Systems" and "Evaluating Financial and Tax Planning Software" in the chapter for a description of financial and tax planning systems and programs and evaluation features that can be applied to these stand-alone programs for focus planning.

- Aardvark/McGraw-Hill, 1020 N. Broadway, Milwaukee, WI 53202, (800) 292-2962, (414) 225-7500: *Estate Tax Planner*, $795.
- Benefit Analysis, Inc., 996 Old Eagle School Rd., Suite 1105, Wayne, PA 19087, (215) 293-0808, (800) 223-3601: *Family Asset Distribution Plan*, $950–$3,200.
- Berkeley Microsystems, Inc., 1960 Los Angeles Ave., Berkeley, CA 94707, (415) 525-1653: *ESTPLAN* (estate tax), $350.
- BNA Software, 231 25th St., NW, Washington, DC 20037, (800) 372-1033: *BNA Estate Tax Spreadsheet*, $1,295.
- Brentmark Software, 249 E. Main St., Suite 2, P.O. Box 9886, Newark, DE 19714, (302) 366-8160: *Brentmark Charitable Financial Planner*, $199; *NumberCruncher-1* (includes GRITS, split interests, private annuities, charitable remainder trusts, 6166 installments, 303 stock redemptions), $225; *ALR plus* (what-if computations of values of annuities, life estates, remainders, and terms

of years for federal midterm rates, midterm rates above and below the value projected), $49.

- Compu-Tate, Inc., 8231 Devlin Point, San Antonio, TX 78240, (512) 684-2248: *Evaluation of Estate Liability,* $500.
- Computer Decisions Corp., 1301 Redwood Way, Suite 190, Petaluma, CA 94952, (707) 795-7125: *EASY-FIDUCIARY ACCOUNTING,* $3,500 license fee; *EASY-AUTOMATED PRICING,* $495 with *EASY,* $1,400 stand-alone; *EASY-DOCKET,* $495 with *EASY,* $1,400 stand-alone; *EASY-706,* $495 with *EASY,* $1,400 stand-alone.
- Financial Technologies International, Inc., 65 Broadway, New York, NY 10006, (212) 440-8200: *EPLAN* (marital and charitable deductions, split-interest trusts, tax apportionment, asset disposition, liquidity and tax analyses; package includes *Quick Tax*), $1,400.
- Innovative Professional Software, Inc., 6825 E. Tennessee, Suite 441, Denver, CO 80224, (800) 622-4070, (303) 762-1954: *ESTATECALC,* $195.
- Institute for Paralegal Training, 1926 Arch St., Philadelphia, PA 19103, (800) 628-3232, (215) 567-4800: *Fiduciary Accountant,* $1,495; *Tax Module* (tax basis each lot), $300; *Estate Administrator,* $295.
- The Lackner Computer Group, Inc., 309 S. Craig St., Pittsburgh, PA 15213, (412) 681-5548, ABA/net Electronic Mailbox #1050: *The Estate Planning Program,* $195; *6-in-1 Estate Administration Program* (federal and state-specific estate and fiduciary returns and accounting), $1,500 (introductory price includes *Q&A*); $1,300 (introductory price without *Q&A*). Inquire for multiprogram and multistate prices. Built on Symantec's *Q&A* file manager/database and *Lotus 1-2-3.*
- Leland, Inc., 8601 Dunwoody Pl., Suite 626, Atlanta, GA 30350, (800) 535-2634, (404) 998-3500: *Trust Manager* (trust and estate accounting/reporting), $5,900 license fee single-user, $8,900 multiple-user.
- Lincoln National Sales Corp., 1300 S. Clinton St., P.O. Box 1110, Ft. Wayne, IN 46801, (219) 427-3206: *Professional Estate Analysis,* $595.
- Longman Financial Services Publishing, P.O. Box 2200, Vernon, CT 06066, (203) 643-7799: *EstateCalc Plus,* $895.
- PG Calc, Inc., 941 Holyoke Center, Cambridge, MA 02138, (617) 497-4970: *Planned Giving Manager,* $2,400.
- PhilanthroTec, Inc., Two South Executive Park, 6135 Park Rd., Suite 109, Charlotte, NC 28210, (704) 554-1646: *Charitable Scenario,* $1,895; *Philanthropist's Supplemental Income Plan,* $895; *Unitrust Marketing System,* $695.
- Randle, Coray & Associates, P.O. Box 1228, Utah State University, Provo, UT 84322, (801) 753-2020: *Estate Tax Planner,* $95.
- Ryan Software, Inc., 901 North Broadway, North White Plains, NY 10603, (800) 447-8338: *Ryan Estate Tax,* $150. On *Lotus 1-2-3* templates.
- Shepard's/McGraw-Hill, P.O. Box 1235, Colorado Springs, CO 80901, (800) 525-2474, (303) 475-7230: *Estate Planning for Farmers and Ranchers,* $500.
- Synaptic Software, 5628 Linden Circle, Johnston, IA 50131, (515) 225-7144: *EstateCalc Plus,* $895.

- TaxCalc, 4210 W. Vickery Blvd., Fort Worth, TX 76107, (800) 527-2669, (817) 738-3122: *Estate Tax Planner,* $100.
- ViewPlan, Inc., 530 Broadway, Suite 1230, San Diego, CA 92101, (800) 826-2127, (800) 352-6699 (CA): *Estate Forecast Model* (alternative scenarios), $495.
- Noah Weinshel, CPA, 1 Stone Pl., Bronxville, NY 10708, (914) 779-5900: *FAME* ("Fiduciary Accounting Made Easy"; accounting only, no tax returns or 706), $750–$2,750 (depending on emulator needed to run mainframe program on PC).

Employee Benefits and Retirement Planning

These stand-alone programs and online services are designed to support employee benefits and retirement planning. See the sections on "Comprehensive Integrated Systems" and "Evaluating Financial and Tax Planning Software" in the chapter for descriptive features and evaluation criteria for retirement planning applications that can be applied to these programs.

- Alfred E. Crommett, 32 Bruce Ave., Shrewsbury, MA 01545, (617) 263-3119: *IRA Annuity Generator,* $169.
- Benefit Analysis, Inc., 996 Old Eagle School Rd., Suite 1105, Wayne, PA 19087, (215) 293-0808, (800) 223-3601: *PenPro* (proposal generator), $950–$2,100; *401K Designer,* $950–$2,100.
- Benefits Software, Inc., 415 North McKinley, Suite 745, Little Rock, AR 72205, (800) 533-1388, (501) 664-1388: *Fringe Facts Software* (employee benefits analysis), $995.
- Blaze SSI Corporation, Box 333, Brielle, NJ 08730, (201) 223-5575: *BLAZE SSI Distribution Planner,* $1,500 license fee; *BLAZE SSI Government Forms Generator,* $500 annual; *BLAZE SSI EBP Valuation System* (defined-benefit and defined-contribution plans), $25,000 license fee; *BLAZE SSI DC Advanced Valuation System* (defined-contribution plans only), $10,000 license fee; *PENDEAS* (qualified plan proposals), $2,000 license fee.
- Brentmark Software, 249 E. Main St., Suite 2, P.O. Box 9886, Newark, DE 19714, (302) 366-8160: *Brentmark Pension & Excise Tax Planner* (analyzes effects of excise tax on plan distribution options), $225.
- Confidential Planning Services, Financial Planning Building, Middletown, OH 45042-0430, (513) 424-1656: *Defined Contribution Analysis,* $99.
- DATAIR Employee Benefit Systems, Inc., 415 East Plaza Dr., Westmont, IL 60559, (312) 325-2600: *Defined Benefit Pension System,* $7,500 license fee; *Defined Contribution-401K System,* $7,500 license fee; *Cafeteria-Flex Benefit System* (including Sec. 89), $2,750 license fee; *Pension Reporter* (annual govt. forms and reports), $695 license fee; *Plan Accountant,* $1,295 license fee; *Client Manager,* $3,485 license fee; *Qualified Plan Distributions and Tax Analysis System,* $950 license fee; *Retire,* $595 license fee; *Document Generator,* $2,250 license fee.

- Collin W. Fritz and Associates, Ltd., 1100 Highway 210 West, Brainerd, MN 56401, (800) 346-3961, (218) 828-0249: *Mincal* (IRA minimum distribution calculator and database), $195.
- Malina & Associates, 16012 Glen Haven Dr., Tampa, FL 33618, (813) 960-1309: *Retirement* (*1-2-3* templates for SS benefits, retirement plan benefits, 26-year projections of earnings, expenses, cash flows), $89.
- Mayer Hoffman McCann, 420 Nichols Rd., Kansas City, MO 64112, (800) 433-2292, (816) 753-3870: *Cafeteria Plan Proposal System,* $495; *Cafeteria Plan Management System,* $3,450.
- Micro Planning Systems, 1499 Bayshore Highway, Suite 214, Burlingame, CA 94010, (415) 692-0407: *Capital Accumulation Analysis,* $495.
- Money Tree Software, 1753 Wooded Knolls Dr., Suite 200, Philomath, OR 97370, (903) 929-2140: *Retirement Solutions,* $195.
- *PIA Calculation Program,* Room 4N29, Link Building, Baltimore, MD 21235, (301) 965-3014. Call for information to obtain free copy.
- Research Press, 4500 W. 72nd Terr., Prairie Village, KS 66208, (913) 362-9667: *PENPLAN SYSTEM* (*1-2-3* worksheets for analyzing averaging tax, mandatory IRA distributions, excise tax on excess distributions), $395.
- Ryan Software, Inc., 901 North Broadway, North White Plains, NY 10603, (800) 447-8338: *Ryan Retirement,* $295. On *Lotus 1-2-3* templates.

Miscellaneous Applications

The following are specialized, stand-alone programs designed for various applications related to financial planning.

- Aardvark/McGraw-Hill, 1020 N. Broadway, Milwaukee, WI 53202, (800) 292-2962, (414) 225-7500: *Tax Shelter/Investment Planner,* $395.
- ADS Systems, 23586 Calabasas Rd., Calabasas, CA 90254, (818) 347-9100: *Global Trader* (bond calculator), $199.
- BNA Software, 2300 M St., NW, Suite 660, Washington, DC 20037, (800) 424-2938: *Real Estate Investment Spreadsheet,* $595.
- Business Week Mutual Fund Scoreboard, P.O. Box 621, Elk Grove, IL 60009-0621, (800) 553-3575: Annual subscriptions to diskettes for *Equity Income Mutual Fund Scoreboard* (700 funds), *Fixed Income Mutual Fund Scoreboard* (500 funds), $149.95 each ($239.95 for both).
- ChipSoft, Inc., 5045 Shoreham Pl., San Diego, CA 92122, (800) 782-1120, (619) 453-8722: *Tally Ho!* (numerous financial calculations), $100.
- CompuTrac, 1017 Pleasant St., New Orleans, LA 70115, (504) 895-1474, (800) 535-7990: *CompuTrac* (graphic, historical analysis of stocks, futures, cash markets), $1,900; *Intra Day Analyst* (graphic, real-time analysis of stocks, futures, and options), $1,600.
- Confidential Planning Services, Financial Planning Building, Middletown, OH 45042-0430, (513) 424-1656: *Business System Software,* $49 (business valuation); *Financial Text Library System* (284 financial documents in 14 categories, implementation checklist of 700 techniques, client letters, agendas, objectives, and assumptions), $395; *Education Funding Analysis,* $99.

- Dow Jones & Company, Inc., P.O. Box 300, Princeton, NJ 08543-0300, (609) 520-4641, (609) 520-4642. *Market Analyzer* (market technical analysis, 15-year charts of historical data), $349 (online price updating through Dow Jones News/Retrieval).
- Dow Jones-Irwin Publishing Co., 1818 Ridge Rd., Homewood, IL 60430, (800) 448-3343 (ext. 2712): *Time Value of Money Templates* (numerous TVM functions), $17.50 plus $22.50 for accompanying text, *Time and Money*. Based on *Lotus 1-2-3* templates.
- Electrosonics, 36380 Garfield, Suite 1, Fraser, MI 48026, (800) 858-8448, (313) 791-0770: *EXEC-AMORT* (loan amortization plus numerous financial calculations), $149.95.
- EQUIS International, Inc., Box 26743, Salt Lake City, UT 84126, (800) 882-3040, (801) 974-5115: *MetaStock Professional* (charting tools for stocks, bonds, commodities, futures, indices, options, mutual funds), $295.
- Financial Data, Inc., Box 1332, Bryn Mawr, PA 19010, (800) 654-2227, (215) 525-6957: *Graph Pak* (60+ graphs on financial, insurance, estate relationships), $199.
- Financial Functions, Inc., Chicago Board Options Exchange Bldg., 400 S. LaSalle Street, P.O. Box 777, Chicago, IL 60604, (800) 622-4070, (800) 942-7317 (IL), (216) 525-6957: *@OPTION* (36 option analysis functions), $315. On *Lotus 1-2-3* template.
- Finplan Co., 2333 N. Geneva Terr., Suite 5A, Chicago, IL 60614, (800) 852-0852, (312) 549-1008: *Divorce Planner* (*1-2-3* spreadsheets for analyzing divorce property settlements, taxes), $200; network version, $300 (includes tax calculations for 25 states).
- Good Software Corp., 13601 Preston Rd., Suite 500W, Dallas, TX 75240, (800) 272-4663: *Amortizer Plus* (loan calculation, amortization), $99.95; *NumberCruncher* (RAM-resident calculator, rates of return, loans, annuities), $19.95.
- MarketBase, Inc., 250 W. 90th St., Suite 12K, New York, NY 10024, (800) 627-5385: *MOLLY* (historical stock market data, indices, interest rates, and so on), $199.95; *Economic Database* (160 data series), $159.95; *International Index Database* (14 foreign exchanges since 1980), from $200 up. Used for spreadsheets and charting software.
- MECA Ventures, 285 Riverside Ave., Westport, CT 06880, (800) 835-2246 (ext. 12), (203) 226-2400: *Financial Calculator* (numerous what-if financial analysis programs), $44.95.
- Micro Planning Systems, 1499 Bayshore Highway, Suite 214, Burlingame, CA 94010, (415) 692-0407: *Market Selector* (loan amortization), $99.95.
- MoneyCare, Inc., 253 Martens Ave., Mountain View, CA 94040, (800) 824-9827, (415) 962-0333: *TValue* (cash flow, interest rate, present value, periodic payment calculations), $95.
- Parkerware Associates, P.O. Box 6, Franklin Park, NJ 08823, (201) 297-2418: *Real Estate Calculator,* $29.95.
- Powder River Properties, Ltd., 1510 Stone St., Falls City, NE 68355, (402) 245-2029: *Loan Maker* (loan calculation and amortization), $89.95.

- Professional Book Distributors, Inc., P.O. Box 100120, Roswell, GA 30077-7120, (800) 848-0773: *KEYEMP* (valuation of a key employee), $99.
- Quantum Financial, Inc., 1800 30th St., Suite 308, Boulder, CO 80301, (800) 383-2719, (303) 447-1787: *Divorce Plan*, $535.
- Research Press, 4500 W. 72nd Terr., Prairie Village, KS 66208, (913) 362-9667: *DIVORCETAX* (*1-2-3* work sheets for analyzing optimum divorce property settlements, taxes), $395.
- Ryan Software, Inc., 901 N. Broadway, North White Plains, NY 10603, (800) 447-8338: *Ryan S Corp* (S or C corporation analysis), $95; *Ryan Investment Planner*, $249. On *Lotus 1-2-3* templates.
- Savant Corporation, 11211 Katy Freeway, Suite 250, Houston, TX 77079, (800) 231-9900, (713) 973-2400: *Technical Investor* (technical analysis), $395; *Fundamental Investor* (fundamental analysis), $395; *Investor's Portfolio* (portfolio analysis), $495. Programs use integrated database.
- Scherrer Resources, Inc., 8100 Cherokee St., Philadelphia, PA 19118, (215) 242-8740: *Realty Ally* (client management and prospecting), $395; *MATE* (add-on module for appointments, time logging, expense reporting), $99.
- Robert A. Stanger & Co., P.O. Box 7490, Shrewsbury, NJ 07702-7490, (800) 631-2291, (201) 389-3600: *Stanger's Partnership Software System* (matches partnership investments to client suitability), $199.
- Syntex Systems, Inc., 1501 W. Valley Highway, N, Suite 104, Auburn, WA 98001, (206) 833-2525: *Financial Analyst* (17 financial calculations), $75.
- Tax Calc, 4210 W. Vickery Blvd., Fort Worth, TX 76107, (800) 527-2669, (817) 738-3122: *Business Valuation Planner*, $195; *Real Estate Planner*, $195; *Depreciation/Fixed Asset Accounting*, $195. Programs run off *Lotus 1-2-3*.
- Yousoufian Software, Inc., 17230 99th Ave., SW, P.O. Box 950, Vashon, WA 98070, (206) 463-5020: *Real Estate Investment Analysis and Syndication*, $1,375.

Software and Hardware Buying Tips

Dale S. Johnson

The following are some basic general tips for choosing the right software and hardware after the firm has determined all needs for information processing and application support.

- Buy for the long term by choosing software with more sophisticated features than the firm may need (or know how to apply) initially, so that users won't outgrow it too soon as their computer proficiencies, planning knowledge, and practice scope increase. Also, choose software that provides comprehensive solutions to planning needs rather than an isolated application that solves only one major problem and that the planner may not be able to integrate with other stand-alone applications.
- Insist on software accompanied by good documentation that
  - contains full installation instructions
  - explains how it works
  - includes a tutorial for learning how to use it
  - includes a reference list of commands by function
  - contains a diagnostics or troubleshooting utility (or a list of error messages and what to do about them)
  - provides examples of major program features
  - includes a table of contents and topical index
  - is written in clear, nonjargon English
- Look for menu-driven procedures and functions, online help messages, and evidence that data entry requirements and procedures have been simplified. Involve users' reactions to the software in the purchase decision. Avoid programs that require lots of memorization. Look for lots of help screens, screen design, and use of color to help the user efficiently work with the software.
- Thoroughly examine report-generation procedures. Most, if not all, of these procedures should be menu-selectable. Examine the standard reports produced by the software, and determine whether the program provides for user-customized reports.
- Be convinced of the software's claims of ease of use before buying. One indication is the initial training needed. Users should be able to start running most programs and systems within an hour after proceeding through a self-paced tutorial. Complex programs (for example, integrated planning systems, database programs, and spreadsheets) may require 2 to 3 days of formal training, usually at the vendor's location.
- Talk to other users of the program before buying and find out its advantages, disadvantages, and problems. Computer clubs, user groups, and reviews of the program in various publications are good indications. Check out the program thoroughly. Probe. Ask tough questions.

- Try the full program before buying it. Don't be sold by canned demonstration versions that some vendors supply; they are often floppy disk commercials rather than working versions that allow the user to test the software with the jobs you have to do every day. For about $25, some vendors sell limited versions of systems and programs that contain most of the actual applications, with functions such as SAVE or PRINT disabled, or with limitations on the number of cases that can be opened. Others usually provide some risk-free means of testing. A 30-day money-back guarantee is becoming the industry norm.
- Buy software only from vendors that seem relatively well established in what is, at best, a volatile industry. How long the vendor has been in business, how many other programs it sells, how widely its systems have sold, how much consulting it provides on using the system, and whether it provides timely updates and enhancements are indications of whether the vendor will support user needs through the years. Insist on a written commitment (in the license agreement or printed in documentation) of the terms of vendor support for the current version, enhancements, and interface with other planning and practice management software.
- Price should be reasonable relative to general applications software programs (for example, stand-alone databases and word processing programs) and to current price levels for major financial planning systems. Network versions should cost only nominally more than single-user versions. Bargain for the best possible price relative to stated list prices.
- When shopping for a computer, other hardware, and software, use resources such as reviews and evaluations in computer trade journals, computer shows, and the experiences of friends and associates to avoid the mistakes that initial purchasers otherwise inevitably make.
- For inexperienced users of computer equipment, the dealer is one of the most important factors in both presale information and postsale support. Check out the dealer's track record for full support because many do not live up to their claims.
- For the experienced buyer who knows what is needed and how to use it, price and brand shopping can result in considerable savings. Almost any brand of computer, printer, and other peripheral hardware can be purchased somewhere for 20–30 percent off the manufacturer's suggested list price. General application software can be purchased at almost half the list price. Check out computer and software retail outlets and the ads in trade magazines from national discount dealers. Lower prices mean less presale information, less service, less support, and more caution for buyers who are on their own.

  Financial planning software is not as frequently or as steeply discounted. Usually, discounts are vendor specials or are made when add-on modules and applications are selected.
- Make sure that the system or program the firm buys does not require hardware components or additional software that exceeds overall needs or budget. For example, do not buy a program that must be run with more than 640K of system memory, with a specific graphical interface program (such as Microsoft *Windows*), or with a specific spreadsheet or database program *unless* practice

activities really require that overall configuration of equipment and users are willing to bear the additional costs and time required to learn how to use it effectively.
- If the firm's computerization needs are more complex than this survey indicates as typical, it may benefit from engaging a professional consultant to help sort out the issues and make specific recommendations.

Index

Above-the-line deduction, 165
Active participant, 323
Actual cash value, 216–19
Adjusted gross income, 165
Alternative minimum tax (AMT), 171–72
American College, The
    code of ethics, 389–92
    designations, 13–14
    fact finder, 121–62
American Depositary Receipts (ADRs),
    271
American Society of CLU & ChFC
    code of ethics, 393–96
    founding, 14
Annual exclusion, 191, 196–97
Annuities, 257–58
Approximate yield, 284–85
Asset and portfolio allocation, 495–97
Assignment of income, 173
Automobile insurance, 247–52
    damage to auto, 250–52
    liability, 248–49
    medical payments, 249
    no-fault, 252
    uninsured motorists, 249–50
Availability bias, 36–37
Average indexed monthly earnings
    (AIME), 326

Bank deposits, 267
Basis, 178–79
Below-the-line deduction, 165
Bond companies, 273
Brochure rule, 379–80

Capital gain (loss), 180–81
Cash equivalents, 267–68
    bank deposits, 267
    money market instruments, 267–68
Cash-flow analysis, 499–501
Cash-management statement, 102

Cash values, 255–56
Certificates of deposit (CDs), 267, 292
Charitable contributions, 202–3
    gifts, 202
    income interests, 203
    remainder interests, 202–3
Charitable deductions, 193
Client and asset management programs,
    344–46, 497–99
Code of ethics
    American College, The, 389–92
    American Society of CLU & ChFC,
        392–96
Coinsurance, 263
Collision damage waiver (CDW), 251–52
Common stock, 270, 292
Common stock companies, 273
Communication principles, 82–84
Community property, 187
Compounding, 457–58
Compound interest, 292, 456–57
Comprehensive financial plan
    content, 9–10
    standards, 9–10, 449–54
Comprehensive integrated systems,
    353–56, 491–92
Computer configurations, 490
Computerizing a financial planning
    practice, 333–68. *See also* Software
Consequentialists, 399
Constructive receipt doctrine, 173–74
Corporate debt securities, 269–70
Corridor deductible, 262–63
Counseling
    effective, 77–82
    financial. *See* Financial counseling
Current yield, 282–83

Databases, 343–44
Data gathering. *See* Information
    gathering
Dealer markets, 296

Deduction floor, 175–76
Deductions
    above-the-line, 165
    below-the-line, 165
    business, 166
    depreciation, 168–69
    itemized, 165–66
    miscellaneous itemized, 175
    paper, 168–69
    personal, 167
    standard, 165–66
Deferred retirement, 327
Defined-benefit pension plans, 318–19
Defined-benefit plans, 315–17
Defined-contribution plans, 315–17
Depreciation, 216–19
Disability income insurance, 258–61
    benefit amount, 260–61
    benefit period, 260
    elimination period, 260
    partial disability, 259
    residual disability, 259
    terms of renewability, 261
    total disability, 258–59
Discounting, 457–58
Dual-income family, 15
Durable power of attorney, 208

Early retirement, 327
Economic benefit doctrine, 172–73
Employer-maintained plans, 323
Equity securities, 270–73
    American Depositary Receipts
        (ADRs), 271
    common stock, 270
    investment companies, 271–73
    preferred stock, 270–71
Estate planning, 184–209
    charitable contributions, 202–3
    durable power of attorney, 208
    goals, 184–85
    information gathering, 185
    life insurance, 203–5
    lifetime gifts, 196–98
    marital deduction, 198–202
    ownership of property, 186–88

software, 505–7
    taxation of transfers, 190–95
    transfers at death, 188–90
    trusts, 206–8
    unified credit, 200–2
    wills, 205–6
Ethics, 384–405
    codes, 389–96
    decision making, 398–403
    issues, 403–5
    law, 385–88
    professionalism, 396–98
    role, 384–85
    work environment, 388–89
Excess benefit plans, 325
Exemptions
    dependency, 169
    personal, 169
Expense method, 310
    work sheet, 314–15

Fact finder
    computer-based, 100–1
    information gathering, 100–5
    sample, 121–62
Familiarity bias, 37–38
Federal transfer taxes. *See* Transfer tax
    system
Fee simple ownership, 186
Filing status, 170–71
Financial counseling, 71–98
    attending and listening, 88–93
    characteristics, 77–82
    communication principles, 82–85
    essentials, 74–77
    nonverbal behaviors, 85–88
    questions, 95–98
    structured communication, 71–74
Financial planners
    activities, 10–11
    federal regulation, 369–83. *See also*
        Investment Advisers Act of 1940
    professional designations, 10–11
    role, 235–36, 301–7
    state regulation, 383

Financial planning
  client services, 489
  comprehensive-focus view, 3–4. *See also* Comprehensive financial planning
  computerization, 333–68
  consumer needs, 17–23
  defined, 4
  evolution, 13–14
  institutions, 13–14
  narrow-focus view, 2–3
  opportunities and challenges, 14–17
  process, 4–8
  programs and needs analysis, 494–95
  single-purpose view, 2
Financial services professionals. *See* Financial planners
Flat-amount formula, 320
Flat-amount-per-year-of-service formula, 319
Flat-percentage-of-earnings formula, 318
Form ADV, 373–74
401(k) plans, 320–21
403(b) plans, 321
Future interests, 186–87
  remainder interest, 186
  reversionary interest, 186–87
Future value, 462–64, 467–73

Generation-skipping transfer tax (GSTT), 193–94
Gifts
  annual tax exclusion, 196
  federal taxation, 191–92
  lifetime, 196–97
  minors, 197–98
Government debt securities, 268–69
Gross estate, 192
Gross income
  deductions, 164–65
  exclusions, 164–65
  principle, 163–64

Hardware
  buying tips, 511–13

Hindsight bias, 38
Holding-period return (HPR), 283–84
Homeowners insurance, 237–47
  causes of loss, 238–39
  liability coverages, 244–47
  property coverages, 239–44

IAFP survey, 17–23
Illusion of control bias, 38
Income tax planning, 163–83
  avoiding limitations on deductions, 175–76
  deferral and acceleration techniques, 176–77
  income and deduction shifting, 174–75
  nonrecognition transactions, 178–80
  passive loss rules, 177–78
  taxable loss transaction, 180
  tax-exempt transactions, 178
Income tax return preparation, 502–3
Index funds, 273
Individual retirement accounts (IRAs), 321–24
  contributions, 322
  eligibility, 323–24
  spousal, 324
Information gathering, 4–5, 99–120
  fact finder, 100–5
  importance, 99
  prerequisites, 99–100
  sample exercise, 105–20
Insider Trading and Securities Fraud Enforcement Act of 1988, 375–78
Insurance
  automobile, 247–52
  contract components, 228–30
  definition, 226
  disability, 258–61
  homeowners, 237–47
  life, 253–58
  loss adjustments, 231–33
  medical expense, 261–64
  planning and marketing software, 503–5
  principle of indemnity, 230–31
  selection, 228–33

Insurance (*cont.*)
  umbrella liability, 252–53
Interest-rate risk, 277–78
Investment Advisers Act of 1940, 297,
    369–81
  antifraud provisions, 380–81
  applicability. *See* SEC Release No.
    IA-770
  assignability of investment advisory
    agreements, 378
  brochure rule, 379–80
  exemptions, 372–73
  fee restrictions, 378
  prohibition of labels, 379
  record keeping responsibilities, 374–78
  registered investment adviser (RIA),
    373–74
Investment Adviser Self-Regulation Act
    of 1989, 382–83
Investment assets, 267–75
  cash equivalents, 267–68
  equity securities, 270–73
  long-term debt instruments, 268–70
  real estate, 274–75
Investment companies, 271–73
Investment Company Act of 1940, 297
Investment markets, 294–98
  dealer, 296
  negotiated, 295
  organized securities, 296
  regulation, 296–98
  true-auction, 295
Investment planning, 265–300
  definition, 265
  economic environment, 294
  information, 298–300
  markets and regulations, 294–98
  principles, strategies, and tactics,
    288–94
Investment return, 281–85
  approximate yield, 284–85
  current yield, 282–83
  holding-period return (HPR), 283–84
Investment risk, 275–81
  causes, 276–81
  definition, 276

Itemized deductions, 165–66

Junk bonds, 270

Large-loss principle, 227
Law and ethics, 385–88
  business law and business ethics,
    386–87
  conflicting moral rules, 388
  legal rules vs. ethical rules, 387–88
  legislating morality, 387
Law of scarcity, 17
Leveraged buyout (LBO), 280–81
Life estates, 186
Life insurance
  annuities, 257–58
  term, 254–55
  universal, 256–57
  use in estate plans, 203–5
  whole, 255–56
Lifetime gifts, 196–98
Living trusts, 207–8
Living wills, 206
Long-term debt instruments, 268–70
  corporate debt securities, 269–70
  government debt securities, 268–69
Loss adjustments, 231–33
Loss aversion, 27–28
Loss control, 221–24
  loss prevention, 223
  loss reduction, 223–24
  planning, 224
  risk avoidance, 222–23
Loss financing, 224–27
  insurance, 225–26
  noninsurance transfer, 224–25
  planning, 227
  retention, 225

Major medical coverage, 261–63
  coinsurance, 263
  deductibles, 262–63
  maximum limit, 262
Maloney Act of 1938, 297

Marital deduction, 192–93, 198–202
Market risk, 278
Medical expense insurance, 261–64
    major medical coverage, 261–63
    planning for older ages, 263–64
Medicare, 327–30
    eligibility, 327–28
    part A, 328–29
    part B, 329–30
Method of impartial legislation, 399–400
Mini planning systems, 356–57, 492–94
Miscellaneous itemized deductions, 175
Mixed portfolio companies, 273
Money market instruments, 267–68, 273
Money-purchase pension plans, 319
Morals. *See* Ethics
Mutual funds, 292

Negotiated markets, 295
No-fault benefits, 252
Nonconsequentialists, 399
Nonqualified plans, 325–26
    excess benefit plans, 325
    supplemental executive retirement
        plans, 325
    top-hat plans, 325
Nonrecognition transactions, 178–80
Nonverbal behaviors, 85–88
    elements, 85–87
    interpretation, 87–88

Old-age, survivor's, disability, and health
        insurance, 326. *See also* Social
        security
Opportunity cost, 12, 455–56
Ordinary gain (loss), 180–81
Ordinary income, 180–81
Organized securities markets, 296

Passbook savings accounts, 292
Passive loss rules, 177–78
Pass-through entities, 182
Pension plans, 317–19
Personal Auto Policy (PAP), 247–52

Personal financial planning, 416–21
Portfolio analysis, 499
Postretirement employment, 331
Preferred stock, 270–71
Present value, 464–67, 473–78
Primary insurance amount (PIA), 326
Principle of indemnity, 230–31
    duplicate insurance, 231
    insurable interest, 230
    subrogation, 230–31
Probate property, 188–89
Professional designations, 13–14
Professionalism, 396–98
Profit-sharing plans, 317–20
Property ownership, 186–88
    individual, 186–87
    joint, 187
    other, 187–88
Purchasing-power risk, 276–77

QTIP marital deduction, 200
Qualified plans, 313–22
    defined-benefit pension plans, 318–19
    defined-benefit vs. defined-contribution
        plans, 315–17
    401(k) plans, 320–21
    403(b) plans, 321
    money-purchase pension plans, 319
    pension vs. profit-sharing plans, 317–18
    principal types, 322
    profit-sharing plans, 319–20
    target-benefit pension plans, 319
    tax advantages, 316

Rational thinking
    limitations, 32–43
Record keeping responsibilities, 374–78
Registered investment adviser (RIA),
        373–81
Registry of Financial Planning
        Practitioners
    establishment, 14
    standards for financial plans, 9–10,
        449–54
Replacement cost, 216–19

Replacement ratio method, 308–10
  work sheet, 312–13
Retirement income, 313–32
  IRAs, 321–24
  nonqualified plans, 325–26
  pension maximization, 331–32
  postretirement employment, 331
  qualified plans, 313–21
  reverse annuity mortgage, 330–31
  social security, 326–30
  trading down, 330
Retirement planning, 301–32
  effect of inflation, 310–11
  estimating financial needs, 307–11
  holistic, 301–3
  overcoming inadequate resources,
    330–32
  role of planner, 301–7
  software, 507–8
  sources of income, 313–32
Reverse annuity mortgage (RAM),
  330–31
Risk
  concept, 29–32
  denial, 34–36
  perceived vs. objective, 31
  voluntary vs. involuntary, 39–40
Risk analysis, 212–21
  risk evaluation, 220–21
  risk identification, 212–15
  risk measurement, 215–20
Risk identification questionnaire, 481–88
Risk management process, 210–36
  risk analysis, 211–21
  risk treatment planning, 211, 221–33
  risk treatment planning
    implementation, 211–12, 233–36
Risk measurement, 216–20
  liability risks, 219
  personal risks, 219–20
  property risks, 216–19
Risk-return profile, 103–4
Risk-taking
  cultural admiration, 28–29
  group dynamics, 41–42
  life-style characteristics, 45–47

situation specific vs. general
  personality trait, 43–45
Risk tolerance
  assessing, 56–65
  financial decisions, 25–56
Risk treatment planning, 221–33
  loss control, 221–24
  loss financing, 224–27
Risk treatment planning implementation,
  233–36
  preparation, 233–35
  role of financial services professional,
    235–36

Sample planning case, 406–48
S corporations, 182
SEC Release No. IA-770, 369–72
  advice about securities, 370
  business standard, 370
  compensation test, 370–71
  reaffirmation, 371–72
SEC Release No. IA-1092, 371–72
SEC v. Capital Gains Research Bureau,
  371
Sec. 1321 assets, 182
Sec. 2503(b) trusts, 197
Sec. 2503(c) trusts, 197–98
Securities Act of 1933, 297
Securities Exchange Act of 1934, 297,
  376–77
Self-regulatory organizations (SROs),
  382–83
Simple interest, 456–57
Social security, 326–30
  eligibility, 326
  medicare, 327–30
  retirement benefits, 326–27
Software
  buying tips, 511–13
  evaluating, 346–49, 358–67
  financial and tax planning, 353–67,
    501–2
  financial planning, 346–53
  service bureaus, 358
  vendors, systems, and programs,
    491–510

Specialty companies, 273
Speculation, 265–66
Spousal IRAs, 324
Spreadsheets, 344
Stand-alone programs, 357–58
Standard deduction, 165–66
State death taxes, 194–95
   credit estate tax, 195
   estate tax, 195
   inheritance tax, 194
   planning, 195
Structured communication, 71–74
   advising, 73–74
   counseling, 72–73
   interviewing, 72
Subchapter S election, 182
Subrogation, 230–31
Supplemental executive retirement plans,
   325

Target-benefit pension plans, 319
Taxable entities, 182–83
Taxable income, 165, 285–86
Taxable year, 172
Tax credits, 171
Tax-deferred annuities, 321
Tax-exempt income, 178, 285–86
Tax rates, 169–71
Tax shelters, 177–78
Term interests, 186
Term life insurance, 254–55
Thrill-seeker, 50–51
Time-value-of-money analysis
   basics, 455–80
   importance in financial planning, 12–13
   money in vs. money out, 11, 460
   opportunity cost and interest rate, 12
   time lines, 460–61
   variables, 13, 459–60
Top-hat plans, 325
Totten trusts, 190
Transfers at death
   intestacy, 189

operation of contract, 190
operation of law, 189–90
probate property, 188–89
will provisions, 188–89
Transfer tax system, 190–95
   federal estate tax, 192–93
   federal gift tax, 191–92
   generation-skipping transfer tax
      (GSTT), 193–94
   state death tax, 194–95
Treasury bills, 268
True-auction markets, 295
Trusts
   estate, 200
   irrevocable, 205
   living, 207–8
   revocable, 204–5
   Sec. 2503(b), 197
   Sec. 2503(c), 197–98
   testamentary, 208
   Totten, 190

Umbrella liability insurance, 252–53
Unified credit, 191–92, 200–2
Uniform Gifts to Minors Act (UGMA),
   197
Uniform Transfers to Minors Act
   (UTMA), 197
Unit-benefit formula, 318
Universal life insurance, 256–57

Values
   differences, 81–82
   orientations, 80–81

Whole life insurance, 255–56
Wills, 205–6

Zero coupon bonds, 292